HANDGUNS

7th Annual Edition

EDITED BY HAL SWIGGETT

DBI Books, Inc.

TABLE OF CONTENTS

FEATURES

STAFF

EDITOR
Hal Swiggett
SENIOR STAFF EDITORS
Harold A. Murtz
Ray Ordorica
ASSOCIATE EDITOR
Robert S.L. Anderson
PRODUCTION MANAGER
John L. Duoba
EDITORIAL/PRODUCTION ASSOCIATE
Jamie L. Puffpaff
EDITORIAL/PRODUCTION ASSISTANT
Holly J. Porter
ASSISTANT TO THE EDITOR
Lilo Anderson
ELECTRONIC PUBLISHING MANAGER
Nancy J. Mellem
ELECTRONIC PUBLISHING ASSOCIATE
Robert M. Fuentes
ELECTRONIC PUBLISHING ASSISTANT
Edward B. Hartigan
GRAPHIC DESIGN
Jim Billy
John L. Duoba
MANAGING EDITOR
Pamela J. Johnson
PUBLISHER
Sheldon L. Factor

DBI BOOKS, INC.

PRESIDENT
Charles T. Hartigan
VICE PRESIDENT & PUBLISHER
Sheldon L. Factor
VICE PRESIDENT—SALES
John G. Strauss
VICE PRESIDENT/MANAGING EDITOR
Pamela J. Johnson
TREASURER
Frank R. Serpone

ABOUT OUR COVERS

One of the most exciting innovations in the hand-gunning world this year was Sigarms' introduction of the SIG P229 pistol chambered for the new, proprietary 357 SIG cartridge. We are pleased to feature both the pistol and cartridge on our covers.

A bottlenecked round, the 357 SIG is a joint venture between Sigarms and Federal Cartridge Co., and is simply the 40 S&W case necked down to accept a 9mm bullet. Shooting a 125-grain jacketed hollowpoint, the new P229 chambering gives an impressive muzzle velocity of over 1300 fps, and more than 500 foot pounds of energy. And this from a barrel that's less than four inches long! With thirteen shots on tap (twelve in the magazine, one up the spout), the P229 shows a lot of promise and power. In fact, Sigarms' tests show that the 357 SIG cartridge outperforms the 9mm Parabellum, 40 S&W and 45 ACP rounds in both velocity and delivered energy. In addition, accuracy with the new round is exceedingly good, and the recoil impulse quite mild.

Introduced in 1991, the SIG-Sauer P229 was originally chambered for the 40 S&W cartridge. It is very much like the other SIG-Sauer guns in the P220 series (with the exception of the P230 in 380 ACP), but for the slide which is machined from a solid piece of stainless steel in the Sigarms New Hampshire plant. This alloy-framed gun is a double-action design, with no manual safety. Instead, there's a decocking lever just forward of the left grip panel that, when depressed, drops the hammer to a safe position; pulling the trigger completely through fires the gun. In addition, there is an automatic firing pin locking safety for further security against accidental discharge.

The new P229 has an overall matte black finish that's highly resistant to wear. Sights are the familiar white-dot-and-bar type, with the rear adjustable for windage. Grips are stippled black polymer and offer a sure hold on the gun.

The SIG-Sauer P229 has an overall length of 7.08 inches, barrel length of 3.86 inches and an empty weight of 32.5 ounces. It is one of the most reliable and functional autoloading handguns on today's market.

Photo by John Hanusin.

ISBN 0-87349-159-9

Library of Congress Catalog #88-72115

HANDGUNS 95

SECTION 1
The Handgun Scene

James profiles the new Sigma and others, page 6.

The DA revolver run-down from Trzoniec, page 14.

Taffin details the best ol' wheelguns, page 21.

The Handgun Scene

AUTOLOADERS

by FRANK JAMES

New gun law sparks skyrocketing demand for handguns, and many makers respond with brand-new self-loader designs.

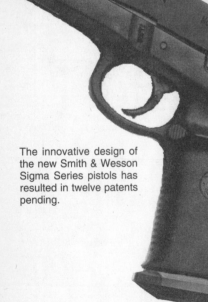

The innovative design of the new Smith & Wesson Sigma Series pistols has resulted in twelve patents pending.

THIS LAST YEAR was a watershed year for the firearms industry. At the beginning of the year, sales were down and business was lethargic, but by the end of the year, the efforts of the Clinton Administration in pushing for more gun control measures after passage of the Brady Law created a frenzy of sales and economic activity for all firearms manufacturers, but most especially for handgun manufacturers. The resulting new products for 1994 from these firms are coming from companies that, as a general rule, are better funded and better organized for the future.

Smith & Wesson

For 1994, Smith & Wesson has the Backpacker, which is a short-barreled (approximately 2½-inch) stainless steel 44 Magnum revolver, and the reintroduced Model 4516, which is a compact-sized 45 ACP double-action semi-auto pistol. The lower priced 22 pistol, the Model 2206, has been upgraded to a target pistol with the addition of a Millett-style adjustable rear sight.

But, the *reeeally big* news at Smith & Wesson is the introduction of their first polymer production pistol—the Sigma. Introduced in early March at a resort in Ft. Lauderdale, Florida, the Sigma is obviously designed to compete directly against that original polymer import pistol from Austria.

Major features include a polymer frame, a trigger-activated safety with its patented hinged design, and metal magazines of fifteen-round capacity in 40 S&W and seventeen-round capacity in 9mm Luger. The 9mm version of Smith's new Sigma will be introduced during the summer of 1994. Surprisingly, only the barrel for the Sigma is produced in the Springfield, Massachusetts, facility as everything else is manufactured by subcontractors.

Smith & Wesson is having great success with their Model 411 pistol, even if technically speaking it isn't new for 1994. This plain-Jane version of the basic 40-caliber pistol is a lower cost alternative to the more expensive Model 4006, and it is popular. It allows the consumer all the quality of a Smith & Wesson, but without the price of their higher level models.

The Smith & Wesson Performance Center has two new handguns; one is a K-frame revolver with a 3-inch ported

Smith & Wesson reintroduced the Model 4516 at the '94 SHOT Show. The Model 4516 is a 45 ACP "medium" size double-action semi-auto pistol with a 7+1 magazine capacity. It features stainless steel construction and a Novak Lo Mount Carry rear sight. (S&W photo)

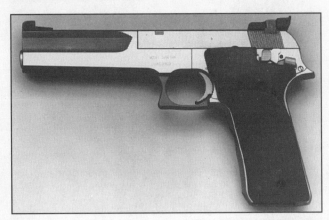

S&W now has what they term the Model 2206 Target Pistol. The basic difference is the addition of thumbrest walnut grips and the installation of an adjustable Millet rear sight. (S&W photo)

The Smith & Wesson Performance Center offers this 356 TSW Compact pistol through their stocking dealer program. The 356 TSW is a new round developed by S&W for competition use, but offers ballistics very close to the 357 Magnum, and this in a large magazine capacity format. (S&W photo)

Colt introduced their new 22 pistol, called simply the Colt 22 Pistol. It features a combination of stainless steel and hard rubber. It is a single-action design, and *not* double-action-only as their '94 catalog states.

barrel and a very slick action, while the second pistol generated true excitement. It is the Performance Center 356 TSW Compact. The 356 TSW cartridge is a 9x22$\frac{1}{2}$mm cartridge that performs close to the 357 Magnum.

Colt

Colt's Manufacturing Company still has a full undiminished presence, this despite the fact the company (at this writing) is still in bankruptcy court. The only new product Colt has is their new 22 semi-auto pistol, which was *not* a double-action-only pistol as their 1994 catalog says it is. The new Colt combines stainless steel construction with hard rubber grips and a heavy barrel with ventilated rib. To be marketed as an entry-level pistol for beginning shooters, it bears an uncanny resemblance to the long-deceased High Standard Sport King. At the 1994 SHOT Show, President Ron Whitaker had a round table discussion with many members of the international firearms press and had an indefinite answer when questioned on this apparent similarity.

Whitaker acknowledged many of the financial difficulties Colt has experienced over the past two years. And, yes, the company is quite concerned about future legislation that would impact negatively upon their product line, specifically

the AR-15, or the Colt Sporter as it is now known, which I believe comprises a significant portion of their civilian sales. He explained that the Colt AA2000 was dropped from production because it was manufactured entirely outside the Hartford, Connecticut, facility (West Hartford now, because they have moved into a new plant), and Colt had difficulty controlling production costs. That related directly to their sales position in terms of the competition. He said they were developing a new pistol to replace the AA2000, but would not commit as to when we might see it.

(Right) Ruger has redesigned their auto pistols into the KP94. The KP94 will be available in a variety of operational styles and two calibers: 9mm Luger and 40 S&W. It features an improved ergonomic grip and a different slide.

(Left) Mitchell Arms unveiled their new high-capacity 45 pistol. It is a single-action design with a 13+1 magazine capacity in 45 ACP. The models on display at the show had ambidextrous safeties, beavertail grip safeties and stainless steel construction.

Llama of Spain has also developed a product to compete in the high-capacity 45 ACP pistol market. It, too, is a single-action design and offers a 13+1 magazine capacity. It is a carbon steel pistol based on the venerable 1911.

Taurus introduced a 45 ACP pistol called the PT-945. This double-action/single-action semi-auto pistol has a single-column magazine holding eight rounds.

Ruger

Sturm, Ruger has introduced their new KP94, which they call a mid-size semi-auto pistol. Ruger recently hired Karl Walter, former president of Glock, to be in charge of their domestic law enforcement sales. Both the introduction of this new pistol and the hiring of a man who knows how to penetrate the American law enforcement market demonstrate just how serious Ruger is about selling service pistols to police officers in America.

Ruger shipped 800,000 firearms last year—300,000 of them semi-auto pistols—so no one can accuse them of being a minor player on the American firearms scene.

The KP94 is available in various firing modes—a manual slide-mounted safety, a decock-only version, and a double-action-only model.

Ruger is the first major firearms manufacturer in America to build a pistol with an integral laser unit. The KP94 Laser Pistol has a Tac-Star R laser unit mounted inside a dust cover forward of the trigger guard. This housing is cast as part of the frame and has windage and elevation adjustments to coordinate the laser beam with point of impact. Ruger feels it is a far more sturdy arrangement than any of the bolt-on models presently being sold.

The KP94 grips have been redesigned for a more ergonomic feel, and the slide has lost its Browning "step."

Mitchell Arms

A number of firms have high-capacity 45s to meet the increasing demand for wide-body 45s. One of the more visually pleasing was the Mitchell Arms Wide Body in stainless steel. Bearing a strong resemblance to the Para-Ordnance

Glock had their latest offering on display. It is a long-slide version of the popular 40-caliber Glock. Called the Model 24, this competition pistol will be offered with either ported or non-ported barrels.

The Glock Model 24 has the front portion of the extended slide cut away for the four ports used to compensate on the factory barrel. The non-ported barrel uses the same slide, but an unmodified barrel.

high-capacity pistols, it is a single-action 1911-type design with the prerequisite thirteen-round magazine and is called the 45 Signature Series.

Mitchell has also resurrected the High Standard line of rimfire target pistols. Twenty-five years ago, High Standard dominated Bullseye precision shooting in America. All of the resurrected models are faithful to the originals, except they are of stainless steel.

Mitchell has also brought back the Victor pistol that High Standard introduced to the Bullseye target market before they went belly-up. Called the Victor II, it features stainless steel construction, optional barrel underweight, and a feature that wasn't found on the original pistol—a barrel with a top rib that will accommodate the mounting of red dot electronic sights.

Formerly, Mitchell Arms offered a stainless steel Luger-clone that was made in Texas. This pistol is now known as the Stoeger American Eagle Luger. Stoeger, who used to import the original back before World War II and trade-marked the name "Luger" in this country, took over distributorship of this stainless steel copy of the toggle-locked single-column 9mm. This new model copies the original in every detail except it is made of stainless steel.

Springfield

Springfield, Inc., the follow-on firm to the earlier Springfield Armory company based in Illinois, has a new high-capacity 45 ACP called the XM-4. Like the Mitchell Wide Body, it, too, is a single-action design based on the 1911 pistol, but employs a polymer Xanex frame made in Israel. Deliveries are expected by mid-summer 1994. It also uses a Para-Ordnance-style magazine, and reportedly Springfield is paying that firm a royalty for the use of their design.

Among the other new Springfield introductions for 1994 are the Mil-Spec Parkerized 1911 pistol in 38 Super and 45 ACP, the Trophy Match 45, and the Lightweight Compact Comp 45.

The Mil-Spec pistols have a Parkerized phosphate finish and feature a commander-style hammer and grip safety. They use a three white-dot sighting system and black rubber grips.

The Trophy Match comes in a lockable blue plastic box, features a commander-style hammer and grip safety, a fully adjustable rear sight, an eight-round magazine, as well as many other extra features.

Browning

Browning for 1994 has added a special nickel-finish version to the popular Buck Mark Target model with 5.5-inch barrel. Made in America, the Browning Buck Mark has proven itself with its inherent accuracy and overall quality. With its ten-shot magazine, the nickel-finish Buck Mark will be an attractive addition to any gun cabinet.

Llama

Llama from Spain is following the high-capacity trend with their single-action 45 pistol called the New Generation. It features a thirteen-round magazine, rubber grips, three-dot sight system, all-steel construction, non-glare finish, extended slide release and a military-type hammer.

Taurus

Taurus, the Brazilian handgun maker, has enjoyed substantial success marketing their look-alike Beretta pistols in the United States, but last year they introduced a new single-column double-action 9mm pistol. This year, they introduced a 45 ACP version of the same pistol called the PT-945. It has an 8+1 magazine capacity and features Taurus' own safety system with On, Off and Decock. It is compact and well balanced.

Glock

Glock introduced a new "long slide" version of their popular Glock 22 in 1994. Called the Glock 24, this new pistol should answer the need of those shooters who want a major caliber handgun in the Glock "race gun" format. The 24 will be available with either ported or non-ported barrel, and will be delivered with the Glock competition trigger as a standard feature.

AMT

One of the bigger pieces of news for something so small is the new 45 ACP Back-Up from AMT. Long known for their 380 ACP Back-Up, this new prototype is the same gun, just made slightly wider to accept the big 45 round. Production is slated for late '94, and the gun on display at the January SHOT Show was a one-of-a-kind model made in AMT's prototype shop. A double-action-only pistol, it will have a 5+1 magazine capacity. Many observers felt it would become the definitive word in small, concealable, self-protection firearms.

AMT has a prototype pistol on display that was on the lips of everyone who saw it—the 45 Back-Up. Everyone is familiar with AMT's 380 Back-Up, and the 45 version is the same pistol only made wider to accept the major caliber round.

Beretta displayed a prototype that is reportedly slated for production in late 1994 to mid-1995—the Beretta 8000. The extraordinary thing about this pistol is it uses a rotating barrel and cam block system very similar to that used on the now defunct Colt AA2000.

The Beretta 8000 was seen in two different examples: one in 9mm Luger and the second in 40 S&W. The 9mm pistol has a fifteen-round magazine, while the 40 version holds only eleven.

Notice the difference between these two Beretta 8000 backstraps. This illustrates some of the differences seen between prototypes. The final production version has yet to be revealed to the press and the public.

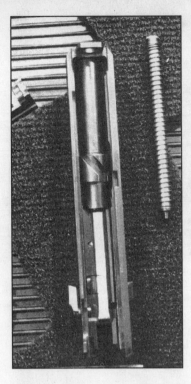

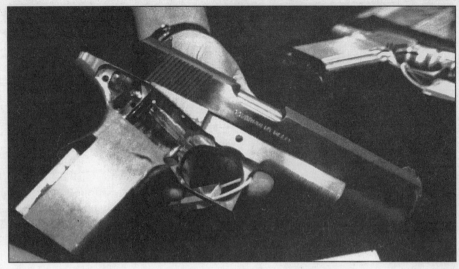

(Left) The cam block that rotates the barrel in and out of "battery" is to the left of the slide/barrel assembly for the Beretta 8000. The cam track can be clearly seen on the bottom of the barrel, but the detent hole to "lock" the gun in battery is less visible.

Chip McCormick had this new prototype pistol on display that featured a removable sideplate on the right side of the frame. This feature allows either single-action or double/single-action mechanisms. It will also use either single-column magazines or a special high-capacity double-stack magazine.

The two guns both featured slide-mounted safeties operated in the conventional manner. The overall size is smaller than the Beretta 92, but magazine capacity remains the same. Colt had an accuracy problem with their rotating barrel pistol, but the Model 8000 prototypes examined each had a detent stop in the cam track on the cam block under the barrel. There is no question this is an improvement over the Colt design as it helps establish an actual "battery" position for the barrel.

Chip McCormick

Chip McCormick is developing a new auto pistol. This comes after the parting of their respective ways with Vigil Tripp last year. What was once known as the McCormick high-capacity frame is now the Tripp, Strayer frame, so McCormick got together with Jim Boland to develop a new 1911 frame with a sideplate on the right side. It is supposed to be capable of accepting either the standard single-column magazine, or a double-stack version of their own design that closely follows the magazine seen on the HK P7M13.

The purpose of the sideplate on the new McCormick/Boland prototype is to allow changeable trigger components. If you want a traditional single-action pistol, those parts can be installed via the sideplate, but if you want a double-action/single-action type of pistol, the sideplate also allows this change-over. I also noticed the grip portions of the prototypes were welded onto the frame after machining.

Al ("Z-Man") Zitta has helped Kleen Bore develop a new compensator system that allows the shooter to change his compensator's position, or even the compensator itself, with great ease. The system employs a male/female coupler and is innovative in its simplicity.

AMT has a new 50-caliber semi-auto pistol for those who feel undergunned. This self-loader in 50 AE represents the largest caliber permitted under domestic U.S. laws. Anything larger is considered a destructive device and must be registered as a piece of artillery, the sole exceptions being shotguns and some African big game rifles.

Beretta

Beretta unveiled their prototype Beretta 8000 in 1994, which in some ways reminds me of the Colt All American 2000. The similarity lies in the fact that the Beretta 8000, like the Colt 2000 before it, uses a rotating barrel. The 8000 rotates the barrel through use of a removable cam block mounted in the frame just above the trigger. It is a double-action/single-action design, but both Beretta 8000 examples on display at the '94 SHOT Show and the European IWA Show were obviously prototypes, because they had different backstraps and grip designs.

Kleen Bore

Another IPSC "racer" who has some interesting new products is Al "Z-Man" Zitta. Working with the Kleen Bore company, Al has developed a series of compensators that can be rotated or removed at leisure. This is accomplished with a spring-loaded coupler and a special female fitting on the muzzle of the barrel. The Kleen Bore comp allows the shooter to adjust his compensator in a manner never before possible. It also makes it easy to clean the gun after the match.

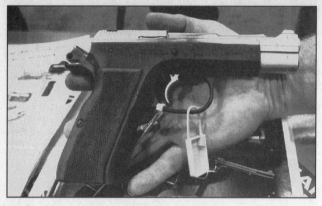

E.A.A. has a 22 rimfire conversion kit available for all E.A.A./Tanfoglio pistols. This conversion kit allows the shooter to get all the benefits associated with a centerfire gun, but also provides inexpensive practice with rimfire ammo.

A new firm called Kahr Arms had this pistol, the K9, on display. It is no bigger than a standard 380 ACP pistol, but holds 7+1 rounds of 9mm Luger. It is a double-action-only pistol with no external safeties.

At the 1994 SHOT Show, Daewoo introduced this new high-capacity 45. It has 13+1 magazine capacity and features a short trigger pull, double-action mechanism and a slide-mounted safety.

Magnum Research

Magnum Research has the new 9mm Baby Eagle Pistol. The MR 9900 FS features a frame-mounted safety and a shorter barrel than the standard MR 9900 pistol, which is now available with a frame-mounted safety under the model designation MR 9900 F. The safety system allows the pistol to be carried cocked and locked or, because it is a double-action design, carried with the hammer down and fired via the double-action trigger pull.

The barrel on the Baby Eagle FS is 3.62 inches, while the standard size has a 4.72-inch barrel. It is available in standard black or two different custom finishes—matte hard chrome and brushed hard chrome.

Action Arms

Action Arms imports the CZ line of pistols from the Czech Republic. At least, they will until September of 1994. While I was at the IWA Show, CZ representatives indicated they would be going to a new importer, but upon my return Action Arms said that while there had been disagreements over production numbers and deliveries, they thought everything could be worked out.

The new products for 1994 include the CZ-75 in 40 S&W and the CZ-75 semi-compact. The CZ-75 in 40 S&W is the same gun as before, but now the barrel sports a bigger hole. The magazine capacity is only two rounds less than the 9mm version. The CZ-75 semi-compact is a version designed for improved concealment and offers a shorter slide and a reduced grip.

The really big news at the '94 IWA was a prototype pistol

that CZ unveiled. They, too, are joining the plastic pistol crowd. They had a plastic-frame 9mm with no external safeties and a long double-action trigger pull. It was a prototype only, and the company director said no decision had been made as to whether it would be produced.

E.A.A.

European American Armory Corporation introduced a neat 22-caliber rimfire conversion kit for all the Tanfoglio series of auto pistols. This makes it possible for the shooter to enjoy both centerfire and rimfire pistol shooting, a great advantage both in terms of economic cost and range versatility.

Kahr Arms

A new company, Kahr Arms, had their Kahr K9 pistol on display. This is certainly one of the smaller 9mm pistols ever built, and it follows the example set previously by Glock in that it has no external safeties and is double-action-only. Magazine capacity is seven rounds, overall length runs 6 inches with a 3½-inch barrel, and the gun weighs 24 ounces. The prototypes looked good and handled well. It is a little gun with a lot of promise.

Daewoo

Daewoo manufactures small arms for South Korea's military. They have recently been exporting a semi-auto 9mm pistol with a "tri-action" firing mechanism. This year they introduced the DH 45, a double-action pistol with a 13+1 capacity in 45 ACP and has an empty weight of 35 ounces.

Caspian

Caspian, long known for their 1911 parts and accessories, had a new slide they manufacture exclusively for Glock guns. It is stainless steel and is combined with a hybrid ported barrel to create a compensated pistol with the same overall length as the factory gun.

Sphinx

Sphinx is a Swiss firm producing CZ-85-style pistols, but there is a difference with these guns over the many others out there—they are definitely the best available. If anything, the quality is superior to the originals. Sphinx this year has introduced the AT 2000 PS. The PS stands for Police Special, and here it denotes the decocking feature of the frame-mounted safety which has three positions: Fire, Safe and Decock. It works much like the Taurus PT-92 or some variations of the H&K USP pistol. Depressing the

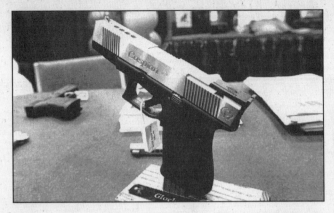

Although they are normally associated with 1911-style pistols, Caspian has developed this after-market stainless steel slide for the Glock pistols. Used in combination with a hybrid ported barrel, the slide will install on the Glock pistol without modification.

Sphinx produces fine-quality Swiss-made pistols that are similar to the original CZ-85, but the Sphinx pistols are, perhaps, even better than the originals. This year Sphinx introduced the AT 2000 PS which has a frame-mounted safety with a decocking feature.

safety-lever when on Safe will decock the hammer and render the pistol safe with the hammer down.

Sigarms

Sigarms 357 SIG made its first appearance at this SHOT Show. The cartridge, a combined effort between Sigarms and Federal Cartridge Company, is a necked-down 40 Smith & Wesson (the P229's original chambering) case to accept a 9mm bullet weighing 125 grains. No reference was made as to why it was named 357 SIG, but, apparently, this came about because its increased velocity (1350 fps from a SAAMI 4-inch standard test barrel) brings it mighty close to 357 Magnum velocity. Read all about this new 357 SIG from Sigarms in our *Handgun Tests* section.

Lorcin

Speaking in terms of economics, Lorcin advertises their products as "the world's most affordable handguns." They now have a thirteen-shot 9mm with a three-dot sighting system and lightweight aluminum alloy frame.

Ram-Line

Ram-Line, manufacturer of those popular aftermarket polymer extra-capacity magazines for 22-caliber firearms, makes an affordable 22 auto in their Ram-Tech pistol. Offered in 1994 in a new short barrel length, the Ram-Tech is available with both fifteen- or twenty-round magazines. The Ram-Tech frame is made from an almost indestructible polymer material that means this pistol will withstand heavy use for anyone, but especially for a first-time shooter.

Star

Star of Spain has two new pistols for 1994, and both look very promising. The first is the Firestar Plus. In a phrase, it is the previous Firestar with a double-column magazine. Everything else remains the same, but the weight doesn't increase significantly as it is 24.5 ounces, and the magazine capacity is now thirteen rounds in 9mm Luger.

The other new Star pistol is the Ultrastar M-205. This is another polymer product, but Star's first. It is a double-action/single-action of the traditional mode. The magazine capacity is nine rounds, and the operating controls mimic those found on the other Star double-action pistols. The slide release is on the left side within very easy reach of the shooter's right thumb, and the safety is slide-mounted and rotates down to the rear to go off Safe.

Mitchell Arms Company is the other firm producing rimfire target pistols that are similar to the old High Standard guns. This cut-away of the Victor demonstrates just how similar the Mitchell guns are to the originals.

Star representatives told us at the IWA Show they are also contemplating manufacture of the same gun with an alloy frame if there is commercial interest. The weight of the Ultrastar is 27.6 ounces.

Armsport

Armsport imports the Bernardelli line of high-quality Italian pistols. The Bernardelli P.One is available in a number of different configurations and employs a forged steel frame, slide and barrel. The magazine latch is reversible, and the pistol is available in either blue or chrome. The Bernardelli P.One is a double-action/single-action semi-auto featuring a frame-mounted safety available in both 9x19mm and 40 S&W. The magazine capacities for the two run sixteen shots in 9mm and twelve rounds in 40 S&W.

The Bernardelli PO18S is similar to the P.One, but features instead a higher capacity magazine, by one round, a matte blue finish and plastic grips.

The Bernardelli Practical VB is an out-of-the-box IPSC race pistol. Fitted with an adjustable Bomar-style rear sight, a frame-mounted gas-pedal safety, and enlarged mag release button, the gun comes equipped for the utmost in factory comp guns. The magazines have plastic factory bumper pads, and the barrel features a multi-port compensator. The magazine capacity for the Practical VB is sixteen rounds in 9mm and twelve rounds in 40.

Depending upon the legislation and how it will ultimately affect all shooters, 1994 will be the year to remember for shooters. In the meantime, the manufacturers around the world are meeting the demand for new pistols and doing it with innovation. ●

The Handgun Scene

DOUBLE ACTION

by STAN TRZONIEC

Autoloaders are fashionable, but double-action six-guns get more jobs done well, and they are as popular as ever.

EVEN WITH THE immense proliferation of new and different semi-automatic pistols in recent years, the double-action revolver is still as strong as it has ever been in the present marketplace.

One of the major reasons is the availability of revolvers in just about every cartridge made for them now and in the past. Over time, we've seen double-action revolvers made in such greats as 44-40, 45 Colt, 32-20, and the newer 357, 41 and 44 Magnums. Sprinkle in the 357 Maximum or the 445 Supermag and you certainly can't complain about choice. Power is another consideration, especially for hunters, and often to contain such brute force the revolver is the only way to go. We've seen cartridges like the 50 Magnum chambered in semi-automatic pistols, but the net result is often a gun so big and heavy that any advantage you might gain with softer recoil is overshadowed by the lack of handiness.

Yet another reason for the guns' popularity is accuracy. Sure, auto pistol proponents say the gun *can* (read expensive) be made as accurate as any wheelgun, but that's the catch. The double action, right out of the box, is still the best choice because the barrel combined with the cylinder is a straight line out to the target—no slide to move back and forth, no cartridge hopping from magazine to barrel. Scope adaptability is still easier on a revolver, with special guns made specifically for such optical use, and these are readily available from production—not custom—sources. Finally, it is still difficult today for any semi-automatic to match the quality or precision of a double-action trigger pull, especially when the shooter is using the single-action mode. The letoff, the feeling, the result—it's all there in today's modern double-action revolver.

Those words were not intended to degrade the present modern lineup of semi-automatic pistols, but to me the best way to enjoy this sport is to use the right tool at the right place and time. In the end, the shooter has the final choice, but let's see if we can just sway you a bit by offering you the best selection of double-action handguns for your consideration. The 1994 SHOT Show, I'm sorry to say, offered nothing radically new in DA technology, but you have the comfort in knowing that there is still a stable and steady supply of

A product of the Smith & Wesson Performance Center, this Model 629 Hunter has a heavy barrel with scope adaptability and barrel porting.

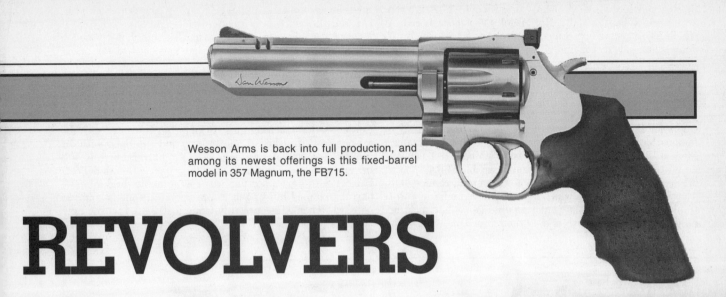

Wesson Arms is back into full production, and among its newest offerings is this fixed-barrel model in 357 Magnum, the FB715.

REVOLVERS

these very safe and traditional guns out there for your immediate use. Let me try to prove the point.

Smith & Wesson

From the master of all double-action manufacturers, at last count Smith & Wesson is still the champ with more than thirty-two models and sixty-eight very different variations chambered for everything from the 22 Long Rifle to 38 Special, 357, 41 and 44 Magnums. One gun, the Model 940, is chambered, of all things, for the 9mm Luger! And that, folks, does not even count the various models produced by their Performance Center over the course of a year in Hunter or special Defense issues. In basic form, Smith & Wesson makes guns in four frame sizes that ascend from the smallest J and move up to K, L and N that handles magnums like the 41 and 44.

Starting with the smallest (J), there is the great Model 36 in 38 Special. As a personal protection gun, it's hard to beat. Smith also makes a very special gun they call the Model 36 LS (LadySmith) for our female sector. This gun has slightly different proportions to better fit a lady's hand. Others in the line chambered for the 38 Special include Models 37, 38, 49, 60, 442, 640 and 649. Some have a concealed hammer, some different sights or grips, and are available in carbon steel, stainless steel or aluminum alloy. Also with this same frame group are models chambered for the 22 Long Rifle or 22 WMR. For hunting small game or

Whether you like to collect or buy new double-action revolvers, companies like Smith & Wesson offer much to the gun enthusiast. Shown here (from top) a nickel-plated Model 27, a blued Model 28 and current-production Model 27 complete with cut-away grip panels for speedloader use. All in all, double-action revolvers never go out of style.

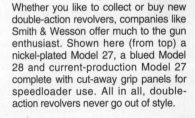

New guns like the LadySmith models are made for females who are not afraid to protect themselves. Smith & Wesson caters to this group by offering no-frills guns that have open sights and smaller grips for petite hands. This one is chambered in 357 Magnum.

light protection while fly-fishing, the Model 63 or 651 are sure hard to beat. Finally, the Model 940 is chambered in the 9mm Luger, which can serve nicely as a backup gun if your prime sidearm is one of the more popular 9mm automatics.

Next up are guns in the K or L frame size. Actually, there is not much difference between them, and there may be somewhat of an overlap within models because S&W introduced the slightly bigger L-frame to give an extra margin of safety for those shooting strictly magnum ammunition. The famous Model 10 is in this line, as are the equally popular Models 13, 14 and 15. Smith & Wesson's Model 19 has been an all-time favorite because it is fully capable of firing both 38 Special and 357 Magnum ammunition on a comfortable mid-weight frame. This was *the* gun some years back, and I think just about every law enforcement agency had most or all officers equipped with one on their hip. This writer has

made in carbon steel (blue) or stainless and may be had in the regular edition, Classic or Classic Deluxe. Barrel lengths are 4, 5, 6, 6½ or 8⅜ inches depending upon model. All Model 29s are factory drilled and tapped for scope mounting which is done by simply removing the rear sight assembly.

There are three new guns in the line that are of interest. One is the Backpacker, a Model 29 in stainless steel with a very short 3-inch barrel. Ouch! Next, from the Performance Center is the 357 Magnum K-Comp, an L-framed gun for serious work finished in matte blue and equipped with an integral compensator to help keep the barrel down during firing. Last, one of my particular favorites, is the Model 629 Hunter with barrel porting, scope adaptability and a heavy barrel. For field hunting or competition, this one is going to be hard to beat. It's currently being distributed by the Lew Horton Company.

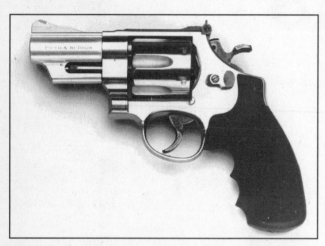

Specialized guns like this S&W Model 29 "Backpacker" make the new year interesting for those of us who may go camping or fishing in the wilds. Chambered for the 44 Magnum, it will be very comfortable on the hip with its 3-inch barrel.

With the medium L-frame, this new entry from Smith, the K-Camp, provides a more manageable gun when shooting the 357 Magnum. With a tritium dot on the front sight, this may be the ideal defense gun for many.

one that is over twenty years old and is still as tight and new as ever.

In stainless, you can choose from the Models 64, 65, 65LS, 66 (the Model 19 as a variation in stainless), the new Model 67 Combat Master Piece and in 22 rimfire as the new 617 Full Lug and the 648. In the slightly larger L-frame, we have the Model 686, almost a custom gun of sorts as the option list is very long. Complete with checkered target-style grips and adjustable sights, this is the king of mid-framed handguns from this Springfield, Massachusetts, company.

For the heavy hitters out there, you can turn to the largest or N-frame guns. The original of all magnum handguns, the Model 27 is regrettably only available in the 6-inch barrel length this year. Upon introduction years back, this was the best 357 Magnum you could buy. Smith & Wesson would allow you to pick your barrel length, sights and other options to make it a very personal gun. They even included a certificate of authenticity to prove you were the original owner. How times change. Next is the Model 657, chambered for the 41 Magnum and available only in stainless steel. The Model 625 is something of an oddball because it is chambered for the 45 ACP. While some may not appreciate its value, I find this gun really useful when hand-loaded with 45 Auto Rim brass. Reason? You don't need those blasted half-moon clips when loading this gun. Finally, the Model 29 in 44 Magnum is currently being

Colt

Further down the river from S&W, but still in "gun valley," is another benchmark of double-action quality, namely Colt's Manufacturing Company. They produce four double-action revolvers that can handle anything from 38 Special to the thundering 44 Magnum. Probably the most famous of all is the Python, a gun noted for quality, accuracy and an uncompromising trigger pull most other makers would die for. Still available in 4-, 6- or 8-inch barrel lengths, the buyer can choose from Royal Blue, stainless or the classy "Ultimate" highly polished guns. The Pythons are very rugged and get their keen looks from the ventilated barrel rib, barrel underlug and distinctive profile.

Within the same frame size is the King Cobra that has grown out of the old Trooper line. Again chambered for the 357 Magnum, the user has the choice of 4- and 6-inch barrels in three finishes much like the Python. For a working gun, the King Cobra represents good value and just might be yet another "snake" to add to your collection. Brought back after some years of absence is the Detective Special, a hideout gun with a short 2-inch barrel for either law enforcement or personal protection. Checking in at only 21 ounces and having the capability of housing six 38 Specials, this is still the choice of many with a knowledge of defensive handguns.

Top of the line is the long-awaited Anaconda in 44 Magnum or 45 Colt. Colt had a void in their line for years in

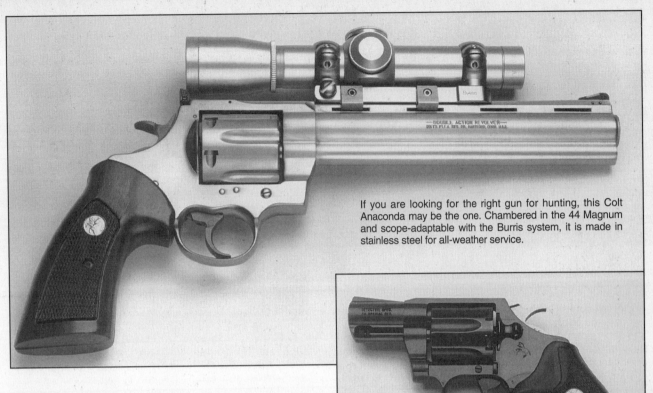

If you are looking for the right gun for hunting, this Colt Anaconda may be the one. Chambered in the 44 Magnum and scope-adaptable with the Burris system, it is made in stainless steel for all-weather service.

the large-frame, large-caliber area, but finally the Anaconda appeared, and to many it was well worth the wait. Almost an identical twin to the Python but on a larger frame, it carries the vent rib, barrel underlug, adjustable sights and a phenomenal trigger pull. My personal sample was very accurate: In a rest, it was no trouble to place five or six shots within a 1-inch circle at 25 yards.

Back by popular demand, the Colt Detective Special is chambered in 38 Special. With new grips and optional finishes, it still is a favorite of many.

For small game, the Ruger SP101 is the ideal trail gun. Here the author tries his luck plinking with the 22 Long Rifle version.

Sturm, Ruger

Sturm, Ruger is another gunmaker who has used modern technology to turn out an assortment of guns that should satisfy the most discriminating of sportsmen. Like others in the fold, Ruger depends upon frame sizes to determine chamberings and the ultimate use. Combining

innovative features in lockup, stainless steel and variety, it's hard to find a Ruger double-action revolver that you can't use!

Within the smallest series, the SP101, we find revolvers chambered for 22 Long Rifle, 32 H&R Magnum, 9mm Luger, 38 Special (+P) and 357 Magnum. Most check in at anywhere from 25 to 34 ounces with the determining factor being the barrel length, underlug or a combination of both. Made of stainless steel and fitted with rubber grips, they could be your first choice when looking for a small-frame, personal-protection handgun. Moving on, the GP100 is a slightly larger, heavier sidearm that—honest—has fifteen variations. Most are chambered for the 357 Magnum, some only for the 38 Special, but all of them feature a close lockup, fixed or adjustable sights, some with interchangeable front sights, and 4140 chrome-moly or 400-series stainless steel.

Naturally everyone has favorites, and for me it's the 44 Magnum Redhawk and Super Redhawk series. The Redhawk is a traditional double-action revolver with a normal frame/barrel configuration, Magna-style grips and barrel lengths of $5^{1}/_{2}$ or $7^{1}/_{2}$ inches. The Super Redhawk, on the other hand, has a novel extended frame for greater strength and comes with Ruger scope rings. Barrel lengths of $7^{1}/_{2}$ or $9^{1}/_{2}$ inches are offered.

Law enforcement personnel might find this particular Ruger handy as a backup gun, as it chambers the 9mm with clips. With an SP101 2-inch barrel, it is darn right handy in a pocket or purse.

As usual, the variations never seem to stop from Ruger. At the top is the GP100 in 38 Special/357 Magnum; underneath the SP101 in 22 Long Rifle. Both are made in stainless and have rubber grips.

Charter Arms

If you thought Charter Arms was defunct, be advised they are back on line and offering some exciting new revolvers. The story is worth a full-sized feature article, but, in short, they are happy to be back in full production and have twenty-seven models to prove it.

Their offerings are chambered for 22 Long Rifle, 32 H&R, 38 and, of all things, 44 Special. Known for their short, undercover-type guns, Charter offers the Off-Duty, Police Undercover and Bulldog. Most are available in blue or stainless; all have fixed sights and neoprene grips. The hammers can be either pocket or spur type, and the newest of the new, the Bulldog Pug, is termed the "lightest and smallest" 44-caliber gun on the market today. According to factory specs, this is a gun weighing 19.5 ounces with a 2½-inch barrel. By the way, inside-the-pants holsters are available from Charter for these guns, and it might be a good idea to buy one when you pick up your gun at the dealer.

Wesson Arms

Sometime back, Wesson Arms (a.k.a. Dan Wesson Arms) fell on some bad times. The founder of the company, Daniel Wesson, had passed away, and through estates and settlements, the company almost ceased operation. But Seth and Carol Wesson have brought back this high-quality company to unheard-of standards, and they offer a list of guns that make even the best wonder how they did it. I've been to the plant, and Wesson is back in full production. They offer guns in calibers from 22 Long Rifle to 445 Super Magnum, and not only their popular interchangeable barrel guns, but new for '94 fixed-barrel (FB) units as well with model numbers like the FB15 (blue 357), FB715 (stainless 357), FB44 and FB744 (blue and stainless 44s). Like others, they build guns in stainless, but their bright blue line is one to behold. The polishing and bluing is absolutely out of this world. They made me a matched pair of guns (they will do that for you, too, complete with your

If you are looking for a good value in magnum double-action revolvers, the Taurus series might be a good place to start. Here the author is shooting the Taurus Model 669 in 357 Magnum.

While some may sneer at the 44 Special's capabilities, new ammunition like CCI's Gold Dot with its huge hollowpoint can sometimes even up the score. That's a Taurus gun in the background.

Wesson Arms has their own claim to fame. With interchangeable barrels, shrouds, sights and grips, you can customize their guns to your tastes very easily.

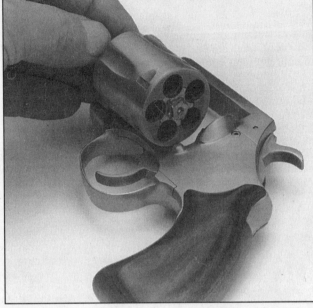

In an effort to break into the defense market, Wesson Arms introduced this small five-shot double-action revolver for those needing such a weapon.

personal serial number if you wish) that will never leave my family.

The Wesson line is a long one. In their fourteen-page catalog, they offer complete guns, barrel or shroud assemblies, frames, Pistol Pacs (that's a gun with four barrel assemblies to include 2½-, 4-, 6- and 8-inch and accessories with an aluminum case), compensated barrel assemblies, 45-caliber pin guns, service guns and brand-new fixed-barrel Hunter guns that include an Open Hunter (sights) and Scoped Hunter (no open sights but drilled and tapped for a scope) all chambered for 41, 44, 357 and 445 Super Mags. Wesson is noted for their specialized handguns, and one prime example is the 45 ACP Pin Gun. Currently, the Pin Gun has a 5-inch barrel with a 1:14 rate of twist, is equipped with the Taylor two-stage forcing cone and has a compensated shroud. And to go one step more, this unique pistol is available in blue or stainless. In addition, all guns are available with either fluted or unfluted cylinders and wood, rubber or Hogue grips.

Taurus

Taurus is another heavy hitter in the league, and while they follow in the footsteps of other makers that offer small, medium and large frame guns, there are some really innovative differences here. In 22 Long Rifle, there are the Models 94 and 96 with 3-, 4- or 6-inch barrels in blue or stainless. Still in the small frame size, the 38 Special is represented by the Model 85, a neat, tidy gun in blue or stainless. Available with or without a hammer spur (85CH), they fill a valuable niche in home-defense armament.

Medium-frame guns include sporting and hunting versions of the Models 65, 66 or 669. With full-length ribs, barrel underlugs, stainless or blued steel, and fancy target-styled Brazilian hardwood grips, Taurus now offers a most unusual twist. With the "CP" or compensated barrel versions, eight round holes at the end of the barrel cushion recoil to a most noticeable effect, especially on the magnum versions. This feature, by the way, will also be available on the newer large-frame 44 Magnum guns coming out this year.

Speaking of large-frame guns, Taurus offers both the 44 Special and 44 Magnum chamberings. With the former, you have a choice of fixed or adjustable sights, and 3-, 4- or 6-inch barrel lengths. All are five-shot guns to keep them compact for on-the-hip use. Again, blue or stainless is available. The newest version, chambered in 44 Magnum, is a first for Taurus, and we all look forward to that gun. The SHOT Show sample was a real beauty, complete with adjustable sights, compensated barrel and a choice of either 6½- or 8⅜-inch barrels. For additional piece of mind after the purchase, Taurus has a *free* repair offer on all of their guns for the lifetime of the handgun.

Rossi

Interarms imports the Rossi line of handguns, and they, too, offer the American shooter quite a choice. New for '94 are the Models 515 and 518 in both the 22 Long Rifle and 22 WMR, made of weather-resistant stainless steel. Next is the Model 851 in 38 Special which has a six-shot cylinder, novel barrel rib and fully adjustable sights. Additionally, the Model 68 (blue and nickel) and the Model 88 (stainless) are good values in the 38-caliber line. If your choice is magnums, the Model 971 might grab your attention. This is considered a medium-frame gun and comes in 2½-, 4- and 6-

In 44 Special, the Rossi Model 720 makes an excellent carry and conceal weapon called the "Covert Special." The gun is double-action-only and has a shrouded hammer for ease of handling in or out of a holster.

inch versions. On top of all this, and new this year, is the 3½-inch compensated barrel for minimal barrel lift with heavy loads.

In large calibers, Rossi offers Models 720 and 720 Covert Special. These are specially built five-shot revolvers made from stainless steel, available with (M720) or without (M720C) the hammer spur, and come in double-action-only for quick drawing out of the holster. I've personally fired these guns and can attest to their good accuracy, finish and quality.

Harrington & Richardson

An old-line company, Harrington & Richardson does not have an extensive line of double-action revolvers, but what they have represents an excellent value for the dollar, not to mention dependability and quality of fit and finish. The top of the line is the Sportsman 999, a break-open gun chambered only in 22 Short, Long and Long Rifle. It comes with either a 4- or 6-inch barrel, polished bright, and with fully adjustable sights. I can't think of a better gun on which to start a youngster. In their other division—New England Firearms—the Standard revolver in blue or stainless can be had in 22 rimfire or 32 H&R Magnum chamberings. With 2½- or 4-inch tubes, and for backpacking, the camp pot or plinking, these are guns that outlast the owner.

New this year from Harrington & Richardson is the 949 Classic Western revolver. Removed from the line for more than a decade now, this nine-shot, double-action, Western revolver is back on the scene. It features a loading gate, case-colored frame and backstrap plus a genuine shrouded ejection rod. It will shoot 22 Short, Long and Long Rifle, and comes complete with two-piece walnut-stained grip panels. This Model 949 comes with a transfer bar-type safety system with H&R proudly stating that it is "100% American made."

E.A.A.

From European American Armory comes the imported Windicator double-action revolvers from Germany. Features like a hammer-block safety; swing-out cylinder; chamberings in 22 rimfire, 32 H&R Magnum, 38 Special and 357 Magnum; adjustable sights; rubber grips; and a choice of barrel lengths make this gun easy on the checkbook while ensuring years of service.

Well, there you have it. A quick, concise rundown on what's out there for the double-action fan. The list is long for sure, but that's great for the consumer. Competition in this market is good for all, and the end result can only be a better product all the way down the line.

Long live the double-action revolver!

●

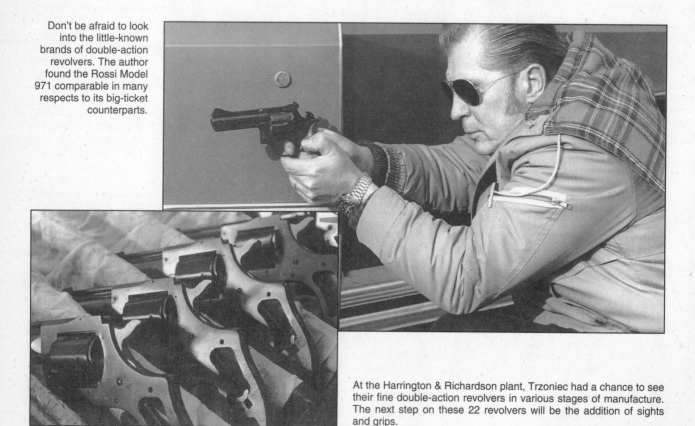

Don't be afraid to look into the little-known brands of double-action revolvers. The author found the Rossi Model 971 comparable in many respects to its big-ticket counterparts.

At the Harrington & Richardson plant, Trzoniec had a chance to see their fine double-action revolvers in various stages of manufacture. The next step on these 22 revolvers will be the addition of sights and grips.

SINGLE ACTION REVOLVERS

by JOHN TAFFIN

Old six-guns never die, they just get resurrected by Ruger, Colt, American Arms, Cimarron, EMF, and a host of others.

Taffin takes aim with Ruger's new Vaquero 45 Colt.

IN 1941 THE single-action revolver died. A few tears were shed, but many were willing to say, "There, that's the end of that!" and be perfectly happy with modern double-action six-guns and semi-automatics. Only one single action was in production then, the 1873 Colt SAA, and with the coming of World War II, production capacity at Hartford was needed for war-time firearms. Only generals like George Patton and Skinny Wainright considered the old Colt suitable for battle; at least they were the only ones with enough rank to get away with packin' one.

The Colt had been in continuous production for sixty-eight years, and since sales hadn't been all that good anyway, the final chapter was finished and the book closed. Well, almost. In 1953, America discovered television in a big way, and much of the black-and-white screen was filled with B-grade Westerns of the 1930s and 1940s. Hoppy, Gene and Roy each made a comeback, and viewers, this then-young teenager included, went nuts over Westerns.

Then there was a young genius in Southport, Connecticut, who stunned the old established firearms firms with the 1949 introduction of a totally new 22-caliber semi-automatic pistol. It was styled after the German Luger and offered at an unbelievably low price. That fellow read the market well, and the Ruger 22 rimfire Single-Six arrrived a short time later. This single-action six-gun was so successful that by 1955 a Los Angeles company, Great Western, was making Colt replicas. In 1957, while working for the magnificent sum of 90 cents an hour, I bought a brand-new, fresh-from-the-factory Colt Single Action Army 45 for $125. The single action was back!

Replicas from Italy joined the Ruger and Colt guns, and the result forty years later is that the single-action six-gun is stronger than ever and definitely here to stay. A mini-

Anyone thinking 45-70 is big need only to take a look at Century's 50-70. Bats, I do believe, could roost in that cavernous barrel.

Century Arms' huge 45-70 five-shot single action is built on a brass frame.

mum of twelve companies either manufacture or import centerfire single actions and, in many cases, simply cannot keep guns in stock. They go out as fast as they are made or received from Europe. What the TV Western did for six-gun sales in the 1950s, handgun hunting and cowboy action, and even just plain good common shootin' sense, are doing for single-action six-gun sales in the 1990s.

American Arms

In addition to blackpowder revolvers patterned after the 1847 Walker, 1851 Navy, 1860 Army and 1858 Remington, American Arms also imports the Buckhorn and Regulator single actions. Buckhorns are built on a larger frame than the original Colts and are chambered for the 44 Magnum. The Regulator in blue, engraved or nickel models comes in 357 Magnum, 44-40, and 45 Colt in standard barrel lengths of 4³/₄, 5¹/₂ and 7¹/₂ inches. The big bores are available as dual-cylinder models with 44 Special and 45 ACP cylinders offered as options.

New from American Arms is one of the slickest little six-guns to come from the Old Country in many a year. The Regulator is now available with a bird's-head grip in either the standard model with ejector rod housing or a shorter barreled Sheriff's Model without an ejector rod. The bird's-head grip gives the old single action a completely new personality and feel. A Sheriff's Model 45 Colt may look like something out of the 1870s, but I know of more than one peace officer and legally licensed citizen now carrying a Sheriff's Model "Colt" as their concealed six-gun.

Century Gun Distributors

Big is beautiful at Century, and this Indiana firm specializes in 6-pound six-guns chambered for rifle cartridges. Five chamberings are available: 30-30, 375 Winchester, 444 Marlin, 45-70 and 50-70. Barrel lengths are 6¹/₂, 8, 10 and 12 inches. Unlike all other six-guns, the Century is not only huge, but the frame is of manganese bronze rather than the

Century's 45-70 single action almost dwarfs this Colt SAA 45.

standard blue or case-colored finish. Sights are ramp front with a Millett adjustable rear.

Having fired the Century extensively in 444, 45-70 and 50-70, I can attest to the fact that this is a lot of gun and very comfortable to shoot in either 444, which I consider best left in a lever gun, or 45-70. Full-house loads in 50-70 are serious to say the least. My own Century is a 45-70 version and a real attention-getter whenever I bring it out.

Cimarron Arms

Before Cimarron, there were the spaghetti Westerns. Not only were the movies made in Italy, the six-guns used in them were also made there, and it showed. With their brass backstrap and trigger guards, and what appeared to be painted-on case coloring, those early "Colt" replicas did not look like Colts SAs at all. Nor did the classic single-action grip feel classic. Enter Mike Harvey and Cimarron and the beginning of a campaign to upgrade the replica single action. This was not only to make it authentic, but also to build it as well as, or better than, those old 19th-century Colts.

A pair of imports: Mike Harvey's Cimarron 44 Special (top) and Boyd Davis' EMF 38-40.

The new Thunderer imported by Mike Harvey's Cimarron Arms. This one is in 45 Colt.

One only has to look at today's offerings from Cimarron and realize that Aldo Uberti-made guns are superb examples of the replica maker's art. Now you have to look twice to make sure the replica is not a true Colt. Cimarrons are offered in standard blue and case coloring of the original, and in nickel or very bright but fragile charcoal blue finish. All standard barrel lengths are offered in 357 Magnum, 44 Special, and the authentic original calibers—45 Colt, 44-40, and 38-40. Sheriff's Models and Storekeeper's Models are also offered.

New from Cimarron this year is the Thunderer. They reached back into history and lifted the grip frame of original Colt double-action six-guns, the 38 Lightning (favored by Billy the Kid) and the 41 Thunderer. Mate this double-action grip frame (with its traditional hump at the top of the backstrap) with a 3½- or 4¾-inch blue or nickel Single Action Army and the Cimarron Thunderer is the result. Grips are one-piece walnut with fine checkering, and the whole package is quite pleasing to the eye as well as the shooting hand.

The Thunderer is available in 357 Magnum, 44 Special, 44-40 and 45 Colt. This is a 19th-century design that will carry well into the 21st century in the holsters and waistbands of dedicated six-gunners.

Colt's Manufacturing Co.

The original Colt Single Action Army, known to collectors now as a First Generation gun, ceased production in 1941, only to be resurrected as the Second Generation in 1956. When the machinery finally wore out, these were removed from production and replaced by the Third Generation six-guns in the late 1970s/early 1980s. After a short run, these also were taken out of production, but consumer demand has resulted in the return of the Colt single action as a Colt Custom Shop offering.

Currently, these revolvers are cataloged in 45 Colt and 44-40 with barrel lengths of 4¾ or 5½ inches, and in blue/case-hardened or nickel finish. Other barrel lengths are

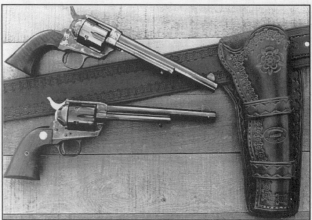

Cimarron's 7½-inch (top) and Colt's 7½-inch, both 45 Colt chambered, with Bull-X Chaparral holster and belt.

available on special order. Newly announced and, hopefully, available as you read this is the first run of 38-40s since before World War II.

Of particular interest to blackpowder shooters is that the blackpowder Colts are back with four models being offered: the 1847 Walker 44, 1849 Pocket Dragoon 31, 1851 Navy 36 and the 1860 Army 44.

European American Armory

The Bounty Hunter, imported from Germany by E.A.A., is made by the Wiehrauch facility in a beautiful pastoral setting outside of Mellrichstadt. Visiting this facility two

European American Armory's Bounty Hunter with Black-Ti finish. Serial number is "JOHN 001." This one was made for our writer.

EMF offers standard barrel lengths of 4³/₄, 5¹/₂ and 7¹/₂ inches on Hartford models in 32-20, 38-40, 44-40, 45 Colt, 357 Magnum and 44 Special. The Bisley model is in 45 Colt only.

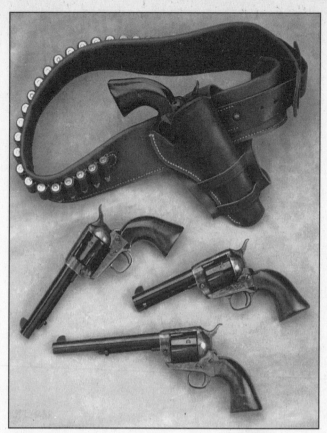

EMF Hartford Models and their cartridge belt/holster rig.

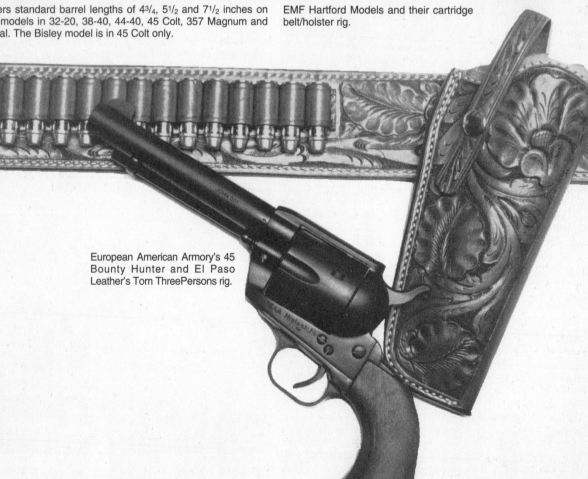

European American Armory's 45 Bounty Hunter and El Paso Leather's Tom ThreePersons rig.

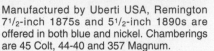

Manufactured by Uberti USA, Remington 7½-inch 1875s and 5½-inch 1890s are offered in both blue and nickel. Chamberings are 45 Colt, 44-40 and 357 Magnum.

EMF's 38-40 shown with Red River belt and holster—a right good-looking combo.

years ago, I was able to shoot the Bounty Hunter prototype in 357 Magnum equipped with a 2x scope. Before I left, I placed an order for the first 45 Colt Bounty Hunter, and a few months later it came, a 5½-inch-barreled gun with serial number JOHN 001.

The Bounty Hunter is a large-frame single action with a transfer bar safety allowing it to be safely carried with six rounds. Present chamberings are 357 Magnum, 41 Magnum, 44 Magnum, 44-40 and 45 Colt, in the three standard single-action barrel lengths. With my heavy 45 Colt load, *for large-frame six-guns only*, of BRP's 305-grain gas-checked bullet over 21.5 grains of WW-296, this gun will group into 1⅝ inches at 25 yards at a very respectable 1015 fps. Recently, the gun was sent off to Ti-Gold to be plated in their Black-Ti finish that will help with cleaning, as my Bounty Hunter has now been relegated to hunting use with blackpowder cartridges.

EMF

Armi San Marco produces some fine replica six-guns that arrive on these shores as the Hartford Model under the EMF banner. In fact, one example fitted with Colt hard rubber grips looks more Colt than a Colt! The Hartfords are offered in three traditional barrel lengths and in 357 Magnum, 38-40, 44-40, 44 Special, 45 Colt and, hooray for EMF, 32-20 as well. New to the line is a bird's-head-gripped Hartford with a 4-inch barrel known as the Pinkerton and an ejectorless 3-inch called the Sheriff's Model.

Not new, but back this year after a few years' absence, is the excellent Bisley Model in all three standard barrel lengths and 45 Colt only chambering. The Bisley is joined

by the newly offered 7½-inch Remington Model 1890 in 44-40 and 45 Colt. These were originally offered by Remington with a 5½-inch barrel length only.

Freedom Arms

Probably the finest, and certainly the strongest, six-guns ever manufactured come out of the Star Valley in Wyoming and bear the Freedom Arms logo. Actually, these guns are really five-shooters, built tank-tough and engineered with Swiss-watch precision. Now into their second decade of production of the 454 Casull, Freedom Arms has added chamberings in 44 Magnum, 22 Long Rifle and 22 WMR in the Model 252, and 357 Magnum in the Model 353. The 252 gives new meaning to accuracy in a 22 wheelgun, and the Model 353 allows heretofore unheard of velocities in a 357 Magnum revolver.

All Freedom Arms guns are built of stainless steel, and cylinders are line-bored to match the barrel and frame of each particular revolver. No mass production here. Freedom Arms' latest offering is their Model 555 that gives us the 50 AE semi-automatic cartridge in a precision revolver. CCI's Lawman 50 AE with its 325-grain hollowpoint bullet does 1342 fps from a 7½-inch barrel and will put its five rounds in 1-inch at 35 yards. Samson's 300-grain softpoint ammunition will stay in 3 inches at 90 yards using the spare tire carrier of my Bronco as a rest.

Mitchell Arms

Tradition is the word at Mitchell Arms with "Colt" replicas being offered in a Cowboy Model with blue finish and brass grip frame, and in 357 Magnum and 45 Colt, both

Freedom Arms' 7¹/₂-inch 50 AE topped with Leupold's 4x scope in Jim Herringshaw's Maxi-Mount.

Freedom Arms' new 50 AE handled mighty nice according to our writer.

with the gunfighter-favored 4³/₄-inch barrel length. A special Cowboy Model in full nickel finish, and in 45 Colt with an extra 45 ACP cylinder, is Mitchell Arms' Bat Masterson Model. Legendary lawman Bat Masterson ordered a special Colt Single Action Army in 1885 with a barrel that was even with the ejector rod housing, nickel finish, special front sight and gutta percha grips.

With a 5¹/₂-inch barrel, the Mitchell Arms single action becomes the U.S. Army Model also available in blue or nickel and both 357 Magnum and 45 Colt. All models wear one-piece walnut grips.

This 45 Cavalry Model is imported by Mitchell Arms.

Navy Arms Co.

For as long as I can remember, Val Forgett of Navy Arms has been providing shooters with replica blackpowder arms. My first Navy Arms six-gun, an 1858 Remington 44 cap-'n'-ball, goes back over thirty years, and I have been shooting a pair of nickeled 1875 Remingtons in 45 Colt and 44-40 for nearly twenty years. In addition to a complete line of blackpowder six-guns and rifles, Navy Arms offers upgraded "1873 Colts" in both blue and nickel finishes in 4³/₄-, 5¹/₂- and 7¹/₂-inch barrel lengths and in 44-40 or 45 Colt. Both calibers are also available as a 3-inch Sheriff's Model.

For military buffs, Navy Arms offers special 45 Colt single actions in 5¹/₂-inch Artillery and 7¹/₂-inch Cavalry Models, complete with arsenal markings and inspector's cartouches. The 1875 and 1890 Remingtons are also available in the same 45 Colt and 44-40 chamberings.

New this year from Navy Arms, and long awaited by single-action six-gunners, is the first replica Smith & Wesson six-gun. Yes, before they became known as the company that built double-action six-guns by which all others are judged, Smith & Wesson made an extremely fine single action. At the 1993 SHOT Show, I tracked down a rumor that the Smith & Wesson Schofield of the 1870s was about to join the swelling ranks of single-action replicas. S&W's

Roy Jinks attested to the fact that the rumor was true and sent us off to the Navy Arms booth. Val Forgett informed us that the Schofield was, indeed, being made by Uberti and would be imported under the Navy Arms banner with shooting models available by late summer. Summer came and went. Fall did the same, and as winter led us into 1994 and the SHOT Show, there were still no Schofields available.

That has now changed, and the hit of the 1994 Show was the first Uberti replica of the Schofield. Both Uberti USA and Navy Arms had real walnut and steel models available for touching, fondling and drooling. My heart did the fast beat normally reserved for Colts and, lately, the Uberti-made replicas. The Italians have done their finest work on the Schofield six-gun.

For a little history, the Schofield was designed by U.S. Army Major Schofield as an improvement on the Smith & Wesson Number Three single action and to compete with the Colt Single Action Army. The top-break Number Three carried the latch on the topstrap and required the use of two hands to operate, a luxury not always available on horseback. Schofield redesigned the latch and placed it on the frame in front of the hammer, allowing its operation with the thumb of the shooting hand. The latch was released, the

Navy Arms' reproduction of Major George W. Schofield's Number Three Schofield which was introduced in 1875 and produced until 1877. Total production was 8969 revolvers. All went to the U.S. Army, except 685 which were sold to civilians. Navy Arms changed the cartridge from 45 S&W, a shorter version, to 45 Colt.

(Clockwise from upper left) The Ruger Vaquero with BluMagnum grips, Colt SAA with BluMagnum grips, Cimarron Calvary, Colt SAA and Cimarron New Thunderer are all chambered to accept 45 Colt cartridges. The holster and cartridge belt set is from Cimarron.

Ruger 44 Blackhawk cylinder compared to Century 45-70 and 50-70 cylinder. Big cartridges do require b-i-g cylinders.

barrel and cylinder pivoted forward, and all six cartridges ejected simultaneously.

The original Schofield was chambered for a 45 "Short Colt" known as the 45 Smith & Wesson, as opposed to the longer 45 Colt, or 45 "Long Colt" used in military-issue guns. The Army purchased both Colt SAAs and Schofields, and issued a 45 cartridge that would work in both. While the short 45 would chamber in the Colt, the 45 Colt would not fit the 45 Schofield. This caused not a few problems when troops found themselves issued Schofield six-guns and 45 Colt ammunition.

It has taken more than 100 years, but that problem has now been addressed, and the new Schofield is built with a longer cylinder and frame chambered for both 45 Colt and 44-40. Both of the models on display at the SHOT Show were in 44-40.

The Schofield is a much more intricate gun than the Colt and required no small expenditure of money and engineering talent to bring to fruition. Both display models were well fitted and finished and, quite simply, beautiful revolvers. Present plans call for both blue and nickle finish and either the standard 7-inch military or Wells Fargo 5-inch barrel lengths. All models should be available as you read this.

These modern Schofields are stronger than their original counterparts, but I cannot stress strongly enough that these are not six-guns for the experimenter. Loads should be kept at present factory levels or lower, and I would not think of trying to hot rod them in the slightest.

Ruger

The company that modernized the single action with the first coil springs and a nearly unbreakable lockwork in its 22 Single-Six in 1953, followed by the adjustable-sighted, flat-topped 357 Blackhawk in 1955, then the 44 Magnum Blackhawk in 1956, has now taken giant backward steps forward the past two years with the introduction of more traditionally styled single actions to warm the hearts of cowboy action shooters and die-hard traditionalists.

First came the Vaquero, a New Model Blackhawk with fixed sights, a case-colored frame and chambered in 45 Colt. Then came high-polish stainless versions, all with a choice of 4⅝-, 5½- and 7½-inch barrel lengths. Though I haven't yet seen any as of this writing, the Vaquero is also to be offered in 44 Magnum and 44-40 chamberings.

Following the Vaqueros came three more "traditional" single actions. Announced in 1993, but still not seen, was the resurrected Bearcat which was dropped more than twenty years ago. The newest Bearcat has a longer cylinder and frame to allow an auxiliary 22 WMR cylinder, and will be available in stainless as well as blue finish.

The newest offerings from Ruger are fixed-sight models of the Old Army and Single-Six, both available in blue or stainless. The original Single-Six wore a windage-adjustable rear sight, and the Old Army has always carried fully

Ruger's New Model Super Blackhawk 44 Magnum with high-gloss stainless finish. Barrel lengths offered are 4⁵/₈ (above), 5¹/₂ and 7¹/₂ inches.

Fixed-sight New Model Single-Six Ruger rimfire is available in blue or high-gloss and 5¹/₂- or 6¹/₂-inch barrel lengths with an extra cylinder—this 22 shoots 22 Long Rifle and 22 WMR.

Ruger's Old Army muzzleloading revolver, with fixed or adjustable sights, is offered in blue or stainless steel. Barrel length is 7¹/₂ inches. Yes, it is a 45: bore diameter .443-inch, groove .451-inch. The suggested pure lead ball or conical is .457-inch.

adjustable sights. Finally from Ruger comes the announcement that 357 Magnum, 45 Colt and 44 Magnum Blackhawks with adjustable sights will be offered in a high-polish stainless finish. Actually, a better term is high gloss, as these are not polished by hand but rather go through a procedure much like brass cartridge cases are tumbled for a bright finish.

The New Model high-gloss 4⁵/₈-Blackhawks in 45 Colt and 44 Magnum are particularly attractive and make especially practical packin' pistols. The 44 Magnum is cataloged as a Super Blackhawk, but comes with the standard Blackhawk grip frame.

Ruger continues to offer their small-frame Bisleys in 22 and 32 Magnum, and big-bore Bisleys only with the 7¹/₂-inch barrel in 357 Magnum, 41 Magnum, 44 Magnum and 45 Colt. Editor Hal Swiggett disagrees with me, but I think the Ruger Bisley grip frame is one of the finest ever offered. It addresses a serious problem I have had, namely getting knuckle-dusted by the Super Blackhawk grip frame.

Texas Longhorn Arms

Tradition with a twist are the watchwords at Texas Longhorn Arms. Master gunmaker Bill Grover has taken the Colt single action built up by Elmer Keith in 1925 and modernized it to his specifications. Grover claims Colt was left-handed, so his Improved Number Five is a mirror image of a gun with the loading gate and ejector rod housing on its left side. This allows right-handed shooters to keep the gun in their right hand while loading and unloading.

Grover's Improved Number Five is a 5¹/₂-inch 44 Magnum, and after many years of backorders, Grover is in a new shop and filling orders. In addition to the Improved Number Five, the company offers the West Texas Flat Top Target Model that I consider one of the finest single actions ever offered.

My particular West Texas Flat Top Target started life as a 7¹/₂-inch 44 Special. Grover requested I send it back to him, and he fitted it with two more cylinders in 44-40 and 44 Magnum. I was able to successfully use the gun on a hunt with Grover in the Texas hill country, taking an animal with each cylinder.

All of Grover's guns are built for right-handers. In addition to the two models mentioned, Grover also offers the Border Special and the South Texas Army.

Shown shooting the Texas Longhorn Arms Improved Number Five 44 Magnum, the author is a great fan of this Bill Grover gun.

Texas Longhorn Arms' 44 Magnums: 5 1/2-inch Improved Number Five and 7 1/2-inch West Texas Flat Top Target.

The author took this Catalina goat while hunting in the Texas Hill Country. His six-gun—Texas Longhorn Arms' 44 Magnum.

Remington 1875 replicas from Uberti and imported by Navy Arms.

Uberti USA

Last, but certainly not least, is Uberti. Not only does Aldo Uberti supply replicas to Cimarron, EMF and Navy Arms, to name a few, they also provide replicas under the Uberti USA banner. A trip through the Uberti model line will bring heartfelt joy to any six-gunner. First come blackpowder guns, Patersons, Walkers, Dragoons, 1851 and 1861 Navys, 1860 Armys, and those first pocket pistols, the 1848 Baby Dragoon, 1849 Pocket, Wells Fargo, Pocket Navy and 1862 Police. These are followed by the Remingtons in blue and stainless with fixed or adjustable sights.

Then come cartridge single actions, known as the 1873 Cattleman. Not to be confused with the Iver Johnson imports of twenty years ago, these examples are totally upgraded and fine spittin' images of the original 1873 Colt Single Action Army. All standard barrel lengths are offered, in blue with case colors or nickel finishes, and also an ejectorless Sheriff's Model with 3-inch barrel. They're offered in 357 Magnum, 38-40, 44-40, 44 Special, 45 Colt and 45 ACP. All carry finely fitted one-piece walnut grips. For those desiring something a little bigger and more powerful, the Buckhorn 44 Magnum is available.

New this year are two models already mentioned. Cimarron's Thunderer and Navy Arms' Schofield Model are both produced by Uberti. The Thunderer is also available from Uberti USA in 44-40, 44 Special, 45 Colt and 45 ACP with 3 1/2-, 4- and 4 3/4-inch barrels with ejector rod housings, and a 3-inch model without ejector rod.

Also new this year is the 1890 Remington, a model without the 1875 web under its barrel, and with 7 1/2- and 5 1/2-inch barrels, both with lanyard rings and steel trigger guard. These are chambered in 357 Magnum, 44-40, 45 Colt and 45 ACP.

Fifty years ago, as World War II ended and Colt announced it would not resume manufacture of the Single Action Army, not even the wisest sage among us could look forward to today and see the tremendous interest in these revolvers. Nor could he forecast the proliferation of models from 22 mini-guns that weigh a few ounces to 6-pound 50-caliber six-guns. The resurrected single action is here to stay, and may it be a great part of the handgunner's battery well into the 21st century. ●

The Handgun Scene

SINGLE SHOT

by MARK HAMPTON

Single-loaders are the ticket when you need just one well-placed shot for hunting, or extreme power or surgical accuracy.

WHY WOULD ANYONE in their right mind want to use a single shot handgun when the availability of revolvers and semi-automatics with multiple-shot capability is almost overwhelming? Well, there is a certain mystique surrounding the single shot handgun. Perhaps it's the lure of filling a deer tag with one well-placed shot, or maybe it's the thrill of knocking over a steel ram from 200 meters in competition. Besides the psychological or emotional reasons for a love affair with single shots, there is also some hard-core evidence, based on facts, why the outdoorsperson should "want" to use these handguns. First of all, single shots are very dependable, regardless of the application, environment or conditions. Many single shots are chambered for bottleneck rifle cartridges capable of delivering large payloads of lead to very specific locations. Yes, these handguns are extremely accurate. Depending on the gun, scope and cartridge combination, many of these fine rigs are capable of outperforming a pile of rifles. Some of the ones I've shot recently will shoot minute of angle on a consistent basis. Folks, that's 1-inch groups at 100 yards, 2-inch groups at 200 yards and, yes, 3-inch groups at the end of three football fields put together. That's using a rock-solid rest, naturally, and my shooting ability has little to do with the groups. The hardware is doing all the work. So, would you like to own a handgun capable of doing a variety of chores from recreational shooting to competition and hunting? Let's take a look at what's new in the single shot lineup.

Thompson/Center

Thompson/Center's Contender has been around for over twenty-five years and needs no introduction at this point. This versatile gun is currently chambered for nineteen calibers including the 410-gauge shotshell. Available in both stainless steel and blue, the T/C is offered in a variety of barrel lengths in seven basic styles.

The only new caliber offering this year is the 300 Whisper, a wildcat based on the 221 Fireball case using a 30-caliber bullet loaded to the same overall length as the 223. SSK Industries will have dies, and Cor-Bon will supply factory ammo in 125-, 150- and 220-grain weights to get started. Ballistics should equal or exceed 30-30 Winchester

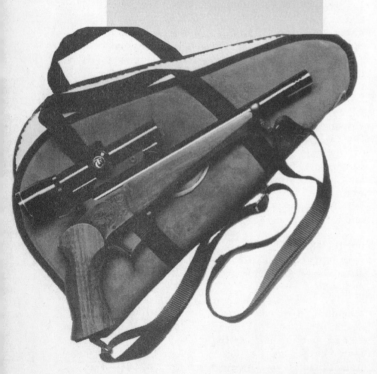

Thompson/Center also offers a "Hunter Package." It includes the pistol, a mounted scope, their muzzlebrake, a sling and carrying case.

PISTOLS

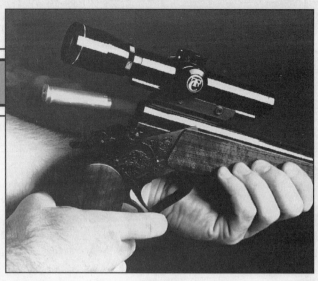

Thompson/Center now offers ejector barrels for their great Contender pistol. It is designed to lift the case back out of the chamber, for those so desiring, or to eject that empty.

factory loads with the same barrel length. I was very skeptical about this offering when Ken French, president of Thompson/Center Arms, came hog hunting with me here in Missouri. To make a long story short, Ken took the biggest tusker on the ranch, an honest 300-pounder, with one well-placed shot. The Nosler 165-grain BT entered just behind the shoulder and exited on the opposite side. Impressive, indeed. If I hadn't seen this incident with my own eyes, I wouldn't have believed it possible. The shot was somewhere around 25 yards and the pig offered a perfect broadside target.

T/C has also equipped some of their 14-inch Hunter barrels with a new automatic ejection system. Available in 30-30 Winchester, 7-30 Waters, 375 Winchester and 45-70, these special barrels will completely throw the empty case out of the chamber. By releasing the trigger guard before the gun is completely broken, it reverts back to partial ejection. When holding the trigger guard rearward until the T/C is completely broken, total ejection of the case is achieved. I'm anxious to try these barrels out in cold weather when my manual dexterity is a little slow.

It's no big secret that the Contender has been one of my favorite hunting handguns for many years, and still is today. This past deer season I carried a stainless 10-inch 44 Magnum around the woods. Using Black Hills 300-grain ammo, this makes a fine close-range whitetail, blackbear or wild hog combination. Other contender fans should look into joining the Thompson/Center Association.

BF Arms

The BF pistol was designed by Bert Stringfellow and had its beginning in the silhouette game. Even though guns from the old BF Arms had a reputation for the actions slamming shut, misfiring, poor sighting systems and being downright ugly to look at, they held an excellent track record in the accuracy department. The single shot falling block design is fairly basic and simple, and the new maker, E.A. Brown Co., has made several improvements in the gun worth mentioning.

First, the grips and forend have been redesigned by Herretts. This move has enhanced the cosmetics as well as

Mark and his wife Karen with an outstanding gemsbok taken with an SSK Industries custom barrel on the Thompson/Center frame.

improved the handling qualities. A custom match-quality barrel from Douglas or Wilson and chambered by Bullberry Barrelworks is now standard. Jim Rock of RPM produces the quality iron sights for the silhouette shooters. Triggers have been improved drastically with standard production guns, running from 12 to 16 ounces. The muzzle crown lets gas escape equally all around the bullet base, ensuring less effect on the bullet, and since BF pistols aren't made on an assembly line, barrels are carefully turned concentric to the bore to ensure a proper crown. All of these handguns include a ram's-head etching on each side of the receiver with premium guns having gold-plated triggers.

For the convenience of competitors as well as handgun hunters, all of the BF guns now have six holes for their tri-

BF Pistols are the brain-child of Bert Stringfellow and are aimed (forgive the pun) at silhouette shooters. E. Arthur Brown now manufactures this falling block design and has vastly increased its models—make that its use.

angle force scope mounts or Scope Rib Sights. They have receiver sight holes for RPM as well as Williams Sights.

It's plain to see these guns have seen some major improvements. The company now offers over sixty chamberings, with or without their muzzlebrake, in blue, electroless nickel or new "French Gray" finishes. The folks at BF Arms are not only manufacturing a handgun, they are selling accuracy, with a guarantee of placing five shots into an inch group at 100 yards, for one year. Sounds like these folks are fairly confident.

Remington

Bolt-action fans have an excellent choice in the Remington XP-100 lineup. Although there is nothing really new for this year, there are a couple of offerings for IHMSA competitors and handgun hunters alike. The XP-100 has now been around for thirty years and is truly a powerful, long-range handgun.

Remington's Silhouette model combines a walnut stock with a 10½-inch barrel chambered for 7mm BR. The stock allows the shooter to grip the gun with one or both hands, yet permits the Creedmoor-style position. The Silhouette comes factory equipped for competition or hunting with adjustable sights. Most hunters I know mount quality optics on these bolt-action beauties.

The XP-100 Hunting Model comes with a 14⅜-inch barrel and wood stock chambered for 223 Remington, 7mm BR, 35 Remington, and, my favorite, the 7mm-08, a superb white-tail cartridge. The gun is drilled and tapped for scope mounts. If you like bolt-action rifles because they are dependable and accurate, you will enjoy the XP-100 for many of the same reasons.

Competitor Corp.

Another unique single shot handgun comes from the Competitor Corp. It seems to have all of the ingredients to do well in the silhouette or hunting arenas. The extremely strong rotating cannon-type breech mechanism allows over 135 possible chamberings, including magnum rifle rounds. The breechblock assembly is located at the rear of the barrel. The barrel is fastened to the stock. The rotary breechblock locks the cartridge into battery, with the action being cocked when rotated, functioning much like a bolt-action rifle. Barrels are available with or without sights, in three lengths: 10½, 14 and 16 inches.

The safety is described as dual. One safety is located in the trigger. A sliding thumb safety in the rear locks the sear. When pushed down, an S tells you it is on safe; pushed upward, the F shows the gun is ready to fire.

Varmint hunting is a great way to get ready for a big game hunt. Mark used his XP-100 223 topped with a Bausch & Lomb 4x scope to take this groundhog.

Remington's XP-100R bolt-action pistol is offered in seven chamberings from 22-250 through 35 Remington. To separate it from their other single shot, the "R" indicates repeater.

Marvin Friedman (from Arad, Israel) took this big South Texas wild hog with a Herrett-stocked 35 Remington XP-100.

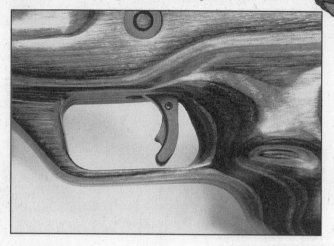

Al Straitiff's Competitor cannon-breeched pistol is offered in at least 135 chamberings—from 17 through 458 Winchester.

Competitor's "other safety" is in its trigger. The pistol can not be fired without pressing this little insert on the face of its trigger.

Three grips are available in synthetic, laminated or a very attractive natural wood. All grips are ambidextrous, so left-hand shooters won't feel left out in the cold. The single-stage trigger is adjustable, too.

One unique design that you don't see every day on a handgun is that this pistol is only 1⅛ inches longer than its 14-inch barrel. A muzzlebrake is optional, and I recommend one for the hard-kicking rounds.

The Competitor comes from the hands of Al Straitiff and is a modestly priced handgun with interchangeable barrel capability. Mounted with quality optics, this should make a fine handgun for the field.

M.O.A.

Another surgically accurate single shot that got its start in the silhouette game is the M.O.A. Maximum. The falling block design found on the M.O.A. makes this handgun capable of nearly unlimited chambering possibilities. Several years ago, I carried an M.O.A. chambered in 250 Savage, and during the winter months I nailed quite a few coyotes with factory Winchester ammo, out to 200 yards or so. A Burris 2½-7x scope aided the process and usually stayed on the 4x setting. I probably could have taken a few more varmints if I just could have remembered to flip the safety switch—that's the mechanism that allows the hammer to fall on the firing pin. I'm a little slow, but after three or four big fat coyotes got away, I caught on real quick.

The handgun comes in 8¾-, 10½-, and 14-inch barrel

lengths with over thirty standard chamberings from 22 rimfire to 454 Casull. My test gun weighed just over 5 pounds with scope and the 14-inch tube. Receivers are drilled and tapped for scope mounts. Walnut grips are available with left- or right-hand thumbrest. The grips on my test gun were smooth on both sides and comfortable to

A good rest is necessary to get the most from any firearm. Here, John Reinhart demonstrates his stainless shooting sticks.

The M.O.A. pistol has built a fine reputation in silhouette shooting and hunting. It is offered in most chamberings suited to its lifestyle.

shoot. Barrels are interchangeable, and if you're buying a used example, just make sure the serial number on the barrel matches the number on the receiver. Prices start at $622, new.

Magnum Research

When shooting Magnum Research's Lone Eagle, the first thing I learned was the importance of ear protection. I thought it would be interesting to play with the Lone Eagle in one of my favorite whitetail deer hunting cartridges, the potent little 308. And it was. Believe it or not, recoil was not a serious problem, especially when equipped with their new muzzlebrake. It tames recoil considerably.

The action, while simple, is a rotary breech, cannon-type design accepting a variety of calibers from 22 Hornet to 444 Marlin. The breech ring rotates clockwise 105 degrees from the locked position to open. It will kick the empty brass out even in cold weather conditions.

The 14-inch barrel assemblies come drilled and tapped for both open sights and universal one-piece scope base, both available from Magnum Research. I mounted a 2½-8x Leupold on my test gun and conducted most of the shooting with the scope set on 4x.

The stock assembly is black in color and made of GE Valox. The trigger comes from the factory set at 5 pounds, but I feel groups could be improved with a lighter pull. I like the cross-bolt safety system found on the Lone Eagle. And for a gun weighing a little over 5 pounds with a scope mounted, it balanced very nicely, not uncomfortable to shoot in the least bit.

This rugged handgun is very affordable and pleasant to shoot. If it were deer season here in Missouri, I would take the gun with me to one of our deer towers and wait for that magic moment. I have faith in this combination of Leupold scope, Lone Eagle and Winchester's 150-grain Supreme ammo, if I will just do my part.

RPM

No stranger to the silhouette world, the XL by RPM is available in over forty calibers from 22 LR to 45-70. My test gun was a 375 Winchester. The XL has really shined in the past, capturing many national championships in IHMSA silhouette competition, NRA Hunters Pistol, Long Range Pistol, and even 22 LR matches.

The author testfires a 308-caliber Lone Eagle pistol from Magnum Research. His target? Yonder rock 150 or so yards out there on a pond dam.

The hinge-type action of the barrel cocks the gun when it's opened. Barrels come in 8 to 14 inches, and the 375 Winchester I was shooting had a muzzlebrake which helped tame recoil. Sights are fully adjustable, and barrels are drilled and tapped for a Weaver base mount. I mounted a Burris 3-9x to check for accuracy. Shooters can exchange many different barrels and calibers on one action.

This gun is always on safe until the shooter depresses the safety-lever. If it is not fully depressed, the safety will catch the hammer and will not allow the firing pin to strike the primer. The trigger pull is adjustable, and I found it easy to shoot consistent groups, even with the potent 250-grain factory Winchester offering, with a light 2-pound trigger pull.

The XL is very accurate and reliable. Jim Rock, the man behind the gun, has been nominated for the Outstanding American Handgunner Award this year. No doubt, Jim has done all of us handgunners a big favor by producing an outstanding pistol.

Ithaca

Ithaca Acquisitions has announced their break-open single shot dubbed the Model 20. It comes in 22 rimfire and 44 Magnum this year, with 10- and 12-inch barrel lengths. I spoke with Eric Neill, spokesperson for Ithaca, and he informed me the company would like to offer two new calibers every year. The gun is equipped with rifle sights, but barrels are drilled and tapped at the factory. The walnut grips that came on the gun were attractive and allowed good control of the test gun. I like the interchangeable barrel system, and the price is quite good at $381 for the two-barrel set.

A unique feature I like about this gun is that it won't close with the hammer cocked, ensuring safety. Another interesting feature is that it has only one firing pin for rimfire and centerfire chamberings. I'm told this gun will be available in June of 1994.

As you can see, the single shot fanatic has quite a selection, whether it's for informal target shooting, silhouette competition or hunting. The single shots simply cannot be beaten in terms of performance, dependability, accuracy and sheer ballistics of powerful cartridges. Find one you like, learn to shoot it safely and properly, and you will receive years of pleasure and enjoyment. I promise. ●

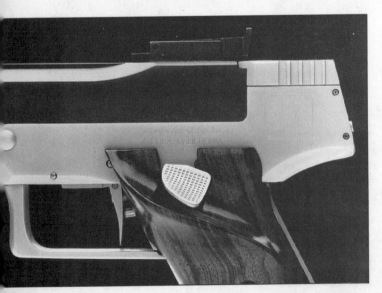

This lever, maybe button is a better description, must be depressed with the thumb to fire XL pistols. A built-in safety for sure.

HANDGUNS 95

SECTION 2
Handgun Tests

A new cartridge and gun, Swiggett reports, page 36.

Ferguson examines Ruger's latest offering, page 46.

The FEG 380 was tested by Murbach, page 77.

FEDERAL'S
FOR SIG-SAUER'S

by HAL SWIGGETT

SIG-SAUER P229 SPECIFICATIONS

Importer: Sigarms Inc.

Action Type: Semi-automatic, Locked-breech, Double-action

Caliber: 357 SIG (40 S&W necked-down)

Capacity: 12+1

Overall length: 7.08 inches

Barrel length: 3.86 inches

Empty Weight: 32.5 ounces

Finish: Matte black stainless steel

Sights: Fixed (windage adj.) White dot front and rear

Grip: Stippled black polymer

Price: $875

WOULD YOU BELIEVE: Thirteen 125-grain 357 SIG bullets spewed out of a barrel barely a fraction of an inch short of 4 inches—without reloading?

SIG-Sauer's P229 autoloader started out as a 40 S&W, but now has a stablemate chambering on that same case that Federal, and SIG, call the 357 SIG. It is so designated on their headstamp—"FC" on top, then "357 SIG" around the lower portion.

I'm not all certain how it acquired the 357 nomenclature, because a pulled bullet mikes .353-inch according to my Lyman dial caliper. Its weight is 125.5 grains. A 9mm bullet for certain, regardless of the name it wears.

But first about the pistol. The slide is blackened stainless steel, I mean black-black and totally non-reflective. A mighty fine finish, for sure. The frame is a lightweight alloy, also black. The grips are of a stippled synthetic material measuring 1.280 inches at their widest point, very comfortable in my size 7 hand. The sights are a square notch rear with a white square directly underneath. Up front there is a white dot.

The double-action P229 weighs 32.5 ounces on my postal scale. Unfortunately, I couldn't check its trigger pull because my scale recently gave up the ghost. The pull, however, is not even a little out of line for a double-action pistol. It's long, but not hefty. In single action, it is downright good—even excellent, and better, by far, than a lot of revolvers coming off assembly lines nowadays.

There is no safety. To lower the hammer, press the drop lever firmly to its bottom and you will feel a "click;" release it and the hammer safely drops to the full rest position.

The twelve-round double-stack magazine has witness holes numbered five, ten and twelve for quickly determining how many rounds it contains. A round in the chamber makes it a thirteen-shooter.

Should there be any negative thoughts concerning bottleneck cartridges in an autoloader, forget them. Bottleneck autoloading ammo is not new. Frank C. Barnes, in his *Cartridges of the World* (DBI Books, Inc.), 7th Edition, page

NEW 357 SIG
P229 AUTOLOADER

216, lists the 5mm Clement auto cartridge as originating in Spain in 1857 for "the obscure Charola-Anitua auto pistol." He goes on to say, "In 1903, the Belgian-made Clement auto-pistol was adapted to this round and this resulted in the change of name. The cartridge is listed in the 1904 and 1934 DWM catalog (No. 484) and was loaded in Germany until about 1938. It was replaced by the more effective 25 ACP."

Take a look at the 30 Luger, along with several other early military autoloaders. More recently, think about Harry Sanford's fine 357 Auto Mag, now collector material.

SIG-Sauer P229 black stainless 357 SIG 12+1 autoloader weighs 32.5 ounces and wears a 3^{15}/$_{16}$-inch barrel.

Federal's cartridge and its headstamp.

That's it in the center: 10mm, 40 S&W, 357 SIG, 357 Magnum and 9mm, left to right.

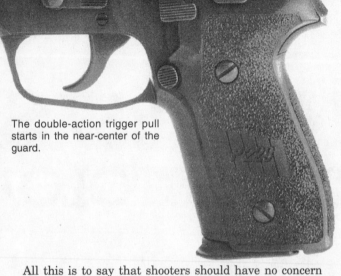

The double-action trigger pull starts in the near-center of the guard.

A wide square notch in the center of the rear sight...

...matches up with a round white dot up front. Both are windage adjustable.

The single-action pull starts way back here and has a surprisingly clean, crisp let-off.

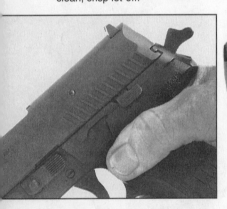

Fully depress the oblong, deeply serrated thumbpiece directly above the magazine release button until it "clicks." Release it and the P229's hammer safely drops. There is no safety—other than this feature.

The 357 SIG's magazine holds twelve rounds, making it a thirteen-shooter when fully loaded.

All this is to say that shooters should have no concern about a necked-down 9mm/40 S&W bottlenecked case called 357 SIG. The ammo is manufactured by Federal.

I don't know who brainstormed this 357 SIG, but Federal and Sigarms got together a year or so ago, settling on the 40 S&W case necked-down to accept 9mm bullets. Why or how it acquired the nomenclature, 357 SIG, makes little difference.

SIG-Sauer's P229 is long-proven and found faultless in every instance of which I know. The manufacturer's name comes from a joint venture between SIG (Schweizerische Industrie-Gesellschaft), Neuhausen, Switzerland, and long-established J.P. Sauer & Sohn based in Germany.

Sigarms, importer of SIG-Sauer pistols, provides documented evidence that their 357 SIG cartridge outperforms 9mm Parabellum, 40 S&W and 45 ACP rounds, not only in velocity but also with regard to energy in foot pounds. Their load starts its 125-grain bullet at 1350 fps, as opposed to the 9mm 124-grain at 1220, 40 S&W's 180-grain at 985 and the 45 ACP's 185 at 950 fps.

As for energy, it's the same story: 357 SIG 125-grain at 510 fpe, 9mm 124-grain at 410, 40 S&W at 390 and 45 ACP at 370 fpe. Rifling twist, by the way, is 1:16 inches, a bit slower than the P229 in 40 S&W.

Testfiring from a machine rest at 25 yards produced 0.7-inch groups, according to literature supplied by Federal. I don't intend to improve on that with my 73-year-old cataract-implanted eyes. Their literature goes on to read, "Three five-round groups with maximum average extreme spread of 2.0 inches at 50 yards, using a Mann Rest Test System."

Chamber pressure, according to Federal, averaged 40,000 psi per ten rounds. Federal's muzzle velocity of 1350 fps comes from a 4-inch SAAMI standard test barrel.

Since SIG-Sauer and Federal have given their cartridge the 357 SIG name, I take it to mean they have confrontation in mind—comparing it to 357 Magnum handguns. The P229 wears a 3.86-inch barrel, so I tested it against a 4-inch Colt Python and a Coonan 357 Magnum autoloader, which has a 7+1 capacity and weighs 45 ounces. Colt's Python is a six-shooter and weighs 39½ ounces.

Since the new 357 SIG is currently offered only with a bullet weight of 125 grains, my choice was to run it against

Remington's 125-grain semi-jacketed hollowpoint. It was the only 125-grain load on my shelves. Its velocity is listed at 1450 fps. I assume this to be from a test barrel, but have no idea as to the length.

My initial thought was that this new 357 SIG just might outrun comparable 357 Magnum loads from a comparable barrel length revolver. Three five-shot strings through my Oehler 35P screens averaged 1387 fps from the Python, with a high of 1392 and low at 1382.

Then I shot three five-shot strings out of the P229. They averaged 1333 fps, with a high of 1349, and low at 1309. Its bullet style, by the way, is "Jacketed Hollow Point Lead Slug," according to information from Federal.

What this shows is the 4-inch Python outran the SIG by 54 fps, in spite of an even 100 fps difference between the two in their factory literature.

357 SIG COMPARABLE BALLISTICS TEST

Handgun	Factory Load/ Bullet Wt. (grs.)	Factory MV (fps)	—Five-shot MV (fps)— High	Low	Avg.
P229	357 SIG/125	1350	1352	1349	1347
Colt Python	357 Mag/125	1450	1392	1382	1387
Coonan	357 Mag/125	1450	1537	1518	1537

The Editor during his visit to SIG's plant, Neuhausen, Switzerland, June 7th, 1971.

The Coonan?

Bear in mind that it has a 5-inch barrel and autoloader configuration, meaning the cartridge is chambered in the barrel (no cylinder gap). With that same 125-grain Remington load, the average of three five-shot strings, I hope you are ready for this, was 1537 fps, a whopping 87 fps above Remington's listing of 1450 fps. Though I've owned this Coonan autoloader a long time, it's been shot very little, but with this "tale of Oehler's tape," it just might make a few trips close at my side.

As this is written, I know of no handloading data for 357 SIG, and no dies with which to use it should there be any.

My guess is this little SIG-Sauer P229 in 357 SIG will find a ready and very willing market. It is light, compact and, in spite of its load, surprisingly easy to handle. For as far back as I can remember, my shooting hand has worn a leather glove, but I found the recoil of this little rascal to be exceptionally light for its performance and didn't need the protection.

If that isn't enough, look at it as 357 Magnum-capable from less than four inches of barrel with thirteen shots on tap.

Some might think of it sort of like having your cake and eating it, too. ●

While testfiring Sigarms P229 357 SIG, recoil was so minimal Hal didn't bother with his usually present Chimere Shooting Glove.

SIG-Sauer's P229 is alongside the Editor's P 210-5 with its extra-length barrel. These P 210-5 autoloaders are often referred to as "the Cadillac of autoloaders"—no slight at all against the P229. There is a trememdous difference in price. Currently, P 210 SIG pistols are imported by Mandall Shooting Supplies, Scottsdale, Arizona.

Since its name is 357 SIG, the Editor chronographed it with a Coonan 357 Magnum 5-inch autoloader and 4-inch Colt Python. His Oehler Model 35P tape told the story.

SMITH & WESSON'S

by FRANK JAMES

S&W SIGMA SPECIFICATIONS

Manufacturer: Smith & Wesson

Model: Sigma, Model SW40F

Caliber: 40 S&W (9mm Luger for Model SW9F)

Slide Length: 7.4 inches

Overall Height: 5.6 inches

Overall Width: 1.3 inches

Sight Radius: 6.4 inches

Barrel Length: 4.5 inches

Barrel Rifling: Left hand (Right hand for the 9mm SW9F)

Rate of Twist: 1:16 (1:18.75 for the 9mm SW9F)

Magazine Capacity: Fifteen rounds (seventeen rounds for the 9mm SW9F)

Empty Weight: 26.36 ounces

Weight Fully Loaded: 34.63 ounces

Trigger Pull: 8 to 10 pounds

Length of Pull: .300-inch

Suggested List Price: $593.00

"WHERE'S WALDO?" IS a popular series of children's books with page after page of cluttered, highly detailed, multi-scene drawings. The objective is to search out the singular figure of "Waldo" among the *many* shown on each page. The name "Waldo" is part of the title of these books, and it is also the name of Smith & Wesson's latest secret product development.

Project Waldo was the final step in the development of a new handgun from Smith & Wesson. It is *not* a Fourth Generation version of S&W's current standard-frame semi-auto pistols, rather it is Smith & Wesson's *first* polymer-framed pistol.

It's name is *Sigma,* and it is the result of a team effort at Smith & Wesson to meet the market demand for a law enforcement/self-protection pistol that is lower in cost and lighter in weight than S&W's previous semi-auto pistols.

It will obviously compete directly with an import from Austria which goes unnamed in presentations made by Smith & Wesson's marketing people, but is referred to simply as the "G-gun." S&W feels that, with the Sigma, they have taken the technology of polymer-framed pistols to the next higher level.

In 1992, Smith & Wesson formulated a marketing analysis as part of a mandated mission statement. The objective was to define the purpose of the company—to make a profit.

A number of things became apparent under this self-scrutiny. The first was they felt the market share for their revolvers was favorable, but there were a number of problems with their semi-automatic pistols.

Smith & Wesson Third Generation pistols were suffering a declining market share, and after interviewing a number of customers, management found their product line was confusing the consumer. (Remember the whiz wheel calculator intended to clarify their maze of model numbers, calibers and extra features?)

Other problems plagued their autoloading pistols as well. There had been too many changes and far too many recalls. The FBI fiasco with S&W 10mm guns did nothing to brighten the polish of their public image.

In response to these difficulties, they formed a team with-

NEW SIGMA

This is serial no. XXX0001, the first Sigma pistol. Although it has all the necessary parts (except for the lower trigger half in this photo), it was not intended to be a firing model. It is just the first assembled working model.

The Sigma design team at Smith & Wesson produced this plastic and Lucite model as they worked toward building the basepad for the Sigma's magazine.

in the company and began work on a new, totally different kind of pistol. Several things were required of this new gun.

It had to have a clear Smith & Wesson identity, both cosmetically and intellectually. They did not want the identity of this product to infer an "ultimate" product, but yet it had to represent a clear departure from past S&W guns.

There were more than 200 names submitted to identify this newcomer. The project name was "Waldo," but the commercial name candidates were wide ranging. We were shown a few of them, and while many borrowed heavily from the names used to identify high-quality automobiles from around the world, that was not true with all of them.

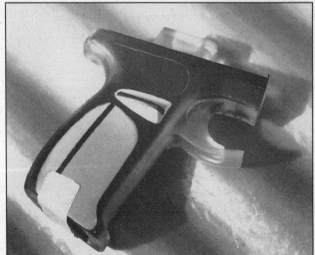

Through use of "human factor analysis," Smith & Wesson worked hard to determine the best grip shape for the new Sigma pistol. This model represents the final shape chosen, one of many made in their search.

The Smith & Wesson Sigma is a polymer frame, high-capacity pistol. It has a trigger-activated safety system and represents a complete departure from Smith & Wesson's previous semi-auto pistol models.

The magazine release on the Sigma is made from polymer and the release button is teardrop shaped. Some of the shooters at the introduction experienced difficulties when they failed to apply a perpendicular force to the release, and the magazine catch trapped the magazine in the grip.

The rear sight on the Sigma is a new design and not the excellent Novak Lo-Mount rear sight. While this sight tries to copy many of the design features of the Novak sight, it doesn't have as distinctive a blade face.

The front sight is plastic, and this, in the opinion of the writer, is a deficiency on the new Sigma, especially for a law enforcement pistol.

Unlike the pistol from Austria, the S&W Sigma doesn't have a safety-lever protruding from the trigger face. It is a trigger activated safety and works through application of a hinged, two-part trigger.

One of the funnier suggestions was "Relentless Redeemer."

This project was named Waldo because of Dean Speir, and his former pseudonym of "Waldo Lydecker." Dean writes a weekly industry intelligence column in *Gun Week* and is reknowned for his exposés of various secret endeavors within the industry. The name of this gun in its prototype phase is simply an indication of their concern (paranoia?) for his possible success. Hence, the question among those working on the project remained, Where's Waldo?

Project Waldo only started a year before introduction, but it was actually the final phase of an ongoing search over a number of years for a different auto pistol within Smith & Wesson. The first project name was "Leader," then "Cop Gun," followed by "Phoenix," "Viper" and "Waldo." Each gun was a different attempt to establish something new and practical for the market.

Smith & Wesson started looking at polymer frames in 1986, and one of the first things done was to machine a copy of the single-column 9mm S&W frame from a polymer compound. It didn't work, but they wanted to verify the stresses involved.

The next project ("Leader") had a fixed barrel in 45 ACP and was blowback operated. It also utilized a viscoelastic dampener to control recoil. Chief Engineer Kevin Foley explained its dismissal by saying, "It satisfied the engineers, but it wouldn't have the customers."

Back to the drawing board. The buzzword in engineering

S&W SIGMA 40 S&W BALLISTICS TEST

Cartridge	Bullet Wgt. (grs.)	Type	Avg. MV (fps)	ES (fps)
Winchester	155	FMJ Match	1131	52
Winchester	155	Silvertip	1161	23
Winchester	180	FMJ (White Box)	955	36
Hornady	155	XTP-HP	1191	72
Hornady	180	XTP-HP	1007	71
Black Hills	155	JHP	1086	49
Black Hills	180	JHP	952	32
Speer CCI Lawman	155	Gold Dot HP	1214	22
Federal Hydra-Shok	155	Hydra-Shok	1148	48
Remington	180	JHP	958	16

ES = Extreme Spead. All testing used ten-shot groups. Chronograph was an Oehler 35P. Air temperature was 62 degrees F, at 676 feet above sea level. Chronograph was ten feet from muzzle of pistol.

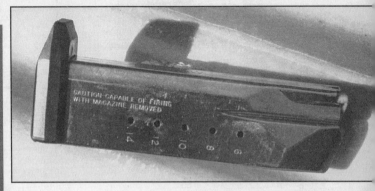

The magazine is a new design and holds fifteen rounds of 40 S&W ammo. The 9mm version holds seventeen rounds. The magazine is made from carbon steel and then given an electroless nickel finish containing Teflon.

The Sigma field-strips for cleaning down to four major components, not counting the magazine. The recoil spring is captured by the guide rod. The field-stripping procedure is identical to the one used on the Glock.

circles today is "concurrent engineering." It means something is designed with a combination of high quality and low price, but not necessarily using the products from the lowest-priced bidder. Smith & Wesson developed the Sigma through application of concurrent engineering.

Their suppliers for this pistol were pre-selected. There was no multiple-bid process used to select the best bid. Neither were any models prepared in S&W's own model shop. Most of the components of the Sigma are manufactured by suppliers outside the Smith & Wesson factory. Only the stainless steel barrel is made there.

Smith & Wesson designed the Sigma primarily for the law enforcement market, with the sporting consumer being solely a secondary market. The primary calibers had to be 40 S&W and 9mm Luger. They wanted a product that would demonstrate ease of operation—no manual safety, no decocking lever and no magazine safety. And they wanted a product that demonstrated superior ergonomics.

To achieve the latter, they retained a consultant on "human factor analysis." They studied the hand sizes of approximately twenty-five people within the company while developing hand size profiles. They built a wooden wing-nut gun that resembled in no small way the "try-guns" used by English gunmakers to build a stock for the perfect fit to the customer. They analyzed the different web angles of the human hand, as well as the average trigger reach.

As a result, they established that the Sigma pistol would have a grip angle of 18 degrees. Additionally, it has two different thicknesses in the grip area to better accommodate the shooter's hand. It is thinner in width above the thumbrest than it is below. Without question, the grip on the Sigma is more comfortable than the G-gun's.

A decision was made to use a striker firing mechanism because this permits greater design freedom. A hammer-activated firing pin system requires more space and, in many instances, raises the pistol's height above the shooting hand.

The Sigma comes in its own polymer box which can be secured with a padlock. This box also serves as the shipping container from the supplier to Smith & Wesson. As shipped, the frame has the trigger components already installed. The recoil spring is captured by the polymer guide rod, and it, too, is shipped in the same box from the supplier to the factory prior to final assembly. If you examine the box, you will notice a small tray above the pistol's slide. It is there to hold the guide rod and spring assembly during shipment to the factory from the outside supplier.

Smith & Wesson gathered a number of gun writers at a resort near Fort Lauderdale, Florida, for the introduction of the Sigma in early March, 1994.

We were taken in the afternoon to the Markham Park range for our first shooting session and given a briefing on the various characteristics of the gun by Smith & Wesson's professional shooter, J. Michael Plaxco.

We weren't allowed to just pot a few rounds as we would have preferred, but rather we had to follow a number of simple drills to get acquainted with the handling characteristics of this new polymer wonder.

As it comes out of the box, the Sigma is a lightweight gun, and despite its differences with the "G-gun," it still resembles the Glock in concept.

Like the Glock, the Sigma uses a trigger-activated safety system, but instead of a protruding lever sticking out away from the trigger face, the Sigma uses a two-piece, hinged trigger to guarantee safety if the gun is dropped.

When pressure is applied to the face of the trigger, the lower half moves rearward slightly, disengaging the internal "trigger safety." As pressure is increased on the trigger, an extension of the trigger moves the striker rearward, compressing a spring.

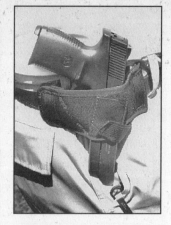

Weighing only 26 ounces, the new Sigma is easy to carry.

The author shot the gun extensively at its unveiling, and found it very controllable. Upon firing, notice the ejected case near his head and the small amount of felt recoil evidenced by the gun, which is already back on target.

When the striker has moved far enough rearward, it is automatically released and flies froward to strike the primer, firing the gun.

As the slide moves rearward about ¼-inch, the disconnector is forced downward by the camming surface on the bottom of the slide. This allows the sear to recover back into position to catch the striker when the slide comes forward. As the slide continues its rearward travel, the spent case is extracted and ejected.

Whenever the trigger is released, the striker safety plunger locks the striker, and the gun cannot fire.

The trigger action was specifically designed to mimic that on the double-action-only Third Generation Smith & Wesson auto pistols. The movement of this trigger is limited to only .300-inch of travel. The listed trigger pull weight is anywhere from 8 to 10 pounds, but Kevin Foley said the ones they checked were running around 8¼ pounds.

The barrel on the Sigma is stainless steel, and it features a left-hand 1:16-inch twist in 40 S&W. The 9mm model features a right-hand 1:18¾-inch twist. The barrel locks to the slide via the forward edge of the barrel's chamber block, engaging a corresponding edge on the slide opening for the ejection port.

The slide is carbon steel and is machined from bar stock.

It is coated with the U.S. equivalent of Tenifer—Melonite.

The sights are Smith & Wesson's own design, and in a departure from those found on the current guns, they are *not* Novak Lo-Mount rear sights. Instead, these new sights have three white dots.

A true weakness on the Sigma, in my opinion, is the installation of a *plastic* front sight with a single white dot. For a pistol designed primarily for the law enforcement market, a plastic front sight is a design denial of the law officer's reality. At some point in a police gun's career, it is going to land on the concrete, and if this one lands on its front sight, it will break and disappear. That is not a good idea, and it doesn't matter if Glock's are also plastic. It still isn't a good idea.

The Sigma rear sight tries to achieve the same features offered by the Novak sight. It is smooth and ramped, but the blade face offered to the shooter is not as distinct as the Novak, and experienced shooters will note the difference.

Shooting the Sigma revealed a trigger pull I thought was heavier than the stated 8¼ pounds. Under concentrated study, I noted a slight, almost imperceptible glitch midway through the trigger stroke. You could actually hear the trigger bar lift the striker safety plunger, before completing the trigger pull.

The gun shot well at short distances. I found my sample shot slightly to the right and a little high. The problem was in the way I worked the trigger and gripped the gun. It was designed for centering in the web of the shooter's hand, and for the pad of the trigger finger to be placed squarely in the center of the trigger face. Due to my foreshortened trigger finger, I can't do that and wound up pulling on the side of the slightly too-wide trigger. Doing so pulled the groups to the right, but I could never figure out why they were going slightly high.

My grip on the gun may have been part of the problem, but I noticed throughout my testing I had a tendency to push the front sight up after recoil, thereby raising my groups.

We used Federal's 180-grain Hydra-Shok during our range session, not pussycat ammunition by anyone's definition. Yet, the gun was easy in recoil. It really was comfortable. No problem whatsoever, and that's more than I can say about some of this pistol's competitors.

Mike Plaxco warned us about coming off the trigger during our rapid-fire sequences, but I did it anyway and, in the process, felt trigger slap on a couple of occasions. I checked with some of the other shooters on the firing line and determined I was the sole one to experience this effect, so all I can say is it was my fault and not the gun's.

The magazine is a new design. Surprisingly, for a polymer-framed gun, it is a metal magazine held in place with a polymer catch assembly. Usually when that happens, the edges on the window eat the magazine latch to the point of severe damage, but S&W, in a secondary operation, polishes the edges on the window so there is nothing to damage the polymer.

The magazine release is located in the appropriate location at the junction of the trigger guard and grip. It has a teardrop shape and is protected by the ridge cast into the grip as a thumbrest. Some of the shooters had trouble with binding of the release during magazine changes, but I didn't. I just pushed in with a positive motion, even if I had to break my grip to reach the button properly. The magazines fell freely from the grip.

The magazine on the 40-caliber pistol holds fifteen rounds, and it has a substantial baseplate. A more subdued or flat baseplate is available as an option to make the pistol easier to conceal. Attention was paid by the designers to the stacking of the rounds to guarantee there was a 45-degree angle between them. If the angle is allowed to be wider or narrower, the rounds will put side forces on the tube walls, and the feeding action of the magazine becomes sluggish.

The magazine body is made from carbon steel, at the supplier's request, and has an electroless nickel coating containing Teflon.

Overall, I like the Sigma, but there are a few things I don't care for in the design. I don't like the plastic front sight, and I'm not real wild about the polymer guide rod and captive recoil spring. It's been my experience that most don't work, and at some point, they will all break and/or malfunction.

In fairness, though, company engineers suggested that all springs in any pistol be replaced every 2500 rounds.

The Sigma is a light pistol, and it's going to prove to be an easy one to carry. Smith & Wesson has done their homework in terms of the grip shape. It is almost that most elusive of all things—one size that fits all. And the gun is a simple design. It contains only forty-two parts, and I am one who believes the fewer the parts, the better the reliability. This gun has the look and feel of a winner.

Project Waldo is now the Smith & Wesson Sigma. My guess is it will prove to be extremely popular...and successful as well.

●

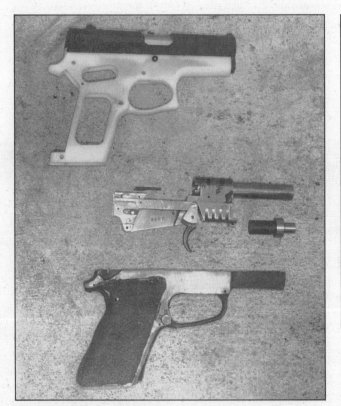

The pistol at the top is the design prototype that had its standard-size frame machined from solid polymer. The lower pistol is the "Project Leader" pistol that was a 45 ACP, had a fixed barrel, and used a viscoelastic dampener for the slide in recoil.

These solid polymer models allowed Smith & Wesson engineers to explore the stresses and other factors affecting this new pistol's design through use of CAD/CAM computers. It is a little slower up front, according to Kevin Foley, but it really saves on the back end. They no longer need to build 'em and then bust 'em.

Handgun Tests

NEWEST FROM

by TOM FERGUSON

RUGER KP94 SPECIFICATIONS

Action: Self-loading; recoil, tilting barrel, link actuated as in M1911A1; double and single action with short throw 45°; safety/decocking levers on both sides of the slide.

Construction: Hard-coated A356T6 aluminum alloy frame, 400-series stainless steel slide and barrel

Finish: Non-glare, matte finish

Caliber: 9mm Luger/9x19m Parabellum (suitable for +P+ ammunition)

Barrel Length: 4¼ inches/108mm

Rifling: 6 groove; 1:10/254mm; right-hand twist

Cartridge Capacity: Fifteen-round staggered column

Safety: Manual ambidextrous safety-levers that, when engaged, push the firing pin forward into the slide, out of reach of the hammer. At the same time, the firing pin is locked firmly in position, preventing forward movement, only then is the hammer decocked.

Sights: Front blade with white dot, rear notch with two white dots, rear sight drift-adjustable for windage. Radius is 5¼ inches

Grips: 6123 Xenoy resin grip panels with non-slip checkered pattern.

Weight unloaded: Approx 33 ounces/935.53 grams

Overall Length: 7½ inches

Suggested Price: $520

IN THE BEGINNING, nearly a hundred years ago, autoloading pistols were carved from solid steel. Firearms designers were cost-conscious even then, but the truth was that even master machinists were paid relatively low wages, and there was little incentive to reduce production costs. The result was that designer and machinist had free rein to exercise their imaginations, and this produced some very fine handguns. The Luger pistol dates from the turn of the century and is a masterpiece of the machinist's art. The Colt M1911 falls into this category as well. During the decades that followed, retail prices rose with wages, but the manufacturing processes remained virtually the same.

By the 1960s, this labor-intensive method of gunmaking was drawing to an end. In the firearms press, shooters began reading of new methods of manufacture which include casting, metal folding (stamping) for frames and slides, and the use of synthetic materials. The actual machining of steel

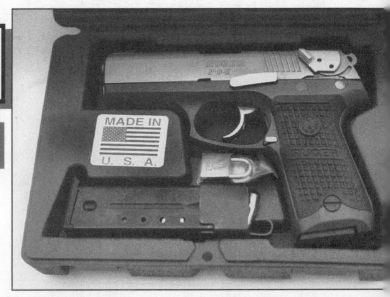

Ruger's new P94 9mm comes with a hard plastic case, extra magazine and loader, and a lock to secure the pistol.

RUGER: P94 9mm

was held to a minimum. The technology was new, or newly adopted from other areas of manufacture, and there were some failures. Most of the mistakes were hastily corrected, however, and today's autoloading pistols are well made, accurate and even more reliable than the revered designs of the past. The single area in which they don't compare well is size. In fact, most modern service-type pistols are larger, bulkier and seemingly more awkward to handle than their predecessors.

Sturm, Ruger & Company, Inc., has directly addressed this problem with its newest autoloader, the P94. This gun is sized mid-way between the bigger P-series and the compact P93, with a grip dimensioned for the shooter who may have small hands. Oddly enough, it doesn't handicap shooters with large hands.

The P94 is available in 9mm Luger and 40 S&W, both of which are favored in law enforcement and defense work. Later, Ruger plans to market the P94L which is equipped with a laser sighting unit forward of the trigger guard.

The P94 has an alloy frame finished in a gray matte color. The material is aircraft-grade aluminum, with heavy slide rails to handle any factory ammo. The slide is stainless, also with a matte finish. At the rear are seven grooves cut deeply to aid in drawing the slide back, and these extend over the top of the slide. The manual safety is slide mounted and ambidextrous. It's the "push-forward" Ruger type with a grooved thumbpiece—shoved upward it puts the pistol in firing mode and exposes a red warning dot. Thumbed downward is safe, with a benevolent white dot showing. The manual safety-lever also acts as a decocker and will drop a cocked hammer. It should be noted this system has the advantage of allowing a cartridge to be chambered or withdrawn from the chamber while the safety-lever is on "Safe."

Thus, while loading or unloading the P94's chamber, there can be no accidental discharges. The decocker provides one-hand return to a safe position after firing, which disconnects the trigger. There is also a passive firing pin block. The P94 can't fire accidentally, even if dropped on the

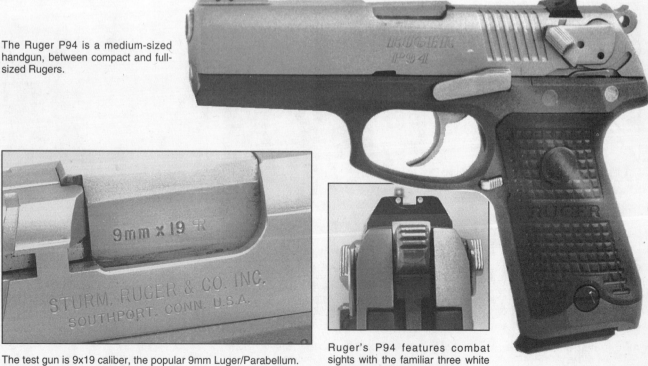

The Ruger P94 is a medium-sized handgun, between compact and full-sized Rugers.

The test gun is 9x19 caliber, the popular 9mm Luger/Parabellum.

Ruger's P94 features combat sights with the familiar three white dot configuration.

The Ruger P94 slide release is in the usual M1911 position on the left side.

The P94's magazine release is ambidextrous and pushes forward to release the magazine.

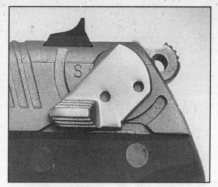

The safety is ambidextrous. Pushed forward, it goes up to fire. Thumbed downward, it will safely drop a cocked hammer.

hammer. There is no magazine safety, however, and the pistol will fire with the magazine removed. This is in keeping with the preferences of a majority, who want to be able to fire the gun as a single shot if the magazine is lost or out of the gun. The two magazines supplied with the P94 carry stick-on labels warning that the P94 will fire with the magazine removed.

The slide release is M1911-style on the left side of the frame. The magazine release is ambidextrous, and pushing forward on the tiny wedge will drop the magazine free of the gun.

The grip area shows the most obvious size reduction in the P94. Although the capacity in 9mm Luger caliber is fifteen rounds, the grip thickness is less than most high-capacity autos, and more nearly resembles "single-stack" pistols. The grip panels are of checkered black Xenoy resin, nearly indestructible, and inletted into the frame to reduce thickness. Trigger reach from backstrap to trigger face is less than 3 inches. Shooters with small hands will find it a more comfortable gun to handle than most "Lotsashots" in 9mm.

Operation of the P94 is of the short recoil, tilting barrel, link-actuated design. The test gun was in 9mm Luger caliber, and the barrel shroud is marked "9x19" to further designate that cartridge. This is a standard DA/SA pistol, with the first shot double action and the remainder fired in single-action mode. From single action, the hammer throw is a short 45 degrees, making for snappier ignition time.

The double-action trigger pull weighs 9 pounds, while in single-action mode the hammer drops at 5. When fired single action, the trigger requires a long takeup, having lots of slack. The sear doesn't release until the trigger is nearly pressed to the frame. To some shooters this may prove annoying, but it won't actually hinder accuracy. Less skilled persons have been given a built-in safety factor because the long takeup prevents premature firing.

In contrast to a couple of decades ago, there are now many good 9mm loads on the market. A recent import from Brazil, MagTech Recreational Products, Inc., offers ammunition in all popular calibers, including some rifle rounds. The P94 was loaded with 124-grain FMJ loads carrying

As a former police officer, the author approves of Ruger's P94 9mm, but prefers their 40 S&W version.

San Antonio Police Officer Charles Burns wears a Glock 40 S&W, but finds the Ruger P94 easy to handle.

The author has a mild objection to the long trigger takeup, or slack, found in the Ruger P94.

RUGER P94 9MM BALLISTICS TEST

Manufacturer	Bullet (grs./type)	Avg. MV (fps)
MagTech	124/FMJ, brass plated	1014
MagTech	115/FMJ	1052
Sure Fire	115/JHP	1232
Black Hills	124/JHP	1109
Black Hills	147/FMJ	899

The Ruger P94 in 9mm is a trim, slick-handling pistol with a fifteen-round magazine. Note the heavy slide rails; the Ruger is rated for +P and +P+ 9mm ammo.

Officer Josie Galindo finds the new Ruger P94 well suited to persons with small hands.

San Antonio police officer Josie Galindo finds the slim grip of the Ruger P94 comfortable to handle.

The author routinely sends any new personally owned autoloader to Teddy Jacobson for tuning.

brass-plated bullets. According to the ballistics chart on the back of the box, velocity is 1100 fps with 333 foot pounds of energy.

When actually chronographed on the Oehler the ammo showed 1002, 1016, 986, 1034 and 1034 fps, averaging 1014 fps. This isn't 1100 fps, but is about right for that bullet. Also on hand was a box of MagTech 115-grain FMJs that chronographed 1049, 1048, 1027, 1074 and 1063, averaging 1052 fps. This is standard-pressure ammo, so higher velocities weren't expected.

Ruger's claim is the P94 is built to handle any factory ammo, including +P or +P+ 9mm loads. Next up was a good-looking 9mm load from Sure Fire. Although the 115-grain JHPs aren't designated +P, the chronograph readout was 1222, 1240, 1224, 1244 and 1232 fps. The average of 1232 fps is fast enough to give good expansion with the JHP bullet and would be a top choice in the new Ruger.

While chronographing these rounds, we fired through a blast screen at a 25-yard ringed target. We made a reasonable effort to shoot good groups, but not an intense one.

The result was 4- and 5-inch groups at this distance, from a sandbag rest. This held true for the 124-grain JHP load from Black Hills. They chronographed 1079, 1150, 1103, 1104 and 1109, for an average 1109 fps. This is good velocity for that bullet, and the Black Hills loads are known to be very accurate.

Still, I turned to another Black Hills load for a maximum effort in the accuracy department, the 147-grain FMJ. Seventy-five feet would be an unusually long shot in a defense scenario, so I set another ringed target at 25 feet. Firing offhand from a two-hand Weaver stance, the Ruger P94 sent five 147-grain JHPs into an inch. Four of the bullet holes were touching, and the point of impact was dead center. I concluded the P94 is sighted for this heavy ammunition, the choice of many police departments. Chronographed afterward, the Black Hills ammo gave 885, 904, 909, 901, and 900 fps, respectively. Averaging 899 fps, this proved by far to be the most accurate load of those I tested in the P94.

Like any other pistol, the mid-sized Ruger has its own ammo preferences. For the shooter, it's only a matter of isolating the brand and bullet weight. The Ruger's front sight sits atop a small ramp, held in place by two tiny roll pins. This means it's easily replaced with a blade height suited to the ammo. Both front and rear are provided with the customary white dots for low-light combat use.

After the paperwork was done, we turned to empty beverage cans for an extended plinking session. The Ruger 9mm did extremely well at 25 yards on the fun targets—not only could I hit the cans, but I picked the end I wanted to hit! The P94 is superbly accurate with these 147-grain JHPs from Black Hills. The bad news is, at 50 yards, the can-hitting accuracy is not so hot. However, this is far beyond any reasonable defense distance and didn't cause great concern.

The outstanding virtue of any Ruger autoloader is reliability—we expected no malfunctions, and none occurred.

In the end, we found little to criticize about the performance of the P94. As a veteran, if not expert, handgunner, I was slightly put off by the long trigger takeup in single-action fire, but tolerated it as a safety measure. As a rule, I send any new personal autoloader to Teddy Jacobson for trigger and action work. Teddy specializes in tuning police handguns and is familiar with all current self-loaders and revolvers. In this case, the long takeup is part of the Ruger design, and there's not much a pistolsmith can do with it. Jacobson could, however, refine the weight of pull in both DA and SA modes.

I welcome this mid-sized Ruger as a remedy to the excessive bulk of most modern pistols. The next version will be a double-action-only (DAO) model, and I look forward to testing that one, too.

A PAIR FROM MINI-MASTER

by HAL SWIGGETT

MINI-MASTER AND BLACK WIDOW SPECIFICATIONS

Manufacturer: North American Arms

Caliber: 22 Long Rifle, 22 WMR, five-shot

Barrel Length: 4 inches (MM); 2 inches (BW)

Weight: 11 ounces (MM); 9.5 ounces (BW)

Grips: Black hard rubber; checkered

Sights: Orange insert front; Millett adjustable or low-profile fixed rear.

Features: Non-fluted cylinder; heavy vent. barrel; interchangable cylinders.

Mini-Master Price:	
Adjustable sight, 22 LR or 22 WMR	$279
With extra LR/WMR cylinder	$317
Fixed sight, 22 LR or 22 WMR	$264
With extra LR/WMR cylinder	$302

Black Widow Price:	
Adjustable sight, 22 LR or 22 WMR	$249
With extra LR/WMR cylinder	$285
Fixed sight, 22 LR or 22 WMR	$235
With extra LR/WMR cylinder	$270

IT'S BEEN SAID many times, "Beware of that little guy in any fight."

A pair of "little guys" from North American Arms brings that old statement to mind.

Weighing in together at 20½ ounces, on first sight these guns would seem to be less than effective in any confrontation. Chambered for 22 Long Rifle (they also accept Short or Long cartridges), an interchangeable cylinder alters their ego to 22 Winchester Magnum Rimfire (WMR), more commonly called 22 Magnum.

Barrel length of the "big" one, the Mini-Master, is 4 inches, with the Black Widow half that at 2 inches. Frames and cylinders are identical; only the shorter barrel separates Widow from Master. Cylinders are 1.422 inches, slightly less than an inch and a half long. Barrel width, including simulated vent rib and full-length underlug, is .404-inch, with a depth of .736-inch. Individual weight: Mini-Master 11 ounces; Black Widow 9½ ounces.

The grips on both are two-piece black rubber, and the Millett sights come in a choice of adjustable or low-profile fixed. Up front, the sight is drift-adjustable and has a bright orange insert. That rear sight, by the way, is white-outlined.

My involvement with mini-revolvers goes back a good many years. There used to be two manufacturers: North American Arms and Freedom Arms. Freedom became so successful with their single-action 454 Casull there ceased to be sufficient hours in the day, so their little mini was dropped. One-horse races are normally not all that exciting, but North American Arms goes on upgrading, adding new models and accessories, and carefully servicing customers as if they had a string of competitors—a sensitivity not all that common in these ever-so-modern times.

I've owned minis from both manufacturers over the years and am seldom all that far away from one. I shouldn't tell this, because now I will very definitely be watched, but the 1½ or 2-inch versions fit mighty comfortable-like behind a small notebook in a shirt pocket. No one would ever expect

NORTH AMERICAN ARMS: AND BLACK WIDOW

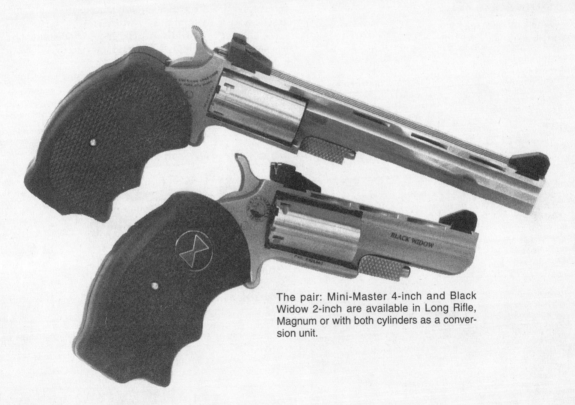

The pair: Mini-Master 4-inch and Black Widow 2-inch are available in Long Rifle, Magnum or with both cylinders as a conversion unit.

any individual to be armed when wearing a short-sleeved shirt and no coat or jacket, but it is possible.

For instance, while attending a shootfest with a group of dedicated handgunners a good many years back, we were shooting at targets of opportunity, a Wyoming mountain serving as our backstop. One of the targets was a not-so-large sheet of steel someone had carried up that mountainside and propped up near 300 yards out. Occasionally, it was hit, but the "boings" of hits were in no way comparable to the number of bullets sent that direction. Feeling fully frustrated, I placed my 7½-inch Ruger Super Blackhawk on the ground and pulled out the little mini 1½-incher from its shirt-pocket hiding place.

All shooting stopped. Every eye was on that tiny little five-gun aimed way up on the side of that Wyoming mountain. Five times it was cocked. Five, carefully as possible,

aimed shots were fired. Every pair of hands applauded and a few of the guys actually pitched their Stetsons in the air. No one could see where any of my 40-grain bullets went, but I knew for sure none hit the steel target.

But it sure did liven up the party.

How do the minis really shoot? For this effort, five different Long Rifle loads were put together along with one box from each manufacturer of 22 WMRs. Here is the "tale of the tape" using an Oehler Model 35P chronograph.

Black Widow is the newest and the first one tested here. With it, I had both the Long Rifle and Magnum cylinders for these tests. The first chrono screen was placed at 8 feet (I use all three screens, not just "start" and "stop" as some do). Remington High Velocity hollowpoints, ten in each string, averaged 814 fps. The string's high was 837, low 782, for an extreme spread of 55 fps. Winchester's 42-grain Super

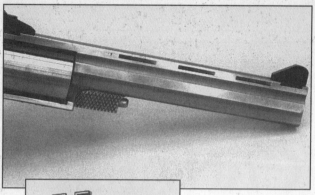

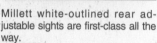

The rib is vented in appearance only and does add greatly to the Mini-Master's and Black Widow's good looks.

Millett white-outlined rear adjustable sights are first-class all the way.

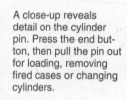

A close-up reveals detail on the cylinder pin. Press the end button, then pull the pin out for loading, removing fired cases or changing cylinders.

The reason my 4-incher doesn't have Mini-Master on its barrel is because it is Experimental 1, as you can see.

North American Arms minis are five-shooters.

Silhouette (most Long Rifle cartridges are 40 grains) topped out at 781 fps. Their low printed 743, which turned in an average of 760 fps. The extreme spread was 38 fps.

Ten CCI Mini-Mag hollowpoints averaged 813 fps. Their high/low was 856/790, making the extreme spread 66 fps. Federal Hi-Power hollowpoints averaged 893 fps with the high 914 and low 864, providing an extreme spread of 50 fps.

Last of the Long Rifles tested was a load I would not have expected to be especially accurate, but it has proved to be almost super in several of my handguns. CCI's 36-grain Mini-Mag+V shot through the three screens at an average of 929 fps. High was 964 and low 896, with 68 fps as the extreme spread. That little flat-nosed rascal did it again.

Changing cylinders to WMR, CCI, Federal and Winchester were put through the same ten-shot routine.

CCI's Maxi-Mag hollowpoint bullets weigh 40 grains. These turned in 990 fps tops, low at 906, making the average 930 fps. The extreme spread was 84 fps.

Federal Classic WMRs are 50-grain jacketed hollowpoints according to information on their box. Ten of them averaged 740 fps with the high 758 and low 722 for only 36 fps extreme spread. This load is superbly accurate in my one-of-a-kind Anschutz Exemplar 22 WMR pistol.

Winchester's WMRs were the most consistent. Only 26 fps separated their high of 862 and low 836 for an average of 850 fps.

Next up was the Mini-Master. I've had this one since

Strip them down and this is what you have. Cylinders are easily removed.

The Editor shows off the pair. All testfiring was at a target 15 yards downrange.

shortly before its commercial release with only the 22 WMR cylinder. This is the 4-inch-barreled version.

Winchester hollowpoints turned in a high of 979 fps, low at 842, with the average at 936 fps. This was 86 fps faster than the Widow's 2-inch barrel.

CCI's Maxi-Mag averaged 1185 fps with high/low of 1322/1089—wild as a March hare with 233 fps extreme spread, but *fast*. A second string, because of that differential, averaged 1146 fps with its high/low of 1204/1081 for 123 fps between them. This was, using the last string, 216 fps ahead of Black Widow and its 2-inch barrel.

Federal 50-grainers topped out at 891 fps with the low at 826 for an average velocity of 858 fps with only 65 fps extreme spread. Consistent for sure.

Accuracy?

I didn't try any of the remaining loads on paper, but had a lot of fun bouncing a soft-drink can hither and yon. At the 15-yard marker, it was absolutely no problem at all hitting them regularly.

If you are into little guns, give this North American Arms pair a look. Probably the 4-inch Mini-Master would be best for most, but the Black Widow has a lot going for it.

Nicely made little holsters are available for both barrel lengths. I mean the real thing—heavy stitching, good leather, the works. Nothing make-believe here.

If your dealer can't show you this pair, drop a note to the factory. They will, for sure, send you literature and probably give you the location of a dealer to aid your cause. •

BLACK WIDOW 22 LR BALLISTICS TEST

Manufacturer	Bullet (grs./type)	—Ten-shot MV (fps)— Avg.	High	Low
Rem. HV	40/HP	814	837	782
Win. Super Sil.	42/LTC	760	781	743
CCI Mini-Mag	40/HP	813	856	790
Fed. Hi-Power	40/HP	893	914	864
CCI Mini-Mag+V	36/FN	929	964	896

HP = Hollowpoint; LTC = Lead Truncated Cone; FN = Flatnose

BLACK WIDOW 22 WMR BALLISTICS TEST

Manufacturer	Bullet (grs./type)	—Ten-shot MV (fps)— Avg.	High	Low
CCI Maxi-Mag	40/HP	930	990	906
Federal Classic	50/JHP	740	758	722
Win. WMR	40/JHP	850	862	836

HP = Hollowpoint; JHP = Jacketed Hollowpoint

MINI-MASTER 22 WMR BALLISTICS TEST

Manufacturer	Bullet (grs./type)	—Ten-shot MV (fps)— Avg.	High	Low
Winchester	40/HP	936	979	842
CCI Maxi-Mag	40/HP	1185	1322	1089
CCI Maxi-Mag	40/HP	1146	1204	1081
Federal Classic	50/JHP	858	891	826

HP = Hollowpoint; JHP = Jacketed Hollowpoint

The Black Widow can be had with two cylinders: Winchester Magnum Rimfire (left) and Long Rifle.

This is the various ammunition used for testing NAA's minis, Long Rifle and WMR, along with the two revolvers and Oehler's 35P printer.

Beautifully made holsters are available from North American Arms for all of their minis. These, obviously, are Black Widow and Mini-Master.

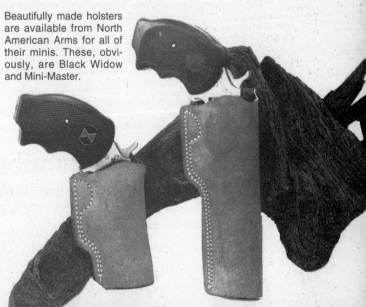

Handgun Tests

THE LONG SLIDE

by FRANK W. JAMES

GLOCK MODEL 24 SPECIFICATIONS

Manufacturer: Glock GmbH, Deutsch-Wagram Austria

Importer: Glock, Inc.

Type: Short recoil operated, Glock "safe" action semi-automatic pistol

Caliber: 40 S&W

Magazine capacity: Fifteen rounds

Weight: 26.5 ounces (751.3 grams) without magazine Empty magazine: 3 ounces (85 grams)

Barrel length: 6 inches (152.4mm)

Rifling Twist: 8 hexagonal lands and grooves, 1:15.75 inches (1 turn in 400mm)

Overall length: 9 inches (228.6mm)

Overall width: 1 1/16 inches (27mm)

Safeties: Three—trigger safety, firing pin safety, drop safety

Price: $806.67

MY FIRST CENTERFIRE handgun was a 38 Special revolver with a 6-inch barrel. It was my initial venture into something beyond 22 rimfire shooting, and I soon learned the advantages found with a long-barreled handgun. The pistol pointed well, and the increased weight of the extra barrel length helped dampen the recoil on some of my hotter handloads. I developed an appreciation for long barrels, and maybe that's why I knew I would like this pistol.

Long-barreled handguns normally are encountered in two types of actions: revolvers and single shot pistols. It isn't very often a long-barreled semi-auto pistol is found under the counter glass at the local gunshop. Long-barrel semi-autos usually require long slides, and long slide auto pistols, in large measure, are custom guns. That is, until now, because the Glock Model 24 follows in the footsteps of the previous Glock 17L, and it's a factory-ready, long barrel/long slide, right-from-the-box gun.

The Glock Model 24 is a long-slide version of the very popular Model 22 in 40 S&W caliber and is built primarily for competition use. Introduced at the 1994 SHOT Show, the gun provides the Glock competition shooter with a high capacity "major" caliber pistol. There is also another version with a ported barrel for those who want the most in terms of recoil control.

I was not able to test the ported Model 24. However, just after the SHOT Show, I was privileged to test-drive the non-ported Model 24 for a couple of days with more than 300 rounds. Since it was in the middle of a deep, cold winter, I was forced to do all my shooting on an indoor range. What I found was an extremely accurate, easy-shooting gun.

Since the introduction of the first Glock pistol, these guns have been the center of various controversies. They were first attacked as horrid "plastic" guns, and the alarm was raised that terrorists would be sneaking them through airport security checkpoints to hijack airliners the world over.

This concern was soon proven bogus because of the amount of steel used in the construction of the Glock's slide and barrel. Steel inserts are even employed as slide rails on

GLOCK MODEL 24

Introduced at the 1994 SHOT Show, the Glock Model 24 provides the competition shooter with a high-capacity "major" caliber long-slide pistol. There are two versions available—one with a ported barrel and those like this one with a non-ported barrel.

the polymer frame, and the entire trigger and firing mechanism is made of steel parts, except for certain components of the magazine assembly.

The next concern was voiced by entrenched old hands who couldn't conceive of a semi-auto pistol without a manual safety. According to their way of thinking, the safety had to be mounted on the frame, but one mounted on the slide would be grudgingly accepted if the situation demanded, whereas a pistol with neither was condemned.

The Glock, of course, doesn't have either of those, and that, to many observers, was just too radical to accept. To this day, many shooters remain unconvinced and out of step. But a large number of law enforcement agencies have eagerly adopted the Glock, and police administrators are some of the most safety-conscious people in the world.

The Glock pistol uses three safeties—two of them non-tra-

The Glock Model 24 is a long-slide version of the very popular Model 22 in 40 S&W caliber. It is built primarily for competition use. This can be verified by examination of the little extras found on this out-of-the-box factory competition pistol.

(Above) The rear sight is made of black plastic and features a wide white-line U-notch outline. This sight is drift-adjustable for windage.

(Left) The Glock Model 24 field-strips the same as the other members of the Glock series of pistols. The major components of the pistol include the polymer frame, captured recoil spring and guide rod, barrel, slide and magazine.

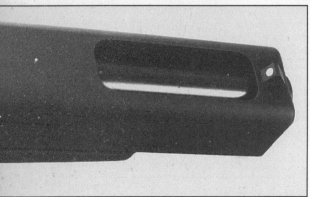

(Right) The magazine release button is the special competition version because it is slightly taller than the normal mag release button. In competition, this button is an asset. On the street, it could prove to be a great liability.

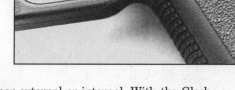

The front sight is a small triangular post with a single white dot. The cut-out portion of the slide indicates the location of the four ports on the ported version of the Glock Model 24.

ditional in engineering and theory, while the third is found on most all popular pistols today.

The first safety is the only one that can be viewed externally. It is the blade-like object protruding from the middle of the trigger. It is disengaged whenever the trigger is depressed, and this created concern among some commentators when the gun was unveiled.

One earnest Glock employee explained it to me, as he compared his pistol to the 1911 with its frame-mounted safety, "Think of your finger as part of the safety. If your finger is inside the trigger guard, the safety is *off!* If your finger is outside of the trigger guard, the safety is *on!* It's that easy and that simple."

He went on to relate how the Glock is always automatically on safe whenever it is in a state of rest. The action isn't even cocked until the trigger pull is partially completed. If you drop the gun, you are dropping an uncocked gun with all safeties engaged. No motion or act, other than removing your finger from the trigger guard, is needed to engage any

of the safeties, either external or internal. With the Glock, you don't have to engage a frame or slide safety to ensure the gun is truly safe.

The remaining two safeties on the Glock are the firing pin and the drop safeties. The first is fairly common and, in a sense, traditional. It is found on a number of different semi-auto pistols, including the Smith & Wesson Third Generation guns, the Series 80 Colts, and the SIG-Sauers, to mention only a few. A firing pin safety requires some positive movement on the part of the trigger mechanism before the firing pin is cleared or released. Otherwise, the firing pin is blocked and inert. The Glock firing pin safety operates in that manner.

The drop safety works off the "cruciform," which is the rear part of the trigger assembly. It prevents the gun from firing should it be dropped and land on the back of the grip or slide. Theoretically, if the gun were dropped in this manner, the mass of the trigger and the connected parts within the mechanism could move rearward with enough force to

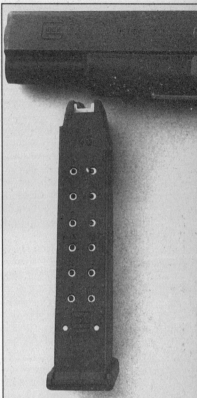

(Above) We found it easy to load fourteen rounds into the Model 24 fifteen-round magazine, but the loading tool provided in the "Tupperware" shipping box proved useful in loading the last round into the magazine.

(Right) Like all Glock magazines, the back of the Model 24 magazine has a series of witness holes to determine the amount of ammunition remaining in the magazine.

(Below) The captured recoil spring and guide rod assembly appears to be the same one used on the Model 22 Glock. The guide rod and spring end just inside the tubular recess on front of the slide as shown here.

fire the gun, if this safety were missing. It isn't, and in this regard, the Glock is an extremely safe pistol.

The main distinguishing feature of all Glocks is the polymer frame. The use of polymer makes it easy to understand why the gun is sometimes referred to as a "plastic" gun.

The outcry over the use of polymer in a handgun is a little difficult to understand when you study the recent history of firearms. Heckler & Koch used polymer as a base material on many of its firearms well before Glock, and Remington made a semi-auto 22 rimfire rifle out of a nylon material to create the highly successful Nylon 66. These small historical notes only reinforce the idea that initial hysteria over the Glock was highly engineered anti-gun hyperbole.

The polymer frame on the Glock pistol has several advantages. The first is the increased ease and speed of manufacture. It only takes the injection mould eighty-five seconds to produce a frame. This runs counter to the many hours of labor and machine time it takes to manufacture the conventional machined steel frame.

This reduction in manufacturing time realizes a significant cost savings for Glock and, ultimately, the consumer.

But there is yet another, *unseen* advantage to the polymer frame, and that is its ability to absorb recoil. It will actually dampen recoil and reduce the sensation of impact from some hard-recoiling calibers.

I say this because I routinely use a Glock Model 23 to test and evaluate various 40 S&W handloads and commercial rounds. Of all the 40-caliber pistols out there, I am utterly convinced the Glock 22 and 23 are the easiest 40s to shoot over a long period of time because of the lessened felt recoil.

This remains true with the Glock Model 24, if not more so. The increased mass of the long slide helps lessen the felt recoil even more.

The ammo companies producing 40 S&W ammunition have increased the power factor of this ammunition since its introduction. In the past, the usual rule was the first pro-

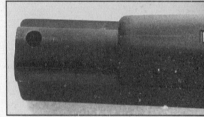

(Right) A mystery is the hole on the bottom of the slide and forward of the captured recoil spring. We were never able to determine the exact purpose of this opening.

duction ammo would be "hot," and then later it would be "cooled" down a bit for greater control.

As interest in the 10mm Auto has waned, there have been increasing demands placed for even hotter 40 S&W loads, and these loads can take their physical toll on the shooter if he has to spend very much time on the firing line.

I can see why Glock makes a ported version of the Model 24. The muzzle does rise in recoil, and although I have never fired the ported version, I'm sure those ports would help to reduce this muzzle flip. They would also prove beneficial in bringing the gun back on target in a much faster and more efficient fashion.

The Glock Model 24 uses what they describe as a "3½-pound connector." That is supposed to translate into a 3½-pound trigger pull, but because of that safety blade protruding from the middle of the trigger, it is very difficult to get an accurate reading as to the actual trigger pull weight.

In any event, I found the test pistol consistently yielded a pull of about 6¾ pounds. That may seem high, but due to the trigger safety, it doesn't really represent the actual pressure needed to make the gun fire.

I took the Model 24 to Don Foreman's new indoor range in Hammond, Indiana, to give the gun a workout. Don, who shoots both revolvers and autos only on single action if he can, soon proved just how accurate this pistol was as he cut a series of very small, almost one-hole groups in the targets at various distances.

The ammo was Black Hills 180-grain JHP and 155-grain JHP. We felt the 180-grain ammo was more accurate than the other with this gun. The Model 24 would easily put five rounds inside 2 inches at 50 feet from a standing position.

I didn't shoot quite as well as Foreman because I have a problem pulling on the side of the Glock trigger with my stub trigger finger. This constantly throws my groups to the right, and when they become large enough to see, my shooting gets even worse.

In fairness to Glock, I must say one of the reasons I like the Glock is because I can *reach* the trigger.

The barrel has eight hexagonal lands and grooves, and the rifling has a twist rate of 1:15.75 inches. Like all Glocks, the barrel locks to the slide via the Pedersen system, where the chamber block of the barrel engages the slide at the ejection port.

The sights consist of a large rear blade with a white outline U-notch and a small triangular front post with a single white dot. I would have preferred a narrower front sight, one that allowed more light on either side of the post when the gun was brought on target. Both front and rear sights are plastic, and the rear is drift-adjustable for windage.

The Model 24 magazine holds fifteen rounds of 40 S&W ammunition and is the same magazine found on the Model 22. It is the newer "fall-free" style. The magazine release button is the competition type, slightly taller than the standard button. This button isn't recommended for guns carried on the street. The chance is too great it will accidentally release the magazine if bumped, but it is an improvement for competition use because it is so much easier to reach.

The Glock 17 was so named because it was the seventeenth product designed and marketed by Gaston Glock. The Model 17L was the first long-slide competition pistol built by the company. Word from sources within the U.S. branch of the firm indicates the 17L will be discontinued once the Model 24 reaches full production. The problem with the Glock 17L is that the 9x19mm cartridge won't make "major" in American IPSC competition—one of the major venues for which this product was designed.

Yet, this still doesn't answer why the Model 24 wasn't called the "22L" instead of the Model 24?

The probable answer is that this model designation adds uniformity to the Glock product line.

The Glock pistols have been controversial, but they have always been revolutionary and innovative. They have also proven to be quite reliable and accurate, and the Model 24 we tested was no exception.

I have always liked long-barreled guns. To me, they just point better. This is especially true for this pistol. In fact, it is a good enough gun that I would purchase it even if I never intended to shoot it in competition. And that's about the highest recommendation I can make. ●

Don Foreman shot this ten-shot group at 25 feet with his second magazine of the test session. The author and Foreman reached the same conclusion: The Glock Model 24 is an accurate pistol.

(Above) We tested the Glock Model 24 during the winter months at Don Foreman's Indoor Range in Hammond, Indiana. Don discovered the Model 24 was an extrememly accurate pistol for something fresh from the box.

(Left) The non-ported version of the Model 24 that we tested did exhibit some muzzle flip while working with the 180-grain Black Hills ammunition. The ported version should prove more efficient and more controllable in terms of returning to the target.

D-MAX INC.'S 45/410 SIDEWINDER
SINGLE ACTION
by LARRY S. STERETT

D-MAX SIDEWINDER SPECIFICATIONS

Caliber: 45 Colt/410-bore

Barrel: 7.5 or 6.5 inches

Capacity: Six rounds

Overall Length: 14.94 inches

Height: 5.79 inches

Width of grip: 1.25 inches

Weight, empty: 63 ounces

Stocks: Pachmayr Presentation

Finish: Satin stainless steel

Sights: Front post; adjustable rear, square notch

Suggested List Price: $700

HANDGUNS CHAMBERED FOR the 410-bore shotshell are not exactly new, but those with a smoothbore barrel were classified by the Bureau of Internal Revenue in 1934 as "any other weapon" under the National Firearms Act. This, in spite of technical testimony by certain experts that such weapons were pistols. Thus, any handgun so chambered today has a rifled barrel and, generally, some means of stopping or slowing down the rotation of the shot charge.

In recent years, the best known of the 45/410 handguns has been the single shot Contender by Thompson/Center. It is chambered for the 45 Colt cartridge, with an elongated chamber to accept 410 shotshells and slug loads. When used with the shotshells, the Contender is fitted with a screw-*in* choke tube that also acts to stop the shot charge rotation. (The early 410-bore pistols had a screw-*on* choke tube.)

A few years back, a five-shot revolver with a short barrel was introduced. Chambered for the 45 Colt/410 and known as the Thunder Five, it could be used for close-in work, as the 2-inch barrel is not long enough to permit both use of a screw-in choke tube and still have much in the way of rifling.

Early in 1993, the Sidewinder appeared on the market. A man-sized revolver with a barrel long enough to make use of both the 45 Colt and 410-bore cartridges, the Sidewinder is manufactured in Bagley, Minnesota, by D-MAX, Inc. This is a new firm that has always been located in Minnesota; it should not to be confused with D-MAX Industries, which is an entirely different firm with no connection and located in the state of Washington.

Made of stainless steel for both strength and weather resistance, the Sidewinder is a single-action design, with a transfer bar system for safety. Unlike the original Colt

SIDEWINDER 410-BORE PATTERNING TESTS

Shell	Pellets (count/size)	Pattern at (yds.)	Pattern % in Circle 30″	20″	15″
Win. AA Skeet 2½″	308/#9	10	—	90	74
Rem. Target 2½″	286/#9	15	75	41	23
Rem. Express 3″	255/#7½	20	46	23	13

Recoil of the Sidewinder, when fired with a heavy 45 Colt load, is similar to that felt when firing a heavy 44 Magnum load in a comparable-weight revolver, and possibly a bit more than when firing the 3-inch 410 shotshell.

The mainspring or hammer spring on the Sidewinder is spiral, not the leaf type as found on the original Colt SAAs.

(Right) The hammer has only two positions—resting against the frame as shown or cocked. There is no half-cock position. Loading is done with the hammer fully down, resting on the frame. Opening the loading gate prevents the hammer from being cocked, and the cylinder is free to rotate clockwise for loading or ejecting empties.

Single Action Army revolver, and many later copies, the Sidewinder has only two hammer positions instead of three. When the hammer is cocked, the transfer bar moves up to a position between the firing pin and hammer. There is no half-cock position on the Sidewinder hammer.

Loading the gun is similar to that of most single-action revolvers. Cylinder rotation is clockwise, and it will hold six rounds. The Sidewinder cylinder is unfluted, and on the test gun it measured 2.950 inches long, with a diameter of 1.732 inches.

Since the 45 Colt cartridge is larger than the 410 shotshell, the rear portion of the cylinder is chambered for 45 Colt, while forward of this chamber, the cylinder is bored to accept the 3-inch 410 shell. When the 410s are fired, the rear portion of each expands to fit the 45 Colt portion of the chamber.

The test gun tipped the scale at 63 ounces, empty, and measured 14¹⁵/₁₆ inches overall with a barrel length of 7½ inches. A 6½-inch barrel is also available. The muzzle is bored and threaded for a Thompson/Center-type choke tube, which must be removed if the gun is to be used with 45 Colt cartridges; it is a good idea to remove the choke tube if 410 rifled slug loads are being used. When shooting 410 shotshells, the choke tube must be installed to reduce shot spin and stabilize patterns out to about 25 yards.

The Sidewinder's trigger measures .284-inch wide and has a smooth, slightly convex face. Let-off was crisp at 3¼ pounds, about right for hunting.

Stocks on the test gun were the black Pachmayr neoprene Presentations with checkered sides and an extension to serve as a filler behind the squared-off trigger guard. They were comfortable and definitely an asset.

Sights on the test gun consisted of an integral base-mounted .145-inch post up front and a white-outlined, square-notch rear, adjustable for windage and elevation. The topstrap is massive—.703-inch wide and .316-inch thick. Sight radius with the 7½-inch barrel length measures 10½ inches.

Sight adjustment is conventional. Rotating the elevation screw clockwise will lower the point-of-impact; counterclockwise will raise it. Rotating the windage screw clockwise will move the point of impact to the left.

The finish on the Sidewinder is satin stainless steel, with the exception of its gray-colored, bead-blasted front sight and black rear sight. Metal-to-metal fit is excellent. The Sidewinder name is etched on the right side of the frame below the cylinder. On the bottom, it reads "D-MAX INC.

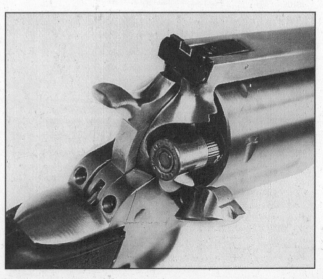

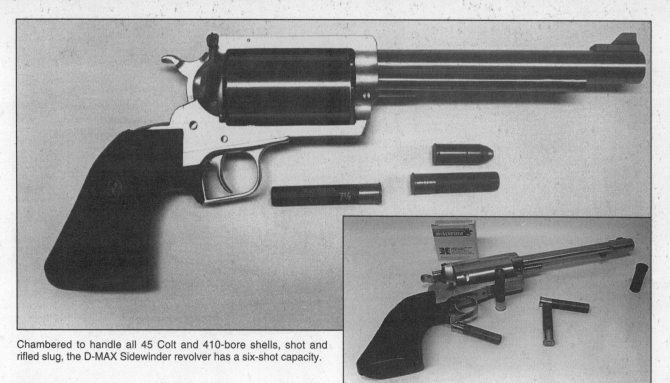

Chambered to handle all 45 Colt and 410-bore shells, shot and rifled slug, the D-MAX Sidewinder revolver has a six-shot capacity.

The Sidewinder tested has a barrel length of 7 1/2 inches; the muzzle end is bored and threaded to accept a Thompson/Center-type screw-in choke, shown here removed.

Bagley MN," with "Cal 45/410" and the serial number below.

I patterened my test gun with 410 shot loads at 10, 15 and 25 yards to determine what could be expected at these distances in the way of a five-shot average. I also tried some crossing and going-away shots on clay targets. At about 10 to 15 or so yards, breaking them wasn't too difficult, after I established a proper follow-through technique. Shooting quail with a Sidewinder might be tough, but busting cottontails could be lots of fun.

The first load patterned was Winchester's 2 1/2-inch AA Skeet round containing an average, by actual count, of 308 #9 pellets per shell. At 10 yards, with the choke tube installed, the gun placed an average of 90 percent of its shot charge inside a 20-inch circle, with 74 percent inside a 15-inch circle. Patterns were centered about an inch above point of aim.

Remington's 410 2 1/2-inch target load, which contained an average of 286 #9 pellets per shot charge, was tried at 15 yards. With this load, the test gun placed an average of 75 percent of its charge inside a 30-inch circle, 41 percent inside a 20-inch circle and 23 percent inside a 15-inch circle. Some holes were starting to show in the patterns at this distance.

Final patterning was done at 20 yards using 3-inch Remington Express loads containing 3/4-ounce of #7 1/2 shot, an average of 255 pellets per charge. At 20 yards, these loads gave an average of 46 percent inside a 30-inch circle, with 23 percent inside a 20-inch circle. The inner 15-inch circle only contained 13 percent of the shot charge, and large holes were present in all patterns. The pattern with the highest percentage was also the one with the most holes. My patterns were a good indication that 20 yards is about the limit for shotshell use, at least with #7 1/2 shot. Using #8 or #9 shot in 3-inch shells might improve pattern averages, but not striking energy.

Rifled slugs were also tried, mainly on ice-filled gallon milk jugs at 25 yards. With the choke tube removed and sights adjusted to place shots 2 inches above point of aim, the Sidewinder made ice fly. It's well worth noting that 45 Colt and 410 rifled slug loads shoot to different points of

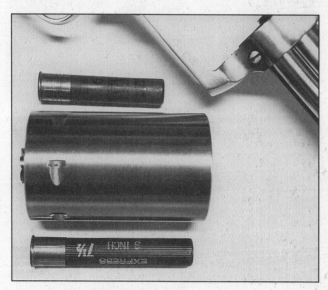

The unfluted cylinder is massive. Fired 3-inch 410-bore shells reach entirely to the muzzle end, but rarely extend beyond; if this should occur, the case is flexible enough to permit cylinder rotation.

impact. Recoil of the test gun, using Winchester's slug load, was not much greater than shooting a revolver chambered for 32 Smith & Wesson; it was possibly even less. Keeping five shots in a palm-sized group at 25 yards with rifled slugs is not difficult. However, there's not much use for rifled slugs weighing 1/5-ounce, and most states do not permit their use on big game, such as whitetail deer.

Most 45 Colt factory cartridges are loaded rather lightly, due to possible use in some pre-1900-era single actions, and generally come with either 225- or 250-grain bullets. Naturally, factory loads will function through the

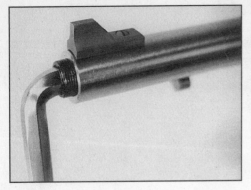

SIDEWINDER 45 COLT BALLISTICS TEST

Manufacturer	Bullet (grs./type)	Powder (grs./type)	Primer	Group avg. @50 yds(ins.)
Federal Factory	225/SWCHP	—	—	7⅝
Handload	300/Hornady XTP	27.5/AA1680	CCI 350 Mag.	3-4
Handload	300/Hornady XTP	20.8/H-4227	CCI 300	3-4

All testing done with three-shot groups at 25 yards.

The screw-in choke tube, shown here partially removed, must be out of the muzzle if 45 Colt cartridges will be used. A hex wrench is provided to aid in choke removal and installation. If removed, accuracy is also better when 410-bore rifled slugs are fired, but should be installed when regular 410 shotshells are used, to reduce pattern swirling. Note the massive front sight on the Sidewinder.

Loading the Sidewinder is done with the hammer resting against the frame, but out of contact with the firing pin. As mentioned, opening this loading gate blocks the hammer from being cocked, but permits the cylinder to be rotated.

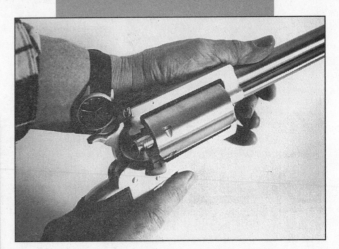

An ejector rod to kick out empties operates the same as on Colt, Ruger and similar single actions. With the hammer down, open the loading gate, rotate the cylinder so it is in line with the notch and move the ejector rod knob, under the barrel, smartly rearward.

Sidewinder, but D-MAX does not recommend using light-weight bullets in this revolver, if handloading.

Using the Federal 225-grain semi-wadcutter hollowpoint load, the Sidewinder shot random dinner-plate-size three-shot groups at 50 yards, even when firing from the bench. The smallest group measured 7⅝ inches, center-to-center.

As mentioned, the Sidewinder prefers heavy bullets, making handloads or custom loads necessary. One such load, consisting of a 300-grain Hornady XTP (.452-inch) bullet ahead of 27.5 grains of Accurate 1680 powder, ignited by CCI's 350 Magnum primer, worked well for this shooter. In a different revolver it might not perform as well, but three-shot groups measuring between 3 and 4 inches, center-to-center, were common. With a scope mounted on the revolver, the groups should shrink even more. Another load that did almost as well consisted of the same bullet ahead of 20.8 grains of H-4227 with CCI 300 primers. At 50 yards, either of these loads would bring down a whitetail.

Factory loads and handloads shot to different points of impact. For this reason, owners would be wise to settle on one specific load, adjusting sights so groups print 1 or 2 inches high using a six o'clock hold. Standard factory loads provide acceptable accuracy for use on deer-size game, but accuracy with my test gun improved when handloads were used.

Recoil with the Sidewinder was mild when firing standard 2½-inch 410 shotshells; 45 Colt factory loads produced a bit more muzzle lift and felt recoil in the palm. The 3-inch 410s and heavy 45 Colt handloads caused the muzzle to lift 3 or 4 inches, and recoil was more pronounced, but not severe. Recoil was considerably less punishing than firing 357 Magnum loads in a lightweight revolver. Part of this is due to the shape of the single-action-style grip, in addition to the weight of the gun, which is an ounce less than 4 pounds, empty. For comparison, recoil seemed more in keeping with that of shooting standard 45 ACP Ball ammo in a M1911 pistol.

Overall, the Sidewinder is an excellent revolver with some unique features. Well designed and crafted, my test gun balanced at about mid-cylinder and handled the same as any single-action revolver based on the Colt SAA. In the hand, it feels like holding a Ruger Super Blackhawk.

As this is written, the stainless steel D-MAX Sidewinder revolver carries a suggested list price of $700 and comes packed in a foam-filled MTM Case-Gard 808 case, complete with instruction manual, screw-in choke tube and tube wrench.

Since the Sidewinder is basically a hunting revolver, packing it afield requires a good holster. A good choice is Michael's of Oregon (Uncle Mike's) No. 4 Sidekick Vertical Shoulder Holster, available in right- or left-hand versions. It has wide web shoulder straps for a comfortable carry and is available in a choice of black or camo at most dealers. •

AT LEAST AS GOOD AS THE COLT
NORINCO'S MODEL 1911A1
by HAL SWIGGETT

NORINCO MODEL 1911A1 SPECIFICATIONS

Caliber: 45 ACP, seven-shot magazine

Barrel: 5 inches

Weight: 39¼ ounces

Length Overall: 8½ inches

Stocks: Checkered wood

Sights: Blade front; adjustable for windage rear

Features: Matte blue finish, delivered with two magazines

Importer: Norinco, ChinaSports, Inc., from China.

Price: $349.95

IT'S ALL JIM Pacheco's fault.

I've known him a good many years. He's retired military. His duty was, primarily, keeping guns spic and span for an Air Force pistol team. He even did a little of the shooting.

After that, he served as a U.S. Customs Inspector on our Texas/Mexico border.

His next undertaking was a deputy sheriff's commission. He still has it. While serving in that capacity, he opened a gun shop, and he still has it. It is his FFL that accounts for every firearm I write about. And besides all that, he has never lied to me.

And that's the reason I got involved with this made-in-China Model 1911A1. He insisted it was good, better, by far, than those currently being turned out in our U.S. of A. by the original manufacturer, I'd best add.

Jim touted that particular Chinese-made Model 1911A1 to the point where he stripped it down, more than once, pointing out those finer points that impressed him. Basically, it was the fit and finish *inside* the autoloader. Search as we did, there were no tool marks to be found. I mean the innermost surfaces were totally free of any tool markings whatsoever. The feed ramp out of the frame and throating into the barrel were finished *a la* custom style here in the U.S.

His efforts toward wearing me down paid off. I agreed to take that new, never-fired 45 ACP autoloader and see if it performed as he insisted it would.

Scrounging through my shelves, I found twelve types/brands of 45 ACP factory loads: Winchester's infamous Black Talon 230-grain SXT HPs; Remington's Golden Saber 230-grain Brass Jacket HPs; Winchester 185-grain Silvertip HP; CCI Lawman 200-grain JHP; Remington 185-

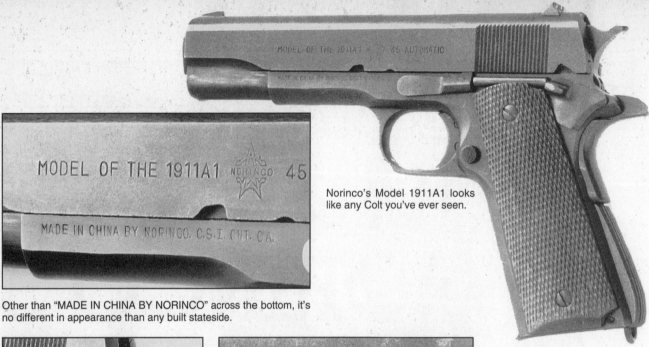

Norinco's Model 1911A1 looks like any Colt you've ever seen.

Other than "MADE IN CHINA BY NORINCO" across the bottom, it's no different in appearance than any built stateside.

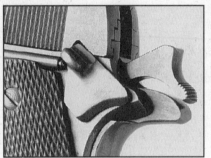

Of course, this insignia on the left side is a bit distinctive.

Hammer, safety, checkered wood grip—all the same as we've known for years.

grain JHP; Federal 185-grain JHP; Federal 185-grain Metal Case Wadcutter Match; Hornady 185-grain JHP; Hornady 230-grain FMJ; GI 1962 WCC 230-grain hardball; GI 1962 FC 230-grain hardball; and fifteen rounds of Super Vel 190-grain HPs. I hated to part with these few Super Vels (*Lee Jurras* Super Vel), but figured it was a good cause.

Considering not all the boxes were full, this adds up to a total of 396 rounds fired. The first five of each went through Oehler's Model 35P chronograph screens. All the rest were shot simply for function. All of this was done in about seven hours.

Believe it or not, Jim had the Norinco back in his hands that same afternoon. It was a thorough workout for me, but near as I could tell, the Norinco didn't even work up a sweat.

All my chronographing, by the way, is done at 8 feet to the first screen with handguns, 10 feet for rifles.

How did they do?

First, a description of the Norinco Model 1911A1 is in order. It weighs 39¼ ounces on my postal scale. Its trigger breaks *real* clean at 5¼ pounds. Barrel length is 5 inches, and magazine capacity is seven rounds, same as Colt Model 1911 autoloaders since their inception. Model 1911 pistols were manufactured from 1911 through 1925 not only by Colt, but, I believe, by Remington-UMC and Springfield Armory to name just a couple.

The military Model 1911A1, a copy of which is the subject here, was made from 1924 through 1945 by not only Colt, but also Ithaca, Union Switch & Signal, Remington Rand (just happen to have one of these in the family) and Singer

The grip safety is the same as on those made in the U.S. of A.

Mfg. Co. There may be others, but these are the ones I specifically know.

It is this one—the military Model 1911A1—Norinco has copied, and very well, I might add. To perfection is an even better description.

Back to what happened through those Oehler screens: Winchester's Black Talon 230 SXT HPs averaged 859 fps with a top of 889 and low 831 fps. Hornady 230 FMJs did 907 top, 876 bottom, for 887 fps average. That company's 185 JHPs topped out at 959 high, 902 low and 924 fps average. Federal 185 Metal Case Wadcutter Match bullets averaged 748 fps with their high at 785 and low at 699. Federal

NORINCO 1911A1 45 ACP BALLISTICS TEST

Manufacturer	Bullet (grs./type)	Five-shot MV (fps) Avg.	High	Low
Win. Black Talon	230/SXT HP	859	889	831
Rem. Golden Saber	230/Brass Jacket HP	824	842	801
Win. Silvertip	185/HP	940	961	926
CCI Lawman	200/JHP	921	930	909
Remington	185/JHP	902	925	889
Federal	185/JHP	937	962	922
Federal	185/Metal Case WC Match	748	785	699
Hornady	185/JHP	924	959	902
Hornady	230/FMJ	887	907	876
GI 1962 WCC	230/Ball	816	867	767
GI 1962 FC	230/Ball	836	872	816
Super Vel	190/HP	1001	1026	966

All shots went into 5¼ inches at 25 yards.

Which is USA-made? China? One is a much-customized 1970 version—which sort of gives it away.

A distinct difference, Colt's Government Model on one...

...Absolutely nothing—other than serial number—on the other.

Inside there are lots of differences. No, not any tool marks anyplace. I mean smooth, smooth throughout its interior.

185 JHPs clocked 937 average with high/low of 962/922. Remington 185 JHPs went from 925 to 889 for a 902 fps average. CCI's Lawman 200-grainers averaged 921 fps with the high/low 930/909. Winchester's 185-grain Silvertip averaged 940 fps with the top at 961 and low 926 fps. Golden Saber 230-grain Brass Jacketed HPs from Remington hit 842 for the high and 801 low with 824 fps average.

How about the thirty-two-year-old GI military issue? Those headstamped WCC averaged 816 fps with 867/767 as high/low. Same year, 1962, but with FC headstamp, turned in 872/816 high/low for 836 fps average. Remember—these are 230-grain hardball match loads.

Last, but far from least, was the Super Vel ammo, because had it not been for Lee Jurras and his Super Vel Cartridge Co., we might still be stumbling along with so-so velocities.

He, alone and for sure, built a fire under the ammunition biggies. His 190-grain HPs averaged, hang on to your chair, 1001 fps. High was 1026 and low 966 fps. This was 61 fps faster than Winchester's 185 Silvertip.

How did the gun shoot?

Other than those sixty chronographing shots, five with each of the dozen loads, my targets were soft-drink cans, several chunks of dirt on the berm, rocks and three sunflower blossoms against that same high dirt bank.

My target, while chronographing, was a 6-inch green bullseye stapled to an 8½x11-inch, rather dark gray sheet of typing paper 25 yards distant. My usual target for chronographing, actually. It was stapled to the plywood target board so I would be aiming slightly above center of the skyscreens. That same target caught all sixty bullets. The perfectly round hole from those many shots measured 5¼ inches across. Its center was 5 inches above my aiming point. All bullets stayed in that 5¼-inch circle.

Not all that bad for, as some folks might say, government work. Bear in mind, please, this is a personal protection, self-defense pistol.

Some of you might be questioning my shooting at small rocks, but allow me to explain. This is a specially-built range for a singular purpose. It has a high dirt bank around all four sides. Cans were bounced hither and yon, small rocks shattered, and those three sunflower blossoms gave

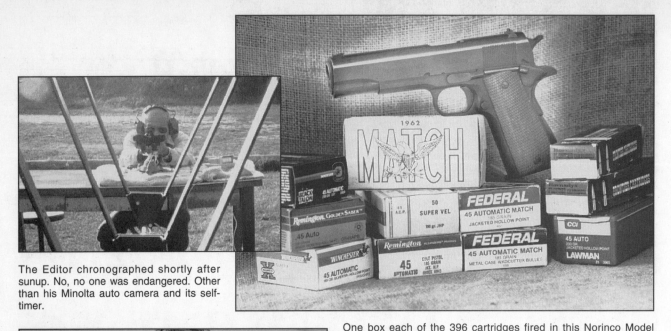

The Editor chronographed shortly after sunup. No, no one was endangered. Other than his Minolta auto camera and its self-timer.

One box each of the 396 cartridges fired in this Norinco Model 1911A1 in a few hours.

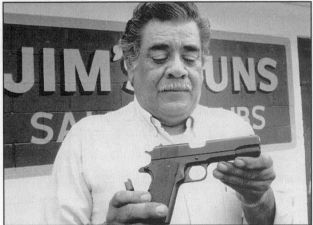

Jim Pacheco, the Editor's FFL dealer, the man who said, "I told you so."

their all. Out to 25 and even 30 yards, by holding a bit low, hits were commonplace.

Then the fun started.

Up to this point, each shot had been aimed, and there had been nary a bobble. So, I set out to foul up this Chinese Model 1911A1.

Seven rounds were stuffed in the magazine, 185s, 190s, 200s and 230s, with no two of the same in sequence. An eighth round was dropped in the chamber, the slide closed, magazine shoved home—and the pistol fired as fast as I could pull the trigger. Not machinegun-like because I'm not that swift, but a whole bunch faster than there ever would be a need. A definite rat-a-tat-tat-tat sort of thing.

I did this five times, forty rounds, with nary hitch in its git-a-long.

No doubt this Norinco Model 1911A1 has a flaw. Everything does.

All I know is I couldn't find it.

Back at Jim's shop, all of the above was related, blow by blow. His grin got wider as details progressed. When finished, I added. "If there is a flaw in that thing I could not find it."

His entire comment included only four words: "I told you so."　　　　●

Norinco's Model 1911A1 fits in the Editor's Roy Baker Pancake Holster as if made for it. Actually, it was—for his 1970 accurized copy. This is an early Roy Baker holster made by Roy himself.

Handgun Tests

AN OLDTIMER RETURNS
HARRINGTON & RICHARDSON'S
MODEL 999 SPORTSMAN

by HAL SWIGGETT

H&R MODEL 999 SPECIFICATIONS

Action: Single or double action

Loading: Top-break with automatic shell ejection

Caliber: 22 Short, Long or Long Rifle

Barrel Length: 4- or 6-inch, both fluted

Capacity: Nine rounds

Sights: Windage-adjustable rear; elevation-adjustable front

Weight: 30 ounces (4-inch); 34 ounces (6-inch)

Grips: Walnut-finished hardwood

Finish: Blue

Price: $279.95

MY FIRST CONTACT with one of Harrington & Richardson's Model 999 Sportsman nine-shot 22 Long Rifle revolvers was in the early 1950s. Bill Freeman, one of several men working the city desk of San Antonio's *Express and Evening News* papers, came into the photo lab one morning, revolver in hand. Back then, folks weren't so sensitive about handguns as they are now. He was looking for me. His first words were, "Hal, I bought this thing from a friend a month or so ago and still don't know why. Would you have any use for it?"

I was still running a trapline then, and had been since Uncle Sam let me out of the Army Air Force (it was Army Air Corps when I enlisted right after Pearl Harbor). Bill had a very fine 22 revolver, didn't have any use for it (and nei-

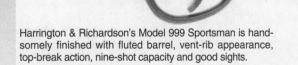

Harrington & Richardson's Model 999 Sportsman is handsomely finished with fluted barrel, vent-rib appearance, top-break action, nine-shot capacity and good sights.

ther did I for that matter, since I was already carrying one when checking my traps), but I bought it for $35.

Wish I still had it.

H&R's Model 999 Sportsman revolvers were introduced in 1933 and were regularly seen in gun shops well into the early 1980s. The company ran into problems, as did many back then. New folks took over, and gradually Harrington & Richardson is becoming, again, a company to watch. I've had the opportunity to work with several of their offerings these past few years and have found no fault with any.

Mine (yes, I bought the test revolver) has a 6-inch barrel, a simulated vent rib (looks great) and fully adjustable sights. Up front, it is adjustable for elevation; the rear for windage. Excellent sights they are, too—same as on any fine revolver. Square, flat-faced blade in front; wide, square-notched back. Very easy for a fast sight picture.

Safety? A transfer bar, as in all better revolvers nowadays. The 999 can be fired single or double action. Mine has a bit of creep in the trigger before it lets off crisply at 5½ pounds. Double action requires a somewhat hefty 16 pounds of pressure to pull it through.

Top-break is their description. Pull up on the wide, grooved "ears" of the rear sight and it opens for loading or ejection. Actually, my method is to push up, from the bottom, with the thumb of my gun hand. About one-third of the way to fully opened, the extraction process begins. Just before the gun is fully open the empties fall clear, and then the extractor pops back into place for reloading. Simple, fast and effective.

The 999 Sportsman is a nine-shot gun that accepts Short, Long or Long Rifle 22 rimfire cartridges. The hammer is 5/16-inch wide and has deep grooves across the spur for positive cocking. The grip is walnut-finished hardwood.

Two barrel lengths are offered, 4 or 6 inches. Their catalog lists the short 4-incher at 30 ounces and the 6-inch version at 34 ounces. My postal scale testifies to their correctness by verifying the 34-ounce figure.

How does it shoot? Right well, thank you.

Though I've shot this one rather extensively, five of the more popular 22 Long Rifle brands went to the range and did their thing through Ken Oehler's Model 35P chronograph. Ten rounds of Federal Hi-Power Long Rifle hollowpoints averaged 990 fps. The high was 1011, low 967—an extreme spread of 44 fps. Winchester's Super Silhouette Long Rifle cartridges feature a 42-grain bullet as opposed to normal 40-grain in most Long Rifle ammunition. High for these ten was 854 fps, low at 752, for an average velocity of 814 fps.

CCI's Mini-Mag Long Rifle hollowpoints topped out at 961 fps. Low for these was 844, for an average of 888 fps. Remington's High Velocity hollowpoints averaged 893 fps with the high at 916 and low 845 fps.

In going back over these four strings, I felt I had to try those Federal Hi-Power loads again. Talk about consistency! High for this second ten was 1013, low 965, and the average, believe it or not, was 990 fps—same as that first string.

Accuracy?

I have no trouble—iron sights, cataract implants in both eyes, seventy-three-year-old hands—keeping a filled cylinder on a playing card at 25 yards. That's almost identical to my very elderly Smith & Wesson K-22.

My bookshelves include a copy of *Shooter's Bible* No. 41, 1950 Edition. Page 101 contains three photographs under the heading "Harrington and Richardson Revolvers." The information includes the fact H&R offered a Model 199, identical to the 999 except that it was single action only, meaning it had to be cocked to fire.

The price in 1950 was $44.95 for the Model 999.

I haven't the vaguest idea as to when the "Sportsman" moniker was added to the Model 999, but it sounds good to me.

Though today's pricing is considerably more than it was back then, at $279.95 it is an excellent value. Really a lot of gun for the money. You won't hear that very often from this old handgunning typewriter jockey. •

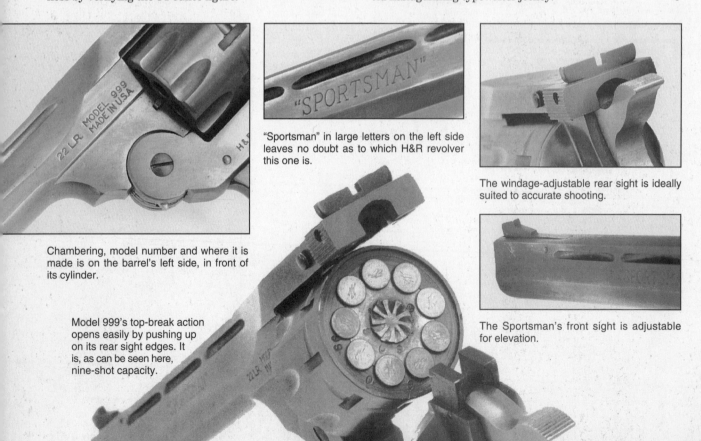

Chambering, model number and where it is made is on the barrel's left side, in front of its cylinder.

"Sportsman" in large letters on the left side leaves no doubt as to which H&R revolver this one is.

The windage-adjustable rear sight is ideally suited to accurate shooting.

Model 999's top-break action opens easily by pushing up on its rear sight edges. It is, as can be seen here, nine-shot capacity.

The Sportsman's front sight is adjustable for elevation.

H&R MODEL 999 SPORTSMAN 22 LR BALLISTICS TEST				
Manufacturer	Bullet (grs./type)	Ten-shot MV (fps) Avg.	High	Low
Fed. Hi-Power	40/HP	990	1011	967
Win. Super Sil.	42/LTC	814	854	752
CCI Mini-Mag	40/HP	888	961	844
Rem. High Vel.	40/HP	893	916	845
HP = Hollowpoint; LTC = Lead Truncated Cone				

Look at his expression and try to convince yourself the Editor wasn't having fun while doing this.

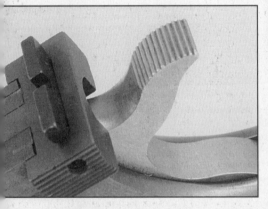

The hammer is 5/16-inch wide and deeply grooved for positive thumbing when shooting single action.

Our writer used these five cartridges for his tests here, and his Oehler 35P chronograph.

The walnut-finished hardwood grip is checkered and small enough for young shooters, yet comfortably fits full-grown hands.

Empties are extracted as the revolver is opened. Push down a tiny bit more with the barrel and these expended cases will fall out.

CONTENDER

by CHRIS CHRISTIAN

T/C CONTENDER SPECIFICATIONS

Manufacturer: Thompson/Center Arms

Action: Single shot, break-open design

Calibers: 22 LR, 22 LR Match, 22 WMR, 17 Rem., 22 Hornet, 222 Rem., 223 Rem., 7mm TCU, 7-30 Waters, 30-30 Win., 32-20 Win., 357 Mag., 357 Rem. Mag., 35 Rem., 375 Win., 44 Mag., 45-70 Gov't, 300 Whisper, 45 Colt/410

Barrel lengths: 10, 12, 14, 16 and 16¼ inches in octagon, bull, Hunter, Super and Vent/Rib configurations

Overall Length: 14 to 20¼ inches

Sights: Adjustable rear and ramped front; vent/rib barrel has beads, front and rear; scope-mountable

Weight: 43 to 65 ounces

Grips: American walnut and rubber Competitor Grip or rubber/Rynite finger-groove model

Finish: High luster blue or satin stainless steel

Price Basic Gun: $435; Extra Barrels: $200+

OVER A QUARTER-CENTURY ago, Thompson/Center shipped their first handgun. It was a rather unpretentious pistol.

Yes, it was a very graceful little gun, with lines reminiscent of some of the classic 18th-century dueling pistols. It came then, as it does now, with one of the finest out-of-the-box triggers you're likely to encounter. The sights were crisp and well-defined, and the little gun (then chambered for the miniscule 22 Long Rifle) took advantage of those factors and delivered uncommonly good accuracy.

But it was just a single shot pistol. In those days, that was not only a rarity, but often considered some sort of abnormal affliction, as well. Not many people gave it much chance to survive.

Today, the Thompson/Center Contender ranks as one of America's classic handguns. In fact, although there are a number of other excellent single shot handguns currently available, when one thinks of "single shot pistols" the ubiquitous Contender is generally the first to spring to mind.

There are some who opine the Contender's success is largely due to the tremendous rise in popularity of both metallic silhouette shooting and handgun hunting. There is no doubt that both played a role. Yet, a more thoughtful observation might bring one to conclude that the Contender, itself, deserves a great deal of credit for that increase in popularity. Here was a gun that was literally "made for games"—accurate, rugged, easy-to-use and capable of exceptional accuracy. All of this, and a modest price tag to boot. If that isn't a formula for success, I don't know what is.

Over the years, the Contender has been chambered for a staggering array of cartridges. Many are no longer offered in the standard line (although they can be had through T/C's custom shop). The current catalog lists eighteen available chamberings in barrels ranging from 10 to 16¼ inches, some in stainless steel and some with T/C's highly effective Muzzle Tamer. While this may sound like a slim selection, one would be hard-pressed to find a noticeable gap in the line.

New this year is an automatic ejection feature for several Contender barrels normally used by hunters. Holding the trigger guard back until the gun is completely broken open will eject the fired case. Or, shooters can opt for extraction, as in the past.

ROUND UP

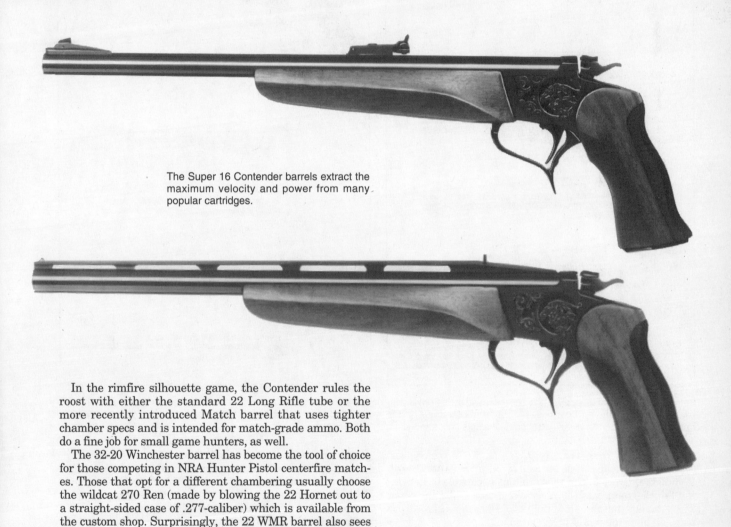

The Super 16 Contender barrels extract the maximum velocity and power from many popular cartridges.

In the rimfire silhouette game, the Contender rules the roost with either the standard 22 Long Rifle tube or the more recently introduced Match barrel that uses tighter chamber specs and is intended for match-grade ammo. Both do a fine job for small game hunters, as well.

The 32-20 Winchester barrel has become the tool of choice for those competing in NRA Hunter Pistol centerfire matches. Those that opt for a different chambering usually choose the wildcat 270 Ren (made by blowing the 22 Hornet out to a straight-sided case of .277-caliber) which is available from the custom shop. Surprisingly, the 22 WMR barrel also sees a lot of use here, especially among shooters who, for one reason or another, do not handload. It has the power to drop 100-meter Hunter Pistol rams, especially with the Federal 50-grain load, and more than ample accuracy. My 10-inch 22 WMR barrel will toss the loads it doesn't like into 1.5-inch groups from a 100-yard bench. You should see what it does with the stuff it likes!

Big bore silhouette shooters have a more than ample

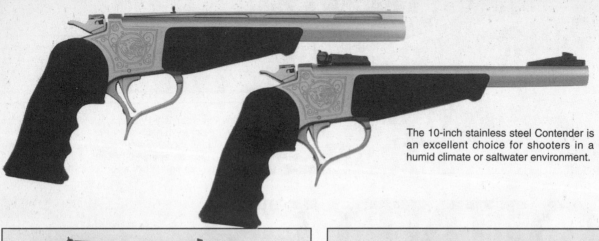

The 10-inch stainless steel Contender is an excellent choice for shooters in a humid climate or saltwater environment.

With a basic Contender receiver, the shooter can select from a variety of barrel lengths and cartridges. This level of versatility has made the Contender America's most popular single shot handgun.

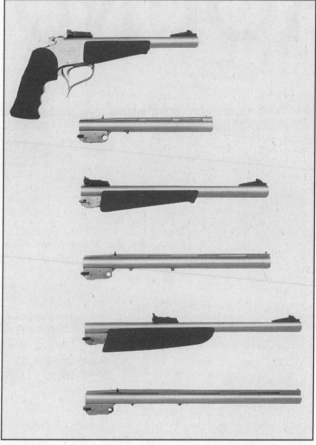

The stainless steel Contender version offers the handgunner a wide selection of barrels and cartridges in a durable, low-maintainance package.

selection in the 7mm TCU, 7-30 Waters, 30-30 Winchester, 357 Magnum, 357 Remington Maximum, and the 35 Remington. Every one of these rounds is capable of delivering 8-inch groups at 200 meters, and some, like the 7mm TCU, can cut that in half. If bullets of 160 grains and up are used, all have the power to level a ram.

Shift to lighter soft-nose ammunition, and each of the above rounds also becomes an excellent hunting number for deer-sized game. Even the 357 Magnum (often considered marginal for deer) can get the job done, thanks to the longer barrel length and the newly available 180-grain JHPs from Federal and Hornady. The Federal round will clock about 1430 fps from my 10-inch barrel and would punch right through a deer on a broadside lung shot. The exit holes show

good expansion, and the venison winds up in the freezer.

If larger game is on the menu, there is the 44 Magnum, 375 Winchester, and the rompin' stompin' 45-70 Government. With the proper bullets, these three rounds will take any animal in North America (and a lot of African game).

Should that selection be not to one's liking, there is always the previously mentioned T/C custom shop, as well as SSK Industries. J.D. Jones, head honcho at SSK, offers a number of highly effective wildcat cartridges in custom T/C barrels that have taken everything up to elephants!

Interestingly, it was Jones (one of the more innovative minds in the firearms business) who created the only new chambering Thompson/Center will be offering in 1994, the 300 Whisper.

CONTENDER STANDARD BARREL SELECTION CHART

Barrel Size (ins.)	Caliber	Gun Stock #	Barrel Stock #	
10 Octagon	22 LR	1010	3010	
10 Bull	22 LR	1013	3013	
	22 LR Match	2257	4257	
	22 Win. Mag.	1023	3023	
	22 Hornet	2013	4013	
	223 Rem.	2045	4045	
	7mm TCU	2250	4250	
	30-30 Win.	2173	4173	
	32-20 Win.	2073	4073	
	357 Mag.	2093	4093	
	357 Rem. Max.	2097	4097	
	44 Mag.	2153	4153	
	300 Whisper	2174	4174	
12 Hunter	223 Rem.		4879	SST 4872
	7-30 Waters		4881	SST 4873
	30-30 Win.		4882	SST 4875
	35 Rem.		4884	SST 4876
	375 Win.		4887	
	44 Mag.		4885	
	45-70 Gov't		4886	SST 4878
14 Hunter	223 Rem.	2800	4101	SST 4611
	7-30 Waters	2810	4102	SST 4612
	30-30 Win.	2820	4103	SST 4614
	35 Rem.	2840	4105	SST 4616
	375 Win.	2930	4108	SST 4619
	44 Mag.	2910	4106	
	45-70 Gov't		4107	SST 4618
14 Super	22 LR	2401	4401	*SST 3201 (SST 4201)
	22 LR Match	2531	531	*SST 3218 (SST 4218)
	17 Rem.	2408	4408	
	22 Hornet	2409	4409	*SST 3208 (SST 4208)
	222 Rem.	2404	4404	
	223 Rem.	2405	4405	*SST 3203 (SST 4203)
	7-30 Waters	2527	4527	*SST 3214 (SST 4214)
	30-30 Win.	2502	4502	*SST 3205 (SST 4205)
	357 Rem. Max.	2517	4517	
	35 Rem.	2505	4505	*SST 3206 (SST 4206)
	375 Win.	2520	4520	*SST 3207 (SST 4207)
	44 Mag.	2508	4508	*SST 3222 (SST 4222)
	300 Whisper	2522	4522	
16 Super	22 LR	2540	4540	*SST 3301 (SST 4301)
	22 Hornet	2545	4545	*SST 3308 (SST 4308)
	223 Rem.	2544	4544	*SST 3302 (SST 4302)
	30-30 Win.	2552	4552	*SST 3306 (SST 4306)
	45-70 Gov't BB with Muzzle Tamer	2551	4551	*SST 3304 (SST 4304)
	45 Colt/410: 10 bull barrel	2138	4138	*SST 2724 (SST 4724)
	10 vent rib	2148	4148	*SST 2725 (SST 4725)
	14 vent rib	2547	4547	*SST 3219 (SST 4219)
	16¼ vent rib	2546	4546	*SST 3303 (SST 4303)

SST = Stainless Steel. * = complete gun. ( ) = accessory barrel only. BB = Bull barrel.

Scope mounting a Contender is a snap, thanks to an excellent selection of mounts from T/C, as well as from most aftermarket mount suppliers.

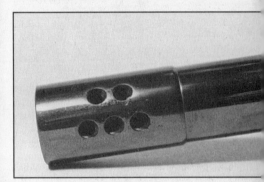

T/C's Muzzle Tamer brake is incredibly effective in taming the muzzle whip associated with hard-kicking calibers.

300 Whisper

According to Jones, the 300 Whisper is a new concept in the development of small case capacity—highly efficient cartridges using heavier bullets of extreme ballistic efficiency.

The Whisper was created to produce extreme accuracy with a heavy projectile moving at subsonic velocities. Its intended function was in suppressed weapons to be used by military special operations units and police counter-sniping teams. In that role it seems to be unmatched. In fact, independent range tests have shown that the 240-grain loading (using the Sierra MatchKing .308-inch bullet at an average velocity of 1040 fps) is capable of sub-MOA accuracy from both bolt-action and semi-auto rifles. Jones markets the round in an M-16 upper receiver package that mates perfectly with the M-16/AR15 rifle lower unit.

More intriguing are the external ballistics of the load. According to figures supplied by Jones, Sierra bullet tests show 1040 fps at the muzzle, 1003 fps at 100 yards and 971 fps at 200 yards! All from a small-cased cartridge of very modest recoil and noise levels. Part of the sound signature of any fired cartridge is the sharp crack as the bullet breaks the sound barrier; that is one reason why a 38 Special wadcutter load is much more pleasant to fire, at least to the ears, than a 22 WMR round, even though their comparative recoil levels are similar.

The extremely high ballistic coefficient of the 240-grain MatchKing bullet allows the 300 Whisper to deliver as

The Contender is offered in a number of calibers that are ideal for small game or varmits. This 18-pound Florida gobbler was taken with a 223 version.

RECOIL PROOF SCOPE CHART

Model	Color	Power	100-yd Field of View (ft.)	Eye Relief (ins.)	Mount Style	Length (ins.)	Wgt. (oz.)
8315	Black	2.5-7x	15-5	8-21	Ring	9.25	9.2
8326*	Black	2.5-7x	15-5	8-21	Ring	9.25	10.5
8316	Silver	2.5-7x	15-5	8-21	Ring	9.25	9.2
8317	Black	2.5-7x	15-5	8-21	Rail	9.25	10.0
8327*	Black	2.5-7x	15-5	8-21	Rail	9.25	11.2
8312	Black	2.5x	15	9-21	Rail	7.25	6.6
8320*	Black	2.5x	15	9-21	Rail	7.25	8.2
8323*	Silver	2.5x	15	9-21	Ring	7.25	7.2
8322*	Black	2.5x	15	9-21	Ring	7.25	7.2

* = Indicates illuminated reticle.

This 300-pound boar required only one shot with a 375 Winchester Contender barrel. This cartridge produces almost the same ballistics in a 14-inch Contender barrel as it does in a 20-inch rifle, making it a top choice for most North American game at ranges under 150 yards.

The 22 LR Contender barrels are top choices for squirrel hunters when equipped with the Recoil Proof 2.5-7x scope. They will often outshoot a 22 rifle!

much, or more, ram-downing power in the silhouette game as the 44 Magnum, but in a much more shooter-friendly package— and a much more accurate one.

The obvious drawback is its trajectory. Sighted in at 200 meters, the bullet will be about 16.5 inches high at 100 meters. Shooting at known distances, however, that does not present a problem as long as the sights have enough movement to correct for it. When one considers the advantages of a low-recoiling, subsonic round using a bullet whose ability to buck the wind and stay on course is legendary (as is its propensity for tossing all its rounds into little 3-inch circles at 200 meters), one would have to conclude the 300 Whisper might well find a role in the IMHSA game.

That's not all the round is capable of, though.

Big bullets at low velocities get the job done, and have been doing so since the old blackpowder days. Combine that with the Whisper's mild manners, and it is not hard to see why some animal control officers have begun using it. Jones, who has tested the round on game animals, tells me the bullet invariably tumbles on impact and does a better job than its paper ballistics would suggest.

Big bullets, however, are not all the Whisper can handle. In fact, this round goes supersonic with the same alacrity as it goes subsonic.

When one substitutes the excellent 125-grain Nosler 30-caliber Ballistic Tip bullet for the heavier MatchKing, the accuracy levels remain similar and the velocity climbs to about 2000 fps from a 10-inch barrel. The Ballistic Tip has an excellent reputation among handgun hunters for its quick and consistent expansion. At 2000 fps, it should do the job quite nicely on deer-sized game inside 200 yards. If slightly tougher game is in the cards, the 150-grain Ballistic Tip can crank out about 1850 fps, providing more penetration before expansion begins and equally good game-downing power.

Those velocity figures may not excite some, but I have "whacked and stacked" a lot of whitetails and wild hogs with a 14-inch Contender in 7mm TCU, using the 120-grain SSP bullets by Speer and Hornady with a velocity of about 2100 fps. It gets the job done in an exemplary fashion, and the 300 Whisper, with either the 125- or 150-grain Ballistic Tips, should do just as well. They should equal the field performance of a 30-30 from a Contender, with about one-third to one-half of the recoil.

The Whisper is a wildcat (although loaded ammunition is available from Cor-Bon and SSK Industries). It is based on the 221 Fireball case, first introduced in 1963 for use in the Remington XP-100 single shot pistol. The brass is readily available.

So, too, are the dies, and loading with them is a snap. The case is first neck-expanded to 6.5mm, then full-length resized to the 300 Whisper dimension with a second die. Small rifle primers are used, and there are no real surprises when loading this round—it goes together easily, like virtu-

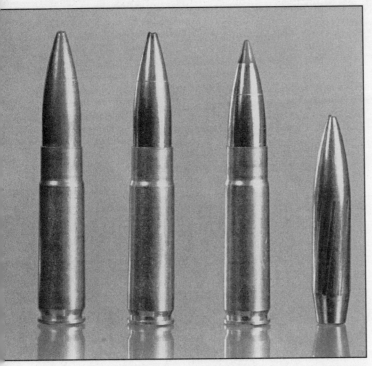

The 300 Whisper is shown (left to right) with 240-, 220- and 125-grain loads. Nosler Ballistic Tip can reach 2000 fps and should equal the field performance of the 30-30 with much less recoil. The 240-grain MatchKing at far right doesn't leave much room for powder.

ally every other round J.D. Jones has created. He designs them to load easily!

On the range, his 300 Whisper proved an accurate and mild-mannered round. On hand were the three Cor-Bon factory loads consisting of 125- and 150-grain Nosler Ballistic Tips and the 220-grain Sierra MatchKing. Although a late spring storm was blowing through, complete with a 20 mph crosswind and intermittent rain (hardly ideal conditions to wring out top accuracy from my backyard 100-yard bench), the factory-supplied 10-inch test barrel mated with T/C's excellent 2.5-7x Recoil Proof scope in Duo Ring mounts displayed accuracy levels with all three rounds that, under the conditions, were outstanding. Cor-Bon's 125-grain load seemed to be the most accurate, routinely producing 1.5-inch groups from the 100-yard bench. Their 150-grain load stayed under 2 inches, while the 220-grain subsonic load just about equalled that performance. Interestingly, despite the wide variation in bullet weights and velocities, when sighted in for 100 yards, points of impact were very close. With the 125-grain load sighted dead-on, the 150-grainer was about 2 inches high. The subsonic load shot to the same

elevation as the 125 load, but about 2 inches to the left.

The recoil was surprisingly light. Both the 125- and 150-grain loads were comparable to a 180-grain 357 Magnum load fired from a similar 10-inch-barreled Contender. The 220-grain load was noticeably softer and should become a real favorite in the silhouette game.

Chronographing these loads showed that velocities from Cor-Bon's ammo were right on the money. The 125-grain Nosler averaged 2057 fps; the 150-grainer came in at 1853 fps; the 220 subsonic load clocked 1004 fps.

Another new feature for the Contender this year is an automatic ejection system on some of the 14-inch Hunter barrels. Available in 30-30, 7-30 Waters and 45-70 Government, they will throw the fired case completely clear of the gun if the shooter holds the trigger guard to the rear until the gun is completely broken open. That should be a big plus for hunters, especially in cold climates where the mandatory mittens can often interfere with a quick reload. If you don't want to send the case flying, just release the trigger guard before the gun is fully broken open and it reverts back to partial ejection, allowing the shooter to manually extract the case. I'd like to see this incorporated into those barrels used for the various silhouette games as well. If time limits are tight, as they are in the Long Range event at the Masters' International, automatic ejection can save valuable seconds, and you can always pick up the brass after the string.

That sums up what is new for the Contender this year, but it is worth mentioning some of the accessory items already in the line.

Iron-sight silhouette shooters will want to take a look at T/C's Silhouette Sight assembly. This precisely machined unit interchanges with the standard rear sight. It allows the shooter to have four different points of impact and access them quickly via a large knurled adjustment dial that does not require the use of a screwdriver. Three rear sight blades of differing widths are available, with a matching front sight assembly that also offers three sight widths. If you shoot iron with your T/C, this is a must-have item.

One of the most popular features on the Contender is the barrel interchangeability. And since the sights are mounted on the barrel, there is no need to re-sight the gun after a barrel change. The only exception to that is if the barrel is installed on a Contender receiver having a different grip style than the one with which it was sighted in. As any experienced handgunner knows, changing the grip can change the shooter's grip pressure, which will affect the recoil forces on the gun and may cause it to shoot to a different point of impact. If you work with several receivers, as I do, it is advisable to equip them all with the same grip. Thompson/Center offers three interchangeable grips, including a recently introduced Rynite model with a sealed air pocket for the web of the hand. This is my favorite for soaking up recoil, as well as creating a non-reflective finish for field use.

Swapping barrels and grips is part of the fun of owning a Contender, and they make it easy with the Contender Combination Tool. This handy little 1.5-ounce gadget contains all that is needed to remove and replace the grip caps and grips, punch out the hinge pin, adjust the trigger and sights, and even remove the choke tube from the 45 Colt/410 barrel.

The current catalog also shows a number of cases, slings and holsters to make your Contender a bit handier in the field.

Mounting a scope on the Contender is a snap. Most makers offer mounts that fit the existing rear sight holes. T/C provides their intregal Duo-Rings, as well as a Rail Mount

300 WHISPER LOAD DATA

Powder	Grs. Wgt	MV (fps)
125-grain Nosler Ballistic Tip (10″ barrel)		
Hodgdon H-110	20.6	2333
WW-296	18.5	2050
150-grain Nosler Ballistic Tip (14″ barrel)		
Hodgdon H110	18.0	2073
AA-1680	20.2	1994
		1850
220-grain Sierra (10″ barrel)		
Hodgdon H-110	9.5	1020
240-grain Sierra MatchKing (10″ barrel)		
AA-2015 BR	18.8	1101
Reloder 7	12.1	1211
AA-1680	13.9	1304

All data utilizes 221 Remington Fireball parent case, Remington 7½ primers. Loads shown were developed in AR-15 rifles and in custom Shilen barrels. Reduce all loads by 10 percent for initial load development on T/C production barrels.

The silhouette rear sight interchanges easily with standard rear sight and offers improved performance for that game.

The Contender Tool has all the required equipment to maintain the handgun and swap barrels and grips. A knurled gold cap unscrews to display allen wrench for adjusting trigger. Handy!

The author relies on Contenders for much of his hunting. Barrels are available in calibers that are more than adequate for most North American big game and have taken animals up to and including elephants!

system. Both are designed for use with T/C's sturdy Recoil Proof scope line. Available in fixed 2.5x models or the popular 2.5-7x variable, these scopes will take the pounding of even the heaviest loads. They can be had in either black or silver finish in both standard 1-inch and rail mount configurations. All of my scope-equiped Contenders wear the 2.5-7x model, and it has performed brilliantly in the field.

One last item of note is the T/C Muzzle Tamer recoil brake, available as standard equipment on the 12- and 14-inch Hunter barrels. There is no question that some of the heavier hunting rounds have more than a little recoil, yet this muzzlebrake does a truly astonishing job at taming it. For example, I had the opportunity to test one of the first 375 Winchester barrels, and muzzle rise with full-power loads was brutal—about 90 degrees! Switching over to the 14-inch Hunter barrel with the Muzzle Tamer was like shooting a different gun. Muzzle rise was reduced to 30 degrees or less. Despite the fact that the 375 Winchester will toss a 220-grain slug at 1980 fps, and put out more energy at 100 yards than the 44 Magnum does at the muzzle, this barrel was more pleasant to fire than my 44 Magnum barrels! In short, the Muzzle Tamer does exactly what the name implies, and very effectively.

That last sentence may also sum up precisely why Thompson/Center has emerged as one of the premier American gunmakers, and it's likely to stay that way. Rugged, accurate, and reliable...at an affordable price. Sounds like a success formula to me! •

CENTURY ARMS'
FEG B9R 380 ACP
PISTOL
by TERRY MURBACH

FEG B9R 380 ACP SPECIFICATIONS

Manufacturer: FEG Hungary

Importer: Century Arms International

Operation: Double Action

Caliber: 380 ACP (9mm Browning Short)

Barrel Length: 4 inches

Weight Empty: 25 ounces

Sights Fixed: Patridge style

Sight Radius: 5.25 inches

Rifling: 7-groove, right-hand twist

Stocks: Checkered wood

Capacity: 15

Price: $312

THIS FEG PISTOL is quaintly marked with an old European name for its cartridge, "9mm Browning Short." It is a name I rather like for our prosaic 380 ACP cartridge, which has acquired more names over the years than any cartridge other than the 9mm Parabellum (9x19, NATO, etc.). Be that as it may, the good ol' 380 is a very popular cartridge, and the pistols that shoot it sell extremely well on this side of the Atlantic.

In the past few years, there has been a concerted effort by several pistol makers to upgrade the firepower of their guns by using double-column magazines. Most others hold twelve or thirteen rounds, but as of this writing, I think FEG is King of the 380 Mountain, as the B9R's magazine holds fifteen rounds. It uses them all in fine style, too. I have yet to have this B9R pistol suffer its first stoppage or jam. It has gobbled up hundreds of factory FMJs and JHPs, plus an even larger number of my handloads using JHP or lead round-nose bullets.

This B9R pistol weighs only 25 ounces. It has an aluminum alloy frame that feels for all the world like a Browning Hi-Power in my hand. The slide and barrel are made of steel, naturally, and are also nearly pure Hi-Power in looks and design. The B9R is not a locked-breech pistol. The slide fits the frame extremely well, and the slide locks up with the barrel in rigid alignment. Yes, indeed, this B9R was set up by someone who knows what shooting is all about, as far as barrels and slides are concerned. The bottom half of the pistol feels "Hi-Powerish" to me, too, but it looks more like a Smith & Wesson frame, and the double action/single action, disconnector, etc., are nearly pure S&W in function.

Both the SA and DA trigger pulls were terrible when the pistol was brand new. The SA trigger has broken in to where it is shootable, but that DA is still one crunchy, tough sonofagun to make go bang. I have dry-fired the dickens out of the DA, but it is still far too heavy. People with weak

FEG B9R 380 ACP wears the good looks of Browning's great Hi-Power 9mm autoloader.

Hundreds of the cartridges shown here were fired with no malfunctions whatsoever after those initial three. A feat mighty hard for any autoloader to top. This, remember, included CCI's Blazer disposable cartridges.

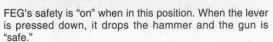

Fifteen rounds of 380 ammo "ain't to be sneezed at." That's what it takes to fill the FEG B9R.

FEG's safety is "on" when in this position. When the lever is pressed down, it drops the hammer and the gun is "safe."

hand strength would have trouble cycling the DA trigger pull, but the gun does have an easy-to-thumb-cock hammer spur.

The B9R's manual safety is a large levered hammer-drop at the left rear of the slide. There is no magazine safety on this pistol.

The magazine release is on the left side at the rear of the trigger guard, right where it's most convenient. It is a bit stiff to operate, but once depressed, the magazine falls away cleanly from the pistol. Other good news is that the gun is furnished with two magazines. Unfortunate for southpaws, the release is not reversible.

The sights on this 380 pistol are quite good, offering a clean, crisp sight picture. The notch in the rear sight was too narrow for my tastes and eyesight, so I opened up the notch by filing about .010-inch off each side. Regulation of the sights was essentially dead on the money with most of the loads we fired. My innate prejudice against fixed sights has eroded a bit further. The B9R's front sight appears to be an integral part of the slide. It won't be falling off any time soon, but if you bang it up, it will be expensive to fix.

Our first testfiring of the pistol produced three misfires in the first fifteen rounds. After that, it never misfired again. Slide stop function was a sometime thing with both magazines. One would work, then quit, then the second would do the same thing. I always had a sneaking hunch it was caused by the slide not being kicked hard enough rearward to engage the stop. A few handloads of stout proportion functioned the slide stop perfectly.

This pistol could really shoot Federal's 95-grain FMJ

FEG B9R 380 ACP BALLISTICS TEST

Manufacturer	Bullet (grs./type)	MV (fps)	ME (fpe)	SD	Group Avg. (ins.)
Blazer	88/JHP	975	185	14	3.27
Blazer	95/FMJ	963	195	16	3.83
Federal	95/FMJ	922	179	13	3.79
Federal	90/JHP	900	161	53	5.25
Federal	90/Hi-Shok	973	189	15	3.00
Hornady	90/XTP	957	183	8	3.31
Hornady	100/FMJ	853	161	11	5.24
Winchester	85/Silvertip	936	165	9	7.25
Hansen	95/FMJ	892	167	19	4.95

All shots taken at 25 yards.

The FEG B9R's barrel is a snug fit to the slide, and that slide beautifully fits to the frame.

FEG B9R's backstrap and slender wood stocks feel good—even when rapid-firing a filled magazine.

The Browning Hi-Power look-alike FEG in front of the test ammo it digested with ease.

The hammer's long spur is easily cocked, but doesn't come near to biting the hand.

The FEG B9R field strips just like 99 percent of all autoloading pistols.

loads as well as the Blazer 88-grain JHPs. It gobbled these up and printed groups that are exceptional for a 380 pistol. When I would really bear down and concentrate, the gun could punch a magazine full of Federal's 95-grain FMJs into one-hole groups at both 7 yards and 50 feet. The 380 cartridge is not noted for target-grade accuracy, and this is usually because the pistols themselves simply are not built to standards tight enough to ensure match accuracy. The cartridge is almost a perfectly scaled-down copy of the 45 ACP and, in guns of equal quality, should shoot just as well as its big brother. It seems to me that the 380 in a good target pistol would be the ideal "centerfire" pistol for NRA bullseye shooting.

The FEG B9R is not a target pistol. It is accurate enough for serious plinking, and I used it for several sessions at my club's plinking range to demolish regimental formations of tin cans before they could move out of their tracks. The inexpensive Blazer ammunition is ideal for such shooting, as the aluminum cases are on a one-way trip to oblivion with each press of the trigger.

I am at a bit of a loss in figuring out how a fifteen-shot 380 pistol fits into the general scheme of defensive handguns. The B9R's grip frame is of 9mm Parabellum proportion without delivering the Parabellum's punch. On the other hand, the fulsome grip allows superb control during rapid-fire, which means you can *really* pour out bursts on this gun while using a firm two-handed grip. A hail of 95-grain bullets is not something one would care to intercept amidships.

The B9R functioned perfectly through my tests, and it was never cleaned. It was literally caked full of crud and just kept chugging away, gobbling up dozens of magazines long after it deserved a thorough cleaning and lubrication. This totaled hundreds of rounds through a filthy, dirty pistol—something I have found in past tests not to the liking of Blazer ammo, where failures to feed were quite common in two of my personal 380 pistols. Generally, Blazers work well in clean guns; it didn't matter one bit in the FEG B9R one way or the other.

The shooting tests started out a bit rough with the gun's heavy trigger pull and three misfires, but once that sorted itself out, the B9R proved to be a proper, upright citizen in the gun world. At less than $250, it is priced most competitively. It's available from Century Arms International. ●

ANOTHER BRAZILIAN HIT
ROSSI'S
by HAL SWIGGETT

ROSSI COVERT SPECIAL MODEL 720C

Manufacturer: Rossi

Importer: Interarms

Caliber: 44 Special, five-shot

Barrel length: 3 inches

Sights: Fixed

Weight: 27.5 ounces

Grips: Combat-style, checkered black rubber

Features: Stainless steel; solid barrel rib; full ejector rod shroud; double-action-only

Price: $312

A SURE-FIRE WINNER is Rossi's newest stainless steel, double-action-only, five-shot 44 Special called the Covert Special.

Weighing in at 30 ounces on my postal scale, it features a full-length ejector rod shroud, fixed rear sight (a square notch in the topstrap) and cross-grooved ramp up front. Their catalog describes the hammer as "shrouded." This must be because it is invisible until the trigger is given a hefty 14-pound pull bringing it out and into firing condition.

The barrel length is 3 inches. The trigger is smooth and somewhat rounded. If it belonged to me, I would make two modifications. One, the rear sight notch would be slightly enlarged. As it is now, the front sight blade fills it completely. That might be the preference of some, but I prefer to see a bit of daylight on each side.

Second, I like an even more rounded trigger. Several years ago, Denver-based 300 Gunsmiths worked over a Model 29 S&W for me. It came back with a very round trigger of which I have become very fond.

Other than those piddlin' modifications, this Rossi fits my way of thinking mighty close.

The grips are described as soft, contoured, combat-style. Whatever the material is, it feels mighty good in my size 7 Cadet hand. The finger grooves fit perfectly.

The 44 Smith & Wesson Special cartridge was introduced shortly after the turn of the century. Both Colt and S&W built revolvers around it. It was, for many years, thought of as the most accurate, most powerful, big-bore handgun cartridge. It isn't, and never was, a cartridge to be taken lightly. Remington and Winchester currently offer this cartridge with a 246-grain lead bullet advertised at 755 fps. Both also offer a 200-grain bullet: Remington a semi-wadcutter, Winchester their Silvertip, at 900 fps. Federal lists a 200-grain semi-wadcutter hollowpoint at 900 fps. Like I said earlier, these are not to be taken lightly.

Since 44 Special happens to be one of my favored cartridges in handguns of this format, I had a few of each maker's 200-grainers on hand. I hasten to add here that in spite

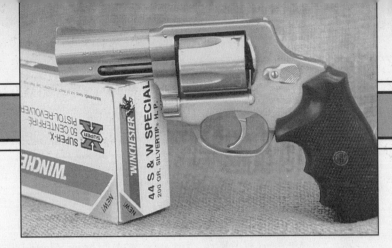

A mighty handsome double-action-only (DAO) 44 Special revolver is this Model 720C from Rossi. Barrel length is 3 inches, and it is all stainless steel. Covert Special is a mighty good name for this one.

COVERT SPECIAL

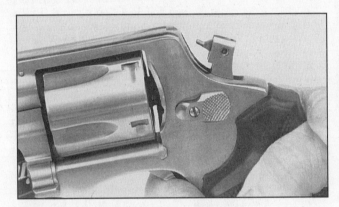

Rossi's Model 720C cannot be cocked. To get this photograph, its trigger had to be pulled and held just short of firing.

Five 44 Special cartridges fill Covert Special's cylinder.

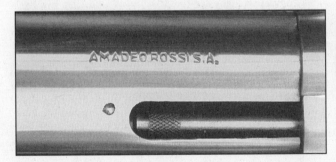

Manufactured by Amadeo Rossi S.A. (Brazil) is imprinted on the barrel's left side.

M720 (its mate is identical except has a hammer and can be cocked) 44 S&W SPL is on its right side.

of what some might tell you, do not fire these shorter cases in your 44 Magnum-chambered handgun. Sooner or later, these shorter cases will score the chambers, and eventually full-length 44 Magnums will stick. You say you've done it with no harm? Keep on and you will find out.

A box each of Federal 200-grain lead semi-wadcutter hollowpoint, Remington 200-grain lead semi-wadcutter and Winchester 200-grain Silvertip went to my gun/ammo/scope testing range. This was enough shooting for this somewhat ancient handgunner to form a firm opinion. Not all that long ago, I took a revolver with the same amount of ammo plus a

box of twenty-five shotshells and fired less than a dozen to convince me the project was in no way worth pursuing. Another way to say this might be, we learn a few things in spite of ourselves.

Be that as it may, ten of the Federals topped at 821 fps with a bottom of 778 fps. The average was 795, meaning a difference of 43 fps, top to bottom. A like number of Remingtons clocked that identical average figure, but with 811 as high and 781 low—only 30 fps variance. What happened with Winchester's Silvertips has occurred more than a few times over these past years. Ten shots went through

ROSSI COVERT SPECIAL 44 SPECIAL BALLISTICS TEST

Manufacturer	Bullet (grs./type)	Ten-shot —MV (fps)—		
		Avg.	High	Low
Federal	200/Lead SWCHP	795	821	778
Remington	200/Lead SWC	795	811	781
Win. Silvertip	200/HP	734	739	725

SWCHP = Semi-wadcutter hollowpoint; HP = Hollowpoint

Testfiring this one was a pleasure because of Hal's deep affection for "chopped," as the calls them, revolvers.

This photo explains itself. Who made it, where, and the importer.

the three screens at an average of 734 fps. That's 61 fps below the other two, even though Federal lists theirs at 900 fps and Remington 1035 fps. Remember, factory figures are at the muzzle, and apparently from test barrels, not actually fired through a handgun anyway. My point here is that those ten Silvertip bullets varied only 14 fps from top to bottom, 739 to 725, mighty consistent for sure.

Accuracy?

This chronographing was done with my target at 15 yards, which is three times as far as from most pillows to the bedroom door. Unusual, admittedly, but all three loads stayed in my green, 6-inch-diameter bullseye target. Regardless of which load you might select, I believe they all

will print relatively close to your point of aim. A different spot for each of us, more likely than not, because no two folks are going to hold the revolver in an identical manner; nor are we going to see sights the same.

Hurriedly aimed shots at 15 feet—not point-shooting, but at the same time not carefully lining up where they were going—kept them within 12 inches. Keep in mind, this is a double-action-only revolver designed specifically for close range and getting shots off as quickly as possible. As I did this, both hands were holding the revolver— same as when chronographing or shooting at animals. My grandfather once said, "God gave you two hands—use both of them when shooting single actions." The term, single actions, was because the gun in hand was Colt's 44-40. I've stuck to that advice all these years in between, and repeat it to every new shooter as the opportunity is offered.

Should it appear I like this Rossi Covert Special, there is a reason. My first of this type was built in 1948 by a smith named Buddy Moreno. His shop was in the back of Toepperwein's Sporting Goods store on West Houston street in downtown San Antonio.

Buddy had to be talked into it because, as he loudly proclaimed, he could see no reason to destroy a perfectly good Model 1917 Smith & Wesson double-action revolver. But he did it, for money—a convincer in many questionable cases.

The main difference between that shortened S&W 45 and this Rossi is the trigger guard. Yes, I still have one of the conversions, the third to be made for me. Barrel length was the same 3 inches. The hammer spur was ground off allowing it to be cocked only with care. By that I mean, its trigger had to be slowly pulled so the thumb could grasp that hammer and bring it back to its cocked position. In essence, it too was double-action-only, as have been the pair that followed. Three deep grooves were cut across the top of that hammer providing better control.

Its trigger guard difference?

The front was cut out to be even with the trigger's tip. Why? I'm really not at all certain, other than that was what I wanted. It did, I guarantee, make the revolver look meaner.

Back then, 45 Auto Rim ammunition was available, designed specifically for the 1917 S&W and Colt revolvers. Without those rimmed cases, a three-round clip had to be used to remove empties. Since ACPs seat on the case mouth, they could be fired either way. Ejection, though slower, was easy—use a pen or pencil to simply punch them out.

In those days, my shooting was done on what was known as the West Avenue Shooting Range. An FBI agent shot there frequently, and over a period of several months, I allowed him to talk me out of that "customized for sure" S&W Model 1917. Actually, that really isn't the truth—his talking became more convincing only as his financial offer increased.

Many years later, I had another one made, identical to that initial chopped version, by putting a photograph of it with another 1917 S&W and issuing the order, "Make this one look like the photograph." Jim Pacheco did exactly that.

There is also a third gun because a burglar took a liking to number two one night as he went through my office desk. In fact, four chopped-style revolvers went with him. One was retrieved in a drug raid by our Sheriff's department. Another was pawned and picked up by the police. Both were returned to me. The other two? Who knows where they are.

Now you know why I whole-heartedly approve of Rossi's Covert Special. Chopped big-bore revolvers have been a way of life for this old handgunner for nigh on to half a century.

Put another way, a lot of "new" things really are not. They are just new to a new generation.

●

HANDGUNS 95

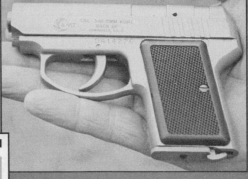

SECTION 3
Custom Handguns

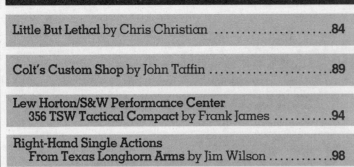

Big things in small packages, says Christian, page 84.

S&W's PC gun gets the once-over from James, page 94.

Wilson checks out Texas Longhorn Arms' SAs, page 98.

LITTLE

CUSTOMIZED AMT DAO
SERIOUS PERFORMANCE IN

by CHRIS CHRISTIAN

Just a touch of custom work turned this palm pistol into pocketable perfection.

T HERE WAS A time when the term "pocket pistol" was in common use. As the name implies, it was a catch-all phrase covering any number of compact handguns that could be slipped into a pocket.

The term is heard less often today, primarily because contemporary fashions leave precious little pocket room. But for those who have a concealed-carry permit, a pistol in the pocket makes as much sense today as it did many years ago.

I'm a firm believer that, when conditions warrant its need, the best place to have a defensive handgun is in the hand. I don't care what type of holster one wears or where it is positioned on the body—having the gun already in your hand beats reaching for one!

The law, however, takes a dim view of "brandishment," or provocative moves. Displaying a handgun (or even placing your hand on a holstered handgun) when only the "potential" for a threat exists can get you into some serious trouble, not to mention escalating a situation that might have been resolved in a more amicable fashion.

That's why pocket pistols make sense.

An individual with a hand slipped casually into an overcoat, windbreaker or trouser's pocket is viewed as perfectly normal and totally non-threatening by the general public. The fact that the hand is wrapped in a firing grip around a handgun ready to be immediately employed doesn't alter that.

It's a very comfortable position to be in when you walk through a dark, deserted parking lot at night. Unfortunately, the selection of handguns suitable for that task is not particularly impressive.

Among semi-autos, most of today's pocket pistols fall into the 22 rimfire or 25 ACP class. Those cartridges don't inspire much confidence, and many of the guns are not par-

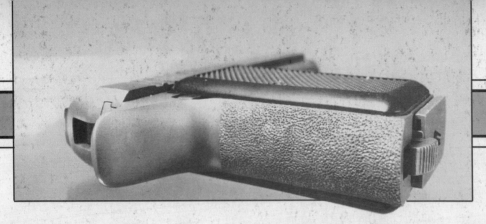

Stippling on the backstrap, as well as the frontstrap, is a big help with small-framed handguns.

BUT LETHAL

BACK UP OFFERS A POCKETABLE PACKAGE

The Art Leckie-installed rear sight is wide, generous and quick to acquire, yet no more prone to snagging than the original milled channel sights on the unaltered gun.

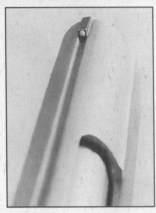

This clever custom front sight, with bright, red plastic bead insert, fits neatly into the existing milled channel.

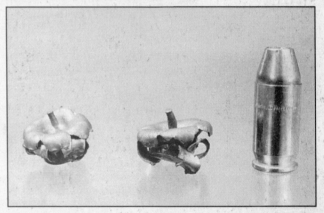

Federal's 90-grain Hyrda-Shok shows excellent expansion in both water and ballistic gelatin. In recent tests involving live targets, it offered performance levels equalling some 38 Special +P loads fired from 4-inch-barreled revolvers! It makes the 380 ACP every bit the equal of the 38 Special snubby.

ticularly well made and have a dubious record of reliability.

The notable exception is the exquisite Seecamp. This little 32 ACP totes comfortably in a Levi's pocket, is made with Swiss-watch precision, and is considered by experts to be state-of-the-art in its class. Unfortunately, they are quite expensive, involve a lengthy wait for delivery, and still only fire a 32 ACP.

If you have b-i-g pockets, there is the 38 snubby revolver alternative. Compact five-shot models, like the J-frame S&Ws or the Taurus Model 85 (with bobbed hammers), pack a better punch and are notable for their reliability. They work well for coat-pocket carry, but are tough on trousers. They are also limited to five rounds, and reloading is an agonizingly slow process if you have to do it quickly. That, of course, assumes you carry extra ammo. I've toted a snubby for ten years and haven't found a convenient way to do it yet. Speedloaders are too bulky, and stripper clips (like

the Bianchi Speed Strip) won't hold the rounds securely enough for pants-pocket carry. My solution is to carry five loose rounds in the right front pants pocket and to hope I never need them.

All of this is why I took a very keen interest in the AMT DAO (double-action-only) Back Up pistol introduced at the 1994 SHOT Show.

Like the Seecamp, it is a double-action-only pistol that carries no safety, levers or controls, and it only fires via a lengthy double-action trigger pull. It is the safest way to carry a loaded handgun in the pocket, yet can be put into immediate use with either hand—just pull the trigger.

With a weight of 18 ounces, overall length of 5 inches, and a width of $^{11}/_{16}$-inch, it is slightly bigger than the Seecamp, yet a lot more compact than a 38 snubby revolver. It takes up little more room in the front pocket of a pair of Levis than does a 4-inch folding knife.

The Back Up is constructed of stainless steel. That's a definite plus for daily pocket carry. And, best of all, it is chambered for the 380 ACP.

That may not excite some. But regardless of whose stopping power theories and tests you look at, they all basically agree the 380 ACP produces the same practical level of power as a 38 Special fired from a 2-inch snubby. One recent test involving live animals (Strasbourg) indicated that the best 380 JHP load (Federal Hydra-Shok) surpassed the snubby loads tested and equalled the performance of a number of 38 Special+P loads fired from 4-inch-barrelled revolvers.

I'll accept the fact that the 380 will at least equal the 38 Special snubby. Once I do that, I'll note that the 380 carries six rounds (five in the magazine plus one in the chamber) instead of the snubby's five rounds. Not only that, a spare loaded magazine for the AMT takes up about as much room as a pack of chewing gum and is a heckuva lot quicker way to reload the gun than digging 38 ammo out of a pocket.

All this went through my mind as I inspected the gun at AMT's SHOT Show booth. The gun had a lot of potential, and I made arrangements to get one.

As it turned out, the little DAO Back Up was immediately available (unlike some guns "introduced" at the SHOT Show and "available" the following year), and it wasn't long before one of my "Buddies In Brown" (as I refer to the local UPS drivers) dropped off one at my FFL address.

Since my shooting range is in my backyard, I popped open the box, grabbed a couple hundred rounds of 380 factory fodder, and went shooting.

At the end of the session I was left with some mixed emotions, including a realization that what often looks promising in the showroom may not always live up to its apparent potential in the real world.

First things first. In terms of reliability—the most critical aspect of any self-defense handgun—the DAO scored an A+! In fact, it was amazing.

I'd grabbed the gun right out of the box and done nothing more than check the bore for an obstruction. Then I ran almost 200 rounds through it, which included virtually every JHP and FMJ currently available from Federal, Hornady, Winchester, CCI and PMC. During the whole time, there was exactly one malfunction, and it was shooter induced. Late in the session, when the gun was really grubby, I sluggishly rode the slide forward to chamber a round from a fresh magazine, and it didn't fully go into battery. A tap to the rear of the slide with the heel of my hand seated it.

That was the total malfunction rate, and pocket-sized semi-autos just aren't supposed to be that good.

There were, however, other features that left me less impressed. The DA-only trigger had about the same length of pull as a Chief's Special revolver, but it was a rather gritty 16 pounds, according to my Brownell's trigger-pull gauge. The trigger was also poorly shaped (it wasn't radiused well) and left a welt on my trigger finger.

I'll be the first to admit that, given the gun's intended use, both of these "problems" are real nit-picking on my part. Many wouldn't consider them drawbacks of any significance, but I'm the one who is going to be carrying this gun.

The biggest problem, however, were the sights—or more precisely, the lack of them. The sights consist of a shallow milled channel running the length of the slide. There is no front reference point. I did not attach any significance to this when I inspected the gun at the SHOT Show. On the range, though, it proved most disconcerting.

During the twenty-eight years I have been involved with

The fully customized AMT DAO Back Up is basically no larger than original gun, yet offers a large increase in performance. With two five-round magazines and one in the chamber, it provides a significant increase in firepower over any revolver.

Federal's 90-grain Hydra-Shok has proven to be the most effective 380 load currently available. The new Starfire 95-grain load from PMC should prove to be as good, giving 380 lovers two truly effective rounds.

handguns (including a ten-year stint in military and civilian law enforcement which included serving as a small arms instructor to both, as well as being an active competitive shooter and handgun hunter), I have developed certain subconscious shooting habits. Any shooter who has been involved with firearms that long on an almost daily basis will have done the same.

These subconscious responses are what allow an experienced shooter to draw a holstered handgun and deliver an accurate 10-yard hit in under a second. This action has to be subconscious, because one cannot consciously think his way through each and every physical action and mental decision required to accomplish that task. This is developed through proper training and repetition.

In my case, a critical subconscious response, the one that will trigger the shot after I have made the conscious deci-

Twelve rounds from a Weaver stance at 15 yards shows a group you can cover with your hand! This is more than adequate combat accuracy and a level that few pocket-sized handguns will achieve.

The unaltered AMT DAO is a convenient palm-sized package that tucks neatly into trouser or jacket pockets. The modifications to the author's gun did not detract from that.

sion to employ a handgun, is to see "sights on target." It doesn't have to be much of a sight picture—at close range, just a glimpse of the front sight alone (called a flash sight picture) will suffice. As the range increases, the sight picture and alignment are refined.

Remove the front sight, however, and almost three decades of training and experience are short-circuited! That's what was happening to me. I was uncomfortable triggering a round without being confident of where it would go.

At close range (inside 7 yards), it wasn't hard to keep a magazine-full in the torso area of a silhouette target—or somewhere in the area. But I was not at all comfortable with "somewhere." I could only imagine how much hesitation on my part might result if I had to use the gun in a self-defense situation where bystanders might be around. Enough to get me hurt?

Moving back to 15 yards really aggravated the problem. It took very careful and slow alignment of the channel to show just a touch of the front of the groove over the rear before I was able to keep five rounds in a 9- or 10-inch group centered on the torso. I developed very little confidence in my ability to deliver a quick and accurate hit at that range.

In all fairness to AMT, I was demanding the gun do something it was never intended to do. This DAO Back Up was designed, manufactured and marketed as nothing more than a deep-concealment back-up gun that could be quickly drawn and put into use at powder-burning range. In that respect, it lived up to everything AMT said about it. I was the one who was pushing the performance envelope.

I could easily envision times when this would be the only handgun I would be carrying, and I knew it had the potential to play that role. I've tested several of their single-action versions, which have rudimentary sights, and found them easily capable of delivering 4-inch point-of-aim groups at 15 to 20 yards. Except for the DAO trigger, this gun is mechanically the same as the others and should be capable of that kind of performance.

With that in mind, I made a phone call to Art Leckie, who has tuned a number of my guns in the past, and I have been

well pleased with the results. The project was, on the surface, a simple one since the gun didn't need major reworking. It functioned quite well as it was. It did, however, need some refinement that would allow me to realize its full potential—basically sights and a better trigger.

Apparently, Leckie had a different definition of "refinement" than I did. What he sent back was as state-of-the-art as you can get! Leckie addressed the trigger problem by completely recontouring it, then carefully smoothing and polishing the action. The end result compared favorably with a quality DA revolver trigger job—a smooth, rounded trigger with an 11-pound pull that is 100-percent reliable. In some respects, it is like a good S&W trigger; it starts light with a smooth stacking at the end, followed by a crisp break.

The gun was then turned over to his associate, gunsmith John Szczepanski, who stippled the front and rear grip straps and forward portion of the trigger guard. Good stippling has the same gripping qualities as 20-line-per-inch checkering and, to my way of thinking, looks just as good.

After that, Leckie got back into it and decided to add a small beavertail to the gun, about which I have mixed emotions. Combined with the excellent stippling job, it does lock the gun firmly in the hand. If you rip off six rounds, this gun finishes in the same position within the hand that it started. This is not to be taken lightly since the gun only allows two fingers on the grip (there ain't room for the pinky).

As a shooting aid it was great, but it might—maybe—possibly—interfere with quickly getting the gun out of a tight pocket.

He also bead-blasted the gun and polished the sides of the slide. Cosmetic, but I can't fault him for that. In addition to being my pistolsmith, he is also a good friend and hunting partner, and he just wanted me to have the best.

The real topper, however, were the sights. A low-profile, fixed rear sight was dovetailed into the rear of the slide. The notch is wide, deep and generous, yet is as snag-free as the original milled channel. Mated to that was a front sight that matched the width of the original channel. Since Leckie

The author found the customized AMT DAO offered more than adequate accuracy, combined with modest recoil. Custom sights and trigger work made this gun a real shooter

Both the DAO and single-action AMT Back Up II proved completely reliable with all currently available 380 rounds.

knows I am a big fan of acquiring the front sight as quickly as possible, he inlaid a bright, red plastic dot into the blade.

The sights did nothing to detract from the pocketability of the gun, but combined with the now-excellent trigger, the difference on the range is incredible! The sights were crisp, sharp and quick to acquire. The red plastic bead leapt out with all the brilliance of the Aimpoint and Simmons LED sights I use on my target pistols. What had been a "point and pray" gun took on a whole new life!

I put up a head and torso target at 7 yards to see if I could get a couple in the head zone; I could have covered the group with a 50-cent piece!

Backing off to 20 yards, I sent two full magazines (twelve rounds) into the torso. The group measured about 2½x4 inches. Elevation was perfect, but windage was a couple inches right.

A few strokes with a Swiss file and a touch of cold blue centered the group. You can't expect a fixed-sighted gun to shoot to the same point of aim for two different people, especially with a gun this small.

Feeling pretty cocky and totally confident, I put up a new head and torso target then backed off to 50 yards. From a Weaver stance, I ran ten rounds downrange. Five were good torso hits. Two were just off the target, low and centered. I couldn't find the other three because the backing paper was badly chewed up from other shooting sessions. I don't think they were very far off, however.

Still, that's pretty good performance for a handgun that you can comfortably carry in a trouser pocket.

Yeah, it took some custom work. But when you stop to consider the total cost of the original gun and the work, it is still less than a Seecamp. And it's stainless steel. And it's a 380. And it will shoot 4-inch groups at 15 yards. And it is available now.

I know what I will be carrying in the future! Anybody interested in a good buy on a used 38 snubby? •

COLT'S CUSTOM SHOP

by JOHN TAFFIN

Super-tuned 1911s, custom SAAs, engraving—all manner of personalized guns are available from Colt.

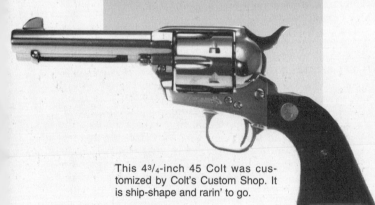

This 4³/₄-inch 45 Colt was customized by Colt's Custom Shop. It is ship-shape and rarin' to go.

THE NEXT BEST thing to shootin' and writin' and talkin' about six-guns is reading about them. A few years ago, a good friend sent me a copy of *Colts From Texas and the Old West*, a unique book full of pictures of First Generation (1873-1941) Colt single actions. Looking through the pages and back into history, one is immediately struck by the fact that famous shootists and six-gunners of yesteryear were not satisfied with plain-Jane, off-the-shelf guns. Lawmen, especially, looked upon their sidearms as badges of office and wanted something that was a cut above the ordinary, with custom grips and engraving being top choices for embellishment.

Texas Rangers like Captain Clint Peoples and Lone Wolf Gonzaullas carried, respectively, a matched pair of Colt single actions and Colt Government Models, fully engraved and ivory stocked, of course. My hero of heroes, Theodore Roosevelt, was particularly fond of a fully engraved Colt Single Action Army. And no "B" Western hero of my misspent youth would have been worth a hoot without his custom Colt.

Probably the most well-known symbol of authority was General George Patton's engraved and ivory-stocked Peacemaker, a 45 Colt purchased just before embarking with Blackjack Pershing into Mexico in 1916. In World War II, Patton's soldiers could always see the Old Man out in front packin' a "matched" pair of fancy revolvers consisting of his famous Colt and a first-year production Smith & Wesson 357 Magnum, also ivory-stocked. Modern-day serious six-gunners of my acquaintance seem to have much of the Roosevelt/Patton/Roy Rogers influence, as not a one carries a stock six-gun or semi-automatic. They may have been personalized only to the point of custom grips, but the shooting personality of the gunner is readily apparent.

The day of the custom handgun is certainly not over, and Colt, which provided so many of these fancy guns to pistoleros of the past, now serves today's shooter from their Custom Shop. Whether it be something as simple as a pair of Single Action Army grips of fancy walnut, rosewood, ebony, stag or ivory, or as extensive as a fully engraved and personalized Python, it is available from the Colt Custom Shop.

All of us have seen examples of exquisite works of art carried out on SAAs in full engraving often matched with gold

One of the Colt Custom Shop mainstays is the Royal Blue/case-hardened with walnut grips 7½-inch 45 Colt single action. First issued in 1875, it served the U.S. Army seventeen years until 1892, when it was replaced by the 38 Long Colt. Peacemaker was its name. Its authority: 40 grains of FFg blackpowder under a 255-grain bullet.

Nickel-finished revolvers are included in Colt's custom work. Barrel length can be 5½ inches like this 44-40, or your choice between 4¾ and 7½ inches.

Single Action Army revolvers never seem quite complete without a good holster. This one is by Bull-X Chaparral.

and silver inlays. Not only does the Custom Shop offer personalized handguns to meet each individual shooter's purse and personality, they also offer custom packages on guns found in the regular catalog. These could be labeled as standard/custom items, much the same as many packages offered by some of the top custom pistolsmiths in the country.

Packages include a Special Combat Government Model Competition Model with skeletonized trigger, custom grip safety, tuned action, polished feed ramp, throated barrel, flared ejection port, cut out Commander hammer, hard-chromed slide and receiver, extended thumb safety, Bo-Mar rear sight, Clark front sight, and flared magazine funnel. Add two magazines and this custom Colt retails for $1518. Changing the finish to Royal Blue, switching the sights to bar-dot night sights, and adding an ambidextrous safety, one has the Special Combat Government Carry Model at $1317. Both guns are fully accurized and come with a certified target attesting to their shooting capability.

A step up the ladder brings us to the Compensated Model 45 ACP with features found on the above two models plus a full-profile BAT compensator for the serious competitive shooter. Particularly appealing to me as a carry gun is a no-nonsense Limited Class M1991A1. It is reminiscent of the type of serious defensive pistol that made the Model 1911 famous, embodying the "essentials" for a carry Government Model, namely lightweight extended trigger mated with a tuned action and a 4-pound trigger pull, upswept grip safety, extended and ambidextrous slide safety, beveled magazine well and an accurizing package.

Commander fanciers have not been left out, and their needs are attended to with the Gold Cup Commander. Basically, a Gold Cup 45 with a Commander-length slide

and barrel, this one carries fully adjustable sights, wide grip safety and beveled magazine well, and is available in either blue or stainless.

The original 38 Special pocket gun, the Detective Special, is back in the Colt catalog and also receives the custom treatment. Available in either blue or hard chrome finish, this double-action-only, bobbed hammer 38 features night sights and a honed action as only the Colt custom smiths can do it.

Now we get to the most interesting, at least to this six-gunner's heart, of the Custom Shop offerings, namely the big-bore six-guns. It took a long time to replace the massive Colt New Service revolver retired in 1941, but when the Colt engineers finally went back to the drawing board in the late 1980s, the result was a superb effort they called the Anaconda.

This big double-action six-gun, available in 44 Magnum or 45 Colt, looks much like an enlarged King Cobra with a Python barrel. I have found the Anaconda in either caliber to be a first-class gun capable of the accuracy needed for hunting. Colt has also recognized this fact and offers the Anaconda Hunter through the Custom Shop.

Packed in a special aluminum carrying case, the Anaconda Hunter has an 8-inch barrel topped with a 2x Leupold scope. For the hunter who prefers iron sights, or who simply wants a powerful packin' pistol with custom touches, Colt fills the bill with the Custom Anaconda. Available in 4-, 6-, and 8-inch barrel lengths, this big snake is custom tuned, fitted with an Elliason rear sight, *black* front sight and, whether chambered for 44 Magnum or 45 Colt, Mag-na-ported barrel to help tame felt recoil and muzzle rise.

(Above) Colt Custom Shop Single Action Armys: 5 1/2-inch nickel 45 with Charles Able grips; 4 3/4-inch nickel 44-40; and 5 1/2-inch 44-40 with BluMagnum grips (top to bottom).

(Left) Taffin in his favorite pose—one-hand, off-hand—and his favorite six-gun, a Colt 7 1/2-inch 45 Single Action Army.

Colt's Custom Shop SAA chamberings are three: 45 Colt, 44-40 and 38-40— all traditional loads for these six-guns.

The heart of the Colt Custom Shop is the ageless Single Action Army. A standard catalog item from 1873 to 1941, the coming of World War II laid the gun to rest. Classic six-guns should not die, and justice demanded its return. It was resurrected in 1956, but since that time it has been an on-again, off-again item going through Second and Third Generation runs. Now, the Third Generation models are back, albeit only through the Custom Shop.

The last run of chamberings for the Colt Single Action Army consisted of 357 Magnum, 44 Special, 44-40 and 45 Colt. Today's offerings from the Custom Shop are 44-40 and 45 Colt. The bad news is the 44 Special is gone; the good news is the Custom Shop will fit 44-40s with extra cylinders in 44 Special. Even the 45s can be had with an auxiliary cylinder in 45 ACP. The third chambering offered this year is the 38 WCF, better known as the 38-40. I have a very special spot in my heart for this one because my first centerfire six-gun was a Colt Single Action Army in this caliber, with the 4 3/4-inch barrel. In a fit of stupidity, I let it get away. Now the 38-40 is back for the first time in more than fifty-five years.

All three chamberings are Custom Shop cataloged with Royal Blue finish mated with the case-hardened frame made famous by Colt, or a full, bright nickel finish. An extra nice custom touch is a nickeled gun with bright blued screws on the frame, backstrap and trigger guard. As this is written, all three chamberings are available with 4 3/4- and 5 1/2-inch barrels. The 45 Colt is the only chambering offered with the Cavalry-length 7 1/2-inch barrel.

All SAAs are coming from the Custom Shop with very nicely shaped but plain-Jane walnut grips with gold-colored Colt medallions. I have replaced the grips on the 5 1/2-inch guns with one-piece bird's-eye maple from BluMagnum on the 44-40 and stags from Charles Able on the 45 Colt. The short-barreled 44-40 now wears Third Generation Colt Eagle grips from my parts box.

Custom six-guns they may be, but as they come from the factory, all Colt single actions could use an action job. I was privileged to host fast-draw expert and gunsmith Bob Munden in my home, and we sat around my workbench and visited as he custom-tuned these guns. Munden replaces the

Factory loads for 45 Colt include CCI 255-grain Blazer, Black Hills 255-grain SWC, Federal 225-grain lead hollowpoint or Winchester 255-grain lead.

Lots of wide open space in Idaho where our writer calls home. Here John has the hammer back, finger on the trigger, and fixin' to fire his 7½-inch 45 Colt SAA.

Nitelite 380 from Colt's Custom Shop.

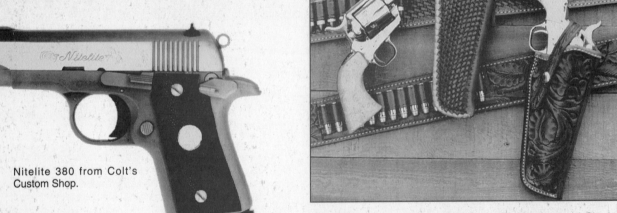

Colt Custom Shop SAAs with grips by BluMagnum and Charles Able. Belts and holsters are from El Paso Leather.

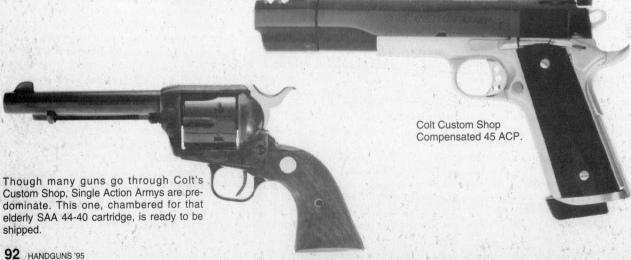

Colt Custom Shop Compensated 45 ACP.

Though many guns go through Colt's Custom Shop, Single Action Armys are predominate. This one, chambered for that elderly SAA 44-40 cartridge, is ready to be shipped.

COLT CUSTOM SHOP SINGLE ACTION ARMY

45 Colt

Cartridge	Bullet (grs./type)	5½" Bbl. MV (fps)	5½" Bbl. Group (ins.)	7½" Bbl. MV (fps)	7½" Bbl. Group (ins.)
Blazer	255/Lead	750	1¾	778	3¾
Winchester	255/Lead	749	3	754	1½
Black Hills	255/SWC	787	2¼	856	1⅝
Oklahoma Ammunition	250/RN	867	2¼	868	1⅜
Federal	225/LSWC-HP	811	2¼	811	2¼
Handload					
9.0/Unique	255/SWC Bull-X	919	2⅝	914	1¾

44-40

Bullet	Powder (grs./type)	4¾" Bbl. MV (fps)	4¾" Bbl. Group (ins.)	5½" Bbl. MV (fps)	5½" Bbl. Group (ins.)
Lyman #429215	8.0/Unique	919	3	904	2
Lyman #427098	9.0/Unique	1106	2⅞	1140	2⅝
Lyman #427098	10.0/Unique	1092	2	1180	3¼
Remington 200/JFP	9.0/Unique	814	2½	950	2

All groups shot at 25 yards. SWC = Semi-wadcutter; RN = Round-nose; LSWC-HP = Lead Semi-wadcutter Hollowpoint; JFP = Jacketed Flatpoint.

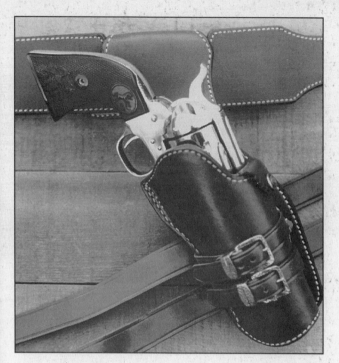

Good leather is mighty important to SAA shooters. A favorite with our author is this Galco Bob Munden rig for his 4¾-inch 44-40 from Colt's Custom Shop.

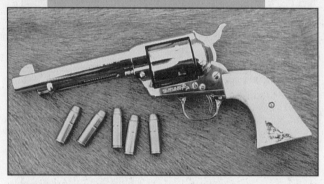

Stag grips by Charles Able add the finishing touch to this nickel Single Action Army 45 from Colt's Custom Shop.

mainsprings and bolt springs with those of his own design, and then works over all of the action parts with file and stone. The result is an incredibly smooth mechanism.

In all my years of shooting Colt single actions, or replicas for that matter, I can recall very few that shot to point of aim with my preferred load. Most have needed the front sight filed down to be brought to point of aim, which is easy to accomplish even by someone as fumble-fingered as me. Sometimes the front sight needs to be built up, which normally requires the aid of a good metalsmith. That takes care of elevation. Windage is accomplished by bending the front sight, turning the barrel or filing the rear notch so the centering of the front sight is changed.

It should come as no great surprise that all four of my test guns needed sight adjustments. Even if they were perfect when they left Hartford, they were that way for someone else's hands and eyes, not mine. However, before adjusting sights on a fixed-sighted gun, you have to decide on the load that will be used and proceed accordingly.

Of the four test guns, two shot low and two shot high. The 7½-inch 45 Colt came in 2 inches low with most loads, and the 4¾-inch 44-40 printed 1½ to 3 inches low. These can easily be corrected by filing the front sight. Not so easy to correct will be the two 5½-inch specimens—with the 45 Colt

shooting an inch high. (I can live with that), and the 44-40 going 3 to 6 inches high. The latter will require the front sight to be built up. One of the best ways to do this is to set a bead on top of the existing sight.

Windage turned out to be a minor problem with one 44-40 shooting dead on and the shorter-barreled 44-40 shooting 1 to 3 inches right, depending on the ammunition used. Both 45s also shot to the right 1 to 2 inches.

Colt single actions are not finely tuned target guns to say the least. The relatively poor sight picture does not aid accuracy. Also, nickel-plated guns with nickel-plated sights mated with bright sunlight are normally more difficult to shoot. As they are now, both 44-40s are 2- to 3-inch shooters at 25 yards, with the 45s doing somewhat better. This is all academic as these guns were created with the idea of an easy-to-pack and even easier-to-shuck-from-leather pistol to be used for close-range encounters where a big-bore six-gun is needed fast.

Somewhat surprising is the fact that the best shooting load in the 5½-inch 45 was the worst in the longer-barreled version, and vice versa. The shorter model liked Winchester's 255-grain lead bullets the best, while the longer one preferred 255-grain Blazers. Best loads for the 44-40s were assembled with the old Lyman #42798, a standard 200-grain flat-nosed cast bullet, and Unique powder. The shorter 44-40 liked 10.0 grains of Unique at 1100 fps, while the other did its best work with 8.0 grains of Unique for 900 fps.

Five dollars to Colt's Custom Shop will bring a Custom Gun brochure and outline the procedure for buying a standard Custom Package item, be it a Single Action Army, double-action revolver or semi-automatic.

I have found only one thing disappointing about the Colt Custom Shop. When I visited the factory, I expressed a desire for a Second Generation 44 Special New Frontier barrel. A search was conducted, but none was to be found anywhere. I switched my request to one in 45 Colt. Still no luck. Even the Custom Shop can't provide everything our heart desires. But they come close. Very close. •

LEW HORTON/S&W 356 TSW

by FRANK JAMES

Hottest 9mm performance comes from the Smith Shooting Team's special gun. This one lays 'em in there at magnum speeds.

At casual glance, the Lew Horton/Smith & Wesson Tactical Compact pistol looks like little more than a fancy Model 6906 with its contrasting two-tone black and bright stainless steel, but looks are deceiving.

A FEW YEARS back, Smith & Wesson announced a number of ambitious plans. One of them was to organize their own shooting team. The purpose of the team was not only to demonstrate and exhibit S&W handguns in various tournaments across the country, but also, as a means of showing the superiority of their pistols, to win and win *big*.

To build the all-out, full-race, really high-performance pistols required by the Smith & Wesson "race" team, a custom shop was created within the factory. That was the start of the Smith & Wesson Performance Center.

However, the Smith & Wesson Shooting Team had a few difficulties on their road toward tournament success. Except for the Sportsman Team Challenge and the International Revolver Championship, the victories were few, and the momentary thrills fleeting.

Whenever things go wrong, fingers tend to point. And one of the directions in which they were pointed was the Performance Center, because on at least one occasion there was a scarcity of race guns for the team. The situation became farcical at a past USPSA national championship, when two of Smith & Wesson's professional and well-esteemed factory shooters were forced to use *a single pistol in the same match*. Obviously, the S&W race team had difficulties—either of an organizational or a technical nature.

However, I have just completed a test of the Lew Horton/Smith & Wesson Performance Center 356 Tactical Compact and found it to be a superior piece of equipment. If their few competition pistols shot like this one, they had little room for complaint, other than a concern for spares.

At a casual glance, the Tactical Compact looks like little more than a fancy Model 6906 with its contrasting two-tone black and bright stainless steel. That is, until you read the script on the top of the barrel, ".356 TSW PERFORMANCE." Then you discover this is far from an ordinary 9mm Smith & Wesson pistol.

This pistol uses the 356 TSW, a cartridge introduced for the Smith & Wesson shooting team. It was supposed to cir-

PERFORMANCE CENTER TACTICAL COMPACT

The Lew Horton Tactical Compact field-strips down to five major components, not counting the twelve-round magazine. The guide rod features two recoil springs to handle the increased forces generated by this mid-caliber thunderbolt.

cumvent the problems with 9mm Major in USPSA competition, while also providing an alternative to the 38 Super. Smith & Wesson high-capacity frames aren't long enough for the 38 Super's overall case length, so S&W had to work with something that would fit the envelope developed for the 9x19mm pistols. The result was the 356 TSW, which in metric terms is something like a 9x22.5mm cartridge.

It is also a high-pressure cartridge. It generates chamber pressures far in excess of SAAMI specifications for the 9x19mm or 9mm Luger round. This helps explain the need for the cartridge in the first place. The higher chamber pressure, in this instance, translates into higher muzzle velocities and substantially greater muzzle energies. But first, let's look at the Tactical Compact from the S&W Performance Center.

To start, the skeleton of this animal does not use a standard-production frame and slide. Word has it both units on this pistol are from a special run of frames and slides built specifically for the Performance Center. This explains the different contours seen on the Tactical Compact.

The slide has a subtle difference which is accented by a touch of bright stainless steel. This bright piece of the slide is raised and slightly thicker than that found on my early production Model 6904. The Performance Center slide is approximately .008-inch wider at various contrasting points than the older 6904.

This thicker-is-better philosophy continues with the frame which is approximately .010-inch thicker than that of the Model 6904 at roughly the same locations.

Even the barrel pin/slide release cross-pin is beefed up,

heavier and stronger. If you look carefully, you will find many small areas that have been beefed up, slicked up, or polished and smoothed to create a better pistol.

One of the big differences is the trigger guard. The 6904 has an exaggerated opening with the hooked trigger guard; the Lew Horton gun lacks the hook and features a normal size opening and rounded trigger guard.

Racking the slide, you immediately notice how smooth and effortlessly it glides across the top of the frame. It requires almost no extra effort. This slide is *fitted* to its frame, with no free play or wobble between the two parts.

This is in steep contrast to my well-worn Model 6904. Not to complain about this early Third Generation 9mm pistol, but it has always had a significant amount of slide-to-frame wobble. None of that is present with the well-fitted Lew Horton/S&W pistol.

To get a better understanding of this special gun and cartridge, one really needs to chronograph the 356 TSW ammo. The results of my tests really opened my eyes.

There is only one source for 356 TSW ammunition at present, and to the best of my knowledge only one load. It's Federal's Gold Medal 147-grain FMJ-TC round. Peter Pi at Cor-Bon is reportedly working on a lightweight bullet load

for the 356 TSW. This supposedly will be the answer to those who pray for a light and fast load in an auto pistol that duplicates the success of the 357 Magnum.

(I've even heard rumors that Glock is looking at the 356 TSW cartridge to duplicate the 357 Magnum 125-grain JHP load. Anyone marketing heavily to police agencies in this country is well aware of that load's reputation among law enforcement.)

We will all have to wait and see, but one thing is for sure—the 356 TSW round is a hot load. The ten-round average velocity for the Tactical Compact and the Federal 147-grain Gold Medal load went 1149 fps on one test and 1154 fps on another. The extreme spreads for ten rounds in each instance were unbelievably low—14 fps for one and 17 fps for the second. Also, this match-quality ammunition combined with the pistol produced accuracy that was beyond expectation. Obviously, this is good ammunition, but how do these velocity figures compare against normal 9x19mm ammunition?

I tested 124-grain JHP El Dorado Starfire, 147-grain JHP Black Hills and 124-grain FMJ Samson to gauge the velocity difference over the chronograph. The Black Hills ammo ran 984 fps, while the 9x21mm Samson had an aver-

To start, the skeleton of this animal does not use a standard-production frame and slide. Word has it both units on this pistol are from a special run of frames and slides built specifically for the Performance Center.

The Tactical Compact comes equipped with the extremely good Novak Lo-Mount rear sight. It has been accepted, even demanded, by professionals the world over.

The front sight is installed via a dovetail and features a single white dot.

All Performance Center pistols are shipped in these polymer gun boxes, complete with the Smith & Wesson Performance Center logo on the top lid.

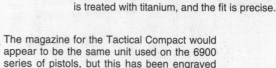

The Briley bushing can be seen clearly in this photo with the barrel removed from the slide. The bushing is treated with titanium, and the fit is precise.

The magazine for the Tactical Compact would appear to be the same unit used on the 6900 series of pistols, but this has been engraved with both the seal of the Performance Center and its caliber to distinguish it from others.

age for ten shots of 1102 fps, and the Starfire averaged 1020 fps.

Despite the bullet weights, it is still obvious the 356 TSW is much faster. Going one step further and examining the difference in projectile weights makes it all the more apparent just how powerful this pistol is over comparable pistols of the same size.

Natural curiosity raises the question of why this pistol is able to handle the much greater forces and pressures of the 356 TSW round when such loads in other pistols would raise concerns over public safety?

The answer is found in a couple of places. The first is the new slide and frame. Both units are stronger than production parts and designed to withstand the stress of this powerhouse, medium-caliber cartridge.

Next is the barrel. The frame and slide may be the skeleton of a pistol, but the barrel is its heart. A poorly fitted barrel is nothing more than a heart with leaky valves. The barrel on a premium-quality pistol must be made of premium-quality materials and fitted with consummate precision—true of the Performance Center gun.

At the rear of the barrel, again going back to my old 6904 "AIP" for a comparison, I found the hood of the Performance Center barrel .115-inch wider than the hood on the older pistol. Also, the PC hood is fitted to the slide with minimum tolerances. Under pressure, it will move slightly from side to side. Compared to the production gun, the difference is dramatic.

At the front of the PC slide, there is a bronze-like Messerschmitt bushing. This thin metal ring is the secret to the precise fit of the barrel at the front. It is tight, yet the fit remains free. There wasn't one malfunction with this pistol throughout my testing. (There is one exception to the previous statement. When firing the normal 9x19mm ammunition, I discovered it lacked the momentum necessary for the slide to lock open after the last round. This never occurred with either the 356 TSW Federal Gold Medal or the 9x21mm Samson, and otherwise the pistol flawlessly handled the lesser powered ammunition.)

Further examination of the Performance Center Tactical

Compact reveals a different guide rod and, instead of the normal recoil spring, two springs—one larger than the other. The guide rod features a heavier spring-loaded center pin that, combined with the additional recoil spring, helps the frame absorb the increase in force.

The magazine on this Lew Horton pistol, even though slightly longer, has the same capacity as the previously mentioned 6904—twelve rounds. It is engraved with the Performance Center logo and caliber to avoid confusion with similar magazines. However, I found the standard 6904 magazine worked well in the PC pistol the few times I used it during testing.

Firing the first twelve rounds at downrange paper demonstrated two things: The first is more recoil than I anticipated, and the second is this pistol is a shooter—it is accurate.

The recoil is not severe; it isn't even as robust as that felt with the normal 40 S&W pistol. There is a louder muzzle report, but again we are entering into an area of relative and *subjective* evaluations. However, it is an easy pistol to shoot, and to shoot well.

I found during my testing it was not at all difficult to keep ten rounds inside a 2½-inch circle at seventy feet with an occasional flyer. For me, that is unusual and normally encountered only when testing the most advanced and exotic of custom pistols.

The Lew Horton/Smith & Wesson Performance Center 356 Tactical Compact has a suggested retail price of $999. That's a lot of money, but this is a lot of pistol. It is an accurate pistol, and the caliber offers the promise of a high-capacity 357 Magnum—something many have been trying to achieve, but few have yet to demonstrate.

The Smith & Wesson Shooting Team disbanded in May of 1994. It is a sad loss, especially for the revolver shooters who enjoyed Jerry Miculek's exceptional and outstanding wheelgun shooting performances.

As for this Smith & Wesson Performance Center product, I rate it highly, and despite its higher retail price, I think it's a good bargain. It would be difficult to find a custom pistol that shoots as well for twice the money. ●

Custom Handguns

RIGHT-HAND FROM TEXAS

by JIM WILSON

He knows that Sam Colt was left-handed, so Bill Grover builds the fine single actions for the rest of us. They shoot, too.

This engraved Grover's Improved #5 has a carved ivory grip.

ONE OF THE greatest benefits of the gun writing business is the opportunity to meet some mighty interesting characters. I am one of those who believes that history is moulded by strong-minded individuals, not the other way around, and firearms history has always been blessed with plenty of these kind of hombres. Elmer Keith, Bill Jordan, Jeff Cooper, Bill Ruger and Skeeter Skelton are just a few who come to mind. To use a border phrase, I sure like a man who wears his own kind of hat.

Couple that with my abiding love of single-action six-guns and you will begin to appreciate my situation. John Taffin once suggested that we form an organization called "Single Actions Anonymous" to address our hopeless addiction. I promptly told him that we ought to call the outfit "Single Actions Unanimous," because I intend to glory in my affliction. Sturdy individuals, with six-guns, are what made this country great.

Bill Grover is one of those sturdy individuals. In the time that we have known each other, we have handgun hunted together, broke bread together, and sat up long into the night talking about those things that really mattered. If you attend the SHOT Show, or a major gun show, just wander around until you spot a fellow who looks exactly like Buffalo Bill Cody. If he looks you straight in the eye and gives you a firm handshake, you've met Bill Grover. And your education about all things single action is just about to truly begin.

Coincidentally, Bill Grover just happens to build some of the best custom single-action handguns I have ever seen. Texas Longhorn Arms is the outfit that was founded, born and nurtured by Grover. It is the culmination of his thirty-year love affair with single actions. It is impossible to talk about Texas Longhorn Arms without talking about Bill Grover, and vice versa.

Like a lot of us, Grover simply can't remember the time when he wasn't interested in six-guns. His Uncle Bill was the shooter in the family, and Grover did some of his earli-

This engraved South Texas Army was custom-made for the founded-in-1880, world-famous Y.O. Ranch located in the Texas Hill Country.

SINGLE ACTIONS LONGHORN ARMS

Bill Grover, on the front porch of his Texas Longhorn Arms factory, holding a Grover's Improved #5 single action in 44 Magnum.

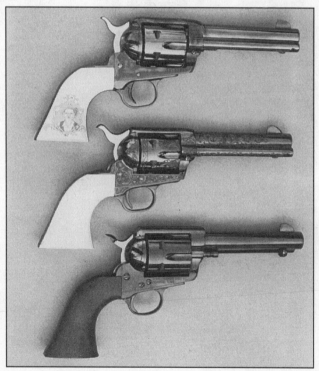

(Top) This Ruger Vaquero features ivory grips with Bill Grover's portrait scrimshawed on them, while the Colt SAA has engraving and one-piece ivory grip. Below is a 4³/₄-inch TLA South Texas Army.

est pistol shooting with the uncle's old Colt New Service. A short time later, Grover discovered Elmer Keith when his uncle loaned him his copy of *Sixguns By Keith*. The boy was hooked.

At the age of sixteen, Grover did some body work on a car in trade for his first handgun, a Colt Scout. After taking this little gun apart numerous times, Bill knew that he wanted to spend his life working with handguns. Later, he even turned down four football scholarships because none of the schools could teach him how to build guns. Instead, he began to hire out to machine shops so he could develop the

machining skills he needed to properly build the kind of handgun that was beginning to take form in his inventive mind.

You see, Grover's main criticism of the traditional single action was that the ejector rod and loading gate seemed to be located on the wrong side of the gun. Their location made loading and unloading pretty clumsy for the right-handed shooter. His research revealed that Sam Colt was left-handed, which may explain the location of these critical parts. (Grover points out that Bill Ruger is another lefty, too.) If the ejector rod and loading gate were located on the left side

SOUTH TEXAS ARMY SPECIFICATIONS

Manufacturer:	Texas Longhorn Arms, Inc.
Caliber:	Most centerfire pistol cartridges
Barrel:	4¾-inch standard (others available)
Weight:	42 ounces
Grips:	Walnut standard
Finish:	Blue (case-coloring optional)
Sights:	Fixed
List Price:	$1500

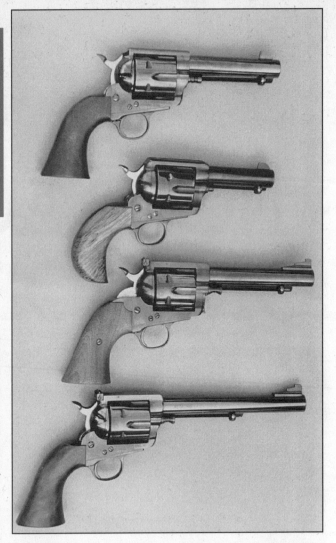

Grover's South Texas Army, Border Special, Improved #5 and Flat Top Target (top to bottom).

South Texas Army six-gun with 4¾-inch barrel and optional case-colored finish.

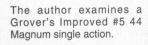

The author examines a Grover's Improved #5 44 Magnum single action.

of the revolver, the thing could be loaded and unloaded without it ever leaving the shooting hand.

Grover took to his machine-shop education with a vengeance. He wasn't just satisfied to design handguns, he had to be able to build them from scratch. Bill didn't want to merely copy someone else's gun designs, he wanted to be a gun inventor. And Grover believes that a true gun inventor is one who can do it all—design work, machine work and quality finishing. It has taken Bill Grover over thirty years of hard work to become an overnight success.

Texas Longhorn Arms began as a one-man operation in a small shop in the Houston area. Grover built each gun completely by hand. His unique six-gun design borrows some of the good points of the Colt and Ruger single actions, together with a few parts that he designed and built himself.

Today, TLA is a modern, up-to-date factory that turns out some of the best single actions money can buy. All of the employees are men that Grover has personally selected and trained, and each one knows that his work is critical to turning out a quality product. Two things impressed me with Texas Longhorn Arms: the pride of the individual employees and the way Grover travels around the work area helping each man with his assigned task.

Texas Longhorn Arms offers four basic models of single-action revolvers. The South Texas Army is a fixed-sight

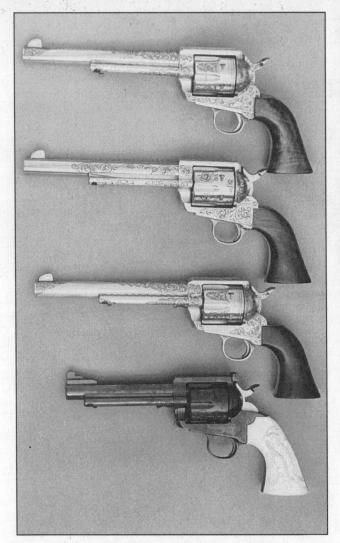

Notice the quality of the engraving and the custom grips from TLA. The top three are South Texas Armys, with Grover's Improved #5 below.

gun offered in most centerfire pistol calibers. It comes standard with a 4³/₄-inch barrel, but can be ordered in 5¹/₂- and 7¹/₂-inch as well. One-piece walnut grips are standard on the Army, but other fancy woods can be used when available.

The Border Special is another fixed-sight model that features a 4-inch barrel and a bird's-head grip. This pistol is a real eye-catcher and looks like a proper gentleman's belly gun if I ever saw one. When Bill visited me a while back, he brought along a Border Special in 44 Magnum. I had gathered together a bunch of single-action enthusiasts who were all dying to shoot Bill's guns. However, they weren't real crazy about firing full-house 44 loads in that little, 40-ounce six-gun. To our surprise, the grip of the Border Special made firing the heavy ammo seem like child's play. The pistol just rolls in your hand and felt recoil is minimal.

The Flat Top Target revolver incorporates all of the modern features of the other two guns and adds adjustable sights as well. Like me, Grover has always appreciated the old steel Micro rear sight that Bill Ruger put on his first centerfire single actions. It was accurate and, being made of steel, plenty durable. The TLA adjustable sight is virtually an exact copy of the fine old Micro. The front sight is Grover's version of the old long-range six-gun sight that Elmer Keith designed years ago. Like the other guns men-

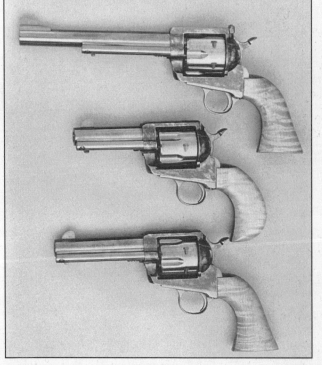

Flat Top Target, Border Special and South Texas Army (top to bottom) featuring fancy wood grips and case-colored frames offered as optional features.

This Grover's Improved #5 (top) has serial number 1 and features fancy engraving and carved ivory grips. An engraved Colt New Frontier displays carved ivory grips and silver buttcap.

tioned, the Flat Top Target is available in most centerfire pistol calibers.

However, the fourth TLA six-shooter is my absolute favorite—Grover's Improved #5. It is Grover's way of paying tribute to Elmer Keith, that grand old gentleman of six-gunning.

In the 1920s, Keith and some friends set out to modify a Colt Single Action Army with all of the custom features they felt the pistol needed. Part of a Bisley grip frame was mated to the Colt trigger guard for an improved grip design that would handle recoil better. Adjustable sights were added, along with a redesigned base pin, base pin latch and Bisley hammer spur. Keith called the results his #5 Colt. It was his favorite single-action revolver.

Bill Grover began by obtaining the exact dimensions of Keith's gun. Then, with the assistance of some talented friends, he set out to incorporate all of Keith's design into a new revolver featuring Grover's standard improvements. Keith's original #5 was chambered for the 44 Special cartridge. Grover's Improved #5 is drilled for the 44 Magnum round. I think Keith would have approved of the caliber change. In fact, I think he would have wanted to buy the first gun that came out of the shop. It's that good.

Bill Grover makes use of coil springs throughout his line. Frames and barrels are made of 4140 chrome-moly certified aircraft steel. His cylinders are crafted from 4340 certified aircraft steel double heat-treated for extra strength. This is the reason the Grover Improved #5 can be safely chambered for 44 Magnum, even though it is the exact same size as Keith's original Colt #5.

I am often asked if custom handguns are really worth the extra cost. When they are hand-fitted from quality materials, the answer is a resounding yes. However, custom work has to manifest itself through improved performance. In this regard, Bill Grover gets an A+ from this shootist.

The cylinders of TLA guns are bored to absolute minimum specifications. Tight cylinder throats result in less stress on the cartridge case and allow the cartridge to use its powder more accurately and efficiently. The cylinder is then tightly fitted to the frame with a minimum of gap between it and the barrel. Internal parts are snugly fitted

The TLA cylinders are bored on modern computer-controlled equipment.

A TLA cylinder is hand-polished by one of Grover's trained employees.

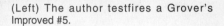
(Left) The author testfires a Grover's Improved #5.

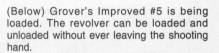
(Below) Grover's Improved #5 is being loaded. The revolver can be loaded and unloaded without ever leaving the shooting hand.

(Left) Texas Longhorn Arms right-hand single-action revolvers are really that—they load on the left side...

...and the trigger is hard against the guard's right side (below). Original Colts are the opposite, indicating that Sam Colt was, in fact, left-handed.

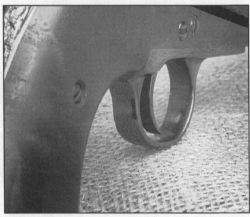

A TLA employee hand-fits a loading gate.

together to allow for minimum play. These are the things custom guns are truly made of, and this is the way Texas Longhorn Arms builds its handguns.

But Bill Grover is not only the inventor at Texas Longhorn Arms, he is also the number one tester. And to Bill Grover, testing his guns means hunting. Over the years, he has used handguns of his manufacture to collect buffalo, bear, elk, whitetail deer, turkey, javelina and numerous exotics.

In March of 1993, I hunted with Bill at the very first Shootists' Safari in Kerrville, Texas. Bill proved his gun that day by taking a very nice Corsican ram with one shot from his Improved #5. Later that year, he was my guest on the Penn Baggett Ranch, at Ozona, Texas, for a go at Rio Grande turkey. His #5 dropped a gobbler sporting a 9-inch beard, another one-shot kill, by the way.

Not to be outdone, I begged, sniveled and groveled to the extent that Grover let me borrow the #5 I photographed for this story. In the next few months, I'll use it during the second annual Shootists' Safari, and for turkey and javelina this spring. My order is already in for a #5 of my very own, you can bet on that.

In this day of mass production and a throw-away market, quality products are like a breath of fresh prairie air. Bill Grover is to be commended in that regard. In spite of personal conflicts and tragedy, he has always managed to keep his goal in mind. Since his childhood, that goal has been to build the best quality handgun that he is capable of making.

In the early days, popularity quickly outdistanced production, and TLA guns were hopelessly backordered. However, with his new factory and trained craftsmen, backorders are rapidly becoming a thing of the past. In fact, on a recent visit to the plant, I was shown prototypes of a single shot pistol and a 22 six-gun that Grover is considering producing. There is also a distinct possibility that TLA will offer stainless steel six-guns in the not-too-distant future.

I wouldn't take a million bucks for my relationship with the handgun fraternity. During the course of this little adventure, I have met a six-gun inventor, toured a modern firearms plant, shot excellent single actions, and made a good friend. It just doesn't get any better than that, I can tell you for sure! •

TLA's number one tester, Bill Grover, puts a Grover's Improved #5 through its paces.

Grover's Improved #5 produced this group fired by the author at 25 yards. Ammunition was Black Hills 300-grain JHP ammo.

See the difference? An engraved Grover's Improved #5 (top) with carved ivory grip lies next to an engraved Colt single action with one-piece ivory grip. Note the ejector rod housings and loading gates are exactly opposite.

HANDGUNS 95

SECTION 4
Hunting Handguns

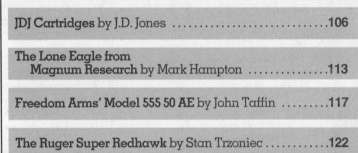

Jones surveys Contender's wildcat
options, page 106.

Taffin goes hunting with the Big 50, page 117.

Field-ready, this Ruger satisfies Trzoniec, page 122.

Hunting Handguns

JDJ CARTRIDGES

by J.D. JONES

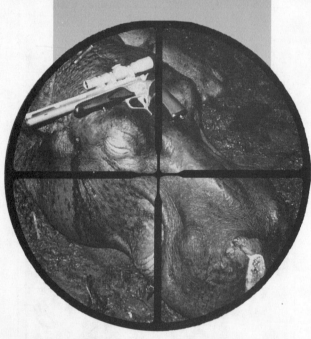

This hippopotamus was taken with SSK's custom 45-70 Thompson/Center Contender barrel shooting Hornady's great 500-grain bullet.

I STARTED EXPERIMENTING with Thompson/Center's Contender pistol in 1969, having no idea it would end up first being an obsession and then a career.

At the time, I worked at the Volunteer Army Ammunition Plant near Chattanooga, Tennessee. At the same time, I was also enamored with fast boats, a water-skiing family, motorcycles and cars, along with working long hours. Maybe better said, "pistol time" was shared with a lot of other things.

(The shortest night of my life was in the home of J.D. Jones during this era. My arrival was around 2 a.m. Talking took up another two hours or so, and we were scheduled for a hog hunt that morning. Finally, he suggested going to bed. All I did was kick off my boots and stretch out on top of the covers. Forty minutes later, he kicked me awake. My immediate question was, "J.D., why did we bother?" His answer was classic J.D. Jones, "I thought you looked tired and needed some rest.—Editor)

In any event, the *hot dog* cartridges of those days were the interesting ones: 256 Winchester, K-Hornet, 221 Fireball, 30-30, 357/44, and others got their share of attention. Since I lived on the edge of the Smoky Mountains and there were plenty of groundhogs in the area, a great deal of time was devoted to chasing them. Plus, I picked up a lot of valuable information about what worked and what didn't.

Back then, and even today, many of the pistol cartridges were damned by writers who claimed rifle bullets won't expand at handgun velocities. Wrong—rifle bullets that work well at handgun velocities have always existed, and today the number of those bullets available to the handloading handgunner is astounding. There is something out there in every caliber that will work for any purpose suited to that cartridge. If major component manufacturers don't make it, there are literally scores of small specialty manufacturers who can and will make most any conceivable projectile for any caliber.

The T/C Contender has had a considerable amount of refinement since its introduction. The influence of custom and factory XP-100s and SSK's line of custom Contenders and barrels has had a profound effect, getting thousands of handgun hunters afield. The development of numerous car-

Four of Jones' JDJ cartridges: 226, 6mm, 257 and 6.5x30, left to right.

tridges and projectiles was carried out with the Contender because the gun is strong, safe and reliable.

In those mid- to late '70s, I was shooting a lot of silhouette and spending a good bit of time hunting big game. I found conventional cartridges and bullets, in some cases, just weren't up to doing a satisfactory job at the things I wanted them to do. One fall, I traveled about seven thousand miles in pursuit of game and fired two shots—got one duck, missed the other. Several other opportunities were presented and passed on because I simply didn't have enough gun or bullet to do the job.

That led to the immediate development of the 375 JDJ, 6.5 JDJ, 7 JDJ and 320-grain 44 Magnum bullets as dual-purpose hunting and silhouette rounds. As I recall, the 375 was first, the 6.5 second and 7mm third.

About that time, the company for which I worked had a change in politics, and both the president and I were fired. I made up my mind never to work for anyone again and started writing about guns and spending more and more time with wildcats and T/Cs. Lee Jurras was fooling with his HOWDAH cartridges in the T/C. We spent many a dollar on telephone service between Ohio and New Mexico.

I made up several T/Cs in 45-70 with different twist rates and throats and, with some help from friends, put about 20,000 test rounds through them. I wrote it up for Howard French, editor of *Guns and Ammo* at the time, and when that article came out, SSK was more than just three letters, it was a business.

Those early days were quite hectic. Phil Crowley, now residing in Stateboro, Georgia, worked with me, and that was it. As I recall, I had about 150-200 orders for 45-70 Contender barrels and about three barrel blanks in stock. It took a couple years to get over that.

The original intent of the JDJ wildcats was to provide more powerful and accurate hunting rounds. Secondarily, the 6.5 and 7mm were, and are, quite good silhouette cartridges. Nowdays, you can knock silhouettes over with a feather, so just about anything that will get there will do the job. Not so in hunting—shot placement, power, reasonable accuracy and bullets well suited for the job are, and forever will be, necessary to do a good job in the field. Other calibers

Larry Kelly, of Mag-na-port International fame and well-known worldwide big game hunter, took this leopard with his 375 JDJ.

J.D., with a 225-yard shot, took this South African blesbok at 225 yards shooting a 165-grain Nosler Ballistic Tip in his 309 JDJ.

The 225 Winchester is a semi-rimmed case, with an unusually large rim. This one became a 6mm JDJ with a 75-grain bullet.

Here we see a 225 Winchester case, left, then opened to accept 6.5mm bullets, and a finished cartridge with 120-grain Nosler Ballistic Tip.

The 225s original diameter was retained here, but its shoulder changed. This is the 226 JDJ.

were developed at customer request. Some because I was curious; some simply to make money.

The 225 Winchester and 444 Marlin cartridge cases were chosen for several reasons—probably the most important was they are very tough and give long case life. Also, they are easily formed with little case loss and are the right capacity to provide the maximum power safely achievable in a T/C.

Let's take a look at the JDJ cartridges and their capabilities; the forming method is indicated by a footnote number after the caliber and described in the corresponding footnote. Incidentally, though they are shot in pistols, none of these cartridges use pistol powder. They are at their best with either medium- or slow-burning rifle powders.

226 JDJ[4]: This is simply the 225 Winchester blown out to maximum case capacity. It was designed at the request of coyote hunters and a few Texas deer hunters (where 22 centerfires are legal for deer, some of which don't go 80 pounds) who wanted the ability to move heavy .224-inch bullets at standard 223 Remington velocities. It's probably at its best with 60- to 70-grain bullets and is about 100 or so fps faster than the 223 with 55-grain loads. Many .224-inch varmint bullets will give positive expansion at over 300 yards. The 223 is a better choice for most individuals; choose the 226 JDJ only if you need or want it. *Do not* shoot 225 Winchester factory ammo in it. SSK uses fast-twist barrels as standard in most of the centerfire 22s.

6mm JDJ #2[4]: The original 6mm, on the 225 Winchester case, was a mistake on the part of the reamer manufacturer. It was simply the 225 necked up to 6mm with no other change. It is no longer available because the #2 version has the improved body taper and shoulder angle. I'm not a 6mm fan. I say that after having shot about thirty deer and deer-sized animals with this caliber, as well as hundreds of varmints. It's OK, but there is better to be had. Bullet selection is critical. Several 70- to 75-grain bullets at around 2800 fps are decent on varmints. I haven't found anything I like about it for deer. The 70-grain Nosler Ballistic Tip is

probably the best varmint/antelope bullet, and their 95-grain Partition is likely the best deer bullet.

257 JDJ[4]: Most varmint bullets from 75 grains and up work well. In my opinion, the best whitetail/antelope/varmint load is the 85-grain Nosler Ballistic Tip at about 2850 fps, or 2900 fps from a 14-inch barrel. Angle shots should be avoided with this blown-out 225 Winchester—only broadside or frontal shots will succeed. This round also will blow up jackrabbits at 300 yards. Dennis Lawrence and I have fourteen straight one-shot kills with this combination and haven't stopped a bullet in an animal yet. Tissue damage is exceptional. For larger deer, I would use 100-grain Nosler Partition bullets at about 2700 fps. Heavyweight 25s are too heavily constructed to give decent long-range performance on game.

6.5 JDJ[4]: This cartridge, another formed from the 225 Winchester case, is exceptionally well-balanced with excellent bullets available in quantity. All 6.5mm bullets not designed for the 6.5 magnums work well. Exceptional are the 85-grain Sierra (varmints only); 100-grain Ballistic Tip (primarily varmints); 120-grain Speer; 120-grain Sierra; 120-grain Ballistic Tip; 120-grain solid-base; 125-grain Nosler Partition (normally at least 30-inch penetration on larger animals); 129-grain Hornady; 139-grain Hornady; 140-grain Ballistic Tip; and 140-grain Partition. Solids are available. When I first started using this round on deer, I thought performance with the 120 Speer was too good to be true. It kills all out of proportion to its paper ballistics. The

---

[1]Form the case neck to proper caliber in the full-length sizing die and load a full charge. (338, 358, 9.3mm, 375, 411, 416)

[2]Form the case neck in the form die, make up a slightly reduced load and fire form the case to final configuration. (6.5x30, 7x30 when making cases from 30-30 or similar, 309, 8mm)

[3]Fire factory ammunition in an improved chamber. (7x30)

[4]Expand the neck to the proper diameter, load and fire form with a slightly reduced load. (226, 6mm, 257, 6.5mm, 270, 7mm #2, 475)

Jones is a great fan of 6.5mm bullets. Shown here are three of his favorites: 6.5 JDJ (225 Winchester case), 6.5x30 JDJ (7x30 Waters case) and 6.5 JDJ #2 (307 Winchester case).

Moving to larger diameters, these four are, left to right: 270 JDJ, 7mm JDJ, 7x30 JDJ and 7mm JDJ #2.

120 Speer at 2400 fps was the first hunting load, and it's still hard to beat. I had about 100 kill reports on this one before I believed it and finally told the public how good it was. I've cleanly taken animals of up to around 600 pounds on many occasions and have a video of my wife dropping a zebra in his tracks with a low shoulder shot with the 125 Partition, which was found under the skin on the off-side. It will do around 2300 fps with the 140 and about 2850 fps with the 85 Sierra. Recoil is negligible. The 120 Ballistic Tip will give positive expansion on an antelope at 300 yards.

6.5x30 JDJ[2]: This one uses more powder than the 6.5 JDJ, and case life is definitely shorter as it uses the 30-30, 7x30 or can be formed from the 375 Winchester case. It was developed only because some customers want to use 30-30 brass—which is not as well-balanced a cartridge as the 225 case.

6.5 JDJ #2[2]: Also developed because of customer's requests—those wanting to use the 307 Winchester case. It will do around 2300 fps with a 140-grainer and not much more than that with a 120. This one suffers from a lack of development.

270 JDJ[4]: Formed from 225 Winchester brass, this cartridge is always accurate, but was troublesome at first due to the lack of proper game bullets. Now, the 130-grain Ballistic Tip, 130-grain solid-base and 130-grain Partition are excellent performers. It will push them at 2400 fps, and if you like the 277-caliber, there is no reason not to choose this one. The 90-grain Sierra and 100-grain Hornady at around 2800 fps do fine on varmints.

7 JDJ[4]: Again formed from 225 Winchester brass. At the same time the 6.5 was performing well, the 7mm was a dog. Only the 120-grain Hornady softpoint and 139-grain Hornady flatpoint came any way near the game performance of the 6.5. The strongly constructed and heavier 7s did great on steel and penciled animals, but not the real ones. That's changed now. The 7mm single shot pistol bul-

A rare photograph: The "fan" seen here is exposed for only 30 seconds or so after death. Jones took this South African springbok at 305 steps with a 6.5 JDJ and 125-grain bullet. A chest shot, but the bullet exited through the right ham.

lets work if you download the JDJ to TCU velocities or use them at long range. The 120-grain Ballistic Tip is probably a better choice. The 140-grain Ballistic Tip or 140-grain Partition will both give positive expansion at 300 yards on deer. All the loads, from the 6.5 through the 7, give very good results on game and steel targets. Recoil is negligible with all of them.

7 JDJ #2[2]: This is based on the 307 Winchester case necked to 7mm. It was designed in an attempt to get 140-grain 7mm bullets to work better. It will do 2400 fps with 140s, which is around 100 fps faster than the 7 JDJ. With bullets lighter than 140 grains, it offers no improvement over the standard 7 JDJ that I've found up to this point. Don't buy it expecting higher velocities with lighter bullets. It hasn't worked out that way in the T/C.

7x30 JDJ[3]: Layne Simpson had more to do with getting this one going than anyone else. The original 7x30 Waters suffers from acute case stretching that requires frequent trimming and usually resorts in short case life. Its case shape isn't the greatest for a T/C action, either. Straightening the case and giving it a sharp shoulder allows better case life as stretching is drastically reduced, but it's still only a 30-30 case. It will do about 2400 fps with a 140-grain, its best loading. It won't give much better velocities than the original version with lighter bullets. SSK rechambers a lot of T/C barrels to this Improved version, but very few people buy it new from SSK. It is a worthwhile improvement over the original.

309 JDJ[2]: Now we get to the first cartridge that shows a lot of improvement in killing power over the 6.5 JDJ. Based on the 444 case necked to 30-caliber, I feel it is at its best with 165-grain bullets at 2300 to 2400 fps. The 165-grain Ballistic Tip, 165-grain Hornady and 165-grain Partition all give exceptional service. Any bullet useful in the 30-30, 30-40 Krag or 300 Savage will give exceptional performance in the 309. Having shot a large number of animals with the 309, I find it visually more powerful at impact than the smaller calibers. Wound channels are larger. Many report excellent results on varmints, antelope and deer with the 125-grain Ballistic Tip at around 2700 fps. Others report several of the softer 180-grain RNs and 180-grain Partitions do very well on larger African animals. It may be the best of the lot as an all-round cartridge. I don't consider it an elk cartridge, but it has dropped a pile of them—yet so has the 6.5. The 309 is unnecessarily powerful for silhouette and a Mag-na-port is recommended to hold down muzzle rise.

8mm JDJ[2]: The 309 and 8mm JDJs, made from the same 444 parent case, parallel the 30-06 and 8x57 Mauser situation. For all practical purposes, the cartridges are ballistically even. This one can definitely be chalked up to satisfying my curiosity. The 8mm favors slightly heavier bullets. The 309 outsells it by one hundred to one, and that's probably the way it should be. Caliber 30 bullets are far easier to find, and the 8mm offers no particular advantage until heavy bullets are used. While all bullets suitable for 8mm Mausers will work fine in the 8mm JDJ, none of the 8mm magnum bullets will expand from the pistol. Fans of the 8mm love this one. With 198-grain boattail surplus bullets, this is an outstanding long-range plinker. The 200-grain Nosler Partition has given really good results on heavier African game. The old 236-grain round-nose Norma bullets with about 3/8-inch of lead exposed on the nose are great in the woods for just about anything.

338 JDJ[1]: Originally based on the 303 British case because of our inability to acceptably form the 444 into a 338 in one step some 10-12 years ago, it is now obsolete and replaced by the...

338 JDJ #2[2]: This one can now be formed in one pass from the 444 case. An excellent and hard-hitting long-range cartridge, the 338 is at its best for deer-sized game with the

Now we are getting into serious hunting cartridges: 309 JDJ with 165-grain bullet, 8mm JDJ with 175-grain bullet, 338 JDJ #2 with 225-grain bullet, and 358 JDJ with 220-grain bullet, left to right.

200-grain Ballistic Tip, 200-grain Hornady flatpoint, 200-grain Hornady spirepoint and 250-grain Nosler Partition. I'm sure others will work, but I don't have firsthand experience with them. The 200s will do 2300 fps and the 250 about 2100 fps. The 200s would be satisfactory for broadside or frontal shots on elk-sized animals. Elk hunters should choose the 250-grain Partition. Doc Rogers loves this one with the 200-grain Ballistic Tip for long-range groundhog and deer, and claims it is the best—and he has shot more of them with handguns than anyone I know.

358 JDJ[1]: This former 444 is quite good with the right bullets: 180-grain single shot pistol bullets and 180-grain Speer for long range; 200-grain Remington Core-Lokt RN; 200-grain Winchester RN and 220-grain Speer. No, the 225-grain Sierra, 225-grain Nosler Partition and various 200- and 250-grain bullets will not give consistent results on game with this cartridge. The 180s will do around 2400 fps and are fragile at close range. The best way to get into trouble with the 358 is to disregard what I've just written. I know of *no* other 358 bullets that have not given erratic results on game. The 220 Speer is my choice for any kind of game heavier than deer. The 250 Speer is a great long-range plinker, but a stinker on game in the velocity range attainable with this cartridge.

9.3 JDJ[1]: The 9.3 (.366-inch) is very popular in Europe, and most JDJs go there, with a few sold to Americans who are familiar with the 9.3's effectiveness. I like Speer's 270-grain SP at about 2075 fps for just about anything. For this wildcat formed from a 444 case, there isn't a big bullet selection, but a large selection isn't necessary. RWS has some neat conepoints, and most of them shoot to the same point

---

[1]Form the case neck to proper caliber in the full-length sizing die and load a full charge. (338, 358, 9.3mm, 375, 411, 416)

[2]Form the case neck in the form die, make up a slightly reduced load and fire form the case to final configuration. (6.5x30, 7x30 when making cases from 30-30 or similar, 309, 8mm)

[3]Fire factory ammunition in an improved chamber. (7x30)

[4]Expand the neck to the proper diameter, load and fire form with a slightly reduced load. (226, 6mm, 257, 6.5mm, 270, 7mm #2, 475)

For "those biggest that walk"—dangerous critters—any of these will take care of the situation. Left to right: 9.3mm JDJ with 286-grain bullet, 375 JDJ with 270-grain, 411 JDJ with 210-grain, 416 JDJ with 400-grain, and 475 JDJ with 500-grain. Probably the best is 375 JDJ. With its 270-grain Hornady spirepoint, muzzle velocity is 2000 fps. That same company's 220-grain starts at 2200 fps. With ease, this one has taken trophies on several continents, from small plains game to that biggest of all—elephant.

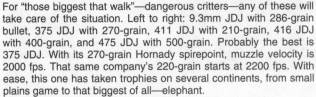

Another trophy with the 375 JDJ. This one a beautiful axis (native to India) deer taken on the famed Y.O. Ranch in Texas—with, what else, a 375 JDJ.

This 300-grain Hornady bullet, fired from a 375 JDJ pistol, was found in the stomach after entering the chest of this big Cape buffalo.

of impact at 100 meters. Leupold Troger, of Austria, has done quite a bit of experimenting with it and finds all hunting bullets and loads group on a cigarette pack at 100 meters without changing the sights.

375 JDJ[1]: There are far more 375 JDJs out in the woods than any of the other cartridges in this series. If I had to choose one cartridge to use the rest of my life, excluding all others, I would not hesitate a bit before picking this one. It does everything. I've taken prairie dogs to elephants, and a great deal of game in between. When I get serious about killing something, the 375 is what's in my hand. The 200-grain Sierra is a little fragile, but works as a great deer bullet if you drop the velocity a little. The 220-grain Hornady is the pick of the litter for deer-sized animals and somewhat larger at about 2250 fps. The 270-grain Hornady spirepoint is extremely accurate and usually shoots *through* a broadside bull elk at 250 yards, though it will take them from any angle. Ditto for the 285-grain Speer Grand Slam. Velocity in this weight range is 2050 to 2100 fps. The Hornady 270- and 300-grain round-noses do well on large animals at close range. On broadside shots, the 300-grain Hornady full metal jacket round-nose almost always shoots clean through buffalo, so be careful of what's on the other side if a herd is present. Any angle except directly astern is OK on them, and it'll work fine if you are close enough to make a spine-tail shot. On frontal chest shots, the bullet will usually be found in the stomach. One buff I shot had his head lowered and the bullet entered and exited the skull, broke up a lot of

neck vertebrae, and ended up inside one of the heart chambers. For this cartridge, another 444, good 375 bullets are available almost anywhere in the world. If equipped with a scope and a brake, most shooters feel it is more comfortable to shoot than a double-action 44 revolver with hunting loads. The 375 JDJ is in use practically around the globe, and most handgun hunters who travel internationally use it extensively. This cartridge has taken far more large African game than any other handgun cartridge.

411 JDJ[1]: After reforming, this old 444 will push a 41-caliber 220-grain Sierra flat-point to 2400 fps, which makes it a very effective deer cartridge. It is at home with most 41-caliber pistol bullets, and 300- to 400-grain Woodleigh and Barnes slugs are fine big game bullets. Like most 41s, the 411 hasn't been really popular, but those who use it swear by it. The 210-grain Sierra in this cartridge is one of the most devastating rounds I've ever used. I won't describe here what it will do inside a deer or on a jackrabbit; however, it will not shoot through a gallon paint can filled with water—the bullet is reduced to small lead and jacket fragments.

416 JDJ[1]: A 300-grainer is the lightest available for this one, and 400 grains is tops. It will do 2000 fps with a 300 and about 1700 to 1750 fps with a 400. It is impressive with

Jones, with a bantang taken in Australia. His cartridge: 411 JDJ with a 400-grain Woodleigh bullet.

the right bullet on big critters. With a 400-grain bullet, the 416 and the 411, both made from the same parent brass, will shoot lengthwise through an adult bull zebra. Using heavy loads with those 400-grain bullets, recoil is pretty strong. A muzzlebrake is definitely recommended. This is about as good as it gets in killing power on large animals from a T/C.

475 JDJ[4]: Less practical than the 45-70 because of bullet availability, this round is simply a 45-70 case blown out straight. Cast bullets are fine, and I've had no trouble taking buffalo with them. I don't mean just one either. I've also done it with the 411 and 45-70. In theory, the slightly larger bullet diameter should be a better killer on large animals than smaller ones. Loaded correctly, I can't see much difference between the 375, 411, 416, 45-70 (in SSK barrels only) and the 475. You can't kill them any deader than dead, and these do it quickly. At close range on large animals, these are probably a bit quicker killing than the 375, but not much. As the range extends, the 375 will do better. It is a great cast bullet gun.

These, then, are the basic JDJ Contender cartridges. They all share several characteristics: All have only slight body taper; most have sharp or fairly sharp shoulders; all give exceptional case life with recommended loads if you do your part by properly loading them (I've gotten over fifty loads out of some brass); all are easy to form. I like to shoot—not reload. Maybe that comes from having loaded a very large number of rounds. We adhere to the KISS (Keep It Simple, Stupid) principle every place we can.

Fire forming should be done with a load that will completely and crisply form the case. Most fire-formed loads are quite accurate—frequently shooting minute of angle—and can be used for practice or hunting.

Generally speaking, consider the 226 and 6mm as varmint cartridges. The 257, 6.5mm, 270, 7mm, 309 and 411 are dual-purpose cartridges for big game and varmints. The 8mm, 338, 358, 9.3mm, 375, 416 and 475 are big game cartridges, which are also fun to shoot for those who like raw power. These are bullets capable of positive expansion on deer at 300 yards in all of the high-velocity cartridges listed.

SSK has chambered T/Cs for a few hundred different cartridges. Many of those reamers will never be used again, because the particular design belonged to a customer who wanted his own specific wildcat. I've designed numerous other cartridges, such as the 338 Woodswalker and the Whisper series of cartridges, that sell well and are in current production. Thompson/Center has adopted the 300 Whisper as a factory chambering as of January '94. Currently, I do not have a complete listing of chamberings as it changes weekly. However, if you are looking for something specific for a T/C, it's quite possible I have the reamer or something like it already. If not, and if I think its safe, I'll get a reamer made and make it up, if you can stand the time lag and money involved—usually about $125 for a reamer and up to six weeks to make it. Then, it'll take several weeks to make the barrel.

There are lots of interesting cartridge designs to come, so put on your thinking cap and give it a try. ●

THE LONE EAGLE
FROM MAGNUM RESEARCH

by MARK HAMPTON

This is how the Lone Eagle comes from the factory—16 inches of barrel, including muzzle-brake drilled and tapped for scope mounting.

WHEN I RECEIVED Magnum Research's Lone Eagle single shot handgun, I couldn't wait to get to the range. I wanted to put this unique pistol through its paces, to see if it lived up to its press release. It's fun getting a new gun and anticipating the first trip to smell burning powder, especially when it's a single shot. I have always had a love affair with accurate handguns capable of cleanly harvesting game from the length of two or three football fields away.

Unfortunately, family commitments that weekend canceled me out, so I called my shooting partner, John Summers, and asked him to give this new gun a workout—a challenge he readily accepted. I welcomed his enthusiasm because I respect John's opinion. He does a good deal of shooting as well as being an avid deer hunter.

My test pistol was chambered for 308 Winchester, the caliber I requested and my favorite whitetail cartridge. Winchester Supreme 150-grain ammo was used exclusively. I have taken a good many whitetails with this load in rifles and was anxious to see what they would do in a handgun. The pistol and two boxes of ammunition were dropped off at John's house, along with a pair of ear muffs. Later that weekend, I learned his findings, along with his general observations and opinion.

John mounted a 2½-8x Leupold. After sighting it in, with most of a box of those factory Winchesters, he was sure proud of those ear muffs. His conclusion: The combo of this cartridge, the mighty 308, and Magnum Research's new muzzlebrake, which very definitely tames felt recoil, sure does make a lot of noise—not a surprising discovery at all.

John also mentioned that the Lone Eagle's 5-pound trigger pull didn't help groups.

The Lone Eagle has a very strong rotary breech, cannon-type action capable of digesting many bottleneck rifle cartridges including 22 Hornet, 22-250, 243, 7mm-08, 30-06 and 444 Marlin, to name a few. Barrel length is 14 inches, and complete barreled actions are interchangeable. The

The Lone Eagle is a very affordable handgun.

This is the "go" button. Push it in and Lone Eagle is on "Safe."

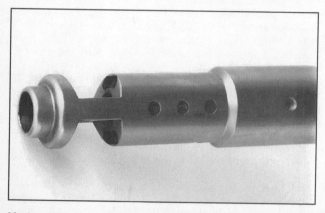

Maybe unusual, but definitely effective, is Lone Eagle's muzzlebrake. Noisy, yes, but then they all are. Make the pistol easier to handle? You bet!

The "leg" sticking down in the cocking lever. Pull it back to its extreme, then let it close, and the pistol is cocked.

breech ring rotates clockwise 105 degrees from locked position to open. The pistol is cocked by pulling out the cocking lever on the forend's left side, then releasing it. Holding the pistol in my right hand while using the left to cock proved to be a simple action. Equipped with a cross-bolt safety, it must be pushed from right to left in order to fire. The operator's manual discourages dry-firing, which could damage the transfer bar and firing pin. When dry-firing, I always insert an empty 308 case.

My test Lone Eagle (LE) arrived with mounts and rings to securely hold the 2½-8x Leupold in place. This scope base is almost 7 inches long with six channels for positioning the rings, which will accept any scope, no matter how short or long. The base came with seven mounting screws to add strength. This provides a very sturdy scope attachment to withstand the most recoil-oriented cartridge a shooter might want to try.

For my accuracy testing, the Leupold was placed on 6x. In the woods, more than likely 2½x, or at the most 4x, would be the choice of most shooters. This variable Leupold, by the way, provided the same clear view, no matter what the setting, an advantage not every scope offers. It is a bit less than 10 inches in length and looks as good as it performs.

Concerning the LE's muzzlebrake, I don't know the cost, but I highly recommend this accessory, especially on heavy kickers. As John had told me, and I found he did not exaggerate, the LE and its muzzlebrake are loud, even with good

According to the author, the muzzle-brake on this Long Eagle 308 Winchester tamed its felt recoil considerably.

Loading the LE is easy: Twist its knurled ring to its extreme right, drop in a cartridge, then turn to the left far as it will go.

This knurled ring makes opening and closing the cannon-type breech easy. Extreme right open, back left far as it will go, and it's ready to shoot.

ear protection. However, the lack of felt recoil was a pleasant surprise. It is extremely controllable with factory ammunition.

The stock assembly is moulded of GE Valox, whatever kind of composition that is, with a right-hand thumbrest. An ambidextrous stock is available for southpaws. Even though my hands are fairly small, this synthetic black stock was easy to grip and hold, all 5+ pounds. Several rounds fired off-hand, at steel silhouettes, proved the big single shot balanced and handled very well.

All of the Lone Eagle's fourteen chamberings are shipped with 14-inch barrels, drilled and tapped for scope mounting, and adjustable sights, for hunting or silhouette, are available. Overall length is 15 1/8 inches, just 1 1/8 inches longer than its barrel, because of the cannon-like breech.

To change barrelled actions, one has only to use the provided hex wrench, remove the cross-bolt, then lift the assembly up out of the stock—not too complicated a maneuver.

Loading and unloading the LE is somewhat different than most handguns. Open the action by rotating its breech ring clockwise far as possible, until the loading slot is aligned with the chamber. At this point, a cartridge can be inserted. To close the action, simply rotate that breech ring counterclockwise to its locked position. Yes, you will still see part of the cartridge rim, but don't panic. Now you are ready to cock the firing pin, disengage the safety and fire.

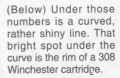

(Left) Here the chamber is open, ready to receive a cartridge.

(Below) Under those numbers is a curved, rather shiny line. That bright spot under the curve is the rim of a 308 Winchester cartridge.

(Above) Offhand shooting showed a lack of recoil because of the use of Magnum Research's muzzlebrake. Downright pleasant to shoot was the verdict.

To change barreled actions remove this through-bolt with a hex wrench...

...and you have a stock ready to install another barreled action. If there is a secret, make certain the action is "cocked" and the safety "on." That action, by the way, doesn't "lift" out. It must be pulled.

After firing, a clockwise turn of the breech ring will eject the spent case. This ejection system functioned perfectly, with those 308 cases popping out clean, even in some mighty cold weather. Once you become accustomed to this procedure, loading and unloading is a piece of cake. With a little practice, a hunter could fire, unload, load and fire again in a matter of seconds, should that be necessary.

I feel the LE's 5-pound trigger pull voided any chance of its best performance. Though, admittedly, once I grew accustomed to its requirements, we got along much better. After all, it's that first shot that counts in any hunting situation, even more so with single shot pistols. One definite dislike: the Lone Eagle's trigger over-travel. This rearward movement must be stopped.

On a cold February day, the first lot of Winchester's Supreme 308s sped across my Oehler 35P skyscreens for an average of 2560 feet per second (fps). Only 260 fps less than the catalog listing from their rifle-length test barrels. Had time permitted, I would like to have tried Nosler's 165-grain Ballistic Tip in some of my handloads. I do know the Nosler BT will expand at this velocity, and shorter pistol barrels have proven more accurate than lengthier rifle tubes. The only loss is velocity, and more often than not, this isn't enough for worry.

Hoping a wild boar would get the test, I took this Lone Eagle to our ranch, where we had some bowhunters seeking boar. In case of a wounded hog, I planned to dispatch him with the LE. Magnum Research had sent a very nice black-nylon shoulder holster, which was worn most of the day. Uncle Mike's also offers a good shoulder rig for these big single shot pistols.

Our bowhunters let me down. They had no cripples. Neither was I able to locate a coyote, so a few steel hogs and a like number of rocks provided a bit of shooting.

Given my druthers, I'd like a chance to try this Lone Eagle out West, perhaps stalking antelope on those wide open plains. Maybe even switching to 243, an ideal "prairie goat" round. Or how about the 22-250 for a bit of varmint shooting, or maybe a 7mm-08 for whitetail. Then, for those brave few looking for a little more "oomph," there is the American favorite 30-06 or, still bigger, the 444 Marlin. Small game hunters haven't been left out, the 22 Hornet is at your disposal.

Whatever application you desire, Lone Eagle offers a rugged, dependable and very affordable single shot handgun. Magnum Research, importers of the Desert Eagle autoloader, have produced another unique handgun for the shooting fraternity.

●

Hunting Handguns

FREEDOM ARMS' MODEL 555 50 AE

by JOHN TAFFIN

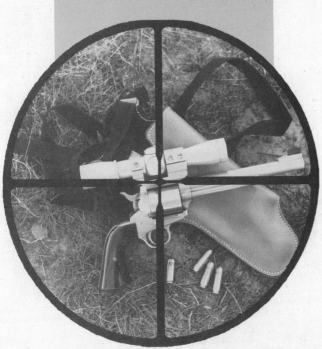

A complete hunting outfit: Freedom Arms' 50 AE with 4x Leupold scope in Jim Herringshaw's Maxi-Mount and FA's shoulder holster.

THE FREEDOM ARMS Casull revolver is one of the finest and strongest revolvers ever built. Freedom Arms' president, Wayne Baker, insists that every 454 Casull be as close to perfection as is humanly possible—nothing less is acceptable. Constructed of 17-4PH stainless steel, the 454 Casull speaks quality from the cylinder/barrel alignment to precise fitting of the specially designed grips, to the 1:24-inch-twist barrel that has proven best for 454 pressures and velocities.

Even before the 44 Magnum became a reality, Dick Casull had started experimenting with heavy-loaded 45 Colt cartridges. Yes, I know that there are many who immediately make the claim that 45 Colt brass is weak. Casull proved the falsity of this statement more than thirty years ago. It was not, and still is not, weak brass. It is only that some revolvers chambered for the 45 Colt have near paper-thin cylinders that contribute to the perpetuation of the myth.

(It is those above-mentioned revolvers that provide evidence disclaiming the "myth." Heavy-loaded 45 Colt cartridges are not for the average 45 Colt-chambered revolver. To prove this, the voice of an authority was needed. I went to Alan Corzine, senior product engineer for Olin/Winchester, manufacturers of a l-o-t of ammunition. Here is what he had to say on this subject.

"Sidewall thickness of the two, 44 Remington Magnum and 45 Colt, is very similar. The 45 Colt is a little thinner, but not enough to make any difference. The web is similar. In their loading, 44 Magnum cartridges are loaded to 36,000 psi; 45 Colt to 14,000 psi. But the offset, which is the measure of strength it takes to bulge a case, is 6100 for the 44 Magnum and 5500 for the 45 Colt. These are psi figures which measure the pressure from inside the case to bulge it against cylinder walls. The 45 Colt case is pretty strong—no problem holding 30,000 psi. Not quite up to 44 Remington Magnum."

The catch is to remember the word revolvers—the guns in

which you are firing those heavy-loaded 45 Colt cartridges. Are they built to take those pressures?

Think on it. Please. —Editor)

The answer seemed to be to turn the old traditional six-gun into a five-gun, that is, make a single-action cylinder with five chambers instead of six. This would allow more metal between the chambers and also permit the bolt slot to be between them instead of over them. It took considerable engineering to change both the ratchet and hand design, but Casull accomplished it, and the new "Most Powerful Revolver in the World" was born—the 454 Magnum as it was called in the 1950s.

Using the new cylinder of 4140 steel, heat-treated to Rockwell 42C, Casull achieved his goal of 1800 fps with the 45 Colt. He wanted a greater margin of safety and soon was building completely custom five-shot revolvers. By the early 1970s, the 454 was a catalog item as a production gun, and a few writers had the privilege of testing it. But it was 1983 before the first factory-produced 454 Casull was sold to the public. It was produced in a totally new plant in Freedom, in the beautiful Star Valley area, in the northwest corner of Wyoming.

The Freedom Arms Casull revolver (I still call it a six-gun even though it only holds five rounds) is a traditionally styled but completely modern single-action revolver. The cylinder allows a lot of beef between its chambers and is fitted so it does not have the "play" that is common to most factory-produced revolvers. The reason is simple: Though they are made in a factory, Freedom Arms' revolvers are, in reality, custom built.

The Freedom Arms grip is not the traditional single-action style that rolls up in the hand on recoil. If it were, some of the heavy loads would probably roll right out of your hand. It is much straighter than either the Colt Single Action Army or Ruger Super Blackhawk, and is engineered to make felt recoil in a 454 Casull feel less than that of a 44 Magnum or heavily loaded 45 Colt in other single-action revolvers.

Loading the Casull is exactly the same as the old-style single actions. Bring the hammer back to half-cock, open the loading gate, and rotate the cylinder to either load or unload. The Freedom Arms revolver is also safe. The safety

bar (actuated by drawing the hammer back about 1/8-inch) holds the hammer away from the frame-mounted firing pin. Since the safety is independent of the trigger, a very smooth pull can be had on these single actions.

Freedom Arms' revolvers are available in the original 454 Casull as well as its less powerful younger brother, the 44 Magnum. Two other excellent big bore cartridges that are long-time favorites of handgunners, 45 Colt and 45 ACP, can be added to the basic 454 through the use of auxiliary cylinders custom fit to each frame. Now, a fourth 45 chambering is available—the 45 Winchester Magnum. Standard barrel lengths for Freedom Arms' revolvers are 4³/₄, 6, 7¹/₂, and 10 inches. The buyer has the option of choosing fixed or adjustable sights, and other barrel lengths are available on special order.

For a number of years, Freedom Arms' revolvers were outlawed from IHMSA silhouette competition under the price-ceiling rule, which excluded pricey revolvers like the Casull. Once this ban was lifted, Freedom Arms started experimenting, and the result was two more chamberings—the Model 353 Casull in 357 Magnum and Model 252 Casull in 22 Long Rifle, with an extra cylinder available in 22 WMR. Both of these are very accurate, and the Model 353

(Above) That's a 44 Magnum, right, and a 454 Casull in the center. Yes, the 50 AE is a big cartridge.

Maybe he should be called "Two-gun Taffin," since he normally has one on his hip while firing another. This time his "shooter" is Freedom Arms' big 50 AE.

allows previously unheard of muzzle velocities from a 357 Magnum revolver.

Now it is time to write a new chapter in the Freedom Arms saga, and that chapter is entitled "Fifty." This past summer, I was privileged to testfire Freedom Arms' latest revolver chambered in 50 Action Express. Meeting with Bob Baker at Freedom, I was able to put the first 7½-inch-barreled gun through its paces. Not only did we have factory ammo from CCI/Speer and Samson, Baker had some "special" loads that he had concocted.

Factory loads for the 50 Action Express will do right at 1300 fps from a Desert Eagle or AMT semi-automatic, with a 300-grain jacketed hollowpoint or softpoint from Samson or a 325-grain jacketed hollowpoint from CCI/Speer. This approximates a heavily loaded 44 Magnum with a 300-grain hard cast bullet in a Ruger Redhawk, Super Blackhawk or Super Redhawk. Baker's special experimental loads far exceeded these in the Freedom 50 Action Express. Only the future will tell what we can expect from the 50 Action Express in a revolver.

Two problems await the reloader of the 50 AE in a revolver. First, semi-automatic cartridges do not have a rim for headspace, but headspace on the front or mouth of the cartridge case, so brass must normally be taper-crimped only. When using 45 ACPs in a six-gun, there is no problem. Pressure and recoil are low, but once they accelerate, inertia kicks in and the movement of the cylinder acts like a bullet puller on the remaining loaded cases in that cylinder. With factory loads in the Freedom Arms 50 AE, the bullet of the fifth cartridge in the chamber will move forward .025- to .030-inch as the other four rounds are fired. Add extra weight in the guise of a mount and scope, plus load only with four rounds, and this is not a problem.

The second problem one encounters requires a little background information. The original 50 Action Express, designed by Evan Whildin and chambered in a Desert Eagle, was a true fifty. Groove diameter was .510-inch as were the bullets, and bore diameter was .500-inch. So, brass was made accordingly. Big Brother stepped in and said semi-automatic handguns may not be more than ½-inch in barrel and bullet diameter. To meet this bureaucratic regulation, barrels were shrunk in diameter, and bullets are now .500-inch.

So what does one use for brass now that bullets are .010-inch smaller? Simple, the beautifully straight case that accepted .510-inch bullets is now tapered. And therein lies

(Left) Freedom Arms' Premier Grade tops their list—the undisputed champion of single-action revolvers.

Taffin appears to come from the "old school" of single-action shooters. Notice he included only four cartridges in this closeup of FA's Model 555 as he tested it. Why four? Old-timers always left an empty chamber under the hammer.

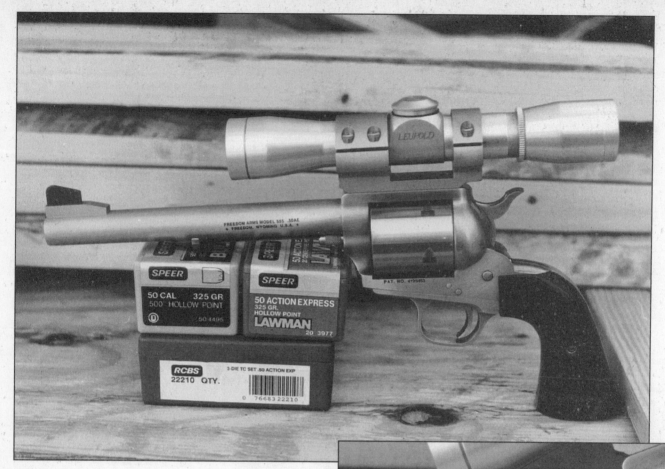

RCBS provides loading dies for the 50 AE. Speer offers 325-grain HP bullets or their Lawman cartridges with that same bullet.

A closeup tells what it is and who made it.

the second problem for reloaders trying to load this cartridge specifically for the Freedom Arms revolver. The higher the velocities, the greater the necessity of a very tight friction fit of bullet to case. With a tapered rather than straight case, the tightest possible fit is impossible to achieve.

These problems are being worked on, and hopefully in the future, we will have moulds for 300-, 350- and 400-grain cast gas-checked bullets with crimp grooves for the 50 AE, as well as a special die that straightens the brass where it meets the bullet. Yes, it is possible to crimp a semi-automatic cartridge for use in a revolver, but it takes a precisely engineered die to do this and still maintain proper headspace.

For testing the Freedom Arms 50 AE, I mounted a 4x Leupold scope using Jim Herringshaw's Maxi-Mount. Temperature was 18 degrees Fahrenheit, and I used the spare tire of my Bronco as a rest, shooting four-shot groups at 35 yards.

Bob Baker had taken their prototype 50 AE to Mark Hampton's Show Me Safaris in Missouri for its baptism as a hunting handgun. On that trip, Bob took a large hog and a larger Barbarosa ram. Since I had a hog hunt with Mark scheduled for New Year's Eve with my good friend Jack Pender, a hunt which some indelicate observer had named Ponderous Pender's Pig Party, we decided I should take the Big Fifty along and try for a big hog.

I testfired some of the original Samson 300-grain softpoint ammunition left over from testing the Desert Eagle a few years back. Setting up a cardboard box with an orange

3-inch square at 90 yards, and using my spare tire on the Bronco once again as a rest, I got the first four rounds in the square. I was ready to go hog hunting.

The last day of the year found me in Missouri. Mark and I were walking down a dirt road looking for hogs. Turning around, we were pleasantly surprised to see a big one on the hill behind us. I wanted to take a frontal shot, and the hog obliged by turning around to face us. Trying like crazy to quiet my inner excitement, I slowly squeezed off a shot. The hog just turned and walked away! But it was walking slowly, as if it were hurt. As it headed for a pond, Mark had me work down and get in front. I was able to do this and squeeze off a second shot. My hog was down!

Shooting uphill, my first shot went through his heart and exited upward through the neck. The second shot did not completely penetrate. Later in the afternoon, Jack Pender took his hog broadside with the 454, loaded with a factory 260-grain softpoint, and it also did not penetrate complete-

John took this Missouri hog with the Freedom Arms Model 555 50 AE using Samson 300-grain JSPs. His scope—Leupold 4x held in Jim Herringshaw's Maxi-Mount.

FREEDOM ARMS' MODEL 555 BALLISTICS TEST

Manufacturer	Bullet (grs./type)	Powder (grs./type)	MV (fps)	Group Avg. (ins.)
CCI Lawman	325/JSP	Factory	1342	1
Speer	325/JHP	26.0/AA#9	1330	1 1/8
Speer	325/JHP	21.0/Blue Dot	1494	2
Speer	325/JHP	31.0/WW-296	1370	2
Speer	325/JHP	26.0/#2400	1335	2
Speer	325/JHP	29.0/H-4227	1196	1 1/8

It takes a dedicated shooter to be out in 18-degree weather, but Taffin did it, and here you can see his 35-yard groups. The velocity of his Lawman 325-grain loads was 1342 fps. Note that four-shot group on top. The lower hole was his aiming point.

ly. The hog was still standing, and Mark did not want us to beat the brush. Earlier I had lent him my custom 4-inch Redhawk with Garrett's heavy 310-grain 44 Magnum loads. One shot with the big 44 in the hog's neck put it down for good. These are tough animals, to say the least. Hampton estimated their weight at 300 and 250 pounds, respectively.

The Freedom Arms 50 AE is built exactly the same as all other Freedom Arms' revolvers. All cylinders are line-bored, meaning, the cylinder is mated with the barreled revolver and chambered in battery. Freedom does not make cylinders and then fit them to a frame and barrel; they are matched before they are chambered.

The sighting system, as on all other adjustable-sighted Freedom Arms revolvers, is unique. Front sight blades are easily interchangeable and available in seven heights, in plain black or orange insert ramp style, a beautiful under-cut Patridge for long-range or target shooting, or a brass bead that mates with a V-notch rear to give Express-style sights that are perfect for close-range hunting with iron sights.

The rear sight is fully adjustable with a locking screw to maintain point of aim. The entire rear sight assembly sits inside a precisely machined recess atop the frame. When that rear sight is removed, the recess accepts a scope mount that is in, rather than on, the frame.

The test gun is the Premier Grade, with highly polished stainless steel. It is also available in Field Grade, a more subdued matte-finished stainless steel. Grips are laminated hardwood with resin bonding.

Carrying a big hunting revolver can be a problem, and I normally opt for a shoulder holster. Freedom Arms offers a beautiful shoulder rig of top-grain cowhide, fully suede-lined with nylon straps that go over the shoulder as well as around the body. The holster also has a strap on the back that fastens to your pants' belt. Fully adjustable, this rig can be worn high or low, at extreme crossdraw angle or nearly straight, and is the best shoulder holster I have encountered for field use. It is available for scoped or iron-sighted Freedom Arms revolvers.

What, then, can we say about the 50 Action Express in a revolver? I like it, plain and simple. I would not choose it ahead of the 454 or even 44 Magnum chamberings, as so many great bullets, both jacketed and hard cast, are available for these two premier six-gun hunting cartridges. However, with enough time to develop bullets and loads for the 50 AE, we may soon see new meaning for the term "big bore revolver."

Hunting Handguns

THE RUGER

by STAN TRZONIEC

This Ruger Super Redhawk with a 9½-inch barrel has a 2x Leupold scope mounted in Ruger rings.

WHEN STURM, RUGER decided to go big-time with a high-class, high-strength, double-action revolver, the Super Redhawk was the result. Noted for its unique profile and 7½- or 9½-inch barrel lengths, the Super Redhawk is also easily adaptable to optical sights with Ruger's integral scope mounting system.

Upon its introduction, the Super Redhawk was the second in the new line of revolvers that started with the GP-100 in the 357 series. This is all part of the ongoing effort by Ruger to provide shooters with the best in design and durability when handling powerful cartridges like the 44 Magnum. Made only of stainless steel, this gun has plenty of features that should please most of the true handgun hunters out there.

Probably the first thing you will notice is the unique profile. Ruger engineers pioneered this design, and basically what it boils down to is an extended frame to offer more strength in critical areas. As you will see, this serves a number of purposes. For one, it adds rigidity to the barrel/frame juncture by way of lengthened bearing surfaces and the relocation of barrel threads for strength. This is really an excellent idea, since the pressure of any high-performance cartridge is greatest at the breech.

In physical appearance, the frame juts forward from the rearmost part of the barrel (at the breech) a full 2½ inches. When you place a micrometer on that part of the frame, it reads .970-inch across the flats—almost a full inch. Where the barrel meets the frame, it tapers down to .955-inch, still leaving a great margin of safety. While the Super Redhawk is an immensely strong revolver, this design feature in no way means that you can hot-rod your handloads to the point of being unsafe. Additional features combined with this frame design make the Super Redhawk one heck of a great field gun.

Another function of this frame design was to make it a perfect platform for mounting a scope. Though the gun comes with a fully adjustable rear sight and an interchangeable-blade ramp front, Ruger has thoughtfully included a pair of rings for the scope mounting. The Redhawk uses the same system as on Ruger's rifles—slots milled into the top of the frame to receive the rings included in the package. There is nothing else to buy. Naturally, this adds weight to

SUPER REDHAWK

If I had to choose a single word that describes the Ruger Super Redhawk it would be "excellent." The large frame is designed to be the ideal platform to mount a scope, making this gun a true hunter's handgun.

the gun, and right out of the box, the Super Redhawk with the 7$\frac{1}{2}$-inch barrel (no scope, rings or ammunition) tips the scale at 53 ounces; with the preferred 9$\frac{1}{2}$-inch tube, it goes a hefty 58 ounces. Add a Leupold 2x scope with Ruger rings and the total now comes to 66 ounces, or 4$\frac{1}{4}$ pounds.

If you were to compare the Super Redhawk with the regular Redhawk, aside from the frame and barrel, both guns are basically the same. As far as I can determine, there has been no change between guns when it comes to the cylinder, its diameter, the type of lockup or the cylinder crane latch. Overall, the cylinder measures 1.780 inches in diameter. When the Redhawk was introduced, the cylinder was said to be 25 percent larger than the nearest competitor. That's great for safety. Cylinder lockup on both guns is at two points. The first is on the front of the cylinder crane, a pivoting latch that mates within a milled recess in the frame. At the rear, the cylinder is held by a spring-loaded pin located dead center within the standing breech. Want still another

safety point? The cylinder bolt has been placed toward the right-hand edge of the frame to allow the locking notches to be milled off-center of the chambers. In this way, more metal has been saved for strength in this highly critical area.

To open or load the gun, merely press inward on the cylinder release button located just rearward of the cylinder. This gun holds six rounds of 44 Magnum ammunition, and close examination of the chambers shows more attention to detail and finish than on some of Ruger's single-action guns. They are going first-class on this one.

The grips are fashioned in the style we've seen on the GP-100 series. In this way, Ruger keeps the "family" appearance of its guns. They are made from rubber and incorporate a wood insert for looks. By the way, there is a New England company by the name of W.F. Lett that makes all kinds of very different grips for Ruger guns, including inserts for the all-weather rifles, single actions and even the

The locking bolt has been moved off-center within the frame to give the locking notches on the cylinder the additional strength needed for this high performance handgun.

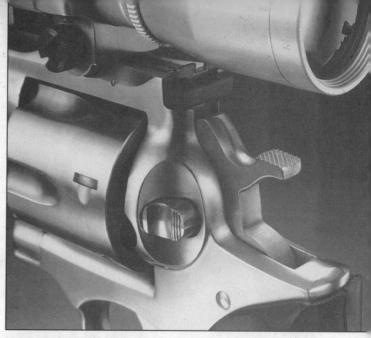

The cylinder release is left of the hammer. Notice the low-slung hammer allowing thumb placement under the scope for cocking. Also note that even with the rear sight down, there is not much room for the scope's eyepiece. Better check that at the dealer before bringing the whole assembly home.

P-series semi-automatic pistols. Contact them for a catalog, I think you'll find it very interesting.

Underneath these grip panels, you'll find the same lockwork as the GP-100 series of medium-frame guns. Whereas the first Redhawks used twin springs mounted in a straight-back horizontal position, with the hammer link pinned around 6 o'clock on the hammer, the Super uses a slightly different approach. With the Super Redhawk, Ruger engineers took the mainspring and mounted it more vertically, which now catches the hammer around 9 o'clock. The trigger latch spring remains in a horizontal plane, but instead of depending upon some complicated leverage to kick the trigger back to its ready position, it ties into the trigger at one rearmost spot and into the frame at another.

The hammer on this model has been lowered, a handy feature especially when you use a scope. With the Leupold mounted, there is about $3/4$-inch space below the eyepiece, which I find more than enough for thumb-cocking even when wearing medium-weight gloves. The hammer spur is checkered for good purchase, even with sweaty hands. The trigger pull on my gun came in at just under 5 pounds in single action; around 13 to 15 pounds double action. This is a bit more than on my plain Redhawk, but since there is very little travel before the sear breaks, it gives the feeling of a much lighter pull. The trigger face is smooth and perfectly formed, and if you had to hang a title on it, you could call it "semi-target."

As for safety within the ignition system, Ruger follows its general policy of the typical transfer bar safety, allowing you to carry a full load of ammunition. At rest, the hammer lies on the frame; when cocking the action, the transfer bar moves upward, allowing contact between the hammer and floating firing pin. When the trigger is released, the bar drops back down, allowing the top part of the hammer to rest on the frame. The hammer can't be cocked when the cylinder is open, preventing an accidental discharge if the cylinder was closed with the hammer at full-cock.

To field-strip the gun, it is best to read the instruction book first. Like other Ruger DA revolvers, the Redhawk and Super can be taken down to basic components without the aid of any fancy tools. All you really need is one dime to remove the stocks, but be careful after parting the grip halves. There is a disassembly pin in the left stock. This is an important part of the disassembly process, for it holds the mainspring in the cocked position for easy removal. However, don't fret if you lose this pin, because a common finishing nail can take its place.

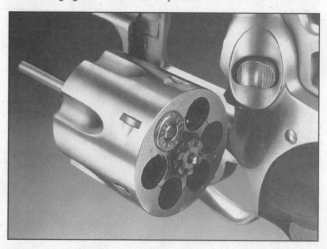

The Super Redhawk is a six-shot. Notice how the locking notches on the cylinder are off-center of the chambers for greater strength in this critical area.

For cylinder lockup, Ruger has chosen to incorporate a front lock on the crane. In addition, the rear of the cylinder locks securely within the standing breech for one rigid assembly when closed.

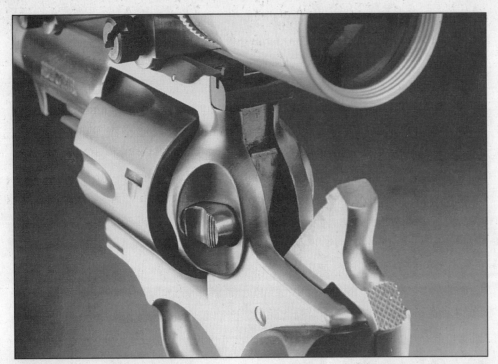

Ruger's safety feature: Under the hammer is the transfer bar assembly that, when the hammer drops, transfers the force to the firing pin. The upper notch on the hammer rests on the frame after the round has been fired.

(Below) The front sight consists of a ramp complete with an insert. Additional front sight blades can be purchased as aftermarket accessories. To remove, push the pin inward on the front part of the base. The small black hole just above the muzzle is where you will find this front sight release.

Ruger rings are included in the package. They are made just like their rifle counterparts, and they attach the same rigid way.

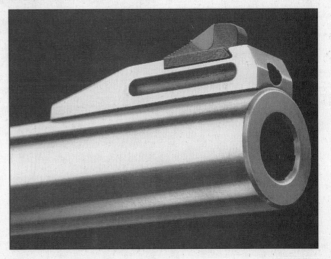

Chambered for the very popular 44 Magnum, this gun finds itself equally at home in the field or at the range. Many forget, but revolvers chambered for the Magnum can also handle the 44 Special, which is great for plinking or taking small game at close range. With the right kind of reloads, the 44 Special can be quite mild for sighting-in or training sessions without the stress of firing full-house loads. Lead bullets as light as 200 grains can be used, and powder charges of around 15.0 to 18.0 grains of 2400 propellant will yield anywhere from 1000 to 1200 fps.

Moving up to magnum power can be easily done with either factory ammo or handloads. I find that commercial loads are fine, but tend to be a bit expensive, especially if you are to become proficient enough for field hunting. The 44 Magnum is good out to about 100 yards. If you don't shoot every week on a regular schedule, don't even think about going further than that. In fact, if you are a first-time handgunner and can't stay within a 4-inch circle (a clay pigeon is fine for this), I'd opt for distances under the century mark. Even when I go varmint hunting with a handgun, the conditions have to be just right (no wind, a good rest, a perfect sight picture) before I pull the trigger. Keep in mind that a 44 Magnum 240-grain bullet traveling at around 1400 fps and sighted in for 50 yards will drop almost $1\frac{1}{2}$ inches at 75 yards, and more than $4\frac{3}{4}$ inches at 100.

With the winter upon us here in New England, range testing of the Super Redhawk consisted of some commercial loads as well as some homebrews in both 44 Special and Magnum. With 240-grain samples, Hornady ammo made nice, tight 1-inch groups at the 25-yard marker, from a rest, averaging 1350 fps. Remington's loads gave me 2-inch groups at 1325 fps, and Winchester came in with $2\frac{3}{4}$-inch

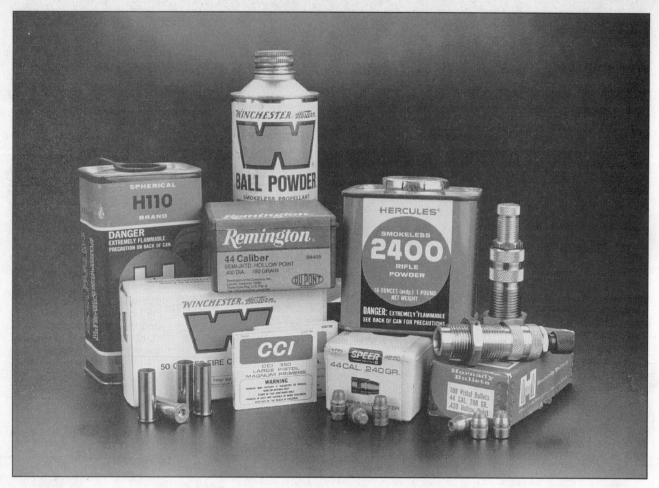

The 44 Magnum is adaptable because of the many loads, bullets and powder combinations available for it. Although factory ammunition is fine, handloads are the best way to get the most from your Super Redhawk.

groups averaging 1375 fps. All were jacketed bullets shot over an Oehler Chronotach.

But as they say in the luxury car commercials, the best is yet to come. The 44 Magnum is a great cartridge, no doubt, but when you start to handload it for the Super Redhawk, big things start to happen. Versatility is the buzzword here, and with brass being turned out by just about everyone, bullet choices by the dozens and propellants without end, one could spend his life just shooting the 44 Magnum.

When loading the 44, always start with clean, fresh cases either new in the box or from a prior loading/shooting session. Stay away from 44 Special brass. It's OK for shooting 44 Specials, but for the heavy hitters, go with the longer 44 Magnum brass, especially for serious hunting duties in a gun like the Redhawk. The shorter cases can lead to what many call "ringing." When the case is shorter than the chamber in the cylinder, residue from the powder and lead bullets will build up in front of the case, making it difficult to chamber the longer, more desirable 44 Magnum cases later. If I had to shoot one type of case, it would be the 44 Mag brass for both the Special and Magnum loads. For better terminal results, use fresh propellant and magnum primers for hard to ignite powders like 2400, H-110 or Olin's 296. Crimp heavy, watch for pressure signs and range-test until you get it right. This Super will take it.

In general terms, the Sierra 180-grain bullet and 27.0 grains of H-110 will give you a very honest 1680 fps in the Ruger. Moving up, we find a 200-grain bullet like

those from Speer or Hornady charged with 26.0 grains of Olin 296 will put you over the 1400 fps mark with little effort. With the popular 240-grain bullets, 22.0 grains of 2400 will nudge around 1370 and 23.0 grains of Olin 296 will hit around 1360, both without any undue pressure problems. Any of these loads will get you started on your way, but if you're looking for more specific information, we can turn to some of my personal records for better answers.

With favored handloads, again with 240-grain bullets from Hornady, Sierra and Speer, velocities were nothing to sneeze at. But again, these rounds were shot in 30-degree weather, so I recommend dropping the charges just a bit when shooting in warmer weather, then work them up. With a Hornady 240-grain jacketed hollowpoint and 21.0 grains of 2400 powder, I saw 1315 fps with 1¼-inch groups. The Sierra FPJ and 24.0 grains of Olin 296 propellant reached 1444 fps, giving 1¼-inch groups. Finally, with the Olin 296 and a Speer magnum hollowpoint over 24.5 grains, the Oehler read 1425 fps with 1½-inch groups. For plinking, I loaded some Hornady 240-grain jacketed hollowpoints over 13.0 grains of 2400 for a velocity of 750 fps. Groups here came in with a mean of 1½ inches. I could not have been more pleased.

In a nutshell, the Ruger Super Redhawk is a fine choice for field hunting. Combined with the 44 Magnum cartridge and rigged with a scope, you could hardly ask for anything more.

•

HANDGUNS 95

SECTION 5
Handgunning Today

Get a grip on it from Sterett, page 128.

More women are shooting, says Ayoob, page 141.

Learn the basics and be a champ like
Plaxco, page 158.

AFTER-MARKET

by LARRY S. STERETT

Here's the lowdown on getting a new handle for your gun from an abundance of makers.

This early Merrill single shot pistol has a custom, fitted-to-the-hand Herrett Target stock.

THERE ARE A NUMBER of interchangeable—even confusing—terms used in the gun world, and what we call the part of a handgun the shooter wraps his hand around is one of them.

The words "grip" and "stock" have been used to mean the same thing for years, although "stock" is generally reserved for long gun usage by most shooters.

In this report we will use the two interchangeably, though they both refer to handguns, of course. So, here is what we've been able to find in the way of the most popular add-on grips and stocks commercially available to handgunners today.

Ajax Custom Grips features their own line of stocks and grips, in addition to selling those from other firms, including the Jay Scott Armarc line, which will be no more since the Scott plant recently closed. Ajax has been in business for thirty-five years, manufacturing stocks and grips of genuine stag, ivory, ivory polymer, exotic woods and plastics for pistols and revolvers. Versions are available to fit most currently manufactured handguns and a few of the golden oldies. Factory medallions for Colt, Ruger, and Smith & Wesson handguns can be installed for an additional $10 per pair, subject to availability. The ivory or ivory polymer stocks look exceptionally good on blued handguns, as do stag and Staglite stocks. White Pearlite, which looks like real mother-of-pearl, and Black Pearlite stocks are made only in the Magna Service type to fit most Colt, Ruger, and Smith & Wesson handguns, plus a few others including AMT, Browning, Beretta, Llama, Walther and Virginian models. In the exotic woods, only super walnut, cherry and black silverwood are regularly available.

In addition, Ajax also has pewter stocks in full scroll, scroll with nameplate, and diamond-checkered versions for the Colt M1911 and Ruger Mark II pistols, plus a line of checkered rubber stocks to fit some Beretta, Charter Arms, Colt, Ruger, and Smith & Wesson handguns. Shooters wanting a pair of S&W Goncalo Alves Combat stocks for N- and K-frame round-butt revolvers might find them at Ajax, just as owners of one or more of the Excam handguns might find wood, plastic or rubber replacement stocks to fit their particular model.

Altamont Design & Manufacturing has been manu-

HANDGUN GRIPS

The Hogue Handall grip sleeve positioned on a Glock pistol.

This Hogue Monogrip one-piece stock rides on a Smith & Wesson revolver. Note there are no screws on the side of the grip.

This Colt M1911 has been fitted with one of the new Hogue rubber wraparounds with finger grooves on the frontstrap.

facturing grips for more than fifteen years. (Anyone who has a John Wayne single-action revolver with ivory stocks owns an Altamont product, since they manufacture the stocks for Colt.) Altamont advertises their products as being from classic to custom, and the raw materials include woods, ivory, stag and bonded ivory, with such options as scrimshaw, engraving, checkering and inlays. Woods include burled walnut, bocote (golden with black stripes) and rosewood. Generally, stocks are left smooth to show off the figure in the wood, although checkering is an option. Altamont is mainly a contract manufacturer, producing stocks for handgun makers, but is getting more into the individual market, particularly on the custom end. Models are available to fit most handguns, from Browning Buckmark and Hi-Power to Dan Wesson revolvers. Between are many: Beretta, Colt, Llama, Luger, Ruger, Smith & Wesson, Taurus, Tanfoglio

and Walther models. Imagine the Colt Single Action Army fitted with a bonded ivory grip that features checkering in a fleur-de-lis pattern or super walnut featuring an oval inlay of a landing eagle, or the M1911 fitted with bonded ivory stocks scrimshawed with a black widow spider or the head of a whitetail buck.

Barami Corporation manufacturers what the firm calls the "Hip-Grip" or pistol handle-holster, which replaces the factory stocks on some small-frame Smith & Wesson, Colt and Charter Arms revolvers. The right stock features an extended lip allowing the revolver to be hooked inside the waistband or belt. It permits a fairly secure carrying position, with only the revolver's grip visible. Barami stocks are smoothly finished and black in color.

Farrar Tool Company makes what some consider the finest line of pliable rubber handgun stocks on the market today. Manufactured to the same size and shape as original factory wooden stocks, Farrar stocks are reinforced with a sturdy spring-steel plate to assure a tight stock-to-frame fit. Models are currently available to fit most current Smith & Wesson handguns, and some Beretta, Colt, Ruger and Walther pistols. UniGrips for S&W's 5900/4000 autos feature a slip-on, one-piece grip with frontstrap and a replacement mainspring housing of tough, heavy-duty polycarbonate. For the Beretta 92F pistols, Farrar also has magazine bumpers, in addition to a sleeve/frame extension for the compact 92F series. By the time this is read, there should also be stocks available for S&W's 45/10 series, in addition to the 59/40, and possibly later for the 69/39. For S&W revolvers, the Farrar UniGrip is available to fit J, K, L and N frames.

Herrett's Stocks produces over a dozen different stock styles, all manufactured from select walnut. These include a rear grip for the Remington XP-100 with a special Timney trigger available in right- or left-hand versions, as well as an ambidextrous design. For the Ruger Mark II, Hi-Standard, Colt M1911 and S&W M41, adjustable target-type Nationals stocks are available, in addition to a 45 Trainer design for the S&W M41 and the Hi-Standard 106-107 Military pistols. The Trainer faithfully duplicates characteristics of the M1911 grip to provide that familiar feel. Regulation, Diamond and Shooting Star stocks, differing mainly in checkering pattern, thumbrest or memory grooves, are available for Colt M1911 autoloaders in 45 and 38 Super chamberings. Combat Camp Perry, Camp Perry, Field and Target stocks with a flared heel are available for most autoloading centerfire and rimfire pistols, including the older Colt Woodsman models; Ruger Standard, Mark I and Mark II; and AMT Lightning. Target stocks are also available for Colt, Ruger and S&W double-action revolvers. Since stocks are made-to-measure, a traced outline of the shooter's hand, right or left, is required, along with a tracing of the outside and inside of the butt frame, including the back portion of the trigger guard and the serial number.

Trooper stocks, including the Jordan Trooper design, are recommended by many law enforcement officers for heavy calibers, such as 44 Magnum. This design is especially suited to PPC shooting, as it can be used right-, left- or two-handed. There are four other variations of the Trooper design—Single Action Trooper, Double Action Trooper, Trooper with Finger Grooves and High Thumbrest Trooper. All Trooper stocks cover the backstrap, but can be made with an open back upon request. Two other Herrett stocks are available for revolvers and are ideal for shooters having small hands—the Detective, designed for small-frame Colt and S&W revolvers, and the Roper, a smooth-finish minimum-dimension design that also fits well in a shoulder holster. Herrett stocks have been used by shooters for more than forty years, and as the firm advertises, their stocks are incomparable.

Hogue Grips feature the Monogrip one-piece revolver stocks designed and patented by Guy Hogue. Secured by a patented steel "stirrup" device that clips over the bottom strap or the existing stock pin, the Monogrips require no modifications to the revolver. Stocks for semi-auto pistols are also available, including models with finger grooves on the frontstrap and smooth or checkered side panels. Manufac-tured of soft rubber, nylon or fancy hardwoods, Hogue stocks feature orthopedic handshape, proportioned finger grooves and, where necessary, relieved surfaces for speedloaders. The black soft-rubber stocks are chemically bonded to a lightweight, synthetic insert to help retain shape and ensure correct fit. Exterior surfaces on the soft-rubber and nylon Monogrips have a cobblestone finish, which is somewhere between a smooth and a checkered surface. Nylon Monogrips are made from 40-percent fiberglass-reinforced nylon which can be worked like wood and will not wear out; these grips are guaranteed for as long as the purchaser owns them, but are not available for all models.

Hogue fancy hardwood stocks are available in more than the usual number of beautiful, hard and durable woods commonly seen, including rosewood laminate, Pau Ferro, Goncalo Alves, tulipwood, kingwood, cocobolo and Lamo Camo. Rosewood laminate and Lamo Camo are lightweight laminated hardwoods and, like other hardwoods, will vary in

Uncle Mike's three-piece set of Custom Grade Moulded Grips for the Third Generation S&W 5900- and 4000-series pistols are moulded of a controlled-density elastomer. Complete with backstrap, these grip are easy to install.

Uncle Mike's new Slip-On grips, complete with finger grooves, improve the gripping surface on most compact and full-size autoloaders, such as the S&W and Glock models shown here.

These Pachmayr Decelerator grips, Gripper on the Colt Anaconda (above) and Compac on the S&W, are 50 percent softer than a regular grip and reduce felt recoil accordingly.

Pachmayr wraparound Full Signature Grips with backstrap on the S&W pistol (above) and the Compac Grips on the Ruger revolver provide a secure, non-slip grasping surface.

The new Pachmayr Slip-On grips with finger grooves will fit most compact and full-size autoloading pistols, such as the Glock (above) and AMT Back Up.

figure and color. Hogue Monogrips have been recently introduced for the Ruger SP-101, V-frame Colt King Cobra and Anaconda, Sig/Sauer P228 and P229, and the various CZ, E.A.A., Tanfoglio and Springfield pistols. There's also a new rubber wraparound with finger grooves for Beretta's 92F series, and the latest on the market are the Handall and Handall Jr. soft-rubber universal grip sleeves. These sleeves are designed to slip over the regular factory stocks and feature ambidextrous palm swells, proportioned finger grooves and the famous cobblestone finish. The Handall will fit most medium- to full-size autoloaders not having a grip safety. The Handall Jr., which has a single finger groove, fits most 22, 25 and 380 pocket-size pistols.

Michaels of Oregon is probably best known for their sling swivels, slings, holsters and blackpowder accessories, but also manufactures an excellent line of Custom Grade Moulded Grips to fit many popular pistols and revolvers. New to the marketplace, Boot Grips fit some twenty different S&W K- and L-frame (square butt) revolvers and probably some clones, and the new Universal Slip-On Grip will fit medium- and full-size autoloaders and comes in two sizes. Injection-moulded of Santoprene to the exact specs of the originals, both styles feature sharp-checkered side panels and finger grooves on the frontstrap. Boot Grips feature a slight ambidextrous palm swell and do not increase the length of pull. Slip-On Grips cannot be used on pistols with grip safeties, such as Colt M1911 and its clones. A Slip-On definitely improves the grip on Glock pistols in any caliber.

Michaels also has a unique three-piece set of grips to replace the hard-plastic factory stocks on most S&W Third Generation 9mm and 40 S&W pistols, except for the 5926 and 4020 pistols. Moulded from a controlled-density elastomer, they provide a firm grip. The two side stocks, which have metal inserts to prevent warping, lock together with a backstrap and are secured by a single pin at the grip's base. The bottom of the backstrap has a integral pocket which holds the pistol's mainspring. As with "Uncle Mike's" other grips, these have no advertising on the surface, nor are they affected by weather conditions.

Pachmayr, Ltd. has been producing soft, real rubber pistol and revolver grips for over thirty years. According to Pachmayr, real rubber offers better gripping and recoil absorption, attractive appearance and improved gun control. Currently, Pachmayr offers five different designs for S&W's K-frame revolvers, and their Signature line for pistols has both frontstrap and backstrap checkered to reduce slippage. Four different types of rubber are used in the manufacture of their grips, depending on grip design. For exam-

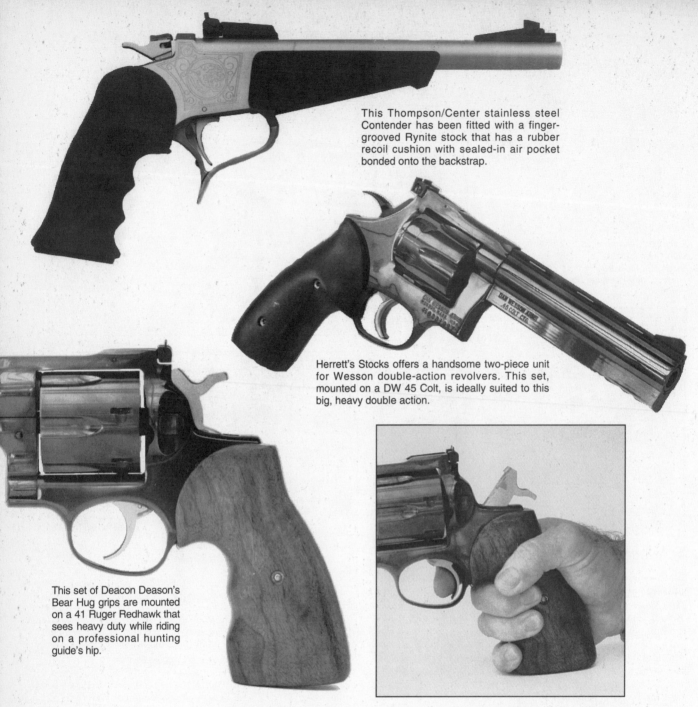

This Thompson/Center stainless steel Contender has been fitted with a finger-grooved Rynite stock that has a rubber recoil cushion with sealed-in air pocket bonded onto the backstrap.

Herrett's Stocks offers a handsome two-piece unit for Wesson double-action revolvers. This set, mounted on a DW 45 Colt, is ideally suited to this big, heavy double action.

This set of Deacon Deason's Bear Hug grips are mounted on a 41 Ruger Redhawk that sees heavy duty while riding on a professional hunting guide's hip.

As can be seen here, Bear Hug Grips comfortably fill the hand yet provide excellent control. This hand wears a size 7 glove, yet Bear Hug fits it perfectly.

ple, the Decelerator elastomer is used where maximum recoil absorption is desired, while a different blend is used in the new Slip-On designs. Decelerator grips are offered in Compac, Gripper and Presentation lines, but they cannot be used for all handguns. Among the sixteen different selections, including the four lines mentioned above, plus the Bill Jordan Combat, Sure-Grip and Slip-On, there should be something to fit most handguns manufactured in the past century.

The newest Pachmayr grips are Slip-Ons in four styles and three sizes. These include small, medium, and large, with finger-groove, and large with plain front or frontstrap surface. To provide a bit more secure gripping surface on

Glocks, or some small 25, 32 and 380 pistols, this is the route to go, and it is more economical than a new pair of stocks.

Three different add-on grips are available for the Thompson/Center Contender, two walnut and one Rynite. Rynite and Competitor grips both feature a rubber recoil cushion bonded to the back of the grip. This protects the hand from the pounding effect of recoil. Both grips also feature a sealed-in air pocket in the sensitive web area. The third grip is their finger groove model with notches and thumbrest to provide consistent hand positioning. (The Rynite stock also has finger grooves.) Finger groove walnut stocks are available in right or left-hand versions; the other

Uncle Mike's latest offering is a design for Smith & Wesson K and L frames. Called the Boot Grip, it offers a slight ambidextrous palm swell that increases the gripping surface without making the revolver hard to hold. The open backstrap design does not add to the length of the trigger pull.

two grips are designed to fit either hand. Some earlier Contender grips were checkered, but current production models are smooth.

Wesson Firearms Co. offers seven different interchangeable grips which can be purchased as options or accessory grips for their Dan Wesson revolvers, in addition to Hogue Gripper models. The Wesson grips include a Wayland Custom walnut grip with smooth finish; a Target grip in walnut or exotic wood, smooth or checkered; a checkered Undercover grip; and a Combat grip with three finger grooves. Unlike some grips, which are actually two separate stocks fitting onto the side of the frame, the Wesson models are one-piece units solidly held to the frame extension by a heavy bolt.

Bear Hug Grips produces one of the most comfortable handgun stocks on the market today—the Skeeter Skelton Style with open back, slim sides, properly placed palm swell and a smooth finish.

A Bear Hug exclusive, the Skeeter Skelton Style is available for both round- or square-butt Smith & Wesson K-, L- and N-frame revolvers.

Two smaller stock styles—the Coyote and RB-LS—designed for comfort and concealment are also available, with the Coyote being available only for S&W J-frame revolvers. Both stocks are also available in custom wood.

Bear Hug also offers custom grips in fancy walnut, rosewood, curly maple, bird's-eye maple, cordia or figured walnut, while standard grips are produced from StaminaWood. Weather resistant and tough, StaminaWood is a resin-impregnated hardwood laminate that takes a high polish and is beautiful in appearance, whether it is mesquite, ebony, ash, rosewood, walnut or cocobolo.

Custom stocks are available to fit all J-, K-, L- and N-frame revolvers, with square or round butt, plus the Ruger Redhawk, Colt Anaconda, King Cobra, Python and D-frame revolvers. The wood is hand-fitted one at a time to each individual's hand tracing and carnuba wax-finished to a satin sheen. Open-back finger groove, wraparound finger groove, wraparound plain front, target styles, and thumbrest stocks are custom options for shooters having large hands, long fingers or both.

Pistol shooters wanting to add a touch of class to their favorite M1911 or clone; S&W Models 41, 422 and 622; High Standard or Ruger Mark II autoloader will find the answer in Bear Hug Grips produced for these pistols. The standard grips have a smooth-finished double palm swell that looks and feels good in any of the StaminaWood types, starting at $55.95, with checkering extra. The M1911-style with checkering looks excellent in ebony, rosewood or mesquite on any stainless or nickel finish. ●

EL VAQUERO
RUGER LIGHTNING

by JERRY BURKE

Today's "young guns" call for genuine-looking six-shooters, and Ruger answers again, in black and white.

Introduced to meet the needs of today's cowboy action shooter, Ruger's new Vaquero is equally adept as a work-a-day for handgunners who prefer the single action.

THE MARSHAL STOOD tall in the dusty street, grimly facing his opponent in the traditional gunfighter's stance, ready and waiting.

The lawman's opponent made a move for his six-gun. The Marshal cleared leather with a long-barreled Colt Peacemaker, wincing slightly as his opponent's shot rang-out—a split-second before his own bullet found its mark...

The brash sound of a car horn brought me back to reality. It was a Saturday evening in August of 1955, and my entire family sat silently in the darkened living room watching "Gunsmoke" on TV. There we would remain, completely transfixed, for the next half-hour.

Following WWII, grassroots interest in the Old West was fanned into a national passion through television programming like "Gunsmoke." The Main Street gunfight previously described opened two decades of "Gunsmoke" episodes. U.S. Marshal Matt Dillon, portrayed by James Arness, always won that weekly shooting contest with the "bad guy," renowned shooting coach Arvo Ojala.

My interest in the Old West goes back to a time before I'd ever heard of television. Western radio dramas, "B" movies on the silver screen and 10-cent comic books brought me the thrilling exploits of Roy Rogers, Gene Autry, the Lone Ranger and Hopalong Cassidy, plus a host of lesser-knowns from Red Ryder to Lash LaRue. But it was the new-found adult-male interest in old-time gunfighting, as seen on television, that would alter the balance of power in the firearms industry.

Colt Single Action Army revolvers in excellent condition were few and far between in the early 1950s. Those that were available became increasingly high-priced as demand skyrocketed. The switch-over from production of the old thumb-buster to make way for more modern military hardware at the start of World War II must have seemed a blessing to Colt management at the time. After all, sales of the old-fashioned Model P single action had been on a downhill run for many years.

The Ruger Vaquero is based on the New Model Blackhawk, but with the rear sight cut into the frame, plain front sight blade and case-colored frame. Although attractive hardwood stocks are standard, this gun sports custom stocks by W.F. Lett Manufacturing and original schrimshaw work by Bill Lett, III.

STRIKES TWICE

In spite of shooter demand after WWII, Colt steadfastly declared that the SAA would never again be produced. The anticipated postwar selling price would be very high, and Colt thought that no one would be willing to part with that much cash.

As a result, our border with Old Mexico became the last source of bargain Colt SAAs and Bisleys in the early 1950s. Steely eyed *gringo* "horse traders" from Tijuana to Matamoros turned to gun haggling. For the gun scrounger

(Below) A collection that would make any single-action fan proud: Ruger's new Vaqueros, blue with case-colored frame (top left) and polished stainless steel; Colt's Single Action Armys, early Post-War model (top right) and nickel-plated model of current manufacture.

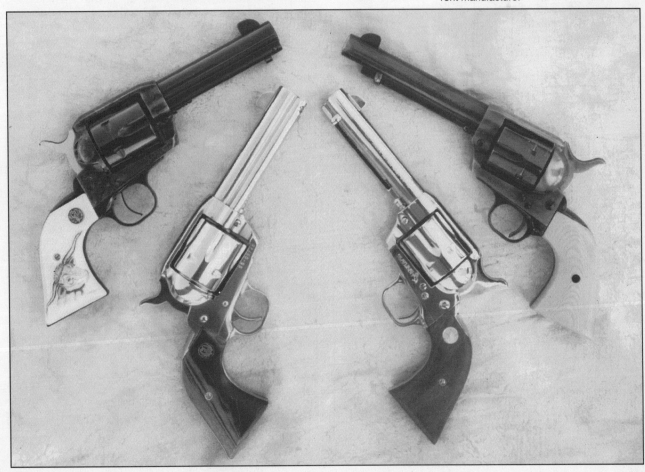

not well grounded in the Spanish language, only two basic words were (and still are) required to communicate one's single-action handgun interest along the Rio Bravo: *"pistola Tejana."* The vigorous, often violent history of Texans and their Colts explains the connection.

All this scrambling for six-guns did not go unnoticed. The then-fledgling firm of Sturm, Ruger & Company broke the deadlock between single-action fanciers and firearms manufacturers in 1953 with the introduction of their superb 22-caliber Single-Six, a slightly scaled-down SA obviously inspired by Colt's original. Single-Six sales soared at a brisk rate and haven't slowed down since. Even so, demand continued to run high for something more—a full-frame, single-action revolver in centerfire caliber.

In 1955, Ruger struck like lightning with the introduction of their single-action Blackhawk revolver in 357 Magnum. It was the same size as the classic Colt SA and included a number of modern features, some at the urging of the legendary Elmer Keith. Amidst all the commotion, Colt relented in 1956 and again offered the historic Peacemaker, thrilling both experienced SA handgunners and greenhorns alike.

Sparked by the many TV Westerns, the "quick draw" hobby became very popular in the late '50s. Armed with the single action of their choice, grown men from soda jerks to

bank presidents slapped leather in many mock gun battles, and the demand for good single-action six-guns grew ever stronger.

The early 1960s found situation comedies and police dramas taking the place of many TV Westerns, and although the general public's interest in their frontier heritage waned, American handgunner enthusiasm for Ruger's Blackhawk steadily increased.

Even with the advent of Ruger's Blackhawk and reintroduction of the incomparable Colt SA, the decades which followed continued to see a significant level of demand for moderately priced single actions in the traditional fixed-sight configuration.

About thirteen years ago, a small group of California *pistoleros* known as "The Wild Bunch" grew tired of the rabid competitiveness and equipment races associated with many organized shooting sports. The group not only decided to march to a different drummer, they designed their own drum as well! They founded the Single Action Shooting Society, which now boasts cowboy action shooting affiliates from coast to coast and beyond our borders. Their credo insists on safe gun handling, and only firearms of the Old West variety are allowed. Participants in SASS events dress the part of their late 19th-century aliases and engage targets in non-traditional ways, such as through the open door of an outhouse from the sitting position! As you might imagine, right after safety, the emphasis is on fun.

More recently, big screen and TV filmmakers fanned the flames of cowboyism once again with productions like "Lonesome Dove I and II," Clint Eastwood's "Unforgiven," Kevin Costner's "Dances With Wolves," "Young Guns I and II," "The Young Riders," and more Old West offsprings.

With the continuing growth of cowboy action shooting and the entertainment industry's focus on the Old West, the demand for traditional single-action handguns skyrocketed. Yet there was no hope in sight for a moderately priced American-made big-bore single action with those practical plain-vanilla sights. Suddenly, in 1993, Ruger officially

An original Ruger 357 Magnum Flattop Blackhawk, produced in 1959. The author credits Bill Ruger for inventing the first SA tool for modern handgunning (top). Ruger's new Vaquero—available in three calibers, as many barrel lengths and two finishes—brings the sport full-circle.

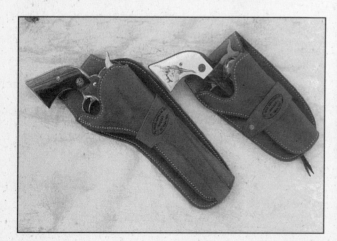

This top-quality, authentic 1890s leather was made by El Paso Saddlery and holds a pair of Ruger Vaqueros in blue and stainless.

Ruger's new Vaquero was introduced to meet the needs of cowboy action shootist groups like the Single Action Shooting Society.

Ruger's Vaquero sports a rear sight notch cut into the frame. The standard front sight blade replaces the typical ramped version found on other Ruger Blackhawk models.

Ruger's latest classic is the fixed-sighted Vaquero here with 7½-inch barrel for the cowboy action shooter seeking the original cavalry-length gun. The Vaquero is also available in 4⅝- and 5½-inch barrel lengths.

announced their second lightning-like reaction to rekindled interest in the Old West, the Vaquero. The Vaquero is designed to meet the needs of today's cowboy action shooter, and Ruger also hoped to interest the single-action "traditionalist."

Fixed sights on such a handgun greatly reduce the chance of the gun shooting around corners after some rough handling. They limit the chance of a hangup while bringing the shootin' iron into action and have the added advantage of eliminating the rips and scratches high-profile sights often cause to clothing and equipment.

Generally speaking, the Vaquero is a Ruger New Model Blackhawk through and through. This includes a number of features we've come to take for granted, such as the beefed-up cylinder and cylinder frame, the long easy-to-grip cylinder pin head, and a grip shape most shooters find better than the original design. When you add Ruger's use of coil

springs and a frame-mounted firing pin, there's plenty for a modern shooter to enjoy. The Vaquero also includes Ruger's patented New Model mechanism, which allows the gun to be safely carried with all six chambers loaded when both the hammer and trigger are in their farthest-forward positions. Even so, many savvy shooters still prefer to load only five rounds in *any* six-shooter, ensuring the chamber under the firing pin is always empty.

The Vaquero has a series of features never before seen on a production big-bore Ruger single action. The top of the frame is rounded and grooved to provide a built-in rear sight. The front sight is a basic blade. In addition, both of the Vaquero's finish options are new to Ruger. The "blued" version includes a blued steel grip frame, with the barrel, ejector rod housing and cylinder also blued. The cylinder frame and loading gate are "color case-finished." The finish provides the multi-colored, swirled appearance of case-hard-

Oklahoma Ammunition Company's 45 Long Colt ammunition performed well in the blued Ruger Vaquero. Fixed sights on this model are pre-set at the factory for 25 yards.

The Vaquero by Ruger shoots as good as it looks. Economical CCI Blazer ammunition performed very well in this polished stainless steel version in 45 Long Colt.

FACTORY AMMO BALLISTICS TEST
RUGER VAQUERO (4⁵/₈-inch Bbl.)

Brand	Case Material	Bullet (grs./type)	MV (fps)	Group (ins.)
CCI Blazer	Aluminum (NR)	200/JHP	975	2.00
CCI Blazer	Aluminum (NR)	255/LRN	842	2.10
Federal	Brass (R)	225/LSWCHP	885	1.80
Oklahoma Ammo	Brass (R)	250/LRN	844	2.15

Results are the average of ten-shot strings fired at 20 yards from a rest. (NR) = Non-reloadable; (R) = Reloadable; JHP = Jacketed Hollowpoint; LRN = Lead Round-Nose; LSWCHP = Lead Semi-Wadcutter Hollowpoint.
Shooting Chrony chronograph used to determine velocity; equipment placed 6 feet from gun muzzle. Group size measured from center-to-center of two widest shots.

Ruger's new Vaquero was designed for the growing cowboy action shooting crowd, like Ron Blaschke, a.k.a. "The Durango Kid," member of the Texas Historical Shootists Society.

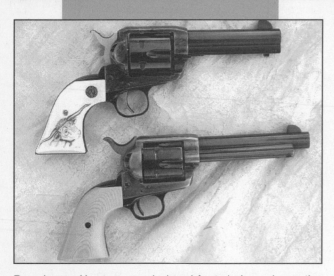

Ruger's new Vaquero was designed for today's cowboy action shooter (top). The post-WWII Colt Single Action Army revolver was resurrected by that firm in response to the first resurgence in the Old West nearly forty years earlier.

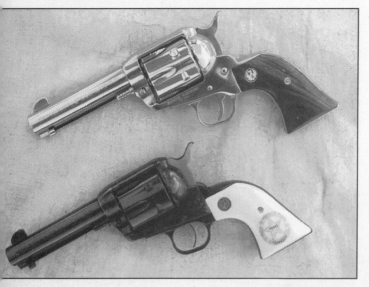

The new Vaqueros come in polished stainless steel with well-fitting standard factory grips (top) or blued with a case-colored frame. Custom grips by W.F. Lett Company add the final touch.

ening, but is a cosmetic feature only. Vaquero owners should pay special attention to this old-timey effect, as it is not as durable a finish as that on the gun's conventional blued parts.

The Vaquero is also offered in stainless steel. Ruger has long been an industry leader in the production of top-quality firearms manufactured from that tough-to-handle material. But the unique feature of the stainless Vaquero is its high-gloss finish—a machine-generated polish that has the appearance of a good nickel-plate job, without any rounded-off corners where they don't belong.

I'm not fond of long-barreled handguns except for hunting, so I got my hands on a pair of Vaqueros—one finished in blue with "color case-finish," the other in high-gloss stainless—with short 4⁵/₈-inch barrels. An intermediate 5¹/₂-inch version and a traditional cavalry-length barrel of 7¹/₂ inches are also available in either finish option.

The first Vaquero chambering was the 45 Long Colt, and the 44-40 WCF, especially popular with cowboy action shooters, is a welcome recent addition. For those who prefer a more modern cartridge, the Vaquero is also available in 44 Magnum. In all, sixteen different Vaqueros are available when you consider two finish options, three calibers and the three barrel lengths available. The 44 Magnum is not offered with a 4⁵/₈-inch barrel.

Fit of parts and overall finish on both test guns were excellent, even in areas where no one usually looks. I detest burred screw heads, and the brace of Vaqueros had nary a one. I also expect cylinders that lock up tight and have minimal clearance with the base of the barrel. Again, the Vaqueros passed with flying colors. In fact, these guns are produced to standards that surpass some handguns with suggested retail prices more than three times higher.

Stock panels on all Vaqueros are fashioned from a dense durable rosewood, which is attractively figured and bound to last a lifetime or two. However, knowing how special these shootin' irons are, I immediately contacted W.F. Lett Manufacturing, which has been the principal original equipment supplier to Sturm, Ruger & Company since 1955. Bill Lett, III, is a talented scrimshander whose work is absolutely first-rate.

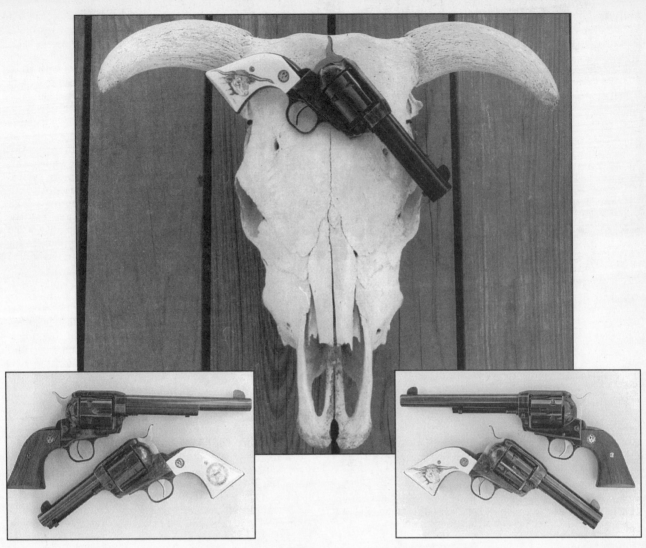

The Ruger Vaquero comes with a choice of barrel lengths, from
7½ inches on down to 4⅝ inches.

Although there were plenty of alternatives, I chose Lett's ivory-like material for the blued/color-case Vaquero; it looks, feels and has the weight of genuine ivory, but is much more stable than the real thing. For scrimshaw, we settled on a Texas longhorn steer for one panel and a replica Texas Ranger badge for the other. The new grips are a perfect fit on the Vaquero and a work of art as well!

Next came the uncontrollable urge to get my hands on custom leather for these very special Ruger six-guns. My first call was to El Paso Saddlery. They have a history of top-quality leather making that dates back to 1889. I requested one of their Hardin shoulder holsters, just like the one they built for John Wesley Hardin in 1895, and an 1890-style single-loop belt holster.

Master gunmaker Bill Grover, of Texas Longhorn Arms, markets a unique multi-purpose outfit he calls the High Rider. It is incredibly practical, being adaptable to standard or crossdraw for both right- and left-handed shooters. Bill agreed to develop the first High Rider ever created for a Ruger Vaquero. Grover's system combines a beautifully crafted holster with matching belt slide which allows the gun to be carried up and out of the way when wearing the holster in a car.

I also obtained Galco International's Trail Boss outfit, which consists of a superb 3-inch-wide money belt, fully

lined holster, and a bronze belt buckle crafted in their own foundry. Finish is a beautiful rich-looking walnut of the same quality shooters have come to expect and appreciate from Galco.

All of the previously mentioned leather products are top-drawer in design, materials and craftsmanship. Selecting one over the other is a matter of personal need and style preference.

Ruger announced the Vaquero as a shootist's gun, whether or not you prefer to dress for the part. So the final phase of getting to know these two "shootin' irons" was seeing how they would perform downrange. The factory ammo I selected for testing was CCI's economical Blazer ammunition. I chose their 200-grain jacketed hollowpoint and their 255-grain round-nose lead bullet loads. Produced with non-reloadable aluminum cases, Blazer ammo has provided a legion of shooters with top performance over the years, at an attractive price.

I also chose Federal's excellent 225-grain lead hollow-points and Oklahoma Ammunition Company's 250-grain conical-style lead projectile loads. Both of these cartridges are manufactured with reloadable brass cases.

Because the Vaquero was introduced as something of a big-bore "fun gun," testing a series of pleasurable 45 LC handloads also seemed in order. The cowboy action shooter

HANDLOAD BALLISTICS TEST
RUGER VAQUERO (4⅝-inch Bbl.)

Brass	Primer	Powder (grs./type)	Bullet (grs./type)	MV (fps)	Group (ins.)
W-W	CCI/LP	6.6/Bullseye	250/Speer LSWC	795	1.81
W-W	CCI/LP	6.2/Red Dot	250/Speer LSWC	790	1.72
W-W	CCI/LP	7.5/Unique	250/Speer LSWC	785	1.76

Results are the average of ten-shot strings fired at 20 yards from a rest. Shooting Chrony chronograph used to determine velocity; equipment placed 6 feet from gun muzzle. Group size measured from center-to-center of two widest shots.

W-W = Winchester-Western; LP = Large Pistol; LSWC = Lead Semi-Wadcutter.

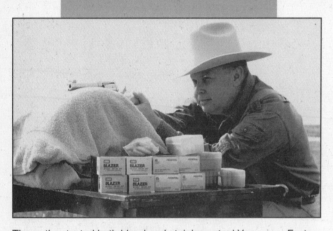

The author tested both blued and stainless steel Vaqueros. Factory ammunition from CCI, Federal and Oklahoma Ammunition Company were included as well as handloads. The author removed his shooting glasses and hearing protection for this photo.

doesn't need barn-burner loads, and neither does the six-gunner who trails around with a traditional single action for the pure and simple joy that experience can bring.

Over the last several decades, I've been a consistent user of Hercules powder. I achieved first-rate success with these powders from the "get-go," so I've found little need to experiment further. I selected Bullseye, Unique and Red Dot powders for use in the 4⅝-inch Vaqueros.

I did all my shooting over my "never-patented-but-quite-effective" benchrest system—an old towel flopped over an even older rolled-up sleeping bag. Vaqueros are pre-set at the Ruger factory to be on target at 25 yards while using the six o'clock hold. However, 20 yards is a more typical shooting distance for casual blasting, so I tried all four types of factory ammunition in each of the Vaqueros from that distance. The results were outstanding, much to the credit of Ruger's gunmaking expertise and the quality of the test ammunition. Typical five-shot factory ammo groups ran 2 inches, measured center-to-center between the widest hits.

For my reloads, I selected Speer's 250-grain lead SWCs, virgin brass by Winchester-Western and CCI primers. In these short barrels, those components, along with the three different Hercules powders, produced average muzzle velocities of just under 800 fps. Attention to detail, including weighing each powder charge and applying a uniform crimp to case mouths, produced groups about ¼-inch tighter than those produced with factory ammunition—not very significant considering the Vaquero's intended purposes.

Many thanks to Bill Ruger for his timely response to consumers' desires and to the Single Action Shooting Society for their devotion to shooting safety and for fostering an appreciation for Old West ways and wardrobes. For those who want a solid, top-quality single action that shoots where you point it without the need for modern high-profile sights, the Vaquero is just what you've been waiting for. Priced at a suggested retail of only $394 for any of the sixteen variations offered, this new Ruger revolver represents the finest of values in a single-action six-gun. ●

First-rate shootin' irons—Ruger's stainless steel Vaquero (left) and blued version with case-colored frame. The blued gun and five rounds of Federal ammunition combined to make this group.

The author used Shooting Chrony Model F-1 to record velocities produced by all loads tested in both Ruger Vaqueros.

PISTOLERA

by MASSAD AYOOB

Today's women take active roles in the shooting sports as competitors and self-defense instructors, and they use guns that fit them.

Women are built to take cover more efficiently...and, psychologically, they're less hesitant to do so. Cathy Ayoob, then fifteen, makes good use of a tree with her S&W LadySmith 357 Magnum.

THERE WAS AN occasion coming up, and I'd bought a gift for my eight-year-old daughter. A friend not involved in the firearms field asked me what I'd bought her.

"A little Ruger Bearcat 22 revolver," I told him.

He was aghast. He blurted, "You mean, a *real* gun?"

My kids have never been permitted to play with the toy ones.

He was almost sputtering, and I was having a little fun. "But, she's *eight*! Do you think that's an appropriate age for a *revolver*?"

"I don't know why not," I answered nonchalantly. "She's had her own *semi-automatic* since she was six..."

I guess he and I just weren't on the same wavelength.

This society still gets shocked about women having guns. Many people got all adither at the thought of S&W and, later, Colt advertising defensive handguns to the distaff market. Of course, it was a sexist reaction; in another generation, those with the same attitude turned up their noses at females who dared have careers and looked with scorn on single mothers. And it's not just women who are locked into those obsolete gender role models. More recently, I remember a clerk in a bookstore who was genuinely offended to learn there was a periodical called *Women and Guns*.

The law itself recognizes, in its explanation of the principle of disparity of force, that men are bigger, stronger and, generally, meaner than women. Unfortunately, it is a fact of life that brutal men have beaten defenseless women to death. But some of these brutal men have learned another fact the hard way.

That fact is, when even an unarmed man violently attacks a woman, the likelihood of her suffering death or grave bodily harm from the beating becomes so great that his male strength is seen as a deadly weapon. She is authorized by the law to put such an attacker on a stainless steel table with a tag on his big toe.

And more than one has done so.

Training the Female

The gender of the instructor is sometimes a factor here. One West Coast instructor who seems self-appointed—there's no evidence he's ever actually taught a full firearms class or been certified to teach—has some extremely vitu-

Seen from this angle, a female contestant at the Bianchi Cup effortlessly negotiates the awkward Barricade Event. Women's lower center of gravity and greater lower body flexibility can, with proper techniques, give them advantages over male counterparts.

perative words for any female student who insists on a female instructor. I can't quite buy that.

I was still fairly young when the first female student looked at me and sighed, "You stand there with your mustache and your leather jacket and your baritone voice and your 45 automatic, and you don't *begin* to relate to my fears."

I thought she was wrong, then. I still hope she was. But that wasn't the point. Her perception was her reality, and if I couldn't get past those perceptions, it was my fault, not hers.

A number of women pick up the gun *because* they've been brutalized. It's confusing enough when credentialled people like Susan Brownmiller urge victimized women *not* to arm themselves because the gun is "an icon of male brutality" and owning one somehow forfeits the moral victory; it is worse to *force* a woman in this unenviable position to accept her training from a teacher who is an alpha male.

For several years, I've experimented at my training school, Lethal Force Institute (LFI), with women-only classes. Success has been mixed. The classes worked out very well and the students loved them, but they were never commercially successful. A lot of strong women refused to take the single-sex program, stating determinedly, "I want the real one, the same one you give the men."

Of course, our course was "the real one," plus many hours of women's issues (guns that fit smaller hands, holsters that fit their anatomies and wardrobes, and the moods of the courts on using a handgun in self-defense). But again, the perception had become the functional reality. So, those women who felt that way were simply plugged into the co-ed classes.

Today, our format is to occasionally offer a one-day "testosterone-free environment"—all female students, all female instructors—the day before the full class begins. This familiarizes the female student with those subjects more specific to her than her brother and creates more of a level playing field the first morning of the regular program.

"Home alone?" Not hardly. Shown at age ten, Cathy Ayoob had mastered both her Fred Sadowsky Custom Colt Police Positive 38 Special and her Akita. Note the custom revolver stocks by "Fuzzy" Farrant.

An aggressively forward isosceles position gives this LFI student excellent control of her SIG P-225 9mm auto, which fits her hand well. A high speed camera has caught the gun just coming back into battery during firing cycle; note the muzzle has barely risen from point of aim with a full power load.

LFI was the first of the mainstream schools to begin using women as full instructors. Past and present staff have included such fine trainers as Kate Alexander, Gila May-Hayes, Graciela Casillas, Diana Smith, Tambra Leslie, Gail Burton, Leah Garlichs, Gail Devoid, Ruth Warners and Linda Pendleton. Running the all-women classes with great success were former Second Chance women's champion Lyn Bates and crack USPSA competitor Laurie Kraynick.

The Female as Trainer

Valerie Atkins runs firearms training at the Federal Law Enforcement Training Center. I invited her to teach firearms for the American Society of Law Enforcement Trainers, and her students' critiques were among the most complimentary ever submitted in that demanding *creme de la creme* atmosphere.

Anyone who thinks women cannot successfully teach strong men has not met Atkins. Nor have they met Pamela

An aggressive stance gives Barbara Budnar, shown here competing at Second Chance, excellent rapid-fire control. The pistol is a Wilson Custom Colt with hot +P 45 ACP ammo.

Graciela Casillas, undefeated women's World Kickboxing Champion, prefers a Colt 45 auto for serious business. (Photo courtesy BC Academy)

J. Miller. Barely 5 feet tall and less than 100 pounds, Miller wields a baton with such authority that she is at the highest level, International Instructor, that a baton trainer can earn with the potent PR-24. Nearly 10 percent of PR-24 internationals are female; Miller is joined by Cat Kelley and Missy O'Linn. O'Linn is also one of the nation's leading authorities on police civil liability and is an ex-cop turned trial attorney who represents policemen in excessive force cases.

What about firearms? John Farnam's wife, Vicki, began in her famous husband's shadows, but quickly developed her own reputation as an excellent trainer and diagnostician who could help the problem shooter. I've noticed that the female firearms coach will tend to be more compassionate and more patient than her male counterpart. She'll also be less clinical, going for core problems that lie beyond the easy diagnoses of heeling or jerking or not watching the front sight.

Do some males have problems taking direction from females in a discipline they've been conditioned by childhood play and a lifetime of entertainment media to see as macho? I ain't gonna lie to you. It happens, though not as often as a woman who has not been in a structured shooting environment might fear. Every now and then, though, the testosterone does get a little bit thick.

In 1993, my sixteen-year-old daughter, Cathy, began interning with me on the range. Having been in shooting and martial arts all her life, her strong foundation in body mechanics made her an excellent diagnostician of tech-

nique. She had also been raised not to take anything from males, in general, and adult males, in particular.

One of her students was an instructor in a police academy. He was firing from what I call the "feeb Weaver," the pathetically weak and off-balance parody of the Weaver stance developed by the FBI in 1981 and, thankfully, abandoned as soon as John Hall became head of the Bureau's firearms training unit. The man wasn't shooting nearly as well as he could have with proper techniques.

Cathy calmly and quietly (but drastically) altered his position. She took his feet from their pedestal position and gave him a wide pyramidal base, brought his shoulders aggressively forward out of his backward lean, and locked his weakly bent gun arm.

This did not sit well with the man at all. In a voice loud enough for all to hear, he remarked sharply, "I didn't pay all this money for a little girl to teach me to shoot!"

Such a comment from an adult would have been devastating to the average sixteen-year-old. Mine just looked at me and rolled her eyes.

I let the student know that the kid was actually a very credible authority.

He listened. He did what she told him. His scores shot upward, better hits in faster times. He kept doing it and finished at the top of a very good body of students. On his critique, he wrote the high point was realizing he could learn something from a teenage girl that was better than what a prestigious academy had given him in instructors' school.

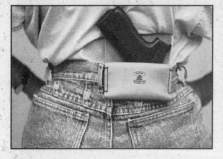

Far-back belt carry works better for women than men, as do shoulder and crossdraw holsters. This Law Concealment holster, formerly known as the Shadow, holds a high-capacity Glock. An S&W Bodyguard 38 inside the breast pocket of a lady's jacket is also held in place with a Law Concealment holster. (Photo courtesy Law Concealment Systems)

Under the watchful eye of Ray Saltzman, Ashley Reichard (age fourteen, 5-feet tall, 110 pounds) fires a full-power 45 round from an S&W auto. Though the spent casing is just above the rear sight at 1 o'clock, the muzzle is still on target for next shot. (LFI photo)

The kid took that in stride, too, but her dad's hat size expanded by about four.

Perhaps some men never will allow themselves to learn from women. But the ones who do will remember the lessons all the more.

Guns for Women

Given lesser upper body strength and particularly smaller hands, the average-size woman will not always be comfortable with the same handgun designed for the average to large male hand. The petite female shooting a full-size service revolver or, worse, double-action autoloader with a long reach to the trigger for the first DA shot is going to have trouble.

Guys, triple-check that your favorite handgun is unloaded and do a little dry fire with me. Point it in a safe direction, take a good hold, and place your trigger finger on... *the front edge of the trigger guard.* Ask yourself what your trigger control would be like if your trigger were suddenly moved to that position. That's not far off from what a petite female with short fingers experiences when she has to use a handgun designed for a big man's hand.

And shall we talk pull weight? Take a hand dynamometer and measure your own hand strength. Now give it to your wife, sister, daughter or mom. If your hand strength goes about 120 pounds, don't be surprised if hers runs maybe half that, 60 pounds.

What's the corollary? Well, if your pet double-action auto requires 16 pounds of pressure for the first shot, ask yourself what your hit probability would be if it were suddenly doubled to a 32-pound pull. Half the strength demands twice the effort.

Now, picture that 32-pound pull on a trigger positioned out to the front of the trigger guard. This will give you a graphic understanding as to why some women can't control man-size guns and, in some cases, can't even fire them.

Women's guns shouldn't be short on power. They should be short only in the dimension of trigger reach. The first of the new generation S&W LadySmith handguns was built on

The author instructs his nieces in handgun safety. They're getting used to the earmuffs in dry fire; when live work starts, they'll don eye protection as well.

the J-size revolver, a 38 Special on a 32 frame. It was superbly designed to fit fingers about one knuckle shorter than the average male's. (This is why so many of you guys with J-frames had to buy bigger grips to be comfortable with them.)

The same thing occurs with the venerable Colt 45 automatic and its many clones. Get the 1911 pistol with the *short* trigger (the one so many of you *guys* have to replace with a long trigger to get the right feel) and *voila*: We have a gun exquisitely suited for the hand of a woman 5 feet tall or so, with proportional finger length.

The same is true of Browning's Hi-Power, which may well be the gun best suited to the female hand. I now keep a couple of Novak Custom Browning 9mms on hand. More than once, a small woman who couldn't qualify with the oversize gun she brought has easily "gone over the top" when she switched to one of my Hi-Powers.

HK's P7 squeeze-cocker is another excellent gun for the female shooter. It forces a firm grip, has perhaps the lightest recoil of any carry-size 9mm and is superbly reliable. The M8 version with the single-stack magazine is best, or the grip girth is likely to be too much. There are exceptions, however; Nancy Bittle, the violence survivor who founded Arming Women Against Rape and Endangerment (AWARE) can shoot "300 possible" scores on demand in police qualifications with her fat-gripped, high-capacity P7M13.

The Glock has gained a reputation for not working well for any shooter who holds the gun with a limp wrist, male or female. This has erroneously been determined by some to mean that women shouldn't use Glocks. *Au contraire*; it means that weak-wristed shooters should not have Glocks. Some of the top female firearms authorities (Sonny Jones and Gila May-Hayes to name but a couple) swear by these polymer pistols, and many of my female students have done their best work with Glocks.

Colt is now pushing its reintroduced D-frame, six-shot 38 Special revolvers rated for +P ammo. The female officer or security professional required to carry a gun fitting those specs will be splendidly served by the 4-inch-barreled Police Positive. The 2-inch concealment version, the Detective

Women are increasingly involved in the firearms industry. Jackie Udell (far left), a sales rep for Springfield Armory, and Mark Stuart (far right) present the 1990 award for top retailer of Springfield Armory guns. (Photo courtesy Springfield Armory))

Special, is the choice of a number of gun-wise women, including my wife.

Gotta have a magnum, but you're 5 feet tall and 90 pounds? Ruger's SP101 will do the job splendidly, but it's a five-shot. If your job requirements demand a half-dozen 357 rounds, the same firm's GP100 is the choice, because its stud-type grip frame allows a pistolsmith to "hog out" a recoil shelf beneath the back of the frame, bringing the web of the hand more into the gun and allowing proper index finger placement on the trigger.

Holsters for Women

The general rule is, "If it won't work for men, it'll work for women, and vice versa." Most males wind up with strong-side hip carry holsters which for the female, with higher hips that swell outward, cause the gun butt to dig into the body and bring it up level with the shoulder blade. You have to be double-jointed to quick-draw from there if you're a woman. Lower carry on the hip is fine for an exposed-duty weapon, but it won't conceal.

The shoulder and crossdraw holsters are ideal for women: narrower bodies and relatively more flexible arms allow drawing from them with ease. The crossdraw usually works better for women than for men for the same reasons. Middle-of-the-back carry, which I consider a terrible idea for men, is a less terrible idea for women because of their body dynamics.

The Mind of the Armed Woman

A strong woman—the kind who accepts responsibility for her life and her family in America in the '90s—can handle a threatening situation.

If all else is equal, women seem to handle post-shooting trauma better than men primarily because society views men and women differently. To the man who shoots a guy coming at him with a knife, society says, "Why didn't you just kick it out of his hand like on TV?" To the woman under the same circumstances, society doesn't expect a TV reaction and judges her less harshly.

Stress studies at LFI, using devices to monitor stress signs (the blood pressure cuff or full cardiac telemetry) as students go through role play, showed that the stress indicators of women rose less precipitously and plateaued sooner than those of males in the same age group.

Cathy Ayoob is shown at age fifteen with her 3-inch S&W firing full-power 357 Magnum loads from an aggressive Chapman stance. Her motto is, "Guns that don't recoil are boring!"

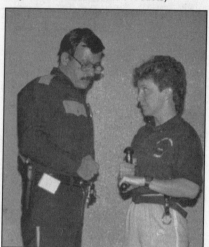

The author talks with P.J. Miller, master instructor of the PR-24 baton. (Photo courtesy Monadnock Lifetime Products)

Male and female instructors share duties at the Lethal Force Institute. Shooting a pace-setter qualifier demonstration for students are (left to right) Laurie Kraynick, Lyn Bates, Roger Lanny and the author. (LFI photo)

Who says women can't conceal guns. Lyn Bates has just drawn these fourteen combat handguns from complete concealment.

Most firearms instructors agree that female students have a faster learning curve with the handgun. The sidearm demands fine motor dexterity, of which women seem to have more. And women don't suffer from the macho psychological baggage men bring with them, so they stay open to lessons and absorb them faster. In awkward shooting postures, such as shooting from behind cover, their much greater lower-body flexibility gives them an enormous balance advantage.

Resources

For the woman considering a gun, there are several sources of positive role modeling and reinforcement of the decision.

Paxton Quigley's book, *Armed and Female,* remains the strongest manifesto of the concept. If your local bookstore or local gun shop doesn't carry it, it can be ordered from Police Bookshelf for $8.45.

Sonny Jones founded *Women and Guns,* and the Second Amendment Foundation has kept it going under the able editorship of Peggy Tartaro.

Nancy Bittle is executive director of AWARE, Arming Women Against Rape and Endangerment. They've done a lot of great work in raising the consciousness of mainstream women from all walks of life as to their options in defending themselves. And they offer training seminars.

AWSDA, the American Women's Self Defense Association, doesn't do that much with firearms, but concentrates on realistic unarmed combat and less lethal force options. They do an excellent job.

Massad Ayoob's Lethal Force Institute offers training around the United States for armed citizens who can show clean criminal records. Write for information. Ayoob's testimony in the famous case of *Christine Hansen, et. al. v. FBI* several years ago resulted in the rehiring of several female agents fired for failure to qualify on the range and the court's order to the FBI to "revise and update its obsolete and sexist firearms training." He has taught some of the nation's leading *pistoleras,* including Lyn Bates, Laurie Kraynick and Barbara Budnar.   •

Handgunning Today

MITCHELL ARMS'
HIGH STANDARD PISTOLS

by FRANK JAMES

These stainless Bullseye guns are familiar shades from the past with a new lease on life.

I**N** 1984 HIGH STANDARD succumbed to economic inevitability and closed their doors. Poor marketing, diminished cash flow, and other management problems contributed to the death of this manufacturer that was once an essential element on the American firearms scene. Although the loss was noted by shooters across many different disciplines, it was especially felt by rimfire target shooters in America. They would sorely miss the Citation and Victor models of High Standard target pistols.

Happily, the days of target shooters yearning for a newly manufactured Victor or Citation have come to an end. Mitchell Arms has introduced a line of semi-auto rimfire pistols that duplicate many of the excellent features of the original High Standard pistols, with one major improvement—these new pistols are manufactured from stainless steel.

Life is a continual evolution of people and trends, and the trends in handgun competition the past couple of decades have been moving in a direction away from the traditional marksmanship venues. A number of different and fresh styles were developed during the 1970s and 1980s.

IPSC shooting is the first that comes to mind, because it enjoys such worldwide success. Another discipline is bowling pin shooting. Called Skittles in Europe, it, too, has become a shooting regimen with universal acceptance. The same to a lesser extent can be said for PPC- and Bianchi Cup-style contests.

The only problem with all these different disciplines is, as each one grew in popularity, the traditional styles became less popular. While not insignificant, they certainly are no longer the center of attention they once were. The emphasis has moved to different kinds of handguns and calibers, and not one of the preceding shooting regimens offers a division or course of fire for the rimfire pistol shooter.

The result is that relatively few people are interested in rimfire marksmanship competition. This obviously created problems for High Standard, and their marketing people were not quick enough to monitor the changing trends.

Mitchell Arms has introduced a line of semi-auto rimfire pistols that duplicate many of the excellent features of the original High Standard pistols, with one major improvement—these new pistols are manufactured from stainless steel.

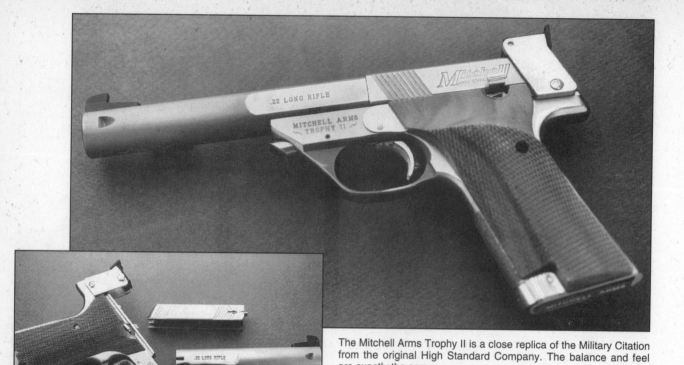

The Mitchell Arms Trophy II is a close replica of the Military Citation from the original High Standard Company. The balance and feel are exactly the same.

One of the outstanding features of the new Mitchell Arms pistols is their ability to change barrels at will, just like the old High Standards. The barrel release sticks out of the frame at its very front. The rear sight is mounted via a bridge.

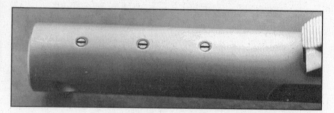

The Trophy II barrel is drilled and tapped for the easy installation of barrel weights. This is an option many experienced Bullseye shooters prefer.

The rear sight is mounted to the frame via a bridge. This is identical to the original installation. A hex screw adjusts trigger pull.

The magazine latch is located on the bottom-front of the grip frame. Pulling the latch forward releases the ten-shot magazine.

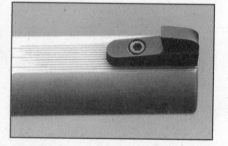

The front sight is a thick undercut blade. The author would have preferred something a little narrower to allow a little more light on either side.

Is there a need for rimfire target pistols today? I believe there most certainly is. Nothing has regenerated my interest in competitive shooting like rimfire precision competition, and I've shot them all.

The most memorable occasion I can think of is the Masters Tournament in Barry, Illinois. It consists of three stages—Action, Long Range and Precision. The Action stage is a form of speed shooting against steel, and if you like the Steel Challenge and other similar events, you will most likely prefer this third of the tournament.

The Long Range stage at the Masters uses "long range" pistols, which are really nothing more than handheld rifles with pistol grip stocks. (*Short rifles.*—Ed.) One-third of this stage is shot standing and two-thirds is shot "freestyle." That is a nice way of saying the competitor shoots from a very uncomfortable and contorted firing position. This stage required an expensive, accurate pistol built specifically to the Masters' rules, and the gun is basically good for nothing else. That's the main reason I quit shooting the tournament.

However, the one thing that really turned me on at the Masters was the Precision stage. It was shot with rimfire pistols, and when I first fired it, I thought I would hate it forever and ever, but I didn't. It was a return to the old-fashioned, stand-on-your-back-legs-and-shoot-one-handed target

The Mitchell Arms Victor we received for testing was equipped with a "red dot" optical sight. It mounted to a full rib which held both the front and rear iron sights. This is a copy of the Weaver scope mounting system.

The Victor, like the Trophy II, had the same barrel changing feature as the original High Standard pistols. This facilitates easy cleaning and allows a convenient means of changing barrels.

competition. It was such a kick to hit a disc approximately ¾-inch in diameter at 164 feet that I became hooked once again on precision competition.

Granted, it was a cheap thrill, but it was tough. For example, shooters who qualify on our Olympic team are usually considered the best precision shots in the world, yet they can't "clean" the course of fire. If they score 75 percent of the possible, it's considered a good run.

Precision rimfire marksmanship is a challenging test of hand and eye coordination. There are no arguments or subterfuge about whether or not the pistol is appropriate for hunting or self-defense. The essence of the whole thing: How well can you shoot with one hand?

Another major part of the allure is that this contest can be shot with a relatively low-cost rimfire pistol, not some custom gun that is good for only one purpose. It doesn't take $3000 to purchase a competitive rimfire target pistol. You can spend $3000 on a precision rimfire pistol if you want to, but it's going to take more than an expensive handgun to outshoot someone like Allan Fulford, Ken Tapp or Capt. McNally.

Many of the better Precision shooters at the Masters still use their old High Standard rimfire target pistols, and they shoot amazing scores. Those old guns have been built and rebuilt, but the frame is still the same High Standard.

That's where Mitchell Arms comes in. Don Mitchell was president of High Standard in 1974, so he is certainly aware of the circumstances that surrounded the company when it failed. He is also aware of its excellent reputation for fine products, and that's what he is trying to resurrect and build upon.

For our testing, we obtained two different Mitchell Arms High Standard pistols—a Trophy II and a Victor.

In the first fifty rounds through the Trophy II, we started having problems that were traced to the magazine sent with the pistol.

A call to Mitchell Arms resulted in two spare magazines, and with their substitution many of the difficulties disappeared. What few problems remained were partly because each test pistol was finicky about the particular brand of ammunition it was fed. But that isn't unusual with rimfire

pistols and shouldn't be construed as a criticism, because these are well-made guns.

The Mitchell Arms High Standard pistols are single-action semi-automatics. They are large pistols, not lightweight guns. Just like their predecessors, they balance well. Of the two test pistols, I particularly liked the balance of the Trophy II.

The Mitchell Arms guns mimic the original High Standards in every detail, including all controls and their operation. The magazine release is found on the bottom-front of the pistol grip. Pulling the release forward drops the magazine. The slide locks open after the last round is fired. The slide release is on the right side. Depressing this lever will release the slide and allow it to go forward when a fresh magazine is loaded into the pistol.

The grip panels reflect the demands of American precision shooting. They are made from American walnut with a thumbrest on the left panel. These are not the "glove" design that wraps around the palm of the hand and is so favored in international competition. Mitchell's catalog lists an optional wood grip that essentially duplicates every aspect of the glove grip, but most American competitions prohibit its use.

Visually, the Mitchell Arms High Standard pistols are attractive. The safety, trigger, magazine release and slide

The Trophy II is a single-action semi-auto rimfire pistol, representing an era in rimfire pistol shooting from two decades ago.

The Mitchell Arms Victor has a frame-mounted safety, shown here in the "off" position.

When the Victor has the safety engaged, the red-colored dot on the slide can't be seen and the safety button is up.

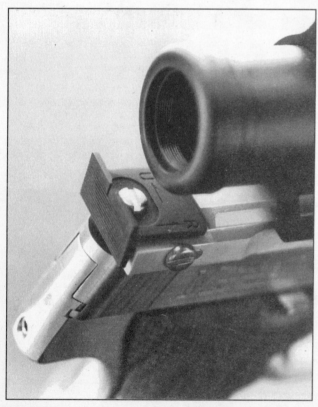

The Mitchell Arms Weaver-style full-length rib contains a rear sight that is adjustable for windage and elevation.

release are gold plated, and they contrast dramatically with the polished stainless steel on the remainder of the pistol.

The heart and lungs of any target pistol, no matter what the discipline, are the sights and the trigger. The trigger is one area where both the Mitchell and earlier High Standard target pistols excel. At the rear of either frame is a set-screw to adjust the weight of the trigger pull. The Trophy II had a $3\frac{1}{2}$-pound trigger pull, while the Victor we tested had an even 2-pound trigger pull, but either could be altered with ease.

The trigger itself has an adjustment screw to manage the degree of over-travel with which the competitor feels most comfortable.

The iron sights on our Trophy II didn't work properly. The adjustment screw for windage simply backed out of the bridge whenever we tried to achieve proper adjustment. We had difficulty with the elevation screw as well, but not as severe.

The Victor we tested came complete with a "red dot" optical sight bearing the name Mitchell Arms. The Victor was equipped with a Weaver rib that contained both the front and rear iron sights as well as mounting points for the scope rings on the "red dot" scope.

If ever I felt a bit of nostalgia when shooting a pistol, it happened during this testing. I remembered that I never really cared for the Victor when it was first introduced, but the Mitchell Arms Trophy II reminded me of the High Standard Military Citation I traded years ago. That was one gun I wished I'd never let go.

The Victor repeatedly shot the best groups. Neither test pistol liked CCI rimfire ammunition. In fact, the Victor malfunctioned with all the CCI ammunition we used and that

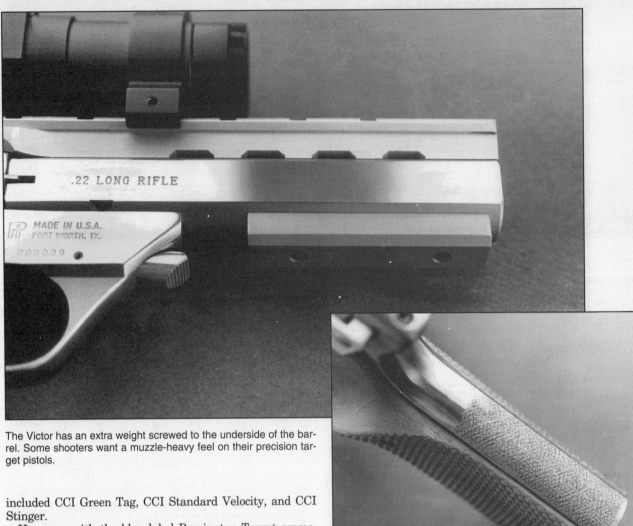

The Victor has an extra weight screwed to the underside of the barrel. Some shooters want a muzzle-heavy feel on their precision target pistols.

The rear of the grip frame on both pistols is stippled. This increases the shooter's purchase on the grip and reduces the possibility of the gun slipping.

included CCI Green Tag, CCI Standard Velocity, and CCI Stinger.

However, with the blue label Remington Target ammo, the Victor worked like a champ. Our best accuracy with the traditional one-hand standing position was five shots inside 1¼-inch at 50 feet on an indoor range. We could have put the gun in a machine rest and achieved a much tighter group, but at some point someone has to replicate reality and try the gun as it will be used in competition. There are many, many others who are better shots than I am, but if I can do this well with the pistol...well, you get the idea.

Both pistols had stippling on the front and rear of the grip portion of the pistol frame. This, combined with the 1911-style grip-to-frame angle, made both pistols feel especially good during our testing. Even though we could only get the iron-sighted Trophy II to put five shots inside 2 inches at the same 50-foot distance, it was the gun that felt the best.

A surprise to us during our testing was the fact the Trophy II, like the Victor, didn't like most CCI ammo, although it worked perfectly with CCI Stinger. I have no explanation or theory why.

My overall impression of the Mitchell Arms High Standard pistols is they are well made, even if somewhat ammo sensitive. We had problems with the magazines, but that was corrected. We also had some difficulties with the sights, but I think these could be easily corrected as well.

In comparison to the prices I paid for my original High Standard pistols, these guns are not inexpensive, but they do offer something above average—the return of the High Standard rimfire target pistol. Oh, to be young again. ●

The full-length rib has "wings" that protect the front sight. The sight picture contrast is good.

Handgunning Today

ALL THAT'S NEW IN

HANDGUN

by LARRY S. STERETT

A scope on your handgun makes hitting easy, so let's take a clear look at your optical options.

USING A SCOPE with a handgun has been done for at least six decades, and possibly longer. I recall reading an article written about 1930 by a gentleman who managed to mount a 10x Fecker target scope on a 6-inch Colt Official Police revolver chambered for the 32-20 WCF. The combination appeared a bit ridiculous, with the long tube of the scope extending well to the rear of the revolver, but it apparently worked. The shooter used it to take groundhogs, making him one of the earlier handgun varmint hunters. My first attempt at using a scoped handgun for hunting consisted of drilling and tapping one of the $37.50 Ruger Auto pistols to accept a one-piece 3/8-inch mount base; it was probably a base for the Marlin Model 39 rifle. No handgun scopes were readily available, so a Weaver J2.5x was used; the eye relief was too short for extended arm use, but with the left elbow wedged against the body, and the hand cupping the pistol, it worked well enough to bag a few squirrels and groundhogs. Ruger's only products at the time were the Auto pistol and the Single-Six revolver, and the rimfire pistol was the best available at the time for mounting a scope. When the short-lived Lightning pistol was produced a few years back, AMT machined grooves on it so tip-off mounts could be used, without having to install a separate base. Ideal!

Scoping handguns really started coming into its own a bit more than two decades back, but who really pioneered it is not known. Prior to his early demise, the late Al Goerg promoted hunting with handguns, and he possibly scoped a few. In later years, Larry Kelly, the Michigan inventor of the Mag-Na-Port system of integral muzzlebrakes for handguns, rifles and shotguns, became a premiere handgun hunter. He was the first to take Africa's big five—lion, leopard, elephant, rhino and Cape buffalo—with a handgun. He has received the Outstanding American Handgunner Award and is in Safari Club International's Hall of Fame.

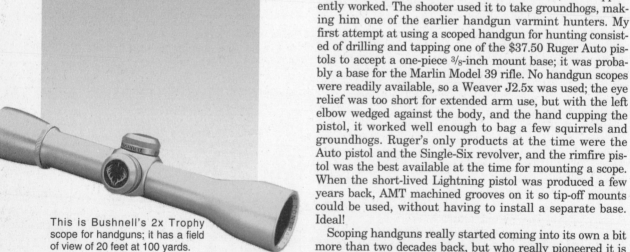

This is Bushnell's 2x Trophy scope for handguns; it has a field of view of 20 feet at 100 yards.

SCOPES

One of the newest members of the Bausch & Lomb/Bushnell line of handgun scopes is this 2x B&L Elite 3000 with a 28mm objective lens and a field of view of 23 feet at 100 yards.

The B&L Series 3000 Elite 2-6x variable handgun scope has a 32mm objective lens and a constant eye relief of 20 inches throughout the power range.

Also available in black, this silver-finish 2-6x Trophy handgun scope by Bushnell will complement any of the current stainless steel handguns.

There were also a few other shooters scattered around who managed to adapt rifle scopes to handgun use, but it really took off when Thompson/Center introduced the single shot Contender and Remington brought forth their XP-100. These two pistols literally begged for scopes.

Finding true pistol scopes presented a major problem. They simply were not available, although W.R. Weaver Co. in El Paso had apparently built one or two experimentally during the 1930s. But it was really Bushnell and their 1.3x Phantom, with integral mount, and Leupold's excellent 2x that provided the needed boost.

Today, there are more than a dozen firms producing or importing some excellent handgun scopes, most with better reticles and many with magnifying powers exceeding those most rifle scopes used to have. They all have extended eye relief, and their lengths are considerably shorter than the 20-inch Fecker of yesteryear. Plus, they weigh less.

Bausch & Lomb

Bausch & Lomb has two new handgun scopes in the Elite Series 3000 line. These new models—the 30-2028 and 30-2632—are available with a choice of glossy black or silver finish and are covered by a lifetime limited warranty. The 2028 is a fixed-power 2x with an eye relief of from 9 to 26 inches, while the 2632 is a 2-6x variable with a constant eye relief of 20 inches through the entire power range. As with any rifle or handgun scope, the field of view at 100 yards depends in part on the power of the scope. For B&L scopes, their 2x has a field of 23 feet, while that of the 2-6x ranges from 13.5 (2x) to 4.5 feet at 6x. There are also two similar scopes in the Bushnell Trophy line, both available with black or silver finishes. Eye relief for both is similar, and the field of view for the 2x is 20 feet at 100 yards, with the 2-6x going from 21 feet (2x) to 7 feet at 6x. Bushnell also has an Illuminated Dot 1x scope. With a 25mm tube, it has a 61-foot field of view at 100 yards and an eye relief suitable for any distance at which a handgun would normally be used.

Beeman

Beeman Precision Airguns is best known for their top-quality airguns, but they do have a line of scopes suitable for use on rimfire and centerfire rifles and handguns. The Model 25 (2x) Blue Ribbon and Model 20 (1.5x) Blue Ring are strictly handgun scopes. The latter model has a 3/4-inch tube diameter and cast tip-off mounts, making it most suitable for rimfire pistols with either machined mount grooves or those on which such bases can be mounted. It would have been perfect for that 6-inch-barreled Ruger I used many years ago, although the J2.5x had more magnification.

Eye relief for the Model 20 is 11 to 16 inches, 10 to 24 inches for the Model 25. The latter has a 1-inch tube and is a modified version of a Leupold handgun scope. The reticle for both scopes is what Beeman calls the 5 pt. TL or "thin-line," which is very similar to the Leupold Duplex. Field of view for the 1.5x is only 14 feet at 100 yards, or 13.5 feet less than Ruko's 1.5x, which is about the same as Burris' 1x scope.

Burris

Burris is the premiere handgun scope manufacturer in the world. This Colorado firm has more handgun models than any of the other firms manufacturing or importing handgun scopes—nine, the highest power being 10x and the highest power variable at 3-9x. According to Burris, they also designed and built the first variable-power handgun scopes and the first ones with target knobs. Counting some models with a choice of black, matte or silver finish, and with Posi-Lock as an option on some models, Burris currently has forty-two handgun scopes available. These include six fixed-power models in 1x, 2x, 3x, 4x, 7x and 10x, and three variables in 1.5-4x, 2-7x, and 3-9x. Some firms refer to their handgun scopes as being EER (Extended Eye Relief) models, while others use LER (Long Eye Relief) and/or IER (Intermediate Eye Relief), or use no such nomenclature at all. All Burris handgun scopes are LER models, except the 7x and 10x, which are IER. The standard reticle is their Plex, except for the 3-9x, which is available in a black-finish version with the Peep Plex. This is the Plex with a small circle or peep at the intersection of the crosshairs. Actual magnification on Burris handgun scopes range from 1.1x to 9.5x, and eye relief ranges from 7.27 to 24 inches, depending on the model. Burris also offers two Scout scopes with powers of 1.5x and a 2.75x. These have eye reliefs of from 7 to 18 inches and from 7 to 14 inches, respectively. Only the matte or glossy black finishes are available, and Plex or Heavy Plex reticles.

Emerging Technologies

Better known as the home of Laseraim sights, Emerging Technologies also has scopes available, including two handgun models, LPIS 2.5-8x and LPS 2x, both made by Hakko. The LPIS scope features a TriColor lighted reticle, permitting it to be either black, green or red. The intensity of the color can be increased or decreased, depending on outside light conditions. The LPS 2x is a 2x scope and laser in one unit, with the laser having a 300-yard range. The laser and scope have separate windage/elevation adjustments, and the laser uses a 6-volt alkaline battery. Both scopes come with a matte black finish.

Leupold

Leupold & Stevens was the first to produce a top-quality handgun scope capable of withstanding the recoil some magnum handguns can produce; imagine recoil from a 50 BMG cartridge in a custom handgun! Currently, there are three Leupold handgun scopes, 2x, 4x and Vari-X 2.5-8x, with actual magnifications of 1.7x, 3.7x and 2.55-8x. All three are available with black or silver finish; the 4x is matte black, the others shiny black. Eye relief is from 12 to 24 inches, and reticles are all the Duplex design, invented by Leupold more than twenty years ago and currently used by many other scope manufacturers but by other names, hence it is an industry classic. The heavy outer posts stand out against thick cover and in twilight or dusk conditions, and point toward the center intersection, while the thin crosshairs are easy to use under full light conditions.

Nikon

Nikon Sport Optics has two EER handgun scopes, a fixed-power 2x and a variable 1.5-4.5x. Both models are available with a choice of satin silver or black luster anodized finish. Eye reliefs are from 10.5 to 26.4 inches, depending on the model, with a parallax setting of 100 yards. Both scopes have their Nikoplex reticle. Nikon guarantees their scopes for a lifetime of use, and to ensure they are waterproof, the scopes are plunged into a sealed tank of 115-degree

The Burris 2-7x LER handgun scope with black finish is one of their many scopes available with the Posi-lock feature. It has a field of view of 21 and 7 feet at 100 yards, when set at 2x and 7x, respectively.

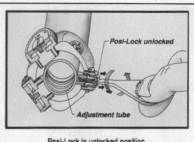

Posi-Lock in unlocked position

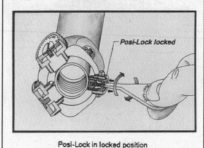

Posi-Lock in locked position

The Burris Posi-lock has been called the most significant advancement in scope design in the last fifty years. It's really a retractable screw that locks in the scope's zero. It's simple and definitely an asset when using a scope on a magnum-caliber handgun.

Introduced in 1993 on rifle scopes, the Burris Peep Plex reticle is now available in their 3-9x handgun scope. The inside of the circle covers one minute of angle at 100 yards at 9x, or about 1 inch, while at 3x, it covers about 3 inches.

Fahrenheit water and are subjected to pressures equivalent to 11,500 feet of altitude.

Pentax

Into handgun scopes only a decade or so, Pentax offers three, one fixed-power 2x and two variables, 1.5-4x and 2.5-7x. Eye relief ranges from 10 to 24 inches, depending on the model, and the scopes are nitrogen filled and leakproof. All three models are super-hard anodized black, with matte black, satin chrome or camouflage available, depending on the model. The lenses have a seven-layer multi-coating, and the reticle is the Penta-Plex, four heavy posts with fine crosshairs in the center.

Redfield

Capable of standing up to the recoil of the most powerful handguns, Redfield's new Golden Five Star handgun scope line includes two fixed-power (2x and 4x) scopes and one variable, a 2.5-7x. All three are available in black or nickel-plated finish, with the variable also available in matte

(Above) This Pentax 2.5-7x handgun scope has an eye relief of from 9 to 28 inches, depending on the power setting. At 100 yards, the field of view of this scope is 7.5 feet at 7x.

(Right) The Smith & Wesson revolvers have been mounted with complementary Pentax 1.5-4x variables, while the Thompson/Center Contender and stainless steel Freedom Arms 454 Casull revolver have Pentax 2x scopes.

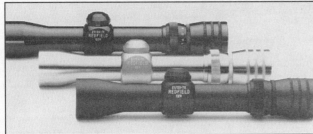

Redfield's new Golden Five 2.5-7x variable handgun scopes (top to bottom) in black, nickel and black matte finishes. The new scopes all come with a free set of flip-up lens covers.

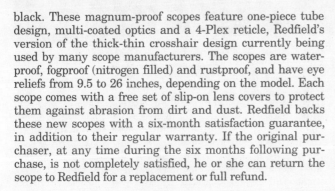

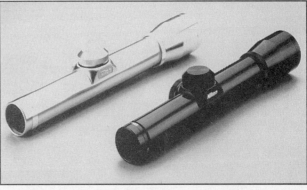

Nikon's 1.5-4.5x EER handgun scope comes in a choice of satin silver or black luster finish. It has a field of view of 17.3 feet at 100 yards on the 1.5x setting.

black. These magnum-proof scopes feature one-piece tube design, multi-coated optics and a 4-Plex reticle, Redfield's version of the thick-thin crosshair design currently being used by many scope manufacturers. The scopes are water-proof, fogproof (nitrogen filled) and rustproof, and have eye reliefs from 9.5 to 26 inches, depending on the model. Each scope comes with a free set of slip-on lens covers to protect them against abrasion from dirt and dust. Redfield backs these new scopes with a six-month satisfaction guarantee, in addition to their regular warranty. If the original purchaser, at any time during the six months following purchase, is not completely satisfied, he or she can return the scope to Redfield for a replacement or full refund.

Ruko

Ruko Products offers three handgun scopes, the 2.5x PC-2520, HE1.5x and HE2.5x. The PC-2520, known as the Mono Color model, has multi-coated optics, plus is fogproof, waterproof, scratchproof and shockproof. It has an eye relief of 11 to 20 inches and a reticle with only the horizontal portion of the crosshairs, similar to half of Leupold's Duplex,

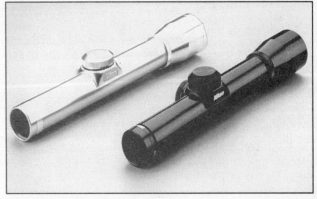

The Nikon 2x fixed-power handgun scopes have fields of view of 22 feet at 100 yards, and an eye relief of from 10.5 to 26.4 inches.

Simmons' new 22001 Gold Medal 2.5-7x variable handgun scope, with a polished black finish, has a 28mm objective lens and eye relief from 15.7 to 19.7 inches. The field of view at 100 yards is 22 feet at 2.5x and drops to 4.8 feet at 7x.

Simmons' new 22006 Gold Medal 4x handgun scope features a silver finish, but is also available in polished black. The objective lens is 32mm, and eye relief is from 10.5 to 26.4 inches.

Williams' Twilight 2x handgun scope, as shown here, and their 1.5x scope are similar, having the same eye relief, but the 1.5x scope has a 1.5-foot larger field of view and is slightly shorter and lighter.

Swift Instruments' 2x handgun scope has a length of 7.2 inches and a field of view of 18.3 feet at 100 yards. It features the Swift Quadraplex reticle, which consists of heavy posts to line up the point-of-aim and fine crosshairs to help you find it. (Also available with a silver finish.)

Swift Instruments' Model 662 2.5x handgun scope has an eye relief of 12 inches and a field of view of 14.3 feet at 100 yards.

but with thicker outer posts and a short vertical mark in the center. Mono Color means interchangeable color filters and a lamp attachment can be used; the scope comes with a red filter and protective filter cap. HE scopes are made by Hakko and feature "Electropoint" reticles. The reticle consists of a center circle with a dot and three tapered posts pointing to the circle or center. By rotating a switch ring, located in front of the eyepiece housing, to the "on" position, the posts and dot are illuminated to permit aiming under poor light conditions. It's not an entirely new idea, but there are not many handgun scopes so designed.

Simmons

Simmons Outdoor Corp. has three new Gold Medal handgun scopes. The result of three years of research, the two fixed powers (2x and 4x) and one variable (2.5-7x) are said to be more durable than handgun scopes previously available. In addition to having multi-coated lenses, the scopes are fogproof, waterproof and shockproof with eye reliefs ranging from 8.6 to 19.7 inches, depending on the model. All three are available with a choice of high gloss black or silver finish, and the Truplex reticle is standard. This is Simmons' version of the Leupold Duplex design. The fields of view vary from 4.8 feet to 22.1 feet at 100 yards, depending on the model and power setting.

Swift

Swift Instruments currently has three fixed-power pistol scopes, 4x, 2.5x and 2x, all nitrogen-filled with multi-coated glass. Eye reliefs vary from 12 to 14.5 inches, and the reticle is a Quadraplex with fine center hairs having heavy outer portions for use under poor light conditions. Swift scopes are hard-anodized black, with one-piece monobloc tube, and are considered to be waterproof and parallax-free at 50 yards. The 2x is also available with a silver finish.

Tasco

Tasco currently has three scopes in their line of World Class pistol scopes, including 2x, 4x and a 1.25-4x variable. According to Tasco, these have multi-coated optics and are hermetically sealed to be waterproof and fogproof. All three are available with a choice of matte black or matte aluminum finish. The reticles are all Tasco's 30/30, which is basically the same as Leupold's Duplex, except for four picket-shaped posts set so the crosshair lines represent an area 30 inches across when on 4x at 100 yards. This is the distance from chest to rump of an average-size deer, so the reticle can be used as a rangefinger. Eye relief ranges from 11 to 23 inches, depending on the model.

Thompson/Center

Thompson/Center, home of the Contender pistol, is also home to the Recoil Proof pistol scope line. Currently, there are nine different models, or more correctly seven, since two of them are available with a choice of black or silver finish. The scopes include 2.5x fixed power with integral mounting rail and Duplex reticle, and with or without mounting rail and a lighted Duplex reticle; plus 2-7x vari-

Tasco's latest additions to their World Class line of handgun scopes are shown here on S&W revolvers. The blued S&W has a matte black 1.25-4x variable, the PWC1.25-4x28, while the custom S&W has been fitted with the aluminum 2x (PWC2x22).

able, with or without mounting rail and with Duplex reticle, with or without mounting rail and with lighted Duplex reticle. Eye relief varies from 8 to 21 inches depending on the model, and field of view varies from 15 to 5 feet at 100 yards, at 2 and 7x, respectively. Field of view for their 2.5x scopes is 15 feet at the same distance. Thompson/Center got into the handgun scope business many years ago to provide Contender shooters with suitable glass for their pistols; the first models were variations of the Bushnell 1.3x Phantom scopes, which did not always handle the recoil of some chamberings. Today's Recoil Proof line is a considerable improvement, not only in increased power and ability to withstand recoil, but also in optics. All T/C scopes are nitrogen-filled and have multi-coated lenses. The Duplex reticle is always centered in the field of view, and the Lighted Duplex reticle permits shooting under low-light conditions. The intensity of the lighted reticle is adjusted by rotating a rheostat on the left side of the adjustment's turret.

Williams Gunsight

Williams Gun Sight Co. is well known for their line of scope mounts, receiver sights, open sights (rifle, shotgun and handgun) and sling swivels, plus gunsmithing services, but they also have a line of rifle and handgun scopes. Two scopes, both fixed power—1.5x and 2x—are classed as handgun models. They have coated lenses and are nitrogen filled, waterproof and shockproof. With parallax corrected at 50 yards, eye relief is from 18 to 25 inches. The scopes are known as the Twilight Series and have T-N-T reticles (Thick 'N' Thin), making them more usable under dusky conditions.

Any shooter buying a handgun scope needs to consider several features prior to making that final decision. Most of today's handgun scopes are purged to remove any internal moisture and are sealed to make them waterproof and fogproof. Most such scopes also have multi-coated optics. Although the amount and type of coating may vary, magnesium fluoride is usually used to reduce reflective glare and light loss. The majority of today's handgun scopes use aluminum alloy tubes with an anodized coating, and many feature one-piece tube construction, without a separate objective lens housing. In addition, most handgun scopes, being less than 10x magnification, are factory-set to be parallax-free at 50 or 100 yards. Parallax is the condition that occurs when the eye is moved away from the bore-line of the scope, causing the reticle to appear to change position relative to the target. Sharpness and brightness of the image depend on the quality of the optics, and generally you get the quality for which you pay. For this shooter, the scope must have an eye relief ranging from 12 to 20 inches, depending on the shooting position being used. Most of the scopes reviewed in this report fall within this range. Magnification of a handgun scope does not need to be high, unless targets will be extremely small, stationary and far away. The higher the magnification, the smaller the field of view; the field of view is the width of the field seen through the scope at 100 yards. Thus, depending on the scope, a variable set at 10x might permit the shooter to see an area 7 feet wide at 100 yards, while the same scope set at 2x might permit him to see an area 50 feet wide at the same distance. For large moving targets, a 2x or 4x is fine, while something a bit higher could be used on ground squirrels and prairie dogs. Just remember, the higher the power, the less you see, but what you do see is enlarged. And, depending on the cartridge used, and its trajectory, the higher magnification might not be a worthwhile choice. Check the eye relief and field of view of the scope. You sure can't hit it if you can't see it. ●

HOW TO GET IN PISTOL

by J. MICHAEL PLAXCO

This world-class shooter tells how to handle your auto pistol for best results at any speed.

IF YOU WANT to learn how to get the most from your handgun (which means getting the most from yourself), the following material will get you started. If you've ever wondered why some people seem to excel in handgun shooting, the answer is that good shooters have a mastery of the fundamentals.

The material in this article is strongly influenced by my background as a "practical" handgun shooter. By my definition, practical handgun shooting is not limited to organized IPSC-type events, rather it is being able to hit your target in the necessary time frame while adhering to the fundamentals required to hit the target. An IPSC competitor may need to hit his targets in fractions of a second; a hunter needs to hit his target while the target is available; an Olympic shooter might have hours to fire all his shots—yet all three share the same, common fundamentals.

Getting Started

Range Safety

There is no more important skill than safe gun handling. Obeying or violating a safety rule can, literally, be a matter of life or death. *Safety is a state of mind.* Your actions regarding firearms safety must become a habit, but they must also never be taken for granted.

- Treat every firearm as if it is loaded! Repeat—*firearms are always considered loaded!* Do not point a firearm at anything you are not willing to see destroyed.
- Eye and ear protection are mandatory.
- The best safety is your trigger finger (which is connected to your brain). If you can see the sights, your finger should be on the trigger; if you cannot see the sights, your finger should be off the trigger.
- At the conclusion of a shooting exercise, unload your pistol and verify that it is empty by *looking into the chamber.*

STARTED SHOOTING

Accuracy is the foundation of a shooting education. Without developing the ability to place shots exactly where you want them, you will not progress to the higher levels.

The safest way to load an auto pistol is to hold the hammer back while releasing the slide on a full magazine. Remember that safety is a state of mind—pay attention!

Loading the Auto Pistol

At all times during this process, the trigger finger is off the trigger and is held outside the trigger guard.

- With the gun pointed in a safe direction, hold it with the shooting grip and cock the hammer with the thumb of the weak hand.
- Pull the slide to the rear using the weak hand and engage the slide stop with the master thumb.
- Insert a loaded magazine, making sure the magazine locks into place.
- Holding the hammer back with the thumb of your shooting hand, release the slide stop with the thumb of the weak hand.
- Engage the thumb safety.

This is the safest way to load an auto pistol. This process fully protects the hammer and sear from damage and should be followed anytime the gun is being loaded. Never allow your hand to pass in front of the muzzle as you are loading or unloading the gun. When removing a round, do not place your hand on the top of the slide so that it covers the ejection port. If your gun has an extended ejector, it is possible for the tip of the ejector to fire the round as it is extracted.

Attaining Accuracy

Hitting your target on demand starts with sighting in. It takes more than two or three shots close to the center of the target to say the gun is "sighted-in." It takes a minimum of ten shots carefully fired at a target, with the ammo you're planning to use, to verify point of impact. After shooting these ten shots, note the impact point and make your sight corrections based on this. Disregard any shots that are well outside that point—wild shots, or flyers, are the result of shooter error, not improper sight adjustment.

Sight Adjustments

When you make a sight correction, make a *positive* correction. For example, if you're shooting a 6-inch group, move a minimum of 3 inches at a time (half the group size) so you can see a definite shift in the location of the next group.

I zero my pistols to hit point of aim at 35 yards for general shooting—from IPSC competition to plinking. At this distance, most shooters will be able to shoot a good enough group to confirm zero. A scoped pistol for hunting might need to be zeroed at a longer range. If I'm shooting a scoped pistol that's in a standard handgun caliber, I'll zero at 75 yards.

To help verify your zero, shoot at the same set of targets for an entire practice session. Afterward, study the patterns to see where the majority of your shots are grouping.

The Base of Accuracy

Accuracy is the foundation of a pistol shooting education. Without it, you will never progress to the higher levels. The inability to fire an accurate shot on demand will hold you back in mastering every other skill you need to acquire. It is critical to any shooting situation. Shooting accurately, and quickly, at extended distances (25-plus yards) is normally the difference between good and great shooters.

Shooters who want to learn how to quickly hit targets must condense the process of firing an accurate shot down to a very short time frame, but the process should be the same as for precision shooting. The faster the shooting speed, the more important it becomes to fire each shot without disturbing the stability and alignment of the pistol.

The ability to hit your target and execute various gun handling skills—such as a draw, reload, engage moving targets, etc.—must coexist. Don't try to develop them together. Each skill has to be developed and practiced separately. Begin and end each range session with precision shooting practice to confirm your ability to place a bullet exactly where you want it.

Some specific skills are more easily acquired through dry firing. Recoil can mask some problems. For instance, you can send your shots left or right by changing your grip pressure as you pull the trigger, which may be hidden by recoil. Dry firing reduces the possibility that feedback from other variables might be misinterpreted and allows you to concentrate on the skill you're learning.

Using the Sights

Sight alignment and sight picture are often confused, but they are not the same. Alignment refers to the relationship between the front and rear sight; the picture is what you see when the gun fires.

Alignment is correct when the top of the front sight is the same height as the top line of the rear sight blade and there is an equal amount of light showing on either side of the front sight. (With optical sights, alignment consists of seeing the dot in the scope—no matter where it appears.) Aligning the sights is a matter of knowing what you need to see, and then seeing it. In order of clarity from best to least, the "classic" sight picture is front sight, rear sight, target.

Next time you handle your gun, notice how clearly you can focus on the front sight. Do you just see it, or do you see it in detail? The front sight should be crystal-clear to fire an accurate shot. This probably isn't the first time you've been given this description of the classic sight picture, and it's a pretty easy concept to understand, but can you see it on demand? Are you fully aware of when you see it and when you don't see it? You must see it well as you fire the shot.

For optical sights, the same principles apply. To fire your most accurate shot, you must focus on the dot, or crosshair, rather than on the target.

Firing Techniques

Prepping the Trigger

You can have the best sight alignment possible, but if you jerk the trigger you'll probably miss the target. Pulling an auto trigger has two steps: prep and squeeze. I've found the weakest area in most shooters is the ability to prep the trigger.

A single-action auto trigger has some amount of pre-travel, that little bit of free movement until the trigger stops against the hammer/sear engagement point. Prepping the trigger means learning to pull through that free movement and hold against the weight of the hammer/sear engagement. You should be aware of this on every shot you fire, no matter how rapidly you shoot. For instance, in a "double tap" (two shots on one target in rapid succession), the gun fires and goes up in recoil, so you prep the trigger as the gun returns back into alignment for the next shot.

It takes time to learn this, and it is a progressive skill: You'll first be able to do it while dry firing, then on one-shot draws, then between shots on double taps. Eventually, it will become a conditioned reflex. Prepping the trigger gives you the best assurance of executing proper trigger control.

Squeezing the Trigger

Once an auto's trigger is prepped, pulling through to fire the shot must be done quickly and without disrupting sight alignment. Your trigger finger should pull straight back and not touch the frame of the gun at any point. Ideally, the middle of the pad of the fingertip should be 90 degrees to the trigger, which enables you to pull the trigger straight to the rear. Then, release the trigger at the same speed in which it's squeezed, keeping the finger in contact as it returns. The term "squeeze" should not be misinterpreted as being a slow-moving process. "Squeeze" implies that increasing the level of pressure against the trigger is done as a smooth acceleration.

As you're learning trigger control, pay attention to sight alignment when putting pressure on the trigger. Both must be done at the same time. After you've acquired the ability to squeeze the trigger without moving the sights, start decreasing the time frame. Experiment to see how quickly you can squeeze the trigger without disrupting alignment.

For optimum trigger control, the first pad of the finger should touch the trigger at a 90-degree angle. Make sure that no other part of the trigger finger touches the gun. The trigger pull itself is a smooth acceleration.

The correct shooting grip has both hands as high on the gun as possible and both thumbs extended forward. The pressure should feel like holding a hammer while driving a nail. The master hand grips the gun front to back, and the support hand grips the gun side to side.

As an illustration, think of two balls rolling down two inclines, one steep and one shallow. In both cases, the balls would start at zero velocity and then accelerate to maximum velocity by the time they reach the bottom of the inclines. Although the time frames would be different, both balls would exhibit a predictable, progressive rate of acceleration. The trigger squeeze must also be a predictable pattern, regardless of its time frame: Pressure increases progressively until the shot breaks.

The characteristics of a good trigger are predictability, repeatability and safety. In general, I prefer my pistols to have a single-action trigger pull weight that's approximately half the weight of the gun itself. If proper trigger control is used, it is not necessary to have an extremely light pull.

Double-Action Revolver Triggers

For revolver shooters, almost all of the same principles apply. When shooting double action, it is imperative that you keep your finger in contact with the trigger on the pull and release stroke. The most important fundamental is fluid acceleration in the trigger pull, described earlier. Prepping an auto trigger *does not* apply to double action revolvers. Many try to "stage" a double-action trigger by pulling it through until they sense the point just before the hammer falls. Then, they stop their pull and squeeze out the last bit of travel when the sight picture is correct. If you find you need or want to pull the trigger in that fashion, you'll be better off cocking the revolver before each shot and shooting it as a single action. It takes a lot of dry firing to master a double-action trigger, but when you can quickly stroke the trigger without disturbing the sights, you're on your way.

To improve double-action trigger control, move your finger in until the first joint contacts the trigger. Also, while a wide trigger might make the pull seem lighter, you'll find that a narrow trigger gives better results.

Shooting Grip

Most people over-grip the handgun. The proper grip tension is about the same pressure you'd feel when holding a hammer to drive a nail. Also, the pressure in both hands

must be equal, to help ensure the gun tracks consistently straight up and down during recoil.

Many believe a death grip on the pistol will prevent recoil. However, no matter how tightly you grip it, the handgun will still recoil—you don't have the strength to prevent it. Gripping the gun with correct tension will allow the hand to recoil intact with the pistol and the pistol then to return back into alignment. With practice, the recoil pattern should become predictable and the handgun should track more consistently.

Concern over the amount of muzzle rise should not be your sole focus. When you're shooting well, you may be aware of more muzzle rise, but with proper recoil control, you should see the gun travel throughout the full arc of movement. Normally, most shooters see the gun start up in recoil and then in several stages as it cycles. As you relax and see a predictable pattern, you will start to see the sights throughout the full arc of motion.

Shooters often have the misconception that locking down the gun to reduce muzzle rise will let them shoot faster, but it's really the speed and consistency with which the gun *returns* to the target that determines how quickly the next shot can be fired. With practice, the sights will return back into alignment after each shot. This is the key to accurate high-speed shooting.

Also, correct grip tension allows proper trigger control. When the hand isn't locked down on the gun, the trigger finger is free to move smoothly, quickly and precisely.

Grip Mechanics

Grip the gun as high on the frame as possible with the shooting hand indexing against the beavertail and making full contact with the rear of the frame.

If I'm shooting a gun with a conventional thumb safety (such as an M1911 Government Model), my thumb rides on top of the safety. Otherwise, the thumb of my shooting hand lies on top of the thumb of my support hand. Extend both thumbs toward the target. Be careful not to press them inward against the slide or frame. This can influence the tracking of the gun in recoil and cause malfunctions.

Place the index finger of the support hand under the trigger guard. You may get a higher hand position if you place it on the front of the trigger guard, but that technique makes it difficult to equally distribute the mass of the support hand on each side of the gun. Having the proper weight balance on each side allows the gun to track more consistently in recoil. The shooting hand squeezes the gun from front to rear; the support hand squeezes side to side. This "clam-shelling" effect puts four-way, equal pressure on the gun.

Placing the finger under the trigger guard positions the hand/wrist for holding the gun down and forward against muzzle rise. Correct grip tension allows the gun to lift and return smoothly; the correct grip position allows the gun to return quickly and consistently.

All fundamentals of the proper grip apply to revolvers as well as autos. With a double-action trigger, get the trigger finger and master thumb as close as possible to parallel.

Shooting Stance

The correct stance is a *progressively aggressive* stance: shoulders in front of ankles, ears in front of shoulders. This posture ensures that the majority of the body weight is forward, braced against the rearward recoil of the gun. In the correct stance, there is an overall feeling of balance. It is an athletic position of readiness.

Your spine should be relatively straight, while your knees are flexed and the upper body bends slightly forward at the ankles, not the waist. If you're doing it correctly, you'll feel tension in your calf muscles. The wider the swing needed to shoot multiple targets, the more the knees should be flexed. It is important to remain flat-footed while the upper body is leaning toward the target.

A common mistake is putting too much weight on the balls of your feet, which causes you to sway back and forth. While shooting, you should feel as though you're walking into a strong headwind. As a test, have someone hold his hand against your upper chest and push. You will have to take a progressively aggressive stance to resist the push and maintain your balance. The upper body must be flexed as if you were anticipating a punch. In a good stance, you won't see the effects of recoil in the shooter's lower body; the recoil is contained by his upper body.

Your feet should be shoulder-width apart. A stance that's too wide will inhibit your ability to swing and shoot multiple targets. A too narrow stance can cause you to lose your balance upon recoil.

Use a neutral body alignment—face straight downrange with your upper body directly facing the target and the gun straight out from the body's centerline. Being square to the target allows equal range of motion to the left and right, which makes it easier to shoot widely spaced targets. Since the arms and shoulders form a triangle with the gun in the

The principles of handgun shooting must always be adhered to, no matter how fast you're shooting. Even at this speed, I am aware of each fundamental described in this article on every shot.

center, the gun recoils back toward the master eye rather than off to either side. But most of all, this is a more natural way to direct a gun toward the target: The eyes are looking straight ahead; the head is erect; the gun is centered.

While my upper body faces the target and my shoulders and hips are parallel in alignment, my feet aren't exactly parallel to the rest of my body. My left foot is slightly forward of my right (for a right-handed shooter, the toes of the right foot should be approximately in line with the ball of the left foot). This gives me a slightly more aggressive stance.

Your arms should mirror each other as much as possible in the degree of bend and the relative levelness. This helps ensure the gun recoils consistently. Arms should be extended, but not locked. It may feel stronger to lock the elbow joint, but your arms are actually in a stronger position when they're not locked. When a joint is locked, it loses its strength throughout the full range of motion.

Gun Mount

The term "gun mount" defines the entire upper body form in its final, ready position. Mounting the gun means indexing on a target in preparation to shoot.

The shoulder area, which includes the large muscles around the back of the shoulder, not just the joint, supplies the majority of your upper body strength while shooting. The shoulders should be slightly adducted—drawn together and pressed inward—for maximum strength. This stabilizes the shoulder area by bringing the strong pectoral and upper back muscles into play.

Shooting Index

Stance and gun mount combine to determine your shooting index, as it is called in practical shooting. Your index results in a natural point of aim where the sights automatically align on a target that's straight ahead. To find your natural point of aim, face the target and assume your shooting stance. Mount the gun and move it left and right a few times to get a feel for where the gun centers. If you are consistently off left or right, you need to shift your entire stance alignment.

It is important to develop a neutral alignment: Face the targets and center the gun. Combined with a neutral grip, this allows for a predictable recoil pattern. Ideally, the gun will recoil and return consistently on target.

The correct shooting stance is a progressively aggressive stance—shoulders in front of ankles, ears in front of shoulders. This ensures that the majority of the body weight is forward, bracing the body against recoil.

Shooting Skills

Handgun skills can be separated into two main categories: shooting skills and gun-handling skills. The former is what you use to actually fire each shot, while the latter is what you use to get to the next shot. Depending on the application, gun handling skills can include the draw, magazine reloading, single-hand shooting, target acquisitions, etc. I don't have enough space in this article to discuss each gun-handling skill. To learn these, I recommend you purchase books and videos on the subject or take a class taught by a qualified instructor.

As far as shooting skills go, develop them first. Learning to shoot accurately on demand is the most important skill you need to develop. This is the basis for all other necessary skills. Regardless of the application, hitting the target always comes first. No matter if you've been shooting for years or are just beginning, don't start practicing gun-handling skills until you can shoot accurately.

Following are a few basics you must be able to apply. No matter what classification level you've attained, if you can't do these things on demand, learn to do them. (Note: Optical sight users should replace "front sight" with "dot or crosshair.")

Focus on the Front Sight, Not the Target

One of the most common mistakes made in pistol shoot-ing is looking at the target instead of the sights. Sometimes you think you're looking at the sights, but you're really looking through them. As you aim, you should be able to see the front sight in perfect detail. If you see holes appearing in the target as you're shooting, you're looking through your sights.

Learn to Read the Sights

Recognize where the sights are the exact instant the gun fires—this is the sight picture. You are never able to hold a handgun perfectly still; you have to squeeze the trigger as the gun is moving within an area near the center of the target. You must overcome the movement and concentrate on sight alignment and trigger control. If the sights were positioned 2 inches high and right, and the bullets hit there, you had proper sight alignment and trigger control as you fired the shot. The gun was just pointed at the wrong place. Through practice, you will improve your ability to hold longer on the center of the target.

It is very important that you call the shot when the gun lifts in recoil. Don't call the shot when you start the trigger pull. Unless you can call the shot at the instant of firing, you may not see if your trigger pull influences the sights.

Focus Throughout Its Arc of Recoil

By watching your front sight you should be able to diagnose what is going on during recoil. Is the front sight moving straight up and back down, or is it lifting to the right or left? The gun must travel up and down at the same speed, allowing the sights to come back into alignment on target at the end of the recoil cycle. Many shooters stop the gun at the highest point in the arc of recoil and look to see if they hit the target.

Execute Proper Trigger Control

Prep and squeeze the trigger when shooting an auto; stroke the trigger through in one smooth motion when shooting a double action. Regardless of the trigger type, once you start your trigger pull, continue to smoothly and progressively accelerate the pressure until the gun fires, pulling straight to the rear. Don't try to start and stop your trigger pull depending upon what your sights are doing. When your sights are aligned on the target within the aiming area, start your trigger pull. Trying to "freeze" the gun and "pick off" the shot will never allow you to develop the fundamentals of sight alignment and trigger control. •

About the Author

The preceding was a specially adapted excerpt from Shooting From Within, by J. Michael Plaxco. For more than fifteen years, Plaxco has been a world-class shooter, winning the World Speed Shooting Championship (Steel Challenge), USA National IPSC Championship, World 3-Gun Championship, Soldier of Fortune 3-Gun Championship, Canadian IPSC National Championship, four NSSF Sportsman's Team Challenge Championships, International Revolver Championship, and Second Chance Grand Champion title. He's also been Team Captain of the World Champion USA IPSC Gold Team, of which he's been a member for twelve years. In addition, Plaxco is a renown pistolsmith, author and shooting instructor, and was a member of Team Smith & Wesson (S&W's professional shooting team).

Handgunning Today

SINGLE ACTIONS

by JOHN TAFFIN

A search for authenticity led this maker to produce perfect replicas of the old SA Colt...and then some.

Cimarron's little Thunderer seems even smaller in the hand of our writer. Idaho's wide-open country provides lots of shootin' space.

MY POPCORN BUCKET is full. I have enough ice-cold Coke to last at least two hours. The seating arrangement is perfect—right side, almost all the way in the back. I'm ready to enjoy that epitome of entertainment—the Western movie. My hopes are high, but I have been disappointed before. Not by the story nor the characters, but by their six-guns. Others may go to the movies; I buy a ticket to a gun show. If the guns are authentic, I'm happy. If those guns are not true single actions, no matter how good the story line nor how realistic the acting, I'm not.

During the 1950s, replica single actions began to arrive from Belgium and Italy. The first were cap-and-ball revolvers on both Colt and Remington patterns, and could be had as Remington Model 1858s in 36- and 44-caliber, and Colt types in the Dragoon, Walker, 1851 and 1860 styles as well as some lesser-known models. All were faithful recreations of the originals.

When the metallic cartridge replicas started to arrive, something went haywire. The replica Colt SAAs carried brass backstraps and trigger guards, and the case-colored frames looked like a poor spray-on finish. Much cheaper than original Colts, the spaghetti six-guns, as I call them, filled the screens of the period as most of the Westerns of the time were made in Italy or Spain.

Every gun-store shelf featured Italian-made six-shooters, mostly in 45 Colt and 357 Magnum, that were supposedly authentic "Colt" copies. They were not bad shooters, generally speaking, but they made a traditional six-gunner shudder, to say the least.

Now all that has changed, and the major credit goes to Mike Harvey and Cimarron Arms. Harvey, an old Western buff himself, purchased the defunct Allen Firearms and began the long, arduous process of convincing the Italians, in this case Aldo Uberti, to upgrade their guns to be true copies of the original 19th-century Colt.

Gone are the brass backstraps and trigger guards. They are now made the way they were meant to be—of steel. Cimarrons from Uberti are finished exceptionally well. Blues are deep, and case-coloring is now as good as any ever seen on Colt guns. Uberti case-colors the hammers just like those found on the original Colts. Grip frames feel like Colts, and one-piece-style walnut grips are very well shaped

FROM CIMARRON

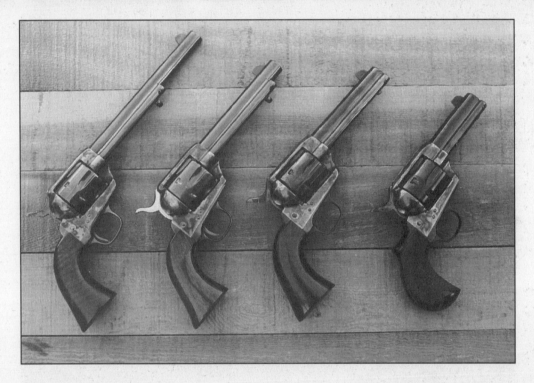

Four from Cimarron: 7½-inch (Single Action Army) 45 Colt, 5½-inch (Frontier Six-Shooter) 45 Colt, 4¾-inch (Peacemaker) 44 Special and 3½-inch (Thunderer) 45 Colt.

and rounded in the right places with no blocky feel or high spots. Fit, finish and feel of the grips have to be rated as excellent.

Handguns cannot be imported without a safety that will survive the drop test, and original Colt safeties will not pass. Cimarron opts for a safety on the hammer that operates as a block when the hammer is drawn to the safety notch. This is a real safety, unlike the false and very weak one found on the old Colt that used the safety notch on the hammer. Always have an empty chamber beneath the hammer on a Colt, as a heavy blow will cause the hammer's safety notch to shear, and the gun could fire. Even with the Uberti safety, I feel it is better to use the old tried-and-true six-gunners' method of carrying an empty chamber under the hammer.

A trip through the Cimarron catalog will make the traditional six-gunner's heart leap for joy. Just as with the original Colt single actions, three standard barrel lengths are offered: the Peacemaker 4¾-inch, Frontier Six Shooter 5½-inch and Single Action Army at 7½ inches. Chamberings are 357 Magnum, 38-40 (38 WCF), 44-40 (44 WCF), 44 Special and 45 Colt. The 45 Colt is *the* chambering for the

original Colt single action and certainly the number one favorite with replicas. With blue and case-colored finish, and one-piece walnut grips, Cimarron single actions retail for $430, or right at one-third the cost of a new Colt SAA from the Colt Custom Shop. If that doesn't get a single-action six-gunner's attention, nothing will.

All barrel lengths and calibers are available as a Black Powder Model with screw-in retainer for the cylinder pin and a Bullseye ejector rod head. Or, you can have the Pre-War Model with half-moon ejector rod head and spring-loaded cross-pin cylinder latch. Black Powder Models are not relegated to the exclusive use of blackpowder only. The designation denotes a look of authenticity, not a strength factor.

Black Powder Models may be ordered in charcoal blue or fire blue finish. The latter is a true blue finish, rather than black, and is very bright. It also is quite fragile and soon wears off a gun that is used extensively. For the fancy-minded among us, or those who simply prefer a little more durability to their gun finish, all models are also available in full nickel finish. Charcoal blue is $15 extra, and $90 is the price tag above normal retail for nickel.

CIMARRON ARMS' SAA 44-40 BALLISTICS TEST
(7½-inch Bbl.)

Bullet Type	Powder (grs./type)	MV (fps)	Group (ins.)
Lyman #429215	10.0/Unique	1204	2¼
Lyman #429215	6.0/Bullseye	825	2
Lyman #429215	7.0/WW-231	884	1¾
Lyman #42798	8.0/Unique	948	2⅝
Lyman #42798	9.0/Unique	1064	2½
Lyman #42798	10.0/Unique	1197	2¼

All groups fired in five-shot strings at 20 yards.

This Cimarron 7½-inch blued six-gun has a Texas Longhorn carved grip and light engraving.

The storekeepers and sheriffs among us have not been forgotten, and the same retail price will get any caliber in a 3½-inch barrel length model with ejector and housing. These "little" six-guns are considered particularly attractive among the crowd of shootists with which I prefer to ride the river.

Any model may be ordered with full cattle brand engraving or A, B or C engraving, consisting of one-fourth, one-half or full coverage, respectively. For those among us who grew up watching Wild Bill Elliott play Red Ryder and other characters dear to the heart of a 1950s pre-teenager, the Wild Bill Elliott Texas Cattle Brand 45 Colt replica can be purchased for $1395.

Most Cimarrons will shoot low for the majority of six-gunners, but the front sight can be filed to fit each particular shooter's point of aim. This is a vast improvement over just a few years back when all replicas were coming through with too little front sight, causing them to shoot high. It is very difficult to fix a high-shooting gun. On the other hand, one that shoots low can be easily adjusted to its owner's hold, sight picture and load with a little file work applied to the top of the front sight.

A good sight picture with the Cimarron replicas is very difficult, because they are authentic right down to the original Colt-style shallow V-notch rear sight made for sharp young eyes. Couple this with the fact that all these Cimarron six-guns were test-fired in freezing weather, and the results look grand to say the least. Here's how my shooting tests panned out:

My first centerfire six-gun was a 38-40 Pre-War Colt Single Action Army with 4¾-inch barrel in better than 90 percent condition. The Cimarron 38-40, which is really 40-caliber, shot better than any Colt 38-40 I have ever experienced. In one test string, I was able to put four shots in ⅝-inch with Winchester factory ammunition.

Unlike the 45 Colt, 38-40 and 44-40 chamberings, the 44 Special is a 20th-century chambering introduced by Smith

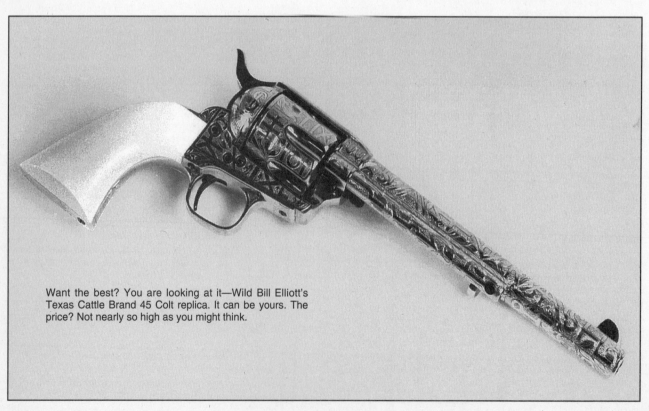

Want the best? You are looking at it—Wild Bill Elliott's Texas Cattle Brand 45 Colt replica. It can be yours. The price? Not nearly so high as you might think.

Cartridge	Bullet (grs./type)	Powder (grs./type)	Single Action Army 7½-inch MV (fps)	Group (ins.)	Frontier Six Shooter 5½-inch MV (fps)	Group (ins.)
Blazer	255/Lead	—	765	2³/₄	749	1¹/₂
Federal	225/LSWCHP	—	904	2⁷/₈	873	1¹/₂
Winchester	255/Lead	—	787	1³/₈	754	1⁷/₈
Handload	SWC/Bull-X 255	9.0/Unique	1015	1¹/₂	928	2
Handload	SWC/Bull-X 255	20.0/H-4227	1010	2	906	1³/₄
Handload	Lyman #454424	9.5/Unique	1059	1³/₄	971	2⁵/₈

All groups fired in five-shot strings at 20 yards.

The barrel's left side, hard against the frame, reveals its chambering—45 Colt. Never has the designation "Long Colt" been seen on any early six-gun.

Cimarron's Cavalry 7¹/₂-inch (top) and Artillery 5¹/₂-inch are replicas of the 1873 and 1895 issued Colt Single Actions.

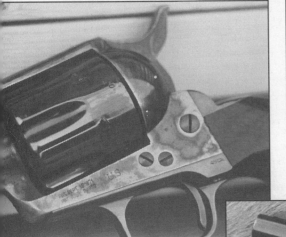

"U.S." stamped on the frame's left side authenticates Cimarron's replicas. This is identical to my friend's documented-by-Colt Artillery 45 Colt.

A lot of Cavalry 7¹/₂-inch 45 Colts were called in and redone with 5¹/₂-inch barrels. These shorter six-guns became known as Artillery Models. No effort was made to keep serial-numbered parts together. A friend happens to own one, documented by Colt, on which *all* serial numbers match, including the one-piece grip—except for the barrel, of course.

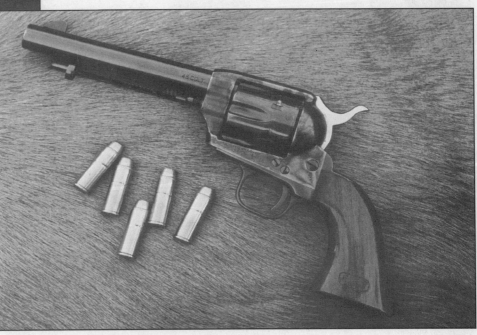

CIMARRON ARMS' PEACEMAKER 38-40 BALLISTICS TEST (4³/₄-inch Bbl.)

Cartridge	Bullet (grs./type)	Powder (grs./type)	MV (fps)	Group (ins.)
Winchester	180/JSP	—	779	³/₄
Handload	Lyman #401452	8.0/Unique	985	3¹/₂
Handload	Lyman #401043	8.0/Unique	863	2¹/₂
Handload	Lyman #401043	10.0/Unique	1233	2¹/₂
Handload	Lyman #401043	5.8/Bullseye	827	2⁷/₈

All groups fired in five-shot strings at 20 yards.

CIMARRON ARMS' PEACEMAKER 44 SPECIAL BALLISTICS TEST (4³/₄-inch Bbl.)

Cartridge	Bullet (grs./type)	Powder (grs./type)	MV (fps)	Group (ins.)
Federal	200/LSWCHP	—	915	⁷/₈
Hornady	240/LSWC	6.0/Unique	777	1⁷/₈
Handload	Lyman #429215GC	8.9/Unique	1049	1⁷/₈

All groups fired in five-shot strings at 20 yards.

Top-quality engraving on this 4³/₄-inch SAA is well-displayed with the addition of the ivory grip. If it's not top quality, Mike Harvey will not put the name Cimarron on it.

The Black Powder Model's trademark is this cylinder pin screw. Cimarron retained all these early characteristics.

& Wesson for their Triple-Lock New Century in 1907. The original chambering for the Colt Single Action Army was 45 Colt, and the 38 WCF (38-40) and 44 WCF (44-40) were chamberings originally found in Winchester's Model '73 lever gun. All three of these early cartridges were loaded with 40 grains of black; the 44 Special was first loaded with 26 grains of black. Cimarron's rendition of the 44 Special in a single action is guaranteed to make a six-gunner's heart beat just a little faster.

To round out the quartet of Cimarron calibers tested, we have the 44-40, originally chambered in the Winchester lever gun and first offered in the Colt SAA in 1878. The old 44 never had a great reputation for accuracy, but like the 38-40, this old round had a surprise in store. Some handloads were assembled with .428-inch bullets, and surprisingly, the Cimarron shot to point of aim.

Ten grains of Unique with the 200-grain flat-nose cast bullet has long been a standard loading with the 44-40 in Colt guns. This load does 1200 fps and will group extremely well. Not bad for a 100-plus-year-old cartridge that was buried in a dual funeral with the 38-40 more than fifty years ago!

To come up with something just a little different for modern six-gunners with 19th-century mindsets, Harvey studied the single-action grip. The improved result fit an old 1873 Colt-style action with a grip frame that is a dead ringer for the 1877 Colt 38 Lightning/41 Thunderer double actions.

It was my good fortune to be able to spend a few months last summer shooting the original prototype Peacekeepers as they were called then. They are now known as the New Thunderer Model to avoid the confusion that could be caused by stocking a Peacekeeper and a Peacemaker. I found these original Peacekeepers to be superb guns, and they were obviously action-tuned by someone who knew single actions. Both proved to be excellent shooters, especially when I tailored loads with cast bullets sized to .454-inch, instead of the standard but smaller .452-inch normally used for 45 Colt loads. This is one of the great benefits afforded reloaders.

Both prototypes did not want to leave Idaho, but I received a call from Cimarron in late summer and they were hastily returned. The guns were still the only ones in the country, and they needed them as samples to show prospective customers.

My production New Thunderer in 45 Colt is extremely well finished with deep, dark bluing on all parts except the

Both ends of Cimarron's line: U.S. Cavalry Model with 7¹/₂-inch barrel and New Thunderer with its 3¹/₂-inch tube.

hammer and frame, which are case-colored. Metal-to-wood fit is excellent, and the dark walnut grips are fine-line checkered and look and feel very good. A nice touch is the use of charcoal-blued screws for the grip frame and frame. These provide a subtle contrast to the dark blue of the rest of the gun.

The New Thunderer grip frame starts out as a round butt, but as it curves up, it features a pronounced double-action-style hump. It looks strange at first, but it is highly functional in controlling 45 Colt loads. Instead of the rolling-in-the-hand feeling afforded by the standard single-action grip, the Thunderer feels more like a double-action grip, and the gun does not twist or roll in the hand.

Shooting the New Thunderer gave me a chance to try out my first 45 Colt reloads with Hodgdon's Universal and Clays powders. All loads performed very well with 255-grain cast semi-wadcutters from Bull-X. Winchester brass and CCI 300 primers were used to assemble all loads.

Factory loads with 255-grain lead bullets from Blazer, Black Hills and Winchester all shot as if they were custom-made for the gun. Add 225-grain Federal hollowpoints to the good-shootin' factory loads, and they should make an excellent choice as a defensive load for the New Thunderer.

This is only the beginning of the Cimarron story. A look at their catalog also reveals a full line of blackpowder percussion revolvers and some of the finest looking lever guns this side of the 19th century. On top of that, great looking leather is also available from Cimarron. ●

CIMARRON ARMS' NEW THUNDERER 45 COLT BALLISTICS TEST (3½-inch Bbl.)

Cartridge	Bullet (grs./type)	Powder (grs./type)	MV (fps)	Group (ins.)
Winchester	255/Lead	—	698	1 3/8
Black Hills	255/Lead	—	778	1 3/8
Blazer	255/Lead	—	713	1 7/8
Federal	225/Lead	—	753	1 7/8
Handload	255/Bull-X	8.5/Universal	699	2 1/2
Handload	255/Bull-X	10.0/Universal	930	2 1/4
Handload	255/Bull-X	6.0/Clays	726	1 3/8
Handload	300/Bull-X	7.5/Universal	651	2 3/4
Handload	Lach. #454255LC	7.1/WW-231	838	2
Handload	Lyman #452424	7.1/WW-231	783	2

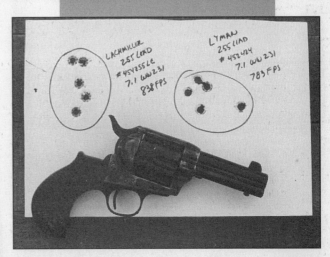

Two of Taffin's 20-yard groups, each measuring 1 3/8 inches, with Cimarron's New Thunderer.

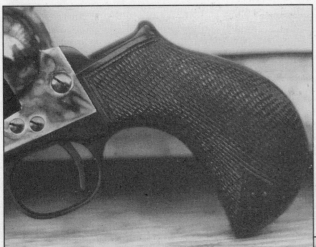

A closeup view shows Cimarron's New Thunderer grip and excellent fine-line checkering.

Often referred to, in those beginning days, as Peacekeeper, the Colt 41 Thunderer was revamped by Cimarron's Mike Harvey. A little from here, a little from someplace else, and Cimarron now offers a New Thunderer. It is the grip that makes this difference.

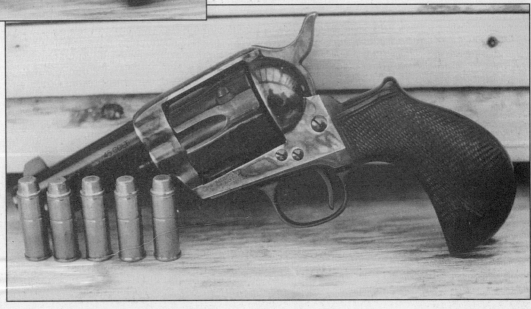

THOSE WONDERFUL WESSON

by STAN TRZONIEC

One of the world's best double-action designs is again available and, with family ties to Dan, better than ever.

In the field, Trzoniec preferred the 8-inch-barreled version. The gun balanced perfectly and, with a 10-inch sighting radius, is ideal for most hunting conditions.

IF SOMEONE WALKED up to you and mentioned the name "Wesson" as it relates to firearms, would you immediately think of the manufacturing firm in Springfield, Massachusetts? If you would, you're not alone, but what about the *other* gunmaker just down the road with almost the same name. Wesson Firearms has now, over the past year or so, done a complete reorganization and is back into full production. They offer more double-action revolvers, in more choices, than most ever dream about.

I'm sure you remember the original Dan Wesson company. When Daniel Wesson introduced his new double-action revolver with interchangeable barrels, shrouds, sights and grips, many turned away laughing. The concept at the time was new, and many thought the idea would never get off the ground. It was a different concept, and while shooters were willing to try almost anything, the first series of Dan Wessons turned off many people. Maybe it was that horrible nut sticking out the end of the barrel, or the design of the original grips. In short, it was a love-hate affair.

As time wore on, so did the Dan Wesson guns. The quality got better, accuracy was the best in any double-action revolver bar none, that fanned barrel nut disappeared into the shroud giving a more streamlined look, and stainless guns appeared. The overhead was small and the guns were getting better. Things were looking up for Dan and his crew. His guns were winning medals for shooters in IHMSA Championship matches, more calibers were on the way and his Pistol-Pacs were starting to be available.

Then it started to tumble. The worst thing was, Daniel B. Wesson (great-grandson of D.B. Wesson, co-founder of Smith & Wesson) died in 1978 just eight short years after he started the company. I talked with Seth and Carol Wesson, and these two friends of mine told me that at the time of D.B.'s death he held only roughly 25 percent of the stock. Two other investors (partners) held the rest. After the estate was settled, his share was taken out of the proceeds, leaving the Wesson family with little. Seth and Carol stayed

The very low curved hammer is a genuine asset to the cocking of the revolver for single-action shooting. Note also the rugged rear sight assembly adjustable for both windage and elevation.

DOUBLE-ACTION REVOLVERS

Novel in its own right is the cylinder latch. Placed on the crane, it is secure and adds to the accuracy of the revolver.

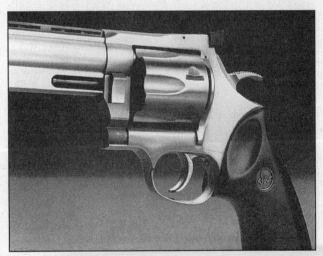

The 6-inch Wesson revolver in stainless with heavy vent barrel (left) and the 8-inch model with vent barrel in blue are both 44-caliber.

With walnut grips, the 44 Wesson poses a very rugged profile. The gun is beautifully finished, and if you look close, you can see the over-travel adjustment just behind the trigger.

with the company for a few more years and finally left. The company went to pot, to put it mildly.

In 1990 Seth and Carol Wesson and some of the employees got together, purchased the company, and started getting Wesson Firearms back on the right track.

Today they have a twelve-page catalog that lists everything the double-action fan could ever want. They list thirteen cartridge offerings, for example. The line is full of choices, starting with the 22 Long Rifle. It progresses to the 22 WMR, 32 Magnum, 32-20, 38 Special, 357 Magnum, 357 Maximum, 375 Supermag, 41 and 44 Magnums, 445 Supermag and 45 Colt. I lost count of the revolver options, but if you add all the barrel lengths in each caliber, all the guns——both fixed and interchangeable barrel assemblies—Pistol-Pacs and whatever, the combinations number in the hundreds. For example, in the popular 357 Magnum, with different barrels—carbon or stainless, vented or heavy ribs—and with lengths from $2\frac{1}{2}$ to 10 inches, there are over thirty different variations. Whew!

Specialty guns help fill the needs of shooters engaging in various sports, and Wesson is there with 22 silhouette guns with 10-inch barrels. They have a five-shot gun (738P) with a 2-inch barrel that has a "footprint" of less than 5x7 inches. They offer compensated barrel assemblies that take the kick out of the heavier calibers like the 44 and 445 Supermag. Also listed is a 45 ACP pin gun with a 5-inch barrel and a Taylor forcing cone. Next came the popular Hunter and Pistol-Pacs. The Hunter is available in most heavy-caliber models with forty-four combinations of barrels, calibers and scope mounting options. The Pistol-Pac is offered in both small- and big-bore models and includes an assortment of barrel lengths ($2\frac{1}{2}$-, 4-, 6- and 8-inch) plus extra sights and grips, all packaged in an aluminum case.

The good folks at Wesson sent me a 44 Magnum Pistol-Pac that included a revolver frame, zebrawood grips, 6- and 8-inch barrels, extra sights, an extra set of grips, a Wesson patch, a feeler gauge, instruction book and shroud assemblies, all packed in an aluminum aircraft case. Plastic cases are available with some options. The heavy vent rib barrel set, like my sample, costs around $815. Considering the versatility offered with each set, the pricing is not out of line.

My gun came with the 8-inch barrel attached. It is a well-balanced piece especially suited for the hard-hitting 44 Magnum cartridge. Picking up the gun, one is amazed how nicely it sits in one's hand. It weighs 60 ounces. With one hand the gun tends to be just a tad muzzle heavy, but with a two-hand hold, it is perfect. For hunting without a scope, this just might be the perfect combination between weight and sight radius. My eyes just ain't what they used to be; however, thanks to the Wesson arrangement of excellent sights and the 10-inch sighting radius, I can handle my own in any given situation.

The rear sight assembly is one heavy-duty affair with both windage and elevation adjustments. The blade is tipped back slightly, maybe 30 degrees from vertical, to keep sunlight glare to a bare minimum. The rear blade measures $\frac{3}{8}$-inch high by $\frac{3}{4}$-inch wide. The front sight blade is slotted into the ventilated rib and is interchangeable. Choice of colors includes red, yellow and white, and for only $2.35 each, you can afford to mix and match to suit weather or brush conditions. Wesson also offers Patridge front sights in six different heights.

As mentioned, Wesson offers barrels from $2\frac{1}{2}$ to 10 inches long. The barrel shrouds are offered in several weights. All are fully interchangeable within frame size and cartridge.

To remove the barrel, unscrew the barrel nut, pull off the

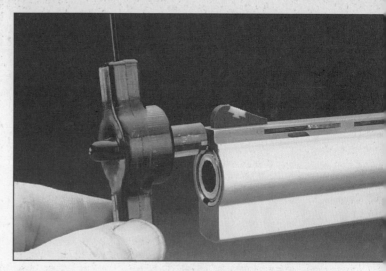

Front sight blades are easily changed by using the smallest Allen wrench bit on the barrel wrench. Loosen the screw, remove the sight blade, insert a new one and tighten it down.

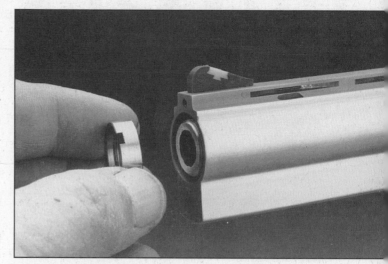

The barrel nut secures the barrel and shroud. It also squares up the whole assembly for greatest accuracy potential.

When installing a new barrel, screw it in so it just touches the feeler gauge. Add the shroud and the nut, and you're in business.

If you want to change barrels, these are the parts needed: (from the bottom) the barrel wrench, barrel shroud, barrel, feeler gauge and barrel nut. Those extra pieces at the bottom are front sight inserts.

shroud, and unscrew the barrel from the frame. To change to another length, reverse the procedure with a few exceptions. Screw the barrel into the frame so it almost touches the cylinder face. Insert the feeler gauge (included with each gun) and adjust the barrel so it just "kisses" the gauge. Now install the shroud, locking it in place via the indexing pin, replace the barrel nut and snug it down. That's it.

All barrels for Wesson revolvers are made from aircraft-quality heat-treated steel and use cut or broached rifling. The end result is a sharper, more defined rifling pattern within the barrel so the lands and grooves can "bite" the bullet better for enhanced accuracy. One other item the Wesson firm touts is that the muzzle is absolutely square, which in their terms allows the bullet to exit the muzzle perfectly, thus helping accuracy. This, in concert with the way the barrel is tensioned between the barrel nut and frame, plus the unique cylinder latch, makes the Wesson revolver very different from its peers.

While other guns in its class use a rear lockup, the Wesson has a front or cylinder latch-type system. This helps keep the shooter's hand from accidentally opening the cylinder. The front locking system keeps the cylinder and barrel (at the breech) in better alignment (*theoretically—Ed.*) than might be the case with a rear pin/front ejector rod lockup. It may take a bit of getting used to in the beginning, but with practice it becomes natural and second-nature to charge or unload the weapon.

When you place an order for your "custom" Wesson revolver, you have the choice of either a fluted or non-fluted cylinder.

The guns have the now-standard-fare safety transfer bar arrangement. The hammer contacts the frame while at rest. Cock the gun and the bar rises, waiting for contact by the hammer. The hammer in newer production guns has been lowered and swept back for easier cocking. In fact, I find that I hardly have to move my hand when shooting single action. Trigger pull on this sample (and others over the years) is nothing short of outstanding. This one went $3^1/_2$ pounds single action and about 12 pounds double action, with a preset overtravel adjustment. The double action is one of the smoothest in the industry. The hammer is checkered, and the trigger face is smooth and of target width.

Last is the matter of grips. Grip design is very personal, and Wesson is here to help. You can choose from walnut, fancy zebrawood or weather-resistant neoprene. They are also available in target or combat styles, checkered or smooth, or in small- or large-frame Hogue-type "Gripper" grips. At one time Wesson would sell you a wood blank so you could carve your own style, but I don't see it listed within the pages of their newest catalog.

In shooting Wesson guns I never have been disappointed in their performance. At 25 yards, groups with the 6-inch barrel and CCI Lawman or Remington ammo never went over the magical inch if I did my part. With the 8-inch tube, groups ranged from $1^1/_2$ to 2 inches, depending upon the ammunition I was using. Past records seem to indicate that commercial loadings from Federal, CCI, Remington and Hydra-Shok turned in the best performances. Naturally, handloaders can do much better as they can tailor the load (powder, primer, bullet) to the gun. It was also interesting to note that with one load, the 6-inch barrel gave 1497 feet per

Both the Fixed Barrel Scoped Hunter (top) and the Fixed Barrel Open Hunter are vented for recoil reduction.

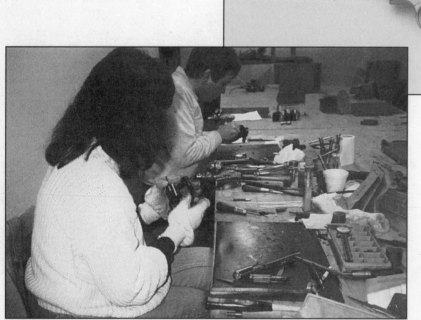

The author has visited the Wesson plant on numerous occasions and has found their work force dedicated to quality in the end product. Here we see the final assembly of Wesson guns. Note the gloves so as to not scratch the high shine on blued guns.

second. Moving up to the 8-inch barrel, we saw 1549 on the screen with the same load. So the old law holds true: For every inch of barrel add 25 fps.

Wesson Arms has made a remarkable comeback, especially in today's economy. They offer guns at fair prices, with excellent quality and in enough combinations to make a man's head swim. For the 1994 model year, the Wesson establishment is not sitting on its laurels. A new line of *fixed-barrel*, compensated and scope-mounted revolvers are being introduced—so new, in fact, that I've only had a brief time to look them over for this report. For the hunter, these guns just might be the way to go.

Currently, the Fixed Barrel series is available in four models: Open Hunter, Compensated Open Hunter, Scoped Hunter and Compensated Scoped Hunter. Open Hunter models are those guns equipped with open sights for those not wanting (or needing) optical hardware. They come with a rugged Iron Sights Gunworks rear sight adjustable for both elevation and windage, and include a dovetailed blade for quick sight acquisition. The Scoped Hunters, on the other hand, adapt to a handgun scope within minutes. If you think I'm joking, keep reading. Should you opt for a Scoped Hunter, pay your money, take the gun home and open the case supplied with your purchase. In it you'll find a Wesson revolver with a Burris mount and rings all screwed down to the barrel rib for almost instant (about five minutes) installation of your favorite optical product. With this gun you receive *no* sights. This just has to be one of the best revolvers around for this type of field duty.

Wesson Hunters come chambered for 41 and 44 Magnums plus 357 and 445 SuperMags. These last two are

finally coming of age for those demanding power and accuracy over the long haul. Marketing executive Carol Wesson told me that these guns are literally being custom built on a one-on-one basis for the owner-to-be. For instance, in addition to the various calibers, all guns in the series will be available with the choice of carbon blue or stainless steel finish. Because these guns have a fixed barrel, the length is quoted at being around $7\frac{1}{2}$ inches for non-compensated guns and around 6 inches with the compensated addition. All barrels will be "Taylor Throated." (*Allen Taylor described his "Taylor Throat" as nothing more than removing the lands from the rifling to the bottom of the groove for approximately $\frac{3}{4}$ inch.—Editor*)

I managed to get in some testing of the guns before another snowstorm came in, and I found there is a slight accuracy advantage in the fixed-barrel guns over those with removable barrels.

Groups averaged around 2 inches with the fixed-barrel gun. With the interchangeable gun, my groups averaged $2\frac{1}{4}$ to $2\frac{1}{2}$ inches at 25 yards.

The Fixed Barrel series comes in either single or double action. The shroud is either a full round (on compensated guns) or a slightly modified Vent Heavy (on non-compensated guns). Grip options run from the traditional Wesson "target" style to Hogue grips in either rubber or hand-rubbed wood. Price is from $805 to $914, depending upon options and your finish preference.

These new Fixed Barrel offerings, like the standards in their line, are designed to shoot and keep on shooting. To drive the point home, Wesson offers a ten-year warranty on their product. ●

HANDGUNS
95

SECTION 6
Handgun Reloading

They're economical and accurate, and that's why Venturino likes 'em, page 176.

Exploding the myths about swaging, as only Corbin can do, page 183.

Handgun Reloading

WHY I SHOOT

by MIKE VENTURINO

OFTEN I AM asked, "Why do you bother to sit in front of a hot lead furnace, pouring molten alloy into bullet moulds? Especially when so many varieties of high-tech bullets can be bought at any modestly stocked gun store?"

The answer is that I simply like doing it. Not being a television watcher, I find the time spent casting bullets to be relaxing. My mind can work actively while my hands are still doing something productive. Furthermore, I like the independence casting my own bullets gives me. How many times have you wandered down to your local gun store to find they are fresh out of exactly the type of bullet you need? I'm never without bullets for any of my guns if I fire up the lead pot and make them.

What do you do if you have a gun for which the factories no longer produce bullets? Have you tried to buy a projectile for, say, the 41 Long Colt or 40-82 Winchester anytime lately? I shoot those calibers and dozens more antique and obsolete cartridges many thousands of rounds a year. All I had to do was buy the proper bullet mould.

Cast bullets are available in an amazing variety of designs, calibers and shapes. They can be had to fit every firearm made.

CAST BULLETS

I also like the versatility that casting my own bullets allows me. I can adapt sizing diameters, alloy hardness and lube to fit any type of gun I might be shooting.

For example, I shoot the old 38-40 cartridge in both rifles and handguns. For cowboy action shooting, I like to load 38-40s with blackpowder and shoot them in one of my several Colt Single Action Armys and Winchester Model 1873 rifles and carbines. Then the bullets are cast of 1:20 tin/lead alloy. These are soft with a Brinnell hardness number (BHN) of about 8, but work well at the low speeds of blackpowder loads—800 fps for handgun and 1200 fps for rifle. However, I also have a smokeless-vintage Winchester Model 1892 rifle which is capable of taking much higher pressure loads. In it, I can load the 38-40 to 1600 fps. Then I use the same bullet as with the other 38-40s, but this time it is cast of Lyman #2 alloy formula which has a BHN of about 14 or 15. Lyman's current formula is now 9 pounds of wheelweight alloy mixed with 1 pound of 50/50 solder.

Another way I can be versatile is with sizing diameters. Here again I will use 38-40 as an example. I have a 1914-vintage Colt SAA that requires .403-inch bullets for best accuracy, but the brand-new 1994 Colt SAA 38-40 which I just acquired has barrel groove and chamber mouth diameters of .401-inch. Therefore, I can use the same bullet mould for both guns, and just appropriately size them. The ease of

Casting bullets is considered by many to be a hot, obnoxious chore, but when using good equipment, the product performs very well.

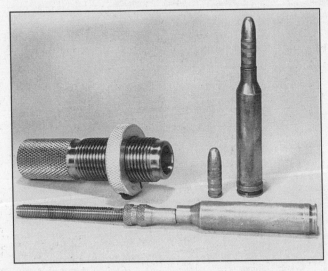

In loading cast bullets, the use of a case mouth belling die is necessary, so that the bullet's base can be started easily.

These four companies produce moulds for off-the-shelf distribution.

For cast bullets to give the best results in autoloading handguns, they should be shaped similarly to the bullets used in hardball factory ammo. Shown are a round of 32 Auto hardball (left), a bullet cast in RCBS mould #32-77RN and a round reloaded with the cast slug.

Cast bullets are perfect for practicing with autoloading handguns, according to the author.

Venturino working his lead pot. Eye protection and a good apron are mandatory.

The author holds a Montana mule deer taken with 50-90 Sharps.

This is how accurate cast bullets can be from big bore blackpowder cartridge rifles.

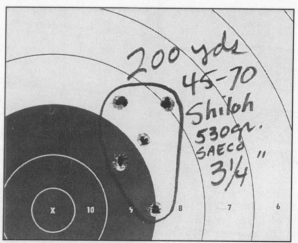

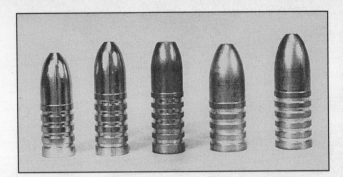

The author had a hand in developing all of these cast bullet designs for blackpowder cartridge rifles: (From left) Redding/SAECO #640 40-caliber 370 grains, Redding/SAECO #740 40-caliber 410 grains, Lyman #410655 40-caliber 400 grains, Redding/SAECO #645 45-caliber 480 grains, and Redding/SAECO #745 45-caliber 520 grains.

Cast bullets are sized and lubed after being poured from molten alloy. This machine is the Redding/SAECO lube/sizer.

This is a custom Hoch mould supplied by Colorado Shooter's Supply. Hoch makes almost anything a customer designs, so cast bullet shooters can experiment with various shapes and calibers. This mould is for a 450-grain, gas-checked 45-caliber bullet.

The true size of a 50-caliber cast bullet is seen when compared with a round of 22 Long Rifle ammunition. The bullet is from RCBS mould #45-450FN.

perfectly fitting the bullet to the bore makes bullet casting especially suited to all the new 40-caliber handguns by different makers that have slightly different bore sizes.

Now, for what purposes are cast bullets good, and for what are they not good? As much as I like and use cast bullets, I must be honest and say they don't fit every bill. For instance, you will never get them to behave at varmint rifle or ultra-high-speed handgun velocities. They will work fine up to about 2000 fps and 100 yards in your 222 or 223 Remington, but they will never be true long-range varmint bullets. On the other hand, they may be entirely adequate in Thompson/Center Contenders chambered for those two cartridges. Cast bullets don't work too well in high-power big game rifles operating at muzzle velocities in excess of about 2200 fps. However, up to that approximate velocity level and out to 150 yards or so, they will do fine.

For just about any other centerfire shooting purpose in metallic cartridge firearms, cast bullets will do just fine. Today's modern handguns will almost never need better bullets than you can cast yourself. Once you're set up to cast your own handgun bullets, you'll find you can easily make bullets for many rifles, carbines and blackpowder guns, and that's another reason to become a bullet caster.

Hunting

Achieving reliable expansion with cast handgun bullets is difficult at best. A flat-nose bullet imparts maximum shock to game animals and, combined with an adequate caliber, one can get quick, reliable kills on deer-sized game.

I've taken pronghorn antelope, deer, elk and even bison with cast bullets at very moderate velocities (around 1300 to 1400 fps), and they do a fine job. Probably, the best combination I have ever used is the 50-90 Sharps from a Shiloh Rifle Mfg. reproduction Sharps. The RCBS #50-450 flat-nose cast of 1:30 tin/lead alloy weighs about 475 grains. Loaded over 100 grains of FFg blackpowder, it will give about 1400 fps from a 30-inch barrel, and nothing I have ever shot with it has moved out of its tracks. These bullet weights and velocities are available out of modern handguns made by John Linebaugh (475 and 500) and others, and the cast bullets don't care if they're launched by rifle or handgun. The terminal performance is identical.

Antique blackpowder calibers such as these are best loaded only with cast bullets: (from left) 40-70 Bottleneck, 40-70 Straight, 44-77, 45-70, 50-70 and 50-90.

The author likes shooting cast bullets in his Model 29 Smith & Wesson 44 Magnum.

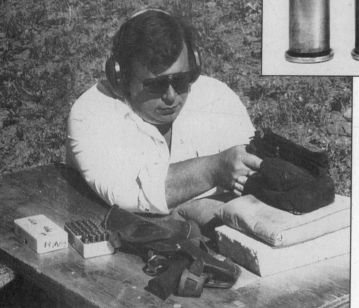

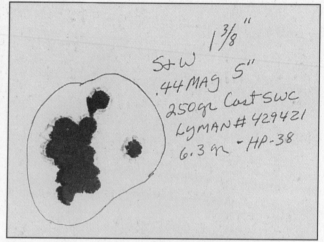

Cast bullets work very well in magnum handguns at either mild or heavy velocities. This group was fired by the author using a Smith & Wesson Model 29 44 Magnum.

Autoloading Handguns

Now let's consider cast bullets for autoloading pistols. This type of firearm is very popular, and more and more handloaders are casting for them. Some have given up that endeavor as hopeless and have gone back to jacketed bullets in their autoloaders. The cast bullet shooter will run into more problems with semi-auto handguns than with most any other type, but good results can be had. My motto on this is, "Make them big enough, make them hard enough, and make them shaped like factory hardball ammo." Do those three things and, most likely, cast bullets in autoloaders will do the job.

One of the major problems I have encountered comes with 9mms. Nominal bullet diameter for 9mm is .355-inch, but the barrels I have slugged have measured from .355- to .357-inch. A cast bullet even .0005 undersize will give lousy results. Once I tried a popular make of imported 9mm with .355-inch cast bullets. They keyholed. Next I tried it with .356 bullets. They grouped, but not tightly. Then I loaded some rounds with .357-inch bullets. They functioned perfectly and would group about 3 inches at 25 yards, or roughly equal to hardball factory ammo. I slugged that gun's bar-

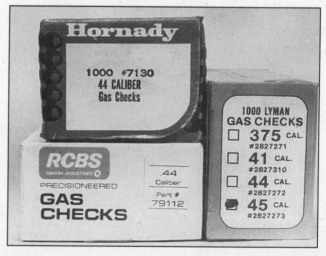

A gas check helps the performance of cast bullets used in magnum handguns.

This Shiloh Sharps 45-70 was used by Monty Merritt for cast bullet shooting.

(Below) Montana building contractor Monty Merritt fires the author's Shiloh Sharps 45-70 at a metallic silhouette of a buffalo placed 956 yards away.

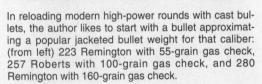

In reloading modern high-power rounds with cast bullets, the author likes to start with a bullet approximating a popular jacketed bullet weight for that caliber: (from left) 223 Remington with 55-grain gas check, 257 Roberts with 100-grain gas check, and 280 Remington with 160-grain gas check.

This is the buffalo silhouette used for target practice with cast bullets. The author is on the left, and Merritt is holding the rifle.

rel and found it to measure .3565-inch. The moral is, slug your gun's barrel before you buy your sizing die.

The other two parts of my motto, hard enough and shaped like hardball bullets, concern feeding. Soft cast bullets are "grabby" when sliding from magazine to chamber. They often hang up. So I cast all my autoloader bullets of Lyman #2 alloy (BHN 14 to 15), at least, and sometimes up to linotype (BHN 22). Also, if they are shaped like factory bullets—either round noses or flat noses with rounded edges—they are more apt to chamber well. Because all my cast bullet shooting in autoloading handguns is strictly for fun, I have no concerns about bullet expansion.

I've never loaded a single round with jacketed bullets in all my 45 ACP handloading, and darned few in any other autoloader caliber. The only place where I would shy away from using cast bullets in autoloading handguns is with those new gas-operated types. Pieces of lead are apt to be shaved off and can clog the gas port.

Magnum Handguns

What about magnum handguns? Cast bullets are a natural in magnum six-guns, perfectly suited to their velocity levels. Such guns are meant to be used on big game, and cast bullets provide the needed penetration. Whether I'm loading 357, 41 or 44 Magnum, I use the same formula for casting magnum six-gun bullets. They are cast of a hard alloy. Again, Lyman #2 formula is a good choice. Bullet shape is always semi-wadcutter, and whenever possible, I like to use gas checks. They almost always result in tighter groups as evidenced by my own testing.

An added bonus with cast bullets is that they are fine for use in reduced plinking and practice loads. Cast bullets can serve well at 1500 fps in magnum handguns, and the exact same bullet can be used at 700 fps with fine results. A jacketed bullet at 700 fps is apt to stick in the barrel!

Another type of cast bullet that I use occasionally in magnum six-guns is the hollowpoint. Again, I like to use a semi-wadcutter shape with a gas check, but here I brew them up with a soft 1:20 tin/lead alloy and try to keep velocities at about the 1250 fps level. There will be some leading, but it is minor. This type of bullet expands very well and is ideal on small deer.

Cast Bullet Moulds

Pistol shooters should buy a mould with as many cavities as possible. In my early years, I bought many single-cavity moulds, and I discovered it was simply too much work to produce any large quantity of bullets. I would never consider handgun moulds with less than two cavities, and my favorites are those with three or four.

I can heartily recommend the Magma casting machine sold by Magma Engineering. Although it is hand-operated, it immensely enhances output. The first day I used mine I turned 20 pounds of alloy into many hundreds of good 45-caliber pistol bullets in less than one hour.

I recommend bullet casting to avid handloaders, but one must use some common sense about the matter. For instance, I cast my own 38-40 and 44-40 bullets for handguns, round-nose 45-caliber 255-grain bullets for 45 Colt, and 246-grain round-noses for 44 Special. I cast many of my own rifle bullets. However, I have poured my last 38 Special 158-grain semiwadcutter, 44-caliber 240-grain semiwadcut-

ter, and 45 ACP 230-grain round-nose bullets. When I need them, I'll buy them cast, sized and lubed, ready to load, from any number of custom casting companies. I'll save my time for the ones I must make myself.

Here's my secret for making the many hours spent over that hot lead pot so much more enjoyable. I read books! Actually I listen to verbatim readings of full-length books on cassette tapes that I rent from Books On Tape. For instance, *Lonesome Dove* is recorded on twenty-seven hour-and-a-half tapes. I enjoyed it so much, I was searching for more moulds so I could spend more time at the pot. Listening to those books turns a chore into a relaxing experience, and afterward you would be amazed at what a pile of glistening fresh projectiles you then have ready to shoot.

As you can see, casting my own bullets for a wide array of guns is not a hot, smelly, obnoxious chore, although I must admit that many times it is easier to buy than make many types of them. However, I have turned bullet casting into something positive, and I'll do it until the end! ●

In magnum handgun calibers like the 357 Magnum, cast bullets can be used either at low velocities for target shooting, like the 150-grain wadcutter (left), or for high-velocity hunting loads, like with the gas-checked 146-grain hollowpoint.

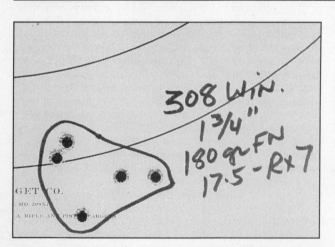

Cast bullets at moderate velocities in modern high-power calibers can be very accurate with a little work. This 100-yard group was fired with a Model 70 Winchester 308 with an RCBS 180-grain bullet #30-180FN.

Cast bullets for use in modern guns and with smokeless powders are usually cast hard. The flat-nose design is an aid to performance if these bullets are used for hunting.

MODERN BULLET SWAGING

by DAVID CORBIN

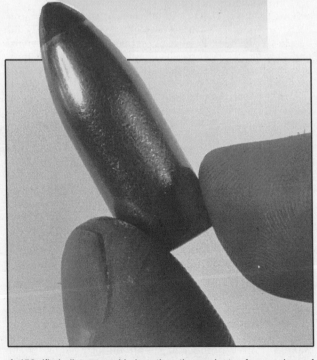

A 458 rifle bullet swaged in less than three minutes from a piece of copper tubing and some scrap range lead that had been cast into a core (cylinder shape).

IN THE 1890s, precision rifle shooters and gunmakers discovered it was practical to make bullets without using hot lead. By pressing room-temperature lead slugs into a polished steel die under tons of pressure, they made bullets which took on the exact shape of the die every time. No air pockets, bubbles or voids remained. The solid steel cylindrical die with a perfectly round hole didn't have parts that snap open and clang shut with every bullet, or hinges that wear down allowing the pouring hole to become oblong. Rather, the bullet was pushed out by its nose through the same hole it entered. Since the swage die operated at room temperature, there was no thermal expansion and contraction with every pour, no variation caused by heating and cooling of the mould, no warpage or shrinkage of either the bullet or the tool.

Bullet swaging in those days was a slow process. The original dies were operated with brass mallets. The bullet maker would pound on a tough steel punch which was fitted to the matching cylinder more accurately than today's high performance car engines. The hammer blows developed the tons of pressure required to cold-flow the lead and form a precise bullet shape. Not surprisingly, this kind of die became known as a "pound die." The people who generally appreciated them most were slug gun shooters firing big-bore rifles at ranges up to 1000 yards, the forerunners of today's benchrest competitors.

In the 1940s, when factory bullets were either hard to find or of mediocre quality, a number of firms built special bullet swage dies to experiment with higher quality projectiles and unusual bullet designs. The Rock Chuck Bullet Swage Company developed a set of tooling that used a powerful lever-operated press to redraw fired 22 rimfire cases into 224 rifle jackets and then apply high pressure to a cold bit of lead wire placed within the jacket, thus forming a 224 centerfire bullet. A two-piece design, like many of that era, the die had a threaded cylinder and a matching nose section that unscrewed so the bullet maker could push the finished

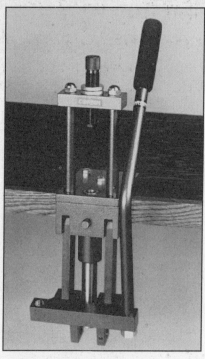

Corbin's CSP-3 silver press is the least expensive bullet swaging press ($189.50) and makes lead or jacketed bullets from 14- to 458-caliber.

The CSP-1 Series II press can handle harder alloys in the range from 14- to 458-caliber. It doubles as a 200,000 psi reloading press and runs on roller bearings.

bullet all the way through. An operator had to screw the two parts together, put the material inside, apply pressure with the press, and then unscrew the top and push out the finished bullet.

The problem with this design was twofold: It was slow, and eventually the wear of the threads would cause the bullet ogive to be offset from the shank. The two centerlines would not necessarily line up, and the bullet would wobble in flight. But it was good enough to launch the RCBS firm, which soon abandoned the difficult-to-make swage dies in favor of more simply manufactured reloading tools.

One of the most famous of the short-lived swaging firms of the 1950s was Biehler and Astles, a couple of fellows who actually used tools belonging to a technical school shop class to make a vastly better kind of bullet swage system. Instead of using one die that came apart, they designed a three-die operation. Each die was solid and had a punch through both ends. The final die had a small spring-steel ejection pin that pushed the bullet out by its nose. The first die swaged the lead core to proper shape and weight. Then the core and jacket were put together and expanded upward in diameter by pressure applied to the core in a second, larger die. Finally, the precise cylinder with its balloon-tight jacket, expanded by internal lead pressure, was put into the ogive or point-forming die and shaped into a bullet.

The advantages of this system were versatility, speed and precision—the ogive and shank were always in perfect alignment. The B&A company didn't last very long, and its prices were quite high, even with the use of virtually free tooling from a school shop to make the dies, but it established without a doubt that the handloader, working with simple equipment, could create bullets of greater accuracy than any punched out by high-speed machinery. The era of benchrest bullet swaging had begun in earnest.

Over the years, a handful of die makers have built swaging equipment, but this type of bullet making suffers from two problems. First, there has been a lack of widespread information about the process, tools and techniques. Most handloaders have misconceptions about the process perpetuated by those who don't keep up with the latest developments. Second, the three vastly different marketing concepts among the major swaging toolmakers keep handloaders from seeing the benefits of swaging.

Some of the old ideas still influencing handloaders incorrectly include: 1) Swaging is too expensive and only for benchrest shooters; 2) Swaging is too involved, meticulous and slow for practical handloading; 3) Swaged bullets have to be made of soft lead and limited design; 4) Swaging is too hard to learn.

All these perceptions used to be true at one time. Back before there were books, articles and the people willing to share information, swaging was very hard to learn. Those who did learn it generally kept their secrets in order to improve their own shooting or to sell bullets. Die makers generally didn't care to tell very much about how they did it, which once again made swaging a rather dark business full of secrets. When Charlie Heckman, founder of C-H Tool and Die Company, began marketing low-cost, simple swage dies for basic pistol bullet designs in the half-jacket style, many shooters thought this was the only thing swaging tools could make. Indeed, unless one spent the equivalent of a few thousand of today's dollars for better equipment, that *was* all swaging could do! But times have changed.

Today, there are still firms which market very simple and inexpensive swage dies that make soft-lead half-jacket-style bullets. The marketing philosophy is that the dies are secondary to the sales of handloading presses and are accessories which might help reduce the cost of shooting. The dies make a limited number of simple bullet designs which account for a majority of the lead found in target range backstops around the country. The dies fit into a standard reloading press, screwing into the top of the press like a

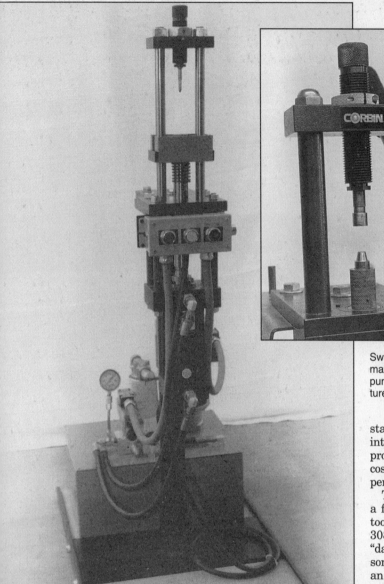

The Corbin CSP-2H Hydraulic Mega Mite can form a solid piece of brass or copper rod into a precision bullet in one stroke.

Bullet swaging is the method used by nearly all of the world's top bullet makers. This book, *World Directory of Custom Bullet Makers*, details products, people and technique.

Swaging is a fast and simple process: Put material into a die and squeeze it between punch ends until it flows at room temperature to take on the die shape.

Swaging can make an inexpensive bullet that can be fired without lubricant at speeds up to 1400 fps without leading, and with soft pure lead serving as the basic material.

standard reloading die, and the punch generally slipping into the ram like a shellholder. Someone seeing only these products advertised would quickly assume swaging is a low-cost way to make soft-lead pistol bullets with half-jackets—period.

The extreme other end of the swaging spectrum involves a few people building extremely expensive, high-quality tools to make precision benchrest bullets in 224, 243 and 308 calibers. These tools plunge the handloader into the "dark side" of swaging, where things are done just because someone once said it tightened the group by a thousandth of an inch. This is the involved, slow, difficult (probably much more so than it need be) aspect of bullet swaging.

The truth is, swaging encompasses far more territory than either of these extremes. In between the low-cost, limited-capability bullets and the super-precision, voodoo rituals is the entire "rest of the story," as Paul Harvey would say. Building cheap mass-market tools and custom-only tools are just two of three ways to market swaging equipment. The third is to make them available to everyone else on a semi-custom basis, where the presses and dies are standardized to interchange within broad groups of calibers (from 14 to 458, for example), yet the shapes and calibers can be tailored to individual shooters' needs. This method makes high-precision equipment available in a price range closer to the low end of the scale. The volume helps reduce the cost of making precision equipment even further, so that benchrest-quality equipment can be offered at closer to the half-jacket handgun die prices.

Today, you can make any caliber of bullet, from the tiny .145-inch rifle bullets to the 10-gauge shotgun slug, with equipment that fits into a corner of the garage or den. Several specialized swaging presses, including both hand-operated and hydraulic-powered, are available. Using a standard reloading press for swaging has always been somewhat like using a 22 rimfire to hunt bear. You can do it, but it's not the best way.

(Above) Now well-known commercial products, these prototypes of high-performance swaged bullets were made on the same swaging equipment a handloader can obtain.

The Corbin Hydro-Press forms the basis for most of the world's custom bullet businesses (over 200 people swage bullets for a living and work at home).

The Corbin CSP-2 Mega Mite Press can reload up to 50 BMG caliber and takes dies that handle any alloy of lead—even pure copper rod.

Bullet jackets can now be easily made at home with the proper jacket drawing tools, using flat strips of copper. The strips are cut into disks, cupped, drawn and trimmed.

Swaging presses accept the dies in a different manner than standard reloading presses with the dies screwing into the ram rather than the top of the press. This design allows the ram to take the force applied to the internal punch and to move the punch forward on the downstroke, resulting in automatic ejection of the bullet. Swaging presses are generally more powerful, tougher and have shorter strokes (on hand-operated models) than standard reloading presses. Today there are swaging press designs that convert into a longer stroke with lower leverage for use with reloading dies, which may be like using a 460 Weatherby to shoot field mice, but it gets the job done!

Besides swaging bullets, most handloaders don't know that they can make their own bullet jackets, since this is something that has not been widely available until recent years. There are three ways to make bullet jackets. The oldest is somewhat of a war-time expedient—using empty cartridge cases. During periods of ammo shortages, empty military cartridge cases have been filled with lead and swaged into larger-caliber bullets (which shoot better than you might expect).

The 30 Carbine case can be used to make a 375-caliber bullet, for instance. Just about any straight-walled pistol case can be made into some caliber of rifle bullet jacket. Fired 22 rimfire cases make very good jackets for 224 rifle bullets and can also be used for 243 and even 25 ACP jackets, using some interesting techniques to pinch-trim the jacket and to expand it. It is even possible to make 257, 264, 270, 284 and even 308 bullets using fired 22 Magnum cases, but it isn't easy enough to recommend doing so on a daily

This set of dies turns fired 22 cases into 224- or 243-caliber bullet jackets for a lifetime of free materials!

A basic but complete bullet swaging "factory on a bench"—core cutter, press, dies, lube, jackets and lead wire.

Pre-serrated jackets aid in fast expansion. One stoke of the swaging press transforms a regular jacket into a serrated one, using a special punch.

basis. The brass will expand that much under internal pressure if you use several short lengths of lead and expand each one separately, so the brass takes on the larger diameter in short sections, like a rattlesnake digesting a rabbit.

The second way to make jackets is to use copper tubing. Barnes Bullets originally popularized this concept, followed by a number of other firms making specialty bullets (such as Cor-Bon and Grizzly). Copper tubing can be partially rolled over and closed at one end using a hand press, or it can be completely swaged into a closed cup in a hydraulic press (a small one that is practical for any reasonably advanced handloader to acquire).

The old idea that a copper tubing jacket is open on both ends is wrong. It's also well proven by now, with hundreds of thousands of bullets fired, that a regular "pure" copper jacket, using the same kind of material as ordinary plumbing, air conditioner and boiler tubing, won't cause any more fouling than a typical factory bullet provided the surface finish is as good. When you hear complaints about fouling from pure copper jackets, the odds are extremely high that the bullet was not polished or burnished by the tooling to remove the loose oxide layer which always forms when the tube is heat-treated (as it must be to form the base without cracking the edges). It is this loose, powdery surface that comes off in the bore and contributes heavily to fouling. A well-finished, reasonably work-hardened tubing jacket is as clean-shooting as anyone would want.

The third way involves tooling just now finding its way into the marketplace, which allows the use of flat sheet copper (or gilding metal, commercial bronze, aluminum sheet or even mild steel). These tools have taken a long time to evolve, since a number of technical problems had to be solved to produce a homemade jacket as high in quality as one made on $250,000 transfer presses and progressive dies. But now, the only difference between the two is the speed with which they are produced.

Using 1-inch-wide, .030-inch-thick roofing copper, you can punch out a disk, turn the disk into a shallow cup like a gas check or half-jacket, then redraw the cup in one or more stages, to make it longer and smaller in diameter and to adjust the taper and wall thickness, depending on the design of the punches and dies. Each set of jacket drawing tooling works as a closely matched package and is designed for a given kind of material. You can't throw just any old sheet of metal in the process and expect it to produce a good jacket, but you can buy modest quantities of the right material at a reasonable price (even as little as 5 pounds, which in the above dimensions would give you 42.5 feet of strip and make about 550 jackets for around $35).

The advantage of home jacket making is that you can have virtually any caliber, length and wall thickness you desire. This helps control the performance of the bullet in ways previously available only to the research departments of the military and large ammunition companies. The jacket design is probably the single most critical element in the terminal performance of ammunition other than the velocity of the bullet. By giving control of jacket design to the handloader, swaging breaks down the last barrier between true ballistic engineering and the home construction of ammunition by recipe. In fact, the control over performance is so vast that, without some background and written guidelines, most handloaders would be in over their heads. Fortunately, the information available today is as complete as the swaging field is wide.

If you have been casting bullets, you know how time-consuming, potentially dangerous and equipment-laden casting can be. With swaging, only a single die or set of dies is required for each diameter of bullet. But within that diameter, you can produce nearly infinite weights and styles. Using a spool of lead wire removes any need for hot lead, so you and your family are not exposed to burns, explosions or toxic fumes. Since you won't have to wait for a pot to melt, you can come home, screw the die in the press and make a dozen bullets in any desired weight or style in just a few minutes time. In fact, you can probably swage a box of bullets and reload them before a lead pot would have time to liquefy its lead!

If you have casting equipment, you can use the pot and a special, top-ejecting core mould to produce lead cores instead of using lead wire. Casting cores has the same drawbacks as casting bullets except you don't have to worry so much about perfect casts. The piston and cylinder type of

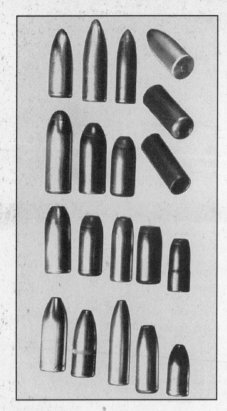

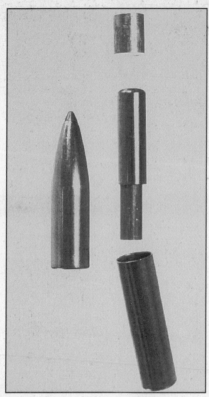

The author, David R. Corbin, is the president of Corbin Mfg. and owner of Corbin Software.

Bullets can be swaged from ordinary materials such as copper tubing and scrap lead. These rifle bullets range from 30- to 458-caliber—all are made from ordinary water tubing.

A swaged double-jacketed bullet uses a smaller caliber jacket to protect the core within a longer, larger jacket. These are easily made at home.

Here are a few of the books available on the subject of bullet swaging. Only in the past twenty years have instructions been readily available to handloaders.

mould is considerably faster than a butterfly-type bullet mould. And, of course, once the cores are formed, you can turn them into any number of different styles of bullets later on. Most bullet swagers use both lead wire and cast cores. The wire is used for making a limited number of some experimental-weight bullets, and the cores are made in the summer, outdoors, and used the rest of the year for the "old standby" bullet weights.

Because swaging is more precise than casting, there is no need to resize, so you eliminate not only the lead pot, ladle, moulds and handles, but also the sizer-lubricator and lubricant. In exchange, you have a swaging press, dies and a lead wire cutter, and either jackets, a jacket-maker kit, a base-guard kit (similar to gas checks but far more effective at removing fouling and eliminating the need for lubricant) or a liquid dip-lube. The net cost for one caliber, weight and style favors casting, but if you want to experiment with various weights and styles, the cost for swaging equipment is far less. How much would it cost for moulds to make every weight of 38-caliber semi-wadcutter bullet from 80 to 250 grains? One swage die does that. Changing the nose or base shape only requires a different punch, typically $20. You can make hollow base and hollowpoint at the same time with a swage die, something quite difficult to do with most moulds.

Some of the other advantages of swaging are: 1) The ability to turn commonly available materials into bullets without the need for components that would otherwise be considered "reloading supplies," which means that taxes and any future restrictions on your handloading would be reduced; 2) The power to design and build bullets that perform as well as or better than those of current manufacture,

even exotic designs made of solid copper or with extreme serrations or hollowpoint features; 3) Technical advantages that allow diameter and weight control to tolerances that average 100 times closer than cast bullets; 4) The ability to use the same tooling to make other designs, other weights and use other materials, if the need arises. For instance, if a high tax on lead is imposed, the right swage tools let you make high quality bullets of solid copper, brass or aluminum.

The wide array of swaging tools, supplies and information available to the handloader covers everything from the making of precision air gun pellets to the production of superior 50 BMG bullets. Partitioned or multiple-jacketed bullets; bonded cores (where jacket and lead core are fused into a monolithic solid that cannot separate on impact); fouling-scraper "base guards" that make shooting soft lead slugs at jacketed bullet velocities possible without any lubrication; lightweight plastic balls that compress within the jackets to shift the balance and produce stable, lightweight bullets within the airframe of a heavy, slow projectile—all these are just the barest glimpse of what handloaders are doing with swaging today. Some have found that swaging turns the shooting hobby into a source of income, as the demand for custom bullets continues to skyrocket. It might be worth your while to take a look! ●

HANDGUNS 95

SECTION 7
A Touch of Nostalgia

An old gun that led to new ideas, as seen by Swiggett, page 190.

An innovation gone, but not forgotten by Dickson, page 193.

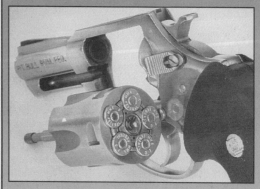

It had a short life, yet impressed Swiggett, page 196.

A Touch of Nostalgia

SMITH & WESSON'S TRIPLE LOCK

by HAL SWIGGETT

What Smith & Wesson started, Elmer Keith perfected.

AT AGE FIFTEEN, Chris King had never fired any handgun bigger than a 22, yet he successfully dropped a handsome blackbuck antelope with my scoped Smith & Wesson Classic DX 44 Magnum.

Eighty-eight years before Chris got his antelope, S&W started working on their first N-frame double-action revolver. As time passed, S&W perfected it into their current Model 629 Classic DX, a big gun so easy to shoot that a fifteen-year-old who had never fired a powerful handgun was able to hunt successfully with it.

But to truly appreciate this gun, you must know something of its history.

The year was 1905. Smith & Wesson's goal was to produce a large-frame double action to handle a new cartridge that was to be known as the 44 S&W Special. The new loading used 26 grains of blackpowder and a bullet weighing 246 grains.

This new revolver was a design departure. Roy Jinks' great book, *History of Smith & Wesson*, published in 1977, tells the story.

The new double action was called the 44 Hand Ejector, and it made its debut in early 1908. It was chambered for the 44 Special, but would also shoot the older 44 Russian. To the usual locking system, S&W added a third lock. Here is the way Roy describes it: "The new revolver was to be designed for maximum tightness and positive alignment of the cylinder. Therefore, the firm added an additional locking device to the revolver frame. This new revolver now locked the cylinder at the breech by means of the center pin protruding into the frame, at the front of the extractor rod, and at the yoke where the yoke and barrel meet when the yoke is closed."

Now you know why it became known as the Triple Lock.

Chris King (left), fifteen years old, took this trophy blackbuck antelope with an 8³/₈-inch S&W Model 629 Classic DX. His guide was Doug Luger of Safaris Plus. The 629 evolved from the Triple Lock, thanks to the efforts of Elmer Keith.

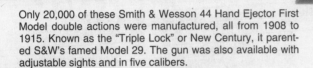

Only 20,000 of these Smith & Wesson 44 Hand Ejector First Model double actions were manufactured, all from 1908 to 1915. Known as the "Triple Lock" or New Century, it parented S&W's famed Model 29. The gun was also available with adjustable sights and in five calibers.

The projection seen in the center of the photograph is the third lock. It holds the crane snugly against the frame for improved strength and accuracy.

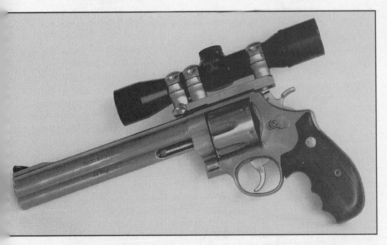

Smith & Wesson's Model 629 Classic DX is the ultimate evolution of the Triple Lock. It is also the result of Elmer Keith's persistence. Bausch & Lomb's 4x scope is firmly held by Redfield's very sturdy three-ring mount.

The hole, visible under the ejection rod in the center of photograph, accepts the pin protruding from the barrel lug. This third lock gave the gun the nickname "Triple Lock."

During the few years it was manufactured, 1908 to 1915, approximately 20,000 were made, including more than 5000 that were sent to England. It was offered in a variety of chamberings including 44 Special, 455 MK II, 38-40, 44-40, 44 Russian and 45 Colt, and with either fixed or adjustable sights. The price was $21.

Next came S&W's 44 Hand Ejector Second Model. This model did not have the shrouded extractor rod or the triple locking system. It was this very expensive machining feature that brought about the First Model's demise.

Elmer Keith owned a Triple Lock S&W 44 Special, but he wasn't exactly happy with it. Nothing was wrong with with the gun, but Keith felt it was capable of much more performance than offered by factory loads. So, being Elmer Keith, he stuffed more and more powder into his Triple Lock cartridges. He made the gun do things S&W never dreamed of. Keith was convinced he was on the right track and that he really had something. He went to the S&W factory and, for lack of a better way to say it, told them how the cow ate that cabbage. He convinced Carl R. Hellstrom, president of the company, who had read Elmer's writings, that he, Keith, knew what he was talking about.

Mr. Hellstrom contacted R.H. Coleman of Remington Arms Co. requesting they consider manufacturing a hot 44 load. Keith wanted it to be called the 44 Special Magnum. In the summer of 1954, Remington supplied case dimensions for this new cartridge. It would be $1/8$-inch longer than the 44 Special and would be called the 44 Remington Magnum. In July of 1954, S&W produced a very limited number of heat-treated Model 1950s in the year of their model number, 1950. This was a progressive step up from our subject Triple Lock.

The Editor's Smith & Wesson 6½-inch Model 29, his personal Elmer Keith "Commemorative," was retrofitted with custom Herrett walnut stocks.

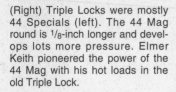

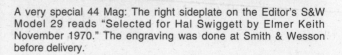

(Right) Triple Locks were mostly 44 Specials (left). The 44 Mag round is ⅛-inch longer and develops lots more pressure. Elmer Keith pioneered the power of the 44 Mag with his hot loads in the old Triple Lock.

A very special 44 Mag: The right sideplate on the Editor's S&W Model 29 reads "Selected for Hal Swiggett by Elmer Keith November 1970." The engraving was done at Smith & Wesson before delivery.

(Left) Elmer Keith holds Swiggett's Model 29 in one hand and the Editor in the other. The photo was taken during the NRA annual meeting in 1971.

At one of the Remington Arms Company seminars, Elmer and I were enjoying our evening meal. Most of our conversation was about Remington Farms' fabulous goose and duck hunting. However, our conversation eventually turned, as always, to handguns and, as always, to S&W 29s. Elmer insisted I didn't own a 44 Magnum unless I owned a Model 29. I made an honest statement, "Elmer, even if I wanted a Model 29 I couldn't afford it." Dishes rattled as he hit the table with his clenched fist, and he said, "By golly, I'm going to have Smith & Wesson send you one."

And, by golly, he did.

A couple of weeks later, I received a letter from Mr. William G. Gunn, president of S&W, asking for a copy of my FFL. He went on to say Elmer Keith had ordered his company to send me a Model 29. I did the same thing any of you would have, I sent him a copy of my FFL.

A few weeks later, my 6½-inch Model 29 Smith & Wesson arrived. On the right sideplate was engraved: "Selected for Hal Swiggett by Elmer Keith November 1970."

The following spring, I took my very special M29 to the annual meeting of the National Rifle Association in Washington, DC, to get a photograph of Elmer, me and my 29 together.

All of you who shoot the Smith & Wesson Model 29 or 629 double-action revolvers owe Elmer Keith a very big "thank you" every time you use the gun.

Both Remington and S&W extensively tested these toughened 1950s. Though everything seemed to be OK, both firms felt that the revolver needed to be heavier.

Smith & Wesson added weight to both the barrel and frame, and produced a new double-action revolver that they called the Model 29. The first one ever made went to Remington, number two to the National Rifle Association, and the third to the father of the 44 Magnum, Elmer Keith.

Eventually the Model 29 was brought out in stainless steel and became the 629. Bolt cuts were widened a bit, and with some cosmetic changes, it became the Model 629 Classic DX. Mine was delivered with a full-length underlug, 8⅜-inch barrel, two sets of grips and five interchangeable front sights. I fitted it with a Bausch & Lomb 4x scope in Redfield mounts, and young Chris King used it to take his trophy blackbuck.

Smith & Wesson's 44 Hand Ejector—known as the Triple Lock, New Century or First Model 44 Hand Ejector—had come a long, long, way.

When the Model 29 came out, it was the only double-action handgun Elmer would carry. Other than that, he was single actions all the way.

Elmer Keith was responsible for getting S&W to upgrade their 44 Hand Ejector First Model. Had it not been for the strength built into that Triple Lock, we might not have the great 44 Remington Magnum cartridge today.

I feel truly blessed that Elmer had one, and that I, too, am lucky enough to own one of only 20,000 Triple Locks made.

I'm luckier still to own a Model 29 that bears the name of the father of the 44 Magnum—Elmer Keith. It's a grand example of the evolution of the Triple Lock S&W.   ●

A Touch of Nostalgia

THE MANN 25 ACP

by JIM DICKSON

From an era when every good man carried a small pistol, this mini-gun survives.

THE SMALLEST PRACTICAL pistol ever made is the Mann 25 ACP, made by Mann Werkzeugfabrik of Suhl, Germany. Fritz Mann was a WWI and prewar supplier of parts and components to the Suhl trade. Miniatures were all the rage in those days, and the company had experience in making miniature watches and lockets. In 1918 Mann entered the pistol business with this little gem. At a time when pistol buyers leaned toward the smallest and cheapest, Mann was determined to outdo all other makers. The price was $12, a good price back then. Quality was also considered good. The gun is made of milled forgings and is hand-fitted and rust blued.

Fritz Mann had met all his design criteria and eagerly awaited throngs of buyers to break down his doors to get at his advanced design. Unfortunately, it was too advanced, and like the M1941 Johnson rifle and M1944 Johnson light machinegun, it went largely unappreciated. Disappointing sales followed, and Fritz learned to his sorrow just how conservative the gun-buying public can be. Advanced designs can be too much for many of them to comprehend, as history has proven over the years.

The Mann is a vest pocket pistol. It was made from 1918-1924, a period when nearly everyone in Europe carried a small pocket pistol. The odd shape of the Mann is as user friendly and ergonomically successful as they come, which is particularly noticeable when carrying the gun. The Mann rests securely upside-down in the vest pocket with the butt always in exactly the same position, waiting for the thumb and forefinger to pluck it out and flip it into firing position. It is fast and sure on the draw. By comparison, a pistol like the Browning Baby 25 ACP, when placed in a vest pocket, is unbalanced, wants to tilt, and is cumbersome to draw.

The thin, flat shape of the Mann also makes it more concealable than other vest pocket pistols. Its 8$\frac{7}{8}$-ounce weight and overall length of 4 inches is complemented by the flattest mechanism ever put on a pocket auto. Rather than use a boxy conventional slide, Fritz Mann designed the gun with an internal bolt and an annular ring in the chamber to retard blowback, since the tiny gun lacked sufficient bolt

The Mann 25 ACP is perhaps the world's smallest practical pistol. It holds five shots in the magazine plus one chambered. Weight is 8$\frac{7}{8}$ ounces; length 4 inches. Though weird-shaped, it is well thought out and practical.

weight for straight blowback operation. It is the only retarded blowback 25 ACP to achieve production status. The thinness resulted in some interesting carries, such as inside the wallet with the money, its butt always sticking unobtrusively up for instant withdrawal.

Smaller pistols have been made, but they fire miniature cartridges instead of standard calibers, or are too misshapen for accurate pointing. The latter is important because small calibers require precise shot placement, and there is no place for sights worthy of the name on guns of this scale. The Mann is a natural pointer. Its odd-looking shape enables it to rest naturally in the hand. Punch your fist, pull the trigger and you are on target. Like the Webley 455 automatic, the Mann is held straight-wristed, with the fist in a boxing position.

Almost everything about the gun is unique. With the bolt pulled back, the barrel is easily turned and withdrawn for cleaning. Further disassembly is not so easy, and the mainspring is ferocious when unleashed. After cleaning the barrel, many users opt to put off further disassembly as long as possible.

The magazine release is on the front of the frame under the second finger—an odd place, but a practical one that works well. The safety is under the thumb. It only blocks the trigger. A striker-fired gun needs a striker-blocking safety to be trustworthy if the gun is dropped. The gun is cocked by pulling the ribbed bolt extension as though it were a M96 Mauser military pistol.

The operating sequence of the Mann starts when finger pressure pivots the trigger against the trigger bar. This tips the sear out of engagement with the striker, releasing the striker to fire the cartridge. On firing, the annular chamber groove is gripped by the expanded brass cartridge case as it acts as a movable piston against the bolt face. As the bolt face is driven back, the ejector knocks the case out of the gun. At the end of the stroke, the recoil spring drives the slide forward again, stripping a new cartridge out of the magazine and into the chamber. A spring acting on the sear causes it to catch the striker and hold it back in position, awaiting the next trigger pull.

Accuracy and reliability are on a par with its competitors, and the well-thought-out grip shape, coupled with the mild-mannered 25 ACP cartridge, make it a pleasure to shoot. It is easy to hit with the Mann.

Like all pocket pistols of its day, the Mann was equipped with thin hard rubber grips that sometimes broke. Mann made some guns with aluminum grips for those who kept dropping their guns. Today, one can get new perfect reproduction replacement grips for this and virtually every other old pistol ever made from Gun Parts Co., West Hurley, New York.

In 1924, the 25 ACP was dropped from the line and replaced with the more conventional-appearing 32 ACP and 380 ACP that still managed to be the smallest guns of their caliber ever made. Price and quality went up on these guns as well.

Like most gunmakers of that era, Mann also made his own ammunition. It carried a circle-and-gate headstamp. He developed a 6.33mm high-velocity bottle-necked cartridge with a 62-grain bullet at 1050 fps. Fritz always strove to invent a better way to do things. The company continued until about 1929 and left the world an enduring legacy of engineering ingenuity.

Today, the Mann is treated as a curiosity, but its unique features remain unduplicated and unsurpassed. As I write this, a Mann 25 sits straight up on the desk before me. Its perfect balance enables it to stand on its magazine bottom like a wine glass on its stem. An unusual sight, it is nonetheless practical, for it can be snatched up from this position far more surely and quickly than can a gun that is lying flat.

A 25 ACP vest pocket pistol should never be anyone's choice for a first-line weapon, despite its popularity as such in post-WWI Europe. Its legitimate place is as a second gun, secreted in unexpected places, and only used for last-ditch desperate emergency use. While it is no manstopper, it sure beats relying on a knife or your fists. The 25 ACP should always be loaded with FMJ ammo, *never* soft-nose or hollowpoints. This round needs all the help it can get penetrating to the vitals. Over the years, 25 ACPs have often failed to penetrate sufficiently. However, they have also saved the lives of a great many 25 owners. The 25 auto is a legitimate special purpose pistol, and the Mann is among the best of the lot. ●

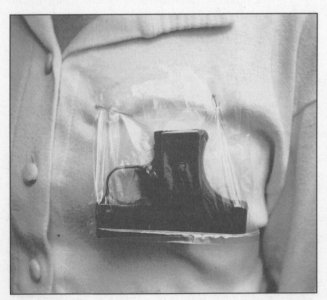

The little Mann 25 ACP is the only vest pocket pistol that settles down securely when carried in a vest. A clear plastic "vest pocket" demonstrates this quality.

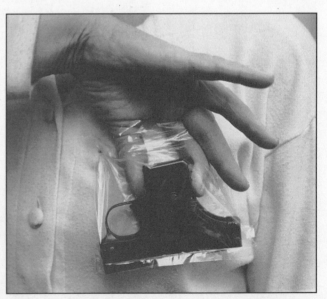

Easily extracted from a vest pocket by the thumb and forefinger, the little Mann can be instantly flipped into firing position. Other more conventional designs are far slower and fumble-prone when drawn from a vest pocket.

The Mann's vertical grip axis means the gun points accurately when you make a fist and punch the gun towards the target. Betty has her eyes locked on her target and had no trouble hitting it. Note the wrist is straight as though she were punching, not bent in the late 19th-Century style.

Note the solid frame and separate bolt with its retracting ridges like a M96 Mauser pistol. Firing the little Mann is fun.

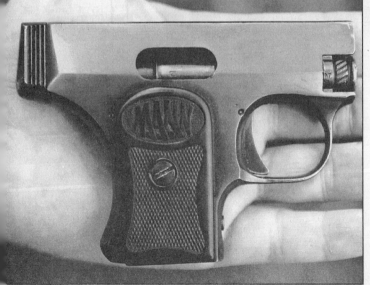

The tiny Mann autoloading 25 ACP easily disappears in the palm of a 5-foot-2-inch girl's hand.

Stripping for cleaning is simple. Pull back the bolt, turn the knurled muzzle and withdraw the barrel. It can't get any simpler.

A Touch of Nostalgia

SHORT OF LIFE IT WAS:
CHARTER ARMS' PIT

by HAL SWIGGETT

This rimmed 9mm wasn't a good enough idea to catch on. Collectors, take note!

IT DIDN'T LAST long, Charter Arms' Pit Bull 9mm Federal. My test revolver, dreamed up in 1988, wore an "X" serial number. This meant it was not yet introduced to the shooting public.

Federal Cartridge Co. listed the loading in their 1989 catalog, and both the revolver and cartridge were on display at the SHOT Show that year. Then Federal stopped manufacturing the cartridge in 1992 and sold all of their considerable inventory.

S.P. Fjestad's *Fourteenth Edition Blue Book Of Gun Values* lists the Pit Bull 9mm Federal as having a life span of three years, 1989-1991. Obviously, it was not well received by the shooting public.

I'm not certain why.

Federal's catalog lists its 115-grain Hi-Shok JHP bullet at 1280 feet per second (fps). A bit higher on that same catalog page, under Automatic Pistol Ballistics, it lists that same bullet at 1160 fps.

Ten shots through my Oehler 35P chronograph averaged 1173 fps from my 2½-inch test revolver.

I was told the same powder was used in both cartridges, but there was a little more in the rimmed (revolver) version.

My X-numbered Pit Bull has a barrel length of 2½ inches and a weight of 25 ounces. Its grooved trigger pulled through at 14 pounds, or, cocked, 4 pounds. Sights are fixed. Its finger-grooved rubber grip is very comfortable and perfectly fits my hand. This 9mm Federal Pit Bull is, by the way, identical in frame size, cylinder length, grip and trigger as Charter's Bulldog Pug 44 Special.

How did it shoot? As usual, better than its handler of the moment. I am, by nature, a center-hold shooter. I put my sights where I want to hit. With this gun, my groups printed about 5 inches above point of aim, shooting from 15 yards. I do not think of this type of gun as a long-range shooter. Group size? A playing card would have covered every five-shot group, and I fired 100 rounds.

The Pit Bull will fire 9mm Luger rounds, but getting the empties out can be a problem. I use a ballpoint pen.

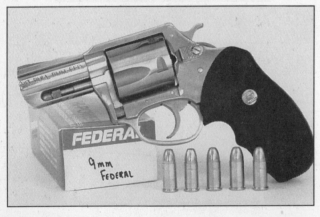

Charter Arms' Pit Bull 9mm Federal 2½-inch-barreled, stainless steel, five-shot, fixed-sight revolver didn't last long.

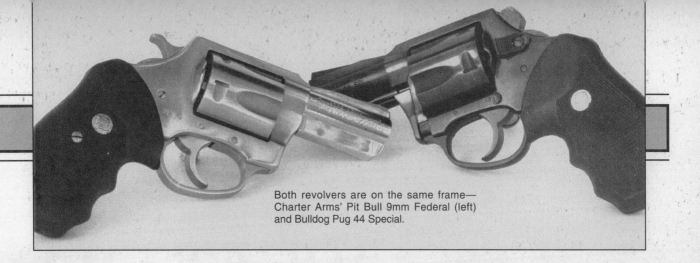

Both revolvers are on the same frame—Charter Arms' Pit Bull 9mm Federal (left) and Bulldog Pug 44 Special.

BULL 9MM FEDERAL

Those first boxes of 9mm Federal ammo were in red and white boxes minus printing on the ends. That blank white space was filled with heavy black penned letters saying simply "9mm Federal," on two lines. By SHOT Show time, the ammo was in regulation boxes with official printing on the ends reading "9mm Federal, 115 gr. J.H.P. No. 9FA," and in heavier type across the bottom, "FOR USE IN REVOLVERS ONLY."

Though I never saw one, I understand Ruger made a few 9mm Federal revolvers. Must have been on the SP101 +P 38 Special frame.

Why was this autoloader cartridge produced in a rimmed version for use in revolvers? Can't say for sure, but there are a lot of folks who prefer wheel-guns over self-shuckers. Rimmed cases allow the shooter to load and unload the gun more conveniently without the need for two- or three-round clips. The venerable 45 ACP round is offered in a rimmed format called the 45 Auto Rim, for Model 1917 Smith & Wesson and Colt revolvers designed to accept 45 ACP cartridges in two-, three-, or six-round clips. Those clips permitted easy extraction, and so do rimmed cases.

One more fact: This 9mm Federal (rimmed) cartridge *will* chamber in older 38 S&W revolvers. That's not a good idea, however. These 9mm Federals are loaded to much higher pressures and could be dangerous as well.

Maybe that's one more reason this gun and cartridge did not make it. ●

(Right) Note the headstamp—9mm Federal—on each case in its five-round cylinder. The guns and ammo will quickly become collector's items.

(Right) The 9mm Federal (left) has a decidedly larger rim than 9mm Luger cartridges.

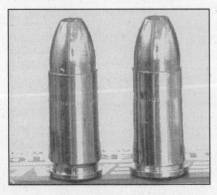

Federal's 9mm Luger (left) and rimmed 9mm Federal—both use the same 115-grain JHP bullet.

Each has its own headstamp—9mm Federal (left) and 9mm Luger.

The 9mm Federal case (left) has a hefty rim.

A Touch of Nostalgia

COLT'S GREAT OLD

by HAL SWIGGETT

The best of Colt's hand fitting might have been done before the Python was born.

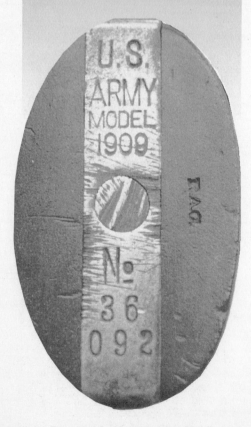

The butt of the Editor's U.S. Army Model 1909 tells its own story. Note "R.A.C.," the inspector's initials, on the grip. Also, the gun appears to have had its lanyard ring sawed off.

COLT'S NEW SERVICE double-action revolvers were manufactured from 1898 to 1942. I happen to own a pair—one made near the beginning of production and the other near the end, both 45 Colt chambered. New Service double actions were, except for their Python, Colt's finest effort.

My 1909 New Service is marked on the barrel's left side "Colt D.A. 45." The rampant colt insignia is so badly worn it is not photographable. The inspector's initials, "R.A.C.," are on the right side of its frame at the lower left corner and again on the left grip panel. On that same side, barely below the topstrap, are the letters "F B." There seems to have been a period after each, but obvious hard use makes this uncertain.

The grip frame's bottom reads: "U.S. ARMY MODEL 1909," four lines, one for each word. This is above the lanyard ring mount. Beneath that used-to-be ring is the serial number, on three lines: "No. 36092."

According to a letter of documentation from Colt, dated August 23, 1989, this 1909 was one of 200 sold to the United States government and shipped to the Commanding Officer, Ordnance Depot, Manila, P.I., December 18, 1909. The letter added, "It is interesting to note that the records also indicate that this revolver was equipped with a lanyard ring when originally shipped from the factory."

Though not so designated, I believe it to be among the first of the New Service revolvers. How good is the quality of workmanship compared with modern guns? High-priced machinery will never, ever, replace hands-on fitting of parts. Actually, no one expects that to happen. That modern revolvers are well made is beyond question. Current Colt wheel-guns will withstand loads far beyond the reaches of my ancient 1909.

However, this three-quarters-of-a-century old 45 Colt double action, that has not only been used but, from its appearance, badly abused, is still tight as that proverbial drum. Its hammer spring is downright powerful. Drop the hammer, hold its trigger back as when firing, and there is absolutely no movement of the cylinder no matter how much pressure you might apply.

The same can be said about my 1937 New Service 45 Colt.

The left side of M1909's barrel is marked "Colt D. A. 45."

NEW SERVICE

This 7½-inch 45 Colt New Service was first shipped to a dealer in Kansas. How it ended up in Georgia is not known. That's where the Editor got it. It left the factory in early 1937 and found its final home in 1967. It is still in 99.8 percent perfect condition, and the Editor even has a factory box for it.

This Model 1909, though there is no such identification on it, was among the first New Service double-action revolvers ever made. This is one of 200 shipped to: Commanding Officer, Ordnance Depot, Manila, Philippine Islands, December 18, 1909. It is chambered in 45 Colt.

Admittedly, however, this one is 99.8 percent perfect and was in a factory box when I acquired ownership. It, too, is literally "tight as a drum."

Those previous descriptions are not to belittle modern production. I'm simply pointing out how things used to be done, be it rifles, shotguns, autoloading pistols or revolvers. I'm shooting loads in both of my Anacondas, 44 Remington Magnum and 45 Colt, that would leave this pair of dearly loved "oldies" in shreds. This is made possible through the use of modern technology, both in materials and production methods.

Back to our subject. Research tells me New Service revolvers were manufactured with 4½-, 5½- and 7½-inch barrels. Chamberings were 38 Special, 357 Magnum, 38-40, 44-40, 44 Russian, 44 Special, 45 ACP, 45 Colt, 450 Eley

and 476 Eley. Finish was either blue or nickel and with hard rubber grips. In the late 1920s, these hard rubber grips were replaced with walnut. However, my research might be questionable because my 7½-inch 45 Colt made in 1937 wears hard rubber grips.

Colt's New Service revolvers were designed for the greatest possible strength. The bolt cuts are not directly over each chamber, but are offset to allow more metal between the bottom of the cut and the cartridge. This excellent feature has continued into modern production.

Since that 1898 beginning, Colt's New Service revolvers have gone through many steps. I'm not a collector, but have friends who are, so with their help maybe we can walk through some of those New Service "renovations." My two six-guns cover both ends of the production spectrum,

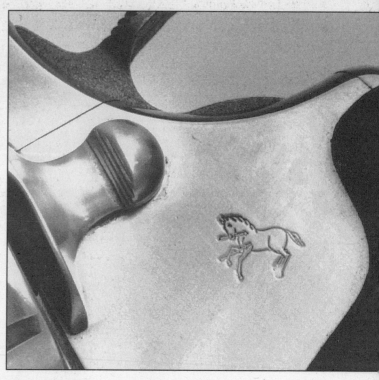

Colt's insignia, the rampant colt, looked like this in 1937. It is identical to the almost-worn-off one on the 1909, that is beyond photography.

Note the change in the company's rampant colt—on current Anaconda 45 Colt double actions.

because the 1909 military issue wasn't all that far from the beginning and my 1937 New Service was made about five years before production ended.

Colt's very successful 38s, brought out in 1889, led the way for their larger-frame 445 and 455. The big guns firmly held their own until World War II brought a halt to production of the New Service and to many other lines of guns as well.

Research revealed early New Service double actions wore firing pins machined as part of the hammer. Later, individ-

ually machined firing pins were pinned into the hammer, a feature that remains to this day.

It was in this same era that a Target Model was added to the New Service line. The new revolver had a flat-topped frame with a windage-adjustable rear sight. Up front, its sight was elevation-adjustable. A side note: A few months ago I allowed a close friend to talk me out of a very early Colt Woodsman 22 autoloader with a sighting system identical to the New Service guns.

One source indicates "Colt's New Service" was stamped

M1909's cylinder latch is square-cut, has checkering inside, and carries the letter "K"—probably the initial of an inspector.

Headstamp of the 1909 cartridge (left) reads: "W.R.A. CO." across its top and "45 COLT" around its lower portion. "W-W 45 COLT" is on the bottom of current manufacture. Note the thinness of the chamber walls and the offset bolt notch.

on the sideplate around that rampant colt on early issue revolvers. In some instances, the letter "C" circled Colt's trademark rearing colt.

It was in this period of time that Colt changed both their bolt and hammer-strut flat springs to coil springs. Soon the Colt "Positive Lock" made its appearance. Its advantage? Less chance of an accidental discharge should the revolver be dropped in such manner as to hit on its hammer. A steel bar blocked the hammer from making contact until the trigger was in its most rearward position. This feature was

Initially, there was a problem getting 45 Colt cartridges to extract from the M1909, so the Army had their own version manufactured with a larger rim. The rim of the early 45 Colt cartridge (left) measures .500-inch in diameter. The rim of a recent cartridge made by Winchester (right) measures .512-inch.

Colt's alone until 1926, and then Smith & Wesson added it to their production.

World War I's issue of Colt's Model 1917 brought about a change in appearance from a straight-tapered barrel to one with a shoulder where the barrel meets the frame. This was the result of military orders and gave a better barrel fit plus an improved appearance. Colt retained the feature on subsequent New Service revolvers.

Between World War I and 1928, production of New Service revolvers was limited to about 2000 a year.

In 1928 Colt changed the frame design. New Service Colt revolvers with serial numbers higher than about 328,000 have a newly contoured frame, a feature Colt carried over into other double actions in their line at about that time. The new look features the rear sight notch milled with square corners, plus a dull matte finish on the topstrap.

Colt added another patent date to the barrel in 1926. It was at this time Colt saw fit to change the cylinder latch from square to a rounded and checkered design. Front sights were changed a bit, basically made thicker on regulation models. Target New Service models were rigged with square post front and Patridge-style rear sights. These guns were, as I understand it, of very limited issue.

During this period, Colt opted to use a lot of leftover Model 1917 parts from World War I to make big-frame guns, and then commercially sold them. Most were chambered in 45 ACP and had barrels marked "COLT MODEL 1917 45 ACP CTGE." These guns didn't have the usual lanyard swivel. A few were chambered 44-40 and, just maybe, some in 38-40. Total production may have been no more than 1000.

The 357 Magnum, developed by Douglas B. Wesson and Philip B. Sharpe, was introduced in 1935, and New Service double actions were then chambered for this new cartridge. About 1940, the British Purchasing Commission was in need of new handguns. As a result, a good many New

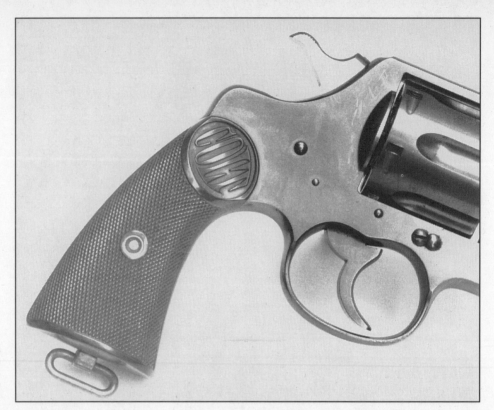

Though one source says grips were changed to walnut in the late 1920s, the editor's 1937-issue gun is still fitted with early hard rubber grips.

Service revolvers will be found with British proof marks and a Parkerized finish. A friend of mine owns one that is so marked and documented by Colt.

Breaking this New Service dissertation down into categories starts with military U.S. Model 1909s. The Army's experience in the Philippines with the inadequacy of 38-caliber revolvers brought about the adoption of the M1909 in 45 Colt. This predated Colt's 45 autoloader which, at that time, was in development stages. The 45 auto was not adopted as the official Army sidearm until 1911.

Because the narrow rim of standard 45 Colt cartridges allowed them to occasionally slip under the ejector, the Army manufactured their own rounds with larger rims for their new revolver. How do I know this? Long, long years ago I acquired my M1909. I fired a good many 45 Colt factory cartridges in it with no problem whatever. Back then, I told a close friend, L.L. "Les" Cline, about my "new" old double action. He said, "Go out back in that cluttered room and check out those shelves. Someplace there you will find part of a box of 'catiges'," as he referred to them, "made by the Army for your old revolver."

He was right—and I still have them someplace in my val-

"NEW SERVICE 45 COLT" is stamped on this 7½-inch barrel. This one was shipped from Colt's factory in 1937.

"UNITED STATES PROPERTY" is clearly stamped on the underside of this U.S. Army 1909 barrel.

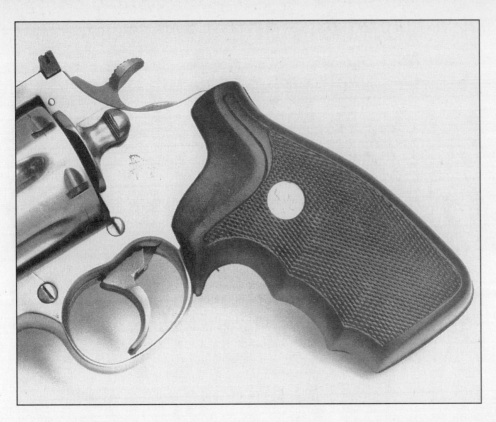

No longer are grips hard rubber, nor walnut for that matter. Now it's Neoprene. The Editor still likes walnut.

ued collection of things dear to me, but that I haven't seen in years. Wherever it is, there are still nine rounds in that little, tattered white box.

I've seen the Model 1909 identified in print as basically an improved model New Service with a 5¹/₂-inch barrel. My source for some of this information is Chuck Karwan's great dissertation on the New Service Colt revolver published in the 1989 issue of this book, HANDGUNS '89. Chuck *is* an authority on guns of yesteryear. Me, I can best categorize my leanings in this direction as an acquirer of elderly firearms. According to Chuck, somewhere between 13,000 and 18,000 of these revolvers were built. Most were sent directly to the Philippines. Mine, the one pictured here, was in a shipment of 200 shipped there December 18, 1909, as mentioned earlier. It is, apparently, one of not very many to have been returned to this country. Most of them were turned over to the Philippine constabulary, to use Chuck's words.

Both our Marines and Navy got into this act with their own versions. Thirteen hundred or so were produced for Marines and a couple hundred less for the Navy. No big numbers, for certain.

The New Service double action was a favorite with many police officers from as early as 1904 through the end of its era. Among their distinguished, and most famous, users were the Royal Canadian Mounted Police. They didn't replace them until the mid-'50s. New York's state troopers depended on their New Service DAs during the same time-span as the RCMPs. And yes, our own Border Patrol depended on them until those mid-'50s. Unlike the Canadians, who used both 455s and 45 Colts, and NYSTs who depended on 45 Colts, our Border Patrol held out for the minuscule 38 Special. Several state police agencies used New Service revolvers including the San Antonio Police Department.

There were Target Models, Shooting Masters and Fitz Specials. J. Henry Fitzgerald, Colt's representative at the National Matches and also an exhibition shooter for his company, is credited as being the first to "chop" a New

Service revolver. He cut his barrels to about 2 inches, bobbed the hammers, and cut away the trigger guard from in front of the trigger. He may have even had the butts shortened, but I'm not certain of this.

In 1947 I had never heard of J. Henry Fitzgerald. I was a twenty-one-year-old newspaper photographer for the *San Antonio Express/News*. I already had a love of big-bore handguns. I acquired a M1917 and took it to Buddy Moreno, the gunsmith at Toepperwein's sporting goods store on West Houston Street, here in San Antonio. My instructions were to turn it into what turned out to be a near exact copy of a Fitz Special. I found this out on a local shooting range while trying it out. An FBI agent happened to be there, saw what I was shooting, and commented, "That looks like a Fitz Special."

Over the years, I've had several "chopped" to that configuration, sold them, then acquired another. One was stolen from my office along with three other handguns. Police found one of my guns in a local pawn shop. Another was picked up by our sheriff's department in a drug raid. My "chopped" M1917 and one other gun never surfaced. I replaced the "chopped" gun, and the new one is identical in shape and form to its predecessors—but you probably already assumed that.

This pair of models, 1917 and New Service, have led to finer production by Colt. Their newest Anaconda is heavier, more sturdily built, and is chambered for the two finest revolver cartridges ever dreamed up—44 Remington Magnum and 45 Colt. These new offerings are made of stainless steel, already have excellent triggers, and come with an additional option never before offered to handgunners, at least not to my knowledge. There is a tiny screw in back of the trigger that allows adjustment from the outside. The adjustment on my Anacondas has never been touched. I couldn't ask for better-than-issued, but it's there for those desiring to "tinker."

What more can we ask or expect from the company that produced the great old New Service. ●

CENTERFIRE HANDGUN CARTRIDGES—BALLISTICS AND PRICES

Caliber	Bullet Wgt. Grs.	Velocity (fps) MV	Velocity 50 yds.	Velocity 100 yds.	Energy (ft. lbs.) ME	Energy 50 yds.	Energy 100 yds.	Mid-Range Traj. (in.) 50 yds.	Mid-Range Traj. 100 yds.	Bbl. Lgth. (in.)	Est. Price /box
221 Rem. Fireball	50	2650	2380	2130	780	630	505	0.2	0.8	10.5"	$15
25 Automatic	35	900	813	742	63	51	43	NA	NA	2"	$18
25 Automatic	45	815	730	655	65	55	40	1.8	7.7	2"	$21
25 Automatic	50	760	705	660	65	55	50	2.0	8.7	2"	$17
7.5mm Swiss	107	1010	NA	NA	240	NA	NA	NA	NA	NA	NEW
7.62mm Tokarev	87	1390	NA	NA	365	NA	NA	0.6	NA	4.5"	NA
7.62mm Nagant	97	1080	NA	NA	350	NA	NA	NA	NA	NA	NEW
7.63mm Mauser	88	1440	NA	NA	405	NA	NA	NA	NA	NA	NEW
30 Luger	93†	1220	1110	1040	305	255	225	0.9	3.5	4.5"	$34
30 Carbine	110	1790	1600	1430	785	625	500	0.4	1.7	10"	$28
32 S&W	88	680	645	610	90	80	75	2.5	10.5	3"	$17
32 S&W Long	98	705	670	635	115	100	90	2.3	10.5	4"	$17
32 Short Colt	80	745	665	590	100	80	60	2.2	9.9	4"	$19
32 Long Colt	82	755	715	675	100	95	85	2.0	8.7	4"	Disc.
32 H&R Magnum	85	1100	1020	930	230	195	165	1.0	4.3	4.5"	$21
32 H&R Magnum	95	1030	940	900	225	190	170	1.1	4.7	4.5"	$19
32 Automatic	60	970	895	835	125	105	95	1.3	5.4	4"	$22
32 Automatic	71	905	855	810	130	115	95	1.4	5.8	4"	$19
8mm Lebel Pistol	111	850	NA	NA	180	NA	NA	NA	NA	NA	NEW
8mm Steyr	113	1080	NA	NA	290	NA	NA	NA	NA	NA	NEW
8mm Gasser	126	850	NA	NA	200	NA	NA	NA	NA	NA	NEW
380 Automatic	85/88	990	920	870	190	165	145	1.2	5.1	4"	$20
380 Automatic	90	1000	890	800	200	160	130	1.2	5.5	3.75"	$10
380 Automatic	95/100	955	865	785	190	160	130	1.4	5.9	4"	$20
38 Automatic	130	1040	980	925	310	275	245	1.0	4.7	4.5"	Disc.
38 Super Auto +P	115	1300	1145	1040	430	335	275	0.7	3.3	5"	$26
38 Super Auto +P	125/130	1215	1100	1015	425	350	300	0.8	3.6	5"	$26
9x18mm Makarov	95	1000	NA	NA	NA	NA	NA	NA	NA	NA	NEW
9x18mm Ultra	100	1050	NA	NA	240	NA	NA	NA	NA	NA	NEW
9mm Steyr	115	1180	NA	NA	350	NA	NA	NA	NA	NA	NEW
9mm Luger	88	1500	1190	1010	440	275	200	0.6	3.1	4"	$24
9mm Luger	90	1360	1112	978	370	247	191	NA	NA	4"	$26
9mm Luger	95	1300	1140	1010	350	275	215	0.8	3.4	4"	NA
9mm Luger	115	1155	1045	970	340	280	240	0.9	3.9	4"	$21
9mm Luger	123/125	1110	1030	970	340	290	260	1.0	4.0	4"	$23
9mm Luger	140	935	890	850	270	245	225	1.3	5.5	4"	$23
9mm Luger	147	990	940	900	320	290	265	1.1	4.9	4"	$26
9mm Luger +P	115	1250	1113	1019	399	316	265	0.8	3.5	4"	$27
9mm Federal	115	1280	1130	1040	420	330	280	0.7	3.3	4"V	$24
38 S&W	146	685	650	620	150	135	125	2.4	10.0	4"	$19
38 Short Colt	125	730	685	645	150	130	115	2.2	9.4	6"	$19
38 Special	110	945	895	850	220	195	175	1.3	5.4	4"V	$23
38 Special	130	775	745	710	175	160	120	1.9	7.9	4"V	$22
38 (Multi-Ball)	140	830	730	505	215	130	80	2.0	10.6	4"V	$10**
38 Special	148	710	635	565	165	130	105	2.4	10.6	4"V	$17
38 Special	158	755	725	690	200	185	170	2.0	8.3	4"V	$18
38 Special	200	635	615	595	180	170	155	2.8	11.5	4"V	Disc.
38 Special +P	95	1175	1045	960	290	230	195	0.9	3.9	4"V	$23
38 Special +P	110	995	925	870	240	210	185	1.2	5.1	4"V	$23
38 Special +P	125	945	900	860	250	225	205	1.3	5.4	4"V	$23
38 Special +P	129	945	910	870	255	235	215	1.3	5.3	4"V	$11
38 Special +P	147/150(c)	884	NA	NA	264	NA	NA	NA	NA	4"V	$27
38 Special +P	158	890	855	825	280	255	240	1.4	6.0	4"V	$20
357 Magnum	110	1295	1095	975	410	290	230	0.8	3.5	4"V	$25
357 (Med. Vel.)	125	1220	1075	985	415	315	270	0.8	3.7	4"V	$25
357 Magnum	125	1450	1240	1090	585	425	330	0.6	2.8	4"V	$25
357 (Multi-Ball)	140	1155	830	665	420	215	135	1.2	6.4	4"V	$11**

Caliber	Bullet Wgt. Grs.	Velocity (fps) MV	Velocity 50 yds.	Velocity 100 yds.	Energy (ft. lbs.) ME	Energy 50 yds.	Energy 100 yds.	Mid-Range Traj. (in.) 50 yds.	Mid-Range Traj. 100 yds.	Bbl. Lgth. (in.)	Est. Price /box
357 Magnum	140	1360	1195	1075	575	445	360	0.7	3.0	4"V	$25
357 Magnum	145	1290	1155	1060	535	430	360	0.8	3.5	4"V	$26
357 Magnum	150/158	1235	1105	1015	535	430	360	0.8	3.5	4"V	$25
357 Magnum	180	1145	1055	985	525	445	390	0.9	3.9	4"V	$25
357 Rem. Maximum	158	1825	1590	1380	1170	885	670	0.4	1.7	10.5"	$14**
40 S&W	155	1140	1026	958	447	362	309	0.9	4.1	4"	$14***
40 S&W	165	1150	NA	NA	485	NA	NA	NA	NA	4"	$18***
40 S&W	180	985	936	893	388	350	319	1.4	5.0	4"	$14***
10mm Automatic	155	1125	1046	986	436	377	335	0.9	3.9	5"	$26
10mm Automatic	170	1340	1165	1145	680	510	415	0.7	3.2	5"	$31
10mm Automatic	175	1290	1140	1035	650	505	420	0.7	3.3	5.5"	$11**
10mm Auto.(FBI)	180	950	905	865	361	327	299	1.5	5.4	4"	$16**
10mm Automatic	180	1030	970	920	425	375	340	1.1	4.7	5"	$16**
10mm Auto H.V.	180†	1240	1124	1037	618	504	430	0.8	3.4	5"	$27
10mm Automatic	200	1160	1070	1010	495	510	430	0.9	3.8	5"	$14**
10.4mm Italian	177	950	NA	NA	360	NA	NA	NA	NA	NA	NEW
41 Action Exp.	180	1000	947	903	400	359	326	0.5	4.2	5"	$13**
41 Rem. Magnum	170	1420	1165	1015	760	515	390	0.7	3.2	4"V	$33
41 Rem. Magnum	175	1250	1120	1030	605	490	410	0.8	3.4	4"V	$14**
41 (Med. Vel.)	210	965	900	840	435	375	330	1.3	5.4	4"V	$30
41 Rem. Magnum	210	1300	1160	1060	790	630	535	0.7	3.2	4"V	$33
44 S&W Russian	247	780	NA	NA	335	NA	NA	NA	NA	NA	NA
44 S&W Special	180	980	NA	NA	383	NA	NA	NA	NA	6.5"	NA
44 S&W Special	200†	875	825	780	340	302	270	1.2	6.0	6"	$13**
44 S&W Special	200	1035	940	865	475	390	335	1.1	4.9	6.5"	$13**
44 S&W Special	240/246	755	725	695	310	285	265	2.0	8.3	6.5"	$26
44 Rem. Magnum	180	1610	1365	1175	1035	745	550	0.5	2.3	4"V	$18***
44 Rem. Magnum	200	1400	1192	1053	870	630	492	0.6	NA	6.5"	$20
44 Rem. Magnum	210	1495	1310	1165	1040	805	635	0.6	2.5	6.5"	$18***
44 (Med. Vel.)	240	1000	945	900	535	475	435	1.1	4.8	6.5"	$17
44 R.M.(Jacketed)	240	1180	1080	1010	740	625	545	0.9	3.7	4"V	$18***
44 R.M. (Lead)	240	1350	1185	1070	970	750	610	0.7	3.1	4"V	$29
44 Rem. Magnum	250	1180	1100	1040	775	670	600	0.8	3.6	6.5"V	$21
44 Rem. Magnum	300	1200	1100	1026	959	806	702	NA	NA	7.5"	$17
450 Short Colt	226	830	NA	NA	350	NA	NA	NA	NA	NA	NEW
45 Automatic	185	1000	940	890	410	360	325	1.1	4.9	5"	$28
45 Auto. (Match)	185	770	705	650	245	204	175	2.0	8.7	5"	$28
45 Auto. (Match)	200	940	890	840	392	352	312	2.0	8.6	5"	$20
45 Automatic	200	975	917	860	421	372	328	1.4	5.0	5"	$18
45 Automatic	230	830	800	675	355	325	300	1.6	6.8	5"	$27
45 Automatic	Shot	This data not available									
45 Automatic +P	185	1140	1040	970	535	445	385	0.9	4.0	5"	$31
45 Win. Magnum	230	1400	1230	1105	1000	775	635	0.6	2.8	5"	$14**
45 Win. Magnum	260	Ballistics not yet announced by manufacturer								NA	$16**
45 Auto. Rim	230	810	775	730	335	305	270	1.8	7.4	5.5"	Disc.
455 Webley MKII	262	850	NA	NA	420	NA	NA	NA	NA	NA	NA
45 Colt	200	1000	938	889	444	391	351	1.3	4.8	5.5"	$21
45 Colt	225	960	890	830	460	395	345	1.3	5.5	5.5"	$22
45 Colt	250/255	860	820	780	410	375	340	1.6	6.6	5.5"	$27
50 Action Exp.	325	1400	1209	1075	1414	1055	835	0.2	2.3	6"	$24**

Notes: Blanks are available in 32 S&W, 38 S&W, and 38 Special. V after barrel length indicates test barrel was vented to produce ballistics similar to a revolver with a normal barrel-to-cylinder gap. Ammo prices are per 50 rounds except when marked with an ** which signifies a 20 round box; *** signifies a 25-round box. Not all loads are available from all ammo manufacturers. Listed loads are those made by Remington, Winchester, Federal, and others. DISC. is a discontinued load. Prices are rounded to nearest whole dollar and will vary with brand and retail outlet. †= new bullet weight this year; "c" indicates a change in data.

RIMFIRE AMMUNITION—BALLISTICS AND PRICES

Cartridge type	Bullet Wt. Grs.	Velocity (fps) 22½" Barrel Muzzle	Velocity 22½" 50 Yds.	Velocity 22½" 100 Yds.	Energy (ft. lbs.) 22½" Barrel Muzzle	Energy 22½" 50 Yds.	Energy 22½" 100 Yds.	Velocity (fps) 6" Barrel Muzzle	Velocity 6" 50 Yds.	Energy (ft. lbs) 6" Barrel Muzzle	Energy 6" 50 Yds.	Approx. Price Per Box 50 Rds.	100 Rds.
22 Short Blank		Not applicable										$4	NA
22 CB Short	30	725	667	610	34	29	24	706	—	32	—	$2	NA
22 Short Match	29	830	752	695	44	36	31	786	—	39	—	—	NA
22 Short Std. Vel.	29	1045	—	810	70	—	42	865	—	48	—	Discontinued	
22 Short High Vel.	29	1095	—	903	77	—	53	—	—	—	—	$2	NA
22 Short H.V. H.P.	27	1120	—	904	75	—	49	—	—	—	—	—	NA
22 CB Long	30	725	667	610	34	29	24	706	—	32	—	$2	NA
22 Long Std. Vel.	29	1180	1038	946	90	69	58	1031	—	68	—	—	—
22 Long High Vel.	29	1240	—	962	99	—	60	—	—	—	—	$2	NA
22 L.R. Sub Sonic	38/40	1070	970	890	100	80	70	940	—	—	—	$2	NA
22 L.R. Std. Vel.	40	1138	1047	975	116	97	84	1027	925	93	76	$2	NA
22 L.R. High Vel.	40	1255	1110	1017	140	109	92	1060	—	100	—	$2	NA
22 L.R. H.V. Sil.	42	1220	—	1003	139	—	94	1025	—	98	—	$2	NA
22 L.R. H.V. H.P.	36/38	1280	1126	1010	131	101	82	1089	—	95	—	$2	NA
22 L.R. Shot	#11 or #12	1047	—	—	—	—	—	950	—	—	—	$5	NA
22 L.R. Hyper Vel	36	1410	1187	1056	159	113	89	—	—	—	—	$2	NA
22 L.R. Hyper H.P	32/33/34	1500	1240	1075	165	110	85	—	—	—	—	$2	NA
22 WRF	45	1320	—	1055	175	—	111	—	—	—	—	NA	$5
22 Win. Mag.	30	2200	1750	1373	322	203	127	1610	—	—	—	—	NA
22 Win. Mag.	40	1910	1490	1326	324	197	156	1428	—	181	—	$6	NA
22 Win. Mag.	50	1650	—	1280	300	180	—	—	—	—	—	NA	NA
22 Win. Mag. Shot	#11	1126	—	—	—	—	—	—	—	—	—	NA	NA

Note: The actual ballistics obtained with your firearm can vary considerably from the advertised ballistics. Also ballistics can vary from lot to lot with the same brand and type load. Prices can vary with manufacturer and retail outlet. NA in the price column indicates this size packaging currently unavailable.

HANDGUNS 95

CATALOG

GUNDEX

Includes models suitable for several forms of competition and other sporting purposes.

Accu-Tek AT-9

Accu-Tek AT-380SS

Accu-Tek HC-380SS

American Arms CX-22

American Arms PK22

ACCU-TEK MODEL AT-9 AUTO PISTOL **Caliber:** 9mm Para., 7-shot magazine. **Barrel:** 3.2". **Weight:** 28 oz. **Length:** 6.25" overall. **Stocks:** Black checkered nylon. **Sights:** Blade front, rear adjustable for windage; three-dot system. **Features:** Stainless steel construction. Double action only. Firing pin block with no external safeties. Lifetime warranty. Introduced 1992. Made in U.S. by Accu-Tek.
Price: Satin stainless $270.00
Price: Black finish over stainless $275.00

Accu-Tek AT-40 Auto Pistol Same as the Model AT-9 except chambered for 40 S&W. Introduced 1992.
Price: Stainless $270.00
Price: Black finish over stainless (AT-40B) $275.00

ACCU-TEK MODEL AT-380SS AUTO PISTOL **Caliber:** 380 ACP, 5-shot magazine. **Barrel:** 2.75". **Weight:** 20 oz. **Length:** 5.6" overall. **Stocks:** Grooved black composition. **Sights:** Blade front, rear adjustable for windage. **Features:** Stainless steel frame and slide. External hammer; manual thumb safety; firing pin block, trigger disconnect. Lifetime warranty. Introduced 1992. Made in U.S. by Accu-Tek.
Price: Satin stainless $182.00
Price: Black finish over stainless (AT-380SSB) $187.00

Accu-Tek Model AT-32SS Auto Pistol Same as the AT-380SS except chambered for 32 ACP. Introduced 1990.
Price: Satin stainless $176.00
Price: Black finish over stainless (AT-32SSB) $181.00

Accu-Tek Model AT-25SS Auto Pistol Similar to the AT-380SS except chambered for 25 ACP with 7-shot magazine. Also available with aluminum frame and slide with 11-oz. weight. Introduced 1991.
Price: Satin stainless $158.00
Price: Black finish over stainless (AT-25SSB) $163.00

> Consult our Directory pages for the location of firms mentioned.

ACCU-TEK MODEL HC-380SS AUTO PISTOL **Caliber:** 380 ACP, 13-shot magazine. **Barrel:** 2.75". **Weight:** 28 oz. **Length:** 6" overall. **Stocks:** Checkered black composition. **Sights:** Blade front, rear adjustable for windage. **Features:** External hammer; manual thumb safety with firing pin and trigger disconnect; bottom magazine release. Stainless finish. Introduced 1993. Made in U.S. by Accu-Tek.
Price: $230.00

AMERICAN ARMS MODEL CX-22 DA AUTO PISTOL **Caliber:** 22 LR, 8-shot magazine. **Barrel:** 3⅓". **Weight:** 22 oz. **Length:** 6⅓" overall. **Stocks:** Checkered black polymer. **Sights:** Blade front, rear adjustable for windage. **Features:** Double action with manual hammer-block safety, firing pin safety. Alloy frame. Has external appearance of Walther PPK. Blue/black finish. Introduced 1990. Made in U.S. by American Arms, Inc.
Price: $209.00

AMERICAN ARMS MODEL PK22 DA AUTO PISTOL **Caliber:** 22 LR, 8-shot magazine. **Barrel:** 3.3". **Weight:** 22 oz. **Length:** 6.3" overall. **Stocks:** Checkered plastic. **Sights:** Fixed. **Features:** Double action. Polished blue finish. Slide-mounted safety. Made in the U.S. by American Arms, Inc.
Price: $209.00

CAUTION: PRICES SHOWN ARE SUPPLIED BY THE MANUFACTURER OR IMPORTER. CHECK YOUR LOCAL GUNSHOP.

7th ANNUAL EDITION **211**

AMERICAN ARMS MODEL PX-22 AUTO PISTOL   Caliber: 22 LR, 7-shot magazine. **Barrel:** 2.85". **Weight:** 15 oz. **Length:** 5.39" overall. **Stocks:** Black checkered plastic. **Sights:** Fixed. **Features:** Double action; 7-shot magazine. Polished blue finish. Introduced 1989. Made in U.S. From American Arms, Inc.
Price: **$198.00**

AMERICAN ARMS MODEL P-98 AUTO PISTOL   Caliber: 22 LR, 8-shot magazine. **Barrel:** 5". **Weight:** 25 oz. **Length:** 8⅛" overall. **Stocks:** Grooved black polymer. **Sights:** Blade front, rear adjustable for windage. **Features:** Double action with hammer-block safety, magazine disconnect safety. Alloy frame. Has external appearance of the Walther P-38 pistol. Introduced 1989. Made in U.S. by American Arms, Inc.
Price: **$219.00**

AMT AUTOMAG II AUTO PISTOL   Caliber: 22 WMR, 9-shot magazine (7-shot with 3⅜" barrel). **Barrel:** 3⅜", 4½", 6". **Weight:** About 23 oz. **Length:** 9⅜" overall. **Stocks:** Grooved carbon fiber. **Sights:** Blade front, adjustable rear. **Features:** Made of stainless steel. Gas-assisted action. Exposed hammer. Slide flats have brushed finish, rest is sandblast. Squared trigger guard. Introduced 1986. From AMT.
Price: **$385.95**

AMT AUTOMAG III PISTOL   Caliber: 30 Carbine, 9mm Win. Mag., 8-shot magazine. **Barrel:** 6⅜". **Weight:** 43 oz. **Length:** 10½" overall. **Stocks:** Carbon fiber. **Sights:** Blade front, adjustable rear. **Features:** Stainless steel construction. Hammer-drop safety. Slide flats have brushed finish, rest is sandblasted. Introduced 1989. From AMT.
Price: **$459.99**

AMT AUTOMAG IV PISTOL   Caliber: 10mm Magnum, 45 Winchester Magnum, 6-shot magazine. **Barrel:** 6.5" (45), 8⅝" (10mm only). **Weight:** 46 oz. **Length:** 10.5" overall with 6.5" barrel. **Stocks:** Carbon fiber. **Sights:** Blade front, adjustable rear. **Features:** Made of stainless steel with brushed finish. Introduced 1990. Made in U.S. by AMT.
Price: **$679.99**
Price: Automag V (50 A.E.) **$899.00**

AMT BACKUP II AUTO PISTOL   Caliber: 380 ACP, 5-shot magazine. **Barrel:** 2½". **Weight:** 18 oz. **Length:** 5" overall. **Stocks:** Carbon fiber. **Sights:** Fixed, open, recessed. **Features:** Concealed hammer, blowback operation; manual and grip safeties. All stainless steel construction. Smallest domestically-produced pistol in 380. From AMT.
Price: **$295.99**

AMT Backup II Double Action Only Pistol   Similar to the standard Backup except has double-action-only mechanism, enlarged trigger guard, slide is rounded ar rear. Has 6-shot magazine. Introduced 1992. From AMT.
Price: **$309.99**

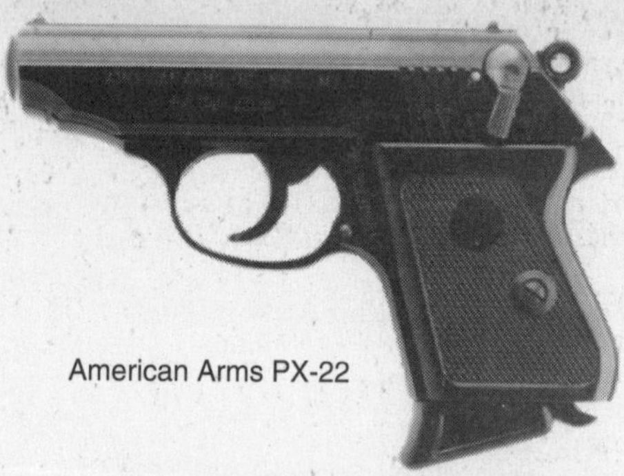

American Arms PX-22

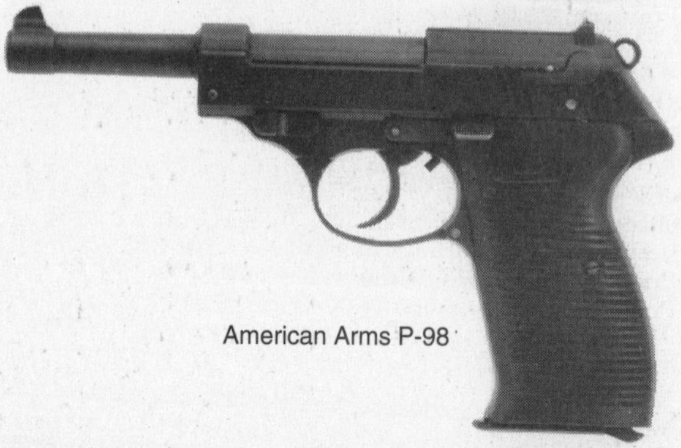

American Arms P-98

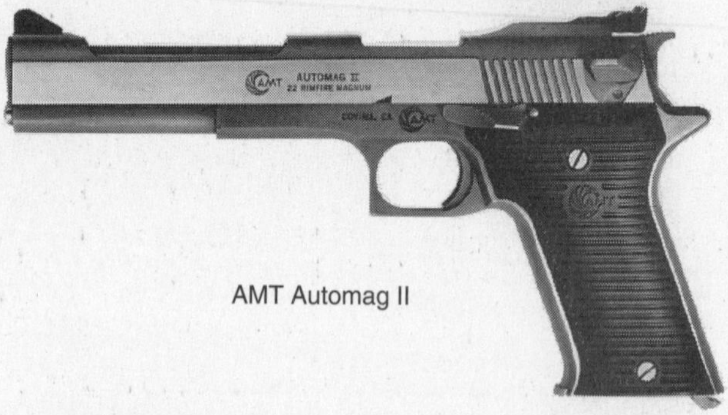

AMT Automag II

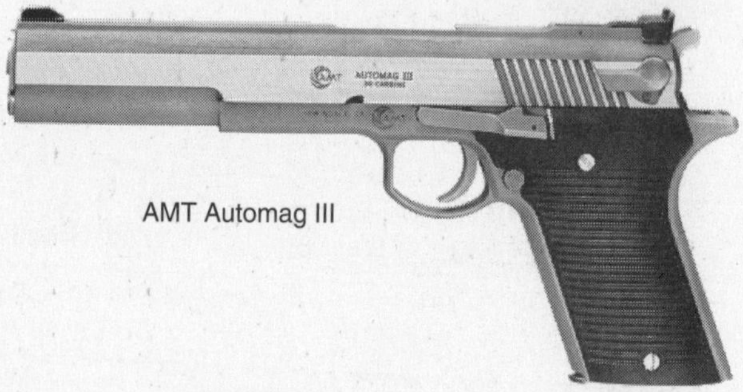

AMT Automag III

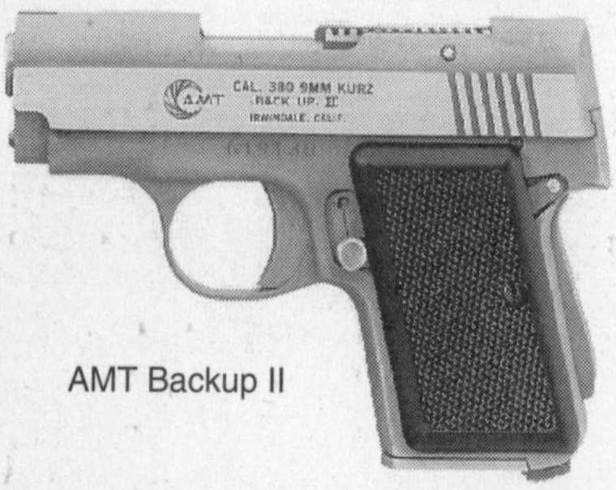

AMT Backup II

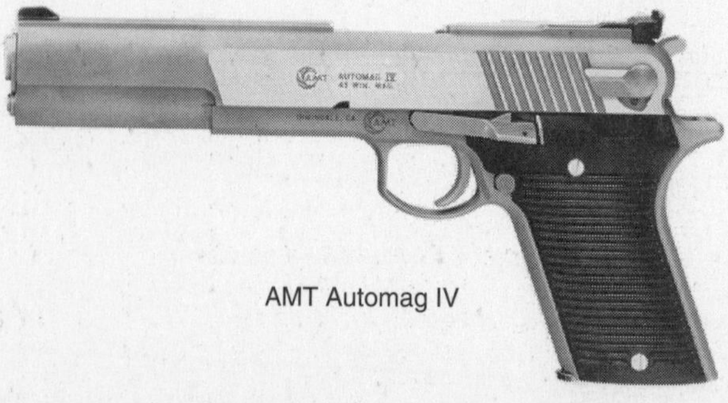

AMT Automag IV

AMT 45 ACP HARDBALLER Caliber: 45 ACP. **Barrel:** 5".
Weight: 39 oz. **Length:** 8½" overall. **Stocks:** Wrap-around rubber.
Sights: Adjustable. **Features:** Extended combat safety, serrated matte
slide rib, loaded chamber indicator, long grip safety, beveled magazine
well, adjustable target trigger. All stainless steel. From AMT.
Price: **$529.99**
Price: Government model (as above except no rib, fixed sights) **$475.95**

AMT 45 ACP HARDBALLER LONG SLIDE Caliber: 45 ACP. **Barrel:** 7". **Length:** 10½" overall. **Stocks:** Wrap-around rubber. **Sights:**
Fully adjustable rear sight. **Features:** Slide and barrel are 2" longer than
the standard 45, giving less recoil, added velocity, longer sight radius. Has
extended combat safety, serrated matte rib, loaded chamber indicator, wide
adjustable trigger. From AMT.
Price: **$575.95**

AMT Hardballer Long Slide

AMT ON DUTY DA PISTOL Caliber: 9mm Para., 15-shot; 40 S&W,
11-shot; 45 ACP, 9-shot magazine. **Barrel:** 4½". **Weight:** 32 oz.
Length: 7¾" overall. **Stocks:** Smooth carbon fiber. **Sights:** Blade
front, rear adjustable for windage; three-dot system. **Features:** Choice
of DA with decocker or double action only. Inertia firing pin, trigger
disconnector safety. Aluminum frame with steel recoil shoulder, stainless
steel slide and barrel. Introduced 1991. Made in the U.S. by AMT.
Price: 9mm, 40 S&W **$469.99**
Price: 45 ACP **$529.99**

AMT On Duty

ARGENTINE HI-POWER 9MM AUTO PISTOL Caliber: 9mm Para.,
13-shot magazine. **Barrel:** 4²¹⁄₃₂". **Weight:** 32 oz. **Length:** 7¾"
overall. **Stocks:** Checkered walnut. **Sights:** Blade front, adjustable
rear. **Features:** Produced in Argentina under F.N. Browning license.
Introduced 1990. Imported by Century International Arms, Inc.
Price: About **$299.95**

Argentine Hi-Power Detective Model Similar to the standard model
except has 3.8" barrel, 6.9" overall length and weighs 33 oz. Grips are
finger-groove, checkered soft rubber. Matte black finish. Introduced 1994.
Imported by Century International Arms, Inc.
Price: About **$310.00**

Argentine Hi-Power

ASTRA A-70 AUTO PISTOL Caliber: 9mm Para., 8-shot; 40 S&W,
7-shot magazine. **Barrel:** 3.5". **Weight:** 29.3 oz. **Length:** 6.5" overall.
Stocks: Checkered black plastic. **Sights:** Blade front, rear adjustable for
windage. **Features:** All steel frame and slide. Checkered grip straps and
trigger guard. Nickel or blue finish. Introduced 1992. Imported from Spain
by European American Armory.
Price: Blue, 9mm Para. **$350.00**
Price: Blue, 40 S&W **$350.00**
Price: Nickel, 9mm Para. **$375.00**
Price: Nickel, 40 S&W **$375.00**
Price: Stainless steel, 9mm **$425.00**
Price: Stainless steel, 40 S&W **$425.00**

Astra A-75

Astra A-75 Decocker Auto Pistol Same as the A-70 except has decocker
system, different trigger, contoured pebble-grain grips. Introduced 1993.
Imported from Spain by European American Armory.
Price: Blue, 9mm or 40 S&W **$395.00**
Price: Nickel, 9mm or 40 S&W **$425.00**
Price: Blue, 45 ACP **$425.00**
Price: Nickel, 45 ACP **$455.00**
Price: Stainless steel, 9mm, 40 S&W **$475.00**
Price: Stainless steel, 45 ACP **$505.00**
Price: Airweight (23.5 oz.), 9mm, blue **$425.00**

ASTRA A-100 AUTO PISTOL Caliber: 9mm Para., 17-shot; 40 S&W,
13-shot; 45 ACP, 9-shot magazine. **Barrel:** 3.9". **Weight:** 29 oz.
Length: 7.1" overall. **Stocks:** Checkered black plastic. **Sights:** Blade
front, interchangeable rear blades for elevation, screw adjustable for
windage. **Features:** Selective double action. Decocking lever permits
lowering hammer onto locked firing pin. Automatic firing pin block. Side
button magazine release. Introduced 1993. Imported from Spain by European American Armory.
Price: Blue, 9mm, 40 S&W, 45 ACP **$425.00**
Price: As above, nickel **$450.00**

Astra A-100

AUTO-ORDNANCE 1911A1 AUTOMATIC PISTOL   Caliber: 9mm Para., 38 Super, 9-shot; 10mm, 45 ACP, 7-shot magazine.   **Barrel:** 5".   **Weight:** 39 oz.   **Length:** 8½" overall.   **Stocks:** Checkered plastic with medallion.   **Sights:** Blade front, rear adjustable for windage.   **Features:** Same specs as 1911A1 military guns—parts interchangeable. Frame and slide blued; each radius has non-glare finish. Made in U.S. by Auto-Ordnance Corp.
Price: 45 cal. **$388.95**
Price: 9mm, 38 Super **$415.00**
Price: 10mm (has three-dot combat sights, rubber wrap-around grips) **$420.95**
Price: 45 ACP General Model (Commander style) **$427.95**
Price: Duo Tone (nickel frame, blue slide, three-dot sight system, textured black wrap-around grips) **$405.00**

Auto-Ordnance ZG-51 Pit Bull Auto   Same as the 1911A1 except has 3½" barrel, weighs 36 oz. and has an over-all length of 7¼". Available in 45 ACP only; 7-shot magazine. Introduced 1989.
Price: **$420.95**

Auto-Ordnance 1911A1 Competition Model   Similar to the standard Model 19911A1 except has barrel compensator. Commander hammer, flat mainspring housing, three-dot sight system, low-profile magazine funnel, Hi-Ride beavertail grip safety, full-length recoil spring guide system, black-textured rubber, wrap-around grips, and extended slide stop, safety and magazine catch. Introduced 1994. Made in U.S. by Auto-Ordnance Corp.
Price: **$615.00**

BABY EAGLE AUTO PISTOL   Caliber: 9mm Para., 40 S&W, 41 A.E.   **Barrel:** 4.37".   **Weight:** 35 oz.   **Length:** 8.14" overall.   **Stocks:** High-impact black polymer.   **Sights:** Combat.   **Features:** Double-action mechanism; polygonal rifling; ambidextrous safety. Model 9mm F has frame-mounted safety on left side of pistol; Model 9mm FS has frame-mounted safety and 3.62" barrel. Introduced 1992. Imported by Magnum Research.
Price: 9mm Para., 40 S&W, 41 A.E., black finish **$569.00**
Price: Conversion kit, 9mm Para. to 41 A.E. **$239.00**
Price: Matte or brushed chrome, add **$149.00**

BAIKAL IJ-70 AUTO PISTOL   Caliber: 9x18mm Makarov, 380 ACP, 8-shot magazine.   **Barrel:** 4".   **Weight:** 25 oz.   **Length:** 6.25" overall.   **Stocks:** Checkered composition.   **Sights:** Blade front, rear adjustable for windage and elevation.   **Features:** Double action; all-steel construction; frame-mounted safety with decocker. Comes with two magazines, cleaning rod, universal tool and leather holster. Introduced 1994. Imported from Russia by K.B.I., Inc.
Price: 9x18mm, blue **$199.00**
Price: 380 ACP, blue **$219.00**
Price: 380 ACP, nickel **$234.00**

Auto-Ordnance 1911A1

Baby Eagle

Baikal IJ-70

Beretta 85 Cheetah

> Consult our Directory pages for the location of firms mentioned.

BERETTA MODEL 80 CHEETAH SERIES DA PISTOLS   Caliber: 380 ACP, 13-shot magazine (M84); 8-shot (M85); 22 LR, 7-shot (M87), 22 LR, 8-shot (M89).   **Barrel:** 3.82".   **Weight:** About 23 oz. (M84/85); 20.8 oz. (M87).   **Length:** 6.8" overall.   **Stocks:** Glossy black plastic (wood optional at extra cost).   **Sights:** Fixed front, drift-adjustable rear.   **Features:** Double action, quick takedown, convenient magazine release. Introduced 1977. Imported from Italy by Beretta U.S.A.
Price: Model 84 Cheetah, plastic grips **$525.00**
Price: Model 84 Cheetah, wood grips **$555.00**
Price: Model 84 Cheetah, wood grips, nickel finish **$600.00**
Price: Model 85 Cheetah, plastic grips, 8-shot **$485.00**
Price: Model 85 Cheetah, wood grips, 8-shot **$510.00**
Price: Model 85 Cheetah, wood grips, nickel, 8-shot **$550.00**
Price: Model 87 Cheetah wood, 22 LR, 7-shot **$490.00**

Beretta 87 Cheetah

Beretta Model 86 Cheetah   Similar to the 380-caliber Model 85 except has tip-up barrel for first-round loading. Barrel length is 4.33", overall length of 7.33". Has 8-shot magazine, walnut or plastic grips. Introduced 1989.
Price: $510.00

BERETTA MODEL 92FS PISTOL   **Caliber:** 9mm Para., 15-shot magazine.   **Barrel:** 4.9".   **Weight:** 34 oz.   **Length:** 8.5" overall.   **Stocks:** Checkered black plastic; wood optional at extra cost.   **Sights:** Blade front, rear adjustable for windage. Tritium night sights available.   **Features:** Double action. Extractor acts as chamber loaded indicator, squared trigger guard, grooved front- and backstraps, inertia firing pin. Matte finish. Introduced 1977. Made in U.S. and imported from Italy by Beretta U.S.A.
Price: With plastic grips $625.00
Price: With wood grips $645.00
Price: Tritium night sights, add $85.00

Beretta 86 Cheetah

Beretta Models 92FS/96 Centurion Pistols   Identical to the Model 92FS and 96F except uses shorter slide and barrel (4.3"). Trijicon or three-dot sight systems. Plastic or wood grips. Available in 9mm or 40 S&W. Also available in D Models (double action only). Introduced 1992.
Price: Model 92FS Centurion, three-dot sights, plastic grips . . $625.00
Price: Model 92FS Centurion, wood grips $645.00
Price: Model 96 Centurion, three-dot sights, plastic grips . . . $640.00
Price: Model 92D Centurion $585.00
Price: Model 96D Centurion $605.00
Price: For Trijicon sights, add $65.00

Beretta 92D Centurion

Beretta Model 92F Stainless Pistol   Same as the Model 92FS except has stainless steel barrel and slide, and frame of aluminum-zirconium alloy. Has three-dot sight system. Introduced 1992.
Price: $755.00
Price: Model 92F-EL Stainless (gold trim, engraved barrel, slide, frame, gold-finished safety-levers, trigger, magazine release, grip screws) $1,240.00
Price: For Trijicon sights, add $65.00

Beretta Model 96F Auto Pistol   Same as the Model 92F except chambered for 40 S&W. Ambidextrous safety mechanism with passive firing pin catch, slide safety/decocking lever, trigger bar disconnect. Has 10-shot magazine. Available with Trijicon or three-dot sights. Introduced 1992.
Price: Model 96F, plastic grips $640.00
Price: Model 96D, double action only, three-dot sights $605.00
Price: For Trijicon sights, add . . . . $80.00 to $90.00

Beretta 92D

Beretta Model 92D Pistol   Same as the Model 92FS except double action only and has bobbed hammer, no external safety. Introduced 1992.
Price: With plastic grips, three-dot sights $585.00
Price: As above with Trijicon sights $680.00

BERETTA MODEL 950BS JETFIRE AUTO PISTOL   **Caliber:** 25 ACP, 8-shot.   **Barrel:** 2.5".   **Weight:** 9.9 oz.   **Length:** 4.5" overall.   **Stocks:** Checkered black plastic or walnut.   **Sights:** Fixed.   **Features:** Single action, thumb safety; tip-up barrel for direct loading/unloading, cleaning. From Beretta U.S.A.
Price: Jetfire wood, blue $180.00
Price: Jetfire wood, nickel $210.00
Price: Jetfire wood, engraved $260.00
Price: Jetfire plastic, matte blue $150.00

Beretta 92F Stainless

Beretta 950 BS Jetfire

Beretta 96D

CAUTION: PRICES SHOWN ARE SUPPLIED BY THE MANUFACTURER OR IMPORTER. CHECK YOUR LOCAL GUNSHOP.

7th ANNUAL EDITION   **215**

Beretta Model 21 Bobcat Pistol Similar to the Model 950 BS. Chambered for 22 LR or 25 ACP. Both double action. Has 2.5" barrel, 4.9" overall length; 7-round magazine on 22 cal.; available in nickel, matte, engraved or blue finish. Plastic or walnut grips. Introduced in 1985.
Price: Bobcat wood, 22-cal. $235.00
Price: Bobcat wood, nickel, 22-cal. $247.00
Price: Bobcat wood, 25-cal. $235.00
Price: Bobcat wood, nickel, 25-cal. $247.00
Price: Bobcat wood, engraved, 22 or 25 . . . . $285.00
Price: Bobcat plastic matte, 22 or 25 . . . . $185.00

Beretta 21 Bobcat

BERETTA MODEL 8000/8040 COUGAR PISTOL **Caliber:** 9mm Para., 15-shot, 40 S&W, 11-shot magazine. **Barrel:** 3.5". **Weight:** 33.5 oz. **Length:** NA. **Stocks:** Textured composition. **Sights:** Blade front, rear drift adjustable for windage. **Features:** Slide-mounted safety; exposed hammer. Matte black Bruniton finish. Announced 1994. Imported from Italy by Beretta U.S.A.
Price: . . . . **NA**

Beretta 8000

BERNARDELLI PO18 DA AUTO PISTOL **Caliber:** 9mm Para., 16-shot magazine. **Barrel:** 4.8". **Weight:** 34.2 oz. **Length:** 8.23" overall. **Stocks:** Checkered plastic; walnut optional. **Sights:** Blade front, rear adjustable for windage and elevation; low profile, three-dot system. **Features:** Manual thumb half-cock, magazine and auto-locking firing pin safeties. Thumb safety decocks hammer. Reversible magazine release. Imported from Italy by Armsport.
Price: Blue $505.00
Price: Chrome $568.00

Bernardelli PO18 Compact DA Auto Pistol Similar to the PO18 except has 4" barrel, 7.44" overall length, 14-shot magazine. Weighs 31.7 oz. Imported from Italy by Armsport.
Price: Blue $552.00
Price: Chrome $600.00

BERNARDELLI P. ONE DA AUTO PISTOL **Caliber:** 9mm Para., 16-shot, 40 S&W, 12-shot magazine. **Barrel:** 4.8". **Weight:** 34 oz. **Length:** 8.35" overall. **Stocks:** Checkered black plastic. **Sights:** Blade front, rear adjustable for windage and elevation; three dot system. **Features:** Forged steel frame and slide; full-length slide rails; reversible magazine release; thumb safety/decocker; squared trigger guard. Introduced 1994. Imported from Italy by Armsport.
Price: 9mm Para., blue/black $530.00
Price: 9mm Para., chrome $580.00
Price: 40 S&W, blue/black $530.00
Price: 40 S&W, chrome $580.00

Bernardelli P018

Bernardelli P. One Practical VB Pistol Similar to the P. One except chambered for 9x21mm, two- or four-port compensator, straight trigger, micro-adjustable rear sight. Introduced 1994. Imported from Italy by Armsport.
Price: Blue/black, two-port compensator $1,425.00
Price: As above, four-port compensator $1,475.00
Price: Chrome, two-port compensator $1,498.00
Price: As above, four-port compensator $1,540.00
Price: Customized VB, four-plus-two-port compensator . . . $2,150.00
Price: As above, chrome $2,200.00

Bernardelli USA

BERNARDELLI MODEL USA AUTO PISTOL **Caliber:** 22 LR, 10-shot, 380 ACP, 7-shot magazine. **Barrel:** 3.5". **Weight:** 26.5 oz. **Length:** 6.5" overall. **Stocks:** Checkered plastic with thumbrest. **Sights:** Ramp front, white outline rear adjustable for windage and elevation. **Features:** Hammer-block slide safety; loaded chamber indicator; dual recoil buffer springs; serrated trigger; inertia-type firing pin. Imported from Italy by Armsport.
Price: Blue, either caliber $387.00
Price: Chrome, either caliber $412.00
Price: Model AMR (6" barrel, target sights) $440.00

BERSA MODEL 23 AUTO PISTOL **Caliber:** 22 LR, 10-shot magazine. **Barrel:** 3.5". **Weight:** 24.5 oz. **Length:** 6.6" overall. **Stocks:** Walnut with stippled panels. **Sights:** Blade front, notch rear adjustable for windage; three-dot system. **Features:** Double action; firing pin and magazine safeties. Available in blue or nickel. Introduced 1989. Distributed by Eagle Imports, Inc.
Price: Blue $287.95
Price: Nickel $321.95

CAUTION: PRICES SHOWN ARE SUPPLIED BY THE MANUFACTURER OR IMPORTER. CHECK YOUR LOCAL GUNSHOP.

AUTOLOADERS, SERVICE & SPORT

BERSA MODEL 83, 85 AUTO PISTOLS **Caliber:** 380 ACP, 7-shot (M83), 13-shot magazine (M85). **Barrel:** 3.5". **Weight:** 25.75 oz. **Length:** 6.6" overall. **Stocks:** Walnut with stippled panels. **Sights:** Blade front, notch rear adjustable for windage; three-dot system. **Features:** Double action; firing pin and magazine safeties. Available in blue or nickel. Introduced 1989. Distributed by Eagle Imports, Inc.
Price: Model 85, blue **$339.95**
Price: Model 85, nickel **$386.95**
Price: Model 83 (as above, except 7-shot magazine), blue . . . **$287.95**
Price: Model 83, nickel **$321.95**

Bersa 85

Bersa 86

BERSA MODEL 86 AUTO PISTOL **Caliber:** 380 ACP, 13-shot magazine. **Barrel:** 3.5". **Weight:** 22 oz. **Length:** 6.6" overall. **Stocks:** Wraparound textured rubber. **Sights:** Blade front, rear adjustable for windage; three-dot system. **Features:** Double action; firing pin and magazine safeties; combat-style trigger guard. Matte blue or satin nickel. Introduced 1992. Distributed by Eagle Imports, Inc.
Price: Matte blue **$374.95**
Price: Satin nickel **$403.95**

BERSA THUNDER 9 AUTO PISTOL **Caliber:** 9mm Para., 15-shot magazine. **Barrel:** 4". **Weight:** 30 oz. **Length:** 7⅜" overall. **Stocks:** Checkered black polymer. **Sights:** Blade front, rear adjustable for windage and elevation; three-dot system. **Features:** Double action. Ambidextrous safety, decocking levers and slide release; internal automatic firing pin safety; reversible extended magazine release; adjustable trigger stop; alloy frame. Link-free locked breech design. Matte blue finish. Introduced 1993. Imported from Argentina by Eagle Imports, Inc.
Price: Blue only **$414.95**

Bersa Thunder 9

BROWNING BDA-380 DA AUTO PISTOL **Caliber:** 380 ACP, 13-shot magazine. **Barrel:** 3¹³⁄₁₆". **Weight:** 23 oz. **Length:** 6¾" overall. **Stocks:** Smooth walnut with inset Browning medallion. **Sights:** Blade front, rear drift-adjustable for windage. **Features:** Combination safety and de-cocking lever will automatically lower a cocked hammer to half-cock and can be operated by right- or left-hand shooters. Inertia firing pin. Introduced 1978. Imported from Italy by Browning.
Price: Blue **$592.95**
Price: Nickel **$624.95**

Browning BDA 380

BROWNING BDM DA AUTO PISTOL **Caliber:** 9mm Para., 15-shot magazine. **Barrel:** 4.73" **Weight:** 31 oz. **Length:** 7.85" overall. **Stocks:** Moulded black composition; checkered, with thumbrest on both sides. **Sights:** Low profile removable blade front, rear screw adjustable for windage. **Features:** Mode selector allows switching from DA pistol to "revolver" mode via a switch on the slide. Decocking lever/safety on the frame. Two redundant, passive, internal safety systems. All steel frame; matte black finish. Introduced 1991. Made in the U.S. From Browning.
Price: **$573.95**

Browning BDA 380 Nickel

Browning BDM

Browning Hi-Power Adjustable Sight

BROWNING HI-POWER 9mm AUTOMATIC PISTOL **Caliber:** 9mm Para., 13-shot magazine. **Barrel:** $4^{21}/_{32}$". **Weight:** 32 oz. **Length:** $7^3/_4$" overall. **Stocks:** Walnut, hand checkered, or black Polyamide. **Sights:** $^1/_8$" blade front; rear screw-adjustable for windage and elevation. Also available with fixed rear (drift-adjustable for windage). **Features:** External hammer with half-cock and thumb safeties. A blow on the hammer cannot discharge a cartridge; cannot be fired with magazine removed. Fixed rear sight model available. Ambidextrous safety available only with matte finish, moulded grips. Imported from Belgium by Browning.
Price: Fixed sight model, walnut grips **$537.95**
Price: 9mm with rear sight adj. for w. and e., walnut grips . . **$585.95**
Price: Mark III, standard matte black finish, fixed sight, moulded grips,
    ambidextrous safety **$506.95**
Price: Silver chrome, adjustable sight, Pachmayr grips **$596.95**

Browning Hi-Power Silver Chrome

Browning 40 S&W Hi-Power Pistol Similar to the standard Hi-Power except chambered for 40 S&W, 10-shot magazine, weighs 35 oz., and has $4^3/_4$" barrel. Comes with matte blue finish, low profile front sight blade, drift-adjustable rear sight, ambidextrous safety, moulded polyamide grips with thumb rest. Introduced 1993. Imported from Belgium by Browning.
Price: **$506.95**

Browning Capitan Hi-Power Pistol Similar to the standard Hi-Power except has adjustable tangent rear sight authentic to the early-production model. Also has Commander-style hammer. Checkered walnut grips, polished blue finish. Reintroduced 1993. Imported from Belgium by Browning.
Price: **$634.95**

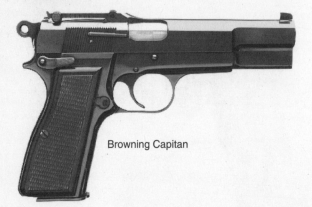

Browning Capitan

Browning Hi-Power HP-Practical Pistol Similar to the standard Hi-Power except has silver-chromed frame with blued slide, wrap-around Pachmayr rubber grips, round-style serrated hammer and removable front sight, fixed rear (drift-adjustable for windage). Introduced 1991.
Price: **$579.95**
Price: With fully adjustable rear sight **$627.95**

BROWNING BUCK MARK 22 PISTOL **Caliber:** 22 LR, 10-shot magazine. **Barrel:** $5^1/_2$". **Weight:** 32 oz. **Length:** $9^1/_2$" overall. **Stocks:** Black moulded composite with skip-line checkering. **Sights:** Ramp front, Browning Pro Target rear adjustable for windage and elevation. **Features:** All steel, matte blue finish or nickel, gold-colored trigger. Buck Mark Plus has laminated wood grips. Made in U.S. Introduced 1985. From Browning.
Price: Buck Mark, blue **$241.95**
Price: Buck Mark, nickel finish with contoured rubber stocks . **$282.95**
Price: Buck Mark Plus **$293.95**

Browning HP Practical

Browning Buck Mark Plus

CAUTION: PRICES SHOWN ARE SUPPLIED BY THE MANUFACTURER OR IMPORTER. CHECK YOUR LOCAL GUNSHOP.

AUTOLOADERS, SERVICE & SPORT

Browning Micro Buck Mark

Browning Micro Buck Mark Nickel

Browning Buck Mark Varmint

Bryco 48

Calico M-950

CALICO MODEL M-950 AUTO PISTOL   **Caliber:** 9mm Para., 50- or 100-shot magazine.   **Barrel:** 7.5".   **Weight:** 2.25 lbs. (empty). **Length:** 14" overall (50-shot magazine).   **Stocks:** Glass-filled polymer. **Sights:** Post front adjustable for windage and elevation, fixed notch rear. **Features:** Helical feed 50- or 100-shot magazine. Ambidextrous safety, static cocking handle. Retarded blowback action. Glass-filled polymer grip. Introduced 1989. From Calico.
Price: $518.80

Browning Micro Buck Mark   Same as the standard Buck Mark and Buck Mark Plus except has 4" barrel. Available in blue or nickel. Has 16-click Pro Target rear sight. Introduced 1992.
Price: Blue $241.95
Price: Nickel $282.95
Price: Micro Buck Mark Plus $293.95

Browning Buck Mark Varmint   Same as the Buck Mark except has $9\frac{7}{8}$" heavy barrel with .900" diameter and full-length scope base (no open sights); walnut grips with optional forend, or finger-groove walnut. Overall length is 14", weight is 48 oz. Introduced 1987.
Price: $365.95

BRYCO MODEL 38 AUTO PISTOLS   **Caliber:** 22 LR, 32 ACP, 380 ACP, 6-shot magazine.   **Barrel:** 2.8".   **Weight:** 15 oz.   **Length:** 5.3" overall.   **Stocks:** Polished resin-impregnated wood.   **Sights:** Fixed. **Features:** Safety locks sear and slide. Choice of satin nickel, bright chrome or black Teflon finishes. Introduced 1988. From Jennings Firearms.
Price: 22 LR, 32 ACP, about $109.95
Price: 380 ACP, about $129.95

BRYCO MODEL 48 AUTO PISTOLS   **Caliber:** 22 LR, 32 ACP, 380 ACP, 6-shot magazine.   **Barrel:** 4".   **Weight:** 19 oz.   **Length:** 6.7" overall.   **Stocks:** Polished resin-impregnated wood.   **Sights:** Fixed. **Features:** Safety locks sear and slide. Choice of satin nickel, bright chrome or black Teflon finishes. Announced 1988. From Jennings Firearms.
Price: 22 LR, 32 ACP, about $139.00
Price: 380 ACP, about $139.00

BRYCO MODEL 59 AUTO PISTOL   **Caliber:** 9mm Para., 13-shot magazine.   **Barrel:** 4".   **Weight:** 33 oz.   **Length:** 6.5" overall.   **Stocks:** Black composition.   **Sights:** Blade front, fixed rear.   **Features:** Striker-fired action; manual thumb safety; polished blue finish. Comes with two magazines. Introduced 1994. From Jennings Firearms.
Price: About $169.00
Price: Model 58 (5.5" overall length, 30 oz.) $169.00

CALICO MODEL 110 AUTO PISTOL   **Caliber:** 22 LR, 100-shot magazine.   **Barrel:** 6".   **Weight:** 3.7 lbs. (loaded).   **Length:** 17.9" overall.   **Stocks:** Moulded composition.   **Sights:** Adjustable post front, notch rear.   **Features:** Aluminum alloy frame; flash suppressor; pistol grip compartment; ambidextrous safety. Uses same helical-feed magazine as M-100 Carbine. Introduced 1986. Made in U.S. From Calico.
Price: $268.30

Calico Model 110

Bryco 38

CAUTION: PRICES SHOWN ARE SUPPLIED BY THE MANUFACTURER OR IMPORTER. CHECK YOUR LOCAL GUNSHOP.

7th ANNUAL EDITION **219**

CENTURY FEG P9R PISTOL   Caliber: 9mm Para., 15-shot magazine. **Barrel:** 4.6". **Weight:** 35 oz. **Length:** 8" overall. **Stocks:** Checkered walnut. **Sights:** Blade front, rear drift adjustable for windage. **Features:** Double action with hammer-drop safety. Polished blue finish. Comes with spare magazine. Imported from Hungary by Century International Arms.
Price: About **$263.00**
Price: Chrome finish, about **$375.00**

Century FEG P9RK Auto Pistol   Similar to the P9R except has 4.12" barrel, 7.5" overall length and weighs 33.6 oz. Checkered walnut grips, fixed sights, 15-shot magazine. Introduced 1994. Imported from Hungary by Century International Arms, Inc.
Price: About **$290.00**

COLT'S 22 AUTOMATIC PISTOL   Caliber: 22 LR, 11-shot magazine. **Barrel:** 4.5". **Weight:** 33 oz. **Length:** 8.62" overall. **Stocks:** Textured black polymer. **Sights:** Blade front, rear drift adjustable for windage. **Features:** Stainless steel construction; ventilated barrel rib; single action mechanism; cocked striker indicator; push-button safety. Introduced 1994. Made in U.S. by Colt.
Price: . . . . **NA**

Century FEG P9RK

Colt's 22 Automatic

Colt Combat Comm. STS

Colt Double Eagle

COLT COMBAT COMMANDER AUTO PISTOL   Caliber: 38 Super, 9-shot; 45 ACP, 8-shot. **Barrel:** 4¼". **Weight:** 36 oz. **Length:** 7¾" overall. **Stocks:** Rubber combat. **Sights:** Fixed, glare-proofed blade front, square notch rear; three-dot system. **Features:** Long trigger; arched housing; grip and thumb safeties.
Price: 45, blue **$707.00**
Price: 45, stainless **$759.00**
Price: 38 Super, stainless **$759.00**

Colt Lightweight Commander MK IV/Series 80   Same as Commander except high strength aluminum alloy frame, rubber combat grips, weight 27½ oz. 45 ACP only.
Price: Blue **$707.00**

COLT DOUBLE EAGLE MKII/SERIES 90 DA PISTOL   Caliber: 45 ACP, 8-shot magazine. **Barrel:** 4½", 5". **Weight:** 39 ozs. **Length:** 8½" overall. **Stocks:** Black checkered Xenoy thermoplastic. **Sights:** Blade front, rear adjustable for windage. High profile three-dot system. Colt Accro adjustable sight optional. **Features:** Made of stainless steel with matte finish. Checkered and curved extended trigger guard, wide steel trigger; decocking lever on left side; traditional magazine release; grooved frontstrap; bevelled magazine well; extended grip guard; rounded, serrated combat-style hammer. Announced 1989.
Price: **$697.00**
Price: Combat Comm., 45, 4½" bbl. **$697.00**

Colt Double Eagle Officer's ACP   Similar to the regular Double Eagle except 45 ACP only, 3½" barrel, 34 oz., 7¼" overall length. Has 5¼" sight radius. Also offered in Lightweight version weighing 25 oz. Introduced 1991.
Price: Standard or Lightweight **$697.00**

COLT GOVERNMENT MODEL 380   Caliber: 380 ACP, 7-shot magazine. **Barrel:** 3¼". **Weight:** 21¾ oz. **Length:** 6" overall. **Stocks:** Checkered composition. **Sights:** Ramp front, square notch rear, fixed. **Features:** Scaled-down version of the 1911A1 Colt G.M. Has thumb and internal firing pin safeties. Introduced 1983.
Price: Blue **$443.00**
Price: Nickel **$504.00**
Price: Stainless **$473.00**
Price: Pocketlite 380, blue **$443.00**

Colt Mustang Plus II   Similar to the 380 Government Model except has the shorter barrel and slide of the Mustang. Introduced 1988.
Price: Blue **$443.00**
Price: Stainless **$473.00**

Colt Goverment Model Pocketlite 380

CAUTION: PRICES SHOWN ARE SUPPLIED BY THE MANUFACTURER OR IMPORTER. CHECK YOUR LOCAL GUNSHOP.

AUTOLOADERS, SERVICE & SPORT

Colt Mustang 380, Mustang Pocketlite Similar to the standard 380 Government Model. Mustang has steel frame (18.5 oz.), Pocketlite has aluminum alloy (12.5 oz.). Both are ½" shorter than 380 G.M., have 2¾" barrel. Introduced 1987.
Price: Mustang 380, blue $443.00
Price: As above, nickel $504.00
Price: As above, stainless $473.00
Price: Mustang Pocketlite, blue $443.00
Price: Mustang Pocketlite STS/N $473.00

COLT GOVERNMENT MODEL MK IV/SERIES 80 **Caliber:** 38 Super, 9-shot; 45 ACP, 8-shot magazine. **Barrel:** 5". **Weight:** 38 oz. **Length:** 8½" overall. **Stocks:** Rubber combat. **Sights:** Ramp front, fixed square notch rear; three-dot system. **Features:** Grip and thumb safeties and internal firing pin safety, long trigger.
Price: 45 ACP, blue $707.00
Price: 45 ACP, stainless $759.00
Price: 45 ACP, bright stainless $829.00
Price: 38 Super, blue $707.00
Price: 38 Super, stainless $759.00
Price: 38 Super, bright stainless $829.00

Colt 10mm Delta Elite Similar to the Government Model except chambered for 10mm auto cartridge. Has three-dot high profile front and rear combat sights, rubber combat stocks with Delta medallion, internal firing pin safety, and new recoil spring/buffer system. Introduced 1987.
Price: Blue $774.00

Colt Combat Elite MK IV/Series 80 Similar to the Government Model except has stainless frame with ordnance steel slide and internal parts. High profile front, rear sights with three-dot system, extended grip safety, beveled magazine well, rubber combat stocks. Introduced 1986.
Price: 45 ACP, STS/B $860.00
Price: 38 Super, STS/B $860.00

COLT MODEL 1991 A1 AUTO PISTOL **Caliber:** 45 ACP, 7-shot magazine. **Barrel:** 5". **Weight:** 38 oz. **Length:** 8.5" overall. **Stocks:** Checkered black composition. **Sights:** Ramped blade front, fixed square notch rear, high profile. **Features:** Parkerized finish. Continuation of serial number range used on original G.I. 1911-A1 guns. Comes with one magazine and moulded carrying case. Introduced 1991.
Price: $517.00

Colt Model 1991 A1 Compact Auto Pistol Similar to the Model 1991 A1 except has 3½" barrel. Overall length is 7", and gun is ⅜" shorter in height. Comes with one 6-shot magazine, moulded case. Introduced 1993.
Price: $517.00

Colt Model 1991 A1 Commander Auto Pistol Similar to the Model 1991 A1 except has 4¼" barrel. Parkerized finish. 7-shot magazine. Comes in moulded case. Introduced 1993.
Price: $517.00

Colt Mustang Pocketlite

Colt Mustang 380

Colt Government Model

Colt Delta Elite

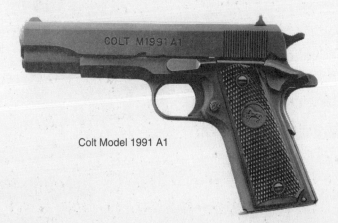

Colt Model 1991 A1

Colt Combat Elite

CAUTION: PRICES SHOWN ARE SUPPLIED BY THE MANUFACTURER OR IMPORTER. CHECK YOUR LOCAL GUNSHOP.

7th ANNUAL EDITION **221**

COLT OFFICER'S ACP MK IV/SERIES 80 **Caliber:** 45 ACP, 6-shot magazine. **Barrel:** 3½". **Weight:** 34 oz. (steel frame); 24 oz. (alloy frame). **Length:** 7¼" overall. **Stocks:** Rubber combat. **Sights:** Ramp blade front with white dot, square notch rear with two white dots. **Features:** Trigger safety lock (thumb safety), grip safety, firing pin safety; long trigger; flat mainspring housing. Also available with lightweight alloy frame and in stainless steel. Introduced 1985.
Price: Blue **$707.00**
Price: L.W., blue finish **$707.00**
Price: Stainless **$759.00**
Price: Bright stainless **$829.00**

Colt Officer's ACP

COONAN 357 MAGNUM PISTOL **Caliber:** 357 Mag., 7-shot magazine. **Barrel:** 5". **Weight:** 42 oz. **Length:** 8.3" overall. **Stocks:** Smooth walnut. **Sights:** Interchangeable ramp front, rear adjustable for windage. **Features:** Stainless and alloy steel construction. Unique barrel hood improves accuracy and reliability. Linkless barrel. Many parts interchange with Colt autos. Has grip, hammer, half-cock safeties, extended slide latch. Made in U.S. by Coonan Arms, Inc.
Price: 5" barrel **$720.00**
Price: 6" barrel **$755.00**
Price: With 6" compensated barrel **$1,400.00**

Coonan 357 Magnum

Coonan 357 Magnum
Compensated

Coonan Compact 357 Magnum Cadet Pistol Similar to the 357 Magnum full-size gun except has 3.9" barrel, shorter frame, 6-shot magazine. Weight is 39 oz., overall length 7.8". Linkless bull barrel, full-length recoil spring guide rod, extended slide latch. Introduced 1993. Made in U.S. by Coonan Arms, Inc.
Price: **$841.00**

CZ 75 AUTO PISTOL **Caliber:** 9mm Para., 40 S&W, 15-shot magazine. **Barrel:** 4.7". **Weight:** 34.3 oz. **Length:** 8.1" overall. **Stocks:** High impact checkered plastic. **Sights:** Square post front, rear adjustable for windage; three-dot system. **Features:** Single action/double action design; choice of black polymer, matte or high-polish blue finishes. All-steel frame. Imported from the Czech Republic by Magnum Research.
Price: 9mm, black polymer finish **$479.00**
Price: 40 S&W, SA/DA or DAO, black polymer finish **$519.00**
Price: 9mm, matte blue **$499.00**
Price: 40 S&W, SA/DA or DAO, matte blue **$539.00**
Price: High-polish blue **$519.00**
Price: 40 S&W, SA/DA or DAO, high-polish blue **$559.00**

Coonan Compact 357 Cadet

CZ 75 Compact Auto Pistol Similar to the CZ 75 except has 13-shot magazine, 3.9" barrel and weighs 32 oz. Has removable front sight, non-glare ribbed slide top. Trigger guard is squared and serrated; combat hammer. Introduced 1993. Imported from the Czech Republic by Magnum Research.
Price: Black polymer finish **$519.00**
Price: Matte blue **$539.00**
Price: High-polish blue **$559.00**

CZ 75 Semi-Compact Auto Pistol Uses the shorter slide and barrel of the CZ 75 Compact with the full-size frame of the standard CZ 75. Has 15-shot magazine; 9mm Para. only. Introduced 1994. Imported from the Czech Republic by Magnum Research.
Price: Black polymer finish **$519.00**
Price: Matte blue finish **$539.00**
Price: High-polish blue finish **$559.00**

CZ 75 Compact

CZ 75

CAUTION: PRICES SHOWN ARE SUPPLIED BY THE MANUFACTURER OR IMPORTER. CHECK YOUR LOCAL GUNSHOP.

CZ 83

CZ 85

CZ 85 Combat

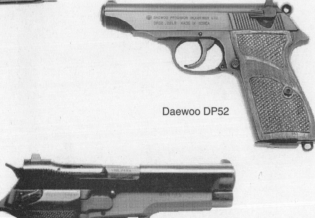

Daewoo DP52

Daewoo DH40

Daewoo DP51

CZ 83 DOUBLE-ACTION PISTOL Caliber: 32, 380 ACP, 12-shot magazine. **Barrel:** 3.8". **Weight:** 26.2 oz. **Length:** 6.8" overall. **Stocks:** High impact checkered plastic. **Sights:** Removable square post front, rear adjustable for windage; three-dot system. **Features:** Single action/double action; ambidextrous magazine release and safety. Blue finish; non-glare ribbed slide top. Imported from the Czech Republic by Magnum Research.
Price: **$389.00**

CZ 85 Auto Pistol Same gun as the CZ 75 except has ambidextrous slide release and safety-levers; non-glare, ribbed slide top; squared, serrated trigger guard; trigger stop to prevent overtravel. Introduced 1986. Imported from the Czech Republic by Magnum Research.
Price: Black polymer finish **$515.00**
Price: Matte blue **$537.00**
Price: High-polish blue **$559.00**

CZ 85 Combat Auto Pistol Same as the CZ 85 except has walnut grips, round combat hammer, fully adjustable rear sight, extended magazine release. Trigger parts coated with friction-free beryllium copper. Introduced 1992. Imported from the Czech Republic by Magnum Research.
Price: Black polymer finish **$619.00**
Price: Matte blue **$645.00**
Price: High-polish blue **$669.00**

DAEWOO DP51 FASTFIRE AUTO PISTOL Caliber: 9mm Para., 13-shot magazine. **Barrel:** 4.25". **Weight:** 28.2 oz. **Length:** 7" overall. **Stocks:** Checkered composition. **Sights:** $\frac{1}{8}$" blade front, square notch rear drift adjustable for windage. Three dot system. **Features:** Patented Fastfire mechanism. Ambidextrous manual safety and magazine catch, automatic firing pin block. No magazine safety. Alloy frame, squared trigger guard. Matte black finish. Introduced 1991. Imported from Korea by Nationwide Sports Dist.
Price: DP51 . . . . **$390.00**
Price: DH40 (40 S&W, 12-shot magazine) **$420.00**

DAEWOO DP52 AUTO PISTOL Caliber: 22 LR, 10-shot magazine. **Barrel:** 3.8". **Weight:** 23 oz. **Length:** 6.7" overall. **Stocks:** NA. **Sights:** $\frac{1}{8}$" blade front, rear drift adjustable for windage; three-dot system. **Features:** Polished blue finish. Comes with two magazines. Introduced 1994. Imported from Korea by Nationwide Sports Distributors.
Price: **$320.00**

DAEWOO DH45 HIGH CAPACITY PISTOL Caliber: 45 ACP, 13-shot magazine. **Barrel:** 5". **Weight:** 35 oz. **Length:** 8.1" overall. **Stocks:** NA. **Sights:** $\frac{1}{8}$" blade front, rear drift adjustable for windage; three-dot system. **Features:** Short-stroke double-action mechanism; hammerless striker design; ambidextrous external safety with internal firing pin lock. Announced 1994. Imported from Korea by Nationwide Sports Distributors.
Price: **$500.00**

DAVIS P-32 AUTO PISTOL **Caliber:** 32 ACP, 6-shot magazine. **Barrel:** 2.8". **Weight:** 22 oz. **Length:** 5.4" overall. **Stocks:** Laminated wood. **Sights:** Fixed. **Features:** Choice of black Teflon or chrome finish. Announced 1986. Made in U.S. by Davis Industries.
Price: **$87.50**

DAVIS P-380 AUTO PISTOL **Caliber:** 380 ACP, 5-shot magazine. **Barrel:** 2.8". **Weight:** 22 oz. **Length:** 5.4" overall. **Stocks:** Black composition. **Sights:** Fixed. **Features:** Choice of chrome or black Teflon finish. Introduced 1991. Made in U.S. by Davis Industries.
Price: **$98.00**

DESERT EAGLE MAGNUM PISTOL **Caliber:** 357 Mag., 9-shot; 41 Mag., 44 Mag., Mag.—8-shot; 50 Magnum, 7-shot. **Barrel:** 6", 10", 14" interchangeable. **Weight:** 357 Mag.—62 oz.; 41 Mag., 44 Mag.—69 oz.; 50 Mag.—72 oz. **Length:** 10¼" overall (6" bbl.). **Stocks:** Wraparound plastic. **Sights:** Blade on ramp front, combat-style rear. Adjustable available. **Features:** Rotating three-lug bolt; ambidextrous safety; combat-style trigger guard; adjustable trigger optional. Military epoxy finish. Satin, bright nickel, hard chrome, polished and blued finishes available. Imported from Israel by Magnum Research, Inc.
Price: 357, 6" bbl., standard pistol **$789.00**
Price: As above, stainless steel frame **$839.00**
Price: 41 Mag., 6", standard pistol **$799.00**
Price: 41 Mag., stainless steel frame **$849.00**
Price: 44 Mag., 6", standard pistol **$899.00**
Price: As above, stainless steel frame **$949.00**
Price: 50 Magnum, 6" bbl., standard pistol **$1,249.00**

DESERT INDUSTRIES DOUBLE DEUCE, TWO BIT SPECIAL PISTOLS **Caliber:** 22 LR, 6-shot; 25 ACP, 5-shot. **Barrel:** 2½". **Weight:** 15 oz. **Length:** 5½" overall. **Stocks:** Rosewood. **Sights:** Special order. **Features:** Double action; stainless steel construction with matte finish; ambidextrous slide-mounted safety. From Desert Industries, Inc.
Price: 22 . . . . **$399.95**
Price: 25 (Two-Bit Special) **$399.95**

DESERT INDUSTRIES WAR EAGLE PISTOL **Caliber:** 380 ACP, 8- or 13-shot; 9mm Para., 14-shot; 10mm, 13-shot; 40 S&W, 14-shot; 45 ACP, 12-shot. **Barrel:** 4". **Weight:** 35.5 oz. **Length:** 7.5" overall. **Stocks:** Rosewood. **Sights:** Fixed. **Features:** Double action; matte-finished stainless steel; slide mounted ambidextrous safety. Announced 1986. From Desert Industries, Inc.
Price: **$795.00**
Price: 380 ACP **$725.00**

E.A.A. WITNESS DA AUTO PISTOL **Caliber:** 9mm Para., 16-shot magazine; 10mm Auto, 10-shot magazine; 38 Super, 40 S&W, 12-shot magazine; 45 ACP, 10-shot magazine. **Barrel:** 4.50". **Weight:** 35.33 oz. **Length:** 8.10" overall. **Stocks:** Checkered rubber. **Sights:** Undercut blade front, open rear adjustable for windage. **Features:** Double-action trigger system; round trigger guard; frame-mounted safety. Introduced 1991. Imported from Italy by European American Armory.
Price: 9mm, blue **$399.00**
Price: 9mm, satin chrome **$425.00**
Price: 9mm, blue slide, chrome frame **$425.00**
Price: 9mm Compact, blue, 13-shot **$399.00**
Price: As above, blue slide, chrome frame, or all-chrome . . **$425.00**
Price: 40 S&W, blue **$425.00**
Price: As above, blue slide, chrome frame, or all-chrome . . **$450.00**
Price: 40 S&W Compact, 8-shot, blue **$425.00**
Price: As above, blue slide, chrome frame, or all-chrome . . **$450.00**
Price: 45 ACP, blue **$495.00**
Price: As above, blue slide, chrome frame, or all-chrome . . **$525.00**
Price: 45 ACP Compact, 8-shot, blue **$495.00**
Price: As above, blue slide, chrome frame or all-chrome . . . **$525.00**
Price: 9mm/40 S&W Combo, blue, compact or full size **$560.00**
Price: As above, blue/chrome, compact or full size **$585.00**
Price: 9mm or 40 S&W Carry Comp, blue **$550.00**
Price: As above, blue/chrome **$575.00**

Davis P-32

Davis P-380

Desert Eagle 6"

Desert Industries Double Deuce

E.A.A. Witness

CAUTION: PRICES SHOWN ARE SUPPLIED BY THE MANUFACTURER OR IMPORTER. CHECK YOUR LOCAL GUNSHOP.

E.A.A. EUROPEAN MODEL AUTO PISTOLS **Caliber:** 32 ACP or 380 ACP, 7-shot magazine. **Barrel:** 3.88". **Weight:** 26 oz. **Length:** 7⅜" overall. **Stocks:** European hardwood. **Sights:** Fixed blade front, rear drift-adjustable for windage. **Features:** Chrome or blue finish; magazine, thumb and firing pin safeties; external hammer; safety-lever takedown. Imported from Italy by European American Armory.
Price: Blue **$150.00**
Price: Blue/chrome **$165.00**
Price: Chrome **$165.00**
Price: Ladies Model **$225.00**

E.A.A. European 380/DA Pistol Similar to the standard European except in 380 ACP only, with double-action trigger mechanism. Available in blue, chrome or blue/chrome finish. Introduced 1992. From European American Armory.
Price: Blue **$185.00**
Price: Chrome **$199.00**
Price: Blue/chrome **$199.00**

> Consult our Directory pages for the location of firms mentioned.

ERMA KGP68 AUTO PISTOL **Caliber:** 32 ACP, 6-shot, 380 ACP, 5-shot. **Barrel:** 4". **Weight:** 22½ oz. **Length:** 7⅜" overall. **Stocks:** Checkered plastic. **Sights:** Fixed. **Features:** Toggle action similar to original "Luger" pistol. Action stays open after last shot. Has magazine and sear disconnect safety systems. Imported from Germany by Mandall Shooting Supplies.
Price: **$795.00**

FEG B9R AUTO PISTOL **Caliber:** 380 ACP, 15-shot magazine. **Barrel:** 4". **Weight:** 25 oz. **Length:** 7" overall. **Stocks:** Hand-checkered walnut. **Sights:** Blade front, drift-adjustable rear. **Features:** Hammer-drop safety; grooved backstrap; squared trigger guard. Comes with spare magazine. Introduced 1993. Imported from Hungary by Century International Arms.
Price: About **$312.00**

FEG FP9 AUTO PISTOL **Caliber:** 9mm Para., 14-shot magazine. **Barrel:** 5". **Weight:** 35 oz. **Length:** 7.8" overall. **Stocks:** Checkered walnut. **Sights:** Blade front, windage-adjustable rear. **Features:** Full-length ventilated rib. Polished blue finish. Comes with extra magazine. Introduced 1993. Imported from Hungary by Century International Arms.
Price: About **$269.00**

FEG GKK-45 DA AUTO PISTOL **Caliber:** 45 ACP, 8-shot magazine. **Barrel:** 4.6". **Weight:** 34 oz. **Length:** 8.06" overall. **Stocks:** Hand-checkered walnut. **Sights:** Blade front, rear adjustable for windage; three-dot system. **Features:** Combat-type trigger guard. Polished blue or hard chrome finish. Comes with two magazines, cleaning rod. Introduced 1994. Imported from Hungary by K.B.I., Inc.
Price: Blue **$449.00**
Price: Hard chrome **$499.00**

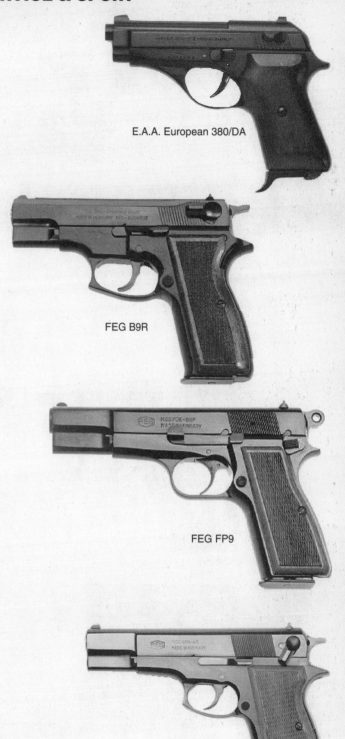

E.A.A. European 380/DA

FEG B9R

FEG FP9

FEG GKK 45

FEG PJK-9HP

FEG PJK-9HP AUTO PISTOL **Caliber:** 9mm Para., 13-shot magazine. **Barrel:** 4.75". **Weight:** 32 oz. **Length:** 8" overall. **Stocks:** Hand-checkered walnut. **Sights:** Blade front, rear adjustable for windage; three dot system. **Features:** Single action; polished blue or hard chrome finish; rounded combat-style serrated hammer. Comes with two magazines and cleaning rod. Imported from Hungary by K.B.I., Inc.
Price: Blue **$349.00**
Price: Hard chrome **$429.00**

CAUTION: PRICES SHOWN ARE SUPPLIED BY THE MANUFACTURER OR IMPORTER. CHECK YOUR LOCAL GUNSHOP.

7th ANNUAL EDITION **225**

AUTOLOADERS, SERVICE & SPORT

FEG SMC-22

Glock 17

Glock 19

Glock 22

Glock 21

Glock 20

FEG SMC-22 DA AUTO PISTOL **Caliber:** 22 LR, 8-shot magazine. **Barrel:** 3.5". **Weight:** 18.5 oz. **Length:** 6.12" overall. **Stocks:** Checkered composition with thumbrest. **Sights:** Blade front, rear adjustable for windage. **Features:** Patterned after the PPK pistol. Alloy frame, steel slide; blue finish. Comes with two magazines, cleaning rod. Introduced 1994. Imported from Hungary by K.B.I., Inc.
Price: **$299.00**

FEG SMC-380 AUTO PISTOL **Caliber:** 380 ACP, 6-shot magazine. **Barrel:** 3.5". **Weight:** 18.5 oz. **Length:** 6.1" overall. **Stocks:** Checkered composition with thumbrest. **Sights:** Blade front, rear adjustable for windage. **Features:** Patterned after the PPK pistol. Alloy frame, steel slide; double action. Blue finish. Comes with two magazines, cleaning rod. Imported from Hungary by K.B.I.
Price: **$279.00**

GLOCK 17 AUTO PISTOL **Caliber:** 9mm Para., 17-shot magazine. **Barrel:** 4.49". **Weight:** 21.9 oz. (without magazine). **Length:** 7.28" overall. **Stocks:** Black polymer. **Sights:** Dot on front blade, white outline rear adjustable for windage. **Features:** Polymer frame, steel slide; double-action trigger with "Safe Action" system; mechanical firing pin safety, drop safety; simple takedown without tools; locked breech, recoil operated action. Adopted by Austrian armed forces 1983. NATO approved 1984. Imported from Austria by Glock, Inc.
Price: With extra magazine, magazine loader, cleaning kit . . **$608.95**
Price: Model 17L (6" barrel) **$806.67**

Glock 19 Auto Pistol Similar to the Glock 17 except has a 4" barrel, giving an overall length of 6.85" and weight of 20.99 oz. Magazine capacity is 15 rounds. Fixed or adjustable rear sight. Introduced 1988.
Price: **$608.95**

Glock 20 10mm Auto Pistol Similar to the Glock Model 17 except chambered for 10mm Automatic cartridge. Barrel length is 4.60", overall length is 7.59", and weight is 26.3 oz. (without magazine). Magazine capacity is 15 rounds. Fixed or adjustable rear sight. Comes with an extra magazine, magazine loader, cleaning rod and brush. Introduced 1990. Imported from Austria by Glock, Inc.
Price: **$670.41**

Glock 21 Auto Pistol Similar to the Glock 17 except chambered for 45 ACP, 13-shot magazine. Overall length is 7.59", weight is 25.2 oz. (without magazine). Fixed or adjustable rear sight. Introduced 1991.
Price: **$670.41**

Glock 22 Auto Pistol Similar to the Glock 17 except chambered for 40 S&W, 15-shot magazine. Overall length is 7.28", weight is 22.3 oz. (without magazine). Fixed or adjustable rear sight. Introduced 1990.
Price: **$670.41**

Glock 23 Auto Pistol Similar to the Glock 19 except chambered for 40 S&W, 13-shot magazine. Overall length is 6.85", weight is 20.6 oz. (without magazine). Fixed or adjustable rear sight. Introduced 1990.
Price: **$608.95**

GRENDEL P-12 AUTO PISTOL **Caliber:** 380 ACP, 11-shot magazine. **Barrel:** 3". **Weight:** 13 oz. **Length:** 5.3" overall. **Stocks:** Checkered DuPont ST-800 polymer. **Sights:** Fixed. **Features:** Double action only with inertia safety hammer system. All steel frame; grip forms magazine well and trigger guard. Introduced 1992. Made in U.S. by Grendel, Inc.
Price: Blue **$175.00**
Price: Electroless nickel **$195.00**

GRENDEL P-30 AUTO PISTOL **Caliber:** 22 WMR, 30-shot magazine. **Barrel:** 5", 8". **Weight:** 21 oz. (5" barrel). **Length:** 8.5" overall (5" barrel). **Stocks:** Checkered Zytel. **Sights:** Blade front, fixed rear. **Features:** Blowback action with fluted chamber; ambidextrous safety, reversible magazine catch. Scope mount available. Introduced 1990.
Price: With 5" barrel **$225.00**
Price: With removable muzzlebrake (Model P-30M) **$235.00**
Price: With 8" barrel (Model P-30L) **$280.00**

HAMMERLI MODEL 212 AUTO PISTOL **Caliber:** 22 LR, 8-shot magazine. **Barrel:** 4.9". **Weight:** 31 oz. **Stocks:** Checkered walnut. **Sights:** Blade front, rear adjustable for windage only. **Features:** Polished blue finish. Imported from Switzerland by Mandall Shooting Supplies and Hammerli Pistols USA.
Price: About **$1,395.00**

HECKLER & KOCH P7M8 AUTO PISTOL **Caliber:** 9mm Para., 8-shot magazine. **Barrel:** 4.13". **Weight:** 29 oz. **Length:** 6.73" overall. **Stocks:** Stippled black plastic. **Sights:** Blade front, adjustable rear; three dot system. **Features:** Unique "squeeze cocker" in frontstrap cocks the action. Gas-retarded action. Squared combat-type trigger guard. Blue finish. Compact size. Imported from Germany by Heckler & Koch, Inc.
Price: P7M8, blued **$1,100.00**
Price: P7M13 (13-shot capacity, ambidextrous magazine release, forged steel frame), blued **$1,330.00**
Price: P7M13, nickel **$1,330.00**

Heckler & Koch P7M10 Auto Pistol Similar to the P7M8 except chambered for 40 S&W with 10-shot magazine. Weighs 43 oz., overall length is 6.9". Introduced 1992. Imported from Germany by Heckler & Koch, Inc.
Price: Blue **$1,315.00**
Price: Nickel **$1,315.00**

Glock 23

Grendel P-12

Grendel P-30

Hammerli Model 212

Heckler & Koch P7M10

Heckler & Koch P7M8

Heckler & Koch P7K3 Auto Pistol   Similar to the P7M8 and P7M13 except chambered for 22 LR or 380 ACP, 8-shot magazine. Uses an oil-filled buffer to decrease recoil. Introduced 1988.
Price: **$1,100.00**
Price: 22 LR conversion unit **$525.00**
Price: 32 ACP conversion unit **$228.00**

HECKLER & KOCH USP AUTO PISTOL   **Caliber:** 9mm Para., 15-shot magazine, 40 S&W, 13-shot magazine.   **Barrel:** 4.25".   **Weight:** 28 oz. (USP40).   **Length:** 6.9" overall.   **Stocks:** Non-slip stippled black polymer.   **Sights:** Blade front, rear adjustable for windage.   **Features:** New HK design with polymer frame, modified Browning action with recoil reduction system, single control lever. Special "hostile environment" finish on all metal parts. Available in SA/DA, DAO, left- and right-hand versions. Introduced 1993. Imported from Germany by Heckler & Koch, Inc.
Price: Right-hand **$635.00**
Price: Left-hand **$655.00**

HELWAN "BRIGADIER" AUTO PISTOL   **Caliber:** 9mm Para., 8-shot magazine.   **Barrel:** 4.5".   **Weight:** 32 oz.   **Length:** 8" overall.   **Stocks:** Grooved plastic.   **Sights:** Blade front, rear adjustable for windage.   **Features:** Polished blue finish. Single-action design. Cross-bolt safety. Imported by Interarms.
Price: **$260.00**

HERITAGE MODEL HA25 AUTO PISTOL   **Caliber:** 25 ACP, 6-shot magazine.   **Barrel:** 2½".   **Weight:** 12 oz.   **Length:** 4⅝" overall.   **Stocks:** Smooth or checkered walnut.   **Sights:** Fixed.   **Features:** Exposed hammer, manual safety; open-top slide. Polished blue or blue/gold finish. Introduced 1993. Made in U.S. by Heritage Mfg., Inc.
Price: Blue **$64.95**
Price: Blue/gold **$79.95**

HI-POINT FIREARMS JS-9MM AUTO PISTOL   **Caliber:** 9mm Para., 9-shot magazine.   **Barrel:** 4.5".   **Weight:** 41 oz.   **Length:** 7.72" overall.   **Stocks:** Textured acetal plastic.   **Sights:** Fixed, low profile.   **Features:** Single-action design. Scratch-resistant, non-glare blue finish. Introduced 1990. From MKS Supply, Inc.
Price: Matte black **$139.95**

HI-POINT FIREARMS MODEL JS-9MM COMPACT PISTOL   **Caliber:** 380 ACP, 9mm Para., 8-shot magazine.   **Barrel:** 3.5".   **Weight:** 35 oz.   **Length:** 6.7" overall.   **Stocks:** Textured acetal plastic.   **Sights:** Combat-style fixed three-dot system; low profile.   **Features:** Single-action design; frame-mounted magazine release. Scratch-resistant matte finish. Introduced 1993. From MKS Supply, Inc.
Price: **$124.95**
Price: With polymer frame (32 oz.) **$132.95**
Price: 380 ACP . . . . **NA**

Heckler & Koch USP

Heckler & Koch P7K3

Helwan Brigadier

Hi-Point JS-40

Hi-Point JS-9mm

Heritage HA25

HI-POINT FIREARMS JS-40 S&W AUTO   **Caliber:** 40 S&W, 8-shot magazine.   **Barrel:** 4.5".   **Weight:** 44 oz.   **Length:** 7.95" overall.   **Stocks:** Checkered acetal resin.   **Sights:** Fixed; low profile.   **Features:** Internal drop-safe mechansim; all aluminum frame. Introduced 1991. From MKS Supply, Inc.
Price: Matte black **$148.95**

Intratec TEC-DC9MS

Jennings J-25

Kahr K9

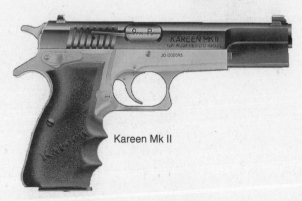

Kareen Mk II

HI-POINT FIREARMS JS-45 CALIBER PISTOL **Caliber:** 45 ACP, 7-shot magazine. **Barrel:** 4.5". **Weight:** 44 oz. **Length:** 7.95" overall. **Stocks:** Checkered acetal resin. **Sights:** Fixed; low profile. **Features:** Internal drop-safe mechanism; all aluminum frame. Introduced 1991. From MKS Supply, Inc.
Price: Matte black **$148.95**

HUNGARIAN T-58 AUTO PISTOL **Caliber:** 7.62mm and 9mm Para., 8-shot magazine. **Barrel:** 4.5". **Weight:** 31 oz. **Length:** 7.68" overall. **Stocks:** Grooved composition. **Sights:** Blade front, rear adjustable for windage. **Features:** Comes with both barrels and magazines. Thumb safety locks hammer. Blue finish. Imported by Century International Arms.
Price: About **$187.00**

INTRATEC TEC-DC9 AUTO PISTOL **Caliber:** 9mm Para., 32-shot magazine. **Barrel:** 5". **Weight:** 50 oz. **Length:** 12½" overall. **Stock:** Moulded composition. **Sights:** Fixed. **Features:** Semi-auto, fires from closed bolt; firing pin block safety; matte blue finish. Made in U.S. by Intratec.
Price: **$269.00**
Price: TEC-DC9S (as above, except stainless) **$362.00**
Price; TEC-DC9K (finished with TEC-KOTE) **$297.00**

Intratec TEC-DC9M Auto Pistol Similar to the TEC-DC9 except smaller. Has 3" barrel, weighs 44 oz.; 20-shot magazine. Made in U.S. by Intratec.
Price: **$245.00**
Price: TEC-DC9MS (as above, stainless) **$339.00**
Price: TEC-DC9MK (finished with TECKOTE) **$277.00**

INTRATEC CATEGORY 9 AUTO PISTOL **Caliber:** 9mm Para., 8-shot magazine. **Barrel:** 3". **Weight:** 21 oz. **Length:** 5.5" overall. **Stocks:** Textured black polymer. **Sights:** Fixed channel. **Features:** Black polymer frame. Announced 1993. Made in U.S. by Intratec.
Price: About **$225.00**

INTRATEC PROTEC-22, 25 AUTO PISTOLS **Caliber:** 22 LR, 10-shot; 25 ACP, 8-shot magazine. **Barrel:** 2½". **Weight:** 14 oz. **Length:** 5" overall. **Stocks:** Wraparound composition in gray, black or driftwood color. **Sights:** Fixed. **Features:** Double-action only trigger mechanism. Choice of black, satin or TEC-KOTE finish. Announced 1991. Made in U.S. by Intratec.
Price: 22 or 25, black finish **$102.00**
Price: 22 or 25, satin or TEC-KOTE finish **$107.95**

INTRATEC TEC-22T AUTO PISTOL **Caliber:** 22 LR, 30-shot magazine. **Barrel:** 4". **Weight:** 30 oz. **Length:** 11³⁄₁₆" overall. **Stocks:** Moulded composition. **Sights:** Protected post front, front and rear adjustable for windage and elevation. **Features:** Ambidextrous cocking knobs and safety. Matte black finish. Accepts any 10/22-type magazine. Introduced 1988. Made in U.S. by Intratec.
Price: **$161.00**
Price: TEC-22TK (as above, TEC-KOTE finish) **$183.50**

JENNINGS J-22, J-25 AUTO PISTOLS **Caliber:** 22 LR, 25 ACP, 6-shot magazine. **Barrel:** 2½". **Weight:** 13 oz. (J-22). **Length:** 4¹⁵⁄₁₆" overall (J-22). **Stocks:** Walnut on chrome or nickel models; grooved black Cycolac or resin-impregnated wood on Teflon model. **Sights:** Fixed. **Features:** Choice of bright chrome, satin nickel or black Teflon finish. Introduced 1981. From Jennings Firearms.
Price: J-22, about **$79.95**
Price: J-25, about **$79.95**

KAHR K9 DA AUTO PISTOL **Caliber:** 9mm Para., 7-shot magazine. **Barrel:** 3.5". **Weight:** 24 oz. **Length:** 6" overall. **Stocks:** Smooth wood; wrap-around design. **Sights:** Blade front, rear drift adjustable for windage; bar-dot combat style. **Features:** Trigger-cocking double-action mechanism with passive firing pin block. Made of 4140 ordnance steel with blue finish. Introduced 1994. Made in U.S. by Kahr Arms.
Price: **$595.00**

KAREEN MK II AUTO PISTOL **Caliber:** 9mm Para., 13-shot magazine. **Barrel:** 4.75". **Weight:** 32 oz. **Length:** 8" overall. **Stocks:** Textured composition. **Sights:** Blade front, rear adjustable for windage. **Features:** Single-action mechanism; external hammer safety; magazine safety; combat trigger guard. Blue finish standard, optional two-tone or matte black. Optional Meprolight sights, improved rubberized grips. Introduced 1969. Imported from Israel by J.O. Arms & Ammunition.
Price: . . . . **$425.00 to $575.00**
Price: Barak 9mm (3.25" barrel, 28 oz., 6.5" overall length) . . . . **$425.00 to $575.00**

KIMEL AP9 AUTO PISTOL **Caliber:** 9mm Para., 20-shot magazine. **Barrel:** 5". **Weight:** 3.5 lbs. **Length:** 11.8" overall. **Stocks:** Checkered plastic. **Sights:** Adjustable post front in ring, fixed open rear. **Features:** Matte blue/black or nickel finish. Lever safety blocks trigger and sear. Fires from closed bolt. Introduced 1988. Made in U.S. Available from Kimel Industries.
Price: Matte blue/black $264.00
Price: Nickel finish $274.00
Price: Mini AP9 (3" barrel) $258.00
Price: Nickel finish $268.00
Price: Target AP9 (12" bbl., grooved forend), blue $279.00

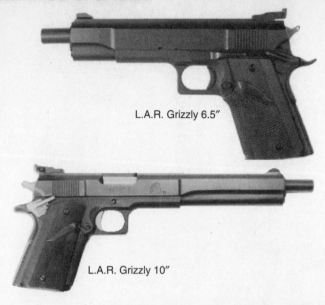

L.A.R. Grizzly 6.5"

L.A.R. GRIZZLY WIN MAG MK I PISTOL **Caliber:** 357 Mag., 357/45, 10mm, 44 Mag., 45 Win. Mag., 45 ACP, 7-shot magazine. **Barrel:** 5.4", 6.5". **Weight:** 51 oz. **Length:** 10½" overall. **Stocks:** Checkered rubber, non-slip combat-type. **Sights:** Ramped blade front, fully adjustable rear. **Features:** Uses basic Browning/Colt 1911A1 design; interchangeable calibers; beveled magazine well; combat-type flat, checkered rubber mainspring housing; lowered and back-chamfered ejection port; polished feed ramp; throated barrel; solid barrel bushings. Available in satin hard chrome, matte blue, Parkerized finishes. Introduced 1983. From L.A.R. Mfg., Inc.
Price: 45 Win. Mag. $920.00
Price: 357 Mag. $933.00
Price: Conversion units (357 Mag.) $228.00
Price: As above, 45 ACP, 10mm, 45 Win. Mag., 357/45 Win. Mag. $214.00

L.A.R. Grizzly 10"

L.A.R. Grizzly Win Mag 8" & 10" Similar to the standard Grizzly Win Mag except has lengthened slide and either 8" or 10" barrel. Available in 45 Win. Mag., 45 ACP, 357/45 Grizzly Win. Mag., 10mm or 357 Magnum. Introduced 1987.
Price: 8", 45 ACP, 45 Win. Mag., 357/45 Grizzly Win. Mag. **$1,313.00**
Price: As above, 10" $1,375.00
Price: 8", 357 Magnum $1,337.50
Price: As above, 10" $1,400.00

L.A.R. Grizzly 50

L.A.R. Grizzly 50 Mark V Pistol Similar to the Grizzly Win Mag Mark I except chambered for 50 Action Express with 6-shot magazine. Weight, empty, is 56 oz., overall length 10⅝". Choice of 5.4" or 6.5" barrel. Has same features as Mark I, IV pistols. Introduced 1993. From L.A.R. Mfg., Inc.
Price: $1,060.00

L.A.R. Grizzly 44 Mag MK IV Similar to the Win. Mag. Mk I except chambered for 44 Magnum, has beavertail grip safety. Matte blue finish only. Has 5.4" or 6.5" barrel. Introduced 1991. From L.A.R. Mfg., Inc.
Price: $933.00

Laseraim Series I

LASERAIM ARMS SERIES I AUTO PISTOL **Caliber:** 10mm Auto, 8-shot, 45 ACP, 7-shot magazine. **Barrel:** 6", with compensator. **Weight:** 46 oz. **Length:** 9.75" overall. **Stocks:** Pebble-grained black composite. **Sights:** Blade front, fully adjustable rear. **Features:** Single action; barrel compensator; stainless steel construction; ambidextrous safety-levers; extended slide release; matte black Teflon finish; integral mount for laser sight. Introduced 1993. Made in U.S. by Emerging Technologies, Inc.
Price: Standard, fixed sight $552.95
Price: Standard, Compact (4⅜" barrel), fixed sight $552.95
Price: Adjustable sight $579.95
Price: Standard, fixed sight, Auto Illusion red dot sight system $649.95
Price: Standard, fixed sight, Laseraim Laser with Hotdot . . . $694.95

Laseraim Series III

Laseraim Arms Series II Auto Pistol Similar to the Series I except without compensator, has matte stainless finish. Standard Series II has 5" barrel, weighs 43 oz., Compact has 3⅜" barrel, weighs 37 oz. Blade front sight, rear adjustable for windage or fixed. Introduced 1993. Made in U.S. by Emerging Technologies, Inc.
Price: Standard or Compact (3⅜" barrel), fixed sight $399.95
Price: Adjustable sight, 5" only $429.95
Price: Standard, fixed sight, Auto Illusion red dot sight $499.95
Price: Standard, fixed sight, Laseraim Laser $499.95

Laseraim Arms Series III Auto Pistol Similar to the Series II except has 5" barrel only, with dual-port compensator; weighs 43 oz.; overall length is 7⅝". Choice of fixed or adjustable rear sight. Introduced 1994. Made in U.S. by Emerging Technologies, Inc.
Price: Fixed sight $533.95
Price: Adjustable sight $559.95
Price: Fixed sight Dream Team Laseraim laser sight $629.95

CAUTION: PRICES SHOWN ARE SUPPLIED BY THE MANUFACTURER OR IMPORTER. CHECK YOUR LOCAL GUNSHOP.

LLAMA XV, III-A SMALL FRAME AUTO PISTOLS   Caliber: 22 LR, 380.   **Barrel:** 3$^{11}/_{16}$".   **Weight:** 23 oz.   **Length:** 6½" overall.   **Stocks:** Checkered polymer, thumbrest.   **Sights:** Fixed front, adjustable notch rear.   **Features:** Ventilated rib, manual and grip safeties. Imported from Spain by SGS Importers International, Inc.
Price: Blue **$248.95**
Price: Satin Chrome **$341.95**

LLAMA COMPACT FRAME AUTO PISTOL   Caliber: 45 ACP, 7-shot.   **Barrel:** 4$^{5}/_{16}$".   **Weight:** 37 oz.   **Stocks:** Checkered polymer.   **Sights:** Blade front, rear adjustable for windage.   **Features:** Scaled-down version of the Large Frame gun. Locked breech mechanism; manual and grip safeties. Introduced 1985. Imported from Spain by SGS Importers Int'l., Inc.
Price: Model IX-B, blue **$299.95**
Price: As above, nickel **$363.95**

LLAMA LARGE FRAME AUTO PISTOL   Caliber: 45 ACP.   **Barrel:** 5".   **Weight:** 40 oz.   **Length:** 8½" overall.   **Stocks:** Checkered polymer.   **Sights:** Fixed.   **Features:** Grip and manual safeties, ventilated rib. Imported from Spain by SGS Importers Int'l., Inc.
Price: Model IX-A, blue **$299.95**
Price: As above, nickel **$363.95**

Llama New Generation Auto Pistols   Similar to the Large and Compact frame 45 automatics except has 13-shot magazine, anatomically designed rubber grips, three-dot combat sights, non-glare matte finish. Chambered only for 45 ACP. Introduced 1994. Imported from Spain by SGS Importers International, Inc.
Price: Compact or Large frame **$391.95**
Price: Max-I (7-shot magazine) **$324.95**

LORCIN L-22 AUTO PISTOL   Caliber: 22 LR, 9-shot magazine.   **Barrel:** 2.5".   **Weight:** 16 oz.   **Length:** 5.25" overall.   **Stocks:** Black combat, or pink or pearl.   **Sights:** Fixed three-dot system.   **Features:** Available in chrome or black Teflon finish. Introduced 1989. From Lorcin Engineering.
Price: About **$89.00**

LORCIN L-25, LT-25 AUTO PISTOLS   Caliber: 25 ACP, 7-shot magazine.   **Barrel:** 2.4".   **Weight:** 14.5 oz.   **Length:** 4.8" overall.   **Stocks:** Smooth composition.   **Sights:** Fixed.   **Features:** Available in choice of finishes: chrome, black Teflon or camouflage. Introduced 1989. From Lorcin Engineering.
Price: L-25 . . . . **$69.00**
Price: LT-25 . . . . **$79.00**

LORCIN L-32, L-380 AUTO PISTOLS   Caliber: 32 ACP, 380 ACP, 7-shot magazine.   **Barrel:** 3.5".   **Weight:** 27 oz.   **Length:** 6.6" overall.   **Stocks:** Grooved composition.   **Sights:** Fixed.   **Features:** Black Teflon or chrome finish with black grips. Introduced 1992. From Lorcin Engineering.
Price: L-32 32 ACP **$89.00**
Price: L-380 380 ACP **$100.00**

Llama Small Frame

Llama Compact Frame

Llama Large Frame

Llama Large Frame Chrome

Lorcin L-25

Llama New Generation

LORCIN L9MM AUTO PISTOL **Caliber:** 9mm Para., 13-shot magazine. **Barrel:** 4.5". **Weight:** 31 oz. **Length:** 7.5" overall. **Stocks:** Grooved black composition. **Sights:** Fixed; three-dot system. **Features:** Matte black finish; hooked trigger guard; grip safety. Introduced 1994. Made in U.S. by Lorcin Engineering.
Price: **$159.00**

MITCHELL ARMS AMERICAN EAGLE AUTO **Caliber:** 9mm Para., 7-shot magazine. **Barrel:** 4". **Weight:** 29.6 oz. **Length:** 9.6" overall. **Stocks:** Checkered walnut. **Sights:** Blade front, fixed rear. **Features:** Recreation of the American Eagle Parabellum pistol in stainless steel. Chamber loaded indicator. Made in U.S. From Mitchell Arms, Inc.
Price: **$695.00**

MITCHELL ARMS SHARPSHOOTER II AUTO PISTOL **Caliber:** 22 LR, 10-shot magazine. **Barrel:** 5.5" bull. **Weight:** 45 oz. **Length:** 10.25" overall. **Stocks:** Checkered walnut with thumbrest. **Sights:** Ramp front, slide-mounted square notch rear adjustable for windage and elevation. **Features:** Military grip. Slide lock; smooth gripstraps; push-button takedown. Announced 1992. From Mitchell Arms, Inc.
Price: Stainless steel **$379.00**

MITCHELL ARMS SPORT-KING II AUTO PISTOL **Caliber:** 22 LR, 10-shot magazine. **Barrel:** 4.5", 6.75". **Weight:** 39 oz. (4.5" barrel). **Length:** 9" overall (4.5" barrel). **Stocks:** Checkered black plastic. **Sights:** Blade front, rear adjustable for windage. **Features:** Military grip; standard trigger; push-button barrel takedown. All stainless steel. Announced 1992. From Mitchell Arms, Inc.
Price: **$312.00**

MITCHELL HIGH STANDARD 45 SIGNATURE SERIES **Caliber:** 45 ACP, 8-shot magazine. **Barrel:** 5". **Weight:** NA. **Length:** 8.75" overall. **Stocks:** Checkered American walnut. **Sights:** Interchangeable blade front, drift adjustable combat rear or fully adjustable rear. **Features:** Royal blue or stainless steel. Introduced 1994. Made in U.S. From Mitchell Arms, Inc.
Price: Blue, drift adjustable sight **$529.00**
Price: As above, stainless **$559.00**
Price: Blue, fully adjustable sight **$569.00**
Price: As above, stainless **$599.00**
Price: Blue, drift adjustable sight, 13-shot magazine **$679.00**
Price: As above, stainless **$709.00**
Price: Blue, fully adjustable sight, 13-shot magazine **$719.00**
Price: As above, stainless **$749.00**

MITCHELL ARMS TROPHY II AUTO PISTOL **Caliber:** 22 LR, 10-shot magazine. **Barrel:** 5.5" bull, 7.25" fluted. **Weight:** 44.5 oz. (5.5" barrel). **Length:** 9.75" overall (5.5" barrel). **Stocks:** Checkered walnut with thumbrest. **Sights:** Undercut ramp front, click-adjustable frame-mounted rear. **Features:** Grip duplicates feel of military 45; positive action magazine latch; front- and backstraps stippled. Trigger adjustable for pull, over-travel; gold-filled roll marks, gold-plated trigger, safety, magazine release; push-button barrel takedown. Available in stainless steel. Announced 1992. From Mitchell Arms, Inc.
Price: Stainless steel **$494.00**

Lorcin L9MM

Mitchell American Eagle

Mitchell Sharpshooter II

Mitchell 45 Signature

Mitchell 45 Signature, 13-shot

Mitchell Trophy II

Mitchell Sport-King II

AUTOLOADERS, SERVICE & SPORT

Mountain Eagle

Navy Arms TT-Olympia

Norinco 1911A1

Para-Ordnance P14.45

Para-Ordnance P12.45

Mitchell Arms Citation II Auto Pistol Same as the Trophy II except has nickel-plated trigger, safety and magazine release, and has silver-filled roll marks. Available in stainless steel. Announced 1992. From Mitchell Arms, Inc.
Price: Stainless steel **$468.00**

MOUNTAIN EAGLE AUTO PISTOL **Caliber:** 22 LR, 15-shot magazine. **Barrel:** 6.5", 8". **Weight:** 21 oz., 23 oz. **Length:** 10.6" overall (with 6.5" barrel). **Stocks:** One-piece impact-resistant polymer in "conventional contour"; checkered panels. **Sights:** Serrated ramp front with interchangeable blades, rear adjustable for windage and elevation; interchangeable blades. **Features:** Injection moulded grip frame, alloy receiver; hybrid composite barrel replicates shape of the Desert Eagle pistol. Flat, smooth trigger. Introduced 1992. From Magnum Research.
Price: Mountain Eagle Standard **$239.00**
Price: Mountain Eagle Target Edition (8" barrel) **$279.00**

NAVY ARMS TT-OLYMPIA PISTOL **Caliber:** 22 LR. **Barrel:** 4.6". **Weight:** 28 oz. **Length:** 8" overall. **Stocks:** Checkered hardwood. **Sights:** Blade front, rear adjsutable for windage. **Features:** Reproduction of the Walther Olympia pistol. Polished blue finish. Introduced 1992. Imported by Navy Arms.
Price: **$290.00**

NORINCO MODEL 59 MAKAROV DA PISTOL **Caliber:** 9x18mm, 380 ACP, 8-shot magazine. **Barrel:** 3.5". **Weight:** 21 oz. **Length:** 6.3" overall. **Stocks:** Checkered plastic. **Sights:** Blade front, adjustable rear. **Features:** Blue finish. Double action. Introduced 1990. Imported from China by China Sports, Inc.
Price: . . . . **NA**

NORINCO NP-15 TOKAREV AUTO PISTOL **Caliber:** 7.62x25mm, 8-shot magazine. **Barrel:** 4.5". **Weight:** 29 oz. **Length:** 7.7" overall. **Stocks:** Grooved black plastic. **Sights:** Fixed. **Features:** Matte blue finish. Imported from China by China Sports, Inc.
Price: . . . . **NA**

NORINCO MODEL 77B AUTO PISTOL **Caliber:** 9mm Para., 8-shot magazine. **Barrel:** 5". **Weight:** 34 oz. **Length:** 7.5" overall. **Stocks:** Checkered wood. **Sights:** Blade front, adjustable rear. **Features:** Uses trigger guard cocking, gas-retarded recoil action. Front of trigger guard can be used to cock the action with the trigger finger. Introduced 1989. Imported from China by China Sports, Inc.
Price: . . . . **NA**

NORINCO M93 SPORTSMAN AUTO PISTOL **Caliber:** 22 LR, 10-shot magazine. **Barrel:** 4.6". **Weight:** 26 oz. **Length:** 8.6" overall. **Stocks:** Checkered composition. **Sights:** Blade front, rear adjustable for windage. **Features:** All steel construction with blue finish, Introduced 1992. Imported from China by Interarms.
Price: . . . . **NA**

NORINCO M1911A1 AUTO PISTOL **Caliber:** 45 ACP, 7-shot magazine. **Barrel:** 5". **Weight:** 39 oz. **Length:** 8.5" overall. **Stocks:** Checkered wood. **Sights:** Blade front, rear adjustable for windage. **Features:** Matte blue finish. Comes with two magazines. Imported from China by China Sports, Inc.
Price: . . . . **NA**

PARA-ORDNANCE P14.45 AUTO PISTOL **Caliber:** 45 ACP, 14-shot magazine. **Barrel:** 5". **Weight:** 28 oz. (alloy frame). **Length:** 8.5" overall. **Stocks:** Textured composition. **Sights:** Blade front, rear adjustable for windage. High visibility three-dot system. **Features:** Available with alloy, steel or stainless steel frame with black finish (silver or stainless gun). Steel and stainless steel frame guns weigh 38 oz. (P14.45), 35 oz. (P13.45), 33 oz. (P12.45). Grooved match trigger, rounded combat-style hammer. Double column, high-capacity magazine gives 15-shot total capacity (P14.45). Beveled magazine well. Manual thumb, grip and firing pin lock safeties. Solid barrel bushing. Introduced 1990. Made in Canada by Para-Ordnance.
Price: P14.45E (steel) **$716.25**
Price: P12.45R (12-shot magazine, 3½" bbl., 24 oz., alloy) . . **$650.00**
Price: P13.45R (13-shot magazine, 4¼" barrel, 28 oz., alloy) . **$650.00**
Price: P14.45E steel frame **$716.25**
Price: P12.45E steel frame **$708.75**

Phoenix Arms HP22

Phoenix Arms HP25

Phoenix Arms Raven

Ram-Line Ram-Tech

Ruger P89

Ruger P89 DAO

PHOENIX ARMS HP22, HP25 AUTO PISTOLS **Caliber:** 22 LR, 11-shot (HP22), 25 ACP, 10-shot (HP25). **Barrel:** 3". **Weight:** 20 oz. **Length:** $5\frac{1}{2}$" overall. **Stocks:** Checkered composition. **Sights:** Blade front, adjustable rear. **Features:** Single action, exposed hammer; manual hold-open; button magazine release. Available in satin nickel, polished blue finish. Introduced 1993. Made in U.S. by Phoenix Arms.
Price: **$99.95**

PHOENIX ARMS MODEL RAVEN AUTO PISTOL **Caliber:** 25 ACP, 6-shot magazine. **Barrel:** $2\frac{7}{16}$". **Weight:** 15 oz. **Length:** $4\frac{3}{4}$" overall. **Stocks:** Ivory-colored or black slotted plastic. **Sights:** Ramped front, fixed rear. **Features:** Available in blue, nickel or chrome finish. Made in U.S. Available from Phoenix Arms.
Price: **$69.95**

PSP-25 AUTO PISTOL **Caliber:** 25 ACP, 6-shot magazine. **Barrel:** $2\frac{1}{8}$". **Weight:** 9.5 oz. **Length:** $4\frac{1}{8}$" overall. **Stocks:** Checkered black plastic. **Sights:** Fixed. **Features:** All steel construction with polished finish. Introduced 1990. Made in the U.S. under F.N. license; distributed by K.B.I., Inc.
Price: Blue **$249.00**
Price: Hard chrome **$299.00**

RAM-LINE RAM-TECH AUTO PISTOL **Caliber:** 22 LR, 15-shot magazine. **Barrel:** 4.5". **Weight:** 19.3 oz. **Length:** NA. **Stocks:** One-piece injection moulded with checkered panels. **Sights:** Ramp front, rear adjustable for windage. **Features:** Compact frame; easy take-down. Injection moulded grip frame, alloy receiver; hybrid composite barrel. Constant force sear spring gives 3-lb. trigger pull. Comes with carrying case. Introduced 1994. Made in U.S. by Ram-Line, Inc.
Price: **$179.00**

ROCKY MOUNTAIN ARMS PATRIOT PISTOL **Caliber:** 223, 5-, 20-, 30-shot magazine. **Barrel:** 7", with Max Dynamic muzzle brake. **Weight:** 5 lbs. **Length:** 20.5" overall. **Stocks:** Black composition. **Sights:** None furnished. **Features:** Milled upper receiver with enhanced Weaver base; milled lower receiver from billet plate; machined aluminum National Match handguard. Finished in DuPont Teflon-S matte black or NATO green. Comes with black nylon case, one magazine. Introduced 1993. From Rocky Mountain Arms, Inc.
Price: **$1,995.00**

RUGER P89 AUTOMATIC PISTOL **Caliber:** 9mm Para., 15-shot magazine. **Barrel:** 4.50". **Weight:** 32 oz. **Length:** 7.84" overall. **Stocks:** Grooved black Xenoy composition. **Sights:** Square post front, square notch rear adjustable for windage, both with white dot inserts. **Features:** Double action with ambidextrous slide-mounted safety-levers. Slide is 4140 chrome moly steel or 400-series stainless steel, frame is a lightweight aluminum alloy. Ambidextrous magazine release. Blue or stainless steel. Introduced 1986; stainless introduced 1990.
Price: P89, blue, with extra magazine and magazine
loading tool, plastic case **$410.00**
Price: KP89, stainless, with extra magazine and magazine loading tool,
plastic case **$452.00**
Price: KP89X Convertible 30 Luger/9mm Para. **$497.00**

Ruger P89 Double-Action Only Automatic Pistol Same as the KP89 except operates only in the double-action mode. Has a bobbed, spurless hammer, gripping grooves on each side of the rear of the slide; no external safety or decocking lever. An internal safety prevents forward movement of the firing pin unless the trigger is pulled. Available in 9mm Para., stainless steel only. Introduced 1991.
Price: With lockable case, extra magazine, magazine loading
tool **$452.00**

Ruger P89D Decocker Automatic Pistol Similar to the standard P89 except has ambidextrous decocking levers in place of the regular slide-mounted safety. The decocking levers move the firing pin inside the slide where the hammer can not reach it, while simultaneously blocking the firing pin from forward movement—allows shooter to decock a cocked pistol without manipulating the trigger. Conventional thumb decocking procedures are therefore unnecessary. Blue or stainless steel. Introduced 1990.
Price: P89D, blue with extra magazine and loader, plastic case **$410.00**
Price: KP89D, stainless, with extra magazine, plastic case . . **$452.00**

Ruger P93 Compact Automatic Pistol Similar to the P89 except has 3.9" barrel, 7.3" overall length, and weighs 31 oz. The forward third of the slide is tapered and polished to the muzzle. Front of the slide is crowned with a convex curve. Slide has seven finger grooves. Trigger guard bow is higher for better grip. Square post front sight, square notch rear drift adjustable for windage, both with white dot inserts. Slide is 400-series stainless steel, black-finished alloy frame. Available as decocker-only or double action-only. Introduced 1993.
    Price: KP93DAO (double action only), KP93 (decocker) . . . **$452.00**

Ruger KP93

Consult our Directory pages for the location of firms mentioned.

RUGER P90 AUTOMATIC PISTOL **Caliber:** 45 ACP, 7-shot magazine. **Barrel:** 4.50". **Weight:** 33.5 oz. **Length:** 7.87" overall. **Stocks:** Grooved black Xenoy composition. **Sights:** Square post front, square notch rear adjustable for windage, both with white dot inserts. **Features:** Double action with ambidextrous slide-mounted safety-levers which move the firing pin inside the slide where the hammer can not reach it, while simultaneously blocking the firing pin from forward movement. Stainless steel only. Introduced 1991.
    Price: KP90 with lockable case, extra magazine **$488.65**

Ruger P90 Decocker Automatic Pistol Similar to the P90 except has a manual decocking system. The ambidextrous decocking levers move the firing pin inside the slide where the hammer can not reach it, while simultaneously blocking the firing pin from forward movement—allows shooter to decock a cocked pistol without manipulating the trigger. Available only in stainless steel. Overall length 7.87", weight 34 oz. Introduced 1991.
    Price: P90D with lockable case, extra magazine, and magazine loading tool **$488.65**

Ruger KP90

RUGER P91 DECOCKER AUTOMATIC PISTOL **Caliber:** 40 S&W, 11-shot magazine. **Barrel:** 4.50". **Weight:** 33 oz. **Length:** 7.87" overall. **Stocks:** Grooved black Xenoy composition. **Sights:** Square post front, square notch rear adjustable for windage, both with white dot inserts. **Features:** Ambidextrous slide-mounted decocking levers move the firing pin inside the slide where the hammer can not reach it while simultaneously blocking the firing pin from forward movement. Allows shooter to decock a cocked pistol without manipulating the trigger. Conventional thumb decocking procedures are therefore unnecessary. Stainless steel only. Introduced 1991.
    Price: KP91D with lockable case, extra magazine, and magazine loading tool **$488.65**

Ruger P91 Double-Action-Only Automatic Pistol Same as the KP91D except operates only in the double-action mode. Has a bobbed, spurless hammer, gripping grooves on each side at the rear of the slide, no external safety or decocking levers. An internal safety prevents forward movement of the firing pin unless the trigger is pulled. Available in 40 S&W, stainless steel only. Introduced 1992.
    Price: KP91DAO with lockable case, extra magazine, and magazine loading tool **$488.65**

Ruger KP91 DAO

Ruger KP94 Automatic Pistol Sized midway between the full-size P-Series and the compact P93. Has 4.25" barrel, 7.5" overall length and weighs about 33 oz. KP94 is manual safety model; KP94DAO is double-action-only (both 9mm Para., 15-shot magazine); KP94D is decocker-only in 40 S&W with 11-shot magazine. Slide gripping grooves roll over top of slide. KP94 has ambidextrous safety-levers; KP94DAO has no external safety, full-cock hammer position or decocking lever; KP94D has ambidextrous decocking levers. Matte finish stainless slide, barrel, alloy frame. Introduced 1994. Made in U.S. by Sturm, Ruger & Co.
    Price: KP94 (9mm), KP944 (40 S&W) $520.00
    Price: KP94DAO (9mm), KP944DAO (40 S&W) $520.00
    Price: KP94D (40 S&W) $520.00

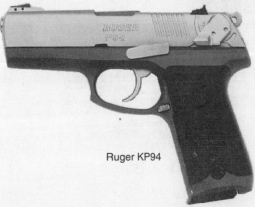

Ruger KP94

CAUTION: PRICES SHOWN ARE SUPPLIED BY THE MANUFACTURER OR IMPORTER. CHECK YOUR LOCAL GUNSHOP.

7TH ANNUAL EDITION   **235**

Ruger P94L Automatic Pistol Same as the KP94 except mounts a laser sight in a housing cast integrally with the frame. Allen-head screws control windage and elevation adjustments. Announced 1994. Made in U.S. by Sturm, Ruger & Co.

Price: . . . . **NA**

Ruger KP94L

RUGER MARK II STANDARD AUTO PISTOL **Caliber:** 22 LR, 10-shot magazine. **Barrel:** 4¾" or 6". **Weight:** 36 oz. (4¾" bbl.). **Length:** 8⁵⁄₁₆" (4¾" bbl.). **Stocks:** Checkered plastic. **Sights:** Fixed, wide blade front, square notch rear adjustable for windage. **Features:** Updated design of the original Standard Auto. Has new bolt hold-open latch. 10-shot magazine, magazine catch, safety, trigger and new receiver contours. Introduced 1982.

Price: Blued (MK 4, MK 6) **$252.00**
Price: In stainless steel (KMK 4, KMK 6) **$330.25**

Ruger 22/45 Mark II Pistol Similar to the other 22 Mark II autos except has grip frame of Zytel that matchs the angle and magazine latch of the Model 1911 45 ACP pistol. Available in 4¾" standard, 5¼" tapered and 5½" bull barrel. Introduced 1992.

Price: KP4 (4¾" barrel) **$280.00**
Price: KP514 (5¼" barrel) **$330.00**
Price: KP512 (5½" bull barrel) **$330.00**

Ruger Mark II Standard

SAFARI ARMS CREST SERIES PISTOLS **Caliber:** 9mm Para., 38 Super, 45 ACP, 7-shot magazine (standard), 6-shot (4-Star). **Barrel:** 5" (standard), 4.5" (4-Star); 416 stainless steel. **Weight:** 39 oz. (standard), 35.7 oz. (4-Star). **Length:** 8.5" overall (standard). **Stocks:** Checkered walnut. **Sights:** Ramped blade front, fully adjustable rear. **Features:** Right- or left-hand models available. Long aluminum trigger, long recoil spring guide, extended safety and slide stop. Stainless steel. Introduced 1993. Made in U.S. by Safari Arms, Inc.

Price: Crest Reliable Right-hand, standard **$740.00**
Price: Crest Renegade Left-hand, standard **$880.00**
Price: Right-hand, 4-Star **$770.00**
Price: Left-hand, 4-Star **$910.00**

Ruger Mark II Standard Stainless

SAFARI ARMS ENFORCER PISTOL **Caliber:** 45 ACP, 6-shot magazine. **Barrel:** 3.8". **Weight:** 36 oz. **Length:** 7.5" overall. **Stocks:** Smooth walnut with etched black widow spider logo. **Sights:** Ramped blade front, rear adjustable for windage and elevation. **Features:** Extended safety, extended slide release; Commander-style hammer; beavertail grip safety; throated, ported, tuned, with cone-shaped barrel, no bushing. Parkerized matte black or satin stainless steel. From Safari Arms, Inc.

Price: **$690.00**

Ruger 22/45 Mark II

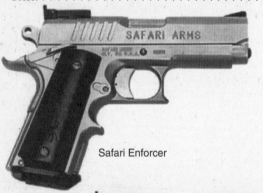

Safari Enforcer

Safari Crest Reliable

Safari Crest Renegade

AUTOLOADERS, SERVICE & SPORT

Safari Enforcer Carrycomp II

Safari G.I. Safari

Seecamp LWS 32

SIG Sauer P225

Safari Arms Enforcer Carrycomp II Pistol Similar to the Enforcer except has Wil Schueman-designed hybrid compensator system. Introduced 1993. Made in U.S. by Safari Arms, Inc.
Price: **$1,010.00**

SAFARI ARMS G.I. SAFARI PISTOL **Caliber:** 45 ACP, 7-shot magazine. **Barrel:** 5". **Weight:** 39.9 oz. **Length:** 8.5" overall. **Stocks:** Checkered walnut. **Sights:** Blade front, fixed rear. **Features:** Beavertail grip safety, extended safety and slide release, Commander-style hammer. Barrel is chrome-lined 4140 steel; National Match 416 stainless optional. Parkerized matte black finish. Introduced 1991. Made in U.S. by Safari Arms, Inc.
Price: **$430.00**

SEECAMP LWS 32 STAINLESS DA AUTO **Caliber:** 32 ACP Win. Silvertip, 6-shot magazine. **Barrel:** 2", integral with frame. **Weight:** 10.5 oz. **Length:** 4⅛" overall. **Stocks:** Glass-filled nylon. **Sights:** Smooth, no-snag, contoured slide and barrel top. **Features:** Aircraft quality 17-4 PH stainless steel. Inertia-operated firing pin. Hammer fired double-action only. Hammer automatically follows slide down to safety rest position after each shot—no manual safety needed. Magazine safety disconnector. Polished stainless. Introduced 1985. From L.W. Seecamp.
Price: **$375.00**

SIG P-210-2 AUTO PISTOL **Caliber:** 7.65mm or 9mm Para., 8-shot magazine. **Barrel:** 4¾". **Weight:** 31¾ oz. (9mm). **Length:** 8½" overall. **Stocks:** Checkered black composition. **Sights:** Blade front, rear adjustable for windage. **Features:** Lanyard loop; matte finish. Conversion unit for 22 LR available. Imported from Switzerland by Mandall Shooting Supplies.
Price: P-210-2 Service Pistol **$3,500.00**

SIG P-210-6 AUTO PISTOL **Caliber:** 9mm Para., 8-shot magazine. **Barrel:** 4¾". **Weight:** 36.2 oz. **Length:** 8½" overall. **Stocks:** Checkered black plastic; walnut optional. **Sights:** Blade front, micro. adjustable rear for windage and elevation. **Features:** Adjustable trigger stop; target trigger; ribbed frontstrap; sandblasted finish. Conversion unit for 22 LR consists of barrel, recoil spring, slide and magazine. Imported from Switzerland by Mandall Shooting Supplies.
Price: P-210-6 . . . . **$3,500.00**
Price: P-210-5 Target **$3,700.00**

SIG SAUER P225 DA AUTO PISTOL **Caliber:** 9mm Para., 8-shot magazine. **Barrel:** 3.8". **Weight:** 26 oz. **Length:** 7³⁄₃₂" overall. **Stocks:** Checkered black plastic. **Sights:** Blade front, rear adjustable for windage. Optional Siglite night sights. **Features:** Double action. Decocking lever permits lowering hammer onto locked firing pin. Square combat-type trigger guard. Shortened, lightened version of P220. Imported from Germany by SIGARMS, Inc.
Price: **$780.00**
Price: With Siglite night sights **$880.00**
Price: K-Kote finish **$850.00**
Price: K-Kote with Siglite night sights **$950.00**

SIG SAUER P220 "AMERICAN" AUTO PISTOL **Caliber:** 38 Super, 45 ACP, (9-shot in 38 Super, 7 in 45). **Barrel:** 4⅜". **Weight:** 28¼ oz. (9mm). **Length:** 7¾" overall. **Stocks:** Checkered black plastic. **Sights:** Blade front, drift adjustable rear for windage. **Features:** Double action. De-cocking lever permits lowering hammer onto locked firing pin. Squared combat-type trigger guard. Slide stays open after last shot. Imported from Germany by SIGARMS, Inc.
Price: "American," blue (side-button magazine release, 45 ACP only) **$805.00**
Price: 45 ACP, blue, Siglite night sights **$905.00**
Price: K-Kote finish **$850.00**
Price: K-Kote, Siglite night sights **$950.00**

SIG Sauer P220

SIG Sauer P226

SIG Sauer P229

SIG Sauer P230

Smith & Wesson .356 TSW

Smith & Wesson 2214

SIG Sauer P226 DA Auto Pistol   Similar to the P220 pistol except has 15-shot magazine, 4.4" barrel, and weighs 26½ oz. 9mm only. Imported from Germany by SIGARMS, Inc.

Price: Blue **$825.00**
Price: With Siglite night sights **$930.00**
Price: Blue, double-action only **$825.00**
Price: Blue, double-action only, Siglite night sights **$930.00**
Price: K-Kote finish **$875.00**
Price: K-Kote, Siglite night sights **$975.00**
Price: K-Kote, double-action only **$875.00**
Price: K-Kote, double-action only, Siglite night sights **$975.00**

SIG Sauer P228 DA Auto Pistol   Similar to the P226 except has 3.86" barrel, with 7.08" overall length and 3.35" height. Chambered for 9mm Para. only, 13-shot magazine. Weight is 29.1 oz. with empty magazine. Introduced 1989. Imported from Germany by SIGARMS, Inc.

Price: Blue **$825.00**
Price: Blue, with Siglite night sights **$930.00**
Price: Blue, double-action only **$825.00**
Price: Blue, double-action only, Siglite night sights **$930.00**
Price: K-Kote finish **$875.00**
Price: K-Kote, Siglite night sights **$975.00**
Price: K-Kote, double-action only **$875.00**
Price: K-Kote, double-action only, Siglite night sights **$975.00**

SIG Sauer P229 DA Auto Pistol   Similar to the P228 except chambered for 9mm Para., 40 S&W with 12-shot magazine. Has 3.86" barrel, 7.08" overall length and 3.35" height. Introduced 1991. Frame made in Germany, stainless steel slide assembly made in U.S.; pistol assembled in U.S. From SIGARMS, Inc.

Price: Blue **$875.00**
Price: Blue, double-action only **$875.00**
Price: With Siglite night sights **$975.00**

SIG SAUER P230 DA AUTO PISTOL   Caliber: 380 ACP, 7-shot. **Barrel:** 3¾". **Weight:** 16 oz. **Length:** 6½" overall. **Stocks:** Checkered black plastic. **Sights:** Blade front, rear adjustable for windage. **Features:** Double action. Same basic action design as P220. Blowback operation, stationary barrel. Introduced 1977. Imported from Germany by SIGARMS, Inc.

Price: Blue **$510.00**
Price: In stainless steel (P230 SL) **$595.00**

SMITH & WESSON MODEL .356 TSW LIMITED PISTOL   Caliber: 356 TSW, 15-shot magazine. **Barrel:** 5". **Weight:** 44 oz. **Length:** 8.5" overall. **Stocks:** Checkered black composition. **Sights:** Blade front drift adjustable for windage, fully adjustable Bo-Mar rear. **Features:** Single action trigger. Stainless steel frame and slide, hand-fitted titanium-coated stainless steel bushing, match grade barrel. Extended magazine well and oversize release; magazine pads; extended safety. Checkered front strap. Introduced 1993. Available from Lew Horton Dist.

Price: About **$1,349.00**

Smith & Wesson Model .356 TSW Compact Pistol   Similar to the .356 TSW Limited except has 3½" barrel, 12-shot magazine, Novak LoMount combat sights. Overall length 7", weight 37 oz. Introduced 1993. Available from Lew Horton Dist.

Price: **$999.00**

SMITH & WESSON MODEL 422, 622 AUTO   Caliber: 22 LR, 12-shot magazine. **Barrel:** 4½", 6". **Weight:** 22 oz. (4½" bbl.). **Length:** 7½" overall (4½" bbl.). **Stocks:** Checkered simulated woodgrain polymer. **Sights:** Field—serrated ramp front, fixed rear; Target— serrated ramp front, adjustable rear. **Features:** Aluminum frame, steel slide, brushed stainless steel or blue finish; internal hammer. Introduced 1987. Model 2206 introduced 1990.

Price: Blue, 4½", 6", fixed sight **$235.00**
Price: As above, adjustable sight **$290.00**
Price: Stainless (Model 622), 4½", 6", fixed sight **$284.00**
Price: As above, adjustable sight **$337.00**

CAUTION: PRICES SHOWN ARE SUPPLIED BY THE MANUFACTURER OR IMPORTER. CHECK YOUR LOCAL GUNSHOP.

Smith & Wesson Model 2214 Sportsman Auto Similar to the Model 422 except has 3" barrel, 8-shot magazine; dovetail Patridge front sight with white dot, fixed rear with two white dots; matte blue finish, black composition grips with checkered panels. Overall length 6⅛", weight 18 oz. Introduced 1990.
Price: **$269.00**
Price: Model 2213 (stainless steel) **$314.00**

Smith & Wesson Model 2206 Auto Similar to the Model 422/622 except made entirely of stainless steel with non-reflective finish. Weight is 35 oz. with 4½" barrel, 39 oz. with 6" barrel. Introduced 1990.
Price: With fixed sight **$327.00**
Price: With adjustable sight **$385.00**

Smith & Wesson Model 2206 Target Auto Same as the Model 2206 except 6" barrel only; Millett Series 100 fully adjustable sight system; Patridge front sight; smooth contoured Herrett walnut target grips with thumbrest; serrated trigger with adjustable stop. Frame is bead-blasted along sighting plane, drilled and tapped for optics mount. Introduced 1994. Made in U.S. by Smith & Wesson.
Price: **$433.00**

SMITH & WESSON MODEL 915 DA AUTO PISTOL **Caliber:** 9mm Para., 15-shot magazine. **Barrel:** 4". **Weight:** 28.5 oz. **Length:** 7.5" overall. **Stocks:** One-piece Xenoy, wraparound with straight backstrap. **Sights:** Post front with white dot, fixed rear. **Features:** Alloy frame, blue carbon steel slide. Slide-mounted decocking lever. Introduced 1992.
Price: **$467.00**

Smith & Wesson 915

Smith & Wesson Model 411 DA Auto Pistol Same as the Model 915 except chambered for 40 S&W, 11-shot magazine. Alloy frame, blue carbon steel slide. Introduced 1994. Made in U.S. by Smith & Wesson.
Price: **$525.00**

SMITH & WESSON MODEL 3913/3914 DOUBLE ACTIONS **Caliber:** 9mm Para., 8-shot magazine. **Barrel:** 3½". **Weight:** 26 oz. **Length:** 6¹³⁄₁₆" overall. **Stocks:** One-piece Delrin wraparound, textured surface. **Sights:** Post front with white dot, Novak LoMount Carry with two dots, adjustable for windage. **Features:** Aluminum alloy frame, stainless slide (M3913) or blue steel slide (M3914). Bobbed hammer with no half-cock notch; smooth .304" trigger with rounded edges. Straight backstrap. Extra magazine included. Introduced 1989.
Price: Model 3913 . . . . **$622.00**
Price: Model 3914 . . . . **$562.00**

Smith & Wesson 3913

Smith & Wesson Model 3953DA Pistol Same as the Models 3913/3914 except double-action only. Model 3953 has stainless slide with alloy frame. Overall length 7"; weight 25.5 oz. Extra magazine included. Introduced 1990.
Price: **$622.00**

Smith & Wesson Model 3913 LadySmith Auto Similar to the standard Model 3913/3914 except has frame that is upswept at the front, rounded trigger guard. Comes in frosted stainless steel with matching gray grips. Grips are ergonomically correct for a woman's hand. Novak LoMount Carry rear sight adjustable for windage, smooth edges for snag resistance. Extra magazine included. Introduced 1990.
Price: **$640.00**

Smith & Wesson 3913 LadySmith

Smith & Wesson Model 3913-NL Pistol Same as the 3913/3914 LadySmith autos except without the LadySmith logo and it has a slightly modified frame design. Right-hand safety only. Has stainless slide on alloy frame; extra magazine included. Introduced 1990.
Price: **$622.00**

Smith & Wesson Model 4046 DA Pistol Similar to the Model 4006 except is double-action only. Has a semi-bobbed hammer, smooth trigger, 4" barrel; Novak LoMount Carry rear sight, post front with white dot. Overall length is 7½", weight 28 oz. Extra magazine included. Introduced 1991.
Price: **$745.00**
Price: With fixed night sights **$855.00**

Smith & Wesson 4006

SMITH & WESSON MODEL 4006 DA AUTO **Caliber:** 40 S&W, 11-shot magazine. **Barrel:** 4". **Weight:** 38.5 oz. **Length:** 7⅞" overall. **Stocks:** Xenoy wraparound with checkered panels. **Sights:** Replaceable post front with white dot, Novak LoMount Carry fixed rear with two white dots, or micro. click adjustable rear with two white dots. **Features:** Stainless steel construction with non-reflective finish. Straight back-strap. Extra magazine included. Introduced 1990.
Price: With adjustable sights **$775.00**
Price: With fixed sight **$745.00**
Price: With fixed night sights **$855.00**

CAUTION: PRICES SHOWN ARE SUPPLIED BY THE MANUFACTURER OR IMPORTER. CHECK YOUR LOCAL GUNSHOP.

7TH ANNUAL EDITION **239**

SMITH & WESSON MODEL 4013, 4053 AUTOS Caliber: 40 S&W, 8-shot magazine. **Barrel:** 3½". **Weight:** 26 oz. **Length:** 7" overall. **Stocks:** One-piece Xenoy wraparound with straight backstrap. **Sights:** Post front with white dot, fixed Novak LoMount Carry rear with two white dots. **Features:** Model 4013 is traditional double action; Model 4053 is double-action only; stainless slide on alloy frame. Introduced 1991.
Price: Model 4013 . . . . **$722.00**
Price: Model 4053 . . . . **$722.00**

SMITH & WESSON MODEL 4500 SERIES AUTOS Caliber: 45 ACP, 7-shot (M4516), 8-shot magazine for M4506, 4566/4586. **Barrel:** 3¾" (M4516), 5" (M4506). **Weight:** 41 oz. (4506). **Length:** 7⅛" overall (4516). **Stocks:** Xenoy one-piece wraparound, arched or straight backstrap on M4506, straight only on M4516. **Sights:** Post front with white dot, adjustable or fixed Novak LoMount Carry on M4506. **Features:** M4506 has serrated hammer spur. Extra magazine included. Contact Smith & Wesson for complete data. Introduced 1989.
Price: Model 4506, fixed sight **$774.00**
Price: Model 4506, adjustable sight **$806.00**
Price: Model 4516, fixed sight **$774.00**
Price: Model 4566 (stainless, 4¼", traditional DA, ambidextrous safety, fixed sight) **$774.00**
Price: Model 4586 (stainless, 4¼", DA only) **$774.00**

SMITH & WESSON MODEL 5900 SERIES AUTO PISTOLS Caliber: 9mm Para., 15-shot magazine. **Barrel:** 4". **Weight:** 28½ to 37½ oz. (fixed sight); 38 oz. (adj. sight). **Length:** 7½" overall. **Stocks:** Xenoy wraparound with curved backstrap. **Sights:** Post front with white dot, fixed or fully adjustable with two white dots. **Features:** All stainless, stainless and alloy or carbon steel and alloy construction. Smooth .304" trigger, .260" serrated hammer. Extra magazine included. Introduced 1989.
Price: Model 5903 (stainless, alloy frame, traditional DA, fixed sight, ambidextrous safety) **$690.00**
Price: Model 5904 (blue, alloy frame, traditional DA, adjustable sight, ambidextrous safety) **$642.00**
Price: Model 5906 (stainless, traditional DA, adjustable sight, ambidextrous safety) **$742.00**
Price: As above, fixed sight **$707.00**
Price: With fixed night sights **$817.00**
Price: Model 5946 (as above, stainless frame and slide) **$707.00**

Smith & Wesson Model 6904/6906 Double-Action Autos Similar to the Models 5904/5906 except with 3½" barrel, 12-shot magazine (20-shot available), fixed rear sight, .260" bobbed hammer. Extra magazine included. Introduced 1989.
Price: Model 6904, blue **$614.00**
Price: Model 6906, stainless **$677.00**
Price: Model 6906 with fixed night sights **$788.00**
Price: Model 6946 (stainless, DA only, fixed sights) **$677.00**

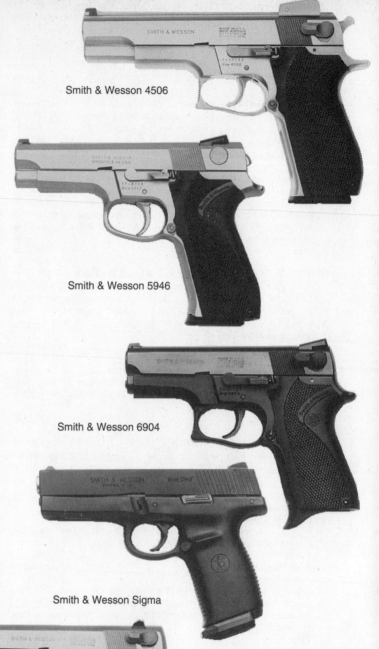

Smith & Wesson 4506

Smith & Wesson 5946

Smith & Wesson 6904

Smith & Wesson Sigma

Smith & Wesson 6906

Smith & Wesson 6946

SMITH & WESSON SIGMA SERIES PISTOLS Caliber: 9mm Para., 17-shot, 40 S&W, 15-shot magazine. **Barrel:** 4.5". **Weight:** 26 oz. **Length:** 7.4" overall. **Stocks:** Integral. **Sights:** White dot front, fixed rear; three-dot system. Tritium night sights available. **Features:** Ergonomic polymer frame; low barrel centerline; internal striker firing system; corrosion-resistant slide; Teflon-filled, electroless-nickel coated magazine. Introduced 1994. Made in U.S. by Smith & Wesson.
Price: Model SW9F (9mm Para.) **$593.00**
Price: Model SW40F (40 S&W) **$593.00**

SPHINX AT-380M AUTO PISTOL Caliber: 380 ACP, 10-shot magazine. **Barrel:** 3.27". **Weight:** 25 oz. **Length:** 6.03" overall. **Stocks:** Checkered plastic. **Sights:** Fixed. **Features:** Double-action-only mechanism, Chamber loaded indicator; ambidextrous magazine release and slide latch. Blued slide, bright Palladium frame, or bright Palladium overall. Introduced 1993. Imported from Switzerland by Sile Distributors, Inc.
Price: Two-tone **$499.95**
Price: Palladium finish **$594.95**

Sphinx AT-380M

SPHINX AT-2000S DOUBLE-ACTION PISTOL Caliber: 9mm Para., 9x21mm, 15-shot, 40 S&W, 11-shot magazine. **Barrel:** 4.53". **Weight:** 36.3 oz. **Length:** 8.03" overall. **Stocks:** Checkered neoprene. **Sights:** Fixed, three-dot system. **Features:** Double-action mechanism changeable to double-action-only. Stainless frame, blued slide. Ambidextrous safety, magazine release, slide latch. Introduced 1993. Imported from Switzerland by Sile Distributors, Inc.
Price: 9mm, two-tone **$902.95**
Price: 9mm, Palladium finish **$989.95**
Price: 40 S&W, two-tone **$911.95**
Price: 40 S&W, Palladium finish **$998.95**

Sphinx AT-2000S

Sphinx AT-2000P, AT-2000PS Auto Pistols Same as the AT-2000S except AT-2000P has shortened frame (13-shot magazine), 3.74" barrel, 7.25" overall length, and weighs 34 oz. Model AT-2000PS has full-size frame. Both have stainless frame with blued slide or bright Palladium finish. Introduced 1993. Imported from Switzerland by Sile Distributors, Inc.
Price: 9mm, two-tone **$858.95**
Price: 9mm, Palladium finish **$945.95**
Price: 40 S&W, two-tone **$867.95**
Price: 40 S&W, Palladium finish **$954.95**

Sphinx AT-2000H Auto Pistol Similar to the AT-2000P except has shorter slide with 3.54" barrel, shorter frame, 10-shot magazine, with 7" overall length. Weight is 32.2 oz. Stainless frame with blued slide, or overall bright Palladium finish. Introduced 1993. Imported from Switzerland by Sile Distributors, Inc.
Price: 9mm, two-tone **$858.95**
Price: 9mm, Palladium finish **$945.95**
Price: 40 S&W, two-tone **$867.95**
Price: 40 S&W, Palladium **$954.95**

Sphinx AT-2000H

SPORTARMS TOKAREV MODEL 213 Caliber: 9mm Para., 8-shot magazine. **Barrel:** 4.5". **Weight:** 31 oz. **Length:** 7.6" overall. **Stocks:** Grooved plastic. **Sights:** Fixed. **Features:** Blue finish, hard chrome optional. 9mm version of the famous Russian Tokarev pistol. Made in China by Norinco. Imported by Sportarms of Florida. Introduced 1988.
Price: Blue, about **$150.00**
Price: Hard chrome, about **$179.00**

SPRINGFIELD INC. 1911A1 AUTO PISTOL Caliber: 9mm Para., 9-shot; 38 Super, 10-shot; 45 ACP, 8-shot. **Barrel:** 5". **Weight:** 35.06 oz. **Length:** 8.59" overall. **Stocks:** Checkered plastic. **Sights:** Fixed low-profile combat-style. **Features:** Beveled magazine well. All forged parts, including frame, barrel, slide. All new production. Introduced 1990. From Springfield Inc.
Price: Basic, 45 ACP, Parkerized **$449.00**
Price: Standard, 45 ACP, blued **$489.00**
Price: Basic, 45 ACP, stainless **$532.00**
Price: Mil-spec (Parkerized), 38 Super **$489.00**

Springfield 1911A1 Factory Comp

Springfield Inc. 1911A1 Factory Comp Similar to the standard 1911A1 except comes with bushing-type dual-port compensator, adjustable rear sight, extended thumb safety, Videki speed trigger, and beveled magazine well. Checkered walnut grips standard. Available in 38 Super or 45 ACP, blue only. Introduced 1992.
Price: 38 Super **$929.00**
Price: 45 ACP **$869.00**

Springfield 1911A1 Mil-spec

Springfield Inc. 1911A1 Custom Carry Gun Similar to the standard 1911A1 except has fixed three-dot low profile sights, Videki speed trigger, match barrel and bushing; extended thumb safety, beavertail grip safety; beveled, polished magazine well, polished feed ramp and throated barrel; match Commander hammer and sear, tuned extractor; lowered and flared ejection port; recoil buffer system, full-length spring guide rod; walnut grips. Comes with two magazines with slam pads, plastic carrying case. Available in all popular calibers. Introduced 1992. From Springfield Inc.
Price: . . . . **P.O.R.**

Springfield Inc. 1911A1 High Capacity Pistol Similar to the Standard 1911A1 except available in 45 ACP and 9x21mm with 10-shot magazine (45 ACP), 16-shot magazine (9x21mm). Has Commander-style hammer, walnut grips, ambidextrous thumb safety, beveled magazine well, plastic carrying case. Blue finish only. Introduced 1993. From Springfield, Inc.
Price: 45 ACP **$999.00**
Price: 9x21mm **$1,099.00**
Price: 45 ACP Factory Comp **$1,225.00**

Springfield Inc. 1911A1 Champion Pistol Similar to the standard 1911A1 except slide is 4.25". Has low-profile three-dot sight system. Comes with Commander hammer and walnut stocks. Available in 45 ACP only; blue or stainless. Introduced 1989.
Price: Blue $529.00
Price: Stainless $558.00
Price: Blue, comp $829.00
Price: Mil-Spec $449.00

Springfield Inc. Product Improved 1911A1 Defender Pistol Similar to the 1911A1 Champion except has tapered cone dual-port compensator system, rubberized grips. Has reverse recoil plug, full-length recoil spring guide, serrated frontstrap, extended thumb safety, Commander-style hammer with modified grip safety to match and a Videki speed trigger. Bi-Tone finish. Introduced 1991.
Price: 45 ACP $959.00

Springfield Inc. 1911A1 Compact Pistol Similar to the Champion model except has a shortened slide with 4.025" barrel, 7.75" overall length. Magazine capacity is 7 shots. Has Commander hammer, checkered walnut grips. Available in 45 ACP only. Introduced 1989.
Price: Blued $529.00
Price: Bi-Tone Comp (blue slide, stainless frame) $829.00
Price: Stainless $558.00
Price: Compact Lightweight $499.00

STAR FIRESTAR AUTO PISTOL **Caliber:** 9mm Para., 7-shot; 40 S&W, 6-shot. **Barrel:** 3.39". **Weight:** 30.35 oz. **Length:** 6.5" overall. **Stocks:** Checkered rubber. **Sights:** Blade front, fully adjustable rear; three-dot system. **Features:** Low-profile, combat-style sights; ambidextrous safety. Available in blue or weather-resistant Starvel finish. Introduced 1990. Imported from Spain by Interarms.
Price: Blue, 9mm $453.00
Price: Starvel finish 9mm $480.00
Price: Blue, 40 S&W $471.00
Price: Starvel finish, 40 S&W $497.00

Star Firestar Plus Auto Pistol Same as the standard Firestar except has 13-shot magazine in 9mm. Also available in 40 S&W and 45 ACP. Introduced 1994. Imported from Spain by Interarms.
Price: Blue $494.00
Price: Starvel $521.00

STAR MEGASTAR 45 ACP AUTO PISTOL **Caliber:** 10mm, 14-shot, 45 ACP, 12-shot magazine. **Barrel:** 4.6". **Weight:** 47.6 oz. **Length:** 8.44" overall. **Stocks:** Checkered composition. **Sights:** Blade front, adjustable rear. **Features:** Double-action mechanism; steel frame and slide; reverse-taper Acculine barrel. Introduced 1992. Imported from Spain by Interarms.
Price: Blue, 10mm $653.00
Price: Starvel finish, 10mm $682.00
Price: Blue, 45 ACP $653.00
Price: Starvel finish, 45 ACP $682.00

Springfield Champion

Star Firestar

Star Firestar Plus

Star Megastar

Star Firestar M45 Auto Pistol Similar to the standard Firestar except chambered for 45 ACP with 6-shot magazine. Has 3.6" barrel, weighs 35 oz., 6.85" overall length. Reverse-taper Acculine barrel. Introduced 1992. Imported from Spain by Interarms.
Price: Blue $494.00
Price: Starvel finish $521.00

Star Ultrastar

Stoeger American Eagle Luger

Sundance A-25

Sundance BOA

STAR ULTRASTAR DOUBLE-ACTION PISTOL **Caliber:** 9mm Para., 9-shot magazine. **Barrel:** 3.57". **Weight:** 26 oz. **Length:** 7" overall. **Stocks:** Checkered black polymer. **Sights:** Blade front, rear adjustable for windage; three-dot system. **Features:** Polymer frame with inside steel slide rails; ambidextrous two-position safety (Safe and Decock). Introduced 1994. Imported from Spain by Interarms.
Price: **$504.00**

STOEGER AMERICAN EAGLE LUGER **Caliber:** 9mm Para., 7-shot magazine. **Barrel:** 4", 6". **Weight:** 32 oz. **Length:** 9.6" overall. **Stocks:** Checkered walnut. **Sights:** Blade front, fixed rear. **Features:** Recreation of the American Eagle Luger pistol in stainless steel. Chamber loaded indicator. Introduced 1994. From Stoeger Industries.
Price: **$695.00**
Price: Navy Model, 6" barrel **$695.00**

SUNDANCE BOA AUTO PISTOL **Caliber:** 25 ACP, 7-shot magazine. **Barrel:** 2½". **Weight:** 16 oz. **Length:** 4⅞". **Stocks:** Grooved ABS or smooth simulated pearl; optional pink. **Sights:** Fixed. **Features:** Patented grip safety, manual rotary safety; button magazine release; lifetime warranty. Bright chrome or black Teflon finish. Introduced 1991. Made in the U.S. by Sundance Industries, Inc.
Price: **$95.00**

> Consult our Directory pages for the location of firms mentioned.

SUNDANCE MODEL A-25 AUTO PISTOL **Caliber:** 25 ACP, 7-shot magazine. **Barrel:** 2.5". **Weight:** 16 oz. **Length:** 4⅞" overall. **Stocks:** Grooved black ABS or simulated smooth pearl; optional pink. **Sights:** Fixed. **Features:** Manual rotary safety; button magazine release. Bright chrome or black Teflon finish. Introduced 1989. Made in U.S. by Sundance Industries, Inc.
Price: **$79.95**

TAURUS MODEL PT 22/PT 25 AUTO PISTOLS **Caliber:** 22 LR, 9-shot (PT 22); 25 ACP, 8-shot (PT 25). **Barrel:** 2.75". **Weight:** 12.3 oz. **Length:** 5.25" overall. **Stocks:** Smooth Brazilian hardwood. **Sights:** Blade front, fixed rear. **Features:** Double action. Tip-up barrel for loading, cleaning. Blue only. Introduced 1992. Made in U.S. by Taurus International.
Price: 22 LR or 25 ACP **$193.00**

TAURUS MODEL PT58 AUTO PISTOL **Caliber:** 380 ACP, 12-shot magazine. **Barrel:** 4.01". **Weight:** 30 oz. **Length:** 7.2" overall. **Stocks:** Brazilian hardwood. **Sights:** Integral blade on slide front, notch rear adjustable for windage. Three-dot system. **Features:** Double action with exposed hammer; inertia firing pin. Introduced 1988. Imported by Taurus International.
Price: Blue **$445.00**
Price: Satin nickel **$477.00**
Price: Stainless steel **$506.00**

Taurus PT22

Taurus PT58

TAURUS MODEL PT 92AF AUTO PISTOL **Caliber:** 9mm Para., 15-shot magazine. **Barrel:** 4.92". **Weight:** 34 oz. **Length:** 8.54" overall. **Stocks:** Brazilian hardwood. **Sights:** Fixed notch rear. Three-dot sight system. **Features:** Double action, exposed hammer, chamber loaded indicator. Inertia firing pin. Imported by Taurus International.

Price: Blue **$492.00**
Price: Blue, Deluxe Shooter's Pak (extra magazine, case) . . . **$521.00**
Price: Nickel **$532.00**
Price: Nickel, Deluxe Shooter's Pak (extra magazine, case) . . **$561.00**
Price: Stainless steel **$559.00**
Price: Stainless, Deluxe Shooter's Pak (extra magazine, case) . **$587.00**

Taurus PT 92AFC Compact Pistol Similar to the PT-92 except has 4.25" barrel, 13-shot magazine, weighs 31 oz. and is 7.5" overall. Available in stainless steel, blue or satin nickel. Introduced 1991. Imported by Taurus International.

Price: Blue **$492.00**
Price: Blue, Deluxe Shooter's Pak (extra magazine, case) . . . **$521.00**
Price: Stainless steel **$559.00**
Price: Stainless, Deluxe Shooter's Pak (extra magazine and case) **$587.00**

Taurus PT 99AF Auto Pistol Similar to the PT-92 except has fully adjustable rear sight, smooth Brazilian walnut stocks and is available in stainless steel, polished blue or satin nickel. Introduced 1983.

Price: Blue **$532.00**
Price: Blue, Deluxe Shooter's Pak (extra magazine, case) . . . **$562.00**
Price: Nickel **$577.00**
Price: Nickel, Deluxe Shooter's Pak (extra magazine, case) . . **$606.00**
Price: Stainless steel **$606.00**
Price: Stainless, Deluxe Shooter's Pak (extra magazine, case) . **$633.00**

TAURUS PT 100 AUTO PISTOL **Caliber:** 40 S&W, 11-shot magazine. **Barrel:** 5". **Weight:** 34 oz. **Stocks:** Smooth Brazilian hardwood. **Sights:** Fixed front, drift-adjustable rear. Three-dot combat. **Features:** Double action, exposed hammer. Ambidextrous hammer-drop safety; inertia firing pin; chamber loaded indicator. Introduced 1991. Imported by Taurus International.

Price: Blue **$502.00**
Price: Blue, Deluxe Shooter's Pak (extra magazine, case) . . . **$530.00**
Price: Nickel **$542.00**
Price: Nickel, Deluxe Shooter's Pak (extra magazine, case) . . **$570.00**
Price: Stainless **$569.00**
Price: Stainless, Deluxe Shooter's Pak (extra magazine, case) . **$595.00**

Taurus PT 101 Auto Pistol Same as the PT 100 except has micro-click rear sight adjustable for windage and elevation, three-dot combat-style. Introduced 1991.

Price: Blue **$542.00**
Price: Blue, Deluxe Shooter's Pak (extra magazine, case) . . . **$571.00**
Price: Nickel **$587.00**
Price: Nickel, Deluxe Shooter's Pak (extra magazine, case) . . **$615.00**
Price: Stainless **$619.00**
Price: Stainless, Deluxe Shooter's Pak (extra magazine, case) . **$648.00**

TAURUS MODEL PT-908 AUTO PISTOL **Caliber:** 9mm Para., 8-shot magazine. **Barrel:** 3.8". **Weight:** 30 oz. **Length:** 7.05" overall. **Stocks:** Checkered black composition. **Sights:** Drift-adjustable front and rear; three-dot combat. **Features:** Double action, exposed hammer; manual ambidextrous hammer-drop; inertia firing pin; chamber loaded indicator. Introduced 1993. Imported by Taurus International.

Price: Blue **$492.00**
Price: Stainless steel **$559.00**

WALTHER PP AUTO PISTOL **Caliber:** 22 LR, 15-shot; 32 ACP, 380 ACP, 7-shot magazine. **Barrel:** 3.86". **Weight:** 23½ oz. **Length:** 6.7" overall. **Stocks:** Checkered plastic. **Sights:** Fixed, white markings. **Features:** Double action; manual safety blocks firing pin and drops hammer; chamber loaded indicator on 32 and 380; extra finger rest magazine provided. Imported from Germany by Interarms.

Price: 22 LR **$783.00**
Price: 32 . . . . **$1,206.00**
Price: 380 . . . . **$1,206.00**
Price: Engraved models . . . . **On Request**

Taurus PT92

Taurus PT99AF

Taurus PT101

Taurus PT-908

Walther PPK/S

Walther PPK/S American Auto Pistol Similar to Walther PP except made entirely in the United States. Has 3.27" barrel with 6.1" length overall. Introduced 1980.
Price: 380 ACP only, blue **$610.00**
Price: As above, stainless **$610.00**

Walther PPK American Auto Pistol Similar to Walther PPK/S except weighs 21 oz., has 6-shot capacity. Made in the U.S. Introduced 1986.
Price: Stainless, 380 ACP only **$610.00**
Price: Blue, 380 ACP only **$610.00**

WALTHER P-38 AUTO PISTOL **Caliber:** 9mm Para., 8-shot. **Barrel:** 4$^{15}/_{16}$". **Weight:** 28 oz. **Length:** 8½" overall. **Stocks:** Checkered plastic. **Sights:** Fixed. **Features:** Double action; safety blocks firing pin and drops hammer. Matte finish standard, polished blue, engraving and/or plating available. Imported from Germany by Interarms.
Price: **$824.00**
Price: Engraved models . . . . **On Request**

Walther P-5 Auto Pistol Latest Walther design that uses the basic P-38 double-action mechanism. Caliber 9mm Para., barrel length 3½"; weight 28 oz., overall length 7".
Price: **$1,096.00**
Price: P-5 Compact **$1,096.00**

WALTHER MODEL TPH AUTO PISTOL **Caliber:** 22 LR, 25 ACP, 6-shot magazine. **Barrel:** 2¼". **Weight:** 14 oz. **Length:** 5⅜" overall. **Stocks:** Checkered black composition. **Sights:** Blade front, rear drift-adjustable for windage. **Features:** Made of stainless steel. Scaled-down version of the Walther PP/PPK series. Made in U.S. Introduced 1987. From Interarms.
Price: Blue or stainless steel, 22 or 25 . . . . **$458.00**

WALTHER P-88 COMPACT AUTO PISTOL **Caliber:** 9mm Para., 14-shot magazine. **Barrel:** 4". **Weight:** 31½ oz. **Length:** 7⅜" overall. **Stocks:** Checkered black composition. **Sights:** Blade front, rear adjustable for windage and elevation. **Features:** Double action with ambidextrous decocking lever and magazine release; alloy frame; loaded chamber indicator; matte finish. Imported from Germany by Interarms.
Price: **$1,725.00**

WILDEY AUTOMATIC PISTOL **Caliber:** 10mm Wildey Mag., 11mm Wildey Mag., 30 Wildey Mag., 357 Peterbuilt, 45 Win. Mag., 475 Wildey Mag., 7-shot magazine. **Barrel:** 5", 6", 7", 8", 10", 12", 14" (45 Win. Mag.); 8", 10", 12", 14" (all other cals.). Interchangeable. **Weight:** 64 oz. (5" barrel). **Length:** 11" overall (7" barrel). **Stocks:** Hardwood. **Sights:** Ramp front (interchangeable blades optional), fully adjustable rear. Scope base available. **Features:** Gas-operated action. Made of stainless steel. Has three-lug rotary bolt. Double or single action. Polished and matte finish. Made in U.S. by Wildey, Inc.
Price: . . . . **$1,175.00 to $1,495.00**

WILKINSON "LINDA" AUTO PISTOL **Caliber:** 9mm Para., 31-shot magazine. **Barrel:** 8⁵/₁₆". **Weight:** 4 lbs., 13 oz. **Length:** 12¼" overall. **Stocks:** Checkered black plastic pistol grip, maple forend. **Sights:** Protected blade front, aperture rear. **Features:** Fires from closed bolt. Semi-auto only. Straight blowback action. Cross-bolt safety. Removable barrel. From Wilkinson Arms.
Price: **$484.84**

WILKINSON "SHERRY" AUTO PISTOL **Caliber:** 22 LR, 8-shot magazine. **Barrel:** 2⅛". **Weight:** 9¼ oz. **Length:** 4⅜" overall. **Stocks:** Checkered black plastic. **Sights:** Fixed, groove. **Features:** Cross-bolt safety locks the sear into the hammer. Available in all blue finish or blue slide and trigger with gold frame. Introduced 1985.
Price: **$179.95**

Walther P-38

Walther P-88 Compact

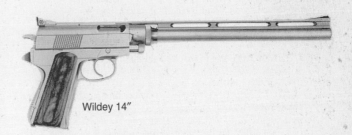
Walther TPH

Wildey 14"

Wilkinson Sherry

CAUTION: PRICES SHOWN ARE SUPPLIED BY THE MANUFACTURER OR IMPORTER. CHECK YOUR LOCAL GUNSHOP.

7TH ANNUAL EDITION **245**

Includes models suitable for several forms of competition and other sporting purposes.

AUTO-ORDNANCE 1911A1 COMPETITION MODEL **Caliber:** 45 ACP. **Barrel:** 5". **Weight:** NA. **Length:** NA. **Stocks:** Black textured rubber wrap-around. **Sights:** Blade front, rear adjustable for windage; three-dot system. **Features:** Machined compensator, combat Commander hammer; flat mainspring housing; low profile magazine funnel; metal form magazine bumper; high-ride beavertail grip safety; full-length recoil spring guide system; extended slide stop, safety and magazine catch; Videcki adjustable speed trigger; extended combat ejector. Introduced 1994. Made in U.S. by Auto-Ordnance Corp.
Price: **$615.00**

BENELLI MP95SE MATCH PISTOL **Caliber:** 22 LR, 10-shot magazine. **Barrel:** 4.33". **Weight:** 38.8 oz. **Length:** 11.81" overall. **Stocks:** Stippled walnut match type; anatomically shaped. **Sights:** Match type. Blade front, click-adjustable rear for windage and elevation. **Features:** Fully adjustable trigger for pull and position, and is removable. Special internal weight box on sub-frame below barrel. Cut for scope rails. Introduced 1993. Imported from Italy by European American Armory.
Price: Blue **$550.00**
Price: Chrome **$625.00**
Price: 10.75", no sights **$529.95**
Price: 10.75", RPM sights **$594.95**
Price: 12", no sights **$562.95**
Price: 12", RPM sights **$643.75**
Price: 15", no sights **$592.95**
Price: 15", RPM sights **$675.00**
Price: 10.75" Ultimate Silhouette (heavy barrel, special forend, RPM rear sight with hooded front, gold-plated trigger) **$687.95**

BERNARDELLI MODEL 69 TARGET PISTOL **Caliber:** 22 LR, 10-shot magazine. **Barrel:** 5.9". **Weight:** 38 oz. **Length:** 9" overall. **Stocks:** Wrap-around, hand-checkered walnut with thumbrest. **Sights:** Fully adjustable and interchangeable target type. **Features:** Conforms to U.I.T. regulations. Has 7.1" sight radius, .27" wide grooved trigger. Manual thumb safety and magazine safety. Introduced 1987. Imported from Italy by Armsport.
Price: **$612.00**

BERETTA MODEL 89 WOOD SPORT GOLD STANDARD PISTOL **Caliber:** 22 LR, 8-shot magazine. **Barrel:** 6" **Weight:** 41 oz. **Length:** 9.5" overall. **Stocks:** Target-type walnut with thumbrest. **Sights:** Interchangeable blade front, fully adjustable rear. **Features:** Single-action target pistol. Matte blue finish. Imported from Italy by Beretta U.S.A.
Price: **$735.00**

BF SINGLE SHOT PISTOL **Caliber:** 22 LR, 357 Mag., 44 Mag., 7-30 Waters, 30-30 Win., 375 Win., 45-70; custom chamberings from 17 Rem. through 45-cal. **Barrel:** 10", 10.75", 12", 15+". **Weight:** 52 oz. **Length:** NA. **Stocks:** Custom Herrett finger-groove grip and forend. **Sights:** Undercut Patridge front, ½-MOA match-quality fully adjustable RPM Iron Sight rear; barrel or receiver mounting. Drilled and tapped for scope mounting. **Features:** Rigid barrel/receiver; falling block action with short lock time; automatic ejection; air-gauged match barrels by Wilson or Douglas; matte black oxide finish standard, electroless nickel optional. Barrel has 11-degree recessed target crown. Introduced 1988. Made in U.S. by E.A. Brown Mfg.
Price: 10", no sights **$499.95**
Price: 10", RPM sights **$564.95**

BROWNING BUCK MARK SILHOUETTE **Caliber:** 22 LR, 10-shot magazine. **Barrel:** 9⅞". **Weight:** 53 oz. **Length:** 14" overall. **Stocks:** Smooth walnut stocks and forend, or finger-groove walnut. **Sights:** Post-type hooded front adjustable for blade width and height; Pro Target rear fully adjustable for windage and elevation. **Features:** Heavy barrel with .900" diameter; 12½" sight radius. Special sighting plane forms scope base. Introduced 1987. Made in U.S. From Browning.
Price: **$401.95**

Auto-Ordnance 1911A1 Competition

Bernardelli Model 69

Beretta Model 89

BF Single Shot

Browning Buck Mark Silhouette

CAUTION: PRICES SHOWN ARE SUPPLIED BY THE MANUFACTURER OR IMPORTER. CHECK YOUR LOCAL GUNSHOP.

Browning Buck Mark Unlimited

Browning Buck Mark Target 5.5

Browning Buck Mark Unlimited Match   Same as the Buck Mark Silhouette except has 14" heavy barrel. Conforms to IHMSA 15" maximum sight radius rule. Introduced 1991.
Price: **$499.95**

Browning Buck Mark Target 5.5   Same as the Buck Mark Silhouette except has a $5\frac{1}{2}$" barrel with .900" diameter. Has hooded sights mounted on a scope base that accepts an optical or reflex sight. Rear sight is a Browning fully adjustable Pro Target, front sight is an adjustable post that customizes to different widths, and can be adjusted for height. Contoured walnut grips with thumbrest, or finger-groove walnut. Matte blue finish. Overall length is $9\frac{5}{8}$", weight is $35\frac{1}{2}$ oz. Has 10-shot magazine. Introduced 1990. From Browning.
Price: **$385.95**
Price: Target 5.5 Gold (as above with gold anodized frame and top rib) **$434.95**
Price: Target 5.5 Nickel (as above with nickel frame and top rib) **$434.95**

Browning Buck Mark Target 5.5 Gold

Browning Buck Mark Target 5.5 Nickel

Browning Buck Mark Field 5.5   Same as the Target 5.5 except has hoodless ramp-style front sight and low profile rear sight. Matte blue finish, contoured or finger-groove walnut stocks. Introduced 1991.
Price: **$385.95**

COLT GOLD CUP NATIONAL MATCH MK IV/SERIES 80   **Caliber:** 45 ACP, 8-shot magazine.   **Barrel:** 5", with new design bushing.   **Weight:** 39 oz.   **Length:** $8\frac{1}{2}$".   **Stocks:** Rubber combat with silver-plated medallion.   **Sights:** Patridge-style front, Colt-Elliason rear adjustable for windage and elevation, sight radius $6\frac{3}{4}$".   **Features:** Arched or flat housing; wide, grooved trigger with adjustable stop; ribbed-top slide, hand fitted, with improved ejection port.
Price: Blue **$899.00**
Price: Stainless **$963.00**
Price: Bright stainless **$1,032.00**
Price: Delta Gold Cup (10mm, stainless) **$987.00**

COMPETITOR SINGLE SHOT PISTOL   **Caliber:** 22 LR through 50 Action Express, including belted magnums.   **Barrel:** 14" standard; 10.5" silhouette; 16" optional.   **Weight:** About 59 oz. (14" bbl.).   **Length:** 15.12" overall.   **Stocks:** Ambidextrous; synthetic (standard) or laminated or natural wood.   **Sights:** Ramp front, adjustable rear.   **Features:** Rotary canon-type action cocks on opening; cammed ejector; interchangeable barrels, ejectors. Adjustable single stage trigger, sliding thumb safety and trigger safety. Matte blue finish. Introduced 1988. From Competitor Corp., Inc.
Price: 14", standard calibers, synthetic grip **$379.90**
Price: Extra barrels, from **$132.95**

Browning Buck Mark Field 5.5

Competitor Single Shot

Colt Gold Cup

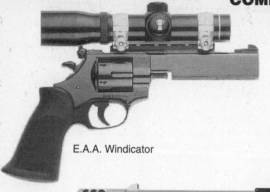

E.A.A. Windicator

E.A.A. Witness Gold Team

Erma ER Match

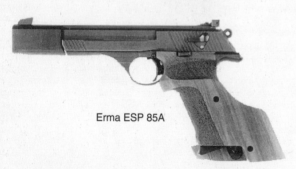

Erma ESP 85A

Erma ESP 85A Golden Target

FAS 602

E.A.A. WINDICATOR TARGET GRADE REVOLVERS **Caliber:** 22 LR, 8-shot, 38 Special, 357 Mag., 6-shot. **Barrel:** 6". **Weight:** 50.2 oz. **Length:** 11.8" overall. **Stocks:** Walnut, competition style. **Sights:** Blade front with three interchangeable blades, fully adjustable rear. **Features:** Adjustable trigger with trigger stop and trigger shoe; frame drilled and tapped for scope mount; target hammer. Comes with barrel weights, plastic carrying box. Introduced 1991. Imported from Germany by European American Armory.
Price: **$299.00**

E.A.A. WITNESS GOLD TEAM AUTO **Caliber:** 9mm Para., 9x21, 10mm Auto, 38 Super, 40 S&W, 45 ACP. **Barrel:** 5.1". **Weight:** 41.6 oz. **Length:** 9.6" overall. **Stocks:** Checkered walnut, competition style. **Sights:** Square post front, fully adjustable rear. **Features:** Triple-chamber compensator; competition SA trigger; extended safety and magazine release; competition hammer; beveled magazine well; beavertail grip. Hand-fitted major components. Hard chrome finish. Match-grade barrel. From E.A.A. Custom Shop. Introduced 1992. From European American Armory.
Price: **$2,195.00**

E.A.A. Witness Silver Team Auto Similar to the Wittness Gold Team except has double-chamber compensator, paddle magazine release, checkered walnut grips, double-dip blue finish. Comes with Super Sight or drilled and tapped for scope mount. Built for the intermediate competition shooter. Introduced 1992. From European American Armory Custom Shop.
Price: 9mm Para., 9x21, 10mm Auto, 38 Super, 40 S&W, 45 ACP . **$1,195.00**

ERMA ER MATCH REVOLVERS **Caliber:** 22 LR, 32 S&W Long, 6-shot. **Barrel:** 6". **Weight:** 47.3 oz. **Length:** 11.2" overall. **Stocks:** Stippled walnut, adjustable match-type. **Sights:** Blade front, micrometer rear adjustable for windage and elevation. **Features:** Polished blue finish. Introduced 1989. Imported from Germany by Precision Sales International.
Price: 22 LR or 32 S&W Long **$1,371.00**

ERMA ESP 85A MATCH PISTOL **Caliber:** 22 LR, 8-shot; 32 S&W, 5-shot magazine. **Barrel:** 6". **Weight:** 39 oz. **Length:** 10" overall. **Stocks:** Match-type of stippled walnut; adjustable. **Sights:** Interchangeable blade front, micrometer adjustable rear with interchangeable leaf. **Features:** Five-way adjustable trigger; exposed hammer and separate firing pin block allow unlimited dry firing practice. Blue or matte chrome; right- or left-hand. Introduced 1988. Imported from Germany by Precision Sales International.
Price: 22 LR **$1,645.00**
Price: 22 LR, left-hand **$1,675.00**
Price: 22 LR, matte chrome **$1,753.00**
Price: 32 S&W **$1,714.00**
Price: 32 S&W, left-hand **$1,744.00**
Price: 32 S&W, matte chrome **$1,822.00**
Price: 32 S&W, matte chrome, left-hand **$1,852.00**

Erma ESP 85A Golden Target Pistol Similar to the ESP-85A Match except has high-polish gold finish on the slide, different adjustable match stocks with finger grooves. Comes with fully interchangeable 6" barrels for 22 LR and 32 S&W. Introduced 1994. Imported from Germany by Precision Sales International.
Price: **$2,100.00**

FAS 602 MATCH PISTOL **Caliber:** 22 LR, 5-shot. **Barrel:** 5.6". **Weight:** 37 oz. **Length:** 11" overall. **Stocks:** Walnut wraparound; sizes small, medium or large, or adjustable. **Sights:** Match. Blade front, open notch rear fully adjustable for windage and elevation. Sight radius is 8.66". **Features:** Line of sight is only $\frac{11}{32}$" above centerline of bore; magazine is inserted from top; adjustable and removable trigger mechanism; single lever takedown. Full 5-year warranty. Imported from Italy by Nygord Precision Products.
Price: **$995.00**

FAS 601 Match Pistol Similar to Model 602 except has different match stocks with adjustable palm shelf, 22 Short only for rapid fire shooting; weighs 40 oz., 5.6" bbl.; has gas ports through top of barrel and slide to reduce recoil; slightly different trigger and sear mechanisms. Imported from Italy by Nygord Precision Products.
Price: **$1,095.00**

FAS 603 Match Pistol Similar to the FAS 602 except chambered for 32 S&W with 5-shot magazine; 5.3" barrel; 8.66" sight radius; overall length 11.0"; weighs 42.3 oz. Imported from Italy by Nygord Precision Products.
Price: **$1,050.00**

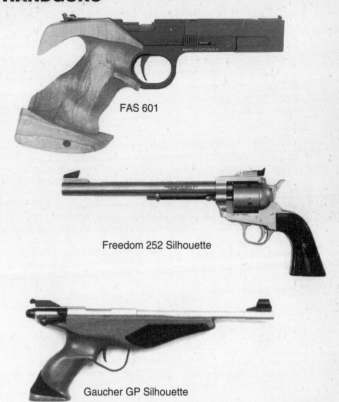

FAS 601

Freedom 252 Silhouette

FREEDOM ARMS CASULL MODEL 252 SILHOUETTE **Caliber:** 22 LR, 5-shot cylinder. **Barrel:** 9.95". **Weight:** 63 oz. **Length:** NA **Stocks:** Black micarta, western style. **Sights:** ⅛" Patridge front, Iron Sight Gun Works silhouette rear, click adjustable for windage and elevation. **Features:** Stainless steel. Built on the 454 Casull frame. Two-point firing pin, lightened hammer for fast lock time. Trigger pull is 3 to 5 lbs. with pre-set overtravel screw. Introduced 1991. From Freedom Arms.
Price: Silhouette Class **$1,350.00**
Price: Extra fitted 22 WMR cylinder **$233.00**

Freedom Arms Casull Model 252 Varmint Similar to the Silhouette Class revolver except has 7.5" barrel, weighs 59 oz., has black and green laminated hardwood grips, and comes with brass bead front sight, express shallow V rear sight with windage and elevation adjustments. Introduced 1991. From Freedom Arms.
Price: Varmint Class **$1,295.00**
Price: Extra fitted 22 WMR cylinder **$233.00**

Gaucher GP Silhouette

GAUCHER GP SILHOUETTE PISTOL **Caliber:** 22 LR, single shot. **Barrel:** 10". **Weight:** 42.3 oz. **Length:** 15.5" overall. **Stocks:** Stained hardwood. **Sights:** Hooded post on ramp front, open rear adjustable for windage and elevation. **Features:** Matte chrome barrel, blued bolt and sights. Other barrel lengths available on special order. Introduced 1991. Imported by Mandall Shooting Supplies.
Price: **$323.00**

GLOCK 17L COMPETITION AUTO **Caliber:** 9mm Para., 17-shot magazine. **Barrel:** 6.02". **Weight:** 23.3 oz. **Length:** 8.85" overall. **Stocks:** Black polymer. **Sights:** Blade front with white dot, fixed or adjustable rear. **Features:** Polymer frame, steel slide; double-action trigger with "Safe Action" system; mechanical firing pin safety, drop safety; simple takedown without tools; locked breech, recoil operated action. Introduced 1989. Imported from Austria by Glock, Inc.
Price: **$806.67**

Glock 17L

GLOCK 24 COMPETITION MODEL PISTOL **Caliber:** 40 S&W, 15-shot magazine. **Barrel:** 6.02". **Weight:** 29.5 oz. **Length:** 8.85" overall. **Stocks:** Black polymer. **Sights:** Blade front with dot, white outline rear adjustable for windage. **Features:** Long-slide competition model available as compensated or non-compensated gun. Factory-installed competition trigger; drop-free magazine. Introduced 1994. Imported from Austria by Glock, Inc.
Price: **$806.67**

Glock 24

Hammerli 208s

HAMMERLI MODEL 208s PISTOL **Caliber:** 22 LR, 8-shot magazine. **Barrel:** 5.9". **Weight:** 37.5 oz. **Length:** 10" overall. **Stocks:** Walnut, target-type with thumbrest. **Sights:** Blade front, open fully adjustable rear. **Features:** Adjustable trigger, including length; interchangeable rear sight elements. Imported from Switzerland by Hammerli Pistols USA, Mandall Shooting Supplies.
Price: About **$1,695.00**

CAUTION: PRICES SHOWN ARE SUPPLIED BY THE MANUFACTURER OR IMPORTER. CHECK YOUR LOCAL GUNSHOP.

7TH ANNUAL EDITION **249**

HAMMERLI MODEL 160/162 FREE PISTOLS Caliber: 22 LR, single shot. **Barrel:** 11.30". **Weight:** 46.94 oz. **Length:** 17.52" overall. **Stocks:** Walnut; full match style with adjustable palm shelf. Stippled surfaces. **Sights:** Changeable blade front, open, fully adjustable match rear. **Features:** Model 160 has mechanical set trigger; Model 162 has electronic trigger; both fully adjustable with provisions for dry firing. Introduced 1993. Imported from Switzerland by Hammerli Pistols USA.

Price: Model 160, about **$1,910.00**
Price: Model 162, about **$2,095.00**

Hammerli 160

Hammerli 162

HAMMERLI MODEL 280 TARGET PISTOL Caliber: 22 LR, 6-shot; 32 S&W Long WC, 5-shot. **Barrel:** 4.5". **Weight:** 39.1 oz. (32). **Length:** 11.8" overall. **Stocks:** Walnut match-type with stippling, adjustable palm shelf. **Sights:** Match sights, micrometer adjustable; interchangeable elements. **Features:** Has carbon-reinforced synthetic frame and bolt/barrel housing. Trigger is adjustable for pull weight, take-up weight, let-off, and length, and is interchangeable. Interchangeable metal or carbon fiber counterweights. Sight radius of 8.8". Comes with barrel weights, spare magazine, loading tool, cleaning rods. Introduced 1990. Imported from Switzerland by Hammerli Pistols USA and Mandall Shooting Supplies.

Price: 22-cal., about **$1,465.00**
Price: 32-cal., about **$1,650.00**

Hammerli 280

McMILLAN SIGNATURE JR. LONG RANGE PISTOL Caliber: Any suitable caliber. **Barrel:** To customer specs. **Weight:** 5 lbs. **Stock:** McMillan fiberglass. **Sights:** None furnished; comes with scope rings. **Features:** Right- or left-hand McMillan benchrest action of titanium or stainless steel; single shot or repeater. Comes with bipod. Introduced 1992. Made in U.S. by McMillan Gunworks, Inc.

Price: **$2,400.00**

McMILLAN WOLVERINE AUTO PISTOL Caliber: 9mm Para., 10mm Auto, 38 Wadcutter, 38 Super, 45 Italian, 45 ACP. **Barrel:** 6". **Weight:** 45 oz. **Length:** 9.5" overall. **Stocks:** Pachmayr rubber. **Sights:** Blade front, fully adjustable rear; low profile. **Features:** Integral compensator; round burr-style hammer; extended grip safety; checkered backstrap; skeletonized aluminum match trigger. Many finish options. Announced 1992. Made in U.S. by McMillan Gunworks, Inc.

Price: Combat or Competition Match **$1,700.00**

McMillan Wolverine

MITCHELL ARMS OLYMPIC II I.S.U. AUTO PISTOL Caliber: 22 Short, 10-shot magazine. **Barrel:** 6.75" round tapered, with stabilizer. **Weight:** 40 oz. **Length:** 11.25" overall. **Stocks:** Checkered walnut with thumbrest. **Sights:** Undercut ramp front, frame-mounted click adjustable square notch rear. **Features:** Integral stabilizer with two removable weights. Trigger adjustable for pull and over-travel; blue finish; stippled front and backstraps; push-button barrel takedown. Announced 1992. From Mitchell Arms.

Price: **$599.00**

Mitchell Olympic II I.S.U.

MITCHELL VICTOR II AUTO PISTOL Caliber: 22 LR, 10-shot magazine. **Barrel:** 4.5" vent rib, 5.5" vent, dovetail or Weaver ribs. **Weight:** 44 oz. **Length:** 9.75" overall. **Stocks:** Military-type checkered walnut with thumbrest. **Sights:** Blade front, fully adjustable rear mounted on rib. **Features:** Push-button takedown for barrel interchangeability. Bright stainless steel combo or royal blue finish. Introduced 1994. Made in U.S. From Mitchell Arms.

Price: Vent rib, 4.5" barrel **$569.00**
Price: Dovetail rib, 5.5" barrel **$599.00**
Price: Weaver rib, 5.5" barrel **$648.00**

Mitchell Victor II

REMINGTON XP-100 SILHOUETTE PISTOL Caliber: 7mm BR Rem., single shot. **Barrel:** 10½". **Weight:** 3⅞ lbs. **Length:** 17¼" overall. **Stock:** American walnut. **Sights:** Blade front, fully adjustable square notch rear. **Features:** Mid-handle grip with scalloped contours for left- or right-handed shooters; match-type trigger; two-position thumb safety. Matte blue finish.

Price: **$625.00**

Remington XP-100 Silhouette

CAUTION: PRICES SHOWN ARE SUPPLIED BY THE MANUFACTURER OR IMPORTER. CHECK YOUR LOCAL GUNSHOP.

COMPETITION HANDGUNS

RUGER MARK II TARGET MODEL AUTO PISTOL **Caliber:** 22 LR, 10-shot magazine. **Barrel:** 5¼", 6⅞". **Weight:** 42 oz. **Length:** 11⅛" overall. **Stocks:** Checkered hard plastic. **Sights:** .125" blade front, micro-click rear, adjustable for windage and elevation. Sight radius 9⅜". **Features:** Introduced 1982.
Price: Blued (MK-514, MK-678) **$310.50**
Price: Stainless (KMK-514, KMK-678) **$389.00**

Ruger Mark II Bull Barrel Same gun as the Target Model except has 5½" or 10" heavy barrel (10" meets all IHMSA regulations). Weight with 5½" barrel is 42 oz., with 10" barrel, 52 oz.
Price: Blued (MK-512) **$310.50**
Price: Blued (MK-10) **$294.50**
Price: Stainless (KMK-10) **$373.00**
Price: Stainless (KMK-512) **$389.00**

Ruger Mark II Government Target Model Same gun as the Mark II Target Model except has 6⅞" barrel, higher sights and is roll marked "Government Target Model" on the right side of the receiver below the rear sight. Identical in all aspects to the military model used for training U.S. armed forces except for markings. Comes with factory test target. Introduced 1987.
Price: Blued (MK-678G) **$356.50**
Price: Stainless (KMK-678G) **$427.29**

Ruger Stainless Government Competition Model 22 Pistol Similar to the Mark II Government Target Model stainless pistol except has 6⅞" slab-sided barrel; the receiver top is drilled and tapped for a Ruger scope base adaptor of blued, chromemoly steel; comes with Ruger 1" stainless scope rings with integral bases for mounting a variety of optical sights; has checkered laminated grip panels with right-hand thumbrest. Has blued open sights with 9¼" radius. Overall length is 11⅛", weight 44 oz. Introduced 1991.
Price: KMK-678GC **$441.00**

SAFARI ARMS MATCHMASTER PISTOL **Caliber:** 45 ACP, 7-shot magazine. **Barrel:** 5"; National Match, stainless steel. **Weight:** 38 oz. **Length:** 8.5" overall. **Stocks:** Smooth walnut with etched scorpion logo. **Sights:** Ramped blade front, rear adjustable for windage and elevation. **Features:** Beavertail grip safety, extended safety, extended slide release, Commander-style hammer; throated, ported, tuned. Finishes: Parkerized matte black, or satin stainless steel. Available from Safari Arms, Inc.
Price: **$670.00**

Safari Arms Matchmaster Carrycomp I Pistol Similar to the Matchmaster except has Wil Schueman-designed hybrid compensator system. Introduced 1993. Made in U.S. by Safari Arms, Inc.
Price: **$1,010.00**

Ruger Mark II Target

Ruger Mark II Bull Stainless

Ruger Mark II Bull Blue

Ruger Mark II Government Target

Safari Matchmaster Carrycomp I

Ruger Mark II Government Competition

Safari Matchmaster

Smith & Wesson 41

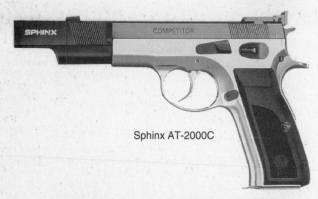

Sphinx AT-2000C

Springfield 1911A1 Trophy
Match Stainless

Springfield 1911A1 Trophy Match Blue

SMITH & WESSON MODEL 41 TARGET **Caliber:** 22 LR, 12-shot clip. **Barrel:** 5½", 7". **Weight:** 44 oz. (5½" barrel). **Length:** 9" overall (5½" barrel). **Stocks:** Checkered walnut with modified thumbrest, usable with either hand. **Sights:** ⅛" Patridge on ramp base; micro-click rear adjustable for windage and elevation. **Features:** ⅜" wide, grooved trigger; adjustable trigger stop.
Price: S&W Bright Blue, either barrel **$753.00**

SPHINX AT-2000C COMPETITOR PISTOL **Caliber:** 9mm Para., 9x21mm, 15-shot, 40 S&W, 11-shot. **Barrel:** 5.31". **Weight:** 40.56 oz. **Length:** 9.84" overall. **Stocks:** Checkered neoprene. **Sights:** Fully adjustable Bo-Mar or Tasco Pro-Point dot sight in Sphinx mount. **Features:** Extended magazine release. Competition slide with dual-port compensated barrel. Two-tone finish only. Introduced 1993. Imported from Switzerland by Sile Distributors, Inc.
Price: With Bo-Mar sights (AT-2000CS) **$1,902.00**
Price: With Tasco Pro-Point and mount **$2,189.00**

Sphinx AT-2000GM Grand Master Pistol Similar to the AT-2000C except has single-action-only trigger mechanism, squared trigger guard, extended beavertail grip, safety and magazine release; notched competition slide for easier cocking. Two-tone finish only. Has dual-port compensated barrel. Available with fully adjustable Bo-Mar sights or Tasco Pro-Point and Sphinx mount. Introduced 1993. Imported from Switzerland by Sile Distributors, Inc.
Price: With Bo-Mar sights (AT-2000GMS) **$2,893.00**
Price: With Tasco Pro-Point and mount (AT-2000GM) . . . **$2,971.00**

SPRINGFIELD INC. 1911A1 BULLSEYE WADCUTTER PISTOL **Caliber:** 45 ACP. **Barrel:** 5". **Weight:** 45 oz. **Length:** 8.59" overall (5" barrel). **Stocks:** Checkered walnut. **Sights:** Bo-Mar rib with undercut blade front, fully adjustable rear. **Features:** Built for wadcutter loads only. Has full-length recoil spring guide rod, fitted Videki speed trigger with 3.5-lb. pull; match Commander hammer and sear; beavertail grip safety; lowered and flared ejection port; tuned extractor; fitted slide to frame; recoil buffer system; beveled and polished magazine well; checkered front strap and steel mainspring housing (flat housing standard); polished and throated National Match barrel and bushing. Comes with two magazines with slam pads, plastic carrying case, test target. Introduced 1992. From Springfield Inc.
Price: . . . . **P.O.R.**

Springfield Inc. 1911A1 Trophy Match Pistol Similar to the 1911A1 except factory accurized, has 4- to 5½-lb. trigger pull, click adjustable rear sight, match-grade barrel and bushing. Comes with checkered walnut grips. Introduced 1994. From Springfield, Inc.
Price: Blue **$899.00**
Price: Stainless steel **$936.00**

Springfield Inc. Trophy Master Expert Pistol Similar to the 1911A1 Trophy Master Competition Pistol except has triple-chamber tapered cone compensator on match barrel with dovetailed front sight; lowered and flared ejection port; fully tuned for reliability. Comes with two magazines, plastic carrying case. Introduced 1992. From Springfield Inc.
Price: 45 ACP, Duotone finish . . . . **P.O.R.**
Price: Trophy Master Expert Ltd. . . . . **P.O.R.**

Springfield Inc. Basic Competition Pistol Has low-mounted Bo-Mar adjustable rear sight, undercut blade front; match throated barrel and bushing; polished feed ramp; lowered and flared ejection port; fitted Videki speed trigger with tuned 3.5-lb. pull; fitted slide to frame; recoil buffer system; Pachmayr mainspring housing; Pachmayr grips. Comes with two magazines with slam pads, plastic carrying case. Introduced 1992. From Springfield Inc.
Price: 45 ACP, blue, 5" only . . . . **P.O.R.**

Springfield Inc. 1911A1 N.M. Hardball Pistol Has Bo-Mar adjustable rear sight with undercut front blade; fitted match Videki trigger with 4-lb. pull; fitted slide to frame; throated National Match barrel and bushing; polished feed ramp; recoil buffer system; tuned extractor; Herrett walnut grips. Comes with two magazines, plastic carrying case, test target. Introduced 1992. From Springfield Inc.
Price: 45 ACP, blue . . . . **P.O.R.**

Springfield Inc. Trophy Master Competition Pistol Similar to the 1911A1 Entry Level Wadcutter Pistol except has brazed, serrated improved ramp front sight; extended ambidextrous thumb safety; match Commander hammer and sear; serrated rear slide; Pachmay flat mainspring housing; extended magazine release; beavertail grip safety; full-length recoil spring guide; Pachmayr wrap-around grips. Comes with two magazines with slam pads, plastic carrying case. Introduced 1992. From Springfield Inc.
Price: 45 ACP, blue . . . . **P.O.R.**

CAUTION: PRICES SHOWN ARE SUPPLIED BY THE MANUFACTURER OR IMPORTER. CHECK YOUR LOCAL GUNSHOP.

T/C Super 14 Contender Blue

Springfield Inc. Trophy Master Distinguished Pistol Has all the features of the 1911A1 Trophy Master Expert except is full-house pistol with Bo-Mar low-mounted adjustable rear sight; full-length recoil spring guide rod and recoil spring retainer; beveled and polished magazine well; walnut grips. Hard chrome finish. Comes with two magazines with slam pads, plastic carrying case. From Springfield Inc.
Price: 45 ACP . . . . **P.O.R.**
Price: Trophy Master Distinguished Limited . . . . **P.O.R.**

THOMPSON/CENTER SUPER 14 CONTENDER **Caliber:** 22 LR, 222 Rem., 223 Rem., 7mm TCU, 7-30 Waters, 30-30 Win., 35 Rem., 357 Rem. Maximum, 44 Mag., 10mm Auto, 445 Super Mag., single shot. **Barrel:** 14". **Weight:** 45 oz. **Length:** 17$\frac{1}{4}$" overall. **Stocks:** T/C "Competitor Grip" (walnut and rubber). **Sights:** Fully adjustable target-type. **Features:** Break-open action with auto safety. Interchangeable barrels for both rimfire and centerfire calibers. Introduced 1978.
Price: **$445.00**
Price: Extra barrels, blued **$210.00**

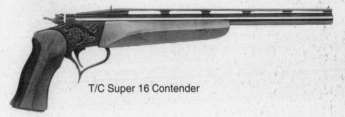

T/C Super 16 Contender

Thompson/Center Super 16 Contender Same as the T/C Super 14 Contender except has 16$\frac{1}{4}$" barrel. Rear sight can be mounted at mid-barrel position (10$\frac{3}{4}$" radius) or moved to the rear (using scope mount position) for 14$\frac{3}{4}$" radius. Overall length is 20$\frac{1}{4}$". Comes with T/C Competitor Grip of walnut and rubber. Available in 22 LR, 22 WMR, 223 Rem., 7-30 Waters, 30-30 Win., 35 Rem., 44 Mag., 45-70 Gov't. Also available with 16" vent rib barrel with internal choke, caliber 45 Colt/410 shotshell.
Price: **$450.00**
Price: 45-70 Gov't **$455.00**
Price: Extra 16" barrels (blued) **$215.00**
Price: As above, 45-70 . . . . **$220.00**
Price: Super 16 Vent Rib (45-410) **$490.00**
Price: Extra vent rib barrel **$245.00**

T/C Super 14 Contender Stainless

Consult our Directory pages for the location of firms mentioned.

Unique D.E.S. 69U

UNIQUE D.E.S. 32U RAPID FIRE MATCH **Caliber:** 32 S&W Long wadcutter. **Barrel:** 5.9". **Weight:** 40.2 oz. **Stocks:** Anatomically shaped, adjustable stippled French walnut. **Sights:** Blade front, micrometer click rear. **Features:** Trigger adjustable for weight and position; dry firing mechanism; slide stop catch. Optional sleeve weights. Introduced 1990. Imported from France by Nygord Precision Products.
Price: Right-hand, about **$1,295.00**
Price: Left-hand, about **$1,345.00**

UNIQUE D.E.S. 69U TARGET PISTOL **Caliber:** 22 LR, 5-shot magazine. **Barrel:** 5.91". **Weight:** 35.3 oz. **Length:** 10.5" overall. **Stocks:** French walnut target-style with thumbrest and adjustable shelf; hand-checkered panels. **Sights:** Ramp front, micro. adj. rear mounted on frame; 8.66" sight radius. **Features:** Meets U.I.T. standards. Comes with 260-gram barrel weight; 100, 150, 350-gram weights available. Fully adjustable match trigger; dry-firing safety device. Imported from France by Nygord Precision Products.
Price: Right-hand, about **$1,195.00**
Price: Left-hand, about **$1,245.00**

Unique 2000-U Match

UNIQUE MODEL 2000-U MATCH PISTOL **Caliber:** 22 Short, 5-shot magazine. **Barrel:** 5.9". **Weight:** 43 oz. **Length:** 11.3" overall. **Stocks:** Anatomically shaped, adjustable, stippled French walnut. **Sights:** Blade front, fully adjustable rear; 9.7" sight radius. **Features:** Light alloy frame, steel slide and shock absorber; five barrel vents reduce recoil, three of which can be blocked; trigger adjustable for position and pull weight. Comes with 340-gram weight housing, 160-gram available. Introduced 1984. Imported from France by Nygord Precision Products.
Price: Right-hand, about **$1,350.00**
Price: Left-hand, about **$1,400.00**

WESSON FIREARMS MODEL 40 SILHOUETTE **Caliber:** 357 Maximum, 6-shot. **Barrel:** 4", 6", 8", 10". **Weight:** 64 oz. (8" bbl.). **Length:** 14.3" overall (8" bbl.). **Stocks:** Smooth walnut, target-style. **Sights:** $\frac{1}{8}$" serrated front, fully adjustable rear. **Features:** Meets criteria for IHMSA competition with 8" slotted barrel. Blue or stainless steel. Made in U.S. by Wesson Firearms Co., Inc.
Price: Blue, 4" **$488.00**
Price: Blue, 6" **$508.00**
Price: Blue, 8" **$550.94**
Price: Blue, 10" **$579.20**
Price: Stainless, 4" **$550.00**
Price: Stainless, 6" **$569.00**
Price: Stainless, 8" slotted **$625.83**
Price: Stainless, 10" **$651.16**

WESSON FIREARMS MODEL 22 SILHOUETTE REVOLVER
Caliber: 22 LR, 6-shot. **Barrel:** 10", regular vent or vent heavy. **Weight:** 53 oz. **Stocks:** Combat style. **Sights:** Patridge-style front, .080" narrow notch rear. **Features:** Single action only. Available in blue or stainless. Introduced 1989. From Wesson Firearms Co., Inc.

Price: Blue, regular vent	$459.72
Price: Blue, vent heavy	$478.10
Price: Stainless, regular vent	$488.84
Price: Stainless, vent heavy	$516.40

Wesson 22 Silhouette

WESSON FIREARMS 45 PIN GUN
Caliber: 45 ACP, 6-shot. **Barrel:** 5" with 1:14" twist; Taylor two-stage forcing cone; compensated shroud. **Weight:** 54 oz. **Length:** 12.5" overall. **Stocks:** Finger-groove Hogue Monogrip. **Sights:** Pin front, fully adjustable rear. Has 8.375" sight radius. **Features:** Based on 44 Magnum frame. Polished blue or brushed stainless steel. Uses half-moon clips with 45 ACP, or 45 Auto Rim ammunition. Introduced 1994. Made in U.S. by Wesson Firearms Co., Inc.

Price: Blue, regular vent	$654.00
Price: Blue, vent heavy	$663.00
Price: Stainless, regular vent	$713.00
Price: Stainless vent heavy	$762.00

Wesson 45 Pin Gun

WESSON FIREARMS MODEL 322/7322 TARGET REVOLVER
Caliber: 32-20, 6-shot. **Barrel:** 2.5", 4", 6", 8", standard, vent, vent heavy. **Weight:** 43 oz. (6" VH). **Length:** 11.25" overall. **Stocks:** Checkered walnut. **Sights:** Red ramp interchangeable front, fully adjustable rear. **Features:** Brigh blue or stainless. Introduced 1991. From Wesson Firearms Co., Inc.

Price: 6", blue	$355.00
Price: 6", stainless	$384.00
Price: 8", vent, blue	$404.55
Price: 8", stainless	$434.71
Price: 6", vent heavy, blue	$412.20
Price: 6", vent heavy, stainless	$441.32
Price: 8", vent heavy, blue	$422.94
Price: 8", vent heavy, stainless	$459.72

WICHITA CLASSIC SILHOUETTE PISTOL
Caliber: All standard calibers with maximum overall length of 2.800". **Barrel:** 11¼". **Weight:** 3 lbs., 15 oz. **Stocks:** AAA American walnut with oil finish, checkered grip. **Sights:** Hooded post front, open adjustable rear. **Features:** Three locking lug bolt, three gas ports; completely adjustable Wichita trigger. Introduced 1981. From Wichita Arms.

Price:	$2,950.00

Wichita Silhouette

WICHITA SILHOUETTE PISTOL
Caliber: 308 Win. F.L., 7mm IHMSA, 7mm-308. **Barrel:** 14¹⁵⁄₁₆". **Weight:** 4½ lbs. **Length:** 21³⁄₈" overall. **Stock:** American walnut with oil finish. Glass bedded. **Sights:** Wichita Multi-Range sight system. **Features:** Comes with left-hand action with right-hand grip. Round receiver and barrel. Fluted bolt, flat bolt handle. Wichita adjustable trigger. Introduced 1979. From Wichita Arms.

Price: Center grip stock	$1,207.00
Price: As above except with Rear Position Stock and target-type Lightpull trigger	$1,207.00

Wichita International

WICHITA INTERNATIONAL PISTOL
Caliber: 22 LR, 22 WMR, 32 H&R Mag., 357 Super Mag., 357 Mag., 7R, 7mm Super Mag., 7-30 Waters, 30-30 Win., single shot. **Barrel:** 10", 10½", 14". **Weight:** 3 lbs. 2 oz. (with 10", 10½" barrels). **Stocks:** Walnut grip and forend. **Sights:** Patridge front, adjustable rear. Wichita Multi-Range sight system optional. **Features:** Made of stainless steel. Break-open action. Grip dimensions same as Colt 45 Auto. Drilled and tapped for furnished see-thru rings. Extra barrels are factory fitted. Introduced 1983. Available from Wichita Arms.

Price: International 10"	$595.00
Price: International 14"	$645.00
Price: Extra barrels, 10"	$365.00
Price: Extra barrels, 14"	$395.00

Wesson Firearms Model 445 Supermag Revolver Similar size and weight as the Model 40 revolvers. Chambered for the 445 Supermag cartridge, a longer version of the 44 Magnum. Barrel lengths of 4", 6", 8", 10". Contact maker for complete price list. Introduced 1989. From Wesson Firearms Co., Inc.

Price: 4", vent heavy, blue	$539.00
Price: As above, stainless	$615.00
Price: 8", vent heavy, blue	$594.00
Price: As above, stainless	$662.00
Price: 10", vent heavy, blue	$615.00
Price: As above, stainless	$683.00
Price: 8", vent slotted, blue	$575.00
Price: As above, stainless	$632.00
Price: 10", vent slotted, blue	$597.00
Price: As above, stainless	$657.00

CAUTION: PRICES SHOWN ARE SUPPLIED BY THE MANUFACTURER OR IMPORTER. CHECK YOUR LOCAL GUNSHOP.

Includes models suitable for hunting and competitive courses of fire, both police and international.

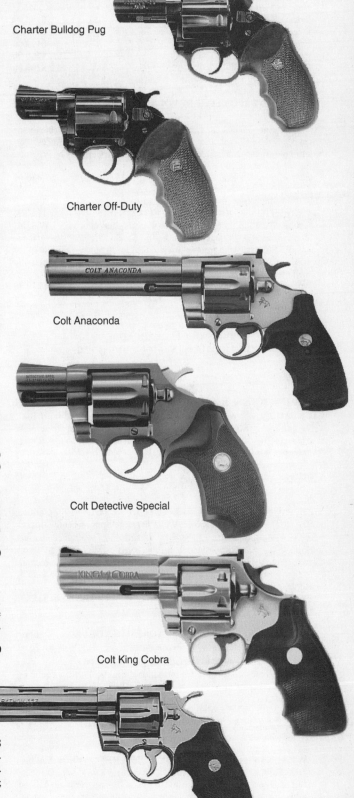

CHARTER BULLDOG PUG REVOLVER **Caliber:** 44 Spec., 5-shot. **Barrel:** 2½". **Weight:** 19½ oz. **Length:** 7" overall. **Stocks:** Checkered walnut Bulldog. **Sights:** Ramp-style front, fixed rear. **Features:** Blue or stainless steel construction. Fully shrouded barrel. Reintroduced 1993. Made in U.S. by Charco, Inc.
Price: Blue $267.60
Price: Nickel $289.51

Charter Bulldog Pug

CHARTER OFF-DUTY REVOLVER **Caliber:** 22 LR, 22 WMR, 6-shot, 38 Spec., 5-shot. **Barrel:** 2". **Weight:** 17 oz. (38 Spec.). **Length:** 6¼" overall. **Stocks:** Checkered walnut. **Sights:** Ramp-style front, fixed rear. **Features:** Available in blue, stainless or electroless nickel. Fully shrouded barrel. Introduced 1993. Made in U.S. by Charco, Inc.
Price: Blue, 22 or 38 Spec. $199.00
Price: Electroless nickel, 22 or 38 Spec. $239.68
Price: Blue, DA only $207.98
Price: Electroless nickel, DA only $247.18

Charter Off-Duty

CHARTER POLICE UNDERCOVER REVOLVER **Caliber:** 32 H&R Mag., 38 Spec., 6-shot. **Barrel:** 2½". **Weight:** 16 oz. (38 Spec.). **Length:** 6¼" overall. **Stocks:** Checkered walnut. **Sights:** Ramp-style front, fixed rear. **Features:** Blue or stainless steel. Fully shrouded barrel. Reintroduced 1993. Made in U.S. by Charco, Inc.
Price: Blue $237.75
Price: Electroless nickel $252.00

Colt Anaconda

COLT ANACONDA REVOLVER **Caliber:** 44 Rem. Magnum, 45 Colt, 6-shot. **Barrel:** 4", 6", 8". **Weight:** 53 oz. (6" barrel). **Length:** 11⅝" overall. **Stocks:** Combat-style black neoprene with finger grooves. **Sights:** Red insert front, adjustable white outline rear. **Features:** Stainless steel; full-length ejector rod housing; ventilated barrel rib; offset bolt notches in cylinder; wide spur hammer. Introduced 1990.
Price: $587.00
Price: 45 Colt, 6" barrel only $587.00

COLT DETECTIVE SPECIAL REVOLVER **Caliber:** 38 Special, 6-shot. **Barrel:** 2". **Weight:** 22 oz. **Length:** 6⅝" overall. **Stocks:** Black composition. **Sights:** Fixed. Ramp front, square notch rear. **Features:** Glare-proof sights, grooved trigger, shrouded ejector rod. Colt blue finish. Reintroduced 1993.
Price: $384.00

Colt Detective Special

COLT KING COBRA REVOLVER **Caliber:** 357 Magnum, 6-shot. **Barrel:** 4", 6". **Weight:** 42 oz. (4" bbl.). **Length:** 9" overall (4" bbl.). **Stocks:** Checkered rubber. **Sights:** Red insert ramp front, adjustable white outline rear. **Features:** Full-length contoured ejector rod housing, barrel rib. Introduced 1986.
Price: Stainless $437.00

Colt King Cobra

COLT PYTHON REVOLVER **Caliber:** 357 Magnum (handles all 38 Spec.), 6-shot. **Barrel:** 4", 6" or 8", with ventilated rib. **Weight:** 38 oz. (4" bbl.). **Length:** 9¼" (4" bbl.). **Stocks:** Rubber wraparound. **Sights:** ⅛" ramp front, adjustable notch rear. **Features:** Ventilated rib; grooved, crisp trigger; swing-out cylinder; target hammer.
Price: Royal blue, 4", 6", 8" $798.00
Price: Stainless, 4", 6", 8" $885.00
Price: Bright stainless, 4", 6", 8" $917.00

Colt Python Stainless

E.A.A. STANDARD GRADE REVOLVERS **Caliber:** 22 LR, 22 LR/22 WMR, 8-shot; 38 Special, 6-shot. **Barrel:** 4", 6" (22 rimfire); 2", 4" (38 Special). **Weight:** 38 oz. (22 rimfire, 4"). **Length:** 8.8" overall (4" bbl.). **Stocks:** Rubber with finger grooves. **Sights:** Blade front, fixed or adjustable on rimfires; fixed only on 32, 38. **Features:** Swing-out cylinder; hammer block safety; blue finish. Introduced 1991. Imported from Germany by European American Armory.
Price: 38 Special 2" **$180.00**
Price: 38 Special, 4" **$199.00**
Price: 22 LR, 6" **$199.00**
Price: 22 LR/22 WMR combo, 4" **$200.00**
Price: As above, 6" **$200.00**

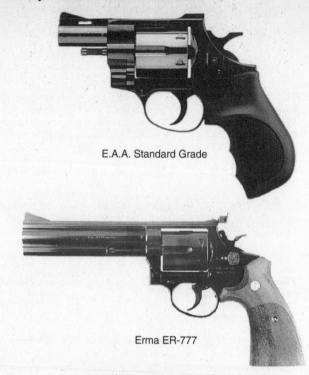

E.A.A. Standard Grade

ERMA ER-777 SPORTING REVOLVER **Caliber:** 357 Mag., 6-shot. **Barrel:** 5½". **Weight:** 43.3 oz. **Length:** 9½" overall (4" barrel). **Stocks:** Stippled walnut service-type. **Sights:** Interchangeable blade front, micro-adjustable rear for windage and elevation. **Features:** Polished blue finish. Adjustable trigger. Imported from Germany by Precision Sales Int'l. Introduced 1988.
Price: **$1,420.00**

HARRINGTON & RICHARDSON SPORTSMAN 999 REVOLVER **Caliber:** 22 Short, Long, Long Rifle, 9-shot. **Barrel:** 4", 6". **Weight:** 30 oz. (4" barrel). **Length:** 8.5" overall. **Stocks:** Walnut-finished hardwood. **Sights:** Blade front adjustable for elevation, rear adjustable for windage. **Features:** Top-break loading; polished blue finish; automatic shell ejection. Reintroduced 1992. From Harrington & Richardson.
Price: **$279.95**

Erma ER-777

Consult our Directory pages for
the location of firms mentioned.

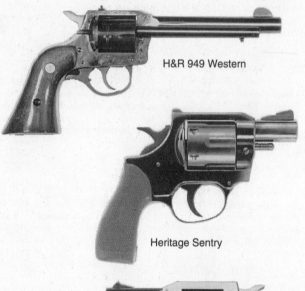

H&R 949 Western

HARRINGTON & RICHARDSON 949 WESTERN REVOLVER **Caliber:** 22 LR, 9-shot cylinder. **Barrel:** 5½". **Weight:** 36 oz. **Length:** NA. **Stocks:** Walnut-stained hardwood. **Sights:** Blade front, adjustable rear. **Features:** Color case-hardened frame and backstrap, traditional loading gate and ejector rod. Introduced 1994. Made in U.S. by Harrington & Richardson.
Price: About **$174.95**

HERITAGE SENTRY DOUBLE-ACTION REVOLVERS **Caliber:** 22 LR, 22 WMR, 32 H&R Mag., 9mm Para., 38 Spec., 6-shot. **Barrel:** 2", 4". **Weight:** 23 oz. (2" barrel). **Length:** 6¼" overall (2" barrel). **Stocks:** Magnum-style round butt; checkered plastic. **Sights:** Ramp front, fixed rear. **Features:** Pill-pin-type ejection; serrated hammer and trigger. Polished blue or nickel finish. Introduced 1993. Made in U.S. by Heritage Mfg., Inc.
Price: . . . . **$109.95 to $119.95**

Heritage Sentry

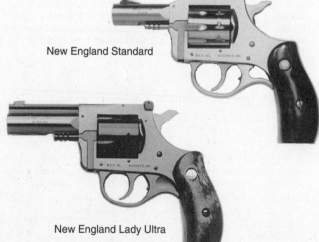

New England Standard

NEW ENGLAND FIREARMS STANDARD REVOLVERS **Caliber:** 22 LR, 9-shot; 32 H&R Mag., 5-shot. **Barrel:** 2½", 4". **Weight:** 26 oz. (22 LR, 2½"). **Length:** 8½" overall (4" bbl.). **Stocks:** Walnut-finished American hardwood with NEF medallion. **Sights:** Fixed. **Features:** Choice of blue or nickel finish. Introduced 1988. From New England Firearms Co.
Price: 22 LR, 32 H&R Mag., blue **$124.95**
Price: 22 LR, 2½", 4", nickel, 32 H&R Mag. 2½" nickel . . . **$134.95**

NEW ENGLAND FIREARMS LADY ULTRA REVOLVER **Caliber:** 32 H&R Mag., 5-shot. **Barrel:** 3". **Weight:** 31 oz. **Length:** 7.25" overall. **Stocks:** Walnut-finished hardwood with NEF medallion. **Sights:** Blade front, fully adjustable rear. **Features:** Swing-out cylinder; polished blue finish. Comes with lockable storage case. Introduced 1992. From New England Firearms Co.
Price: **$149.95**

New England Lady Ultra

DOUBLE-ACTION REVOLVERS, SERVICE & SPORT

NEW ENGLAND FIREARMS ULTRA REVOLVER   Caliber: 22 LR, 9-shot; 22 WMR, 6-shot.   **Barrel:** 4", 6".   **Weight:** 36 oz.   **Length:** $10\frac{5}{8}$" overall (6" barrel).   **Stocks:** Walnut-finished hardwood with NEF medallion.   **Sights:** Blade front, fully adjustable rear.   **Features:** Blue finish. Bull-style barrel with recessed muzzle, high "Lustre" blue/black finish. Introduced 1989. From New England Firearms.
Price: **$149.95**
Price: Ultra Mag 22 WMR **$149.95**

New England Ultra

ROSSI MODEL 68 REVOLVER   Caliber: 38 Spec.   **Barrel:** 2", 3".   **Weight:** 22 oz.   **Stocks:** Checkered wood and rubber.   **Sights:** Ramp front, low profile adjustable rear.   **Features:** All-steel frame, thumb latch operated swing-out cylinder. Introduced 1978. Imported from Brazil by Interarms.
Price: 38, blue, 3", both wood and rubber grips **$218.00**
Price: M68/2 (2" barrel), wood and rubber grips **$231.00**
Price: 3", nickel **$223.00**

Rossi Model 68 2"

ROSSI MODEL 88 STAINLESS REVOLVER   Caliber: 32 S&W, 38 Spec., 5-shot.   **Barrel:** 2", 3".   **Weight:** 22 oz.   **Length:** 7.5" overall.   **Stocks:** Checkered wood, service-style, and rubber.   **Sights:** Ramp front, square notch rear drift adjustable for windage.   **Features:** All metal parts except springs are of 440 stainless steel; matte finish; small frame for concealability. Introduced 1983. Imported from Brazil by Interarms.
Price: 3" barrel, wood and rubber grips **$249.00**
Price: M88/2 (2" barrel), wood and rubber grips **$265.00**

Rossi Model 88 2"

ROSSI MODEL 515, 518 REVOLVERS   Caliber: 22 LR (Model 518), 22 WMR (Model 515), 6-shot.   **Barrel:** 4".   **Weight:** 30 oz.   **Length:** 9" overall.   **Stocks:** Checkered wood and finger-groove wrap-around rubber.   **Sights:** Blade front with red insert, rear adjustable for windage and elevation.   **Features:** Small frame; stainless steel construction; solid integral barrel rib. Introduced 1994. Imported from Brazil by Interarms.
Price: Model 518, 22 LR **$275.00**
Price: Model 515, 22 WMR **$290.00**

ROSSI MODEL 720 REVOLVER   Caliber: 44 Special, 5-shot.   **Barrel:** 3".   **Weight:** 27.5 oz.   **Length:** 8" overall.   **Stocks:** Checkered rubber, combat style.   **Sights:** Red insert front on ramp, fully adjustable rear.   **Features:** All stainless steel construction; solid barrel rib; full ejector rod shroud. Introduced 1992. Imported from Brazil by Interarms.
Price: **$312.00**
Price: Model 720C, spurless hammer, DA only **$312.00**

Rossi Model 88 3"

ROSSI MODEL 851 REVOLVER   Caliber: 38 Special, 6-shot.   **Barrel:** 3" or 4".   **Weight:** 27.5 oz. (3" bbl.).   **Length:** 8" overall (3" bbl.).   **Stocks:** Checkered Brazilian hardwood.   **Sights:** Blade front with red insert, rear adjustable for windage.   **Features:** Medium-size frame; stainless steel construction; ventilated barrel rib. Introduced 1991. Imported from Brazil by Interarms.
Price: **$270.00**

Rossi Model 518

Rossi Model 851

Rossi Model 720C

CAUTION: PRICES SHOWN ARE SUPPLIED BY THE MANUFACTURER OR IMPORTER. CHECK YOUR LOCAL GUNSHOP.

7th ANNUAL EDITION   **257**

Rossi Model 971

Rossi Model 971 Comp

Ruger GP-100 (GP-141)

Ruger Redhawk

Ruger Redhawk 5"

Ruger Redhawk Blue

ROSSI MODEL 971 REVOLVER **Caliber:** 357 Mag., 6-shot. **Barrel:** 2½", 4", 6", heavy. **Weight:** 36 oz. **Length:** 9" overall. **Stocks:** Checkered Brazilian hardwood. Stainless models have checkered, contoured rubber. **Sights:** Blade front, fully adjustable rear. **Features:** Full-length ejector rod shroud; matted sight rib; target-type trigger, wide checkered hammer spur. Introduced 1988. Imported from Brazil by Interarms.

Price: 4", stainless	$301.00
Price: 6", stainless	$301.00
Price: 4", blue	$270.00
Price: 2½", stainless	$301.00

Rossi Model 971 Comp Gun Same as the Model 971 stainless except has 3¼" barrel with integral compensator. Overall length is 9", weight 32 oz. Has red insert front sight, fully adjustable rear. Checkered, contoured rubber grips. Introduced 1993. Imported from Brazil by Interarms.

Price: $301.00

RUGER GP-100 REVOLVERS **Caliber:** 38 Special, 357 Magnum, 6-shot. **Barrel:** 3", 3" heavy, 4", 4" heavy, 6", 6" heavy. **Weight:** 3" barrel—35 oz., 3" heavy barrel—36 oz., 4" barrel—37 oz., 4" heavy barrel—38 oz. **Sights:** Fixed; adjustable on 4" heavy, 6", 6" heavy barrels. **Stocks:** Ruger Santoprene Cushioned Grip with Goncalo Alves inserts. **Features:** Uses action and frame incorporating improvements and features of both the Security-Six and Redhawk revolvers. Full length and short ejector shroud. Satin blue and stainless steel. Introduced 1988.

Price: GP-141 (357, 4" heavy, adj. sights, blue)	$413.50
Price: GP-160 (357, 6", adj. sights, blue)	$413.50
Price: GP-161 (357, 6" heavy, adj. sights, blue)	$413.50
Price: GPF-330 (357, 3"), GPF-830 (38 Spec.)	$397.00
Price: GPF-331 (357, 3" heavy), GPF-831 (38 Spec.)	$397.00
Price: GPF-340 (357, 4"), GPF-840 (38 Spec.)	$397.00
Price: GPF-341 (357, 4" heavy), GPF-841 (38 Spec.)	$397.00
Price: KGP-141 (357, 4" heavy, adj. sights, stainless)	$446.50
Price: KGP-160 (357, 6", adj. sights, stainless)	$446.50
Price: KGP-161 (357, 6" heavy, adj. sights, stainless)	$446.50
Price: KGPF-330 (357, 3", stainless), KGPF-830 (38 Spec.)	$430.00
Price: KGPF-331 (357, 3" heavy, stainless), KGPF-831 (38 Spec.)	$430.00
Price: KGPF-340 (357, 4", stainless), KGPF-840 (38 Spec.)	$430.00
Price: KGPF-341 (357, 4" heavy, stainless), KGPF-841 (38 Spec.)	$430.00

RUGER REDHAWK **Caliber:** 44 Rem. Mag., 6-shot. **Barrel:** 5½", 7½". **Weight:** About 54 oz. (7½" bbl.). **Length:** 13" overall (7½" barrel). **Stocks:** Square butt Goncalo Alves. **Sights:** Interchangeable Patridge-type front, rear adjustable for windage and elevation. **Features:** Stainless steel, brushed satin finish, or blued ordnance steel. Has a 9½" sight radius. Introduced 1979.

Price: Blued, 44 Mag., 5½", 7½"	$458.50
Price: Blued, 44 Mag., 7½", with scope mount, rings	$496.50
Price: Stainless, 44 Mag., 5½", 7½"	$516.75
Price: Stainless, 44 Mag., 7½", with scope mount, rings	$557.25

CAUTION: PRICES SHOWN ARE SUPPLIED BY THE MANUFACTURER OR IMPORTER. CHECK YOUR LOCAL GUNSHOP.

DOUBLE-ACTION REVOLVERS, SERVICE & SPORT

Ruger Super Redhawk Revolver Similar to the standard Redhawk except has a heavy extended frame with the Ruger Integral Scope Mounting System on the wide topstrap. The wide hammer spur has been lowered for better scope clearance. Incorporates the mechanical design features and improvements of the GP-100. Choice of 7½" or 9½" barrel, both with ramp front sight base with Redhawk-style Interchangeable Insert sight blades, adjustable rear sight. Comes with Ruger "Cushioned Grip" panels of Santoprene with Goncalo Alves wood panels. Satin polished stainless steel, 44 Magnum only. Introduced 1987.
Price: KSRH-7 (7½"), KSRH-9 (9½") **$557.25**

Ruger Super Redhawk 7½"

RUGER SP101 REVOLVERS **Caliber:** 22 LR, 32 H&R Mag., 6-shot, 9mm Para., 38 Special +P, 357 Mag., 5-shot. **Barrel:** 2¼", 3$\frac{1}{16}$", 4". **Weight:** 2¼"—25 oz.; 3$\frac{1}{16}$"—27 oz. **Sights:** Adjustable on 22, 32, fixed on others. **Stocks:** Ruger Santoprene Cushioned Grip with Xenoy inserts. **Features:** Incorporates improvements and features found in the GP-100 revolvers into a compact, small frame, double-action revolver. Full-length ejector shroud. Stainless steel only. Introduced 1988.
Price: KSP-821 (2½", 38 Spec.) **$408.00**
Price: KSP-831 (3$\frac{1}{16}$", 38 Spec.) **$408.00**
Price: KSP-221 (2¼", 22 LR) **$408.00**
Price: KSP-240 (4", 22 LR) **$408.00**
Price: KSP-241 (4" heavy bbl., 22 LR) **$408.00**
Price: KSP-3231 (3$\frac{1}{16}$", 32 H&R) **$408.00**
Price: KSP-921 (2¼", 9mm Para.) **$408.00**
Price: KSP-931 (3$\frac{1}{16}$", 9mm Para.) **$408.00**
Price: KSP-321 (2¼", 357 Mag.) **$408.00**
Price: KSP-331 (3$\frac{1}{16}$", 357 Mag.) **$408.00**

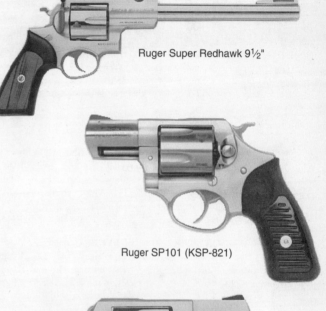
Ruger Super Redhawk 9½"

Ruger SP101 (KSP-821)

Ruger SP101 Double-Action-Only Revolver Similar to the standard SP101 except is double action only with no single-action sear notch. Has spurless hammer for snag-free handling, floating firing pin and Ruger's patented transfer bar safety system. Available with 2½" barrel in 38 Special +P and 357 Magnum only. Weight is 25½ oz., overall length 7.06". Natural brushed satin stainless steel. Introduced 1993.
Price: KSP821L (38 Spec.), KSP321XL (357 Mag.) **$408.00**

SMITH & WESSON MODEL 10 M&P REVOLVER **Caliber:** 38 Special, 6-shot. **Barrel:** 2", 4". **Weight:** 30 oz. **Length:** 9$\frac{5}{16}$" overall. **Stocks:** Soft rubber; round or square butt. Wood optional. **Sights:** Fixed, ramp front, square notch rear.
Price: Blue **$368.00**
Price: With square butt grips **$375.00**

Smith & Wesson Model 10 38 M&P Heavy Barrel Same as regular M&P except has heavy ribbed barrel with square butt grips. Weighs 33½ oz.
Price: Blue **$375.00**

Ruger SP101 DAO (KSP821L)

Ruger SP101 (KSP-831)

Smith & Wesson Model 10

Ruger SP101 (KSP-240)

SMITH & WESSON MODEL 13 H.B. M&P   Caliber: 357 and 38 Special, 6-shot. **Barrel:** 3" or 4". **Weight:** 34 oz. **Length:** $9^5/_{16}$" overall (4" bbl.). **Stocks:** Soft rubber; wood optional. **Sights:** $^1/_8$" serrated ramp front, fixed square notch rear. **Features:** Heavy barrel, K-frame, square butt (4"), round butt (3").
Price: Blue **$386.00**
Price: Model 65, as above in stainless steel **$423.00**

Smith & Wesson Model 14

Smith & Wesson Model 15

Smith & Wesson Model 19 4"

Smith & Wesson Model 629 6"

Smith & Wesson Model 629 Classic

Smith & Wesson Model 629 Classic DX

Smith & Wesson Model 27

SMITH & WESSON MODEL 14 FULL LUG REVOLVER   Caliber: 38 Special, 6-shot. **Barrel:** 6", full lug. **Weight:** 47 oz. **Length:** $11^1/_8$" overall. **Stocks:** Soft rubber; wood optional. **Sights:** Pinned Patridge front, adjustable micrometer click rear. **Features:** Has .500" target hammer, .312" smooth combat trigger. Polished blue finish. Reintroduced 1991. Limited production.
Price: **$461.00**

SMITH & WESSON MODEL 15 COMBAT MASTERPIECE   Caliber: 38 Special, 6-shot. **Barrel:** 4". **Weight:** 32 oz. **Length:** $9^5/_{16}$" (4" bbl.). **Stocks:** Soft rubber; wood optional. **Sights:** Front, Baughman Quick Draw on ramp, micro-click rear, adjustable for windage and elevation.
Price: Blued **$407.00**

SMITH & WESSON MODEL 19 COMBAT MAGNUM   Caliber: 357 Magnum and 38 Special, 6-shot. **Barrel:** $2^1/_2$", 4", 6". **Weight:** 36 oz. **Length:** $9^9/_{16}$" (4" bbl.). **Stocks:** Soft rubber; wood optional. **Sights:** Serrated ramp front $2^1/_2$" or 4" bbl., red ramp on 4", 6" bbl., micro-click rear adjustable for windage and elevation.
Price: S&W Bright Blue, adj. sights . . . . **$408.00** to **$443.00**

SMITH & WESSON MODEL 27 REVOLVER   Caliber: 357 Magnum and 38 Special, 6-shot. **Barrel:** 6". **Weight:** $45^1/_2$ oz. **Length:** $11^5/_{16}$" overall. **Stocks:** Soft rubber; wood optional. Grooved tangs and trigger. **Sights:** Patridge front, micro-click rear adjustable for windage and elevation.
Price: **$486.00**

SMITH & WESSON MODEL 29, 629 REVOLVERS   Caliber: 44 Magnum, 6-shot. **Barrel:** 6", $8^3/_8$". **Weight:** 47 oz. (6" bbl.). **Length:** $11^3/_8$" overall (6" bbl.). **Stocks:** Soft rubber; wood optional. **Sights:** $^1/_8$" red ramp front, micro-click rear, adjustable for windage and elevation.
Price: S&W Bright Blue, 6" **$549.00**
Price: S&W Bright Blue, $8^3/_8$" **$560.00**
Price: Model 629 (stainless steel), 4" **$581.00**
Price: Model 629, 6" **$586.00**
Price: Model 629, $8^3/_8$" barrel **$600.00**

Smith & Wesson Model 29, 629 Classic Revolvers   Similar to the standard Model 29 and 629 except has full-lug 5", $6^1/_2$" or $8^3/_8$" barrel; chamfered front of cylinder; interchangable red ramp front sight with adjustable white outline rear; Hogue round butt Santoprene grips with S&W monogram; the frame is drilled and tapped for scope mounting. Factory accurizing and endurance packages. Overall length with 5" barrel is $10^1/_2$"; weight is 51 oz. Introduced 1990.
Price: Model 29 Classic, 5", $6^1/_2$" **$591.00**
Price: As above, $8^3/_8$", (blue) **$603.00**
Price: Model 629 Classic (stainless), 5", $6^1/_2$" **$623.00**
Price: As above, $8\ ^3/_8$" **$643.00**

Smith & Wesson Model 629 Classic DX Revolver   Similar to the Classic Hunters except offered only with $6^1/_2$" or $8^3/_8$" full-lug barrel; comes with five front sights: 50-yard red ramp; 50-yard black Patridge; 100-yard black Patridge with gold bead; 50-yard black ramp; and 50-yard black Patridge with white dot. Comes with Hogue combat-style round butt grip. Introduced 1991.
Price: Model 629 Classic DX, $6^1/_2$" **$803.00**
Price: As above, $8^3/_8$" **$829.00**

CAUTION: PRICES SHOWN ARE SUPPLIED BY THE MANUFACTURER OR IMPORTER. CHECK YOUR LOCAL GUNSHOP.

DOUBLE-ACTION REVOLVERS, SERVICE & SPORT

SMITH & WESSON MODEL 36, 37 CHIEFS SPECIAL & AIR-WEIGHT **Caliber:** 38 Special, 5-shot. **Barrel:** 2", 3". **Weight:** 19½ oz. (2" bbl.); 13½ oz. (Airweight). **Length:** 6½" (2" bbl. and round butt). **Stocks:** Round butt soft rubber; wood optional. **Sights:** Fixed, serrated ramp front, square notch rear.
Price: Blue, standard Model 36, 2" $374.00
Price: As above, 3" $374.00
Price: Blue, Airweight Model 37, 2" only $408.00
Price: As above, nickel, 2" only $424.00

Smith & Wesson Model 36LS, 60LS LadySmith Similar to the standard Model 36. Available with 2" barrel. Comes with smooth, contoured rosewood grips with the S&W monogram. Has a speedloader cutout. Comes in a fitted carry/storage case. Introduced 1989.
Price: Model 36LS $404.00
Price: Model 60LS (as above except in stainless) $456.00

Smith & Wesson Model 60 3" Full-Lug Revolver Similar to the Model 60 Chief's Special except has 3" full-lug barrel, adjustable micrometer click black blade rear sight; rubber Uncle Mike's Custom Grade Boot Grip. Overall length 7½"; weight 24½ oz. Introduced 1991.
Price: $453.00

Smith & Wesson Model 60 Chiefs Special Stainless Same as Model 36 except all stainless construction, 2" bbl. and round butt only.
Price: Stainless steel $427.00

SMITH & WESSON MODEL 38 BODYGUARD **Caliber:** 38 Special, 5-shot. **Barrel:** 2". **Weight:** 14½ oz. **Length:** 6⁵⁄₁₆" overall. **Stocks:** Soft rubber; wood optional. **Sights:** Fixed serrated ramp front, square notch rear. **Features:** Alloy frame; internal hammer.
Price: Blue $440.00
Price: Nickel $455.00

Smith & Wesson Model 49, 649 Bodyguard Revolvers Same as Model 38 except steel construction, weight 20½ oz.
Price: Blued, Model 49 . . . . $405.00
Price: Stainless, Model 649 . . . . $464.00

SMITH & WESSON MODEL 63 KIT GUN **Caliber:** 22 LR, 6-shot. **Barrel:** 2", 4". **Weight:** 24 oz. (4" bbl.). **Length:** 8³⁄₈" (4" bbl. and round butt). **Stocks:** Round butt soft rubber; wood optional. **Sights:** Red ramp front, micro-click rear adjustable for windage and elevation. **Features:** Stainless steel construction.
Price: 2" $453.00
Price: 4" $458.00

SMITH & WESSON MODEL 64 STAINLESS M&P **Caliber:** 38 Special, 6-shot. **Barrel:** 2", 3", 4". **Weight:** 34 oz. **Length:** 9⁵⁄₁₆" overall. **Stocks:** Soft rubber; wood optional. **Sights:** Fixed, ⅛" serrated ramp front, square notch rear. **Features:** Satin finished stainless steel, square butt.
Price: 2" $411.00
Price: 3", 4" $419.00

SMITH & WESSON MODEL 65LS LADYSMITH **Caliber:** 357 Magnum, 6-shot. **Barrel:** 3". **Weight:** 31 oz. **Length:** 7.94" overall. **Stocks:** Rosewood, round butt. **Sights:** Serrated ramp front, fixed notch rear. **Features:** Stainless steel with frosted finish. Smooth combat trigger, service hammer, shrouded ejector rod. Comes with soft case. Introduced 1992.
Price: $456.00

SMITH & WESSON MODEL 66 STAINLESS COMBAT MAGNUM **Caliber:** 357 Magnum and 38 Special, 6-shot. **Barrel:** 2½", 4", 6". **Weight:** 36 oz. (4" barrel). **Length:** 9⁹⁄₁₆" overall. **Stocks:** Soft rubber; wood optional. **Sights:** Red ramp front, micro-click rear adjustable for windage and elevation. **Features:** Satin finish stainless steel.
Price: 2½" $461.00
Price: 4", 6" $467.00

Smith & Wesson Model 36LS
LadySmith

Smith & Wesson Model 60 3"

Smith & Wesson Model 49

Smith & Wesson Model 63 4"

Smith & Wesson Model
65LS LadySmith

Smith & Wesson Model 66 4"

SMITH & WESSON MODEL 67 COMBAT MASTERPIECE Caliber: 38 Special, 6-shot. **Barrel:** 4". **Weight:** 32 oz. **Length:** $9^5/_{16}$" overall. **Stocks:** Soft rubber; wood optional. **Sights:** Red ramp front, micro-click rear adjustable for windage and elevation. **Features:** Stainless steel with satin finish. Smooth combat trigger, semi-target hammer. Introduced 1994.
Price: **$462.00**

SMITH & WESSON MODEL 586, 686 DISTINGUISHED COMBAT MAGNUMS Caliber: 357 Magnum. **Barrel:** 4", 6", full shroud. **Weight:** 46 oz. (6"), 41 oz. (4"). **Stocks:** Soft rubber; wood optional. **Sights:** Baughman red ramp front, four-position click-adjustable front, S&W micrometer click rear (or fixed). **Features:** Uses new L-frame, but takes all K-frame grips. Full-length ejector rod shroud. Smooth combat-type trigger, semi-target type hammer. Trigger stop on 6" models. Also available in stainless as Model 686. Introduced 1981.
Price: Model 586, blue, 4", from **$457.00**
Price: Model 586, blue, 6" **$461.00**
Price: Model 686, 6", adjustable front sight **$525.00**
Price: Model 686, $8^3/_8$" **$510.00**
Price: Model 686, $2^1/_2$" **$476.00**

SMITH & WESSON MODEL 617 FULL LUG REVOLVER Caliber: 22 LR, 6-shot. **Barrel:** 4", 6", $8^3/_8$". **Weight:** 42 oz. (4" barrel). **Length:** NA. **Stocks:** Soft rubber; wood optional. **Sights:** Patridge front, adjustable rear. **Features:** Stainless steel with satin finish; 4" has .312" smooth trigger, .375" semi-target hammer; 6" has either .312" combat or .400" serrated trigger, .375" semi-target or .500" target hammer; $8^3/_8$" with .400" serrated trigger, .500" target hammer. Introduced 1990.
Price: 4" **$455.00**
Price: 6", semi-target hammer, combat trigger **$460.00**
Price: 6", target hammer, target trigger **$485.00**
Price: $8^3/_8$" **$496.00**

Smith & Wesson Model 648 K-22 Masterpiece MRF Similar to the Model 617 except chambered for 22 WMR cartridge. Available with 6" full-lug barrel only, combat-style square butt grips, combat trigger and semi-target hammer. Introduced 1991.
Price: **$464.00**

SMITH & WESSON MODEL 625 REVOLVER Caliber: 45 ACP, 6-shot. **Barrel:** 5". **Weight:** 46 oz. **Length:** 11.375" overall. **Stocks:** Soft rubber; wood optional. **Sights:** Patridge front on ramp, S&W micrometer click rear adjustable for windage and elevation. **Features:** Stainless steel construction with .400" semi-target hammer, .312" smooth combat trigger; full lug barrel. Introduced 1989.
Price: **$591.00**

SMITH & WESSON MODEL 640, 940 CENTENNIAL Caliber: 38 Special, 9mm Para., 5-shot. **Barrel:** 2", 3". **Weight:** 20 oz. **Length:** $6^5/_{16}$" overall. **Stocks:** Soft rubber; wood optional. **Sights:** Serrated ramp front, fixed notch rear. **Features:** Stainless steel version of the original Model 40 but without the grip safety. Fully concealed hammer, snag-proof smooth edges. Model 640 introduced 1990; Model 940 introduced 1991.
Price: Model 640 (38 Special) **$464.00**
Price: Model 940 (9mm Para., rubber grips) **$470.00**

Smith & Wesson Model 442 Centennial Airweight Similar to the Model 640 Centennial except has alloy frame giving weight of 15.8 oz. Chambered for 38 Special, 2" carbon steel barrel; carbon steel cylinder; concealed hammer; Uncle Mike's Custom Grade Santoprene grips. Fixed square notch rear sight, serrated ramp front. Introduced 1993.
Price: Blue **$423.00**
Price: Nickel **$438.00**

SMITH & WESSON MODEL 651 REVOLVER Caliber: 22 WMR, 6-shot cylinder. **Barrel:** 4". **Weight:** $24^1/_2$ oz. **Length:** $8^{11}/_{16}$" overall. **Stocks:** Soft rubber; wood optional. **Sights:** Red ramp front, adjustable micrometer click rear. **Features:** Stainless steel construction with semi-target hammer, smooth combat trigger. Reintroduced 1991. Limited production.
Price: **$455.00**

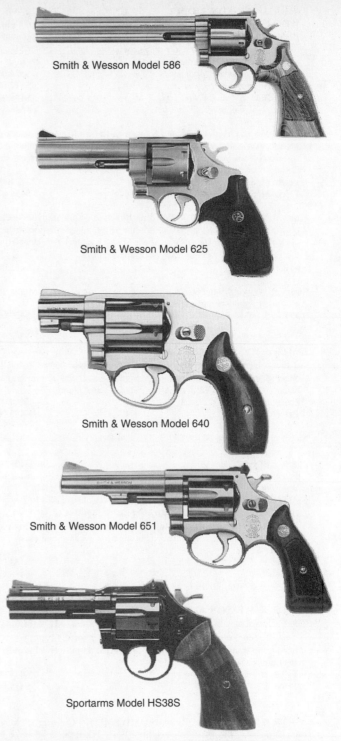

Smith & Wesson Model 586

Smith & Wesson Model 625

Smith & Wesson Model 640

Smith & Wesson Model 651

Sportarms Model HS38S

SMITH & WESSON MODEL 657 REVOLVER Caliber: 41 Magnum, 6-shot. **Barrel:** 6". **Weight:** 48 oz. **Length:** $11^3/_8$" overall. **Stocks:** Soft rubber; wood optional. **Sights:** Pinned $^1/_8$" red ramp front, micro-click rear adjustable for windage and elevation. **Features:** Stainless steel construction.
Price: **$523.00**

SPORTARMS MODEL HS38S REVOLVER Caliber: 38 Special, 6-shot. **Barrel:** 3", 4". **Weight:** 31.3 oz. **Length:** 8" overall (3" barrel). **Stocks:** Checkered hardwood; round butt on 3" model, target-style on 4". **Sights:** Blade front, adjustable rear. **Features:** Polished blue finish; ventilated rib on 4" barrel. Made in Germany by Herbert Schmidt; Imported by Sportarms of Florida.
Price: About **$150.00**

CAUTION: PRICES SHOWN ARE SUPPLIED BY THE MANUFACTURER OR IMPORTER. CHECK YOUR LOCAL GUNSHOP.

DOUBLE-ACTION REVOLVERS, SERVICE & SPORT

TAURUS MODEL 44 REVOLVER **Caliber:** 44 Magnum, 6-shot. **Barrel:** 4", 6½", 8⅜". **Weight:** 44¾ oz. (4" barrel). **Length:** NA. **Stocks:** Checkered Brazilian hardwood. **Sights:** Serrated ramp front, micro-click rear adjustable for windage and elevation. **Features:** Heavy solid rib on 4", vent rib on 6½", 8⅜". Compensated barrel. Blued model has color case-hardened hammer and trigger. Introduced 1994. Imported by Taurus International.
Price: Blue, 4" **$418.00**
Price: Blue, 6½", 8⅜" **$435.00**
Price: Stainless, 4" **$480.00**
Price: Stainless, 6½", 8⅜" **$500.00**

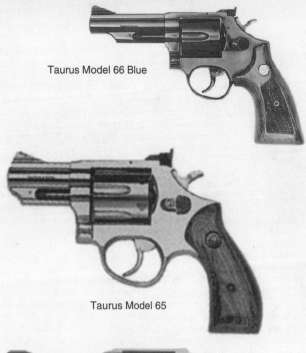

Taurus Model 66 Blue

TAURUS MODEL 66 REVOLVER **Caliber:** 357 Magnum, 6-shot. **Barrel:** 2.5", 4", 6". **Weight:** 35 oz.(4" barrel). **Stocks:** Checkered Brazilian hardwood. **Sights:** Serrated ramp front, micro-click rear adjustable for windage and elevation. Red ramp front with white outline rear on stainlees models only. **Features:** Wide target-type hammer spur, floating firing pin, heavy barrel with shrouded ejector rod. Introduced 1978. Imported by Taurus International.
Price: Blue, 2.5" **$313.00**
Price: Blue, 4", 6" **$313.00**
Price: Blue, 4", 6" compensated **$323.00**
Price: Stainless, 2.5" **$393.00**
Price: Stainless, 4", 6" **$393.00**
Price: Stainless, 4", 6" compensated **$463.00**

Taurus Model 65

Taurus Model 65 Revolver Same as the Model 66 except has fixed rear sight and ramp front. Available with 2.5" or 4" barrel only, round butt grip. Imported by Taurus International.
Price: Blue, 2.5", 4" **$285.00**
Price: Stainless, 2.5", 4" **$355.00**

TAURUS MODEL 80 STANDARD REVOLVER **Caliber:** 38 Spec., 6-shot. **Barrel:** 3" or 4". **Weight:** 30 oz. (4" bbl.). **Length:** 9¼" overall (4" bbl.). **Stocks:** Checkered Brazilian hardwood. **Sights:** Serrated ramp front, square notch rear. **Features:** Imported by Taurus International.
Price: Blue **$248.00**
Price: Stainless **$299.00**

Taurus Model 80

TAURUS MODEL 82 HEAVY BARREL REVOLVER **Caliber:** 38 Spec., 6-shot. **Barrel:** 3" or 4", heavy. **Weight:** 34 oz. (4" bbl.). **Length:** 9¼" overall (4" bbl.). **Stocks:** Checkered Brazilian hardwood. **Sights:** Serrated ramp front, square notch rear. **Features:** Imported by Taurus International.
Price: Blue **$248.00**
Price: Stainless **$299.00**

TAURUS MODEL 83 REVOLVER **Caliber:** 38 Spec., 6-shot. **Barrel:** 4" only, heavy. **Weight:** 34 oz. **Stocks:** Oversize checkered Brazilian hardwood. **Sights:** Ramp front, micro-click rear adjustable for windage and elevation. **Features:** Blue or nickel finish. Introduced 1977. Imported by Taurus International.
Price: Blue **$260.00**
Price: Stainless **$309.00**

Taurus Model 82

Taurus Model 85

Taurus Model 83

TAURUS MODEL 85 REVOLVER **Caliber:** 38 Spec., 5-shot. **Barrel:** 2", 3". **Weight:** 21 oz. **Stocks:** Checkered Brazilian hardwood. **Sights:** Ramp front, square notch rear. **Features:** Blue, satin nickel finish or stainless steel. Introduced 1980. Imported by Taurus International.
Price: Blue, 2", 3" **$276.00**
Price: Stainless steel **$337.00**

Taurus Model 85CH Revolver   Same as the Model 85 except has 2" barrel only and concealed hammer. Smooth Brazilian hardwood stocks. Introduced 1991. Imported by Taurus International.
Price: Blue **$276.00**
Price: Stainless **$337.00**

TAURUS MODEL 86 REVOLVER   **Caliber:** 38 Spec., 6-shot.   **Barrel:** 6" only.   **Weight:** 34 oz.   **Length:** 11¼" overall.   **Stocks:** Oversize target-type, checkered Brazilian hardwood.   **Sights:** Patridge front, micro-click rear adjustable for windage and elevation.   **Features:** Blue finish with non-reflective finish on barrel. Imported by Taurus International.
Price: **$352.00**

TAURUS MODEL 94 REVOLVER   **Caliber:** 22 LR, 9-shot cylinder.   **Barrel:** 3", 4".   **Weight:** 25 oz.   **Stocks:** Checkered Brazilian hardwood.   **Sights:** Serrated ramp front, click-adjustable rear for windage and elevation.   **Features:** Floating firing pin, color case-hardened hammer and trigger. Introduced 1989. Imported by Taurus International.
Price: Blue **$288.00**
Price: Stainless **$339.00**

TAURUS MODEL 96 REVOLVER   **Caliber:** 22 LR, 6-shot.   **Barrel:** 6".   **Weight:** 34 oz.   **Length:** NA.   **Stocks:** Checkered Brazilian hardwood.   **Sights:** Patridge-type front, micrometer click rear adjustable for windage and elevation.   **Features:** Heavy solid barrel rib; target hammer; adjustable target trigger. Blue only. Imported by Taurus International.
Price: **$352.00**

TAURUS MODEL 441/431 REVOLVERS   **Caliber:** 44 Special, 5-shot.   **Barrel:** 3", 4", 6".   **Weight:** 40.4 oz. (6" barrel).   **Length:** NA.   **Stocks:** Checkered Brazilian hardwood.   **Sights:** Serrated ramp front, micrometer click rear adjustable for windage and elevation.   **Features:** Heavy barrel with solid rib and full-length ejector shroud. Introduced 1992. Imported by Taurus International.
Price: Blue, 3", 4", 6" **$307.00**
Price: Stainless, 3", 4", 6" **$386.00**
Price: Model 431 (fixed sights), blue **$281.00**
Price: Model 431 (fixed sights), stainless **$351.00**

TAURUS MODEL 669 REVOLVER   **Caliber:** 357 Mag., 6-shot.   **Barrel:** 4", 6".   **Weight:** 37 oz., (4" bbl.).   **Stocks:** Checkered Brazilian hardwood.   **Sights:** Serrated ramp front, micro-click rear adjustable for windage and elevation.   **Features:** Wide target-type hammer, floating firing pin, full-length barrel shroud. Introduced 1988. Imported by Taurus International.
Price: Blue, 4", 6" **$322.00**
Price: Blue, 4", 6" compensated **$340.00**
Price: Stainless, 4", 6" **$402.00**
Price: Stainless, 4", 6" compensated **$421.00**

Taurus Model 669

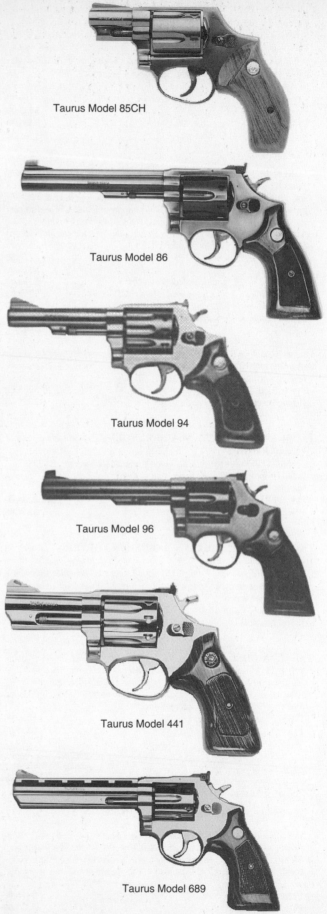

Taurus Model 85CH

Taurus Model 86

Taurus Model 94

Taurus Model 96

Taurus Model 441

Taurus Model 689

Taurus Model 689 Revolver   Same as the Model 669 except has full-length ventilated barrel rib. Available in blue or stainless steel. Introduced 1990. From Taurus International.
Price: Blue, 4" or 6" **$335.00**
Price: Stainless, 4" or 6" **$416.00**

TAURUS MODEL 761 REVOLVER **Caliber:** 32 H&R Magnum, 6-shot. **Barrel:** 6", heavy, solid rib. **Weight:** 34 oz. **Stocks:** Checkered Brazilian hardwood. **Sights:** Patridge-type front, micro-click rear adjustable for windage and elevation. **Features:** Target hammer, adjustable target trigger. Blue only. Introduced 1991. Imported by Taurus International.
Price: **$326.00**

Taurus Model 741 Revolver Same as the Model 761 except with 3" or 4" heavy barrel only, serrated ramp front sight, micro click rear adjustable for windage and elevation. Introduced 1991. Imported by Taurus International.
Price: Blue, 3", 4" **$254.00**
Price: Stainless, 3", 4" **$342.00**

TAURUS MODEL 941 REVOLVER **Caliber:** 22 WMR, 8-shot. **Barrel:** 3", 4". **Weight:** 27.5 oz. (4" barrel). **Length:** NA. **Stocks:** Checkered Brazilian hardwood. **Sights:** Serrated ramp front, rear adjustable for windage and elevation. **Features:** Solid rib heavy barrel with full-length ejector rod shroud. Blue or stainless steel. Introduced 1992. Imported by Taurus International.
Price: Blue **$310.00**
Price: Stainless **$367.00**

THUNDER FIVE REVOLVER **Caliber:** 45 Colt/410 shotshell, 2" and 3"; 5-shot cylinder. **Barrel:** 2". **Weight:** 48 oz. **Length:** 9" overall. **Stocks:** Pachmayr checkered rubber. **Sights:** Fixed. **Features:** Double action with ambidextrous hammer-block safety; squared trigger guard; internal draw bar safety. Made of chrome moly steel, with matte blue finish. Announced 1991. From Holston Ent.
Price: **$549.00**
Price: Model T-70, 45-70 Gov't. (from Dragun Ent.) **$599.00**

> Consult our Directory pages for the location of firms mentioned.

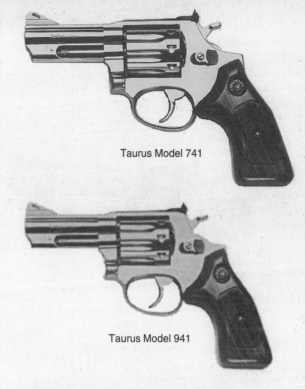

Taurus Model 741

Taurus Model 941

Wesson Model 14

Wesson Model 22

WESSON FIREARMS MODEL 8 & MODEL 14 **Caliber:** 38 Special (Model 8); 357 (Model 14), both 6-shot. **Barrel:** 2½", 4", 6"; interchangeable. **Weight:** 30 oz. (2½"). **Length:** 9¼" overall (4" bbl.). **Stocks:** Checkered, interchangeable. **Sights:** ⅛" serrated front, fixed rear. **Features:** Interchangeable barrels and grips; smooth, wide trigger; wide hammer spur with short double-action travel. Available in stainless or Brite blue. Contact Wesson Firearms for complete price list.
Price: Model 8-2, 2½", blue **$267.00**
Price: As above except in stainless **$311.00**
Price: Model 714-2 Pistol Pac, stainless **$522.00**

Wesson Firearms Model 9, 15 & 32M Revolvers Same as Models 8 and 14 except they have adjustable sight. Model 9 chambered for 38 Special, Model 15 for 357 Magnum. Model 32M is chambered for 32 H&R Mag. Same specs and prices as for Model 15 guns. Available in blue or stainless. Contact Wesson Firearms for complete price list.
Price: Model 9-2 or 15-2, 2½", blue **$338.00**
Price: As above except in stainless **$366.00**

Wesson Firearms Model 15 Gold Series Similar to the Model 15 except has smoother action to reduce DA pull to 8-10 lbs.; comes with either 6" or 8" vent heavy slotted barrel shroud with bright blue barrel. Shroud is stamped "Gold Series" with the Wesson signature engraved and gold filled. Hammer and trigger are polished bright; rosewood grips. New sights with orange dot Patridge front, white triangle on rear blade. Introduced 1989.
Price: 6" . . . . **NA**
Price: 8" . . . . **NA**

WESSON FIREARMS MODEL 22 REVOLVER **Caliber:** 22 LR, 22 WMR, 6-shot. **Barrel:** 2½", 4", 6", 8"; interchangeable. **Weight:** 36 oz. (2½"), 44 oz. (6"). **Length:** 9¼" overall (4" barrel). **Stocks:** Checkered; undercover, service or over-size target. **Sights:** ⅛" serrated, interchangeable front, white outline rear adjustable for windage and elevation. **Features:** Built on the same frame as the Wesson 357; smooth, wide trigger with over-travel adjustment, wide spur hammer, with short double-action travel. Available in Brite blue or stainless steel. Contact Wesson Firearms for complete price list.
Price: 2½" bbl., blue **$349.00**
Price: As above, stainless **$391.00**
Price: With 4", vent. rib, blue **$381.00**
Price: As above, stainless **$423.00**
Price: Blue Pistol Pac, 22 LR **$637.00**

Wesson FB44-5

Wesson FB15

Wesson FB715-6

Wesson 445 Supermag

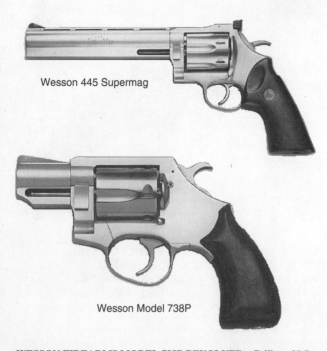

Wesson Model 738P

WESSON FIREARMS FB44, FB744 REVOLVERS **Caliber:** 44 Magnum, 6-shot. **Barrel:** 4", 5", 6", 8". **Weight:** 50 oz. (4" barrel). **Length:** 9¾" overall (4" barrel). **Stocks:** Hogue finger-groove rubber. **Sights:** Interchangeable blade front, fully adjustable rear. **Features:** Fixed, non-vented heavy barrel shrouds, but other features same as other Wesson revolvers. Brushed stainless or polished blue finish. Introduced 1994. Made in U.S. by Wesson Firearms Co., Inc.

Price: FB44-4 (4", blue)	**$400.00**
Price: As above, stainless (FB744-4)	**$442.00**
Price: FB44-5 (5", blue)	**$403.00**
Price: As above, stainless (FB744-5)	**$444.00**
Price: FB44-6 (6", blue)	**$407.00**
Price: As above, stainless (FB744-6)	**$448.00**
Price: FB44-8 (8", blue)	**$414.00**
Price: As above, stainless (FB744-8)	**$455.00**

WESSON FIREARMS FB15, FB715 REVOLVERS **Caliber:** 357 Magnum, 6-shot. **Barrel:** 2½", 4" (Service models), 3", 4", 5", 6" (target models). **Weight:** 40 oz. (4" barrel). **Length:** 9¾" overall (4" barrel). **Stocks:** Service style or Hogue rubber. **Sights:** Blade front, adjustable rear (Target); fixed rear on Service. **Features:** Fixed barrels, but other features same as other Wesson revolvers. Service models in brushed stainless, satin blue, Target in brushed stainless or polished blue. Introduced 1993. Made in U.S. by Wesson Firearms Co., Inc.

Price: FB14-2 (Service, 2½", blue)	**$249.00**
Price: As above, 4"	**$254.00**
Price: FB714-2 (Service, 2½", stainless)	**$268.00**
Price: As above, 4"	**$274.00**
Price: FB15-3 (Target, 3", blue)	**$259.00**
Price: As above, 5"	**$272.00**
Price: FB715 (Target, 4", stainless)	**$284.00**
Price: As above, 6"	**$298.00**

WESSON FIREARMS HUNTER SERIES REVOLVERS **Caliber:** 357 Supermag, 41 Mag., 44 Mag., 445 Supermag, 6-shot. **Barrel:** 6", 7½", depending upon model. **Weight:** About 64 oz. **Length:** 14" overall. **Stocks:** Hogue finger-groove rubber, wood presentation. **Sights:** Blade front, dovetailed Iron Sight Gunworks rear. **Features:** Fixed barrel revolvers. Barrels have 1:18.75" twist, Alan Taylor two-stage forcing cone; non-fluted cylinder; bright blue or satin stainless. Introduced 1994. Made in U.S. by Wesson Firearms Co., Inc.

Price: Open Hunter (open sights, 7½" barrel), blue	**$804.94**
Price: As above, stainless	**$848.63**
Price: Compensated Open Hunter (6" compensated barrel, 7" shroud), blue	**$836.98**
Price: As above, stainless	**$880.65**
Price: Scoped Hunter (7½" barrel, no sights, comes with scope rings on shroud), blue	**$837.97**
Price: As above, stainless	**$880.96**
Price: Compensated Scoped Hunter (6" barrel, 7" shroud, scope rings on shroud), blue	**$870.73**
Price: As above, stainless	**$913.72**

WESSON FIREARMS MODEL 41V, 44V, 45V REVOLVERS **Caliber:** 41 Mag., 44 Mag., 45 Colt, 6-shot. **Barrel:** 4", 6", 8", 10"; interchangeable. **Weight:** 48 oz. (4"). **Length:** 12" overall (6" bbl.). **Stocks:** Smooth. **Sights:** ⅛" serrated front, white outline rear adjustable for windage and elevation. **Features:** Available in blue or stainless steel. Smooth, wide trigger with adjustable over-travel; wide hammer spur. Available in Pistol Pac set also. Contact Wesson Firearms for complete price list.

Price: 41 Mag., 4", vent	**$433.55**
Price: As above except in stainless	**$508.30**
Price: 44 Mag., 4", blue	**$433.55**
Price: As above except in stainless	**$508.30**
Price: 45 Colt, 4", vent	**$433.55**
Price: As above except in stainless	**$508.30**

WESSON FIREARMS MODEL 738P REVOLVER **Caliber:** 38 Special +P, 5-shot. **Barrel:** 2". **Weight:** 24.6 oz. **Length:** 6.5" overall. **Stocks:** Pauferro wood or rubber. **Sights:** Blade front, fixed notch rear. **Features:** Designed for +P ammunition. Stainless steel construction. Introduced 1992. Made in U.S. by Wesson Firearms Co., Inc.
Price: **$285.00**

CAUTION: PRICES SHOWN ARE SUPPLIED BY THE MANUFACTURER OR IMPORTER. CHECK YOUR LOCAL GUNSHOP.

Both classic six-shooters and modern adaptations for hunting and sport.

AMERICAN ARMS REGULATOR SINGLE ACTIONS **Caliber:** 357 Mag.; 44-40, 45 Colt. **Barrel:** 4¾", 5½", 7½". **Weight:** 32 oz. (4¾" barrel) **Length:** 8⅛" overall (4¾" barrel). **Stocks:** Smooth walnut. **Sights:** Blade front, groove rear. **Features:** Blued barrel and cylinder, brass trigger guard and backstrap. Introduced 1992. Imported from Italy by American Arms, Inc.
Price: Regulator, single cylinder **$305.00**
Price: Regulator, dual cylinder (44-40/44 Spec. or 45
Colt/45 ACP) **$349.00**
Price: Regulator DLX (all steel) **$349.00**

American Arms Buckhorn Single Action Similar to the Regulator single action except chambered for 44 Magnum. Available with 4¾", 6" or 7½" barrel. Overall length 11¾", weight is 44 oz. with 6" barrel. Introduced 1993. Imported from Italy by American Arms, Inc.
Price: **$339.00**
Price: Buckhorn Target (with target sights) **$349.00**

CENTURY GUN DIST. MODEL 100 SINGLE ACTION **Caliber:** 30-30, 375 Win., 444 Marlin, 45-70, 50-70. **Barrel:** 6½" (standard), 8", 10", 12". **Weight:** 6 lbs. (loaded). **Length:** 15" overall (8" bbl.). **Stocks:** Smooth walnut. **Sights:** Ramp front, Millett adjustable square notch rear. **Features:** Highly polished high tensile strength manganese bronze frame, blue cylinder and barrel; coil spring trigger mechanism. Calibers other than 45-70 start at $2,000.00. Contact maker for full price information. Introduced 1975. Made in U.S. From Century Gun Dist., Inc.
Price: 6½" barrel, 45-70 . . . . **$1,250.00**

CIMARRON U.S. CAVALRY MODEL SINGLE ACTION **Caliber:** 45 Colt **Barrel:** 7½". **Weight:** 42 oz. **Length:** 13½" overall. **Stocks:** Walnut. **Sights:** Fixed. **Features:** Has "A.P. Casey" markings; "U.S." plus patent dates on frame, serial number on backstrap, trigger guard, frame and cylinder, "APC" cartouche on left grip; color case-hardened frame and hammer, rest charcoal blue. Exact copy of the original. Imported by Cimarron Arms.
Price: **$459.00**

Cimarron Artillery Model Single Action Similar to the U.S. Cavalry model except has 5½" barrel, weighs 39 oz., and is 11½" overall. U.S. markings and cartouche, case-hardened frame and hammer; 45 Colt only.
Price: **$459.00**

CIMARRON 1873 PEACEMAKER REPRO **Caliber:** 38 WCF, 357 Mag., 44 WCF, 44 Spec., 45 Colt. **Barrel:** 4¾", 5½", 7½". **Weight:** 39 oz. **Length:** 10" overall (4" barrel). **Stocks:** Walnut. **Sights:** Blade front, fixed or adjustable rear. **Features:** Uses "old model" black-powder frame with "Bullseye" ejector or New Model frame. Imported by Cimarron Arms.
Price: Peacemaker, 4¾" barrel **$429.95**
Price: Frontier Six Shooter, 5½" barrel **$429.95**
Price: Single Action Army, 7½" barrel **$429.95**

CIMARRON NEW THUNDERER REVOLVER **Caliber:** 357 Mag., 44 WCF, 44 Spec., 45 Colt, 6-shot. **Barrel:** 3½", 4¾", with ejector. **Weight:** 38 oz. (3½" barrel). **Length:** NA. **Stocks:** Hand-checkered walnut. **Sights:** Blade front, notch rear. **Features:** Thunderer grip; color case-hardened frame with balance blued, or nickel finish. Introduced 1993. Imported by Cimarron Arms.
Price: Color case-hardened **$429.95**
Price: Nickeled **$529.95**

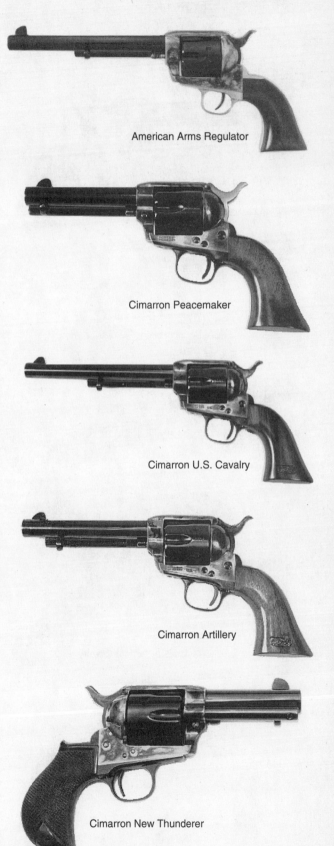

American Arms Regulator

Cimarron Peacemaker

Cimarron U.S. Cavalry

Cimarron Artillery

Cimarron New Thunderer

CAUTION: PRICES SHOWN ARE SUPPLIED BY THE MANUFACTURER OR IMPORTER. CHECK YOUR LOCAL GUNSHOP.

7th ANNUAL EDITION **267**

SINGLE-ACTION REVOLVERS

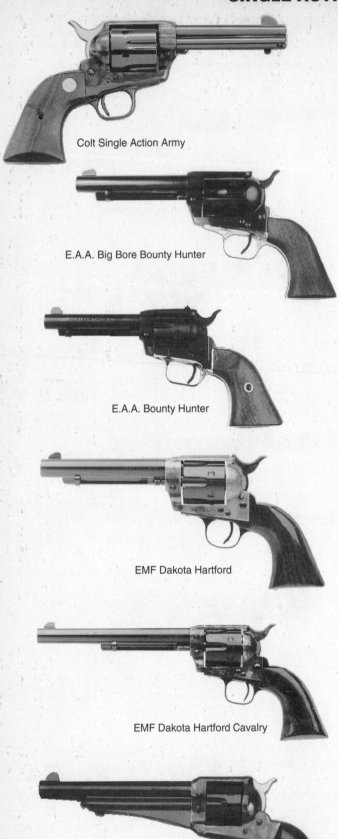

Colt Single Action Army

E.A.A. Big Bore Bounty Hunter

E.A.A. Bounty Hunter

EMF Dakota Hartford

EMF Dakota Hartford Cavalry

EMF 1875 Outlaw

COLT SINGLE ACTION ARMY REVOLVER Caliber: 44-40, 45 Colt, 6-shot. **Barrel:** 4¾", 5½", 7½". **Weight:** 40 oz. (4¾" barrel). **Length:** 10¼" overall (4¾" barrel). **Stocks:** American walnut. **Sights:** Blade front, notch rear. **Features:** Available in full nickel finish with nickel grip medallions, or Royal Blue with color case-hardened frame, gold grip medallions. Reintroduced 1992.
Price: **$1,213.00**

E.A.A. BIG BORE BOUNTY HUNTER SA REVOLVERS Caliber: 357 Mag., 41 Mag., 44-40, 44 Mag., 45 Colt, 6-shot. **Barrel:** 4⅝", 7½". **Weight:** 2.5 lbs. **Length:** 11" overall (4⅝" barrel). **Stocks:** Smooth walnut. **Sights:** Blade front, grooved topstrap rear. **Features:** Transfer bar safety; three position hammer; hammer forged barrel. Introduced 1992. Imported by European American Armory.
Price: Blue **$299.00**
Price: Color case-hardened frame **$310.00**
Price: Chrome-plated **$350.00**

E.A.A. BOUNTY HUNTER REVOLVER Caliber: 22 LR, 22 WMR, 6-shot cylinder. **Barrel:** 4¾", 6", 9". **Weight:** 32 oz. **Length:** 10" overall (4¾" barrel). **Stocks:** European hardwood. **Sights:** Blade front, adjustable rear. **Features:** Available in blue finish only. Introduced 1991. From European American Armory Corp.
Price: 4¾", blue **$80.00**
Price: 4¾", blue, 22 LR/22 WMR combo **$99.00**
Price: 6", blue, 22 LR/22 WMR combo **$125.00**
Price: 9", blue, 22 LR/22 WMR combo **$110.00**

EMF DAKOTA 1875 OUTLAW REVOLVER Caliber: 357, 44-40, 45 Colt. **Barrel:** 7½". **Weight:** 46 oz. **Length:** 13½" overall. **Stocks:** Smooth walnut. **Sights:** Blade front, fixed groove rear. **Features:** Authentic copy of 1875 Remington with firing pin in hammer; color case-hardened frame, blue cylinder, barrel, steel backstrap and brass trigger guard. Also available in nickel, factory engraved. Imported by E.M.F.
Price: All calibers **$465.00**
Price: Nickel **$550.00**
Price: Engraved **$600.00**
Price: Engraved Nickel **$710.00**

EMF Dakota 1890 Police Revolver Similar to the 1875 Outlaw except has 5½" barrel, weighs 40 oz., with 12½" overall length. Has lanyard ring in butt. No web under barrel. Calibers 357, 44-40, 45 Colt. Imported by E.M.F.
Price: All calibers **$470.00**
Price: Nickel **$560.00**
Price: Engraved **$620.00**
Price: Engraved nickel **$725.00**

EMF DAKOTA HARTFORD SINGLE-ACTION REVOLVERS Caliber: 22 LR, 357 Mag., 32-20, 38-40, 44-40, 44 Spec., 45 Colt. **Barrel:** 4¾", 5½", 7½". **Weight:** 45 oz. **Length:** 13" overall (7½" barrel). **Stocks:** Smooth walnut. **Sights:** Blade front, fixed rear. **Features:** Identical to the origianl Colts with inspector cartouche on left grip, original patent dates and U.S. markings. All major parts serial numbered using original Colt-style lettering, numbering. Bullseye ejector head and color case-hardening on frame and hammer. Introduced 1990. From E.M.F.
Price: **$600.00**
Price: Cavalry or Artillery **$655.00**
Price: Nickel plated **$725.00**
Price: Pinkerton (bird's-head grip), 45 Colt, 4" barrel **$680.00**
Price: Bisley Model (45 Colt) **$680.00**
Price: Nickel plated **$805.00**

EMF Dakota New Model Single-Action Revolvers Similar to the standard Dakota except has color case-hardened forged steel frame, black nickel backstrap and trigger guard. Calibers 357 Mag., 44-40, 45 Colt only.
Price: **$460.00**
Price: Nickel **$585.00**

FREEDOM ARMS PREMIER 454 CASULL **Caliber:** 44 Mag., 454 Casull with 45 Colt, 45 ACP, 45 Win. Mag. optional cylinders, 5-shot. **Barrel:** 4¾", 6", 7½", 10". **Weight:** 50 oz. **Length:** 14" overall (7½" bbl.). **Stocks:** Impregnated hardwood. **Sights:** Blade front, notch or adjustable rear. **Features:** All stainless steel construction; sliding bar safety system. Lifetime warranty. Made in U.S. by Freedom Arms, Inc.
Price: Field Grade (matte finish, Pachmayr grips), adjustable sights,
4¾", 6", 7½", 10" **$1,175.00**
Price: Field Grade, fixed sights, 4¾" only **$1,119.00**
Price: Field Grade, 44 Rem. Mag., adjustable sights,
all lengths **$1,175.00**
Price: Premier Grade (brush finish, impregnated
hardwood grips) adjustable sights, 4¾", 6", 7½", 10" **$1,480.00**
Price: Premier Grade, fixed sights, 7½" only **$1,396.00**
Price: Premier Grade, 44 Rem. Mag., adjustable sights,
all lengths **$1,480.00**
Price: Fitted 45 ACP or 45 Colt cylinder, add **$233.00**

Freedom 454 Field Grade

Freedom Arms Casull Model 353 Revolver Similar to the Premier 454 Casull except chambered for 357 Magnum with 5-shot cylinder; 4¾", 6", 7½" or 9" barrel. Weighs 59 oz. with 7½" barrel. Standard model has adjustable sights, matte finish, Pachmayr grips, 7½" or 9" barrel; Silhouette has 9" barrel, Patridge front sight, Iron Sight Gun Works Silhouette adjustable rear, Pachmayr grips, trigger over-travel adjustment screw. All stainless steel. Introduced 1992.
Price: Field Grade **$1,175.00**
Price: Premier Grade (brushed finish, impregnated
hardwood grips, Premier Grade sights) **$1,480.00**
Price: Silhouette **$1,267.05**

Heritage Rough Rider

Freedom Arms Model 555 Revolver Same as the 454 Casull except chambered for the 50 A.E. (Action Express) cartridge. Offered in Premier and Field Grades with adjustable sights, 4¾", 6", 7½" or 10" barrel. Introduced 1994. Made in U.S. by Freedom Arms, Inc.
Price: Premier Grade **$1,480.00**
Price: Field Grade **$1,175.00**

HERITAGE ROUGH RIDER REVOLVER **Caliber:** 22 LR, 22 LR/22 WMR combo, 6-shot. **Barrel:** 3", 4¾", 6½", 9". **Weight:** 31 to 38 oz. **Length:** NA. **Stocks:** Goncolo Alves. **Sights:** Blade front, fixed rear. **Features:** Hammer block safety. High polish blue finish, gold-tone screws, polished hammer. Introduced 1993. Made in U.S. by Heritage Mfg., Inc.
Price: .... **$89.95** to **$129.95**

Mitchell Single Action

MITCHELL SINGLE-ACTION ARMY REVOLVERS **Caliber:** 357 Mag., 45 ACP, 45 Colt, 6-shot. **Barrel:** 4¾", 5½", 7½". **Weight:** NA. **Length:** NA. **Stocks:** One-piece walnut. **Sights:** Serrated ramp front, fixed or adjustable rear. **Features:** Color case-hardened frame, brass or steel backstrap/trigger guard; hammer-block safety. Bright nickel-plated model and dual cylinder models available. Contact importer for complete price list. Imported by Mitchell Arms, Inc.
Price: Cowboy, 4¾", Army 5½", Cavalry 7½", blue, 357,
45 Colt, 45 ACP **$399.00**
Price: As above, nickel **$439.00**
Price: 45 Colt/45 ACP dual cyl., blue **$549.00**
Price: As above, nickel **$588.00**
Price: Bat Masterson model, 45 Colt, 4¾", nickel **$439.00**

Navy Arms 1873

NAVY ARMS 1873 SINGLE-ACTION REVOLVER **Caliber:** 44-40, 45 Colt, 6-shot cylinder. **Barrel:** 3", 4¾", 5½", 7½". **Weight:** 36 oz. **Length:** 10¾" overall (5½" barrel). **Stocks:** Smooth walnut. **Sights:** Blade front, groove in topstrap rear. **Features:** Blue with color case-hardened frame, or nickel. Introduced 1991. Imported by Navy Arms.
Price: Blue **$390.00**
Price: Nickel **$455.00**
Price: Economy model with brass backstrap and trigger guard . **$340.00**
Price: 1873 U.S. Cavalry Model (7½", 45 Colt, arsenal
markings) **$480.00**
Price: 1895 U.S. Artillery Model (as above, 5½" barrel) ... **$480.00**

Navy Arms 1875 Schofield

NAVY ARMS 1875 SCHOFIELD REVOLVER **Caliber:** 44-40, 45 Colt, 6-shot cylinder. **Barrel:** 5", 7". **Weight:** 39 oz. **Length:** 10¾" overall (5" barrel). **Stocks:** Smooth walnut. **Sights:** Blade front, notch rear. **Features:** Replica of Smith & Wesson Model 3 Schofield. Single-action, top-break with automatic ejection. Polished blue finish. Introduced 1994. Imported by Navy Arms.
Price: Wells Fargo (5" barrel, Wells Fargo markings) **$795.00**
Price: U.S. Cavalry model (7" barrel, military markings **$795.00**

CAUTION: PRICES SHOWN ARE SUPPLIED BY THE MANUFACTURER OR IMPORTER. CHECK YOUR LOCAL GUNSHOP.

7th ANNUAL EDITION **269**

SINGLE-ACTION REVOLVERS

North American Mini

North American Mini-Master

North American Black Widow

Phelps Heritage I

Ruger Blackhawk

Ruger Bisley

NORTH AMERICAN MINI-REVOLVERS Caliber: 22 LR, 22 WMR, 5-shot. **Barrel:** 1⅛", 1⅝". **Weight:** 4 to 6.6 oz. **Length:** 3⅝" to 6⅛" overall. **Stocks:** Laminated wood. **Sights:** Blade front, notch fixed rear. **Features:** All stainless steel construction. Polished satin and matte finish. Engraved models available. From North American Arms.

Price: 22 LR, 1⅛" bbl. $157.00
Price: 22 LR, 1⅝" bbl. $157.00
Price: 22 WMR, 1⅝" bbl. $178.00
Price: 22 WMR, 1⅛" or 1⅝" bbl. with extra 22 LR cylinder . $210.00

NORTH AMERICAN MINI-MASTER Caliber: 22 LR, 22 WMR, 5-shot cylinder. **Barrel:** 4". **Weight:** 10.7 oz. **Length:** 7.75" overall. **Stocks:** Checkered hard black rubber. **Sights:** Blade front, white outline rear adjustable for elevation, or fixed. **Features:** Heavy vent barrel; full-size grips. Non-fluted cylinder. Introduced 1989.

Price: Adjustable sight, 22 WMR or 22 LR $279.00
Price: As above with extra WMR/LR cylinder $317.00
Price: Fixed sight, 22 WMR or 22 LR $264.00
Price: As above with extra WMR/LR cylinder $302.00

North American Black Widow Revolver Similar to the Mini-Master except has 2" Heavy Vent barrel. Built on the 22 WMR frame. Non-fluted cylinder, black rubber grips. Available with either Millett Low Profile fixed sights or Millett sight adjustable for elevation only. Overall length 5⅞", weight 8.8 oz. From North American Arms.

Price: Adjustable sight, 22 LR or 22 WMR $249.00
Price: As above with extra WMR/LR cylinder $285.00
Price: Fixed sight, 22 LR or 22 WMR $235.00
Price: As above with extra WMR/LR cylinder $270.00

PHELPS HERITAGE I, EAGLE I, GRIZZLY REVOLVERS Caliber: 444 Marlin, 45-70, 50-70, 6-shot. **Barrel:** 8", 12", 16" (45-70). **Weight:** 5½ lbs. **Length:** 19½" overall (12" bbl.). **Stocks:** Smooth walnut. **Sights:** Ramp front, adjustable rear. **Features:** Single action; polished blue finish; safety bar. From Phelps Mfg. Co.

Price: 8", 45-70 or 444 Marlin, about $1,185.00
Price: 12", 45-70 or 444 Marlin, about $1,265.00
Price: 8", 50-70, about $1,550.00

RUGER BLACKHAWK REVOLVER Caliber: 30 Carbine, 357 Mag./38 Spec., 41 Mag., 45 Colt, 6-shot. **Barrel:** 4⅝" or 6½", either caliber; 7½" (30 Carbine, 45 Colt only). **Weight:** 42 oz. (6½" bbl.). **Length:** 12¼" overall (6½" bbl.). **Stocks:** American walnut. **Sights:** ⅛" ramp front, micro-click rear adjustable for windage and elevation. **Features:** Ruger interlock mechanism, independent firing pin, hardened chrome moly steel frame, music wire springs throughout.

Price: Blue, 30 Carbine (7½" bbl.), BN31 . . . . $328.00
Price: Blue, 357 Mag. (4⅝", 6½"), BN34, BN36 . . . . . . $328.00
Price: Blue, 357/9mm Convertible (4⅝", 6½"), BN34X,
    BN36X $343.50
Price: Blue, 41 Mag., 45 Colt (4⅝", 6½"), BN41, BN42, BN45 $328.00
Price: Stainless, 357 Mag. (4⅝", 6½"), KBN34, KBN36 . . . $404.00
Price: High-gloss stainless, 357 Mag. (4⅝", 6½"), GKBN34,
    GKBN36 . . . . $404.00
Price: High-gloss stainless, 45 Colt (4⅝", 7½"), GKBN44,
    GKBN45 . . . . $404.00

Ruger Bisley Single-Action Revolver Similar to standard Blackhawk except the hammer is lower with a smoothly curved, deeply checkered wide spur. The trigger is strongly curved with a wide smooth surface. Longer grip frame has a hand-filling shape. Adjustable rear sight, ramp-style front. Has an unfluted cylinder and roll engraving, adjustable sights. Chambered for 357, 41, 44 Mags. and 45 Colt; 7½" barrel; overall length of 13". Introduced 1985.

Price: $391.00

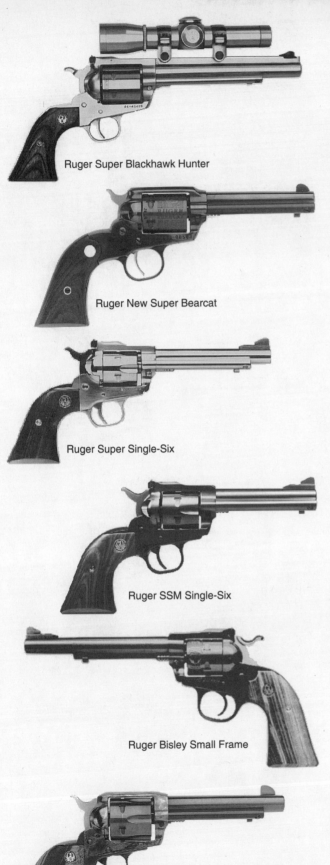

Ruger Super Blackhawk Hunter

Ruger New Super Bearcat

Ruger Super Single-Six

Ruger SSM Single-Six

Ruger Bisley Small Frame

Ruger Vaquero

RUGER SUPER BLACKHAWK **Caliber:** 44 Magnum, 6-shot. Also fires 44 Spec. **Barrel:** 4⅝", 5½", 7½", 10½". **Weight:** 48 oz. (7½" bbl.), 51 oz. (10½" bbl.). **Length:** 13⅜" overall (7½" bbl.). **Stocks:** American walnut. **Sights:** ⅛" ramp front, micro-click rear adjustable for windage and elevation. **Features:** Ruger interlock mechanism, non-fluted cylinder, steel grip and cylinder frame, square back trigger guard, wide serrated trigger and wide spur hammer.
Price: Blue (S45N, S47N, S411N) **$378.50**
Price: Stainless (KS45N, KS47N, KS411N) **$413.75**
Price: Stainless KS47NH Hunter with scope rings, 7½" **$479.50**
Price: High-gloss stainless (4⅝", 5½", 7½"), GKS458N, GKS45N, GKS47N **$413.75**

RUGER NEW SUPER BEARCAT SINGLE ACTION **Caliber:** 22 LR/22 WMR, 6-shot. **Barrel:** 4". **Weight:** 23 oz. **Length:** 8⅞" overall. **Stocks:** Smooth rosewood with Ruger medallion. **Sights:** Blade front, fixed notch rear. **Features:** Reintroduction of the Ruger Super Bearcat with slightly lengthened frame, Ruger patented transfer bar safety system. Comes with two cylinders. Available in blue or stainless steel. Introduced 1993. From Sturm, Ruger & Co.
Price: SBC4, blue **$298.00**
Price: KSBC4, stainless **$325.00**

RUGER SUPER SINGLE-SIX CONVERTIBLE **Caliber:** 22 LR, 6-shot; 22 WMR in extra cylinder. **Barrel:** 4⅝", 5½", 6½", or 9½" (6-groove). **Weight:** 34½ oz. (6½" bbl.). **Length:** 11¹³⁄₁₆" overall (6½" bbl.). **Stocks:** Smooth American walnut. **Sights:** Improved Patridge front on ramp, fully adjustable rear protected by integral frame ribs; or fixed sight. **Features:** Ruger interlock mechanism, transfer bar ignition, gate-controlled loading, hardened chrome moly steel frame, wide trigger, music wire springs throughout, independent firing pin.
Price: 4⅝", 5½", 6½", 9½" barrel, blue, fixed or adjustable sight (5½", 6½") **$281.00**
Price: 5½", 6½" bbl. only, high-gloss stainless steel, fixed or adjustable sight **$354.00**

Ruger SSM Single-Six Revolver Similar to the Super Single-Six revolver except chambered for 32 H&R Magnum (also handles 32 S&W and 32 S&W Long). Weight is about 34 oz. with 6½" barrel. Barrel lengths: 4⅝", 5½", 6½", 9½". Introduced 1985.
Price: **$281.00**

> Consult our Directory pages for the location of firms mentioned.

Ruger Bisley Small Frame Revolver Similar to the Single-Six except frame is styled after the classic Bisley "flat-top." Most mechanical parts are unchanged. Hammer is lower and smoothly curved with a deeply checkered spur. Trigger is strongly curved with a wide smooth surface. Longer grip frame designed with a hand-filling shape, and the trigger guard is a large oval. Adjustable dovetail rear sight; front sight base accepts interchangeable square blades of various heights and styles. Has an unfluted cylinder and roll engraving. Weight about 41 oz. Chambered for 22 LR and 32 H&R Mag., 6½" barrel only. Introduced 1985.
Price: **$328.75**

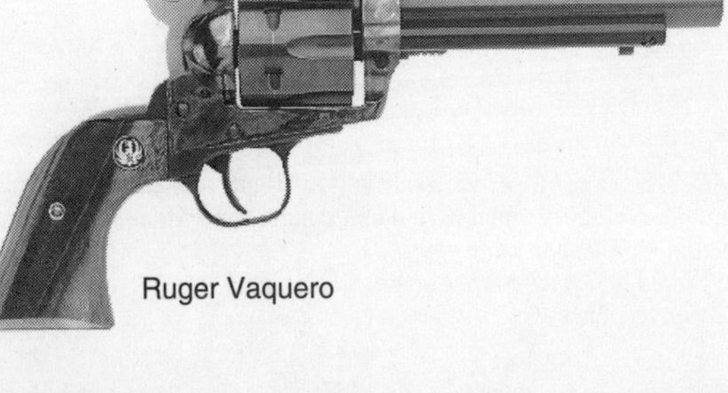

RUGER VAQUERO SINGLE-ACTION REVOLVER **Caliber:** 44-40, 44 Magnum, 45 Colt, 6-shot. **Barrel:** 4⅝", 5½", 7½". **Weight:** 41 oz. **Length:** 13⅜" overall (7½" barrel). **Stocks:** Smooth rosewood with Ruger medallion. **Sights:** Blade front, fixed notch rear. **Features:** Uses Ruger's patented transfer bar safety system and loading gate interlock with classic styling. Blued model has color case-hardened finish on the frame, the rest polished and blued. Stainless model is polished. Introduced 1993. From Sturm, Ruger & Co.
Price: BNV44 (4⅝"), BNV445 (5½"), BNV45 (7½"), blue . **$394.00**
Price: KBNV44 (4⅝"), KBNV455 (5½"), KBNV45 (7½"), stainless **$394.00**

SPORTARMS MODEL HS21S SINGLE ACTION **Caliber:** 22 LR or 22 LR/22 WMR combo, 6-shot. **Barrel:** 5½". **Weight:** 33.5 oz. **Length:** 11" overall. **Stocks:** Smooth hardwood. **Sights:** Blade front, rear drift adjustable for windage. **Features:** Available in blue with imitation stag or wood stocks. Made in Germany by Herbert Schmidt; Imported by Sportarms of Florida.
Price: 22 LR, blue, "stag" grips, about **$100.00**
Price: 22 LR/22 WMR combo, blue, wood stocks, about **$120.00**

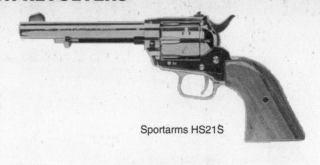

Sportarms HS21S

TEXAS LONGHORN ARMS GROVER'S IMPROVED NO. FIVE
Caliber: 44 Magnum, 6-shot. **Barrel:** 5½". **Weight:** 44 oz. **Length:** NA. **Stocks:** Fancy AAA walnut. **Sights:** Square blade front on ramp, fully adjustable rear. **Features:** Music wire coil spring action with double locking bolt; polished blue finish. Handmade in limited 1,200-gun production. Grip contour, straps, over-sized base pin, lever latch and lockwork identical copies of Elmer Keith design. Lifetime warranty to original owner. Introduced 1988.
Price: **$985.00**

Texas Longhorn Grover's No. Five

TEXAS LONGHORN ARMS RIGHT-HAND SINGLE ACTION
Caliber: All centerfire pistol calibers. **Barrel:** 4¾". **Weight:** NA. **Length:** NA. **Stocks:** One-piece fancy walnut, or any fancy AAA wood. **Sights:** Blade front, grooved topstrap rear. **Features:** Loading gate and ejector housing on left side of gun. Cylinder rotates to the left. All steel construction; color case-hardened frame; high polish blue; music wire coil springs. Lifetime guarantee to original owner. Introduced 1984. From Texas Longhorn Arms.
Price: South Texas Army Limited Edition—handmade, only 1,000 to be produced; "One of One Thousand" engraved on barrel . **$1,500.00**

Texas Longhorn South Texas Army

Texas Longhorn Arms Texas Border Special Similar to the South Texas Army Limited Edition except has 3½" barrel, bird's-head style grip. Same special features. Introduced 1984.
Price: **$1,500.00**

Texas Longhorn Arms Sesquicentennial Model Revolver Similar to the South Texas Army Model except has ¾-coverage Nimschke-style engraving, antique golden nickel plate finish, one-piece elephant ivory grips. Comes with handmade solid walnut presentation case, factory letter to owner. Limited edition of 150 units. Introduced 1986.
Price: **$2,500.00**

Texas Longhorn Flat Top

Texas Longhorn Arms West Texas Flat Top Target Similar to the South Texas Army Limited Edition except choice of barrel length from 7½" through 15"; flat-top style frame; ⅛" contoured ramp front sight, old model steel micro-click rear adjustable for windage and elevation. Same special features. Introduced 1984.
Price: **$1,500.00**

Texas Longhorn Arms Cased Set Set contains one each of the Texas Longhorn Right-Hand Single Actions, all in the same caliber, same serial numbers (100, 200, 300, 400, 500, 600, 700, 800, 900). Ten sets to be made (#1000 donated to NRA museum). Comes in hand-tooled leather case. All other specs same as Limited Edition guns. Introduced 1984.
Price: **$5,750.00**
Price: With ¾-coverage "C-style" engraving **$7,650.00**

Uberti 1873 Cattleman

UBERTI 1873 CATTLEMAN SINGLE ACTIONS **Caliber:** 38 Spec., 357 Mag., 44 Spec., 44-40, 45 Colt/45 ACP, 6-shot. **Barrel:** 4¾", 5½", 7½"; 44-40, 45 Colt also with 3". **Weight:** 38 oz. (5½" bbl.). **Length:** 10¾" overall (5½" bbl.). **Stocks:** One-piece smooth walnut. **Sights:** Blade front, groove rear; fully adjustable rear available. **Features:** Steel or brass backstrap, trigger guard; color case-hardened frame, blued barrel, cylinder. Imported from Italy by Uberti USA.
Price: Steel backstrap, trigger guard, fixed sights **$410.00**
Price: Brass backstrap, trigger guard, fixed sights **$365.00**

Uberti 1873 Buckhorn Single Action A slightly larger version of the Cattleman revolver. Available in 44 Magnum or 44 Magnum/44-40 convertible, otherwise has same specs.
Price: Steel backstrap, trigger guard, fixed sights **$410.00**
Price: Convertible (two cylinders) **$460.00**

CAUTION: PRICES SHOWN ARE SUPPLIED BY THE MANUFACTURER OR IMPORTER. CHECK YOUR LOCAL GUNSHOP.

SINGLE-ACTION REVOLVERS

UBERTI 1875 SA ARMY OUTLAW REVOLVER **Caliber:** 357 Mag., 44-40, 45 Colt, 6-shot. **Barrel:** 7½". **Weight:** 44 oz. **Length:** 13¾" overall. **Stocks:** Smooth walnut. **Sights:** Blade front, notch rear. **Features:** Replica of the 1875 Remington S.A. Army revolver. Brass trigger guard, color case-hardened frame, rest blued. Imported by Uberti USA.
Price: **$405.00**
Price: 45 Colt/45 ACP convertible **$450.00**

Uberti 1875 Outlaw

UBERTI 1890 ARMY OUTLAW REVOLVER **Caliber:** 357 Mag., 44-40, 45 Colt, 6-shot. **Barrel:** 5½". **Weight:** 37 oz. **Length:** 12½" overall. **Stocks:** American walnut. **Sights:** Blade front, groove rear. **Features:** Replica of the 1890 Remington single action. Brass trigger guard, rest is blued. Imported by Uberti USA.
Price: **$410.00**
Price: 45 Colt/45 ACP convertible **$415.00**

Uberti 1890 Army

MISCELLANEOUS

Specially adapted single-shot and multi-barrel arms.

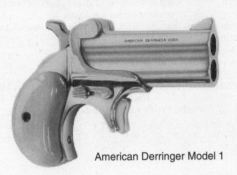
American Derringer Model 1

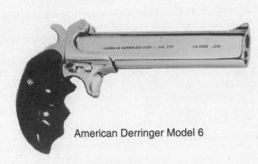
American Derringer Model 6

American Derringer Model 6 Similar to the Model 1 except has 6" barrels chambered for 3" 410 shotshells or 45 Colt, rosewood stocks, 8.2" o.a.l. and weighs 21 oz. Shoots either round for each barrel. Manual hammer block safety. Introduced 1986.
Price: High polish or satin finish **$387.50**
Price: Gray matte finish **$362.50**

American Derringer Model 10 Lightweight Similar to the Model 1 except frame is of aluminum, giving weight of 10 oz. Available in 45 Colt or 45 ACP only. Matte gray finish. Introduced 1989.
Price: 45 Colt **$320.00**
Price: 45 ACP **$257.00**
Price: Model 11 (38 Spec., aluminum bbls., wgt. 11 oz.) **$205.00**

AMERICAN DERRINGER MODEL 1 **Caliber:** 22 LR, 22 WMR, 30 Luger, 30-30 Win., 32 ACP, 380 ACP, 38 Spec., 9mm Para., 357 Mag., 357 Maximum, 10mm, 40 S&W, 41 Mag., 38-40, 44-40 Win., 44 Spec., 44 Mag., 45 Colt, 45 ACP, 410-bore (2½"). **Barrel:** 3". **Weight:** 15½ oz. (38 Spec.). **Length:** 4.82" overall. **Stocks:** Rosewood, Zebra wood. **Sights:** Blade front. **Features:** Made of stainless steel with high-polish or satin finish. Two-shot capacity. Manual hammer block safety. Introduced 1980. Available in almost any pistol caliber. Contact the factory for complete list of available calibers and prices. From American Derringer Corp.
Price: 22 LR or WMR . . . . **$312.00 to $375.00**
Price: 38 Spec. **$225.00**
Price: 357 Maximum **$265.00**
Price: 357 Mag. **$250.00**
Price: 9mm, 380, ... **$224.00**
Price: 10mm, 40 S&W **$257.00**
Price: 44 Spec., ... **$320.00**
Price: 44-40 Win., 45 Colt, 45 Auto Rim **$320.00**
Price: 30-30, 41, 44 Mags., 45 Win. Mag. **$375.00**
Price: 45-70, single shot **$312.00**
Price: 45 Colt, 410, 2½" **$320.00**
Price: 45 ACP, 10mm Auto **$257.00**
Price: 125th Anniversary model (brass frame, stainless bbl., 44-40, 45 Colt, 38 Spec.) **$320.00**

American Derringer Model 4 Similar to the Model 1 except has 4.1" barrel, overall length of 6", and weighs 16½ oz.; chambered for 3" 410-bore shotshells or 45 or 44 Magnum Colt. Can be had with 45-70 upper barrel and 3" 410-bore or 45 Colt bottom barrel. Made of stainless steel. Manual hammer block safety. Introduced 1985.
Price: 3" 410/45 Colt (either barrel) **$352.00**
Price: 3" 410/45 Colt or 45-70 (Alaskan Survival model) . . . **$387.50**
Price: 44 Magnum with oversize grips **$422.00**
Price: Alaskan Survival model (45-70 upper, 410-45 Colt lower) **$387.50**

American Derringer Model 7 Ultra Lightweight Similar to Model 1 except made of high strength aircraft aluminum. Weighs 7½ oz., 4.82" o.a.l., rosewood stocks. Available in 22 LR, 32 H&R Mag., 380 ACP, 38 Spec., 44 Spec. Introduced 1986.
Price: 22 LR **$220.00**
Price: 38 Spec. **$220.00**
Price: 380 ACP **$220.00**
Price: 32 H&R Mag. **$220.00**
Price: 44 Spec. **$500.00**

CAUTION: PRICES SHOWN ARE SUPPLIED BY THE MANUFACTURER OR IMPORTER. CHECK YOUR LOCAL GUNSHOP.

7th ANNUAL EDITION **273**

American Derringer Semmerling

American Derringer Mini COP

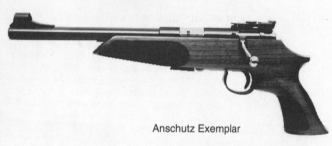

Anschutz Exemplar

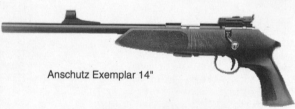

Anschutz Exemplar 14"

Anschutz Exemplar Hornet

High Standard Derringer

American Derringer Lady Derringer Same as the Model 1 except has tuned action, is fitted with scrimshawed synthetic ivory grips; chambered for 32 H&R Mag. and 38 Spec.; 22 LR, 22 WMR, 380 ACP, 357 Mag., 9mm Para., 45 ACP, 45 Colt/410 shotshell available at extra cost. Deluxe Grade is highly polished; Deluxe Engraved is engraved in a pattern similar to that used on 1880s derringers. All come in a French fitted jewelry box. Introduced 1991.
Price: Deluxe Grade **$235.00**
Price: Deluxe Engraved Grade **$750.00**

American Derringer Texas Commemorative A Model 1 Derringer with solid brass frame, stainless steel barrel and rosewood grips. Available in 38 Speical, 44-40 Win., or 45 Colt. Introduced 1987.
Price: 38 Spec. **$225.00**
Price: 44-40 or 45 Colt **$320.00**

AMERICAN DERRINGER DA 38 MODEL **Caliber:** 9mm Para., 38 Spec. **Barrel:** 3". **Weight:** 14.5 oz. **Length:** 4.8" overall. **Stocks:** Rosewood, walnut or other hardwoods. **Sights:** Fixed. **Features:** Double-action only; two-shots. Manual safety. Made of satin-finished stainless steel and aluminum. Introduced 1989. From American Derringer Corp.
Price: 38 Spec. **$250.00**
Price: 9mm Para. **$275.00**

AMERICAN DERRINGER SEMMERLING LM-4 **Caliber:** 9mm Para., 7-shot magazine; 45 ACP, 5-shot magazine. **Barrel:** 3.625". **Weight:** 24 oz. **Length:** 5.2" overall. **Stocks:** Checkered plastic on blued guns, rosewood on stainless guns. **Sights:** Open, fixed. **Features:** Manually-operated repeater. Height is 3.7", width is 1". Comes with manual, leather carrying case, spare stock screws, wrench. From American Derringer Corp.
Price: Blued **$1,750.00**
Price: Stainless steel **$1,875.00**

AMERICAN DERRINGER COP 357 DERRINGER **Caliber:** 38 Spec. or 357 Mag., 4-shot. **Barrel:** 3.14". **Weight:** 16 oz. **Length:** 5.53" overall. **Stocks:** Rosewood. **Sights:** Fixed. **Features:** Double-action only. Four shots. Made of stainless steel. Introduced 1990. Made in U.S. by American Derringer Corp.
Price: **$375.00**

American Derringer Mini COP Derringer Similar to the COP 357 except chambered for 22 WMR. Barrel length of 2.85", overall length of 4.95", weight is 16 oz. Double action with automatic hammer-block safety. Made of stainless steel. Grips of rosewood, walnut or other hardwoods. Introduced 1990. Made in U.S. by American Derringer Corp.
Price: **$312.50**

ANSCHUTZ EXEMPLAR BOLT-ACTION PISTOL **Caliber:** 22 LR, 5-shot; 22 Hornet, 5-shot. **Barrel:** 10", 14". **Weight:** $3\frac{1}{2}$ lbs. **Length:** 17" overall. **Stock:** European walnut with stippled grip and forend. **Sights:** Hooded front on ramp, open notch rear adjustable for windage and elevation. **Features:** Uses Match 64 action with left-hand bolt; Anschutz #5091 two-stage trigger set at 9.85 oz. Receiver grooved for scope mounting; open sights easily removed. The 22 Hornet version uses Match 54 action with left-hand bolt, Anschutz #5099 two-stage trigger set at 19.6 oz. Introduced 1987. Imported from Germany by Precision Sales International.
Price: 22 LR **$499.50**
Price: 22 LR, left-hand **$499.50**
Price: 22 LR, 14" barrel **$522.00**
Price: 22 Hornet (no sights, 10" bbl.) **$899.00**

HIGH STANDARD DERRINGER **Caliber:** 22 LR, 22 WMR, 2-shot. **Barrel:** 3.5". **Weight:** 11 oz. **Length:** 5.12" overall. **Stocks:** Black composition. **Sights:** Fixed. **Features:** Double action, dual extraction. Hammer-block safety. Blue finish. Introduced 1990. Made in U.S. by American Derringer Corp.
Price: **$169.50**

DAVIS DERRINGERS **Caliber:** 22 LR, 22 WMR, 25 ACP, 32 ACP. **Barrel:** 2.4". **Weight:** 9.5 oz. **Length:** 4" overall. **Stocks:** Laminated wood. **Sights:** Blade front, fixed notch rear. **Features:** Choice of black Teflon or chrome finish; spur trigger. Introduced 1986. Made in U.S. by Davis Industries.
Price: **$65.00**

DAVIS D-38 DERRINGER **Caliber:** 32 H&R, 38 Special. **Barrel:** 2.75". **Weight:** 11.5 oz. **Length:** 4.65" overall. **Stocks:** Textured black synthetic. **Sights:** Blade front, fixed notch rear. **Features:** Alloy frame, steel-lined barrels, steel breech block. Plunger-type safety with integral hammer block. Chrome or black Teflon finish. Introduced 1992. Made in U.S. by Davis Industries.
Price: **$98.00**

FEATHER GUARDIAN ANGEL PISTOL **Caliber:** 22 LR/22 WMR. **Barrel:** 2". **Weight:** 12 oz. **Length:** 5" overall. **Stocks:** Black composition. **Sights:** Fixed. **Features:** Uses a pre-loaded two-shot drop-in "magazine." Stainless steel construction; matte finish. From Feather Industries. Introduced 1988.
Price: **$119.95**

GAUCHER GN1 SILHOUETTE PISTOL **Caliber:** 22 LR, single shot. **Barrel:** 10". **Weight:** 2.4 lbs. **Length:** 15.5" overall. **Stock:** European hardwood. **Sights:** Blade front, open adjustable rear. **Features:** Bolt action, adjustable trigger. Introduced 1990. Imported from France by Mandall Shooting Supplies.
Price: About **$289.95**
Price: Model GP Silhouette **$259.95**

HJS FRONTIER FOUR DERRINGER **Caliber:** 22 LR. **Barrel:** 2". **Weight:** 5½ oz. **Length:** 3¹⁵⁄₁₆" overall. **Stocks:** Brown plastic. **Sights:** None. **Features:** Four barrels fire with rotating firing pin. Stainless steel construction. Introduced 1993. Made in U.S. by HJS Arms, Inc.
Price: **$165.00**

HJS Antigua Derringer Same as the Frontier Four except blued stainess barrel, brass frame, brass pivot pins. Brown plastic grips. Introduced 1994. Made in U.S. by HJS Arms, Inc.
Price: **$180.00**

HJS LONE STAR DERRINGER **Caliber:** 380 ACP. **Barrel:** 2". **Weight:** 6 oz. **Length:** 3¹⁵⁄₁₆" overall. **Stocks:** Brown plastic. **Sights:** Groove. **Features:** Stainless steel Construction. Beryllium copper firing pin. Button-rifled barrel. Introduced 1993. Made in U.S. by HJS Arms, Inc.
Price: **$185.00**

ITHACA MODEL 20 SINGLE SHOT **Caliber:** 22 LR, 44 Mag. **Barrel:** 10", 12". **Weight:** 3¼ lbs. **Length:** 15" overall (10" barrel). **Stocks:** American walnut with satin finish. **Sights:** Ithaca Gun Raybar Deerslayer sights or drilled and tapped for scope mounting. **Features:** Single firing pin for RF/CF use. Comes with both barrels matched to one frame. Matte blue finish.
Price: 22 LR/44 Mag. combo, 10" and 12" barrels **$348.65**

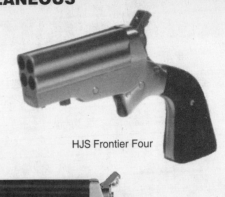

HJS Frontier Four

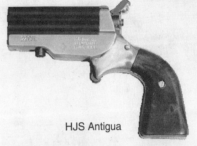

HJS Antigua

Davis 22 Derringer

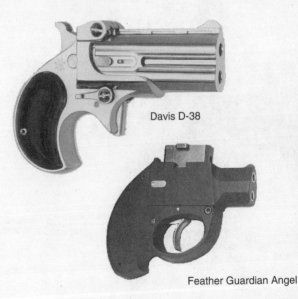

Davis D-38

Feather Guardian Angel

Ithaca Model 20

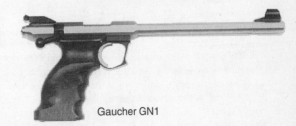

Gaucher GN1

CAUTION: PRICES SHOWN ARE SUPPLIED BY THE MANUFACTURER OR IMPORTER. CHECK YOUR LOCAL GUNSHOP.

7th ANNUAL EDITION **275**

Magnum Research Lone Eagle

Maximum Single Shot

New Advantage Derringer

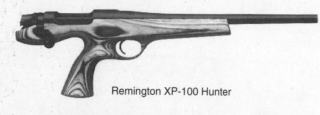

Remington XP-100 Hunter

Remington XP-100R KS

Remington XP-100 Custom HB

Remington XP-100 Custom HB Long Range Pistol Chambered for 223 Rem., 22-250 Rem., 7mm-08 Rem., 35 Rem., 250 Savage, 6mm BR, 7mm BR, 308. Offered with standard 14½" barrel with adjustable rear leaf and front bead sights, or with heavy 15½" barrel without sights. Custom Shop 14½" barrel, Custom Shop English walnut stock in right- or left-hand configuration. Action tuned in Custom Shop. Weight is under 4½ lbs. (heavy barrel, 5½ lbs.). Introduced 1986.

Price: Right- or left-hand **$945.00**

MAGNUM RESEARCH LONE EAGLE SINGLE SHOT PISTOL
Caliber: 22 Hornet, 223, 22-250, 243, 7mm BR, 7mm-08, 30-30, 308, 30-06, 357 Max., 35 Rem., 358 Win., 44 Mag., 444 Marlin. **Barrel:** 14", interchangable. **Weight:** 4lbs., 3 oz. to 4 lbs., 7 oz. **Length:** 15" overall. **Stocks:** Composition, with thumbrest. **Sights:** None furnished; drilled and tapped for scope mounting and open sights. Open sights optional. **Features:** Cannon-type rotating breech with spring-activated ejector. Ordnance steel with matte blue finish. Cross-bolt safety. External cocking lever on left side of gun. Introduced 1991. Available from Magnum Research, Inc.

Price: Complete pistol **$344.00**
Price: Barreled action only **$254.00**
Price: Scope base **$14.00**
Price: Adjustable open sights **$35.00**

MANDALL/CABANAS PISTOL **Caliber:** 177, pellet or round ball; single shot. **Barrel:** 9". **Weight:** 51 oz. **Length:** 19" overall. **Stock:** Smooth wood with thumbrest. **Sights:** Blade front on ramp, open adjustable rear. **Features:** Fires round ball or pellets with 22 blank cartridge. Automatic safety; muzzlebrake. Imported from Mexico by Mandall Shooting Supplies.

Price: **$139.95**

MAXIMUM SINGLE SHOT PISTOL **Caliber:** 22 LR, 22 Hornet, 22 BR, 22 PPC, 223 Rem., 22-250, 6mm BR, 6mm PPC, 243, 250 Savage, 6.5mm-35M, 270 MAX, 270 Win., 7mm TCU, 7mm BR, 7mm-35, 7mm INT-R, 7mm-08, 7mm Rocket, 7mm Super Mag., 30 Herrett, 30 Carbine, 30-30, 308 Win., 30x39, 32-20, 357 Mag., 357 Maximum, 358 Win., 44 Mag., 454 Casull. **Barrel:** 8¾", 10½", 14". **Weight:** 61 oz. (10½" bbl.); 78 oz. (14" bbl.). **Length:** 15", 18½" overall (with 10½" and 14" bbl., respectively). **Stocks:** Smooth walnut stocks and forend. **Sights:** Ramp front, fully adjustable open rear. **Features:** Falling block action; drilled and tapped for M.O.A. scope mounts; integral grip frame/receiver; adjustable trigger; Douglas barrel (interchangeable). Introduced 1983. Made in U.S. by M.O.A. Corp.

Price: Stainless receiver, blue barrel **$622.00**
Price: Stainless receiver, stainless barrel **$677.00**
Price: Extra blued barrel **$164.00**
Price: Extra stainless barrel **$222.00**
Price: Scope mount **$52.00**

NEW ADVANTAGE ARMS DERRINGER **Caliber:** 22 LR, 22 WMR, 4-shot. **Barrel:** 2½". **Weight:** 15 oz. **Length:** 4½" overall. **Stocks:** Smooth walnut. **Sights:** Fixed. **Features:** Double-action mechanism, four barrels, revolving firing pin. Rebounding hammer. Blue or stainless. Reintroduced 1989. From New Advantage Arms Corp.

Price: 22 LR, 22 WMR, blue, about **$199.00**
Price: As above, stainless, about **$229.00**

REMINGTON XP-100 HUNTER PISTOL **Caliber:** 223 Rem., 7mm BR Rem., 7mm-08 Rem., 35 Rem., single shot. **Barrel:** 14½". **Weight:** 4½ lbs. **Length:** 21¼" overall. **Stocks:** Laminated wood with contoured grip. **Sights:** None furnished. Drilled and tapped for scope mounting. **Features:** Mid-handle grip design with scalloped contours for right- or left-handed shooters; two-position safety. Matte blue finish. Introduced 1993.

Price: **$548.00**

Remington XP-100R KS Repeater Pistol Similar to the Custom Long Range Pistol except chambered for 223 Rem., 22-250, 7mm-08 Rem., 250 Savage, 308, 350 Rem. Mag., and 35 Rem., and has a blind magazine holding 5 rounds (7mm-08 and 35), or 6 (223 Rem.). Comes with a rear-handle, synthetic stock of Du Pont Kevlar to eliminate the transfer bar between the forward trigger and rear trigger assembly. Fitted with front and rear sling swivel studs. Has standard-weight 14½" barrel with adjustable leaf rear sight, bead front. The receiver is drilled and tapped for scope mounts. Weight is about 4½ lbs. Introduced 1990. From Remington Custom Shop.

Price: **$840.00**

RPM XL SINGLE SHOT PISTOL **Caliber:** 22 LR, 22 WMR, 225 Win., 25 Rocket, 6.5 Rocket, 32 H&R Mag., 357 Max., 357 Mag., 30-30 Win., 30 Herrett, 357 Herrett, 41 Mag., 44 Mag., 454 Casull, 375 Win., 7mm UR, 7mm Merrill, 30 Merrill, 7mm Rocket, 270 Ren, 270 Rocket, 270 Max., 45-70. **Barrel:** 8" slab, 10¾", 12", 14" bull; .450" wide rib, matted to prevent glare. **Weight:** About 60 oz. **Length:** 12¼" overall (10¾" bbl.). **Stocks:** Smooth Goncalo with thumb and heel rest. **Sights:** Front .100" blade, rear adjustable for windage and elevation. Hooded front with interchangeable post optional. **Features:** Blue finish, hard chrome optional. Barrel is drilled and tapped for scope mounting. Cocking indicator visible from rear of gun. Has spring-loaded barrel lock, positive hammer block thumb safety. Trigger adjustable for weight of pull and over-travel. For complete price list contact RPM.

Price: Regular ¾" frame, right-hand action **$807.50**
Price: As above, left-hand action **$832.50**
Price: Wide ⅞" frame, right-hand action **$857.50**
Price: Extra barrel, 8", 10¾" **$287.50**
Price: Extra barrel, 12", 14" **$357.50**

RPM XL Pistol

SUNDANCE POINT BLANK O/U DERRINGER **Caliber:** 22 LR, 2-shot. **Barrel:** 3". **Weight:** 8 oz. **Length:** 4.6" overall. **Stocks:** Grooved composition. **Sights:** Blade front, fixed notch rear. **Features:** Double-action trigger, push-bar safety, automatic chamber selection. Fully enclosed hammer. Matte black finish. Introduced 1994. Made in U.S. by Sundance Industries.
Price: **$99.00**

Sundance Point Blank

TEXAS ARMS DEFENDER DERRINGER **Caliber:** 9mm Para., 357 Mag., 44 Mag., 45 ACP, 45 Colt/410. **Barrel:** 3". **Weight:** 21 oz. **Length:** 5" overall. **Stocks:** Smooth wood. **Sights:** Blade front, fixed rear. **Features:** Interchangeable barrels; retracting firing pins; rebounding hammer; cross-bolt safety; removable trigger guard; automatic extractor. Blasted finish stainless steel. Introduced 1993. Made in U.S. by Texas Arms.
Price: **$310.00**
Price: Extra barrel **$100.00**

Texas Arms Defender

TEXAS LONGHORN "THE JEZEBEL" PISTOL **Caliber:** 22 Short, Long, Long Rifle, single shot. **Barrel:** 6". **Weight:** 15 oz. **Length:** 8" overall. **Stocks:** One-piece fancy walnut grip (right- or left-hand), walnut forend. **Sights:** Bead front, fixed rear. **Features:** Handmade gun. Top-break action; all stainless steel; automatic hammer block safety; music wire coil springs. Barrel is half-round, half-octagon. Announced 1986. From Texas Longhorn Arms.
Price: About **$250.00**

THOMPSON/CENTER CONTENDER **Caliber:** 7mm TCU, 30-30 Win., 22 LR, 22 WMR, 22 Hornet, 223 Rem., 270 Ren, 7-30 Waters, 32-20 Win., 357 Mag., 357 Rem. Max., 44 Mag., 10mm Auto, 445 Super Mag., 45/410, single shot. **Barrel:** 10", tapered octagon, bull barrel and vent. rib. **Weight:** 43 oz. (10" bbl.). **Length:** 13¼" (10" bbl.). **Stocks:** T/C "Competitor Grip." Right or left hand. **Sights:** Under-cut blade ramp front, rear adjustable for windage and elevation. **Features:** Break-open action with automatic safety. Single-action only. Interchangeable bbls., both caliber (rim & centerfire), and length. Drilled and tapped for scope. Engraved frame. See T/C catalog for exact barrel/caliber availability.
Price: Blued (rimfire cals.) **$435.00**
Price: Blued (centerfire cals.) **$435.00**
Price: Extra bbls. (standard octagon) **$200.00**
Price: 45/410, internal choke bbl. **$205.00**

T/C Contender

Thompson/Center Contender Hunter Package Package contains the Contender pistol in 223, 7-30 Waters, 30-30, 375 Win., 357 Rem. Maximum, 35 Rem., 44 Mag. or 45-70 with 14" barrel with T/C's Muzzle Tamer, a 2.5x Recoil Proof Long Eye Relief scope with lighted reticle, q.d. sling swivels with a nylon carrying sling. Comes with a suede leather case with foam padding and fleece lining. Introduced 1990. From Thompson/Center Arms.
Price: 14" barrel **$740.00**

T/C Contender Hunter

CAUTION: PRICES SHOWN ARE SUPPLIED BY THE MANUFACTURER OR IMPORTER. CHECK YOUR LOCAL GUNSHOP.

7th ANNUAL EDITION **277**

T/C Stainless Contender

T/C Stainless Super 14 Contender

Ultra Light Model 20

Wichita Master

Thompson/Center Stainless Contender Same as the standard Contender except made of stainless steel with blued sights, black Rynite forend and ambidextrous finger-groove grip with a built-in rubber recoil cushion that has a sealed-in air pocket. Receiver has a different cougar etching. Available with 10" bull barrel in 22 LR, 22 LR Match, 22 Hornet, 223 Rem., 30-30 Win., 357 Mag., 44 Mag., 45 Colt/410. Introduced 1993.
Price: **$465.00**
Price: 45 Colt/410 . . . . **$470.00**

Thompson/Center Stainless Super 14, Super 16 Contender Same as the standard Super 14 and Super 16 except they are made of stainless steel with blued sights. Both models have black Rynite forend and finger-groove, ambidextrous grip with a built-in rubber recoil cushion that has a sealed-in air pocket. Receiver has a different cougar etching. Available in 22 LR, 22 LR Match, 22 Hornet, 223 Rem., 30-30 Win., 35 Rem. (Super 14), 45-70 (Super 16 only), 45 Colt/410. Introduced 1993.
Price: 14" bull barrel **$475.00**
Price: 16¼" bull barrel **$480.00**
Price: 45 Colt/410, 14" **$505.00**
Price: 45 Colt/410, 16" **$510.00**

UBERTI ROLLING BLOCK TARGET PISTOL **Caliber:** 22 LR, 22 WMR, 22 Hornet, 357 Mag., single shot. **Barrel:** 9⅞", half-round, half-octagon. **Weight:** 44 oz. **Length:** 14" overall. **Stocks:** Walnut grip and forend. **Sights:** Blade front, fully adjustable rear. **Features:** Replica of the 1871 rolling block target pistol. Brass trigger guard, color case-hardened frame, blue barrel. Imported by Uberti USA.
Price: **$380.00**

ULTRA LIGHT ARMS MODEL 20 REB HUNTER'S PISTOL **Caliber:** 22-250 thru 308 Win. standard. Most silhouette calibers and others on request. 5-shot magazine. **Barrel:** 14", Douglas No. 3. **Weight:** 4 lbs. **Stock:** Composite Kevlar, graphite reinforced. Du Pont Imron paint in green, brown, black and camo. **Sights:** None furnished. Scope mount included. **Features:** Timney adjustable trigger; two-position, three-function safety; benchrest quality action; matte or bright stock and metal finish; right- or left-hand action. Shipped in hard case. Introduced 1987. From Ultra Light Arms.
Price: **$1,600.00**

WICHITA MASTER PISTOL **Caliber:** 6mm BR, 7mm BR, 243, 7mm-08, 22-250, 308, 3-shot magazine. **Barrel:** 13", 14.875". **Weight:** 4.5 lbs. (13" barrel). **Length:** NA. **Stock:** American walnut with oil finish; glass bedded. **Sights:** Hooded post front, open adjustable rear. **Features:** Comes with left-hand action with right-hand grip. round receiver and barrel. Wichita adjustable trigger. Introduced 1991. From Wichita Arms.
Price: **$1,550.00**

BLACKPOWDER PISTOLS—SINGLE SHOT, FLINT & PERCUSSION

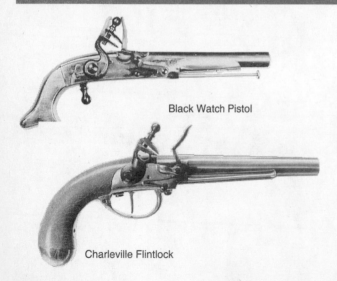

Black Watch Pistol

Charleville Flintlock

BLACK WATCH SCOTCH PISTOL **Caliber:** 577 (.500" round ball). **Barrel:** 7", smoothbore. **Weight:** 1½ lbs. **Length:** 12" overall. **Stock:** Brass. **Sights:** None. **Features:** Faithful reproduction of this military flintlock. From Dixie Gun Works.
Price: **$175.00**

CHARLEVILLE FLINTLOCK PISTOL **Caliber:** 69 (.680" round ball). **Barrel:** 7½". **Weight:** 48 oz. **Length:** 13½" overall. **Stock:** Walnut. **Sights:** None. **Features:** Brass frame, polished steel barrel, iron belt hook, brass buttcap and backstrap. Replica of original 1777 pistol. Imported by Dixie Gun Works.
Price: **$195.00**

CAUTION: PRICES SHOWN ARE SUPPLIED BY THE MANUFACTURER OR IMPORTER. CHECK YOUR LOCAL GUNSHOP.

BLACKPOWDER SINGLE SHOT PISTOLS—FLINT & PERCUSSION

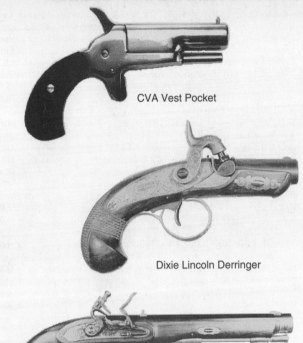

CVA Vest Pocket

Dixie Lincoln Derringer

Dixie Pennsylvania

Dixie Screw Barrel

Dixie Tornado

Navy Arms Kentucky Flintlock

CVA HAWKEN PISTOL Caliber: 50. **Barrel:** 9¾"; ¹⁵⁄₁₆" flats. **Weight:** 50 oz. **Length:** 16½" overall. **Stock:** Select hardwood. **Sights:** Beaded blade front, fully adjustable open rear. **Features:** Color case-hardened lock, polished brass wedge plate, nose cap, ramrod thimble, trigger guard, grip cap. Imported by CVA.
Price: **$149.95**
Price: Kit **$109.95**

CVA VEST POCKET DERRINGER Caliber: 31. **Barrel:** 2½", brass. **Weight:** 16 oz. **Stock:** Two-piece walnut. **Features:** All brass frame and barrel. A muzzle-loading version of the Colt No. 3 derringer. Imported by CVA.
Price: Finished **$69.95**

DIXIE LINCOLN DERRINGER Caliber: 41. **Barrel:** 2", 8 lands, 8 grooves. **Weight:** 7 oz. **Length:** 5½" overall. **Stock:** Walnut finish, checkered. **Sights:** Fixed. **Features:** Authentic copy of the "Lincoln Derringer." Shoots .400" patched ball. German silver furniture includes trigger guard with pineapple finial, wedge plates, nose, wrist, side and teardrop inlays. All furniture, lockplate, hammer, and breech plug engraved. Imported from Italy by Dixie Gun Works.
Price: With wooden case **$285.95**

DIXIE PENNSYLVANIA PISTOL Caliber: 44 (.430" round ball). **Barrel:** 10" (⅞" octagon). **Weight:** 2½ lbs. **Stock:** Walnut-stained hardwood. **Sights:** Blade front, open rear drift-adjustable for windage; brass. **Features:** Available in flint only. Brass trigger guard, thimbles, nosecap, wedgeplates; high-luster blue barrel. Imported from Italy by Dixie Gun Works.
Price: Finished **$149.95**
Price: Kit **$119.95**

> Consult our Directory pages for
> the location of firms mentioned.

DIXIE SCREW BARREL PISTOL Caliber: .445". **Barrel:** 2½". **Weight:** 8 oz. **Length:** 6½" overall. **Stock:** Walnut. **Features:** Trigger folds down when hammer is cocked. Close copy of the originals once made in Belgium. Uses No. 11 percussion caps. From Dixie Gun Works.
Price: **$89.00**
Price: Kit **$74.95**

DIXIE TORNADO TARGET PISTOL Caliber: 44 (.430" round ball). **Barrel:** 10", octagonal, 1:22 twist. **Stocks:** Walnut, target-style. Left unfinished for custom fitting. Walnut forend. **Sights:** Blade on ramp front, micro-type open rear adjustable for windage and elevation. **Features:** Grip frame style of 1860 Colt revolver. Improved model of the Tingle and B.W. Southgate pistol. Trigger adjustable for pull. Frame, barrel, hammer and sights in the white, brass trigger guard. Comes with solid brass, walnut-handled cleaning rod with jag and nylon muzzle protector. Introduced 1983. From Dixie Gun Works.
Price: **$215.50**

FRENCH-STYLE DUELING PISTOL Caliber: 44. **Barrel:** 10". **Weight:** 35 oz. **Length:** 15¾" overall. **Stock:** Carved walnut. **Sights:** Fixed. **Features:** Comes with velvet-lined case and accessories. Imported by Mandall Shooting Supplies.
Price: **$295.00**

HARPER'S FERRY 1806 PISTOL Caliber: 58 (.570" round ball). **Barrel:** 10". **Weight:** 40 oz. **Length:** 16" overall. **Stock:** Walnut. **Sights:** Fixed. **Features:** Case-hardened lock, brass-mounted browned barrel. Replica of the first U.S. Gov't.-made flintlock pistol. Imported by Navy Arms, Dixie Gun Works.
Price: . . . . **$249.95 to $405.00**
Price: Kit (Dixie) **$199.95**

KENTUCKY FLINTLOCK PISTOL   Caliber: 44, 45. **Barrel:** 10⅛". **Weight:** 32 oz. **Length:** 15½" overall. **Stock:** Walnut. **Sights:** Fixed. **Features:** Specifications, including caliber, weight and length may vary with importer. Case-hardened lock, blued barrel; available also as brass barrel flint Model 1821. Imported by Cabela's, Navy Arms (44 only), The Armoury.
Price: . . . . **$145.00 to $207.00**
Price: In kit form, from . . . . **$90.00 to $112.00**
Price: Single cased set (Navy Arms) **$300.00**
Price: Double cased set (Navy Arms) **$515.00**

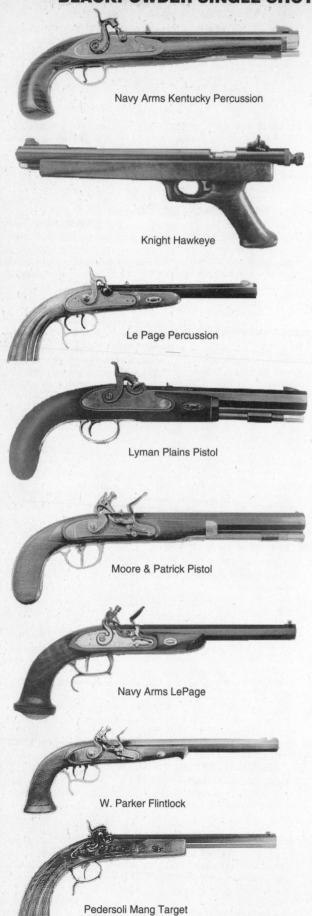

Navy Arms Kentucky Percussion

Knight Hawkeye

Le Page Percussion

Lyman Plains Pistol

Moore & Patrick Pistol

Navy Arms LePage

W. Parker Flintlock

Pedersoli Mang Target

Kentucky Percussion Pistol   Similar to flint version but percussion lock. Imported by The Armoury, Cabela's, Navy Arms, CVA (50-cal.).
Price: . . . . **$129.95 to $250.00**
Price: Steel barrel (Armoury) **$179.00**
Price: Single cased set (Navy Arms) **$290.00**
Price: Double cased set (Navy Arms) **$495.00**

KNIGHT HAWKEYE PISTOL   **Caliber:** 50.   **Barrel:** 12", 1:20" twist.   **Weight:** 3¼ lbs.   **Length:** 20" overall.   **Stock:** Black composite, autumn brown or shadow black laminate.   **Sights:** Bead front on ramp, open fully adjustable rear.   **Features:** In-line ignitiion design; patented double safety system; removeable breech plug; fully adjustable trigger; receiver drilled and tapped for scope mounting. Made in U.S. by Modern Muzzle Loading, Inc.
Price: Blued **$374.95**
Price: Stainless **$424.50**

LE PAGE PERCUSSION DUELING PISTOL   **Caliber:** 45.   **Barrel:** 10", rifled.   **Weight:** 40 oz.   **Length:** 16" overall.   **Stock:** Walnut, fluted butt.   **Sights:** Blade front, notch rear.   **Features:** Double-set triggers. Blued barrel; trigger guard and buttcap are polished silver. Imported by Dixie Gun Works.
Price: **$259.95**

LYMAN PLAINS PISTOL   **Caliber:** 50 or 54.   **Barrel:** 8", 1:30 twist, both calibers.   **Weight:** 50 oz.   **Length:** 15" overall.   **Stock:** Walnut half-stock.   **Sights:** Blade front, square notch rear adjustable for windage.   **Features:** Polished brass trigger guard and ramrod tip, color case-hardened coil spring lock, spring-loaded trigger, stainless steel nipple, blackened iron furniture. Hooked patent breech, detachable belt hook. Introduced 1981. From Lyman Products.
Price: Finished **$219.95**
Price: Kit **$179.95**

MOORE & PATRICK FLINT DUELING PISTOL   **Caliber:** 45.   **Barrel:** 10", rifled.   **Weight:** 32 oz.   **Length:** 14½" overall.   **Stock:** European walnut, checkered.   **Sights:** Fixed.   **Features:** Engraved, silvered lockplate, blue barrel. German silver furniture. Imported from Italy by Dixie Gun Works.
Price: **$335.00**

NAVY ARMS LE PAGE DUELING PISTOL   **Caliber:** 44.   **Barrel:** 9", octagon, rifled.   **Weight:** 34 oz.   **Length:** 15" overall.   **Stock:** European walnut.   **Sights:** Adjustable rear.   **Features:** Single-set trigger. Polished metal finish. From Navy Arms.
Price: Percussion **$475.00**
Price: Single cased set, percussion **$685.00**
Price: Double cased set, percussion **$1,290.00**
Price: Flintlock, rifled **$550.00**
Price: Flintlock, smoothbore (45-cal.) **$550.00**
Price: Flintlock, single cased set **$760.00**
Price: Flintlock, double cased set **$1,430.00**

W. PARKER FLINTLOCK PISTOL   **Caliber:** 45.   **Barrel:** 11", rifled.   **Weight:** 40 oz.   **Length:** 16½" overall.   **Stock:** Walnut.   **Sights:** Blade front, notch rear.   **Features:** Browned barrel, silver-plated trigger guard, finger rest, polished and engraved lock. Double-set triggers. Imported by Dixie Gun Works.
Price: **$310.00**

PEDERSOLI MANG TARGET PISTOL   **Caliber:** 38.   **Barrel:** 10.5", octagonal; 1:15" twist,   **Weight:** 2.5 lbs.   **Length:** 17.25" overall.   **Stock:** Walnut with fluted grip.   **Sights:** Blade front, open rear adjustable for windage.   **Features:** Browned barrel, polished breech plug, rest color case-hardened. Imported from Italy by Dixie Gun Works.
Price: **$749.00**

CAUTION: PRICES SHOWN ARE SUPPLIED BY THE MANUFACTURER OR IMPORTER. CHECK YOUR LOCAL GUNSHOP.

BLACKPOWDER SINGLE SHOT PISTOLS—FLINT & PERCUSSION

QUEEN ANNE FLINTLOCK PISTOL **Caliber:** 50 (.490" round ball). **Barrel:** 7½", smoothbore. **Stock:** Walnut. **Sights:** None. **Features:** Browned steel barrel, fluted brass trigger guard, brass mask on butt. Lockplate left in the white. Made by Pedersoli in Italy. Introduced 1983. Imported by Dixie Gun Works.
Price: $189.95
Price: Kit $138.50

Thompson/Center Scout

THOMPSON/CENTER SCOUT PISTOL **Caliber:** 45, 50 and 54. **Barrel:** 12", interchangeable. **Weight:** 4 lbs., 6 oz. **Length:** NA. **Stocks:** American black walnut stocks and forend. **Sights:** Blade on ramp front, fully adjustable Patridge rear. **Features:** Patented in-line ignition system with special vented breech plug. Patented trigger mechanism consists of only two moving parts. Interchangeable barrels. Wide grooved hammer. Brass trigger guard assembly. Introduced 1990. From Thompson/Center.
Price: 45-, 50- or 54-cal. $340.00
Price: Extra barrel, 45-, 50- or 54-cal. $145.00

Traditions Buckskinner

TRADITIONS BUCKSKINNER PISTOL **Caliber:** 50. **Barrel:** 10" octagonal, ¹⁵⁄₁₆" flats. **Weight:** 40 oz. **Length:** 15" overall. **Stocks:** Stained beech or laminated wood. **Sights:** Blade front, rear adjustable for windage. **Features:** Percussion ignition. Blackened furniture. Imported by Traditions, Inc.
Price: Beech stocks $157.00
Price: Laminated stocks $182.00

Traditions William Parker

TRADITIONS WILLIAM PARKER PISTOL **Caliber:** 45 and 50. **Barrel:** 10³⁄₈", ¹⁵⁄₁₆" flats; polished steel. **Weight:** 40 oz. **Length:** 17½" overall. **Stock:** Walnut with checkered grip. **Sights:** Brass blade front, fixed rear. **Features:** Replica dueling pistol with 1:18" twist, hooked breech. Brass wedge plate, trigger guard, cap guard; separate ramrod. Double-set triggers. Polished steel barrel, lock. Imported by Traditions, Inc.
Price: $265.00

TRADITIONS PIONEER PISTOL **Caliber:** 45. **Barrel:** 9⁵⁄₈", ¹³⁄₁₆" flats. **Weight:** 36 oz. **Length:** 15" overall. **Stock:** Beech. **Sights:** Blade front, fixed rear. **Features:** V-type mainspring; 1:18" twist. Single trigger. German silver furniture, blackened hardware. From Traditions, Inc.
Price: $169.00
Price: Kit $119.00

Traditions Pioneer

TRADITIONS TRAPPER PISTOL **Caliber:** 50. **Barrel:** 9³⁄₄", ⁷⁄₈" flats. **Weight:** 2³⁄₄ lbs. **Length:** 16" overall. **Stock:** Beech. **Sights:** Blade front, adjustable rear. **Features:** Double-set triggers; brass buttcap, trigger guard, wedge plate, forend tip, thimble. From Traditions, Inc.
Price: $170.00
Price: Kit $130.00

Traditions Trapper

BLACKPOWDER REVOLVERS

ARMY 1851 PERCUSSION REVOLVER **Caliber:** 44, 6-shot. **Barrel:** 7½". **Weight:** 45 oz. **Length:** 13" overall. **Stocks:** Walnut finish. **Sights:** Fixed. **Features:** 44-caliber version of the 1851 Navy. Imported by The Armoury, Armsport.
Price: $129.00

Army 1851

CAUTION: PRICES SHOWN ARE SUPPLIED BY THE MANUFACTURER OR IMPORTER. CHECK YOUR LOCAL GUNSHOP.

7th ANNUAL EDITION **281**

BLACKPOWDER REVOLVERS

ARMY 1860 PERCUSSION REVOLVER **Caliber:** 44, 6-shot. **Barrel:** 8". **Weight:** 40 oz. **Length:** 13⅝" overall. **Stocks:** Walnut. **Sights:** Fixed. **Features:** Engraved Navy scene on cylinder; brass trigger guard; case-hardened frame, loading lever and hammer. Some importers supply pistol cut for detachable shoulder stock, have accessory stock available. Imported by American Arms, Cabela's (1860 Lawman), E.M.F., Navy Arms, The Armoury, Cimarron, Dixie Gun Works (half-fluted cylinder, not roll engraved), Euroarms of America (brass or steel model), Armsport, Mitchell, Traditions, Inc. (brass or steel), Uberti USA.
Price: About . . . . $92.95 to $300.00
Price: Single cased set (Navy Arms) $265.00
Price: Double cased set (Navy Arms) $430.00
Price: 1861 Navy: Same as Army except 36-cal., 7½" bbl., wgt. 41 oz., cut for shoulder stock; round cylinder (fluted avail.), from CVA (brass frame, 44-cal.), Mitchell . . . . $99.95 to $249.00
Price: Steel frame kit (E.M.F., Mitchell, Navy, Euroarms) . . . . $125.00 to $216.25
Price: Colt Army Police, fluted cyl., 5½", 36-cal. (Cabela's) . $124.95

American Arms 1860 Army

BABY DRAGOON 1848, 1849 POCKET, WELLS FARGO **Caliber:** 31. **Barrel:** 3", 4", 5", 6"; seven-groove, RH twist. **Weight:** About 21 oz. **Stock:** Varnished walnut. **Sights:** Brass pin front, hammer notch rear. **Features:** No loading lever on Baby Dragoon or Wells Fargo models. Unfluted cylinder with stagecoach holdup scene; cupped cylinder pin; no grease grooves; one safety pin on cylinder and slot in hammer face; straight (flat) mainspring. From Armsport, Dixie Gun Works, Uberti USA, Cabela's.
Price: 6" barrel, with loading lever (Dixie Gun Works) $254.00
Price: 4" (Cabela's, Uberti USA) $179.95

Uberti 1860 Army

CABELA'S PATERSON REVOLVER **Caliber:** 36, 5-shot cylinder. **Barrel:** 7½". **Weight:** 24 oz. **Length:** 11½" overall. **Stocks:** One-piece walnut. **Sights:** Fixed. **Features:** Recreation of the 1836 gun. Color case-hardened frame, steel backstrap; roll-engraved cylinder scene. Imported by Cabela's.
Price: $199.95

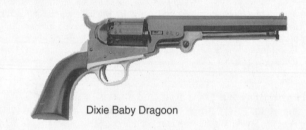

Dixie Baby Dragoon

COLT 1847 WALKER PERCUSSION REVOLVER **Caliber:** 44. **Barrel:** 9", 7 groove, right-hand twist. **Weight:** 73 oz. **Stocks:** One-piece walnut. **Sights:** German silver front sight, hammer notch rear. **Features:** Made in U.S. Faithful reproduction of the original gun, including markings. Color case-hardened frame, hammer, loading lever and plunger. Blue steel backstrap, brass square-back trigger guard. Blue barrel, cylinder, trigger and wedge. From Colt Blackpowder Arms Co.
Price: $442.50

Cabela's Paterson

COLT 1849 POCKET DRAGOON REVOLVER **Caliber:** 31. **Barrel:** 4". **Weight:** 24 oz. **Length:** 9½" overall. **Stocks:** One-piece walnut. **Sights:** Fixed. Brass pin front, hammer notch rear. **Features:** Color case-hardened frame. No loading lever. Unfluted cylinder with engraved scene. Exact reproduction of original. From Colt Blackpowder Arms Co.
Price: $390.00

Colt 1847 Walker

COLT 1851 NAVY PERCUSSION REVOLVER **Caliber:** 36. **Barrel:** 7½", octagonal, 7 groove left-hand twist. **Weight:** 40½ oz. **Stocks:** One-piece oiled American walnut. **Sights:** Brass pin front, hammer notch rear. **Features:** Faithful reproduction of the original gun. Color case-hardened frame, loading lever, plunger, hammer and latch. Blue cylinder, trigger, barrel, screws, wedge. Silver-plated brass backstrap and square-back trigger guard. From Colt Blackpowder Arms Co.
Price: $427.50

Colt 1851 Navy

Uberti 1861 Navy Percussion Revolver Similar to 1851 Navy except has round 7½" barrel, rounded trigger guard, German silver blade front sight, "creeping" loading lever. Available with fluted or round cylinder. Imported by Uberti USA.
Price: Steel backstrap, trigger guard, cut for stock . . . $300.00

CVA Colt Sheriff's Model Similar to the Uberti 1861 Navy except has 5½" barrel, brass or steel frame, semi-fluted cylinder. In 36-caliber only.
Price: Brass frame, finished $149.95
Price: Brass frame (Armsport) $155.00
Price: Steel frame (Armsport) $193.00

CAUTION: PRICES SHOWN ARE SUPPLIED BY THE MANUFACTURER OR IMPORTER. CHECK YOUR LOCAL GUNSHOP.

BLACKPOWDER REVOLVERS

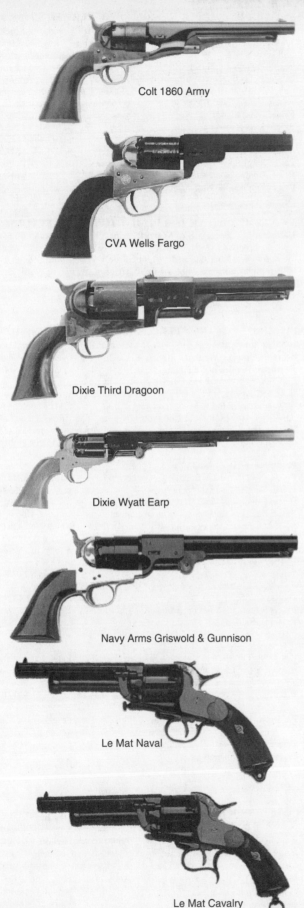

Colt 1860 Army

CVA Wells Fargo

Dixie Third Dragoon

Dixie Wyatt Earp

Navy Arms Griswold & Gunnison

Le Mat Naval

Le Mat Cavalry

COLT 1860 ARMY PERCUSSION REVOLVER   Caliber: 44.   **Barrel:** 8", 7 groove, left-hand twist.   **Weight:** 42 oz.   **Stocks:** One-piece walnut.   **Sights:** German silver front sight, hammer notch rear.   **Features:** Steel backstrap cut for shoulder stock; brass trigger guard. Cylinder has Navy scene. Color case-hardened frame, hammer, loading lever. Reproduction of original gun with all original markings. From Colt Blackpowder Arms Co.
Price: **$427.50**

CVA POCKET REVOLVER   Caliber: 31, 5-shot.   **Barrel:** 4", octagonal.   **Weight:** 15 oz.   **Length:** 7½" overall.   **Stocks:** Two-piece walnut.   **Sights:** Post front, grooved topstrap rear.   **Features:** Spur trigger, brass frame with blued barrel and cylinder. Introduced 1984. Imported by CVA.
Price: Finished **$129.95**

CVA WELLS FARGO MODEL   Caliber: 31, 5-shot.   **Barrel:** 4", octagonal.   **Weight:** 28 oz. (with extra cylinder).   **Length:** 9" overall.   **Stocks:** Walnut.   **Sights:** Post front, hammer notch rear.   **Features:** Brass frame and backstrap; blue finish. Comes with extra cylinder. Imported by CVA.
Price: Brass frame, finished **$129.95**

> Consult our Directory pages for the location of firms mentioned.

DIXIE THIRD MODEL DRAGOON   Caliber: 44 (.454" round ball).   **Barrel:** 7⅜".   **Weight:** 4 lbs., 2½ oz.   **Stocks:** One-piece walnut.   **Sights:** Brass pin front, hammer notch rear, or adjustable folding leaf rear.   **Features:** Cylinder engraved with Indian fight scene. This is the only Dragoon replica with folding leaf sight. Brass backstrap and trigger guard; color case-hardened steel frame, blue-black barrel. Imported by Dixie Gun Works.
Price: **$199.95**

DIXIE WYATT EARP REVOLVER   Caliber: 44.   **Barrel:** 12" octagon.   **Weight:** 46 oz.   **Length:** 18" overall.   **Stocks:** Two-piece walnut.   **Sights:** Fixed.   **Features:** Highly polished brass frame, backstrap and trigger guard; blued barrel and cylinder; case-hardened hammer, trigger and loading lever. Navy-size shoulder stock ($45) will fit with minor fitting. From Dixie Gun Works.
Price: **$130.00**

GRISWOLD & GUNNISON PERCUSSION REVOLVER   Caliber: 36 or 44, 6-shot.   **Barrel:** 7½".   **Weight:** 44 oz. (36-cal.).   **Length:** 13" overall.   **Stocks:** Walnut.   **Sights:** Fixed.   **Features:** Replica of famous Confederate pistol. Brass frame, backstrap and trigger guard; case-hardened loading lever; rebated cylinder (44-cal. only). Rounded Dragoon-type barrel. Imported by Navy Arms (as Reb Model 1860).
Price: About **$229.00**
Price: Single cased set (Navy Arms) **$205.00**
Price: Double cased set (Navy Arms) **$335.00**
Price: As above, kit **$90.00**

LE MAT REVOLVER   Caliber: 44/65.   **Barrel:** 6¾" (revolver); 4⅞" (single shot).   **Weight:** 3 lbs., 7 oz.   **Stocks:** Hand-checkered walnut.   **Sights:** Post front, hammer notch rear.   **Features:** Exact reproduction with all-steel construction; 44-cal. 9-shot cylinder, 65-cal. single barrel; color case-hardened hammer with selector; spur trigger guard; ring at butt; lever-type barrel release. From Navy Arms.
Price: Cavalry model (lanyard ring, spur trigger guard) **$595.00**
Price: Army model (round trigger guard, pin-type barrel release) **$595.00**
Price: Naval-style (thumb selector on hammer) **$595.00**
Price: Engraved 18th Georgia cased set **$795.00**
Price: Engraved Beauregard cased set **$1,000.00**

BLACKPOWDER REVOLVERS

Uberti 1851 Navy

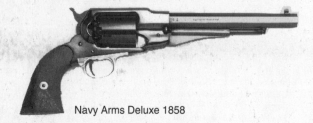

Navy Arms Deluxe 1858

American Arms 1858 Stainless Target

Navy Arms 1858 Army

CVA Bison

Uberti 1862 Police

NAVY MODEL 1851 PERCUSSION REVOLVER   Caliber: 36, 44, 6-shot. **Barrel:** 7½". **Weight:** 44 oz. **Length:** 13" overall. **Stocks:** Walnut finish. **Sights:** Post front, hammer notch rear. **Features:** Brass backstrap and trigger guard; some have 1st Model squareback trigger guard, engraved cylinder with navy battle scene; case-hardened frame, hammer, loading lever. Imported by American Arms, The Armoury, Cabela's, Mitchell, Navy Arms, E.M.F., Dixie Gun Works, Euroarms of America, Armsport, CVA (36-cal. only), Traditions, Inc., Uberti USA.

Price: Brass frame . . . . **$99.95 to $280.00**
Price: Steel frame . . . . **$130.00 to $285.00**
Price: Kit form . . . . **$110.00 to $123.95**
Price: Engraved model (Dixie Gun Works) **$139.95**
Price: Single cased set, steel frame (Navy Arms) **$245.00**
Price: Double cased set, steel frame (Navy Arms) **$405.00**
Price: Confederate Navy (Cabela's) **$69.95**

NAVY ARMS DELUXE 1858 REMINGTON-STYLE REVOLVER   Caliber: 44. **Barrel:** 8". **Weight:** 2 lbs., 13 oz. **Stocks:** Smooth walnut. **Sights:** Dovetailed blade front. **Features:** First exact reproduction—correct in size and weight to the original, with progressive rifling; highly polished with blue finish, silver-plated trigger guard. From Navy Arms.

Price: Deluxe model **$365.00**

NEW MODEL 1858 ARMY PERCUSSION REVOLVER   Caliber: 36 or 44, 6-shot. **Barrel:** 6½" or 8". **Weight:** 38 oz. **Length:** 13½" overall. **Stocks:** Walnut. **Sights:** Blade front, groove-in-frame rear. **Features:** Replica of Remington Model 1858. Also available from some importers as Army Model Belt Revolver in 36-cal., a shortened and lightened version of the 44. Target Model (Uberti USA, Navy Arms) has fully adjustable target rear sight, target front, 36 or 44. Imported by American Arms, Cabela's, Cimarron, CVA (as 1858 Army), Dixie Gun Works, Navy Arms, The Armoury, E.M.F., Euroarms of America (engraved, stainless and plain), Armsport, Mitchell, Traditions, Inc., Uberti USA.

Price: Steel frame, about . . . . **$99.95 to $280.00**
Price: Steel frame kit (Euroarms, Navy Arms) . . . **$115.95 to $242.00**
Price: Single cased set (Navy Arms) **$255.00**
Price: Double cased set (Navy Arms) **$420.00**
Price: Stainless steel Model 1858 (American Arms, Euroarms, Uberti USA, Cabela's, Navy Arms, Armsport, Traditions) **$169.95 to $380.00**
Price: Target Model, adjustable rear sight (Cabela's, Euroarms, Uberti USA, Navy Arms) . . . . **$95.95 to $399.00**
Price: Brass frame (CVA, Cabela's, Traditions, Navy Arms) . . . . **$79.95 to $212.95**
Price: As above, kit (CVA, Dixie Gun Works, Navy Arms) . . . . **$145.00 to $188.95**
Price: Remington "Texas" (Mitchell) **$199.00**
Price: Buffalo model, 44-cal. (Cabela's) **$129.95**

CVA 1858 Target Revolver   Similar to the New Model 1858 Army revolver except has ramp-mounted blade front sight on 8" barrel, adjustable rear sight, overall blue finish. Imported by CVA.
Price: **$204.95**

CVA Bison Revolver   Similar to the CVA 1858 Target except has 10¼" octagonal barrel, 44-caliber, brass frame.
Price: Finished **$194.95**
Price: From Armsport **$222.00**

POCKET POLICE 1862 PERCUSSION REVOLVER   Caliber: 36, 5-shot. **Barrel:** 4½", 5½", 6½", 7½". **Weight:** 26 oz. **Length:** 12" overall (6½" bbl.). **Stocks:** Walnut. **Sights:** Fixed. **Features:** Round tapered barrel; half-fluted and rebated cylinder; case-hardened frame, loading lever and hammer; silver or brass trigger guard and backstrap. Imported by CVA (7½" only), Navy Arms (5½" only), Uberti USA (5½", 6½" only).

Price: About . . . . **$139.95 to $310.00**
Price: Single cased set with accessories (Navy Arms) **$360.00**

CAUTION: PRICES SHOWN ARE SUPPLIED BY THE MANUFACTURER OR IMPORTER. CHECK YOUR LOCAL GUNSHOP.

BLACKPOWDER REVOLVERS

ROGERS & SPENCER PERCUSSION REVOLVER **Caliber:** 44.
Barrel: 7½". **Weight:** 47 oz. **Length:** 13¾" overall. **Stocks:** Walnut. **Sights:** Cone front, integral groove in frame for rear. **Features:** Accurate reproduction of a Civil War design. Solid frame; extra large nipple cut-out on rear of cylinder; loading lever and cylinder easily removed for cleaning. From Euroarms of America (standard blue, engraved, burnished, target models), Navy Arms.
Price: . . . . $160.00 to $276.00
Price: Nickel-plated $215.00
Price: Engraved (Euroarms) $349.00
Price: Kit version . . . . $245.00-$252.00
Price: Target version (Euroarms, Navy Arms) $291.00
Price: Burnished London Gray (Euroarms, Navy Arms) $299.00

Euroarms Rogers & Spencer

RUGER OLD ARMY PERCUSSION REVOLVER **Caliber:** 45, 6-shot. Uses .457" dia. lead bullets. **Barrel:** 7½" (6-groove, 16" twist).
Weight: 46 oz. **Length:** 13¾" overall. **Stocks:** Smooth walnut.
Sights: Ramp front, rear adjustable for windage and elevation; or fixed (groove). **Features:** Stainless steel; standard size nipples, chrome-moly steel cylinder and frame, same lockwork as in original Super Blackhawk. Also available in stainless steel. Made in USA. From Sturm, Ruger & Co.
Price: Stainless steel (Model KBP-7) $428.00
Price: Blued steel (Model BP-7) $378.50
Price: Stainless steel, fixed sight (KBP-7F) $428.00
Price: Blued steel, fixed sight (BP-7F) $378.50

Ruger Old Army Blued

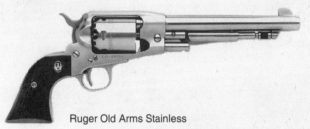

Ruger Old Arms Stainless

SHERIFF MODEL 1851 PERCUSSION REVOLVER **Caliber:** 36, 44, 6-shot. **Barrel:** 5". **Weight:** 40 oz. **Length:** 10½" overall.
Stocks: Walnut. **Sights:** Fixed. **Features:** Brass backstrap and trigger guard; engraved navy scene; case-hardened frame, hammer, loading lever. Imported by E.M.F.
Price: Steel frame $172.00
Price: Brass frame $140.00

Sheriff Model 1851

SPILLER & BURR REVOLVER **Caliber:** 36 (.375" round ball). **Barrel:** 7", octagon. **Weight:** 2½ lbs. **Length:** 12½" overall. **Stocks:** Two-piece walnut. **Sights:** Fixed. **Features:** Reproduction of the C.S.A. revolver. Brass frame and trigger guard. Also available as a kit. From Cabela's, Dixie Gun Works, Mitchell, Navy Arms.
Price: . . . . $89.95 to $199.00
Price: Kit form $95.00
Price: Single cased set (Navy Arms) $230.00
Price: Double cased set (Navy Arms) $370.00

Dixie Spiller & Burr

TEXAS PATERSON 1836 REVOLVER **Caliber:** 36 (.375" round ball).
Barrel: 7½". **Weight:** 42 oz. **Stocks:** One-piece walnut. **Sights:** Fixed. **Features:** Copy of Sam Colt's first commercially-made revolving pistol. Has no loading lever but comes with loading tool. From Dixie Gun Works, Navy Arms, Uberti USA.
Price: About . . . . $335.00 to $395.00
Price: With loading lever (Uberti USA) $450.00
Price: Engraved (Navy Arms) $465.00

Dixie Texas Paterson

UBERTI 1st MODEL DRAGOON **Caliber:** 44. **Barrel:** 7½", part round, part octagon. **Weight:** 64 oz. **Stocks:** One-piece walnut.
Sights: German silver blade front, hammer notch rear. **Features:** First model has oval bolt cuts in cylinder, square-back flared trigger guard, V-type mainspring, short trigger. Ranger and Indian scene roll-engraved on cylinder. Color case-hardened frame, loading lever, plunger and hammer; blue barrel, cylinder, trigger and wedge. Available with old-time charcoal blue or standard blue-black finish. Polished brass backstrap and trigger guard. From Uberti USA.
Price: $325.00

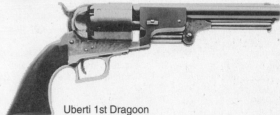

Uberti 2nd Model Dragoon Revolver Similar to the 1st Model except distinguished by rectangular bolt cuts in the cylinder.
Price: $325.00

Uberti 1st Dragoon

BLACKPOWDER REVOLVERS

Uberti 3rd Model Dragoon Revolver   Similar to the 2nd Model except for oval trigger guard, long trigger, modifications to the loading lever and latch. Imported by Uberti USA.
Price: Military model (frame cut for shoulder stock, steel back-strap) **$330.00**
Price: Civilian (brass backstrap, trigger guard) **$325.00**

UBERTI 1862 POCKET NAVY PERCUSSION REVOLVER   Caliber: 36, 5-shot.   **Barrel:** 5½", 6½", octagonal, 7-groove, LH twist.   **Weight:** 27 oz. (5½" barrel).   **Length:** 10½" overall (5½" bbl.).   **Stocks:** One-piece varnished walnut.   **Sights:** Brass pin front, hammer notch rear.   **Features:** Rebated cylinder, hinged loading lever, brass or silver-plated backstrap and trigger guard, color-cased frame, hammer, loading lever, plunger and latch, rest blued. Has original-type markings. From Uberti USA.
Price: With brass backstrap, trigger guard **$310.00**

WALKER 1847 PERCUSSION REVOLVER   Caliber: 44, 6-shot.   **Barrel:** 9".   **Weight:** 84 oz.   **Length:** 15½" overall.   **Stocks:** Walnut.   **Sights:** Fixed.   **Features:** Case-hardened frame, loading lever and hammer; iron backstrap; brass trigger guard; engraved cylinder. Imported by American Arms, Cabela's, CVA, Navy Arms, Dixie Gun Works, Uberti USA, E.M.F., Cimarron, Traditions, Inc.
Price: About . . . . **$225.00** to **$360.00**
Price: Single cased set (Navy Arms) **$385.00**
Price: Deluxe Walker with French fitted case (Navy Arms) . . **$505.00**

Uberti 3rd Dragoon

Dixie Walker 1847

AIRGUNS

AIRROW MODEL 6A AIR PISTOL   Caliber: #2512 10.75" arrow.   **Barrel:** 10.75".   **Weight:** 1.75 lbs.   **Length:** 16.5" overall.   **Power:** CO_2 or compressed air.   **Stocks:** Checkered composition.   **Sights:** Bead front, fully adjustable Williams rear.   **Features:** Velocity to 375 fps. Pneumatic air trigger. Floating barrel. All aircraft aluminum and stainless steel construction; Mil-spec materials and finishes. Announced 1993. From Swivel Machine Works, Inc.
Price: About **$597.00**

BEEMAN P1 MAGNUM AIR PISTOL   Caliber: 177, 5mm, 22, single shot.   **Barrel:** 8.4".   **Weight:** 2.5 lbs.   **Length:** 11" overall.   **Power:** Top lever cocking; spring piston.   **Stocks:** Checkered walnut.   **Sights:** Blade front, square notch rear with click micrometer adjustments for windage and elevation. Grooved for scope mounting.   **Features:** Dual power for 177 and 20-cal.: low setting gives 350-400 fps; high setting 500-600 fps. Rearward expanding mainspring simulates firearm recoil. All Colt 45 auto grips fit gun. Dry-firing feature for practice. Optional wooden shoulder stock. Introduced 1985. Imported by Beeman.
Price: 177, 5mm, 22-cal. **$390.00**
Price: 177, 5mm, stainless/blue finish **$440.00**

Airrow Model 6A

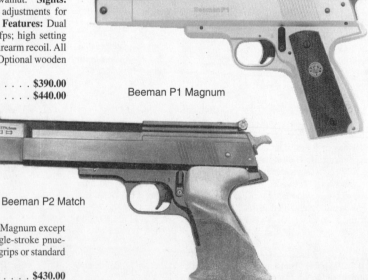
Beeman P1 Magnum

Beeman P2 Match

Beeman P2 Match Air Pistol   Similar to the Beeman P1 Magnum except shoots only 177 or 5mm pellets; completely recoilless single-stroke pneumatic action. Weighs 2.2 lbs. Choice of thumbrest match grips or standard style. Introduced 1990.
Price: 177, 5mm, standard grip **$430.00**
Price: 177, match grip **$460.00**

CAUTION: PRICES SHOWN ARE SUPPLIED BY THE MANUFACTURER OR IMPORTER. CHECK YOUR LOCAL GUNSHOP.

AIRGUNS

Beeman/FWB C20

BEEMAN/FEINWERKBAU C20 CO_2 PISTOL **Caliber:** 177, single shot. **Barrel:** 10.1", 12-groove rifling. **Weight:** 2.5 lbs. **Length:** 16" overall. **Power:** Special CO_2 cylinder. **Stock:** Stippled walnut with adjustable palm shelf. **Sights:** Blade front, open rear adjustable for windage and elevation. Notch size adjustable for width. Interchangeable front blades. **Features:** Fully adjustable trigger; can be set for dry firing. Separate gas chamber for uniform power. Cylinders interchangeable even when full. Short-barrel model also available. Introduced 1988. Imported by Beeman.
Price: Right-hand, regular or Mini **$1,130.00**
Price: Left-hand **$1,195.00**

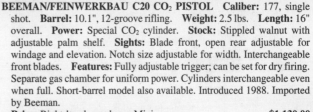

> Consult our Directory pages for the location of firms mentioned.

Beeman/FWB C25

BEEMAN/FEINWERKBAU C25 CO_2 PISTOL **Caliber:** 177, single shot. **Barrel:** 10.1"; 12-groove rifling. **Weight:** 2.5 lbs. **Length:** 16.5" overall. **Power:** Vertical, interchangeable CO_2 bottles. **Stocks:** Stippled walnut with adjustable palm shelf. **Sights:** Blade front, rear micrometer adjustable. Notch size adjustable for width; interchangeable front blades. **Features:** Fully adjustable trigger; can be set for dry firing. Has special vertical CO_2 cylinder and weight rail for balance. Short-barrel model (C25 Mini) also available. Introduced 1992. Imported by Beeman.
Price: Right-hand **$1,295.00**
Price: Left-hand **$1,295.00**
Price: C25 Mini **$1,285.00**

Beeman/FWB C55

BEEMAN/FWB C55 CO_2 RAPID FIRE PISTOL **Caliber:** 177, single shot or 5-shot magazines. **Barrel:** 7.3". **Weight:** 2.5 lbs. **Length:** 15" overall. **Power:** Special CO_2 cylinder. **Stocks:** Anatomical, adjustable. **Sights:** Interchangeable front, fully adjustable open micro-click rear with adjustable notch size. **Features:** Velocity 510 fps. Has 11.75" sight radius. Built-in muzzle brake. Introduced 1993. Imported by Beeman Precision Airguns.
Price: Right-hand **$1,590.00**
Price: Left-hand **$1,665.00**

Beeman/FWB 65 MkII

BEEMAN/FEINWERKBAU 65 MKII AIR PISTOL **Caliber:** 177, single shot. **Barrel:** 6.1" or 7.5", removable bbl. wgt. available. **Weight:** 42 oz. **Length:** 13.3" or 14.1" overall. **Power:** Spring, sidelever cocking. **Stocks:** Walnut, stippled thumbrest; adjustable or fixed. **Sights:** Front, interchangeable post element system, open rear, click adjustable for windage and elevation and for sighting notch width. Scope mount available. **Features:** New shorter barrel for better balance and control. Cocking effort 9 lbs. Two-stage trigger, four adjustments. Quiet firing, 525 fps. Programs instantly for recoil or recoilless operation. Permanently lubricated. Steel piston ring. Special switch converts trigger from 17.6-oz. pull to 42-oz. let-off. Imported by Beeman.
Price: Right-hand **$1,090.00**
Price: Left-hand, 6.1" barrel **$1,160.00**
Price: Model 65 Mk. 1 (7.5" bbl.) **$1,160.00**

Beeman/FWB 102

BEEMAN/FEINWERKBAU 102 PISTOL **Caliber:** 177, single shot. **Barrel:** 10.1", 12-groove rifling. **Weight:** 2.5 lbs. **Length:** 16.5" overall. **Power:** Single-stroke pneumatic, underlever cocking. **Stocks:** Stippled walnut with adjustable palm shelf. **Sights:** Blade front, open rear adjustable for windage and elevation. Notch size adjustable for width. Interchangeable front blades. **Features:** Velocity 460 fps. Fully adjustable trigger. Cocking effort 12 lbs. Introduced 1988. Imported by Beeman.
Price: Right-hand **$1,360.00**
Price: Left-hand **$1,360.00**

Beeman HW70A

BEEMAN HW70A AIR PISTOL **Caliber:** 177, single shot. **Barrel:** $6\frac{1}{4}$", rifled. **Weight:** 38 oz. **Length:** $12\frac{3}{4}$" overall. **Power:** Spring, barrel cocking. **Stocks:** Plastic, with thumbrest. **Sights:** Hooded post front, square notch rear adjustable for windage and elevation. Comes with scope base. **Features:** Adjustable trigger, 24-lb. cocking effort, 410 fps MV; automatic barrel safety. Imported by Beeman.
Price: **$200.00**

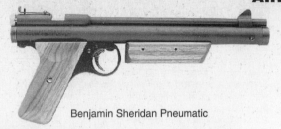

Benjamin Sheridan Pneumatic

BENJAMIN SHERIDAN PNEUMATIC PELLET PISTOLS Caliber: 177, 20, 22, single shot. **Barrel:** 9⅜", rifled brass. **Weight:** 38 oz. **Length:** 13⅛" overall. **Power:** Under-lever pneumatic, hand pumped. **Stocks:** Walnut stocks and pump handle. **Sights:** High ramp front, fully adjustable notch rear. **Features:** Velocity to 525 fps (variable). Bolt action with cross-bolt safety. Choice of black or nickel finish. Made in U.S. by Benjamin Sheridan Co.
Price: Black finish, HB17 (177), HB20 (20), HB22 (22) . . . **$104.95**
Price: Nickel finish, H17 (177), H20 (20), H22 (22) **$111.50**

Benjamin Sheridan CO²

BENJAMIN SHERIDAN CO_2 PELLET PISTOLS Caliber: 177, 20, 22, single shot. **Barrel:** 6⅜", rifled brass. **Weight:** 29 oz. **Length:** 9.8" overall. **Power:** 12-gram CO_2 cylinder. **Stocks:** Walnut. **Sights:** High ramp front, fully adjustable notch rear. **Features:** Velocity to 500 fps. Turn-bolt action with cross-bolt safety. Gives about 40 shots per CO_2 cylinder. Black or nickel finish. Made in U.S. by Benjamin Sheridan Co.
Price: Black finish, EB17 (177), EB20 (20), EB22 (22) **$96.50**
Price: Nickel finish, E17 (177), E20 (20), E22 (22) **$109.50**

BRNO Aeron-Tau

BRNO AERON-TAU CO_2 PISTOL Caliber: 177. **Barrel:** 10". **Weight:** 37 oz. **Length:** 12.5" overall. **Power:** 12.5-gram CO_2 cartridges. **Stocks:** Stippled hardwood with palm rest. **Sights:** Blade front, open fully adjustable rear. **Features:** Comes with extra seals and counterweight. Blue finish. Imported by Century International Arms.
Price: About **$299.00**

Crosman Auto Air II

CROSMAN AUTO AIR II PISTOL Caliber: BB, 17-shot magazine, 177 pellet, single shot. **Barrel:** 8⅝" steel, smoothbore. **Weight:** 13 oz. **Length:** 10¾" overall. **Power:** CO_2 Powerlet. **Stocks:** Grooved plastic. **Sights:** Blade front, adjustable rear; highlighted system. **Features:** Velocity to 480 fps (BBs), 430 fps (pellets). Semi-automatic action with BBs, single shot with pellets. Silvered finish. Introduced 1991. From Crosman.
Price: About **$28.00**

Crosman SSP 250

CROSMAN MODEL SSP 250 PISTOL Caliber: 177, 20, 22, single shot. **Barrel:** 9⅞", rifled steel. **Weight:** 3 lbs., 1 oz. **Length:** 14" overall. **Power:** CO_2 Powerlet. **Stocks:** Composition; black, with checkering. **Sights:** Hooded front, fully adjustable rear. **Features:** Velocity about 560 fps. Interchangeable accessory barrels. Two-stage trigger. High/low power settings. From Crosman.
Price: About **$48.00**

Crosman 357 8"

CROSMAN MODEL 357 AIR PISTOL Caliber: 177, 6- and 10-shot pellet clips. **Barrel:** 4" (Model 357-4), 6" (Model 357-6), rifled steel; 8" (Model 357-8), rifled brass. **Weight:** 32 oz. (6"). **Length:** 11⅜" overall (357-6). **Power:** CO_2 Powerlet. **Stocks:** Checkered wood-grain plastic. **Sights:** Ramp front, fully adjustable rear. **Features:** Average 430 fps (Model 357-6). Break-open barrel for easy loading. Single or double action. Vent. rib barrel. Wide, smooth trigger. Two cylinders come with each gun. Model 357-8 has matte gray finish, black grips. From Crosman.
Price: 4" or 6", about **$45.00**
Price: 8", about **$50.00**
Price: Model 1357 (same gun as above, except shoots BBs, has 6-shot clip), about **$45.00**

Crosman 357 4"

CAUTION: PRICES SHOWN ARE SUPPLIED BY THE MANUFACTURER OR IMPORTER. CHECK YOUR LOCAL GUNSHOP.

AIRGUNS

CROSMAN MODEL 1008 REPEAT AIR **Caliber:** 177, 8-shot pellet clip **Barrel:** 4.25", rifled steel. **Weight:** 17 oz. **Length:** 8.625" overall. **Power:** CO_2 Powerlet. **Stocks:** Checkered plastic. **Sights:** Post front, adjustable rear. **Features:** Velocity about 430 fps. Break-open barrel for easy loading; single or double semi-automatic action; two 8-shot clips included. Optional carrying case available. Introduced 1992. From Crosman.
Price: About **$43.00**
Price: With case, about **$50.00**

Crosman Model 1008

CROSMAN MODEL 1322, 1377 AIR PISTOLS **Caliber:** 177 (M1377), 22 (M1322), single shot. **Barrel:** 8", rifled steel. **Weight:** 39 oz. **Length:** $13\frac{5}{8}$". **Power:** Hand pumped. **Sights:** Blade front, rear adjustable for windage and elevation. **Features:** Moulded plastic grip, hand size pump forearm. Cross-bolt safety. Model 1377 also shoots BBs. From Crosman.
Price: About **$50.00**

Crosman Model 1322

CZ MODEL 3 AIR PISTOL **Caliber:** 177, single shot. **Barrel:** 7.25". **Weight:** 44 oz. **Length:** 13.75" overall. **Power:** Spring piston, barrel cocking. **Stocks:** High-impact plastic; ambidextrous, with thumbrest. **Sights:** Hooded front, fully adjustable rear. **Features:** Velocity about 420 fps. Externally adjustable trigger; removable screwdriver threaded into receiver. Imported from the Czech Republic by Action Arms.
Price: **$79.00**

CZ Model 3

DAISY MODEL 91 MATCH PISTOL **Caliber:** 177, single shot. **Barrel:** 10.25", rifled steel. **Weight:** 2.5 lbs. **Length:** 16.5" overall. **Power:** CO_2, 12-gram cylinder. **Stocks:** Stippled hardwood; anatomically shaped and adjustable. **Sights:** Blade and ramp front, changeable-width rear notch with full micrometer adjustments. **Features:** Velocity to 476 fps. Gives 55 shots per cylinder. Fully adjustable trigger. Imported by Daisy Mfg. Co.
Price: About **$670.00**

Daisy Model 91

DAISY MODEL 288 AIR PISTOL **Caliber:** 177 pellets, 24-shot. **Barrel:** Smoothbore steel. **Weight:** .8 lb. **Length:** 12.1" overall. **Power:** Single stroke spring air. **Stocks:** Moulded resin with checkering and thumbrest. **Sights:** Blade and ramp front, open fixed rear. **Features:** Velocity to 215 fps. Cross-bolt trigger block safety. Black finish. From Daisy Mfg. Co.
Price: About **$26.00**

DAISY/POWER LINE 717 PELLET PISTOL **Caliber:** 177, single shot. **Barrel:** 9.61". **Weight:** 2.8 lbs. **Length:** $13\frac{1}{2}$" overall. **Stocks:** Moulded wood-grain plastic, with thumbrest. **Sights:** Blade and ramp front, micro-adjustable notch rear. **Features:** Single pump pneumatic pistol. Rifled steel barrel. Cross-bolt trigger block. Muzzle velocity 385 fps. From Daisy Mfg. Co. Introduced 1979.
Price: About **$80.00**

Daisy/Power Line 747 Pistol Similar to the 717 pistol except has a 12-groove rifled steel barrel by Lothar Walther, and adjustable trigger pull weight. Velocity of 360 fps. Manual cross-bolt safety.
Price: About **$160.00**

Daisy Model 288

Daisy/Power Line 717

CAUTION: PRICES SHOWN ARE SUPPLIED BY THE MANUFACTURER OR IMPORTER. CHECK YOUR LOCAL GUNSHOP.

7th ANNUAL EDITION **289**

DAISY MODEL 500 RAVEN AIR PISTOL Caliber: 177 pellets, single shot. **Barrel:** Rifled steel. **Weight:** 36 oz. **Length:** 8.5" overall. **Power:** CO_2. **Stocks:** Moulded plastic with checkering. **Sights:** Blade front, fixed rear. **Features:** Velocity up to 500 fps. Hammer-block safety. Resembles semi-auto centerfire pistol. Barrel tips up for loading. Introduced 1993. From Daisy Mfg. Co.
Price: About **$65.00**

DAISY/POWER LINE MATCH 777 PELLET PISTOL Caliber: 177, single shot. **Barrel:** 9.61" rifled steel by Lothar Walther. **Weight:** 32 oz. **Length:** 13½" overall. **Power:** Sidelever, single pump pneumatic. **Stocks:** Smooth hardwood, fully contoured with palm and thumbrest. **Sights:** Blade and ramp front, match-grade open rear with adjustable width notch, micro. click adjustments. **Features:** Adjustable trigger; manual cross-bolt safety. MV of 385 fps. Comes with cleaning kit, adjustment tool and pellets. From Daisy Mfg. Co.
Price: About **$335.00**

DAISY/POWER LINE 44 REVOLVER Caliber: 177 pellets, 6-shot. **Barrel:** 6", rifled steel; interchangeable 4" and 8". **Weight:** 2.7 lbs. **Power:** CO_2. **Stocks:** Moulded plastic with checkering. **Sights:** Blade on ramp front, fully adjustable notch rear. **Features:** Velocity up to 400 fps. Replica of 44 Magnum revolver. Has swing-out cylinder and interchangeable barrels. Introduced 1987. From Daisy Mfg. Co.
Price: **$70.00**

DAISY/POWER LINE 45 AIR PISTOL Caliber: 177, 13-shot clip. **Barrel:** 5", rifled steel. **Weight:** 1.25 lbs. **Length:** 8.5" overall. **Power:** CO_2. **Stocks:** Checkered plastic. **Sights:** Fixed. **Features:** Velocity 400 fps. Semi-automatic repeater with double-action trigger. Manually operated lever-type trigger block safety; magazine safety. Introduced 1990. From Daisy Mfg. Co.
Price: About **$80.00**
Price: Model 645 (nickel-chrome plated), about **$85.00**

DAISY/POWER LINE 93 PISTOL Caliber: 177, BB, 15-shot clip. **Barrel:** 5", steel. **Weight:** 17 oz. **Length:** NA. **Power:** CO_2. **Stocks:** Checkered plastic. **Sights:** Fixed. **Features:** Velocity to 400 fps. Semi-automatic repeater. Manual lever-type trigger-block safety. Introduced 1991. From Daisy Mfg. Co.
Price: About **$80.00**
Price: Model 693 (nickel-chrome plated), about **$85.00**

DAISY/POWERLINE 400 BB PISTOL Caliber: BB, 20-shot magazine. **Barrel:** Smoothbore steel. **Weight:** 1.4 lbs. **Length:** 10.7" overall. **Power:** 12-gram CO_2. **Stocks:** Moulded black checkered plastic. **Sights:** Blade front, fixed open rear. **Features:** Velocity to 420 fps. Blowback slide cycles automatically on firing. Rotary trigger block safety. Introduced 1994. From Daisy Mfg. Co.
Price: About **$83.00**

Daisy Model 500 Raven

Daisy/Power Line Match 777

Daisy/Power Line 44

Daisy/Power Line 45

Daisy/Power Line 400

Daisy/Power Line 93

CAUTION: PRICES SHOWN ARE SUPPLIED BY THE MANUFACTURER OR IMPORTER. CHECK YOUR LOCAL GUNSHOP.

AIRGUNS

Daisy/Power Line 1200

Daisy/Power Line 1700

GAT Pistol

Hammerli 480 Competition

Marksman 1010X

Marksman 1015 Special Edition

Record Jumbo

DAISY/POWER LINE CO_2 1200 PISTOL **Caliber:** BB, 177. **Barrel:** $10\frac{1}{2}$", smooth. **Weight:** 1.6 lbs. **Length:** 11.1" overall. **Power:** Daisy CO_2 cylinder. **Stocks:** Contoured, checkered moulded wood-grain plastic. **Sights:** Blade ramp front, fully adjustable square notch rear. **Features:** 60-shot BB reservoir, gravity feed. Cross-bolt safety. Velocity of 420-450 fps for more than 100 shots. From Daisy Mfg. Co.
Price: About **$37.50**

DAISY/POWERLINE 1700 AIR PISTOL **Caliber:** 177 BB, 60-shot magazine. **Barrel:** Smoothbore steel. **Weight:** 1.4 lbs. **Length:** 11.2" overall. **Power:** CO_2 **Stocks:** Moulded checkered plastic. **Sights:** Blade front, adjustable rear. **Features:** Velocity to 420 fps. Cross-bolt trigger block safety; matte finish. Has $\frac{3}{8}$" dovetail mount for scope or point sight. Introduced 1994. From Daisy Mfg. Co.
Price: About **$40.00**

"GAT" AIR PISTOL **Caliber:** 177, single shot. **Barrel:** $7\frac{1}{2}$" cocked, $9\frac{1}{2}$" extended. **Weight:** 22 oz. **Power:** Spring piston. **Stocks:** Cast checkered metal. **Sights:** Fixed. **Features:** Shoots pellets, corks or darts. Matte black finish. Imported from England by Stone Enterprises, Inc.
Price: **$21.95**

HAMMERLI 480 COMPETITION AIR PISTOL **Caliber:** 177, single shot. **Barrel:** 9.8". **Weight:** 37 oz. **Length:** 16.5" overall. **Power:** Air or CO_2. **Stocks:** Walnut with 7-degree rake adjustment. Stippled grip area. **Sights:** Undercut blade front, fully adjustable open match rear. **Features:** Under-barrel cannister charges with air or CO_2 for power supply; gives 320 shots per filling. Trigger adjustable for position. Introduced 1994. Imported from Switzerland by Hammerli Pistols USA.
Price: **$1,295.00**

MARKSMAN 1010 REPEATER PISTOL **Caliber:** 177, 18-shot repeater. **Barrel:** $2\frac{1}{2}$", smoothbore. **Weight:** 24 oz. **Length:** $8\frac{1}{4}$" overall. **Power:** Spring. **Features:** Velocity to 200 fps. Thumb safety. Black finish. Uses BBs, darts or pellets. Repeats with BBs only. From Marksman Products.
Price: Matte black finish **$24.95**
Price: Model 1010X (as above except nickel-plated) **$33.50**

MARKSMAN 1015 SPECIAL EDITION AIR PISTOL **Caliber:** 177, 24-shot repeater. **Barrel:** 3.8", rifled. **Weight:** 22 oz. **Length:** 10.3" overall. **Power:** Spring-air. **Stocks:** Checkered brown composition. **Sights:** Fixed. **Features:** Velocity about 230 fps. Skeletonized trigger, extended barrel with "ported compensator." Shoots BBs, pellets, darts or bolts. From Marksman Products.
Price: **$30.95**

RECORD JUMBO DELUXE AIR PISTOL **Caliber:** 177, single shot. **Barrel:** 6", rifled. **Weight:** 1.9 lbs. **Length:** 7.25" overall. **Power:** Spring-air, lateral cocking lever. **Stocks:** Smooth walnut. **Sights:** Blade front, fully adjustable open rear. **Features:** Velocity to 322 fps. Thumb safety. Grip magazine compartment for extra pellet storage. Introduced 1983. Imported from Germany by Great Lakes Airguns.
Price: **$110.50**

CAUTION: PRICES SHOWN ARE SUPPLIED BY THE MANUFACTURER OR IMPORTER. CHECK YOUR LOCAL GUNSHOP.

7th ANNUAL EDITION **291**

RWS/DIANA MODEL 5G AIR PISTOL **Caliber:** 177, single shot. **Barrel:** 7". **Weight:** 2¾ lbs. **Length:** 16" overall. **Power:** Spring-air, barrel cocking. **Stocks:** Plastic, thumbrest design. **Sights:** Tunnel front, micro-click open rear. **Features:** Velocity of 410 fps. Two-stage trigger with automatic safety. Imported from Germany by Dynamit Nobel-RWS, Inc.
Price: **$200.00**

RWS/Diana Model 5G

RWS/DIANA MODEL 6M MATCH AIR PISTOL **Caliber:** 177, single shot. **Barrel:** 7". **Weight:** 3 lbs. **Length:** 16" overall. **Power:** Spring-air, barrel cocking. **Stocks:** Walnut-finished hardwood with thumbrest. **Sights:** Adjustable front, micro. click open rear. **Features:** Velocity of 410 fps. Recoilless double piston system, movable barrel shroud to protect from sight during cocking. Imported from Germany by Dynamit Nobel-RWS, Inc.
Price: Right-hand **$475.00**
Price: Left-hand **$530.00**

RWS/Diana Model 6M

RWS/Diana Model 6G Air Pistols Similar to the Model 6M except does not have the movable barrel shroud. Has click micrometer rear sight, two-stage adjustable trigger, interchangeable tunnel front sight. Available in right- or left-hand models.
Price: Right-hand **$350.00**
Price: Left-hand **$390.00**

RWS/Diana Model 6G

RWS GAMO PR-45 AIR PISTOL **Caliber:** 177, single shot. **Barrel:** 8.3". **Weight:** 25 oz. **Length:** 11" overall. **Power:** Pre-compressed air. **Stocks:** Composition. **Sights:** Blade front, adjustable rear. **Features:** Velocity to 430 fps. Recoilless and vibration free. Manual safety. Imported from Spain by Dynamit Nobel-RWS, Inc.
Price: **$130.00**
Price: Compact model (adjustable walnut grips, adjustable trigger, swiveling trigger shoe) **$200.00**

RWS Gamo PR-45 Compact

SHARP MODEL U-FP CO₂ PISTOL **Caliber:** 177, single shot. **Barrel:** 8", rifled steel. **Weight:** 2.4 lbs. **Length:** 11.6" overall. **Power:** 12-gram CO₂ cylinder. **Stocks:** Smooth hardwood. Walnut target stocks available. **Sights:** Post front, fully adjustable target rear. **Features:** Variable power adjustment up to 545 fps. Adjustable trigger. Also available with adjustable field sight. Imported from Japan by Great Lakes Airguns.
Price: **$199.50**
Price: With walnut target grips **$228.50**

STEYR CO₂ MATCH 91 PISTOL **Caliber:** 177, single shot. **Barrel:** 9". **Weight:** 38.7 oz. **Length:** 15.3" overall. **Power:** Pre-compressed CO₂ cylinders. **Stocks:** Fully adjustable Morini match with palm shelf; stippled walnut. **Sights:** Interchangeable blade in 4mm, 4.5mm or 5mm widths, fully adjustable open rear with interchangeable 3.5mm or 4mm leaves. **Features:** Velocity about 500 fps. Adjustable trigger, adjustable sight radius from 12.4" to 13.2". Imported from Austria by Nygord Precision Products.
Price: About **$1,050.00**

Sharp Model U-FP

RWS Gamo PR-45

STEYR LP5 MATCH PISTOL **Caliber:** 177, 5-shot magazine. **Barrel:** NA. **Weight:** 40.2 oz. **Length:** 13.39" overall. **Power:** Pre-compressed CO₂ cylinders. **Stocks:** Adjustable Morini match with palm shelf; stippled walnut. **Sights:** Movable 2.5mm blade front; 2-3mm interchangeable in .2mm increments; fully adjustable open match rear. **Features:** Velocity about 500 fps. Fully adjustable trigger; has dry-fire feature. Barrel and grip weights available. Introduced 1993. Imported from Austria by Nygord Precision Products.
Price: About **$1,250.00**

CAUTION: PRICES SHOWN ARE SUPPLIED BY THE MANUFACTURER OR IMPORTER. CHECK YOUR LOCAL GUNSHOP.

A

A&M Sales, 23 W. North Ave., North Lake, IL 60264/708-562-8190

Accu-Tek, 4525 Carter Ct., Chino, CA 91710/909-627-2404; FAX: 909-627-7817

Accuracy Gun Shop, 1240 Hunt Ave., Columbus, GA 31907/706-561-6386

Accuracy Gun Shop, Inc., 5903 Boulder Highway, Las Vegas, NV 89122/702-458-3330

Action Arms Ltd., P.O. Box 9573, Philadelphia, PA 19124/215-744-0100; FAX: 215-533-2188

Adventure A.G.R., 2991 St. Jude, Waterford, MI 48329/313-673-3090

Ahlman's Custom Gun Shop, Inc., Rt. 1, Box 20, Morristown, MN 55052/507-685-4244

Aimpoint, Inc., 580 Herndon Parkway, Suite 500, Herndon, VA 22070/703-471-6828; FAX: 703-689-0575

Aimtech Mount Systems, P.O. Box 223, Thomasville, GA 31799/912-226-4313; FAX: 912-227-0222

Air Gun Rifle Repair, 6420 1st Ave. W., Sebring, FL 33870/813-655-0516

Air Gun Shop, The, 2312 Elizabeth St., Billings, MT 59102/406-656-2983

Air Guns Unlimited, 15866 Main St., La Puente, CA 91744/818-333-4991

Air Venture, 9752 E. Flower St., Bellflower, CA 90706/310-867-6355

Airgun Repair Centre, 3227 Garden Meadows, Lawrenceburg, IN 47025/812-637-1463

Airgun Repair Centre, Ltd., P.O. Box 6249, Cincinnati, OH 45206-0249/812-637-1463

Alexander, Gunsmith, W.R., 1406 Capitol Circle N.E. #D, Tallahassee, FL 32308/904-656-6176

All Game Sport Center, 6076 Guinea Pike, Milford, OH 45150/513-575-0134

Allison & Carey Gun Works, 17311 S.E. Stark, Portland, OR 97233/503-256-5166

Alpine Arms Corp., 6716 Fort Hamilton Pkwy., Brooklyn, NY 11219/718-833-2228

Alpine Range, 5482 Shelby Rd., Fort Worth, TX 76140/817-478-6613

American Arms, Inc., 715 E. Armour Rd., N. Kansas City, MO 64116/816-474-3161; FAX: 816-474-1225

American Derringer Corp., 127 N. Lacy Dr., Waco, TX 76705/800-642-7817, 817-799-9111; FAX: 817-799-7935

Ammo Load, Inc., 1560 East Edinger, Suite G., Santa Ana, CA 92705/714-558-8858; FAX: 714-569-0319

AMT, 6226 Santos Diaz St., Irwindale, CA 91702/818-334-6629; FAX: 818-969-5247

Andersen Gunsmithing, 2485 Petaluma Blvd. N.,Petaluma, CA 94952/707-763-3852

Anderson Manufacturing Co., Inc., P.O. Box 2640, 2741 N. Crosby Rd., Oak Harbor, WA 98277/206-675-7300; FAX: 206-675-3939

Anschutz GmbH (See U.S. importer—PSI, Inc.)

Antonowicz, Frank, 8349 Kentucky Ave. North, Minneapolis, MN 55445

Apple Town Gun Shop, Rt. 104, Williamson, NY 14589/315-589-3311

Argonaut Gun Shop, 607 McHenry Ave., Modesto, CA 95350/209-522-5876

Armadillo Air Gun Repair, 5892 Hampshire Rd., Corpus Christi, TX 78408/512-289-5458

Armoury, Inc., The, Rt. 202, Box 2340, New Preston, CT 06777/203-868-0001

Armscorp USA, Inc., 4424 John Ave., Baltimore, MD 21227/410-247-6200

Armsport, Inc., 3950 NW 49th St., Miami, FL 33142/305-635-7850; FAX: 305-633-2877

Armurie De L'Outaouqis, 28 Rue Bourque, Hull, Quebec, CANADA J8Y 1X1/819-777-9824

ASI, 6226 Santos Dias St., Irwindale, CA 91706/818-334-6629

Astra-Unceta Y Cia, S.A. (See U.S. importer—E.A.A. Corp.)

Atlantic & Pacific Guns, 4859 Virginia Beach Blvd., Virginia Beach, VA 23462/804-490-1618

Atlantic Guns, Inc., 944 Bonifant St., Silver Springs, MD 20910/301-585-4448/301-279-7963

Atlas Gun Repair, 4908 E. Judge Perez Dr., Violet, LA 70092/504-277-4229

Auto Electric & Parts, Inc., 24 W. Baltimore Ave., Media, PA 19063/215-565-2432

Auto-Ordnance Corp., Williams Lane, West Hurley, NY 12491/914-679-7225; FAX: 914-679-2698

B

B&B Supply Co., 4501 Minnehaha Ave., Minneapolis, MN 55406/612-724-5230

B&W Gunsmithing, 505 Main Ave. N.W., Cullman, AL 35055/205-737-9595

B-Square Co., P.O. Box 11281, 2708 St. Louis Ave., Ft. Worth, TX 76110/817-923-0964, 800-433-2909; FAX: 817-926-7012

Bachelder Custom Arms, 1229 Michigan N.E., Grand Rapids, MI 49503/616-459-3636

Badger Shooters Supply, Inc., 202 N. Harding, Owen, WI 54460/715-229-2101; FAX: 715-229-2332

Baikal (See U.S. importer—K.B.I., Inc.)

Bain & Davis, Inc., 307 E. Valley Blvd., San Gabriel, CA 91776-3522/818-573-4241, 213-283-7449

Bait & Tackle Shop, The, Rt. 1, Box 5B, Fairmont, WV 26554/304-363-0183

Baity's Custom Gunworks, Rt. 4 Box 409-A (old Hwy. 421), North Wilksboro, NC 28659/919-667-8785

Barrows Point Trading Post, Rt. 4 West, Quechee, VT 05059/802-295-1050

Bausch & Lomb, Inc., 42 East Ave., Rochester, NY 14603/800-828-5423

Beard's Sport Shop, 811 Broadway, Cape Girardeau, MO 63701/314-334-2266

Beauchamp & Son, Inc., 160 Rossiter Rd., Richmond, MA 01254/413-698-3822; FAX: 413-698-3866

Bedlan's Sporting Goods, Inc., 1318 E. Street, P.O. Box 244, Fairbury, NE 68352/402-729-6112

Beeman Precision Airguns, Inc., 5454 Argosy Dr., Huntington Beach, CA 92649/714-890-4800; FAX: 714-890-4808

Belleplain Supply, Inc., Box 346, Handsmill Rd., Belleplain, NJ 08270/609-861-2345

Bellrose & Son, L.E., 21 Forge Pond Rd., Granby, MA 01033-0184/413-467-3637

Ben's Gun Shop, 1151 S. Cedar Ridge, Duncanville, TX 75137/214-780-1807

Benjamin/Sheridan Co., Crossman, Rts. 5 and 20, E. Bloomfield, NY 14443/716-657-6161; FAX: 716-657-5405

Benson Gun Shop, 35 Middle Country Rd., Coram L.I., NY 11727/516-736-0065

Beretta Firearms, Pietro (See U.S. importer—Beretta U.S.A. Corp.)

Beretta U.S.A. Corp., 17601 Beretta Drive, Accokeek, MD 20607/301-283-2191

Bernardelli Vincenzo S.p.A., Via Matteotti 125, Gardone V.T., ITALY I-25063/30-8912851-2-3

Bersa S.A. (See U.S. importer—Eagle Imports, Inc.)

Bickford's Gun Repair, 426 N. Main St., Joplin, MO 64801/417-781-6440

Bill Barton Sport Center, 7414 N. Milwaukee Ave., Niles, IL 60648/708-647-8585

Billings Gunsmiths, Inc., 1940 Grand Ave., Billings, MT 59102/406-652-3104

Billy Freds, P.O. Box 7646, 2465 I-40, Amarillo, TX 79109/806-352-2519

Blount, Inc., Sporting Equipment Div., 2299 Snake River Ave., P.O. Box 856, Lewiston, ID 83501/800-627-3640, 208-746-2351

Blue Ridge Outdoor Sports, Inc., 2314 Spartansburg Hwy., E. Flat Rock, NC 28726/704-697-3006

Blythe's Sport Shop, Inc., 2810 N. Calmut Ave., Valparaiso, IN 46383/219-462-4412

Bob's Crosman Repair, 2510 E. Henry Ave., Cudahy, WI 53110/414-769-8256

Bob's Gun & Tackle Shop, (Blaustein & Reich, Inc.), 746 Granby St., Norfolk, VA 23510/804-627-8311/804-622-9786

Bob's Repair, 3127 E. 650 N., Menan, ID 83434/208-754-4664

Boggus Gun Shop, 1402 W. Hopkins St., San Marcos, TX 78666/512-392-3513

Bohemia Arms, 17101 Los Modelos, Fountain Valley, CA 92708/714-963-0809; FAX: 714-963-0809

Bolsa Gunsmithing, 7404 Bolsa Ave., Westminster, CA 92683/714-894-9100

Boracci, E. John, Village Sport Center, 38-10 Merrick Rd., Seaford L.I., NY 11783/516-785-7110

Boudreaux, Gunsmith, Preston, 412 W. School St., Lake Charles, LA 70605/318-478-0640

Bradys Sportsmans Surplus, P.O. Box 4166, Missoula, MT 59806/460-721-5500

Braverman Arms Co., 912 Penn Ave., Wilkinsburg, PA 15221/412-241-1344

Brazdas Top Guns, 307 Bertrand Dr., Lafayette, LA 70506/318-233-4137

Brenner Sport Shop, Charlie, 344 St. George Ave., Rahway, NJ 07065/908-382-4066

Bridge Sportsmen's Center, 1319 Spring St., Paso Robles, CA 93446/805-238-4407

BRNO (See U.S. importers—Action Arms Ltd.; Bohemia Arms Co.)

Broadway Arms, 4116 E. Broadway, N. Little Rock, AR 72117/501-945-9348

Brock's Gunsmithing, Inc., North 2104 Division St., Spokane, WA 99207/509-328-9788

Brown Co., E. Arthur, 3404 Pawnee Dr., Alexandria, MN 56308/612-762-8847

Browning Arms Co. (See page 298)

Brunswick Gun Shop, 31 Bath Rd., Brunswick, ME 04011/207-729-8322

Bryan & Associates, 209 Rushton Rd., Belton, SC 29627/803-338-4786

Bryco Arms (See U.S. distributor—Jennings Firearms, Inc.)

Buffalo Gun Center, Inc., 3385 Harlem Rd., Buffalo, NY 14225/716-833-2581

Bullseye Gun Works, 7949 E. Frontage Rd.. Overland Park, KS 66204/913-648-4867

Burby, Inc. Guns & Gunsmithing, Rt. 7 South RR #3, Box 345, Middlebury, VT 05753/802-388-7365

Burgins Gun Shop, RD #1 Box 66, Mericksville Rd., Sidney Center, NY 13839/607-829-8668

Burris, P.O. Box 1747, Greeley, CO 80631/303-356-1670; FAX: 303-356-8702

Burton Hardware, 200 N. Huntington, Sulphur, LA 70663/318-527-8651

Bushmaster Firearms (See Quality Parts Co.)

Bushnell, Bausch & Lomb Sports Optics Div., 9200 Cody, Overland Park, KS 66214/913-888-0220

C

C-H Tool & Die Corp. (See 4-D Custom Die Co.)

Cabela's, 812-13th Ave., Sidney, NE 69160/308-254-5505; FAX: 308-254-7809

Caddo Arms & Cycle, 1400 Fairfield Ave., Shreveport, LA 71101/318-424-9011

Cal's Customs, 110 E. Hawthorne, Fallbrook, CA 92028/619-728-5230

Calico Light Weapon Systems, 405 E. 19th St., Bakersfield, CA 93305/805-323-1327; FAX: 805-323-7844

Camdex, Inc., 2330 Alger, Troy, MI 48083/313-528-2300

Cape Outfitters, Rt. 2, Box 437C, Cape Girardeau, MO 63701/314-335-4103; FAX: 314-335-1555

Capitol Sports & Western Wear, 1092 Helena Ave., Helena, MT 59601/406-443-2978

Carl's Gun Shop, Route 1, Box 131, El Dorado Springs, MO 64744/417-876-4168

Carpenters Gun Works, RD 1 Box 43D, Newton Rd., Proctorsville, VT 05153/802-226-7690

Carroll's Gun Shop, Inc., 1610 N. Alabama Rd., Wharton, TX 77488/409-532-3175

Carter's Country, 8925 Katy Freeway, Houston, TX 77024/713-461-1844

Casey's Gun Shop, 59 Des E Rables, P.O. Box 100, Rogersville, New Brunswick E0A 2T0 CANADA/506-775-6822

Catfish Guns, 900 Jeffco-Executive Park, Imperial, MO 63052/314-464-1217

Central Ohio Police Supply, c/o Wammes Guns, 225 South Main St., Bellefontaine, OH 43311

Centre Firearms Co., Inc., 10 West 37th St., New York City, NY 10018/212-244-4040

Century Gun Dist., Inc., 1467 Jason Rd., Greenfield, IN 46140/317-462-4524

Century International Arms, Inc., 48 Lower Newton St., St. Albans, VT 05478/802-527-1252; FAX: 802-527-0470

Cervera, Albert J., Rt. 1 Box 808, Hanover, VA 23069/804-994-5783

Chalmette Jewelry & Guns, 507 W. St. Bernard Hwy., Chalmette, LA 70043/504-271-2538

CHARCO, 26 Beaver St., Ansonia, CT 06401/203-735-4686; 203-735-6569

Charlie's Sporting Goods, Inc., 7401 Menaul Blvd. N.E., Albuquerque, NM 87110/505-884-4545

Charlton Co., Ltd., M.D., Box 153, Brentwood Bay, B.C., CANADA V0S 1A0/604-652-5266

Charter Arms (See CHARCO)

Cherry Corners, Inc., 11136 Congress Rd., P.O. Box 38, Lodi, OH 44254/216-948-1238

Cherry's Gun Shop, 302 S. Farmerville St., Ruston, LA 71270/318-255-5678

Chet Paulson Outfitters, 1901 South 72nd St., Suite A-14, Tacoma, WA 98408/206-475-8831

ChinaSports, Inc., 2010 S. Lynx Place, Ontario, CA 91761/714-923-1411; FAX: 714-923-0775

Chuck's Gun Shop, Box 9112 Espinosa Rd., Ranchos De Taos, NM 87557/505-758-8594

Chung, Gunsmith, Mel, 8 Ing Rd., P.O. Box 1008, Kaunakakai, HI 96748/808-553-5888

Cimarron Arms, P.O. Box 906, Fredericksburg, TX 78624-0906/210-997-9090; FAX: 210-997-0802

Clapps Gun Shop, P.O. Box 578, Brattleboro, VT 05302-0578/802-254-4663

Clark Custom Guns, Inc., P.O. Box 530, 11462 Keatchie Rd., Keithville, LA 71047/318-925-0836; FAX: 318-925-9425

Cogdell's, Inc., 615 N. Valley Mills Dr., Waco, TX 76710/817-772-8224

Colabaugh Gunsmith, Inc., Craig, R.D. 4, Box 4168 Gumm St., Stroudsburg, PA 18360/717-992-4499

Coleman, Inc., Ron, 1600 North I-35 #106, Carrollton, TX 75006/214-245-3030

Colt Blackpowder Arms Co., 5 Centre Market Place, New York, NY 10013/212-925-2159; FAX: 212-966-4986

Colt's Mfg. Co., Inc., P.O. Box 1868, Hartford, CT 06144-1868/203-236-6311; FAX: 203-244-1449

Competitor Corp., Inc., P.O. Box 244, 293 Townsend Rd., West Groton, MA 01472/508-448-3521; FAX: 603-673-4540

Coonan Arms, Inc., 1465 Selby Ave., St. Paul, MN 55104/612-646-0902; FAX: 612-646-0902

Corbin, Inc., 600 Industrial Circle, P.O. Box 2659, White City, OR 97503/503-826-5211; FAX: 503-826-8669

Covey's Precision Gunsmith, 700 N. Main St., Roswell, NM 88201/505-623-6565

CR Specialty, 1701 Baltimore Ave., Kansas City, MO 64108/816-221-3550

Creekside Gun Shop, Inc., P.O. Box 100 Main St., Holcomb, NY 14469/716-657-6338; FAX: 716-657-7900

Crosman Airguns (See page 298)

Cumberland Arms, Rt. I, Box 1150 Shafer Rd., Blantons Chapel, Manchester, TN 37355

Cumberland Knife & Gun Works, 5661 Bragg Blvd., Fayetteville, NC 28303/919-867-0009

Custom Firearms Shop, The, 1133 Indiana Ave., Sheboygan, WI 53081/414-457-3320

Custom Gun Shop, 12505 97th St., Edmonton, Alberta, CANADA T5G 1Z8/403-477-3737

Custom Gun Works, 4952 Johnston St., Lafayette, LA 70503/318-984-0721

CVA, 5988 Peachtree Corners East, Norcross, GA 30071/404-449-4687; FAX: 404-242-8546

Cylinder & Slide, Inc., 245 E. 4th St., Fremont, NE 68025/402-721-4277; FAX: 402-721-0263

CZ (See U.S. importer—Action Arms Ltd.)

D

D&D Sporting Goods, 108 E. Main, Tishomingo, OK 73460/405-371-3571

D&J Coleman Service, 4811 Guadalupe Ave., Hobbs, NM 88240/505-392-5318

D&L Gunsmithing/Guns & Ammo, 3615 Summer Ave., Memphis, TN 38122/901-327-4384

D&L Shooting Supplies, 2663 W. Shore Rd., Warwick, RI 02886/401-738-1889

Daenzer, Charles E., 142 Jefferson Ave., Otisville, MI 48463/313-631-2415

Daewoo Precision Industries Ltd., (See U.S. importer—Nationwide Sports Distributors)

Daisy Mfg. Co., P.O. Box 220, Rogers, AR 72756/501-636-1200; FAX: 501-636-1601

Dakota (See U.S. importer—EMF Co., Inc.)

Dale's Guns & Archery Center, 3915 Eighteenth Ave., S.W., Rochester, MN 55902/507-289-8308

Damiano's Field & Stream, 172 N. Highland Ave., Ossining, NY 10562/914-941-6005

Danny's Gun Repair, Inc., 811 East Market St., Louisville, KY 40206/502-583-7100

Darnall's Gun Works, RR #3, Box 274, Bloomington, IL 61704/309-379-4331

Daryl's Gun Shop, Inc., R.R. #2 Highway 30 West, Box 145, State Center, IA 50247/515-483-2656

Davco Stores, 305 Broadway, Box 152, Monticello, NY 12701/914-794-5225

Davidson's of Canada, 584 Neal Dr., Box 479, Peterborough, Ontario, CANADA K9J 6X7/705-742-5408; 800-461-7663

Dayton Traister, P.O. Box 593, Oak Harbor, WA 98277/206-679-4657; FAX:206-675-1114

Delisle Thompson Sporting Goods, Ltd., 1814A Loren Ave., Saskatoon, Saskatchewan, CANADA S7H 1Y4/306-653-2171

Denver Arms, Ltd., P.O. Box 4640, Pagosa Springs, CO 81157/303-731-2295

Denver Instrument Co., 6542 Fig St., Arvada, CO 80004/800-321-1135, 303-431-7255; FAX: 303-423-4831

Desert Industries, Inc., 3245 E. Patrick Ln., Suite H, Las Vegas, NV 89120/702-597-1066; FAX: 702-434-9495

Diana (See U.S. importer—Dynamit Nobel-RWS, Inc.)

Dixie Gun Works, Hwy. 51 South, Union City, TN 38261/901-885-0700, order 800-238-6785; FAX: 901-885-0440

Dillon Precision Products, Inc., 7442 E. Butherus Dr., Scottsdale, AZ 85260/602-948-8009, 800-762-3845; FAX: 602-998-2786

Dollar Drugs, Inc., 15A West 3rd, Lee's Summit, MO 64063/816-524-7600

Don & Tim's Gun Shop, 3724 Northwest Loop 410 and Fredricksburg, San Antonio, TX 78229/512-736-0263

Don's Gun Shop, 1085 Tunnel Rd., Ashville, NC 28805/704-298-4867

Don's Sport Shop, Inc., 7803 E. McDowell Rd., Scottsdale, AZ 85257/602-945-4051

Don's Sporting Goods, 120 Second Ave. South, Lewiston, MT 59457/406-538-9408

Dorn's Outdoor Center, 4388 Mercer University Drive, Macon, GA 31206/912-471-0304

Down Under Gunsmiths, 318 Driveway, Fairbanks, AK 99701/907-456-8500

Dragun Enterprises, P.O. Box 222, Murfreesboro, TN 37133-2222/615-895-7373, 800-467-7375; FAX: 800-829-7536

Dubbs, Gunsmith, Dale R., 32616 U.S. Hwy. 90, Seminole, AL 36574/205-946-3245

Duncan Gun Shop, Inc., 414 Second St., North Wilksboro, NC 28659/919-838-4851

Dynamit Nobel-RWS, Inc., 81 Ruckman Rd., Closter, NJ 07624/201-767-1995; FAX: 201-767-1589

E

E.A.A. Corp., P.O. Box 1299, Sharpes, FL 32959/407-639-7006

Eagle Imports, Inc., 1750 Brielle Ave., Unit B1, Wanamassa, NJ 07712/908-493-0333; FAX: 908-493-0301

Ed's Gun & Tackle Shop, Inc., Suite 90, 2727 Canton Rd. (Hwy. 5), Marietta, GA 30066/404-425-8461

Efinger Sporting Goods, 513 W. Union Ave. Rt. 28, Bound Brook, NJ 08805/908-356-0604

Elbe Arms Co., Inc., 610 East 27th St., Cheyenne, WY 82001/307-634-5731

EMF Co., Inc., 1900 E. Warner Ave. Suite 1-D, Santa Ana, CA 92705/714-261-6611; FAX: 714-956-0133

Enstad & Douglas, 211 Hedges, Oregon City, OR 97045/503-655-3751

Epps "Orillia" Ltd., Ellwood, RR 3, Hwy. 11 North, Orillia, Ont. L3V 6H3, CANADA/705-689-5333

Erma Werke GmbH (See U.S. importers—Mandall Shooting Supplies, Inc.; PSI, Inc.)

Ernie's Gun Shop, Ltd., 1031 Marion St., Winnipeg, Manitoba, CANADA R2J 0L1/204-233-1928

Essex Arms, P.O. Box 345, Island Pond, VT 05846/802-723-4313

Euroarms of America, Inc., 208 E. Piccadilly St., Winchester, VA 22601/703-662-1863; FAX: 703-662-4464

Ewell Cross Gun Shop, Inc., 8240 Interstate 30W, Ft. Worth, TX 76108/817-246-4622

Eyster Heritage Gunsmiths, Inc., Ken, 6441 Bishop Rd., Centerburg, OH 43011/614-625-6131

F

FAS (See U.S. importer—Nygord Precision Products)

Fausti & Figlie s.n.c., Stefano (See U.S. importer—American Arms, Inc.)

Feather Industries, Inc., 2300 Central Ave. K, Boulder, CO 80301/303-442-7021; FAX: 303-447-0944

Federal Firearms Co., Inc., Box 145, Thom's Run Rd., Oakdale, PA 15071/412-221-0300

FEG (See U.S. importers—Century International Arms, Inc.; K.B.I., Inc.)

Felton, James, Custom Gunsmith, 1033 Elizabeth St., Eugene, OR 97402/503-689-1687

Firearms Service Center, 2140 Old Shepherdsville Rd., Louisville, KY 40218/502-458-1148

Firearms Unlimited, Inc., 4360 Corporate Square, Naples, FL 33942/813-643-2922

Fix Gunshop, Inc., Michael D., R.D. 11, Box 192, Reading, PA 19607/215-775-2067

Flaig's Inc., 2200 Evergreen Rd., Pittsburgh, PA 15209/412-821-1717

Flintrop Arms Corp., 4034 W. National Ave., Milwaukee, WI 53215/414-383-2626

Foothills Shooting Center, 7860 W. Jewell Ave., Lakewood, CO 80226/303-985-4417

Forster Products, 82 E. Lanark Ave., Lanark, IL 61046/815-493-6360; FAX: 815-493-2371

4-D Custom Die Co., 711 N. Sandusky St., P.O. Box 889, Mt. Vernon, OH 43050-0889/614-397-7214; FAX: 614-397-6600

Fox & Company, 2211 Dutch Valley Rd., Knoxville, TN 37918/615-687-7411

Franklin Sports, Inc., 3941 Atlanta Hwy., Bogart, GA 30622/706-543-7803

Fred's Gun Shop, 1364 Ridgewood Dr., Mobile, AL 36608/205-344-1079

Freedom Arms, Inc., P.O. Box 1776, Freedom, WY 83120/307-883-2468; FAX: 307-883-2005

Freer's Gun Shop, Building B-1, 8928 Spring Branch Dr., Houston, TX 77080/713-467-3016

Fremont Tool Works, 1214 Prairie, Ford, KS 67842/316-369-2338

Fricano, Gunsmith, J., 15258 Moreland, Grand Haven, MI 49417/616-846-4458

Friedman's Army Surplus, 2617 Nolenville Rd., Nashville, TN 37211/615-244-1653

Frontiersman's Sports, 6925 Wayzata Blvd., Minneapolis, MN 55426/612-544-3775

FWB (See U.S. importer—Beeman Precision Airguns, Inc.)

G

G&S Gunsmithing, 220 N. Second St., Eldridge, IA 52748/319-285-4153

G.H. Gun Shop, 520 W. "B" St., McCook, NE 69001/308-345-1250

G.I. Loan Shop, 1004 W. Second St., Grand Island, NE 68801/308-382-9573

Gander Mountain, Inc., P.O. Box 128, Hwy. "W", Wilmot, WI 53192/414-862-2331,Ext. 6425

Garber & Sams Gunsmithing, 1821 Maytown Rd., Elizabethtown, PA 17022/717-361-7875

Garfield Gunsmithing, 237 Wessington Ave., Garfield, NJ 07026/201-478-0171

Garrett Gunsmiths, Inc., Peter, 838 Monmouth St., Newport, KY 41071-1821/606-261-1855

Gart Brothers Sporting Goods, 1000 Broadway, Denver, CO 80203/303-861-1122

Gary's Gun Shop, 905 W. 41st St., Sioux Falls, SD 57104/605-332-6119

Gaucher Armes, S.A. (See U.S. importer—Mandall Shooting Supplies, Inc.)

Geake & Son, Inc., 23510 Woodward Ave., Ferndale MI 48220/313-542-0498

Gemini Arms Ltd., 79 Broadway, Hicksville, NY 11801/516-931-2641

Gene's Gunsmithing, Box 34 GRP 326 R.R. 3, Selkirk, Manitoba, CANADA R1A 2A8/204-757-4413

Gibbs Rifle Co., Inc., Cannon Hill Industrial Park, Rt. 2, Box 214 Hoffman, Rd./Martinsburg, WV 25401/304-274-0458; FAX: 304-274-0078

Girard, Florent, Gunsmith, 598 Verreault, Chicoutimi, Quebec, CANADA G7H 2B8/418-696-3329

Glenn's Reel & Rod Repair, 2210 E. 9th St., Des Moines, IA 50316/515-262-2990

Glock GmbH (See U.S. importer—Glock, Inc.)

Glock, Inc., 6000 Highlands Parkway, Smyrna, GA 30082/404-433-8719

Gonic Arms, Inc., 134 Flagg Rd., Gonic, NH 03839/603-332-8456, 603-332-8457

Gordon's Wigwam, 501 S. St. Francis, Wichita, KS 67202/316-264-5891

Gorenflo Gunsmithing, 1821 State St., Erie, PA 16501/814-452-4855

Great Lakes Airguns, 6175 S. Park Ave., Hamburg, NY 14075/716-648-6666; FAX: 716-648-5279

Green Acres Sporting Goods, Inc., 8774 Normandy Blvd., Jacksonville, FL 32221/904-786-5166

Greene's Gun Shop, 4778 Monkey Hill Rd., Oak Harbor, WA 98277/206-675-3421

Grenada Gun Works, Hwy. 8 East, Grenada, MS 38901/601-226-9272

Grendel, Inc., P.O. Box 560909, Rockledge, FL 32956-0909/800-274-7427, 407-636-1211; FAX: 407-633-6710

Grice Gun Shop, Inc., 216 Reed St., P.O. 1028, Clearfield, PA 16830/814-765-9273

Grundman's, Inc., 75 Wildwood Ave., Rio Dell, CA 95562/707-764-5744

Gun & Tackle Store, The, 6041 Forrest Ln., Dallas, TX 75230/214-239-8181

Gun Ace Gunsmithing, 3395 So. 5175 West, P.O. Box 1606, Cedar City, UT 84721/801-586-7421

Gun Center, The, 5831 Buckeystown Pike, Frederick, MD 21701/301-694-6887

Gun City USA, Inc., 573 Murfreesboro Rd., Nashville, TN 37210/615-256-6127

Gun City, 212 W. Main Ave., Bismarck, ND 58501/701-223-2304

Gun Corral, Inc., 2827 East College Ave., Decatur, GA 30030/404-299-0288

Gun Doc, Inc., 5405 N.W. 82nd Ave., Miami, FL 33166/305-477-2777

Gun Exchange, Inc., 5317 W. 65th St., Little Rock, AR 72209/501-562-4668

Gun Hospital, The, 45 Vineyard Ave., E. Providence, RI 02914/401-438-3495

Gun Rack, Inc., The, 213 Richland Ave., Aiken, SC 29801/803-648-7100

Gun Room, The, 201 Clark St., Chapin, SC 29036/803-345-2199

Gun Shop, Inc., The, 8945 Biscayne Blvd., Miami Shores, FL 33138/305-757-1422

Gun Shop, The, 5550 S. 900 East St., Salt Lake City, UT 84117/801-263-3633

Gun Shop, The, 5567 Manitou Rd., Excelsior, MN 55331/612-474-2646

Gun World, 392 Fifth Street, Elko, NV 89801/702-738-2666

Guns & Stuff, Inc., 3055 N. Broadway, Wichita, KS 67219/316-838-2448

Gunshop, Inc., The, 44633 N. Sierra Hwy., Lancaster CA 93534/805-942-8377

Gunsmith Co., The, 3435 S. State St., Salt Lake City, UT 84115/801-467-8244

Gunsmith, Inc., The, 1410 Sunset Blvd., West Columbia, SC 29169/803-791-0250

Gunsmith, The, 2205 Nord Ave., Chico, CA 95926/916-343-4550

Gunsmithing Ltd., 57 Unquowa Rd., Fairfield, CT 06430/203-254-0436

Gunsmithing Specialties, Co., 110 North Washington St., Papillion, NE 68046/402-339-1222

H

H&R 1871, Inc., 60 Industrial Rowe, Gardner, MA 01440/508-632-9393; FAX: 508-632-2300

Hagstrom, E.G., 2008 Janis Dr., Memphis, TN 38116/901-398-5333

Hammerli Ltd. (See U.S. importers—Beeman Precision Ariguns, Inc.; Hammerli USA; Mandall Shooting Supplies, Inc.)

Hammerli USA, 19296 Oak Grove Circle, Groveland, CA 95321/209-962-5311

Hampel's, Inc., 710 Randolph, Traverse City, MI 49684/616-946-5485

Harry's Army & Navy Store, 691 NJSH Rt. 130, Yardville, NJ 08620/609-585-5450

Hart & Son, Inc., Robert W., 401 Montgomery St., Nescopeck, PA 18635/717-752-3655; FAX: 717-752-1088

Hart's Gun Supply, Ed, U.S. Route 415, Bath, NY 14810/607-776-4228

Hatfield Gun Co., Inc., 224 N. 4th St., St. Joseph, MO 64501/816-279-8688; FAX: 816-279-2716
Hawken Shop, The (See Dayton Traister)
Heckler & Koch GmbH (See U.S. importer—Heckler & Koch, Inc.)
Heckler & Koch, Inc., 21480 Pacific Blvd., Sterling, VA 20166/703-450-1900; FAX: 703-450-8160
Helwan (See U.S. importer—Interarms)
Hemlock Gun Shop, Box 149, Rt. 590 & Crane Rd., Lakeville, PA 18438/717-226-9410
Henry's Airguns, 1204 W. Locust, Belvidere, IL 61008/815-547-5091
Herold's Gun Shoppe, 1498 E. Main Street, Box 350, Waynesboro, PA 17268/717-762-4010
Hill Top Gunsmithing, Rt. 3, Box 85, Canton, NY 13617/315-386-1165
Hill's Hardware & Sporting Goods, 1234 S. Second St., Union City, TN 38261/901-885-1510
Hill's, Inc., 1720 Capital Blvd., Raleigh, NC 27604/919-833-4884
HJS Arms, Inc., 1515 Oriole Ln., Brownsville, TX 78521H-S Precision, Inc., 1301 Turbine Dr., Rapid City, SD 57701/605-341-3006; FAX: 605-342-8964
Hobb's Bicycle & Gun Sales, 406 E. Broadway, Hobbs, NM 88240/505-393-9815
Hodson & Son Pell Gun Repair, 4500 S. 100 E., Anderson, IN 46013/317-643-2055
Hoffman's Gun Center, Inc., 2600 Berlin Turnpike, Newington, CT 06111/203-666-8827
Hollywood Engineering, 10642 Arminta St., Sun Valley, CA 91352/818-842-8376
Horchler's Gun Shop, 100 Ratlum Rd. RFD, Collinsville, CT 06022/203-379-1977
Hornady Mfg. Co., P.O. Box 1848, Grand Island, NE 68801/800-338-3220, 308-382-1390
Houma Gun Works, 1520 Grand Caillou Rd., Houma, LA 70363/504-872-2782
Hunter's Den, 4000 McLain Rd., North Little Rock, AR 72116-8026/501-771-1675
Huntington Die Specialties, 601 Oro Dam Blvd., Oroville, CA 95965/916-534-1210; FAX: 916-534-1212
Huntington Sportsman's Store, 601 Oro Dam Blvd., P.O. Box 991, Oroville, CA 95965/916-534-8000
Hutch's, 50 E. Main St., Lehi, UT 84043/801-768-3461
Hutchinson's Gun Repair, 507 Clifton St., Pineville, LA 71360/318-640-4315

I

Imbert & Smithers, Inc., 1144 El Camino Real, San Carlos, CA 94070/415-593-4207
IMI (See U.S. importer—Magnum Research, Inc.)
Interarms, 10 Prince St., Alexandria, VA 22314/703-548-1400
Intermountain Arms & Tackle, Inc., 105 E. Idaho St., Meridian, ID 83642/208-888-4911; FAX: 208-888-4381
Intratec, 12405 SW 130th St., Miami, FL 33186/305-232-1821; FAX: 305-253-7207
Ithaca Acquisition Corp., Ithaca Gun Co., 891 Route 34B, King Ferry, NY 13081/315-364-7171; FAX: 315-364-5134

J

J&G Gunsmithing, 625 Vernon St., Roseville, CA 95678/916-782-7075
J.O. Arms & Ammunition Co., 5709 Hartsdale, Houston, TX 77036/713-789-0745; FAX: 713-789-7513
Jack's Lock & Gun Shop, 32 4th St., Fond Du Lac, WI 54935/414-922-4420
Jackalope Gun Shop, 1048 S. 5th St., Douglas, WY 82633/307-358-3441
Jackson, Inc., Bill, 9501 U.S. 19 N., Pinellas Park, FL 34666/813-576-4169
Jason Empire, Inc., 9200 Cody, Overland Park, KS 66214-3259/913-888-0220; FAX: 913-888-0222
Jay's Sports, Inc., North 88 West 15263 Main St., Menomonee Falls, WI 53051/414-251-0550
Jennings Firearms, Inc., 17692 Cowan, Irvine, CA 92714/714-252-7621; FAX: 714-252-7626
Jensen's Custom Ammunition, 5146 E. Pima, Tucson, AZ 85712/602-325-3346; FAX: 602-322-5704
Jim's Sporting Goods, 1307 Malcolm Ave., Newport, AR 72112/501-523-5165
Jim's Trading Post, #10 Southwest Plaza, Pine Bluff, AR 71603/501-534-8591
Joe's Gun Shop, 4430 14th St., Dorr, MI 49323/616-877-4615
Joe's Gun Shop, 5215 W. Edgemont Ave., Phoenix, AZ 85035/602-233-0694
John Q's Quality Gunsmithing, 5165 Auburn Blvd., Sacramento, CA 95841/916-344-7669
Johnson Gunsmithing, Don, N15515 Country Rd. 566, Powers, MI 49874/906-497-5757
Johnson Service, Inc., W., 3654 N. Adrian Rd., Adrian, MI 49221/517-265-2545
Jones, J.D., 721 Woodvue Lane, Wintersville, OH 43952/614/264-0176; FAX: 614-264-2257
Jordan Gun Shop, 28 Magnolia Dr., Tifton, GA 31794/912-382-4251
Jovino Co., Inc., John, 5 Center Market Pl., New York, NY 10013/212-925-4881
JSL (Hereford) Ltd. (See U.S. importer—Specialty Shooters Supply, Inc.)
Junior's Gun & Lock Shop, 100 E. Grand St., Ponca City, OK 74601/405-762-4553

K

K&M Services, 5430 Salmon Run Rd., Dover, PA 17315
K.B.I., Inc., P.O. Box 5440, Harrisburg, PA 17110-0440/717-540-8518; FAX: 717-540-8567
Kahles USA, P.O. Box 81071, Warwick, RI 02888/800-752-4537: FAX: 717-540-8567
Kahr Arms, P.O. Box 220, Blauvelt, NY 10913/914-353-5996; FAX: 914-353-7833/800-453-2767, 210-542-2767
Karrer's Gunatorium, 5323 N. Argonne Rd., Spokane, WA 99212/509-924-3030
Kassnar (See U.S. importer—K.B.I., Inc.)
Keeley, John L., 671 Ridge Rd., Spring City, PA 19475/215-469-6874
Keidel's Gunsmithing Service, 927 Jefferson Ave., Washington, PA 15301/412-222-6379
Keller Gunsmithing, 147 N. Miami Ave., Bradford, OH 45308/513-448-2424
Keller's Co., Inc., Rt. 4, Box 1257, Burlington, CT 06013/203-583-2220
Keng's Firearms Specialty, Inc., 875 Wharton Dr. SW, Atlanta, GA 30336/404-691-7611; FAX: 404-505-8445
Kesselring Gun Shop, 400 Hwy. 99 North, Burlington, WA 98233/206-724-3113; FAX: 206-724-7003
Kick's Sport Center, 300 Goodge St., Claxton, GA 30417/912-739-1734
Kimel Industries, 3800 Old Monroe Rd., P.O. Box 335, Matthews, NC 28105/800-438-9288; FAX: 704-821-6339
King's Gun Shop, Inc., 32301 Walter's Hwy., Franklin, VA 23851/804-562-4725
King's Gun Works, 1837 W. Glenoaks Blvd., Glendale, CA 91201/818-956-6010
Kirkpatrick, Gunsmith, Larry, 707 79th St., Lubbock, TX 79404/806-745-5308
Klelon, Gunsmith, Dave, 57 Kittleberger Park, Webster, NY 14580/716-872-2256
Kopp, Terry K., 1301 Franklin, Lexington, MO 64067/816-259-2636
Korth (See U.S. importer—Mandall Shooting Supplies, Inc.)
Kotila Gun Shop, Rt. #2, Box 212, Cokato, MN 55321/612-286-5636
Krebs Gunsmithing, 7417 N. Milwaukee Ave., Niles, IL 60714/708-647-6994

L

L&M Firing Line, Inc., 20 S. Potomac St., Aurora, CO 80012/303-363-0041
L&S Technologies, Inc. (See Aimtech Mount Systems)
L'Armurier Alain Bouchard, Inc., 420 Route 143, Ulverton, Quebec CANADA J0B 2J0/819-826-6611
L.A.R. Manufacturing, Inc., 4133 W. Farm Rd., West Jordan, UT 84088/801-255-7106; FAX: 801-569-1972
Labs Air Gun Shop, 2307 N. 62nd St., Omaha, NE 68104/402-553-0990
Lafayette Shooters, 3530 Amb Caffrey Parkway, Lafayette, LA 70503/318-988-1191
Laibs Gunsmithing, North Hwy. 23, R.R. 1, Spicer, MN 56288/612-796-2686
Laser Devices, Inc., 2 Harris Ct. A-4, Monterey, CA 93940/408-373-0701; FAX: 408-373-0903
Laseraim Arms, Sub. of Emerging Technologies, Inc., P.O. Box 3548, Little Rock, AR 72203/501-375-2227; FAX: 501-372-1445
Lawson's Custom Firearms, Inc., Art, 313 S. Magnolia Ave., Ocala, FL 32671/904-629-7793
Lee Precision, Inc., 4275 Hwy. U, Hartford, WI 53027/414-673-3075
Leo's Custom Stocks, 1767 Washington Ave., Library, PA 15129/412-835-4126
Leupold, P.O. Box 688, Beaverton, OR 97075/503-526-1491; FAX: 503-526-1475
Levan's Sport Goods, 433 N. Ninth St., Lebanon, PA 17042/717-273-3148
Lew's Mountaineer Gunsmithing, Route 2, Box 330A, Charleston, WV 25314/304-344-3745
Lewis Arms, 1575 Hooksett Rd., Hooksett, NH 03106/603-485-7334
Llama Gabilondo Y Cia (See U.S. importer—SGS Importers International, Inc.)
Loftin & Taylor, 2619 N. Main St., Jacksonville, FL 32206/904-353-9634
Log Cabin Sport Shop, 8010 Lafayette Rd., Lodi, OH 44254/216-948-1082
Lolo Sporting Goods, 1026 Main St., Lewiston, ID 83501/208-743-1031
Lone Star Guns, Inc., 2452 Avenue "K", Plano, TX 75074/214-424-4501; 800-874-7923
Long Beach Uniform Co., Inc., 2789 Long Beach Blvd., Long Beach, CA 90806/310-424-0220
Long Gunsmithing Ltd., W.R., 2007 Brook Rd. North, Cobourg, Ontario CANADA K9A 4S3/416-372-5955
Longacres, Inc., 358 Chestnut St., Abilene, TN 79602/915-672-9521
Lorcin Engineering Co., Inc., 10427 San Sevaine Way, Ste. A, Mira Loma, CA 91752/909-360-1406; FAX: 909-360-0623
Lounsbury Sporting Goods, Bob, 104 North St., Middletown, NY 10940/914-343-1808
Lusignant Armurier, A. Richard, 15820 St. Michel, St. Hyacinthe, Quebec, CANADA, J2T 3R7/514-773-7997
Lutter, Robert E., 3547 Auer Dr., Ft. Wayne, IN 46835/219-485-8319
Lyman Products Corp., Rt. 147 West St., Middlefield, CT 06455/203-349-3421; FAX: 203-349-3586

M

M.O.A. Corp., 2451 Old Camden Pike, Eaton, OH 45320/513-456-3669
Mac-1 Distributors, 13974 Van Ness Ave., Gardena, CA 90249/310-327-3582
Magasin Latulippe, Inc., 637 St. Vallier O, P.O. Box 395, Quest, Quebec, CANADA G1K 6W8/418-529-0024
Magma Engineering Co., P.O. Box 161, Queen Creek, AZ 85242/602-987-9008; FAX: 602-987-0148
Magnum Gun Service, 357 Welsh Track Rd., Newark, DE 19702/302-454-0141
Magnum Research, Inc., 7110 University Ave., Minneapolis, MN 55432/612-574-1868; FAX: 612-574-0109
Mandall Shooting Supplies, Inc., 3616 N. Scottsdale Rd., Scottsdale, AZ 85252/602-945-2553; FAX: 602-949-0734
Magnum Research, Inc., 7110 University Ave., Minneapolis, MN 55432/612-574-1868; FAX: 612-574-0109
Manufacture D'Armes Des Pyrenees Francaises (See Unique/M.A.P.F.)
Marksman Products, 5482 Argosy Dr., Huntington Beach, CA 92649/714-898-7535, 800-822-8005; FAX: 714-891-0782
Marine Gun & Lock Shop, 1525 Piney Green Rd., Jacksonville, NC 28546/919-353-9114
Marshall Gun Shop, 1345 Chambers Rd., Dellwood, MO 63135/314-522-8359
Martin Gun Shop, Henry, 206 Kay Lane, Shreveport, LA 71115/318-797-1119
Martin's Gun Shop, 3600 Laurel Ave., Natchez, MS 39120/601-442-0784
Mashburn Arms Co., Inc., 1218 North Pennsylvania Ave., Oklahoma City, OK 73107/405-236-5151
Master Gunsmiths, Inc., 21621 Ticonderoga, Houston, TX 77044/713-459-1631
Matt's 10X Gunsmithing, Inc., 5906 Castle Rd., Duluth, MN 55803/218-721-4210
May & Company, Inc., P.O. Box 1111, 838 W. Capitol St., Jackson, MS 39209/601-354-5781
McBride's Guns, Inc., 2915 San Gabriel, Austin, TX 78705/512-472-3532
McClelland Gun Shop, 1533 Centerville Rd., Dallas, TX 75228-2597/214-321-0231
McDaniel Co., Inc., B., 8880 Pontiac Tr., P.O. Box 119, South Lyon, MI 48178/313-437-8989
McGuns, W.H., N. 22nd Ave. at Osborn St., Humboldt, TN 38343/901-784-5742
McMillan Gunworks, Inc., 302 W. Melinda Lane, Phoenix, AZ 85027/602-582-9627; FAX: 602-582-5178
MCS, Inc., 34 Delmar Dr., Brookfield, CT 06804/203-775-1013; FAX: 203-775-9462
MEC, Inc., 715 South St., Mayville, WI 53050/414-387-4500
Metro Rod & Reel, 236 S.E. Grand Ave., Portland, OR 97214/503-232-3193
Meydag, Peter, 12114 East 16th, Tulsa, OK 74128/918-437-1928
Miclean, Bill, 499 Theta Ct., San Jose, CA 95123/408-224-1445
Midwest Sporting Goods Co., Inc., 8565 Plainfield Rd., Lyons, IL 60534/708-447-4848
Midwestern Shooters Supply, Inc., 150 Main St., Lomira, WI 53048/414-269-4995
Mike's Crosman Service, 5995 Renwood Dr., Winston-Salem, NC 27106/919-922-1031
Mill Creek Sport Center, 8180 Main St., Dexter, MI 48104/313-426-3445
Miller's Sport Shop, 2 Summit View Dr., Mountaintop, PA 18707/717-474-6931
Millers Gun Shop, 915 23rd St., Gulfport, MS 39501/601-684-1765
Millie "D" Enterprises, 1241 W. Calle Concordia, Tucson, AZ 85737/602-297-4887
Mines Gun Shack, Rt. 4 Box 4623, Tullahoma, TN 37388/615-455-1414
Mirador Optical Corp., P.O. Box 11614, Marina Del Rey, CA 90295-7614/310-821-5587; FAX: 310-305-0386
Mitchell Arms, Inc., 3400 W. MacArthur Blvd., Ste. 1, Santa Ana, CA 92704/714-957-5711; FAX: 714-957-5732
Moates Sport Shop, Bob, 10418 Hull St. Rd., Midlothian, VA 23112/804-276-2293
Modern Guncraft, 148 N. Branford Rd., Collinsville, CT 06492/203-265-1015
Modern MuzzleLoading, Inc., 234 Airport Rd., P.O. Box 130, Centerville, IA 52544/515-856-2626; FAX: 515-856-2628
Montana Armory, Inc., 100 Centennial Dr., Big Timber, MT 59011/406-932-4353

WARRANTY SERVICE CENTER DIRECTORY

Montana Gun Works, 3017 10th Ave. S., Great Falls, MT 59405/406-761-4346

Moreau, Gunsmith, Pete, 1807 S. Erie, Bay City, MI 48706/517-893-7106

Morini (See U.S. importer—Mandall Shooting Supplies.)

Mossberg & Sons, Inc., O.F., 7 Grasso Ave., North Haven, CT 06473/203-288-6491; FAX: 203-288-2404

Mowrey Gun Works, P.O. Box 246, Waldron, IN 46182/317-525-6181; FAX: 317-525-6181

Mueschke Manufacturing Co., 1003 Columbia St., Houston, TX 77008/713-869-7073

Mulvey's Marine & Sport Shop, 994 E. Broadway, Monticello, NY 12701/914-794-2000

N

N.A. Guns, Inc., 10220 Florida Blvd., Baton Rouge, LA 70815/504-272-3620

Nagel Gun Shop, Inc., 6201 San Pedro Ave., San Antonio, TX 78216/210-342-5420; 210-342-9893

Nationwide Sports Distributors, 70 James Way, Southampton, PA 18966/215-322-2050; FAX: 215-322-5972

Navy Arms Co., 689 Bergen Blvd., Ridgefield, NJ 07657/201-945-2500; FAX: 201-945-6859

Nelson's Engine Shop, 620 State St., Cedar Falls, IA 50613/319-266-4497

Nevada Air Guns, 3297 "J" Las Vegas Blvd. N., N. Las Vegas, NV 89115/702-643-8532

New Advantage Arms Corp., 2843 N. Alvernon Way, Tucson, AZ 85712/602-881-7444; FAX: 602-323-0949

New England Firearms, 60 Industrial Rowe, Gardner, MA 01440/508-632-9393; FAX: 508-632-2300

Newby, Stewart, Gunsmith, Main & Cross Streets, Newburgh, Ontario CANADA K0K 2S0/613-378-6613

Nichols Sports Optics, P.O. Box 37669, Omaha, NE 68137/402-339-3530; FAX: 402-330-8029

Nicholson's Gunsmithing, 33 Hull St., Shelton, CT 06484/203-924-5635

Nikon, Inc., 1300 Walt Whitman Rd., Melville, NY 11747/516-547-4200

Norinco (See U.S. importers—Century International Arms, Inc.; ChinaSports, Inc.; Interarms)

North American Arms, 2150 South 950 East, Provo, UT 84606-6285/800-821-5783, 801-374-9990; FAX: 801-374-9998

Northern Precision Airguns, 1161 Grove St., Tawas City, MI 48763/517-362-6949

Northern Virginia Gun Works, Inc., 7518-K Fullerton Road, Springfield, VA 22150/703-644-6504

Northland Sport Center, 1 Mile W. on U.S. 2, Bagley, MN 56621/218-694-2464

Northwest Arms Service, 720 S. Second St., Atwood, KS 67730/913-626-3700

Nu-Line Guns, Inc., 1053 Caulks Hill Rd., Harvester, MO 63304/314-441-4500; FAX: 314-447-5018

Nygord Precision Products, P.O. Box 8394, La Crescenta, CA 91224/818-352-3027; FAX: 818-352-3378

O

Oakland Custom Arms, Inc., 4690 W. Walton Blvd., Waterford, MI 48329/810-674-8261

Old Western Scrounger, Inc., 12924 Hwy. A-I2, Montague, CA 96064/916-459-5445; FAX: 916-459-3944

Olympic Arms, Inc., 624 Old Pacific Hwy. SE, Olympia, WA 98503/206-456-3471; FAX: 206-491-3447

On Target Gunshop, Inc., 6984 West Main St., Kalamazoo, MI 49009/616-375-4570

Oshman's Sporting Goods, Inc., 975 Gessner, Houston, TX 77024/713-467-1155

Ott's Gun Service, Rt. 2, Box 169A, Atmore, AL 36502/205-862-2588

Ott's Gunsmith Service, RR 1, Box 259, Decatur, IL 62526/217-875-3468

Outdoor America Store, 1925 N. MacArthur Blvd., Oklahoma City, OK 73127/405-789-0051

Outdoorsman Sporting Goods Co., The, 1707 Radner Ct., Geneva, IL 60134/708-232-9518

Outdoorsman, Inc., Village West Shopping Center, Fargo, ND 58103/701-282-0131

Outpost, The, 2451 E. Maple Rapids Rd., Eureka, MI 48833/517-224-9562

Ozark Shooters, Inc., P.O. Box 6518, Branson, MO 65616/417-587-3093

P

Pachmayr Ltd., 1875 S. Mountain Ave., Monrovia, CA 91016/818-357-7771, 800-423-9704; FAX: 818-358-7251

Pacific International Service Co., Mountain Way, P.O. Box 3, Janesville, CA 96114/916-253-2218

Paducah Shooters Supply, Inc., 3919 Cairo St., Paducah, KY 42001/502-443-3758

Para-Ordnance Mfg., Inc. (See U.S. importer—Para-Ordnance, Inc.)

Pardini Armi Commerciale Srl (See U.S. importers—MCS, Inc.; Nygord Precision Products)

Pasadena Gun Center, 206 E. Shaw, Pasadena, TX 77506/713-472-0417; FAX: 713-472-1322

Paul Co., The, 27385 Pressonville Rd., Wellsville, KS 66092/913-883-4444; FAX: 913-883-2525

Pedersen & Son, 2717 S. Pere Marquette Hwy., Ludington, MI 49431/616-843-2061

Pedersoli Davide & C. (See U.S. importers—Beauchamp & Son, Inc.; Cabela's; Dixie Gun Works; EMF Co., Inc.; Navy Arms Co.)

Pekin Gun & Sporting Goods, 1304 Derby St., Pekin, IL 61554/309-347-6060

Pentax Corp., 35 Inverness Dr. E., Englewood, CO 80112/303-799-8000

Perry's of Wendell, Inc., P.O. Box 826, Wendell, NC 27591/919-365-6391

Peters Stahl GmbH (See U.S. importers—McMillan Gunworks, Inc.; Olympic Arms)

Phelps Mfg. Co., Box 2266, Evansville, IN 47714/812-476-8791

Phillips, D.J., Gunsmith, Rt. 1, N31-W22087 Shady Ln., Pewaukee, WI 53072/414-691-2165

Phoenix Arms, 1420 S. Archibald Ave., Ontario, CA 91761/909-947-4843; FAX: 909-947-6798

PHOXX Shooters Supply, 5813 Watt Ave., N. Highlands, CA 95660/916-348-9827

Pintos Gun Shop, 835 N. Central Bldg. B, Kent, WA 98032/206-859-6333

Pioneer Arms Co., 355 Lawrence Rd., Broomall, PA 19008/215-356-5203

Plaza Gunworks, Inc., 983 Gasden Highway, Birmingham, AL 35235/205-836-6206

Poly Technologies, Inc. (See U.S. importer—Keng's Firearms Specialty, Inc.)

Ponsness/Warren, P.O. Box 8, Rathdrum, ID 83858/208-687-2231; FAX: 208-687-2233

Poor Borch's, Inc., 1204 E. College Dr., Marshall, MN 56258/507-532-4880

Potter Gunsmithing, 13960 Boxhorn Dr., Muskego, WI 53150/414-425-4830

Powell & Son Ltd., William (See U.S. importers—Bell's Legendary Country Wear)

Precision Airgun Sales, Inc., 5139 Warrensville Center Rd., Maple Hts., OH 44137-1906/216-587-5005

Precision Arms & Gunsmithing Ltd., Hwy. 27 & King Road Box 809, Nobleton, Ontario, CANADA L0G 1N0/416-859-0965

Precision Gun Works, 4717 State Rd. 44, Oshkosh, WI 54904/414-233-2274

Precision Gunsmithing, 2723 W. 6th St., Amarillo, TX 79106/806-376-7223

Precision Pellet, 1018 Erwin Dr., Joppa, MD 21085/410-679-8179

Precision Reloading, Inc., P.O. Box 122, Stafford Springs, CT 06076/203-684-7979; FAX: 203-684-6788

Precision Sales International, Inc., P.O. Box 1776, Westfield, MA 01086/413-562-5055; FAX: 413-562-5056

Precision Sport Optics, 15571 Producer Lane, Unit G, Huntington Beach, CA 92649/714-891-1309; FAX: 714-892-6920

Preuss Gun Shop, 4545 E. Shepherd, Clovis, CA 93612/209-299-6248

Princess Anne Marine & Sport Center, 2371 Virginia Beach Blvd., Virginia Beach, VA 23454/804-340-6269

Professional Armaments, Inc., 4555 S. 300 West, Murray, UT 84107/801-268-2598

Q

Quality Firearms of Idaho, Inc., 114 13th Ave. S., Nampa, ID 83651/208-466-1631

R

R&R Shooters Supply, W6553 North Rd., Mauston, WI 53948/608-847-4562

R.D.P. Tool Co., Inc., 49162 McCoy Ave., East Liverpool, OH 43920/216-385-5129

Rajo Corporation, 2027 W. Franklin St., Evansville, IN 47712/812-422-6945

Ralph's Gun Shop, 200 Fourth St., South, Niverville, Manitoba, CANADA R0A 1E0/204-338-4581

Ram-Line, Inc., 545 Thirty-One Rd., Grand Junction, CO 81504/303-434-4500; FAX: 303-434-4004

Randy's Gun Repair, P.O. Box 106, Tabustinac, N.B. CANADA E0C 2A0/506-779-4768

Ranging, Inc., Routes 5 & 20, East Bloomfield, NY 14443/716-657-6161

Rapids Gun Shop, 7811 Buffalo Ave., Niagara Falls, NY 14304/716-283-7873

Ray's Gunsmith Shop, 3199 Elm Ave., Grand Junction, CO 81504/303-434-6162

Ray's Liquor and Sporting Goods, 1956 Solano St., Box 677, Corning, CA 96021/916-824-5625

Ray's Rod & Reel Service, 414 Pattie St., Wichita, KS 67211/316-267-9462

Ray's Sport Shop, Inc., 559 Route 22, North Plainfield, NJ 07060/908-561-4400

Ray's Sporting Goods, 730 Singleton Blvd., Dallas, TX 75212/214-747-7916

RCBS, Div. of Blount, Inc., 605 Oro Dam Blvd., Oroville, CA 95965/800-533-5000, 916-533-5191

Red's Gunsmithing, P.O. Box 1251, Chickaloon, AK 99674/907-745-4500

Redding Reloading, Inc., 1089 Starr Rd., Cortland, NY 13045/607-753-3331; FAX: 607-756-8445

Redfield, Inc., 5800 E. Jewell Ave., Denver, CO 80224/303-757-6411; FAX: 303-756-2338

Reliable Gun & Tackle, Ltd., 3227 Fraser St., Vancouver, British Columbia CANADA V5V 4B8/604-874-4710

Reloading Center, 515 W. Main St., Burley, ID 83318/208-678-5053

Remington Arms Co., Inc. (See page 298)

Reynolds Gun Shop, Inc., 3502A S. Broadway, Tyler, TX 75702/903-592-1531

Rice Hardware, 15 S.W. First Ave., Gainesville, FL 32601/904-377-0892

Richland Gun Shop, 207 Park St., Richland, PA 17087/717-866-4246

Richmond Gun Shop, 517 E. Main St., Richmond, VA 23219/804-644-7207

River Bend Sport Shop, 230 Grand Seasons Dr., Waupaca, WI 54981/715-258-3583

Ron's Gun Repair, 1212 Benson Rd., Sioux Falls, SD 57104/605-338-7398

Ross Sporting Goods, 204 W. Main St., Farmington, NM 87401/505-325-1062

Rossi S.A., Amadeo (See U.S. importer—Interarms)

Roy's Antiques & Things, Route 1 Box 303, Mountain Rest, SC 29664/803-638-5340

Roy's Sport Shop, 10 Second St. NE, Watertown, SD 57201/605-886-7508

RPM, 15481 N. Twin Lakes Dr., Tucson, AZ 85737/602-825-1233; FAX: 602-825-3333

Rue's Gunsmithing, 664 S. Magnolia, El Cajon, CA 92020/619-447-2169

Rusk Gun Shop, Inc., 6904 Watts Rd., Madison, WI 53719/608-274-8740

Rutko Corp. d/b/a Stonewall Range, 100 Ken-Mar Dr., Broadview Heights, OH 44147/216-526-0029

RWS (See U.S. importer—Dynamit Nobel-RWS, Inc.)

S

S.E.M. Gun Works, 3204 White Horse Rd., Greenville, SC 29611/803-295-2948

S.K. Guns, Inc., 3041A Main Ave., Fargo, ND 58103/701-293-4867; FAX: 701-232-0001

Safari Arms/SGW (See Olympic Arms, Inc.)

Saffle Repair Service, 312 Briar Wood Dr., Jackson, MS 39206/601-956-4968

Sanders Custom Gun Shop, P.O. Box 5967-2031, Bloomingdale Ave., Augusta, GA 30906/706-798-5220

Sanders Gun Shop, 3001 Fifth St., P.O. Box 4181, Meridian, MS 39301/601-485-5301

Saskatoon Gunsmith Shoppe, Ltd., 2310 Avenue "C" N., Saskatoon, Saskatchewan, CANADA S7L 5X5/306-244-2023

Sauer (See U.S. importer—Paul Co., The)

Scalzo's Sporting Goods, 207 Odell Ave., Endicott, NY 13760/607-746-7586

Scharch Mfg., Inc., 10325 Co. Rd. 120, Unit C, Salida, CO 81201/719-539-7242

Schmidt, Herbert (See U.S. importer—Sportarms of Florida)

Schultheis Sporting Goods, 6 Main St., Akrport, NY 14807/607-295-7485

Sea Gull Marina, 1400 Lake, Two Rivers, WI 54241/414-794-7533

Selin Gunsmith, Ltd., Del, 2803 28th Street, Vernon, British Columbia, CANADA V1T 4Z5/604-545-6413

SGS Importers International, Inc., 1750 Brielle Ave., Unit B1, Wanamassa, NJ 07712/908-493-0302; FAX: 908-493-0301

Shaler Eagle, 192 Arrow Wood, Jonesbrough, TN 37659/615-753-7620

Shamburg's Wholesale Spt. Gds., 403 Frisco Ave., Clinton, OK 73601/405-323-0209

Shapel's Gun Shop, 1708 N. Liberty, Boise, ID 83704/208-375-6159

Sharps Arms Co., Inc., C. (See Montana Armory, Inc.)

Shepherd Scope Ltd., Box 189, Waterloo, NE 68069/402-779-2424; FAX: 402-779-4010

Sheridan Gun, Inc., Austin, P.O. Box 577, Durham, CT 06422

Shooters Supply, 1120 Tieton Dr., Yakima, WA 98902

Shooting Gallery, The, 1619 Penna, Weirton, WV 26062/304-723-3298

Siegle's Gunshop, Inc., 508 W. MacArthur Blvd., Oakland, CA 94609/415-655-8789

Sievert's Guns 4107 W. Northern, Pueblo, CO 81005/719-564-0035

SIG (See U.S. importer—Mandall Shooting Supplies, Inc.)

SIG-Sauer (See U.S. importer—Sigarms, Inc.)

Sigarms, Inc., Industrial Drive, Corporate Park, Exeter, NH 03833/603-772-2302; FAX: 603-772-9082

Sile Distributors, Inc., 7 Centre Market Pl., New York, NY 10013/212-925-4389; FAX: 212-925-3149

Sillman, Hal, Associated Services, 1514 NE 205 Terrace, Miami, FL 33179/305-651-4450

Simmons Enterprises, Ernie, 709 East Elizabethtown Rd., Manheim, PA 17545/717-664-4040

Simmons Gun Repair/Sauer, 700 S. Rodgers Rd., Olathe, KS 66062/913-782-3131

Simmons Outdoor Corp., 2120 Killearney Way, Tallahassee, FL 32308-3402/904-878-5100; FAX: 904-878-0300

Sipes Gun Shop, 7415 Asher Ave., Little Rock, AR 72204/501-565-8480

Skeet's Gun Shop, Rt. 3, Box 123, Tahlequah, OK 74464/918-456-4749

Smith & Smith Gun Shop, Inc., 2589 Oscar Johnson Drive, Charleston Heights, SC 29405/803-744-2024

Smith & Wesson (See page 298)

Smith's Lawn & Marine Svc., 9100 Main St., Clarence, NY 14031/716-633-7868

Societa Armi Bresciane Srl (See U.S. importer—Cape Outfitters)

Sodak Sport & Bait, 850 South Hwy 281, Aberdeen, SD 57401/605-225-2737

Solothurn (See U.S. importer—Sile Distributors)

Solvay Home & Outdoor Center, 102 First St., Solvay, NY 13209/315-468-6285

Somerset Sports Shop, 140 W. Sanner St., Somerset, PA 15501/814-445-6214

Southland Gun Works, Inc., 1134 Hartsville Rd., Darlington, SC 29532/803-393-6291

Southwest Airguns, Box 132 Route 8, Lake Charles, LA 70605-9304/318-474-6038

Southwest Shooters Supply, Inc., 1940 Linwood Blvd., Oklahoma City, OK 73106/405-235-4476

Speer Products, Div. of Blount, Inc., P.O. Box 856, Lewiston, ID 83501/208-746-2351; FAx: 208-746-2915

Sport Shop, The, 100 Will Roger Dr., Kingfisher, OK 73750/405-375-5130

Sportarms of Florida, 5555 NW 36 Ave., Miami, FL 33142/305-635-2411; FAX: 305-634-4536

Sporting Goods, Inc., 232 North Lincoln St., Hastings, NE 68901/402-462-6132

Sports Mart, The, 828 Ford St., Ogdensburg, NY 13669/315-393-2865

Sports World, Inc., 5800 S. Lewis Ave., Suite 154, Tulsa, OK 74105/918-742-4027

Sportsman's Center, U.S. Hwy. 130, Box 731, Bordentown, NJ 08505/609-298-5300

Sportsman's Depot, 644 Miami St., Urban, OH 43078/513-653-4429

Sportsman's Haven, RR 4, Box 541, 14695 E. Pike Rd., Cambridge, OH 43725/614-432-7243

Sportsman's Paradise Gunsmith, 640 Main St., Pineville, LA 71360/318-443-6041

Sportsman's Shop, 101 W. Main St., New Holland, PA 17557/717-354-4311

Sportsmen's Exchange & Western Gun Traders, Inc., 560 S. "C" St., Oxnard, CA 93030/805-483-1917

Sportsmen's Repair Ctr., Inc., 106 S. High St., Box 134, Columbus Groves, OH 45830/419-659-5818

Spradlin's, 113 Arthur St., Pueblo, CO 81004/719-543-9462

Springfield, Inc., 420 W. Main St., Geneseo, IL 61254/309-944-5631; FAX: 309-944-3676

Stalwart Corp., P.O. Box 357, Pocatello, ID 83204/208-232-7899; FAX: 208-232-0815

Stan's Gun Repair, RR #2 Box 48, Westbrook, MN 56183/507-274-5649

Star Bonifacio Echeverria S.A. (See U.S. importer—Interarms)

Star Machine Works, 418 10th Ave., San Diego, CA 92101/619-232-3216

Starnes, Ken, 32900 SW Laurelview Rd., Hillsboro, OR 97123/503-628-0705

Steyr Airguns (See U.S. importers—GSI, Inc./Nygord Presion Products)

Steyr-Daimler-Puch (See U.S. importer—GSI, Inc.)

Stocker's Shop, 5199 Mahoning Ave., Warren, OH 44483/216-847-9579

Stoeger Industries (See page 298)

Stratemeyer, H.P., Winch Hill Rd., P.O. Box 489, Langdon, NH 03602/603-835-6130

Sturm, Ruger & Co., Inc., Lacey Place, Southport, CT 06490/203-259-7843

Sundance Industries, Inc., 25163 W. Avenue Stanford, Valencia, CA 91355/805-257-4807

Surplus Center, 621 S.E. Cass, Roseburg, OR 97470/503-672-4312

Swift Instruments, Inc., 952 Dorchester Ave., Boston, MA 02125/617-436-2960; FAX: 617-436-3232

Swivel Machine Works, Inc., 167 Cherry St., Suite 286, Milford, CT 06460/203-926-1840; FAX: 203-726-9431

T

Tanfoglio S.r.l., Fratelli (See U.S. importer—E.A.A. Corp.)

Tapco, Inc., P.O. Box 818, Smyrna, GA 30081/404-435-9782, 800-359-6195; FAX: 404-333-9798

Tasco Sales, Inc., 7600 NW 84th Ave., Miami, FL 33122/305-591-3670; FAX: 305-592-5895

Taurus Firearms, Inc., 16175 NW 49th Ave., Miami, FL 33014/305-624-1115; FAX: 305-623-7506

Taurus International Firearms (See U.S. importer—Taurus Firearms, Inc.)

Taylor & Vadney, Inc., 303 Central Ave., Albany, NY 12206/518-472-9183

Taylor's Sporting Goods, Gene, 445 W. Gunnison Ave., Grand Junction, CO 81505/303-242-8165

Taylor's Technical Gunsmithing Co., 14 Stalwart Industrial Drive, P.O. Box 508, Gormely, Ontario CANADA L0H 1G0/416-888-9391

Techni-Mec (See U.S. importer—Mandall Shooting Supplies, Inc.)

Ted's Gun & Reel Repair, 311 Natchitoches St. Box 1635, W. Monroe, LA 71291/318-323-0661

Ten Ring Service, 2227 West Lou Dr., Jacksonville, FL 32216/904-724-7419

Texas Arms, P.O. Box 154906, Waco, TX 76715/817-867-6972

Texas Gun Shop, Inc., 4518 S. Padre Island Dr., Corpus Christi, TX 78411/512-854-4424

Texas Longhorn Arms, Inc., 5959 W. Loop South, Suite 424, Bellaire, TX 77401/713-660-6323; FAX: 713-660-0493

Theoben Engineering (See U.S. importer—Air Rifle Specialists)

Thompson's Gunshop, Inc., 10254-84th St., Alto, MI 49302/616-891-0440

Thompson/Center Arms (See page 298)

300 Gunsmith Service, Inc. (Wichita Guncraft), 6850 S. Yosemite Ct., Englewood, CO 80112/303-773-0300

Thunder Mountain Arms, P.O. Box 593, Oak Harbor, WA 98277/206-679-4657; FAX: 206-675-1114

Traders, The, 685 E. 14th St., San Leandro, CA 94577/510-569-0555

Trading Post, The, 412 Erie St. S., Massillon, OH 44646/216-833-7761

Traditions, P.O. Box 235, Deep River, CT 06417/203-526-9555; FAX: 203-526-4564

Treaster, Inc., Verne, 3604 West 16th St., Indianapolis, IN 46222/317-638-6921

Treptow, Inc., Herman, 209 S. Main St., Milltown, NJ 08850/908-828-0184

Trijicon, Inc., P.O. Box 6029, Wixom, MI 48393-6029/810-960-7700; FAX: 810-960-7725

U

Uberti USA, Inc., 362 Limerock Rd., P.O. Box 469, Lakeville, CT 06039/203-435-8068; FAX: 203-435-8146

Uberti, Aldo (See U.S. importers—American Arms, Inc.; E. Christopher Firearms Co., Inc.; Cimarron Arms; Dixie Gun Works; EMF Co., Inc.; Mitchell Arms, Inc.; Navy Arms Co; Uberti USA, Inc.)

Ultra Light Arms, Inc., P.O. Box 1270, 214 Price St., Granville, WV 26534/304-599-5687

Unique Sporting Goods, Rd. 1 Box 131 E., Lorreto, PA 15940/814-674-8889

Unique/M.A.P.F. (See U.S. importer—Nygord Precision Products)

Upper Missouri Trading Co., 304 Harold St., Crofton, NE 68730/402-388-4844

Upton's Gun Shop, 810 Croghan St., Fremont, OH 43420/419-332-1326

V

Valley Gun Shop, 7719 Hartford Rd., Baltimore, MD 21234/410-668-2171

Valley Gunsmithing, John A. Foster, 619 Second St., Webster City, IA 50595/515-832-5102

Van Burens Gun Shop, 2706 Sylvania Ave., Toledo, OH 43613/419-475-9526

Van's Gunsmith Service, Rt. 69A, Parish, NY 13131/315-625-7251

W

Walker Arms Co., Inc., 499 County Rd. 820, Selma, AL 36701/205-872-6231

Wallace Gatlin Gun Repair, Rt. 2, Box 73, Oxford, AL 36203/205-831-6993

Walther GmbH (See U.S. importer—Interarms)

Warren's Sports Hdqts., 240 W. Main St., Washington, NC 27889/919-946-0960

Way It Was Sporting, The, 620 Chestnut Street, Moorestown, NJ 08057/609-231-0111

Weapon Works, The, 7017 N. 19th Ave., Phoenix, AZ 85021/602-995-3010

Weaver Scope Repair Service, 1121 Larry Mahan Dr., Suite B, El Paso, TX 79925/915-593-1005

Webley & Scott Ltd. (See U.S. importer—Beeman Precision Airguns, Inc.)

Weihrauch KG, Hermann (See U.S. importers—Beeman Precision Airguns; E.A.A. Corp.)

Weinberger Gunsmithing, Herbert, 30 W. Prospect St., Waldwick, NJ 07436/201-447-0025

Wessel Gun Service, 4000 E. 9-Mile Rd., Warren, MI 48091/313-756-2660

Wesson Firearms Co., Inc., Maple Tree Industrial Center, Rt. 20, Wilbraham, Rd./Palmer, MA 01069/413-267-4081; FAX: 413-267-3601

West Gate Gunsports, Inc., 10116-175th Street, Edmonton, Alberta, CANADA T5S 1A1/403-489-9633

West Luther Gun Repair, R.R. #1, Conn, Ontario, CANADA N0G 1N0/519-848-6260

Wheeler Gun Shop, C., 1908 George Washington Way Bldg. F, Richland, WA 99352/509-946-4634

White Dog Gunsmithing, 62 Central Ave., Ilion, NY 13357/315-894-6211

White Shooting Systems, Inc., P.O. Box 277, Roosevelt, UT 84066/801-722-3085; FAX: 801-722-3054

Wholesale Shooters Supplies, 751 W. Brubaker Valley Rd., Lititz, PA 17543/717-626-8574

Wholesale Sports, 12505 97 St., Edmonton, Alberta, CANADA T5G 1Z8/403-426-4417; 403-477-3737

Wichita Guncraft, Inc., 4607 Barnett Rd., Wichita Falls, TX 76310/817-692-5622

Wilderness Sport & Electronics, 14430 S. Pulaski Rd., Midlothian, IL 60445/708-389-1776

Wildey, Inc., P.O. Box 475, Brookfield, CT 06804/203-355-9000; FAX: 203-354-7759

Wilkinson Arms, 26884 Pearl Rd., Parma, ID 83660/208-722-6771; FAX: 208-722-5197/602-998-3941; FAX: 602-998-3941

Will's Gun Shop, 5603 N. Hubbard Lake Rd., Spruce, MI 48762/517-727-2500

William's Gun Shop, Ben, 1151 S. Cedar Ridge, Duncanville, TX 75137/214-780-1807

Williams Gun Shop, 7389 Lapeer Rd., Davison, MI 48423/313-653-2131

Williams Gun Sight Co., 7389 Lapeer Rd., Box 329, Davison, MI 48423/810-653-2131, 800-530-9028; FAX: 810-658-2140

Williams Gunsmithing, 4955 Cole Rd., Saginaw, MI 48601/517-777-1240

Williamson Gunsmith Service, 117 West Pipeline Rd., Hurst, TX 76053/817-285-0064

Windsor Gun Shop, 8410 Southeastern Ave., Indianapolis, IN 46239/317-862-2512

Wisner's Gun Shop, Inc., 287 NW Chehalis Ave., Chehalis, WA 98532/206-748-8942; FAX: 206-748-7011

Wolf Custom Gunsmithing, Gregory, c/o Albright's Gun Shop, 36 E. Dover St., Easton, MD 21601/410-820-8811

Wolfer Brothers, Inc., 1701 Durham, Houston, TX 77007/713-869-7640

Woodman's Sporting Goods, 223 Main Street, Norway, ME 04268/207-743-6602

Wortner Gun Works, Ltd., 433 Queen St., Chatham, Ont., CANADA N7M 2J1/519-352-0924

Y

Ye Olde Blk Powder Shop, 994 W. Midland Rd., Auburn, MI 48611/517-662-2271

Ye Olde Gun Shop, 12½ Woodlawn Ave., Bradford, PA 16701/814-368-3034

Ye Olde Gun Shoppe, P.O. Box 358, Sitka, AK 99835/907-747-5720

Z

Zabala Hermanos S.A. (See U.S. importer—American Arms, Inc.)

Zanes Gun Rack, 4167 N. High St., Columbus, OH 43214/614-263-0369

WARRANTY SERVICE CENTERS

■BR=Browning ■CR=Crosman ■RE=Remington ■ST=Stoeger ■SW=Smith & Wesson ■TC=Thompson/Center

SERVICE CENTER	CITY	BR	CR	RE	ST	SW	TC
ALABAMA							
B&W Gunsmithing	Cullman			●			
Dubbs, Gunsmith, Dale R.	Seminole			●			
Fred's Gun Shop	Mobile			●			
Ott's Gun Service	Atmore	●		●			
Plaza Gunworks, Inc.	Birmingham			●		●	●
Walker Arms Co., Inc.	Selma	●		●	●	●	
Wallace Gatlin Gun	Oxford			●			
ALASKA							
Down Under Gunsmiths	Fairbanks	●		●			
Red's Gunsmithing	Chickaloon	●		●		●	
Ye Olde Gun Shoppe	Sitka						
ARIZONA							
Don's Sport Shop, Inc.	Scottsdale	●		●			
Jensen's Custom Ammunition/Lathrops	Tucson	●		●		●	●
Joe's Gun Shop	Phoenix		●				
Millie "D" Enterprises	Tucson		●				
Weapon Works, The	Phoenix			●			
ARKANSAS							
Broadway Arms	North Little Rock			●			
Gun Exchange, Inc.	Little Rock			●		●	
Hunters Den	North Little Rock	●					
Jim's Sporting Goods	Newport			●			
Jim's Trading Post	Pine Bluff	●					
Sipes Gun Shop	Little Rock			●			
CALIFORNIA							
Air Guns Unlimited	La Puente		●				
Air Venture Air Guns	Bellflower		●	●			
Andersen Gunsmithing	Petaluma			●			
Argonaut Gun Shop	Modesto			●			
Bain & Davis	San Gabriel						
Beeman Precision Arms, Inc.	Santa Rosa		●				
Bolsa Gunsmithing	Westminster	●		●			
Bridge Sportsman's Ctr.	Paso Robles			●			
Cat's Customs	Fallbrook		●	●			
Grundman's	Rio Dell			●			
Gunshop, Inc., The	Lancaster			●			●
Gunsmith, The	Chico	●		●			
Huntington Sportsman's Store	Oroville	●		●			
Imbert & Smithers, Inc.	San Carlos	●		●			

SERVICE CENTER	CITY	BR	CR	RE	ST	SW	TC
J&G Gunsmithing	Roseville			●			
John Q's Quality Gunsmithing	Sacramento			●			
King's Gun Works, Inc.	Glendale			●			
Long Beach Uniform Co., Inc.	Long Beach		●			●	
Mac-1	Gardena		●				
Miclean, Bill	San Jose		●	●			
Pacific International Service Co.	Janesville	●	●	●	●	●	●
Pachmayr Gun Works	Monrovia	●		●	●	●	
PHOXX Shooters Supply	N. Highlands		●	●			
Preuss Gun Shop	Clovis		●				
Ray's Liquor and Sporting Goods	Corning	●		●			
Rue's Gunsmithing	El Cajon	●					
Siegle's Gunshop, Inc.	Oakland		●	●		●	
Sportsman's Exchange, Inc.	Oxnard		●	●			
Traders, The	San Leandro			●			
COLORADO							
Foothills Shooting Ctr.	Lakewood	●		●			
Gart Brothers Sporting Goods	Denver	●		●			
L&M Firing Line, Inc.	Aurora					●	
Ray's Gunsmith Shop	Grand Junction		●	●			
Sievert's Guns	Pueblo						●
Spradlin's	Pueblo			●			
Taylor's Sporting Goods, Gene	Grand Junction	●		●			
300 Gunsmith Service (Wichita Guncraft)	Englewood			●		●	●
CONNECTICUT							
Gunsmithing Limited	Fairfield	●		●			
Hoffman's Gun Center, Inc.	Newington			●			
Horchler's Gun Shop	Collinsville		●	●			
Keller's Co., Inc.	Burlington						
Modern Guncraft	Collinsville		●	●			
Nicholson's Gunsmithing	Shelton			●			
DELAWARE							
Magnum Gun Service	Newark			●			
FLORIDA							
Air Gun Rifle Repair	Sebring		●				
Alexander, Gunsmith, W.R.	Tallahassee						
Firearms Unlimited, Inc.	Naples		●	●		●	
Green Acres Sporting Goods, Inc.	Jacksonville			●		●	
Gun Doc, Inc.	Miami			●			
Gun Shop, Inc., The	Miami Shores		●	●			
Jackson, Inc., Bill	Pinellas Park			●			

See page 293 for Service Center addresses.

■BR=Browning ■CR=Crosman ■RE=Remington ■ST=Stoeger ■SW=Smith & Wesson ■TC=Thompson/Center

SERVICE CENTER	CITY	BR	CR	RE	ST	SW	TC
Lawsons Custom Firearms, Inc., Art	Ocala			●			
Loftin & Taylor	Jacksonville			●			
Rice Hardware	Gainesville			●			
Sillman, Hal, Associated Services	Miami		●				
Ten Ring Service	Jacksonville						●
GEORGIA							
Accuracy Gun Shop	Columbus	●	●	●			
Dom's Outdoor Center	Macon	●		●			
Ed's Gun & Tackle Shop, Inc.	Marietta	●	●	●			
Franklin Sports, Inc.	Bogart	●		●			
Gun Corral, Inc.	Decatur			●		●	
Jordan Gun & Pawn Shop	Tifton	●		●			
Kick's Sport Center	Claxton			●			
Sanders Custom Gun Shop	Augusta			●			
HAWAII							
Chung, Gunsmith, Mel	Kaunakakai			●		●	
IDAHO							
Bob's Repair	Menan	●	●	●			
Intermountain Arms & Tackle, Inc.	Meridian	●	●	●			●
Lolo Sporting Goods	Lewiston	●	●	●			
Quality Firearms	Nampa		●	●			
Reloading Center	Burley		●	●			
Shapel's Gun Shop	Boise		●	●		●	
ILLINOIS							
A&M Sales	North Lake		●	●			
Bill Barton Sport Center	Niles		●	●			
Darnall's Gun Works	Bloomington		●				
Henry's Airguns	Belvidere		●	●			
Krebs Gunsmithing	Niles		●				
Midwest Sporting Goods Co., Inc.	Lyons		●	●		●	
Ott's Gunsmith Service	Decatur		●				
Outdoorsman Sporting Goods Co.	Geneva		●				
Pekin Gun & Sporting Goods	Pekin		●				
Wilderness Sport & Electronics	Midlothian		●				
INDIANA							
Airgun Centre, Ltd.	Lawrenceburg		●				
Blythe's Sport Shop, Inc.	Valparaiso		●	●			
Hodson & Son Pell Gun Repair	Anderson		●				
Lutter, Robert E.	Ft. Wayne		●				
Rajo Corporation	Evansville		●				
Treaster, Inc.	Indianapolis		●	●			
Windsor Gun Shop	Indianapolis		●				
IOWA							
Daryl's Gun Shop, Inc.	State Center		●	●			
Glenn's Reel & Rod Repair	Des Moines		●				
G&S Gunsmithing	Eldridge			●			

SERVICE CENTER	CITY	BR	CR	RE	ST	SW	TC
Nelson's Engine Shop	Cedar Falls			●			
Valley Gunsmithing, John A. Foster	Webster City		●	●			
KANSAS							
Bullseye Gun Works	Overland Park			●			
Gordon's Wigwam	Wichita	●	●	●			
Guns & Stuff, Inc.	Wichita		●	●			
Northwest Arms Service	Atwood		●	●			
Ray's Rod & Reel Service	Wichita			●			
Simmons Gun Repair	Olathe			●			
KENTUCKY							
Danny's Gun Repair, Inc.	Louisville			●			
Firearms Service Center	Louisville			●			
Garrett Gunsmiths, Inc.	Newport			●			
Paducah Shooters Supply, Inc.	Paducah	●					
LOUISIANA							
Atlas Gun Repair	Violet	●		●			
Boudreaux, Gunsmith	Lake Charles			●			
Brazdas Top Guns	Lafayette			●			
Burton Hardware	Sulphur			●			
Caddo Arms & Cycle	Shreveport			●			
Chalmette Jewelry & Guns	Chalmette	●		●			
Cherry's Gun Shop	Ruston			●			
Clark Custom Guns, Inc.	Keithville					●	
Custom Gun Works	Lafayette			●			
Houma Gun Works	Houma	●		●			
Hutchinson's Gun Repair	Pineville	●		●			
Lafayette Shooters	Lafayette			●			
Martin Gun Shop	Shreveport	●		●			
N.A. Guns, Inc.	Baton Rouge			●			
Southwest Airguns	Lake Charles		●	●			
Sportsman's Paradise Gunsmith	Pineville			●			
Ted's Gun & Reel Repair	W. Monroe			●			
MAINE							
Brunswick Gun Shop	Brunswick	●		●			
Woodman's Sporting Goods	Norway			●		●	
MARYLAND							
Atlantic Guns, Inc.	Silver Springs	●		●			
Gun Center, The	Frederick		●	●			
Precision Pellet	Joppa		●				
Valley Gun Shop	Baltimore	●		●			
Wolf Custom Gunsmithing, Gregory, c/o Albright's Gun Shop	Easton	●	●	●			
MASSACHUSETTS							
Bellrose & Son, L.E.	Granby		●				

See page 293 for Service Center addresses.

■BR=Browning ■CR=Crosman ■RE=Remington ■ST=Stoeger ■SW=Smith & Wesson ■TC=Thompson/Center

SERVICE CENTER	CITY	BR	CR	RE	ST	SW	TC
MICHIGAN							
Adventure A.G.R.	Waterford	•	•				
Bachelder Custom Arms	Grand Rapids	•	•	•		•	
Daenzer, Charles E.	Otisville		•	•	•	•	
Fricano, Gunsmith, J.	Grand Haven		•	•			
Geake & Son, Inc.	Ferndale			• •			
Hampel's, Inc.	Traverse City			•			
Joe's Gun Shop	Dorr		•	•			
Johnson Gunsmithing, Don	Powers			•			
Johnson Service, Inc., W.	Adrian			• •			
McDaniel Co., Inc., B.	South Lyon			• •			
Mill Creek Sport Center	Dexter		•	•			
Moreau, Gunsmith, Pete	Bay City		•	•			
Northern Precision Airguns	Tawas City		•	•			
Oakland Custom Arms	Waterford			•			
On Target Gunshop, Inc.	Kalamazoo	•		• •			
Outpost, The	Eureka	•	•	•			
Pederson & Son, C.R.	Ludington		•	•			
Thompson's Gunshop, Inc.	Alto	•		• •			
Wessel Gun Service	Warren	•		•			
Williams Gun Shop	Davison	•	•	• •			
Williams Gunsmithing	Saginaw		•	•			
Will's Gun Shop	Spruce						
Ye Olde Blk Powder Shop	Auburn						•
MINNESOTA							
Ahlman's Custom Gun Shop, Inc.	Morristown	•	•	•	•	•	
Antonowicz, Frank	Minneapolis	•		•			
B&B Supply Co.	Minneapolis		•				
Dale's Guns & Archery Center	Rochester	•					
Frontiersman's Sports	Minneapolis			–			
Gun Shop, The	Excelsior			•			
Kotla Gun Shop	Cokato		•	•			
Laibs Gunsmithing	Spicer			•			
Matt's 10X Gunsmithing, Inc.	Duluth			•			
Northland Sport Center	Bagley			•			
Poor Borch's, Inc.	Marshall		•	•			
Stan's Gun Repair	Westbrook			•			
MISSISSIPPI							
Grenada Gun Works	Grenada		•	• •			
Martins Gun Shop	Natchez						
May & Company, Inc.	Jackson		•	•			
Millers Gun Shop	Gulfport		•				
Saffle Repair Service	Jackson						•
Sanders Gun Shop	Meridian			•			
MISSOURI							
Beard's Sport Shop	Cape Girardeau		•	•			
Bickford's Gun Repair	Joplin			•			

SERVICE CENTER	CITY	BR	CR	RE	ST	SW	TC
Carl's Gun Shop	El Dorado Springs			•		•	
Catfish Guns	Imperial	•		•		•	
CR Specialty	Kansas City	•	•				
Dollar Drugs, Inc.	Lee's Summit			•			•
Kopp. Prof. Gunsmith, Terry K.	Lexington		•	•		•	
Marshall Gun Shop	Dellwood		•	•		•	
Nu-Line Guns, Inc.	Harvester	•		•			
Ozark Shooters, Inc.	Branson						
MONTANA							
Air Gun Shop, The	Billings	•	•				
Billings Gunsmiths	Billings		•	•		•	
Brady's Sportsmans Surplus	Missoula						•
Capitol Sports & Western Wear	Helena			•			
Don's Sporting Goods	Lewiston	•					
Montana Gun Works	Great Falls		•	•		•	
NEBRASKA							
Bedlan's Sporting Goods, Inc.	Fairbury	•		•			
Cylinder & Slide, Inc.	Fremont			•		•	
G.H. Gun Shop	McCook			•			
G.I. Loan Shop	Grand Island	•		•			
Gunsmithing Specialties, Co.	Papillion			•			
Labs Air Gun Shop	Omaha						
Sporting Goods, Inc.	Hastings		•	•			
Upper Missouri Trading Co., Inc.	Crofton	•	•	•			•
NEVADA							
Accuracy Gun Shop, Inc.	Las Vegas	■		•			
Gun World	Elko			•			
Nevada Air Guns	N. Las Vegas						
NEW HAMPSHIRE							
Lewis Arms	Hooksett	•		•			
Stratemeyer, H.P.	Langdon			•			
NEW JERSEY							
Belleplain Supply, Inc.	Belleplain	•		•			
Brenner Sport Shop, Charlie	Rahway		•	•			
Efinger Sporting Goods	Bound Brook	•		•			
Garfield Gunsmithing	Garfield	•		•			
Harry's Army & Navy Store	Robbinsville	•		•		•	
Ray's Sport Shop, Inc.	Plainfield			•			
Sportsman's Center	Bordentown			•			
The Way It Was Sporting	Moorestown			•			
Treptow, Inc., Herman	Milltown			•			
Weinberger Gunsmithing, Herbert	Waldwick			•			
NEW MEXICO							
Charlie's Sporting Goods, Inc.	Albuquerque		•	•		•	
Chuck's Gun Shop	Ranchos De Taos		•	•			
Covey's Precision Gunsmith	Roswell						

See page 293 for Service Center addresses.

WARRANTY SERVICE CENTERS (cont.)

■BR=Browning ■CR=Crosman ■RE=Remington ■ST=Stoeger ■SW=Smith & Wesson ■TC=Thompson/Center

SERVICE CENTER	CITY	BR	CR	RE	ST	SW	TC
D&J Coleman Service	Hobbs		•				
Hobb's Bicycle & Gun Sales	Hobbs			•			
Ross Sporting Goods	Farmington			•			
NEW YORK							
Alpine Arms Corp.	Brooklyn					•	
Apple Town Gun Shop	Williamson		•	•			
Benson Gun Shop	Coram L.I.		•	•			
Boracci, E. John, Village Sport Ctr.	Seaford L.I.						
Buffalo Gun Center, Inc.	Buffalo			•			
Burgins Gun Shop	Sidney Center		•	•			
Centre Firearms Co., Inc.	New York City			•			
Creekside Gun Shop	Holcomb	•					
Damiano's Field & Stream	Ossining		•	•			
Davco Stores, 305 Broadway	Monticello		•				
Gemini Arms Ltd.	Hicksville		•	•			
Hart's Gun Supply, Ed	Bath			•			
Hill Top Gunsmithing	Canton			•			
Jovino Co., Inc., John	New York					•	
Kielon, Gunsmith, Dave	Webster		•	•			
Lounsbury Sporting Goods, Bob	Middletown		•	•			
Mulvey's Marine & Sport Shop	Monticello		•				
Rapids Gun Shop	Niagra Falls		•				
Scalzo's Sporting Goods	Endicott		•				
Schultheis Sporting Goods	Arkport					•	
Smith's Lawn & Marine Svc.	Clarence		•	•			
Solvay Home & Outdoor Center	Solvay			•			
Sports Mart, The	Ogdensburg	•					
Taylor & Vadney, Inc.	Albany					•	
Van's Gunsmith Service	Parish		•	•			
White Dog Gunsmithing	Ilion		•	•			
NORTH CAROLINA							
Baity's Custom Gunworks	North Wilksboro		•	•			
Blue Ridge Outdoor Sports, Inc.	E. Flat Rock	•		•			
Don's Gun Shop	Ashville		•	•			
Duncan Gun Shop, Inc.	North Wilksboro		•	•			
Hill's, Inc.	Raleigh	•					
Marine Gun & Lock Shop	Jacksonville		•				
Mike's Crosman Service	Winston-Salem		•	•			
Perry's of Wendell, Inc.	Wendell			•			
Warren's Sports Hdqts.	Washington			•			
NORTH DAKOTA							
Gun City, Inc.	Bismarck		•	•			
Outdoorsman, Inc.	Fargo	•	•				
S.K. Guns, Inc.	Fargo		•				
OHIO							
Airgun Centre, Ltd.	Cincinnati		•				
All Game Sport Center	Milford		•				

SERVICE CENTER	CITY	BR	CR	RE	ST	SW	TC
Central Ohio Police Supply, c/o Wammes Guns	Bellefontaine						•
Cherry Corners, Inc.	Lodi			•			
Eyster Heritage Gunsmiths, Ken	Centerburg	•		•			•
Keller Gunsmithing	Bradford			•			
Log Cabin Sport Shop	Lodi		•				
Precision Airgun Sales	Maple Heights		•				•
Rutko Corp. (Stonewall Range)	Broadview Heights					•	
Sportsman's Depot	Urban		•	•			
Sportsman's Haven	Cambridge	•				•	•
Sportsmen's Repair Ctr., Inc.	Columbus Groves		•	•			
Stocker's Shop	Warren			•			
Trading Post, The	Massillon		•				
Upton's Gun Shop	Fremont		•	•			
VanBurne's Gun Shop	Toledo					•	
Zanes Gun Rack	Columbus		•				
OKLAHOMA							
D&D Sporting Goods	Tishomingo			•			
Junior's Gun & Lock Shop	Ponca City		•	•			
Mashburn Arms Co., Inc.	Oklahoma City			•			
Meydag, Peter	Tulsa	•		•			
Outdoor America Store	Oklahoma City		•				
Shamburg's Wholesale Spt. Gds.	Clinton			•			
Skeet's Gun Shop	Tahlequah			•			
Southwest Shooters Supply, Inc.	Oklahoma City	•	•				
Sport Shop, The	Kingfisher					•	
Sports World, Inc.	Tulsa		•	•			
OREGON							
Allison & Carey Gun Works	Portland	•		•			
Enstad & Douglas	Oregon City		•	•			•
Felton, James	Eugene						
Metro Rod & Reel	Portland			•			
Starnes, Gunmaker, Ken	Hillsboro					•	
Surplus Center	Roseburg		•	•			
PENNSYLVANIA							
Auto Electric & Parts, Inc.	Media			•			
Braverman Arms Co.	Wilkinsburg		•	•			
Colabaugh Gunsmith, Inc., Craig	Stroudsburg			•			
Federal Firearms Co., Inc.	Oakdale			•			
Fix Gunshop, Inc., Michael D.	Reading			•			
Flaig's Inc.	Pittsburgh			•			
Garber & Sams Gunsmithing	Elizabethtown			•			
Gorenflo Gunsmithing	Erie			•			
Grice Gun Shop, Inc.	Clearfield					•	
Hart & Son, Robert W.	Nescopeck			•			
Hemlock Gun Shop	Lakeville		•				
Herold's Gun Shoppe	Waynesboro			•			

See page 293 for Service Center addresses.

■BR=Browning ■CR=Crosman ■RE=Remington ■ST=Stoeger ■SW=Smith & Wesson ■TC=Thompson/Center

SERVICE CENTER	CITY	BR	CR	RE	ST	SW	TC
Keeley, John L.	Spring City		●				
Keidel's Gunsmithing Service	Washington	●		●			
Leo's Custom Stocks	Library			●			
Levan's Sport Goods	Lebanon			●			
Miller's Sport Shop	Mountaintop			●			
Richland Gun Shop	Richland	●		●			
Somerset Sports Shop	Somerset		●	●			
Sportsman's Shop	New Holland	●		●			
Unique Sporting Goods	Lorreto		●	●			
Wholesale Shooters Supplies	Lititz			●			
Ye Olde Gun Shop	Bradford						
RHODE ISLAND							
D&L Shooting Supplies	Warwick		●	●			
Gun Hospital, The	E. Providence		●	●			
SOUTH CAROLINA							
Bryan & Associates	Belton						
Gun Rack, Inc., The	Aiken			●			
Gun Room, The	Chapin						
Gunsmith, Inc., The	West Columbia		●	●		●	
Roy's Antiques & Things	Mountain Rest		●	●			
S.E.M. Gun Works	Greenville	●					
Smith & Smith Gun Shop, Inc.	Charleston Hghts.						
Southland Gun Works, Inc.	Darlington			●			
SOUTH DAKOTA							
Gary's Gun Shop	Sioux Falls	●		●			
Ron's Gun Repair	Sioux Falls	●		●			
Roy's Sport Shop	Watertown			●			
Sodak Sport & Bait	Aberdeen	●		●			●
TENNESSEE							
D&L Gunsmithing/Guns & Ammo	Memphis	●		●			
Fox & Company	Knoxville			●			
Friedman's Army Surplus	Nashville						
Gun City USA, Inc.	Nashville	●		●		●	
Hagstrom, E.G.	Memphis						
Hill's Hardware & Sporting Goods	Union City	●		●			
McGuns, W.H.	Humboldt		●	●			
Mines Gun Shack	Tullahoma						
Shafer Eagle	Jonesbrough		●	●			
TEXAS							
Alpine Range	Fort Worth	●	●				
Armadillo Air Gun Repair	Corpus Christi		●				
Ben's Gun Shop	Duncanville						
Billy Freds	Amarillo	●		●			
Boggus Gun Shop	San Marcos						
Carroll's Gun Shop, Inc.	Wharton	●		●			
Carter's Country	Houston			●			
Cogdell's, Inc.	Waco			●			

SERVICE CENTER	CITY	BR	CR	RE	ST	SW	TC
Coleman, Inc., Ron	Carrollton	●		●			
Don & Tim's Gun Shop	San Antonio			●			
Ewell Cross Gun Shop, Inc.	Ft. Worth	●		●			
Freer's Gun Shop	Houston			●			
Gun & Tackle Store, The	Dallas			●			
Kirkpatrick, Gunsmith, Larry	Lubbock			●			
Lone Star Guns, Inc.	Plano			●		●	
Longacres, Inc.	Abilene			●			
Master Gunsmiths, Inc.	Houston	●		●			
McBride's Guns, Inc.	Austin	●		●	●	●	
McClelland Gun Shop	Dallas	●		●			
Mueschke Manufacturing Co.	Houston			●			
Nagel Gun Shop, Inc.	San Antonio	●		●			
Oshman's Sporting Goods, Inc.	Houston	●		●	●		●
Pasadena Gun Center	Pasadena			●			
Precision Gunsmithing	Amarillo						
Ray's Sporting Goods	Dallas			●			
Reynolds Gun Shop, Inc.	Tyler			●			
Texas Gun Shop, Inc.	Corpus Christi			●			●
Wichita Guncraft, Inc.	Wichita Falls			●			
Williamson Gunsmith Service	Hurst		●				
Wolfer Brothers, Inc.	Houston			●			
UTAH							
Gun Ace Gunsmithing	Cedar City			●			
Gun Shop, The	Salt Lake City	●		●			
Gunsmith Co., The	Salt Lake City			●			
Hutch's	Lehi		●	●			
Professional Armaments, Inc.	Murray		●	●		●	
VERMONT							
Barrows Point Trading Post	Quechee			●			
Burby, Inc. Guns & Gunsmithing	Middlebury	●		●			●
Carpenters Gun Works	Proctorsville						
Clapps Gun Shop	Brattleboro		●	●			
VIRGINIA							
Atlantic & Pacific Guns	Virginia Beach			●			
Bob's Gun & Tackle Shop (Blaustein & Reich, Inc.)	Norfolk	●		●		●	
Cervera, Albert J.	Hanover			●			
King's Gun Shop, Inc.	Franklin	●		●			
Moates Sport Shop, Bob	Midlothian	●					
Northern Virginia Gun Works, Inc.	Springfield			●			
Princess Anne Marine & Sport Center	Virginia Beach			●			
Richmond Gun Shop	Richmond		●	●			
WASHINGTON							
Brock's Gunsmithing, Inc.	Spokane			●			
Chet Paulson Outfitters	Tacoma	●		●			

See page 293 for Service Center addresses.

WARRANTY SERVICE CENTERS (cont.)

■BR=Browning ■CR=Crosman ■RE=Remington ■ST=Stoeger ■SW=Smith & Wesson ■TC=Thompson/Center

SERVICE CENTER	CITY	BR	CR	RE	ST	SW	TC
Greene's Gun Shop	Oak Harbor			●			
Karrer's Gunatorium	Spokane			●			
Kesselring Gun Shop	Burlington	●	●	●			
Pintos Gun Shop	Kent						
Shooters Supply	Yakima					●	●
Wisner's Gun Shop, Inc.	Chehalis	●	●	●			
Wheeler Gun Shop, C.	Richland			●		●	●
WEST VIRGINIA							
Bait & Tackle Shop, The	Fairmont		●	●			
Lew's Mountaineer Gunsmithing	Charleston			●			
Shooting Gallery, The	Weirton		●	●			
WISCONSIN							
Badgers Shooters Supply, Inc.	Owen		●	●			
Bob's Crosman Repair	Cudahy		●				
Custom Firearms Shop, The	Sheboygan			●			
Flintrop Arms Corp.	Milwaukee	●	●	●		●	
Gander Mountain, Inc.	Wilmot	●	●	●			
Jack's Lock & Gun Shop	Fond Du Lac			●			
Jay's Sports, Inc.	Menomonee Falls	●		●			
Midwestern Shooters Supply, Inc.	Lomira			●			
Phillips, D.J., Gunsmith	Pewaukee			●			
Potter Gunsmithing	Muskego			●			
Precision Gun Works	Oshkosh			●			
River Bend Sport Shop	Waupaca			●			
R&R Shooters Supply	Mauston		●				
Rusk Gun Shop, Inc.	Madison	●	●				
Sea Gull Marina	Two Rivers						
WYOMING							
Elbe Arms Co., Inc.	Cheyenne			●			

SERVICE CENTER	CITY	BR	CR	RE	ST	SW	TC
Jackalope Gun Shop	Douglas			●			
CANADA							
Armurie De L'Outaouqis	Hull, PQ			●			
Casey's Gun Shop	Rogersville, NB	●		●		●	
Charlton Co., Ltd.	Brentwood Bay, BC					●	
Custom Gun Shop	Edmonton, AB			●			
Davidson's of Canada	Peterborough, ON			●			
Delisle Thompson Sport Goods	Saskatoon, SK			●			
Epps, Ellwood	Orilla, ON			●			
Ernie's Gun Shop, Ltd.	Winnipeg, MB			●			●
Gene's Gunsmithing	Selkirk, MB						●
Girard, Florent, Gunsmith	Chicoutimi, PQ			●			
L'Armurier Alain Bouchard, Inc.	St. Chrysostome, PQ	●					
Long Gunsmithing Ltd., W.R.	Coburg, ON	●		●			
Lusignant Armurier, A. Richard	St. Hyacinthe, PQ			●			
Magasin Latulipe, Inc.	Quest, PQ	●		●			
Newby, Stewart, Gunsmith	New Burgh, ON			●			
Precision Arms & Gunsmithing Ltd.	Nobleton, ON			●			
Ralph's Gun Shop	Niverville, MB			●			
Randy's Gun Repair	Tabustinac, NB			●			
Reliable Gun & Tackle, Ltd.	Vancouver, BC	●		●			
Saskatoon Gunsmith Shoppe, Ltd.	Saskatoon, SK			●			
Selin Gunsmith, Ltd., Del	Vernon, BC			●			
Taylor's Technical Gunsmithing Co.	Gormely, ON					●	
West Gate Gunsports, Inc.	Edmonton, AB			●			
West Luther Gun Repair	Conn, ON			●			
Wholesale Sports	Edmonton, AB	●		●			
Wortner Gun Works, Ltd.	Chatham, ON					●	

See page 293 for Service Center addresses.

METALLIC SIGHTS

Handgun Sights

BO-MAR DELUXE BMCS Gives ⅜" windage and elevation adjustment at 50 yards on Colt Gov't 45; sight radius under 7". For GM and Commander models only. Uses existing dovetail slot. Has shield-type rear blade.
Price: **$65.95**
Price: BMCS-2 (for GM and 9mm) **$65.95**
Price: Flat bottom **$65.95**
Price: BMGC (for Colt Gold Cup), angled serrated blade, rear **$65.95**
Price: BMGC front sight **$12.00**
Price: BMCZ-75 (for CZ-75, TZ-75, P-9 and most clones. Works with factory front. **$65.95**
BO-MAR FRONT SIGHTS Dovetail style for S&W 4506, 4516, 1076; undercut style (.250", .280", 5/16" high); Fast Draw style (.210", .250", .230" high).
Price **$12.00**
BO-MAR BMU XP-100/T/C CONTENDER No gunsmithing required; has .080" notch.
Price: **$77.00**
BO-MAR BMML For muzzleloaders; has .062" notch, flat bottom.
Price: **$65.95**
Price: With ⅜" dovetail **$65.95**
BO-MAR RUGER "P" ADJUSTABLE SIGHT Replaces factory front and rear sights.
Price: Rear sight **$65.95**
Price: Front sight **$12.00**

MMC M/85 ADJUSTABLE REAR SIGHT Designed to be compatible with the Ruger P-85 front sight. Fully adjustable for windage and elevation.
Price: M/85 Adjustable Rear Sight, plain **$52.45**
Price: As above, white outline **$57.70**
MMC STANDARD ADJUSTABLE REAR SIGHT Available for Colt 1911 type, Ruger Standard Auto, and now for S&W 469, and 659 pistols. No front sight change is necessary, as this sight will work with the original factory front sight.
Price: Standard Adjustable Rear Sight, plain leaf **$46.05**
Price: Standard Adjustable Rear Sight, white outline **$51.15**
MMC MINI-SIGHT Miniature size for carrying, fully adjustable, for maximum accuracy with your pocket auto. MMC's Mini-Sight will work with the factory front sight. No machining is necessary; easy installation. Available for Walther PP, PPK, and PPK/S pistols. Will also fit fixed sight Browning Hi-Power (P-35).
Price: Mini-Sight, plain **$58.45**
Price: Mini-Sight, white bar **$63.45**
MEPROLIGHT SIGHTS Replacement tritium open sights for popular handguns and AR-15/M-16 rifles. Both front and rear sights have tritium inserts for illumination in low-light conditions. Inserts give constant non-glare green light for 5 years, even in cold weather. For most popular auto pistols, revolvers, some rifles and shotguns. **Contact Hesco, Inc. for complete details.**
Price: Shotgun bead front sight **$22.95**
Price: M-16 front sight only **$32.95**
Price: H&K SR9, MP5 front sight only **$49.95**
Price: Colt Python, King Cobra, Ruger GP-100 adj. sights ... **$124.95**
Price: Most other front and rear fixed sights **$94.95**
Price: Adj. sights for Beretta, Browning, Colt Gov't., Glock, Ruger P-Series, SIG, Taurus PT-92 .... **$139.95**

Bo-Mar BMSW
(photo: Brownell's, Inc.)

Bo-Mar BMCG Gold Cup

BO-MAR BMR Fully adjustable rear sight for Ruger MKI, MKII Bull barrel autos.
Price: Rear **$65.95**
Price: Undercut front sight **$12.00**
BO-MAR BMSW SMITH & WESSON SIGHTS Replace the S&W Novak-style fixed sights. A .385" high front sight and minor machining required. For models 4506, 4516, 1076; all 9mms with 5¾" and 6³⁄₁₆" radius.
Price: **$65.95**
Price: .385" front sight **$12.00**
Price: BM-645 rear sight (for S&W 645, 745), uses factory front **$65.95**
Price: BMSW-52 rear sight (for Model 52), fits factory dovetail, uses factory front **$65.95**
BO-MAR LOW PROFILE RIB & ACCURACY TUNER Streamlined rib with front and rear sights; 7⅛" sight radius. Brings sight line closer to the bore than standard or extended sight and ramp. Weight 5 oz. Made for Colt Gov't 45, Super 38, and Gold Cup 45 and 38.
Price: **$123.00**
BO-MAR COMBAT RIB For S&W Model 19 revolver with 4" barrel. Sight radius 5¾", weight 5½ oz.
Price: **$110.00**
BO-MAR HUNTER REAR SIGHT Replacement rear sight in two models—S&W K and L frames use 2¾" Bo-Mar base with ⁷⁄₁₆" overhang, has two screw holes; S&W N frame has 3" base, three screw holes. A .200" taller front blade is required.
Price: **$79.00**
BO-MAR WINGED RIB For S&W 4" and 6" length barrels—K-38, M10, HB 14 and 19. Weight for the 6" model is about 7¼ oz.
Price: **$123.00**
BO-MAR COVER-UP RIB Adjustable rear sight, winged front guards. Fits right over revolver's original front sight. For S&W 4" M-10HB, M-13, M-58, M-64 and 65, Ruger 4" models SDA-34, SDA-84, SS-34, SS-84, GF-34, GF-84.
Price: **$117.00**
C-MORE SIGHTS Replacement front sight blades offered in two types and five styles. Made of Du Pont Acetal, they come in a set of five high-contrast colors: blue, green, pink, red and yellow. Easy to install. Patridge style for Colt Python (all barrels), Ruger Super Blackhawk (7½"), Ruger Blackhawk (4⅝"); ramp style for Python (all barrels), Blackhawk (4⅝"), Super Blackhawk (7½" and 10½"). From C-More Systems.
Price: Per set **$19.95**
MMC COMBAT FIXED REAR SIGHT (Colt 1911-Type Pistols) This veteran MMC sight is well known to those who prefer a true combat sight for "carry" guns. Steel construction for long service. Choose from a wide variety of front sights.
Price: Combat Fixed Rear, plain **$18.45**
Price: As above, white outline **$23.65**
Price: Combat Front Sight for above, six styles, from ... **$5.15**

Bo-Mar "P" Series
(photo: Brownell's, Inc.)

MMC Mini Sight
(photo: Brownell's, Inc.)

MILLETT BAR-DOT-BAR TRITIUM SIGHTS Combo set uses the Series 100 fully adjustable sight system with horizontal tritium inserts on the rear, a single insert on the front. Available for: Ruger P-85, SIG Sauer P220, P225/226, Browning Hi-Power, Colt GM, CZ/TZ, TA-90, Glock 17, 19, 20, 21, 22, 23, S&W (2nd, 3rd generations), Beretta 84, 85, 92SB, Taurus PT-92.
Price: **$135.00**
Price: Beretta, Taurus **$143.50**
MILLETT 3-DOT SYSTEM SIGHTS The 3-Dot System sights use a single white dot on the front blade and two dots flanking the rear notch. Fronts available in Dual-Crimp and Wide Stake-On styles, as well as special applications. Adjustable rear sight available for most popular auto pistols and revolvers.
Price: Front, from **$16.00**
Price: Adjustable rear .... **$55.60 to $56.80**
MILLETT REVOLVER FRONT SIGHTS All-steel replacement front sights with either white or orange bar. Easy to install. For Ruger GP-100, Redhawk, Security-Six, Police-Six, Speed-Six, Colt Trooper, Diamondback, King Cobra, Peacemaker, Python, Dan Wesson 22 and 15-2.
Price: .... **$13.60 to $16.00**

CAUTION: PRICES SHOWN ARE SUPPLIED BY THE MANUFACTURER OR IMPORTER. CHECK YOUR LOCAL GUNSHOP.

METALLIC SIGHTS

MILLETT DUAL-CRIMP FRONT SIGHT   Replacement front sight for automatic pistols. Dual-Crimp uses an all-steel two-point hollow rivet system. Available in eight heights and four styles. Has a skirted base that covers the front sight pad. Easily installed with the Millett Installation Tool Set. Available in Blaze Orange Bar, White Bar, Serrated Ramp, Plain Post.
Price: **$16.00**

MILLETT STAKE-ON FRONT SIGHT   Replacement front sight for automatic pistols. Stake-On sights have skirted base that covers the front sight pad. Easily installed with the Millet Installation Tool Set. Available in seven heights and four styles—Blaze Orange Bar, White Bar, Serrated Ramp, Plain Post.
Price: **$16.00**

OMEGA OUTLINE SIGHT BLADES   Replacement rear sight blades for Colt and Ruger single action guns and the Interarms Virginian Dragoon. Standard Outline available in gold or white notch outline on blue metal. From Omega Sales, Inc.
Price: **$8.95**

OMEGA MAVERICK SIGHT BLADES   Replacement "peep-sight" blades for Colt, Ruger SAs, Virginian Dragoon. Three models available—No. 1, Plain; No. 2, Single Bar; No. 3, Double Bar Rangefinder. From Omega Sales, Inc.
Price: Each **$6.95**

P-T TRITIUM NIGHT SIGHTS   Self-luminous tritium sights for most popular handguns, Colt AR-15, H&K rifles and shotguns. Replacement handgun sight sets available in 3-Dot style (green/green, green/yellow, green/orange) with bold outlines around inserts; Bar-Dot available in green/green with or without white outline rear sight. Functional life exceeds 15 years. From Innovative Weaponry, Inc.
Price: Handgun sight sets **$89.95**
Price: Rifle sight sets **$89.95**
Price: Rifle, front only **$32.95**
Price: Shotgun, front only **$18.95**

TRIJICON NIGHT SIGHTS   Three-dot night sight system uses tritium inserts in the front and rear sights. Tritium "lamps" are mounted in silicone rubber inside a metal cylinder. A polished crystal sapphire provides protection and clarity. Inlaid white outlines provide 3-dot aiming in daylight also. Available for most popular handguns with fixed or adjustable sights. From Trijicon, Inc.
Price: . . . . **$19.95 to $175.00**

Millett Dual Crimp (top), Stake-On front sights

Wichita Series 70/80 sight

Meprolight tritrium sights

Trijicon three-dot fixed

Trijicon three-dot adjustable

Merit Optical Attachment

THOMPSON/CENTER SILHOUETTE SIGHTS   Replacement front and rear sights for the T/C Contender. Front sight has three interchangeable blades. Rear sight has three notch widths. Rear sight can be used with existing soldered front sights.
Price: Front sight **$31.95**
Price: Rear sight **$85.00**

WICHITA SERIES 70/80 SIGHT   Provides click windage and elevation adjustments with precise repeatability of settings. Sight blade is grooved and angled back at the top to reduce glare. Available in Low Mount Combat or Low Mount Target styles for Colt 45s and their copies, S&W 645, Hi-Power, CZ 75 and others.
Price: Rear sight, target or combat **$66.75**
Price: Front sight, Patridge or ramp **$10.45**

WICHITA GRAND MASTER DELUXE RIBS   Ventilated rib has wings machined into it for better sight acquisition and is relieved for Mag-Na-Porting. Milled to accept Weaver see-thru-style rings. Made of stainless or blued steel; front and rear sights blued. Has Wichita Multi-Range rear sight system, adjustable front sight. Made for revolvers with 6" barrel.
Price: Model 301S, 301B (adj. sight K frames with custom bbl. of 1" to 1.032" dia. L and N frame with 1.062" to 1.100" dia. bbl.) **$160.00**
Price: Model 303S, 303B (adj. sight K, L, N frames with factory barrel) **$160.00**

Sight Attachments

MERIT IRIS SHUTTER DISC   Eleven clicks give 12 different apertures. No. 3 Disc and Master, primarily target types, 0.22" to .125"; No. 4, ½" dia. hunting type, .025" to .155". Available for all popular sights. The Master Deluxe, with flexible rubber light shield, is particularly adapted to extension, scope height, and tang sights. All Merit Deluxe models have internal click springs; are hand fitted to minimum tolerance.
Price: Master Deluxe **$63.00**
Price: No. 3 Disc **$52.00**
Price: No. 4 Hunting Disc **$45.00**

MERIT LENS DISC   Similar to Merit Iris Shutter (Model 3 or Master) but incorporates provision for mounting prescription lens integrally. Lens may be obtained locally from your optician. Sight disc is 7/16" wide (Model 3), or 3/4" wide (Master). Model 3 Target.
Price: **$65.00**
Price: Master Deluxe **$75.00**

MERIT OPTICAL ATTACHMENT   For revolver and pistol shooters, instantly attached by rubber suction cup to regular or shooting glasses. Any aperture .020" to .156".
Price: Deluxe (swings aside) **$63.00**

Maker and Model	Magn.	Field at 100 Yds. (feet)	Eye Relief (in.)	Length (in.)	Tube Dia. (in.)	W&E Adjustments	Weight (ozs.)	Price	Other Data
ACTION ARMS									
Micro-Dot									
1.5-4.5x LER Pistol	1.5-4.5	80-26	12-24	8.8	1	Int.	9.5	$199.00	Variable intensity LED red aiming dot. Average battery life 20 to 4500 hours. Waterproof, nitrogen-filled aluminum tube. Fits most standard 1" rings. Both Ultra Dot models avail. in black and satin chrome. Imported by Action Arms Ltd.
Ultra-Dot 25 1x	—	—	—	5.1	1	Int.	4.0	139.00	
Ultra-Dot 30 1x	—	—	—	5.1	30mm	Int.	3.9	149.00	
ADCO									
MiRAGE Ranger 1"	0	—	—	5.2	1	Int.	4.5	139.00	[1]Multi-Color Dot system changes from red to green. [2]For airguns, paintball, rimfires. Uses common lithium wafer battery. [3]Comes with standard dovetail mount. [4]3/8" dovetail mount; poly body; adj. intensity diode. All come with extension tube for mounting. Black or matte nickel finish. Optional 2x booster available. Five year warranty. From ADCO Sales.
MiRAGE Ranger 30mm	0	—	—	5.5	30mm	Int.	5.5	149.00	
MiRAGE Sportsman[1]	0	—	—	5.2	1	Int.	4.5	219.00	
MiRAGE Competitor[1]	0	—	—	5.5	30mm	Int.	5.5	249.00	
IMP Sight[2]	0	—	—	4.5	—	Int.	2	19.95	
Square Shooter[3]	0	—	—	5.0	—	Int.	5	98.00	
MiRAGE Eclipse[1]	0	—	—	5.5	30mm	Int.	5.3	215.00	
MiRAGE Champ Red Dot	0	—	—	4.5	—	Int.	2	39.95	
AIMPOINT									
Comp	0	—	—	4.6	30mm	Int.	4.3	308.00	Illuminates red dot in field of view. Noparallax (dot does not need to be centered). Unlimited field of view and eye relief. On/off, adj. intensity. Dot covers 3" @ 100 yds. Mounts avail. for all sights and scopes. [1]Projects red dot of visible laser light onto target. Black finish (LSR-2B) or stainless (LSR-2S); or comes with rings and accessories. Optional toggle switch, **$34.95**. Lithium battery life up to 15 hours. [2]For Beretta, Browning, Colt Gov't., Desert Eagle, Glock, Ruger, SIG-Sauer, S&W. [3]For Colt, S&W. From Aimpoint.
Laserdot[1]	—	—	—	3.5	1	Int.	4.0	319.95	
Autolaser[2]	—	—	—	3.75	1	Int.	4.3	351.00	
Revolver Laser[3]	—	—	—	3.5	1	Int.	3.6	339.00	
APPLIED LASER SYSTEMS									
MiniAimer MA-3[1]	—	—	—	1.36	—	Int.	.88	246.00	[1]Output power 5mW; also MA-35, power less than 3mW, **$350.00**; [2]for HK USP; 5mW; also HK USP 635nm (3mW) **$350.00**; [3]also SP 89/MP5 635nm (3mW) **$350.00**; [4]5mW power. Mounts avail. for Browning Hi-Power, S&W, Colt 1911, Beretta 92F, Glock, SIG-Sauer, Ruger P-85 MkII, Firestor. From Applied Laser Systems.
Custom MiniAimer[2]	—	—	—	1.74	—	Int.	1.6	298.00	
Custom MiniAimer[3]	—	—	—	2.08	—	Int.	1.2	298.00	
T2 Custom Aimer[4]	—	—	—	2.8	—	Int.	2.2	198.00	
AR-15 Custom Aimer[4]	—	—	—	2.0	—	Int.	3.0	279.00	
Custom Glock Mini Laser[4]	—	—	—	.75	—	Int.	.8	385.00	
ARMSON O.E.G.									
Standard	0	—	—	5 1/8	1	Int.	4.3	175.00	Shows red dot aiming point. No batteries needed. Standard model fits 1" ring mounts (not incl.). [1]Daylight Only Sight with 3/8" dovetail mount for 22s. Does not contain tritium. From Trijicon, Inc.
22 DOS[1]	0	—	—	3 3/4	—	Int.	3.0	104.00	
22 Day/Night	0	—	—	3 3/4	—	Int.	3.0	146.00	
Colt Pistol	0	—	—	3 3/4	—	Int.	3.0	209.00	
BAUSCH & LOMB									
Elite 3000 Handgun									
30-2028G[1]	2	23	9-26	8.4	1	Int.	6.9	284.95	[1]Also in silver finish, 303.95. [2]Also in silver finish, **$411.95 Contact Bausch & Lomb Sports Optics Div. for details.**
30-2632G[2]	2-6	10-4	20	9.0	1	Int.	10.0	392.95	
BEEMAN									
Blue Ring 20[1]	1.5	14	11-16	8.3	3/4	Int.	3.6	59.95	All scopes have 5-pt. reticle, all glass, fully coated lenses. [1]Pistol scope; cast mounts included. [2]Pistol scope; silhouette knobs. Imported by Beeman.
Blue Ribbon 25[2]	2	19	10-24	9 1/16	1	Int.	7.4	154.95	
B-SQUARE									
BSL-1[1]	—	—	—	2.75	.75	Int.	2.25	229.95	[1]Blue finish; stainless, **$239.95**. T-slot mount; cord or integral switch. [2]Blue finish; stainless, **$309.95**. T-slot mount; cord or integral switch. Uses common A76 batteries. Dimensions 1.1"x1.1"x.6". From B-Square.
Mini-Laser[2]	—	—	—	1.1	—	Int.	2.9	299.95	
BURRIS									
Handgun									
1 1/2-4x LER[1,5,10]	1.6-3.	16-11	11-25	10 1/4	1	Int.	11	328.95	All scopes avail. in Plex reticle. Steel-on-steel click adjustments. [1]Dot reticle on some models. [2]Matte satin finish. [3]Available with parallax adjustment $28 extra (standard on 10x, 12x, 4-12x, 6-12x, 6-18x, 6x HBR and 3-12x Signature). [4]Silver matte finish $30 extra. [5]Target knobs extra, standard on silhouette models, LER and XER with P.A., 6x HBR. [6]Available with Posi-Lock.
2-7x LER[2,3,4,6]	2-6.5	21-7	7-27	9.5	1	Int.	12.6	321.95	
3-9x LER[3,4,6]	3.4-8.4	12-5	22-14	11	1	Int.	14	359.95	
1x LER[1]	1.1	27	10-24	8 3/4	1	Int.	6.8	202.95	
2x LER[1,4,5]	1.7	21	10-24	8 3/4	1	Int.	6.8	209.95	
3x LER[3,5]	2.7	17	10-20	8 7/8	1	Int.	6.8	226.95	
4x LER[1,3,4,5,6]	3.7	11	10-22	9 5/8	1	Int.	9.0	235.95	
7x IER[1,3,4,5]	6.5	6.5	10-16	11 1/4	1	Int.	10	258.95	
10x IER[1,3,5]	9.5	4	8-12	13 1/2	1	Int.	14	348.95	

CAUTION: PRICES SHOWN ARE SUPPLIED BY THE MANUFACTURER OR IMPORTER. CHECK YOUR LOCAL GUNSHOP.

Maker and Model	Magn.	Field at 100 Yds. (feet)	Eye Relief (in.)	Length (in.)	Tube Dia. (in.)	W&E Adjust-ments	Weight (ozs.)	Price	Other Data
BUSHNELL									[1]Also silver finish, **$204.95**. [2]Also silver finish, **$248.95**. Contact Bausch & Lomb Sports Optics Div. for details.
Trophy Handgun									
73-0232[1]	2	20	9-26	8.7	1	Int.	7.7	189.95	
73-2632[2]	2-6	21-7	9-26	9.1	1	Int.	9.6	235.95	
INTERAIMS									Intended for handguns. Comes with rings. Dot size less than 1½" @ 100 yds. Waterproof. Battery life 50-10,000 hours. Black or nickel finish. 2x booster, 1" or 30mm, **$139.00** Imported by Stoeger.
One V	0	—	—	4.5	1	Int.	4	145.95	
One V 30	0	—	—	4.5	30mm	Int.	4	159.95	
KILHAM									Unlimited eye relief; internal click adjustments; crosshair reticle. Fits Thompson/Center rail mounts, for S&W K, N, Ruger Blackhawk, Super, Super Single-Six, Contender.
Hutson Handgunner II	1.7	8	—	5½	7/8	Int.	5.1	119.95	
Hutson Handgunner	3	8	10-12	6	7/8	Int.	5.3	119.95	
LASERAIM									[1]300-yd. range; 15-hr. batt. [2]Red dot laser; fits Weaver-style mounts; also LA2XM with Hotdot, **$269.95**. [3]300-yd. range; 2" dot at 100 yds.; rechargeable Nicad battery; also LA5 Magnum—1000-yd. range, 1" dot at 100 yds., **$209.95**. [4]500-yd. range; 2" dot at 100 yds.; rechargeable Nicad battery. [5]1.5-mile range; 1" dot at 100 yds.; 20+ hrs. batt. life. [6]1.5-mile range; 1" dot at 100 yds.; rechargeable Nicad battery (comes with in-field charger); [7]Trigger guard mount for S&W 3900, 5900, 6900, Glock, Ruger P-Series, Beretta 93F, FS. All have w&e adj.; black or satin silver finish. From Emerging Technologies, Inc.
LA8[1]	—	—	—	2.94	.74	Int.	NA	139.95	
LA2X Dualdot[2]	—	—	—	NA	30mm	Int.	NA	249.95	
LA5[3]	—	—	—	2	.75	Int.	1.2	199.95	
LA9 Hotdot[4]	—	—	—	2	.75	Int.	NA	239.95	
LA10 Hotdot[5]	—	—	—	3.87	.75	Int.	NA	249.95	
LA11 Hotdot[6]	—	—	—	2.75	.75	Int.	NA	249.95	
LA14[7]	—	—	—	NA	NA	Int.	NA	283.00	
LASER DEVICES									Projects high intensity beam of laser light onto target as an aiming point. Adj. for w. & e. [1]Diode laser system. From Laser Devices, Inc.
He Ne FA-6	—	—	—	6.2	—	Int.	11	229.50	
He Ne FA-9	—	—	—	12	—	Int.	16	299.00	
He Ne FA-9P	—	—	—	9	—	Int.	14	299.00	
FA-4[1]	—	—	—	4.5	—	Int.	3.5	299.00	
LASERSIGHT									Projects a highly visible beam of concentrated laser light onto the target. Adjustable for w.& e. Visible up to 500 yds. at night. For handguns, rifles, shotguns. Uses two standard 9V batteries. From Imatronic Lasersight.
LS45	0	—	—	7.5	—	Int.	8.5	245.00	
LS25	0	—	—	6	3/4	Int.	3.5	270.00	
LS55	0	—	—	7	1	Int.	7	299.00	
LEUPOLD									Constantly centered reticles, choice of Duplex, tapered CPC, Leupold Dot, Crosshair and Dot. CPC and Dot reticles extra. [1]2x and 4x scopes have from 12"-24" of eye relief and are suitable for handguns, top ejection arms and muzzleloaders. [2]Battery life 60 min.; dot size .625" @ 25 yds. Black matte finish Partial listing shown. **Contact Leupold for complete details.**
M8-2X EER[1]	1.7	21.2	12-24	7.9	1	Int.	6.0	257.10	
M8-2X EER Silver[1]	1.7	21.2	12-24	7.9	1	Int.	6.0	278.00	
M8-4X EER[1]	3.7	9	12-24	8.4	1	Int.	7.0	346.40	
M8-4X EER Silver[1]	3.7	9	12-24	8.4	1	Int.	7.0	346.40	
Vari-X 2.5-8 EER	2.5-8.0	13-4.3	11.7-12	9.7	1	Int.	10.9	521.40	
Laser									
LaserLight[7]	—	—	—	1.18	NA	Int.	.5	258.90	
NIKON									Super multi-coated lenses and blackening of all internal metal parts for maximum light gathering capability; positive ¼-MOA; fogproof; waterproof; shockproof; luster and matte finish. From Nikon, Inc.
1.5-4.5x24 EER	1.5-4.4	13.7-5.8	24-18	8.9	1	Int.	9.3	387.00	
2x20 EER	2	22	26.4	8.1	1	Int.	6.3	234.00	
OAKSHORE ELECTRONICS									[1]Variable intensity red dot appears in center of the duplex crosshair. Waterproof; nitrogen filled; coated lenses; ½-MOA dot at 100 yds. From Oakshore Electronic Sights, Inc.
MicroDOT 1.5-4.5x LER[1]	1.5-4.5	14.9-6.9	12-24	9	1	Int.	10	199.00	
PENTAX									Multi-coated lenses, fogproof, waterproof, nitrogen-filled. Penta-Plex reticle. Click ⅓-½-MOA adjustments. Matte finish **$20.00** extra. [1]Also in matte chrome **$260.00**. [2]Also in matte chrome **$380.00**. [3]Chrome-Matte finish **$390.00**. Imported by Pentax Corp.
Pistol									
2x LER[1]	2	21	10-24	8¾	1	Int.	6.8	230.00	
1.5-4x LER[2]	1.5-4	16-11	11-25	10	1	Int.	11	350.00	
2½-7x[3]	2.5-7	12.0-7.5	11-28	12	1	Int.	12.5	370.00	
REDFIELD									4-Plex reticle is standard. [1]Magnum proof. Specially designed for magnum and auto pistols. Uses Double Dovetail mounts. Also in nickel-plated finish, 2x, **$232.95**, 4x, **$232.95**, 2½-7x, **$310.95**, 2½-7x matte black, **$310.95**. [2]All Golden Five Star scopes come with Butler Creek flip-up lens covers. **Contact Redfield for full data.**
Handgun Scopes									
Golden Five Star 2x[1,2]	2	24	9.5-20	7.88	1	Int.	6	216.95	
Golden Five Star 4x[1,2]	4	75	13-19	8.63	1	Int.	6.1	216.95	
Golden Five Star 2½-7x[1,2]	2½-7	11-3.75	11-26	9.4	1	Int.	9.3	295.95	
SIGHTRON									Red dot sights. All come with haze filter caps, polarized lens, ring mounts, two sunshades, 3-volt lithium battery, Allen wrench. Matte black finish; also avail. with stainless finish. [1]3 MOA dot; also 5 MOA dot (S33-5), 12 MOA dot (S33-12). Avail. with interchangeable dot size— 3-5-12 MOA, (S33-3D) **$369.95**. From Sightron, Inc.
S33-3[1]	1	40	—	5.31	33mm	Int.	5.6	259.95	

CAUTION: PRICES SHOWN ARE SUPPLIED BY THE MANUFACTURER OR IMPORTER. CHECK YOUR LOCAL GUNSHOP.

HANDGUN SCOPES

Maker and Model	Magn.	Field at 100 Yds. (feet)	Eye Relief (in.)	Length (in.)	Tube Dia. (in.)	W&E Adjust-ments	Weight (ozs.)	Price	Other Data
SIMMONS									Only selected models shown. Contact Simmons Outdoor Corp. for complete details.
Gold Medal Handgun									
22002	2.5-7	9.7-4.0	8.9-19.4	9.25	1	Int.	9.0	319.95	
22004	2	3.9	8.6-19.5	7.3	1	Int.	7.4	219.95	
22006	4	8.9	9.8-18.7	9	1	Int.	8.8	249.95	
SWIFT									All Swift scopes have Quadraplex reticles and are fogproof and waterproof. [1]Available in black or silver finish—same price. From Swift Instruments.
Pistol Scopes									
661 4x32	4	90	10-22	9.2	1	Int.	9.5	115.00	
662 2.5x32	2.5	14.3	9-22	8.9	1	Int.	9.3	105.00	
663 2x20[1]	2	18.3	9-21	7.2	1	Int.	8.4	110.00	
TASCO									[1]Electronic dot reticle with rheostat; coated optics; adj. for windage and elevation; waterproof, shockproof, fogproof; Lithium battery; 3x power booster avail.; matte black or matte aluminum finish; dot or T-3 reticle. [2]Also matte aluminum finish. [3]Also with crosshair reticle. [4]Dot size 1.5" at 100 yds.; waterproof. [5]Black matte or stainless finish. [6]Available with 5-min. or 10-min. dot. [7]Available with 10, 15, 20-min. dot. **Contact Tasco for details on complete line.**
World Class Pistol									
PWC2x22[2]	2	25	11-20	8.75	1	Int.	7.3	206.00	
PWC4x28[2]	4	8	12-19	9.45	1	Int.	7.9	252.00	
Propoint									
PDP2[1,2,6]	1	40	—	5	30mm	Int.	5	267.00	
PDP3[1,2,6]	1	52	—	5	30mm	Int.	5	367.00	
PDP4[5,7]	1	82	—	—	45mm	Int.	6.1	458.00	
PB1[3]	3	35	3	5.5	30mm	Int.	6.0	183.00	
PB3	2	30	—	1.25	30mm	Int.	2.6	214.00	
LaserPoint[15]	—	—	—	2	5/8	Int.	.75	435.00	
THOMPSON/CENTER RECOIL PROOF PISTOL SCOPES									[1]Also silver finish, **$325.00** (#8316); with rail mount, black, **$308.95** (#8317); with lighted reticle, black, **$359.50** (#8326); with rail, lighted reticle, black, **$370.75** (#8327). [2]With lighted reticle, **$280.90** (#8322); silver, **$292.10** (#8323); with lighted reticle, rail mount, black, **$292.10** (#8320). From Thompson/Center.
8312 Compact Rail[2]	2.5	15	9-21	7.25	1	Int.	6.6	202.00	
8315 Compact[1]	2.5-7	15-5	8-21	9.25	1	Int.	9.2	297.75	
WILLIAMS									TNT models. From Williams Gunsight Co.
Pistol Scopes									
Twilight 1.5x TNT	1.5	19	18-25	8.2	1	Int.	6.4	157.30	
Twilight 2x TNT	2	17.5	18-25	8.5	1	Int.	6.4	159.64	

Leupold LaserLight

Williams Twilight 1.5x

B-Square Mini-Laser

B-Square Mini-Laser

Aimpont Comp

ADCO MiRage Competitor

Redfield 2½-7x Golden Five Star

CAUTION: PRICES SHOWN ARE SUPPLIED BY THE MANUFACTURER OR IMPORTER. CHECK YOUR LOCAL GUNSHOP.

Maker, Model, Type	Adjust.	Scopes	Price
ACTION ARMS	No	1" split rings	From $12.00
For UZI, Ruger Mk. II, and many other popular handguns. Accept Weaver rings. All allow use of iron sights; some include rings; many in satin stainless finish. **Partial list shown.** From Action Arms.			
AIMPOINT	No	1"	49.95-89.95
Laser Mounts[1]	No	1", 30mm	51.95
Mounts/rings for all Aimpoint sights and 1" scopes. For many popular revolvers, auto pistols, shotguns, military-style rifles/carbines, sporting rifles. Most require no gunsmithing. [1]Mounts Aimpoint Laser-dot below barrel; many popular handguns, military-style rifles. Contact Aimpoint.			
AIMTECH			
Handguns			
AMT Auto Mag II, III	No	1"	56.99-64.95
Auto Mag IV	No	1"	64.95
Astra revolvers	No	1"	63.25
Beretta/Taurus auto	No	1"	63.25
Browning Buck Mark/Challenger II	No	1"	56.99
Browning Hi-Power	No	1"	63.25
Glock 17, 17L, 19, 22, 23	No	1"	63.25
Govt. 45 Auto	No	1"	63.25
Rossi revolvers	No	1"	63.25
Ruger Mk I, Mk II	No	1"	49.95
S&W K,L,N frame	No	1"	63.25
S&W Model 41 Target	No	1"	63.25
S&W Model 52 Target	No	1"	63.25
S&W 45, 9mm autos	No	1"	56.99
S&W 422/622/2206	No	1"	56.99
Taurus revolvers	No	1"	63.25
TZ/CZ/P9 9mm	No	1"	63.25
Mount scopes, lasers, electronic sights using Weaver-style base. All mounts allow use of iron sights; no gunsmithing. Available in satin black or satin stainless finish. **Partial listing shown.** Contact maker for full details. From L&S Technologies, Inc.			
B-SQUARE			
Pistols			
Beretta/Taurus 92/99[4]	—	1"	69.95
Browning Buck Mark[4]	No	1"	49.95
Colt 45 Auto	E only	1"	69.95
Colt Python/MkIV, 4",6",8"[1,4]	E	1"	59.95
Dan Wesson Clamp-On[2,4]	E	1"	59.95
Ruger 22 Auto Mono-Mount[3]	No	1"	59.95
Ruger Single-Six	No	1"	59.95
Ruger Blackhawk, Super B'hwk[5]	W&E	1"	59.95
Ruger GP-100[6]	No	1"	59.95
Ruger Redhawk[5]	W&E	1"	59.95
S&W 422/2206[6]	No	1"	59.95
Taurus 66[6]	No	1"	59.95
S&W K, L, N frame[2,4]	No	1"	59.95
T/C Contender (Dovetail Base)	W&E	1"	39.95
BSL Laser Mounts			
Scope Tube Clamp[7,8,9]	No	—	39.95
45 Auto[7,8,9]	No	—	39.95
SIG P226[7,8,9]	No	—	39.95
Beretta 92F/Taurus PT99[7,8,9]	No	—	39.95
Colt King Cobra, Python, MkV[7,8,9]	No	—	39.95
S&W L Frame[8,9]	No	—	39.95
Browning HP[7,8,9]	No	—	39.95
Glock	No	—	39.95
Star Firestar[7,8,9]	No	—	39.95
Rossi small frame revolver[7,8,9]	No	—	39.95
Taurus 85 revolver[7,8,9]	No	—	39.95
[1]Clamp-on, blue finish; stainless finish $59.95. [2]Blue finish; stainless finish $59.95. [3]Clamp-on, blue; stainless finish $59.95. $79.95. [4]Weaver-style rings. Rings not included with Weaver-type bases; stainless finish add $10. [5]Blue; stainless finish $69.95. [6]Blue; stainless $69.95. [7]Stainless finish add $10. [8]Under-barrel mount, no gunsmithing. [9]Used with B-Square BSL-1 Laser Sight only. Mounts for many shotguns, airguns, military and law enforcement guns also available. **Partial listing of mounts shown here. Contact B-Square for more data.**			
BURRIS			
L.E.R. (LU) Mount Bases[1]	W only	1" split rings	23.95
L.E.R. No Drill-No Tap Bases[1,2,3]	W only	1" split rings	23.95-50.95
[1]Universal dovetail; accept Burris, Universal, Redfield, Leupold rings. For Dan Wesson, S&W, Virginian, Ruger Blackhawk, Win. 94. [2]Selected rings and bases available with matte Safari or silver finish. [3]For S&W K,L,N frames, Colt Python, Dan Wesson with 6" or longer barrels.			

Maker, Model, Type	Adjust.	Scopes	Price
CONETROL			
Pistol Bases, 2 or 3-ring[1]	W only	1" scopes	—
[1]For XP-100, T/C Contender, Colt SAA, Ruger Blackhawk, S&W. Three-ring mount available for T/C Contender and other pistols in Conetrol's three grades.			
HOLDEN			
Ironsighter Handguns[1]	No	1" split rings	33.95-58.95
[1]For 1" dia. extended eye relief scopes.			
KRIS MOUNTS			
One Piece (T)[1]	No	1", 26mm split rings	12.98
[1]Blackhawk revolver. Mounts have oval hole to permit use of iron sights.			
LASER AIM	No	Laser Aim	35.00-59.00
Mounts Laser Aim above or below barrel. Avail. for most popular handguns From Emerging Technologies, Inc.			
LASERSIGHT	No	LS45 only	29.95-149.00
For the LS45 Lasersight. Allows LS45 to be mounted alongside any 1" scope. Universal adapter attaches to any full-length Weaver-type base. For most popular handguns including Python, Desert Eagle, S&W N frame, Colt 45ACP. From Imatronic Lasersight.			
LEUPOLD			
STD Handgun mounts[1]	No	—	57.90
[1]Base and two rings; Casull, Ruger, S&W, T/C; add $5.00 for silver finish.			
MILLETT			
One-Piece Bases[2]	Yes	1"	23.95
Handgun Bases, Rings[1]		1"	34.60-69.15
[1]Two and three-ring sets for Colt Python, Trooper, Diamondback, Peacekeeper, Dan Wesson, Ruger Redhawk, Super Redhawk. [2]Turn-in bases and Weaver-style for most popular rifles and T/C Contender, XP-100 pistols. From Millett Sights.			
OAKSHORE			
Handguns			
Browning Buck Mark	No	1"	29.00
Colt Cobra, Diamondback, Python, 1911	No	1"	38.00-52.00
Ruger 22 Auto, GP100	No	1"	33.00-49.00
S&W N Frame	No	1"	45.00-60.00
S&W 422	No	1"	35.00-38.00
From Oakshore Electronic Sights, Inc.			
REDFIELD			
Three-Ring Pistol System SMP[1]	No	1" split rings (three)	56.95-62.95
[1]Used with MP scopes for: S&W K, L or N frame, XP-100, T/C Contender, Ruger receivers.			
SSK INDUSTRIES			
T'SOB	No	1"	65.00-145.00
Quick Detachable	No	1"	From 160.00
Custom installation using from two to four rings (included). For T/C Contender, most 22 auto pistols, Ruger and other S.A. revolvers, Ruger, Dan Wesson, Colt DA revolvers. Black or white finish. Uses Kimber rings in two- or three-ring sets. In blue or SSK Khrome. For T/C Contender or most popular revolvers. Standard, non-detachable model also available, from **$65.00.**			
SPRINGFIELD, INC.			
Competition—Rings[1]	No	30mm	129.95
Competition—Ringless[2]	No	—	129.95
[1]For red dot sights; 3.0 oz. [2]Weaver-style base; 2.16 oz. Drilling, tapping required. From Springfield, Inc.			
TASCO			
Ruger[2]	No	1", 30mm	31.00-73.00
Desert Eagle Ringmount[1]	No	1", 30mm	64.00-90.00
[1]For Desert Eagle pistols, 22s, air rifles with deep dovetails. [2]Low, high only; for Redhawk and Super; blue or stainless. From Tasco.			

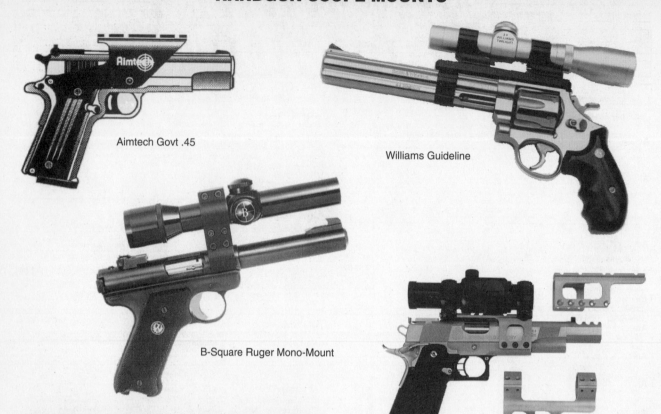

Aimtech Govt .45

Williams Guideline

B-Square Ruger Mono-Mount

Springfield, Inc. Competition mounts

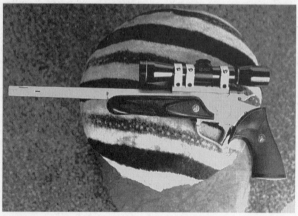

SSK T'SOB three-ring mount

Aimtech Browning Hi-Power

Maker, Model, Type	Adjust.	Scopes	Price
THOMPSON/CENTER			
Contender 9741[1]	No	2½, 4 RP	17.00
S&W 9747[2]	No	Lobo or RP	17.00
Ruger 9748[3]	No	Lobo or RP	17.00
Quick Release System[4]	No	1"	Rings 48.00
			Base 24.50

[1]T/C rail mount scopes; all Contenders except vent. rib. [2]All S&W K and Combat Masterpiece, Hi-Way Patrolman, Outdoorsman, 22 Jet, 45 Target 1955. Requires drilling, tapping. [3]Blackhawk, Super Blackhawk, Super Single-Six. Requires drilling, tapping. [4]For Contender pistol, Carbine, Scout, all M/L long guns. From Thompson/Center.

Maker, Model, Type	Adjust.	Scopes	Price
WEAVER			
Mount Base System[1]			
Blue Finish	No	1"	68.37
Stainless Finish	No	1"	95.63

[1]No drilling, tapping. For Colt Python, Trooper, 357, Officer's Model, Ruger Blackhawk & Super, Mini-14, Security-Six, 22 auto pistols, Single-Six 22, Redhawk, Blackhawk SRM 357, S&W current K, L with adj. sights. From Weaver.

Maker, Model, Type	Adjust.	Scopes	Price
WEIGAND			
1911 PDP4[1]	No	40mm, PDP4	69.95
1911 General Purpose[2]	No		59.95

Maker, Model, Type	Adjust.	Scopes	Price
Weigand (cont.)			
Ruger Mark II[3]	No	—	49.95
3rd Generation[4]	No	—	99.95
Pro Ringless[5]	No	30mm	99.95
Stabilizer I Ringless[6,7]	No	30mm	99.95
Revolver Mount[8]	No		35.50

[1]For Tasco PDP4 and similar 40mm sights. [2]Weaver rail; takes any standard rings. [3]No drilling, tapping. [4]For M1911; grooved top for Weaver-style rings; requires drilling, tapping. [5]Two-piece design; for M1911, P9/EA-9, CZ-75 copies; integral rings; silver alum. finish. [6]Three-piece design; fits M1911, P9/EA-9, TZ, CZ-75 copies; silver alum. finish. [7]Stabilizer II —more forward position; for M1911, McCormick frames. [8]Frame mount. From Weigand Combat Handguns, Inc.

Maker, Model, Type	Adjust.	Scopes	Price
WILLIAMS			
Guideline Handgun[1]	No	1" split rings.	79.95

[1]No drilling, tapping required; heat treated alloy. For Ruger Blackhawk, Super Blackhawk, Redhawk; S&W N frame, M29 with 10⅝" barrel ($79.95); S&W K, L frames; Colt Python, King Cobra; Ruger MkII Bull Barrel; Streamline Top Mount for T/C Contender. From Williams Gunsight Co.

NOTES

(S)—Side Mount (T)—Top Mount; 22mm=.866"; 25.4mm=1.024"; 26.5mm=1.045"; 30mm=1.81"

CAUTION: PRICES SHOW ARE SUPPLIED BY THE MANUFACTURER OR IMPORTER. CHECK YOUR LOCAL GUNSHOP.

PERIODICAL PUBLICATIONS

Action Pursuit Games Magazine (M)
CFW Enterprises, Inc., 4201 W. Vanowen Pl., Burbank, CA 91505. $2.95 single copy U.S., $3.50 Canada. Editor: Randy Kamiya, 818-845-2656. World's leading magazine of paintball sports.

Airgun World
10 Sheet St., Windsor, Berks., SL4 1BG, England. £19.20 (£26.00 overseas) for 12 issues. Monthly magazine catering exclusively to the airgun enthusiast.

Alaska Magazine
Alaska Publishing Properties Inc., 808 E St., Suite 200, Anchorage, AK 99501. $24.00 yr. Hunting, Fishing and Life on the Last Frontier articles of Alaska and western Canada. Outdoors Editor, Ken Marsh.

American Firearms Industry
Nat'l. Assn. of Federally Licensed Firearms Dealers, 2455 E. Sunrise Blvd., Suite 916, Ft. Lauderdale, FL 33304. $25.00 yr. For firearms retailers, distributors and manufacturers.

American Handgunner*
591 Camino de la Reina, Suite 200, San Diego, CA 92108. $16.75 yr. Articles for handgun enthusiasts, competitors, police and hunters.

American Hunter (M)
National Rifle Assn., 11250 Waples Mill Rd., Fairfax, VA 22030 (Same address for both.) Publications Div. $25.00 yr. Wide scope of hunting articles.

American Survival Guide
McMullen and Yee Publishing, Inc., 774 S. Placentia Ave., Placentia, CA 92670-6846. 12 issues $26.95/714-572-2255; FAX: 714-572-1864.

American West*
American West Management Corp., 7000 E. Tanque Verde Rd., Suite #30, Tucson, AZ 85715. $15.00 yr.

Arms Collecting (Q)
Museum Restoration Service, P.O. Box 70, Alexandria Bay, NY 13607-0070. $20.00 yr.; $54.00 3 yrs.; $100.00 5 yrs.

Australian Shooters Journal
Sporting Shooters' Assn. of Australia, Inc., P.O. Box 2066, Kent Town SA 5071, Australia. $45.00 yr. locally; $55.00 yr. overseas surface mail only. Hunting and shooting articles.

The Backwoodsman Magazine
P.O. Box 627, Westcliffe, CO 81252. $15.00 for 6 issues per yr.; $28.00 for 2 yrs.; sample copy $2.50. Subjects include muzzle-loading, woodslore, primitive survival, trapping, homesteading, blackpowder cartridge guns, 19th century how-to.

Black Powder Times
P.O. Box 1131, Stanwood, WA 98292. $15.00 yr.; add $2 per year for Canada, $5 per year other foreign. Tabloid newspaper for blackpowder activities; test reports.

Caliber
GFI-Verlag, Theodor-Heuss Ring 62, 50668 Köln, Germany. For hunters, target shooters and reloaders.

The Caller (Q) (M)
National Wild Turkey Federation, P.O. Box 530, Edgefield, SC 29824. Tabloid newspaper for members; 4 issues per yr.

The Cast Bullet*(M)
Official journal of The Cast Bullet Assn. Director of Membership, 4103 Foxcraft Dr., Traverse City, MI 49684. Annual membership dues $14, includes 6 issues.

Combat Handguns*
Harris Publications, Inc., 1115 Broadway, New York, NY 10010. Single copy $2.95 U.S.A.; $3.25 Canada.

The Derringer Peanut (M)
The National Association of Derringer Collectors, P.O. Box 20572, San Jose, CA 95160. A newsletter dedicated to developing the best derringer information. Write for details.

Deutsches Waffen Journal
Journal-Verlag Schwend GmbH, Postfach 100340, D-74523 Schwäbisch Hall, Germany/0791-404-500; FAX:0791-404-505. DM97.10 yr. (interior); DM114.60 (abroad), postage included. Antique and modern arms and equipment. German text.

The Engraver (M) (Q)
P.O. Box 4365, Estes Park, CO 80517. Mike Dubber, editor. The journal of firearms engraving.

The Field
Astley House, 33 Notting Hill Gate, Notting Hill, London W11 3JQ, England. £35.00 sterling U.S. (approx. $70.00) yr. Hunting and shooting articles, and all country sports.

Field & Stream
Times Mirror Magazines, Two Park Ave., New York, NY 10016. $11.94 yr. Monthly shooting column. Articles on hunting and fishing.

FIRE
Euro-Editions, Boulevard Lambermont 140, B1030 Brussels, Belgium. Belg. Franc 1500 for 6 issues. Arms, shooting, ammunition. French text.

Fur-Fish-Game
A.R. Harding Pub. Co., 2878 E. Main St., Columbus, OH 43209. $15.95 yr. "Gun Rack" column by Don Zutz.

Gray's Sporting Journal
Gray's Sporting Journal, Inc., P.O. Box 1207, Augusta, GA 30903. $35.95 per yr. for 6 consecutive issues. Hunting and fishing journals. Expeditions and Guide Book (Annual Grouse Guide).

Gun List
700 E. State St., Iola, WI 54990. $27.95 yr. (26 issues); $52.00 2 yrs. (52 issues). Indexed market publication for firearms collectors and active shooters; guns, supplies and services.

The Gun Report
World Wide Gun Report, Inc., Box 38, Aledo, IL 61231-0038. $29.95 yr. For the antique and collectable gun dealer and collector.

Gunmaker (M)†
ACGG, P.O. Box 812, Burlington, IA 52601-0812. The journal of custom gunmaking.

The Gunrunner
Div. of Kexco Publ. Co. Ltd., Box 565G, Lethbridge, Alb., Canada T1J 3Z4. $23.00 yr. Monthly newspaper, listing everything from antiques to artillery.

Gun Show Calendar (Q)
700 E. State St., Iola, WI 54990. $12.95 yr. (4 issues). Gun shows listed chronologically by date, and alphabetically by state.

Gun Tests
11 Commerce Blvd., Palm Coast, FL 32142. The consumer resource for the serious shooter. Write for information.

Gun Week†
Second Amendment Foundation, P.O. Box 488, Station C, Buffalo, NY 14209. $32.00 yr. U.S. and possessions; $40.00 yr. other countries. Tabloid paper on guns, hunting, shooting and collecting.

Gun World
Gallant/Charger Publications, Inc., 34249 Camino Capistrano, Capistrano Beach, CA 92624. $20.00 yr. For the hunting, reloading and shooting enthusiast.

Guns & Ammo
Petersen Publishing Co., 6420 Wilshire Blvd., Los Angeles, CA 90048. $21.94 yr. Guns, shooting, and technical articles.

Guns
Guns Magazine, P.O. Box 85201, San Diego, CA 92138. $19.95 yr.; $34.95 2 yrs.; $46.95 3 yrs. In-depth articles on a wide range of guns, shooting equipment and related accessories for gun collectors, hunters and shooters.

Guns and Gear
Creative Arts, Inc., 4901 Northwest 17th Way, Fort Lauderdale, FL 33309/305-772-2788; FAX: 305-351-0484. Single copy $4.95. Covering all aspects of the shooting sports.

Guns Review
Ravenhill Publishing Co. Ltd., Box 35, Standard House, Bonhill St., London EC 2A 4DA, England. £20.00 sterling (approx. U.S. $38 USA & Canada) yr. For collectors and shooters.

Handgunning (Q)
PJS Publications, News Plaza, P.O. Box 1790, Peoria, IL 61656. Cover price $3.95; subscriptions $19.98 for 6 issues. Premier journal for multi-sport handgunners: hunting, reloading, law enforcement, practical pistol and target shooting, and home defense.

Handgun Times
Creative Arts, Inc., 4901 NW 17th Way, Fort Lauderdale, FL 33309/305-772-2788; FAX: 305-351-0484. Single copy $4.95. Technical evaluations, detailed information and testing by handgun experts.

Handloader*
Wolfe Publishing Co., 6471 Airpark Dr., Prescott, AZ 86301. $29.00 yr. The journal of ammunition reloading.

Hunting Horizons
Wolfe Publishing Co., 6471 Airpark Dr., Prescott, AZ 86301. $34.00 yr. Dedicated to the finest pursuit of the hunt.

The Insider Gun News
The Gunpress Publishing Co., 1347 Webster St. NE, Washington, DC 20017. Editor, John D. Aquilino. $50.00 yr. (12 issues). Newsletter by former NRA communications director.

INSIGHTS*
NRA, 11250 Waples Mill Rd., Fairfax, VA 22030. Editor, John E. Robbins. $15.00 yr., which includes NRA junior membership; $10.00 for adult subscriptions (6 issues). Plenty of details for the young hunter and target shooter; emphasizes gun safety, marksmanship training, hunting skills.

International Shooting Sport*/UIT Journal
International Shooting Union (UIT), Bavariaring 21, D-80336 Munich, Germany. Europe: (Deutsche Mark) DM44.00 yr.; outside Europe: DM50.00 yr. (air mail postage included.) For international sport shooting.

Internationales Waffen-Magazin
Habegger-Verlag Zürich, Postfach 9230, CH-8036 Zürich, Switzerland. SF 91.00 (approx. U.S. $61.00) surface mail for 10 issues. Modern and antique arms, self-defense. German text; English summary of contents.

The Journal of the Arms & Armour Society (M)
E.J.B. Greenwood (Hon. Sec.), Field House, Upper Dicker, Hailsham, East Sussex, BN27 3PY, England. £15.00 surface mail; £20.00 airmail sterling only yr. Articles for the historian and collector.

Law and Order
Law and Order Magazine, 1000 Skokie Blvd., Wilmette, IL 60091. $20.00 yr. Articles for law enforcement professionals.

Man At Arms*
P.O. Box 460, Lincoln, RI 02865. $24.00 yr.; $46.00 2 yrs. plus $8.00 for foreign subscribers. The N.R.A. magazine of arms collecting-investing, with excellent articles for the collector of antique arms and militaria.

MAN/MAGNUM
S.A. Man (Pty) Ltd., P.O. Box 35204, Northway, Durban 4065, Republic of South Africa. SA Rand 100.00 for 12 issues. Africa's only publication on hunting, shooting, firearms, bushcraft, knives, etc.

Muzzle Blasts (M)
National Muzzle Loading Rifle Assn., P.O. Box 67, Friendship, IN 47021. $30.00 yr. annual membership. For the blackpowder shooter.

Muzzleloader Magazine*
Rebel Publishing Co., Inc., Dept. Gun, Route 5, Box 347-M, Texarkana, TX 75501. $16.00 U.S.; $19.00 U.S. for foreign subscribers a yr. The publication for blackpowder shooters.

National Defense (M)*
American Defense Preparedness Assn., Two Colonial Place, Suite 400, 2101 Wilson Blvd., Arlington, VA 22201-3061/703-522-1820; FAX: 703-522-1885. $35.00 yr. Articles on both military and civil defense field, including weapons, materials technology, management.

PERIODICAL PUBLICATIONS

National Rifle Assn. Journal (British) (Q)
Natl. Rifle Assn. (BR.), Bisley Camp, Brookwood, Woking, Surrey, England. GU24, OPB. £19.00 Sterling including postage.

National Wildlife*
Natl. Wildlife Fed., 1400 16th St. NW, Washington, DC 20036, $16.00 yr. (6 issues); *International Wildlife*, 6 issues, $16.00 yr. Both, $22.00 yr., includes all membership benefits. Write attn.: Membership Services Dept., for more information.

New Zealand GUNS*
Waitekauri Publishing, P.O. 45, Waikino 3060, New Zealand. $NZ90.00 (6 issues) yr. Covers the hunting and firearms scene in New Zealand.

New Zealand Wildlife (Q)
New Zealand Deerstalkers Assoc., Inc., P.O. Box 6514, Wellington, N.Z. $30.00 (N.Z.). Hunting, shooting and firearms/game research articles.

North American Hunter* (M)
P.O. Box 3401, Minnetonka, MN 55343. $18.00 yr. (7 issues). Articles on all types of North American hunting.

Outdoor Life
Times Mirror Magazines, Two Park Ave., New York, NY 10016. Special 1-yr. subscription, $11.97. Extensive coverage of hunting and shooting. Shooting column by Jim Carmichel.

La Passion des Courteaux (Q)
Phenix Editions, 25 rue Mademoiselle, 75015 Paris, France. French text.

Petersen's HUNTING Magazine
Petersen Publishing Co., 6420 Wilshire Blvd., Los Angeles, CA 90048. $19.94 yr.; Canada $29.34 yr.; foreign countries $29.94 yr. Hunting articles for all game; test reports.

P.I. Magazine
America's Private Investigation Journal, 755 Bronx Dr., Toledo, OH 43609. Chuck Klein, firearms editor with column about handguns.

Point Blank
Citizens Committee for the Right to Keep and Bear Arms (sent to contributors), Liberty Park, 12500 NE 10th Pl., Bellevue, WA 98005

POINTBLANK (M)
Natl. Firearms Assn., Box 4384 Stn. C, Calgary, AB T2T 5N2, Canada. Official publication of the NFA.

The Police Marksman*
6000 E. Shirley Lane, Montgomery, AL 36117. $17.95 yr. For law enforcement personnel.

Police Times (M)
Membership Records, 3801 Biscayne Blvd., Miami, FL 33137.

Popular Mechanics
Hearst Corp., 224 W. 57th St., New York, NY 10019. $15.94 yr. Firearms, camping, outdoor oriented articles.

Safari* (M)
Safari Magazine, 4800 W. Gates Pass Rd., Tucson, AZ 85745/602-620-1220. $30.00 (6 times). The journal of big game hunting, published by Safari Club International. Also publish *Safari Times*, a monthly newspaper, included in price of $30.00 field membership.

Second Amendment Reporter
Second Amendment Foundation, James Madison Bldg., 12500 NE 10th Pl., Bellevue, WA 98005. $15.00 yr. (non-contributors).

Shooting Industry
Publisher's Dev. Corp., 591 Camino de la Reina, Suite 200, San Diego, CA 92108. $50.00 yr. To the trade $25.00.

Shooting Sports Retailer*
SSR Publishing, Inc., P.O. Box 25, Cuba, NY 14727-0025/716-968-3858. 6 issues yr. Free to qualifying retailers, wholesalers, manufacturers, distributors; $30 annually for all other subscribers; $35 for foreign subscriptions; single copy $5.

Shooting Sports USA
National Rifle Assn. of America, 11250 Waples Mill Road, Fairfax, VA 22030. Annual subscriptions for NRA members are $5 for classified shooters and $10 for non-classified shooters. Non-NRA member subscriptions are $15. Covering events, techniques and personalities in competitive shooting.

The Shooting Times & Country Magazine (England)†
Astley House, 33 Notting Hill Gate, Notting Hill, London W11 3JQ, England. £65 (approx. $98.00) yr.; £79 yr. overseas (52 issues). Game shooting, wild fowling, hunting, game fishing and firearms articles. Britain's best selling field sports magazine.

Shooting Times
PJS Publications, News Plaza, P.O. Box 1790, Peoria, IL 61656. $21.98 yr. Guns, shooting, reloading; articles on every gun activity.

The Shotgun News‡
Snell Publishing Co., Box 669, Hastings, NE 68902. $20.00 yr.; all other countries $100.00 yr. Sample copy $3.00. Gun ads of all kinds.

SHOT Business
Flintlock Ridge Office Center, 11 Mile Hill Rd., Newtown, CT 06470-2359/203-426-1320; FAX: 203-426-1087. For the shooting, hunting and outdoor trade retailer.

The Sixgunner (M)
Handgun Hunters International, P.O. Box 357, MAG, Bloomingdale, OH 43910

Soldier of Fortune
Subscription Dept., P.O. Box 348, Mt. Morris, IL 61054. $24.95 yr.; $34.95 Canada; $45.95 foreign.

SPG Lubricants/BP Cartridge (Q)
SPG Lubricant, P.O. Box 761, Livingston, MT 59047. $13 yr. For the blackpowder cartridge enthusiast.

Sporting Goods Business
Miller Freeman, Inc., 1515 Broadway, New York, NY 10036. Trade journal.

Sporting Goods Dealer
Two Park Ave., New York, NY 10016. $100.00 yr. Sporting goods trade journal.

Sporting Gun
Bretton Court, Bretton, Peterborough PE3 8DZ, England. £27.00 (approx. U.S. $36.00), airmail £35.50 yr. For the game and clay enthusiasts.

Sports Afield
The Hearst Corp., 250 W. 55th St., New York, NY 10019. $13.97 yr. Tom Gresham on firearms, ammunition; Grits Gresham on shooting and Thomas McIntyre on hunting.

The Squirrel Hunter
P.O. Box 368, Chireno, TX 75937. $14.00 yr. Articles about squirrel hunting.

TACARMI
Via E. De Amicis, 25; 20123 Milano, Italy. $120.00 yr. approx. Antique and modern guns. (Italian text.)

The U.S. Handgunner* (M)
U.S. Revolver Assn., 40 Larchmont Ave., Taunton, MA 02780. $10.00 yr. General handgun and competition articles. Bi-monthly sent to members.

U.S. Airgun Magazine
2603 Rollingbrook, Benton, AR 72015. Cover the sport from hunting, 10-meter, field target and collecting. Write for details.

The Varmint Hunter Magazine (Q)
The Varmint Hunters Assn., Box 759, Pierre, SD 57501/800-528-4868. $24.00 yr.

Waffenmarkt-Intern
GFI-Verlag, Theodor-Heuss Ring 62, 50668 Köln, Germany. Only for gunsmiths, licensed firearms dealers and their suppliers in Germany, Austria and Switzerland.

Wild Sheep (M) (Q)
Foundation for North American Wild Sheep, 720 Allen Ave., Cody, WY 82414. Official journal of the foundation.

Women & Guns
P.O. Box 488, Sta. C, Buffalo, NY 14209. $24.00 yr. U.S.; (12 issues). Only magazine edited by and for women gun owners.

---

*Published bi-monthly †Published weekly ‡Published three times per month. All others are published monthly.
M=Membership requirements; write for details. Q=Published Quarterly.

HANDGUNNER'S LIBRARY

ABC's of Reloading, 5th Edition, by Dean A. Grennell, DBI Books, Inc., Northbrook, IL, 1993. 288 pp., illus. Paper covers. $18.95.

The definitive guide to every facet of cartridge and shotshell reloading.

*Air Gun Digest, 3rd Edition, by J.I. Galan, DBI Books, Inc., Northbrook, IL, 1995. 288 pp., illus. Paper covers. (February '95)

Everything from A to Z on air gun history, trends and technology.

America's Great Gunmakers, by Wayne van Zwoll, Stoeger Publishing Co., So. Hackensack, NJ, 1992. 288 pp., illus. Paper covers. $16.95.

This book traces in great detail the evolution of guns and ammunition in America and the men who formed the companies that produced them.

The American Cartridge, by Charles R. Suydam, Borden Publishing Co., Alhambra, CA, 1986. 184 pp., illus. $12.50.

An illustrated study of the rimfire cartridge in the United States.

Ammunition Making, by George E. Frost, National Rifle Association of America, Washington, D.C., 1990. 160 pp., illus. Paper covers. $17.95.

Reflects the perspective of "an insider" with half a century's experience in successful management of ammunition manufacturing operations.

Antique Guns: The Collector's Guide, by John E. Traister, Stoeger Publishing Co., So. Hackensack, NJ, 1988. 320 pp., illus. Paper covers. $16.95.

Covers all categories, history, craftsmanship, firearms components, gunmakers and values on the gun-trading market.

Arms & Accoutrements of the Mounted Police 1873-1973, by Roger F. Phillips and Donald J. Klancher, Museum Restoration Service, Ont., Canada, 1982. 224 pp., illus. $49.95.

A definitive history of the revolvers, rifles, machine guns, cannons, ammunition, swords, etc. used by the NWMP, the RNWMP and the RCMP during the first 100 years of the Force.

Arms Makers of Maryland, by Daniel D. Hartzler, George Shumway, York, PA, 1975. 200 pp., illus. $45.00.

A thorough study of the gunsmiths of Maryland who worked during the late 18th and early 19th centuries.

The Art of Engraving, by James B. Meek, F. Brownell & Son, Montezuma, IA, 1973. 196 pp., illus. $33.95.

A complete, authoritative, imaginative and detailed study in training for gun engraving. The first book of its kind—and a great one.

*Artistry in Arms: The Guns of Smith & Wesson, by Roy G. Jinks, Smith & Wesson, Springfield, MA, 1991. 85 pp., illus. Paper covers. $19.95.

Catalog of the Smith & Wesson International Museum Tour 1991-1995 organized by the Connecticut Valley Historical Museum and Springfield Library and Museum Association.

Artistry in Arms, The R. W. Norton Gallery, Shreveport, LA, 1970. 42 pp., illus. Paper covers. $9.95.

The art of gunsmithing and engraving.

Astra Automatic Pistols, by Leonardo M. Antaris, FIRAC Publishing Co., Sterling, CO, 1989. 248 pp., illus. $45.00.

Charts, tables, serial ranges, etc. The definitive work on Astra pistols.

Basic Handloading, by George C. Nonte, Jr., Outdoor Life Books, New York, NY, 1982. 192 pp., illus. Paper covers. $6.95.

How to produce high-quality ammunition using the safest, most efficient methods known.

Beginner's Guide to Guns and Shooting, Revised Edition, by Clair F. Rees, DBI Books, Inc., Northbrook, IL, 1988. 224 pp., illus. Paper covers. $15.95.

The "how to" book for beginning shooters. The perfect teaching tool for America's youth, the future of our sport, for novices of any age.

Beretta Automatic Pistols, by J.B. Wood, Stackpole Books, Harrisburg, PA, 1985. 192 pp., illus. $24.95.

Only English-language book devoted entirely to the Beretta line. Includes all important models.

Black Powder Hobby Gunsmithing, by Sam Fadala and Dale Storey, DBI Books, Inc., Northbrook, IL., 1994. 256 pp., illus. Paper covers. $17.95.

A how-to guide for gunsmithing blackpowder pistols, rifles and shotguns from two men at the top of their respective fields.

Black Powder Loading Manual, Revised Edition, by Sam Fadala, DBI Books, Inc., Northbrook, IL, 1991. 320 pp., illus. Paper covers. $16.95.

Revised and expanded edition of this landmark loading book first published in 1982. Covers 600 loads for 120 of the most popular blackpowder rifles, handguns and shotguns.

*The Blackpowder Notebook, by Sam Fadala, Wolfe Publishing Co., Prescott, AZ, 1994. 212 pp., illus. $22.50.

For anyone interested in shooting muzzleloaders, this book will help improve scores and obtain accuracy and reliability.

Blacksmith Guide to Ruger Flat-top & Super Blackhawks, by H.W. Ross, Jr., Blacksmith Corp., Chino Valley, AZ, 1990. 96 pp., illus. Paper covers. $9.95.

A key source on the extensively collected Ruger Blackhawk revolvers.

Blue Book of Gun Values, 14th edition, compiled by S.P. Fjestad, Investment Rarities, Inc., Minneapolis, MN, 1993. 621 pp., illus. Soft covers. $24.95.

Uses percentage grading system to determine each gun's value based on its unique condition.

Blue Steel and Gun Leather, by John Bianchi, Beinfeld Publishing, Inc., No. Hollywood, CA, 1978. 200 pp., illus. $19.95.

A complete and comprehensive review of holster uses plus an examination of available products on today's market.

*Boarders Away, Volume II: Firearms of the Age of Fighting Sail, by William Gilkerson, Andrew Mowbray, Inc. Publishers, Lincoln, RI, 1993. 331 pp., illus. $65.00.

Covers the pistols, muskets, combustibles and small cannon used aboard American and European fighting ships, 1626-1826.

*British Small Arms Ammunition, 1864-1938, by Peter Labett, Armory Publications, Oceanside, CA, 1994. 352 pp., illus. $75.00.

The military side of the story illustrating the rifles, carbines, machine guns, revolvers and automatic pistols and their ammunition, experimental and adopted, from 577 Snider to modern times.

Browning Dates of Manufacture, compiled by George Madis, Art and Reference House, Brownsboro, TX, 1989. 48 pp. $5.00.

Gives the date codes and product codes for all models from 1824 to the present.

Browning Hi-Power Pistols, Desert Publications, Cornville, AZ, 1982. 20 pp., illus. Paper covers. $9.00.

Covers all facets of the various military and civilian models of the Browning Hi-Power pistol.

The Bullet Swage Manual. MDSU/I, by Ted Smith, Corbin Manufacturing and Supply Co., White City, OR, 1988. 45 pp., illus. Paper covers. $10.00.

A book that fills the need for information on bullet swaging.

Burning Powder, compiled by Major D.B. Wesson, Wolfe Publishing Company, Prescott, AZ, 1992. 110 pp. Soft cover. $10.95.

A rare booklet from 1932 for Smith & Wesson collectors.

Cartridge Case Measurements, by Dr. Arthur J. Mack, Amrex Enterprises, Vienna, VA, 1990. 300 pp., illus. Paper covers. $49.95.

Lists over 5000 cartridges of all kinds. Gives basic measurements (rim, head, shoulder, neck, length, plus bullet diameter) in both English and Metric. Hundreds of experimental cartridges and wildcats.

Cartridges of the World, 7th Edition, by Frank Barnes, edited by Mike Bussard, DBI Books, Inc., Northbrook, IL, 1993. 464 pp., illus. Paper covers. $21.95

Completely revised edition of the general purpose reference work for which collectors, police, scientists and laymen reach first for answers to cartridge identification questions. (September '93)

Cast Bullets, by Col. E. H. Harrison, A publication of the National Rifle Association of America, Washington, DC, 1979. 144 pp., illus. Paper covers. $12.95.

An authoritative guide to bullet casting techniques and ballistics.

Civil War Pistols, by John D. McAulay, Andrew Mowbray Inc., Lincoln, RI, 1992. 166 pp., illus. $38.50.

A survey of the handguns used during the American Civil War.

Colt Automatic Pistols, by Donald B. Bady, Borden Publ. Co., Alhambra, CA, 1974, 368 pp., illus. $19.95.

The rev. and enlarged ed. of a key work on a fascinating subject. Complete information on every automatic marked with Colt's name.

The Colt Double Action Revolvers: A Shop Manual, Volume 1, by Jerry Kuhnhausen, VSP Publishers, McCall, ID, 1988. 224 pp., illus. Paper covers. $22.95.

Covers D, E, and I frames.

The Colt Double Action Revolvers: A Shop Manual, Volume 2, by Jerry Kuhnhausen, VSP Publishers, McCall, ID, 1988. 156 pp., illus. Paper covers. $17.95.

Covers J, V, and AA models.

The Colt .45 Auto Pistol, compiled from U.S. War Dept. Technical Manuals, and reprinted by Desert Publications, Cornville, AZ, 1978. 80 pp., illus. Paper covers. $9.95.

Covers every facet of this famous pistol from mechanical training, manual of arms, disassembly, repair and replacement of parts.

The Colt .45 Automatic Shop Manual, by Jerry Kuhnhausen, VSP Publishers, McCall, ID, 1987. 200 pp., illus. Paper covers. $19.95.

Covers repairing, accurizing, trigger/sear work, action tuning, springs, bushings, rebarreling, and custom .45 modification.

Colt 45 Service Pistol Models of 1911 and 1911A1, by Charles W. Clawson, Charles W. Clawson, Fort Wayne, IN, 1991. 429 pp., illus. $65.00.

Complete military history, development and production 1900 through 1945 plus foreign pistols, gallery pistols, revolvers, cartridge development, and much more.

Colt Heritage, by R.L. Wilson, Simon & Schuster, 1979. 358 pp., illus. $75.00.

The official history of Colt firearms 1836 to the present.

Colt Peacemaker British Model, by Keith Cochran, Cochran Publishing Co., Rapid City, SD, 1989. 160 pp., illus. $35.00.

Covers those revolvers Colt squeezed in while completing a large order of revolvers for the U.S. Cavalry in early 1874, to those magnificent cased target revolvers used in the pistol competitions at Bisley Commons in the 1890s.

Colt Peacemaker Encyclopedia, by Keith Cochran, Keith Cochran, Rapid City, SD, 1986. 434 pp., illus. $59.95.

A must book for the Peacemaker collector.

Colt Peacemaker Encyclopedia, Volume 2, by Keith Cochran, Cochran Publishing Co., SD, 1992. 416 pp., illus. $60.00.

Included in this volume are extensive notes on engraved, inscribed, historical and noted revolvers, as well as those revolvers used by outlaws, lawmen, movie and television stars.

Colt Peacemaker Yearly Variations, by Keith Cochran, Keith Cochran, Rapid City, SD, 1987. 96 pp., illus. $17.95.

A definitive, precise listing for each year the Peacemaker was manufactured from 1873-1940.

Colt Pistols 1836-1976, by R.L. Wilson in association with R.E. Hable, Jackson Arms, Dallas, TX, 1976. 380 pp., illus. $125.00.

A magnificently illustrated book in full color featuring Colt firearms from the famous Hable collection.

Colt Revolvers and the Tower of London, by Joseph G. Rosa, Royal Armouries of the Tower of London, London, England, 1988. 72 pp., illus. Soft covers. $15.00.

Details the story of Colt in London through the early cartridge period.

Colt Revolvers and the U.S. Navy 1865-1889, by C. Kenneth Moore, Dorrance and Co., Bryn Mawr, PA, 1987. 140 pp., illus. $29.95.

The Navy's use of all Colt handguns and other revolvers during this era of change.

Colt Single Action Army Revolvers and the London Agency, by C. Kenneth Moore, Andrew Mowbray Publishers, Lincoln, RI, 1990. 144 pp., illus. $35.00.

Drawing on vast documentary sources, this work chronicles the relationship between the London Agency and the Hartford home office.

The Colt U.S. General Officers' Pistols, by Horace Greeley IV, Andrew Mowbray Inc., Lincoln, RI, 1990. 199 pp., illus. $38.00.

These unique weapons, issued as a badge of rank to General Officers in the U.S. Army from WWII onward, remain highly personal artifacts of the military leaders who carried them. Includes serial numbers and dates of issue.

Colt's Dates of Manufacture 1837-1978, by R.L. Wilson, published by Maurie Albert, Coburg, Australia; N.A. distributor I.D.S.A. Books, Hamilton, OH, 1983. 61 pp. $10.00.

An invaluable pocket guide to the dates of manufacture of Colt firearms up to 1978.

Colt's 100th Anniversary Firearms Manual 1836-1936: A Century of Achievement, Wolfe Publishing Co., Prescott, AZ, 1992. 100 pp., illus. Paper covers. $12.95.

Originally published by the Colt Patent Firearms Co., this booklet covers the history, manufacturing procedures and the guns of the first 100 years of the genius of Samuel Colt.

Colt's SAA Post War Models, George Garton, revised edition, Gun Room Press, Highland Park, NJ, 1987. 166 pp., illus. $29.95.

The complete facts on Colt's famous post war single action army revolver using factory records to cover types, calibers, production numbers and many variations of this popular firearm.

The Colt Whitneyville-Walker Pistol, by Lt. Col. Robert D. Whittington, Brownlee Books, Hooks, TX, 1984. 96 pp., illus. Limited edition. $20.00.

A study of this fascinating pistol and associated characters 1846-1851.

Combat Handgunnery, 3nd Edition, The Gun Digest Book of by Chuck Karwan, DBI Books, Inc., Northbrook, IL, 1992. 256 pp., illus. Paper covers. $16.95.

This all-new edition looks at real world combat handgunnery from three different perspectives—military, police and civilian.

Combat Pistols, by Terry Gander, Sterling Publishing Co., Inc., 1991. Paper covers. $9.95.

The world's finest and deadliest pistols are shown close-up, with detailed specifications, muzzle velocity, rate of fire, ammunition, etc.

*Combat Raceguns: The World's Best Custom Pistols, by J.M. Ramos, Paladin Press, Boulder, CO, 1994. 168 pp., illus. Paper covers. $25.00.

Learn how to put together your own precision combat racegun with the best compensators, frames, controls, sights and custom accessories.

Competitive Pistol Shooting, by Laslo Antal, A&C Black, Cambs, England, 1989. 176 pp., illus. Soft covers. $24.00

Covers free pistol, air pistol, rapid fire, etc.

Competitive Shooting, by A.A. Yuryev, introduction by Gary L. Anderson, NRA Books, The National Rifle Assoc. of America, Wash., DC, 1985. 399 pp., illus. $29.95.

A unique encyclopedia of competitive rifle and pistol shooting.

The Complete Book of Combat Handgunning, by Chuck Taylor, Desert Publications, Cornville, AZ, 1982. 168 pp., illus. Paper covers. $16.95.

Covers virtually every aspect of combat handgunning.

Complete Book of Shooting: Rifles, Shotguns, Handguns, by Jack O'Connor, Stackpole Books, Harrisburg, PA, 1983. 392 pp., illus. $24.95.

A thorough guide to each area of the sport, appealing to those with a new or ongoing interest in shooting.

The Complete Handloader, by John Wootters, Stackpole Books, Harrisburg, PA, 1989. 224 pp., illus. $29.95.

One of the deans of gun writers shares a lifetime of experience and recommended procedures on handloading for rifles, handguns, and shotguns.

HANDGUNNER'S LIBRARY

The Complete Handloader for Rifles, Handguns and Shotguns, by John Wootters, Stackpole Books, Harrisburg, PA, 1988. 214 pp., $29.95.

Loading-bench know-how.

The Complete Metal Finishing Book, by Harold Hoffman, H&P Publishers, San Angelo, TX, 1992. 364 pp., illus. Paper covers. $28.95.

Instructions for the different metal finishing operations that the normal craftsman or shop will use. These are primarily firearm related.

Compliments of Col. Ruger: A Study of Factory Engraved Single Action Revolvers, by John C. Dougan, Taylor Publishing Co., El Paso, TX, 1992. 238 pp., illus. $46.50.

Clearly detailed black and white photographs and a precise text present an accurate history of the Sturm, Ruger & Co. single-action revolver engraving project.

Confederate Revolvers, by William A. Gary, Taylor Publishing Co., Dallas, TX, 1987. 174 pp., illus. $45.00.

Comprehensive work on the rarest of Confederate weapons.

Cowboy Collectibles and Western Memorabilia, by Bob Bell and Edward Vebell, Schiffer Publishing, Atglen, PA, 1992. 160 pp., illus. Paper covers. $29.95.

The exciting era of the cowboy and the wild west collectibles including rifles, pistols, gun rigs, etc.

The Custom Government Model Pistol, by Layne Simpson, Wolfe Publishing Co., Prescott, AZ, 1992. 639 pp., illus. $24.50.

This book is about one of the world's greatest firearms and the things pistolsmiths do to make it even better.

The CZ-75 Family: The Ultimate Combat Handgun, by J.M. Ramos, Paladin Press, Boulder, CO, 1990. 100 pp., illus. Soft covers. $16.00.

And in-depth discussion of the early-and-late model CZ-75s, as well as the many newest additions to the Czech pistol family.

The Deringer in America, Volume 1, The Percussion Period, by R.L. Wilson and L.D. Eberhart, Andrew Mowbray Inc., Lincoln, RI, 1985. 271 pp., illus. $48.00.

A long awaited book on the American percussion deringer.

*****The Deringer in America, Volume 2, The Cartridge Period,** by L.D. Eberhart and R.L. Wilson, Andrew Mowbray Inc., Publishers, Lincoln, RI, 1993. 284 pp., illus. $65.00.

Comprehensive coverage of cartridge deringers organized alphabetically by maker. Includes all types known by the authors to have been offered to the American market.

Encyclopedia of Modern Firearms, Vol. 1, compiled and publ. by Bob Brownell, Montezuma, IA, 1959. 1057 pp. plus index, illus. $60.00. Dist. By Bob Brownell, Montezuma, IA 50171.

Massive accumulation of basic information of nearly all modern arms pertaining to "parts and assembly." Replete with arms photographs, exploded drawings, manufacturers' lists of parts, etc.

Encyclopedia of Ruger Rimfire Semi-Automatic Pistols: 1949-1992, by Chad Hiddleson, Krause Publications, Iola, WI, 1993. 250 pp., illus. $29.95.

Covers all physical aspects of Ruger 22-caliber pistols including important features such as boxes, grips, muzzlebrakes, instruction manuals, serial numbers, etc.

English Pistols: The Armories of H.M. Tower of London Collection, by Howard L. Blackmore, Arms and Armour Press, London, England, 1985. 64 pp., illus. Soft covers. $14.95.

All the pistols described are from this famed collection.

Experiments of a Handgunner, by Walter Roper, Wolfe Publishing Co., Prescott, AZ, 1989. 202 pp., illus. $37.00.

A limited edition reprint. A listing of experiments with functioning parts of handguns, with targets, stocks, rests, handloading, etc.

Exploded Handgun Drawings, The Gun Digest Book of, edited by Harold A. Murtz, DBI Books, Inc., Northbrook, IL. 1992. 512 pp., illus. Paper covers. $19.95.

Exploded or isometric drawings for 494 of the most popular handguns.

Fast and Fancy Revolver Shooting, by Ed. McGivern, Anniversary Edition, Winchester Press, Piscataway, NJ, 1984. 484 pp., illus. $18.95.

A fascinating volume, packed with handgun lore and solid information by the acknowledged dean of revolver shooters.

'51 Colt Navies, by Nathan L. Swayze, The Gun Room Press, Highland Park, NJ, 1993. 243 pp., illus. $59.95.

The Model 1851 Colt Navy, its variations and markings.

Firearms Assembly/Disassembly, Part I: Automatic Pistols, Revised Edition, The Gun Digest Book of, by J.B. Wood, DBI Books, Inc., Northbrook, IL, 1990. 480 pp., illus. Soft covers. $18.95.

Covers 58 popular autoloading pistols plus nearly 200 variants of those models integrated into the text and completely cross-referenced in the index.

Firearms Assembly/Disassembly Part II: Revolvers, Revised Edition, The Gun Digest Book of, by J.B. Wood, DBI Books, Inc., Northbrook, IL, 1990. 480 pp., illus. Soft covers. $18.95.

Covers 49 popular revolvers plus 130 variants. The most comprehensive and professional presentation available to either hobbyist or gunsmith.

Firearms Assembly 4: The NRA Guide to Pistols and Revolvers, NRA Books, Wash., DC, 1980. 253 pp., illus. Paper covers. $13.95.

Text and illustrations explaining the takedown of 124 pistol and revolver models, domestic and foreign.

Firearms Engraving as Decorative Art, by Dr. Fredric A. Harris, Barbara R. Harris, Seattle, WA, 1989. 172 pp., illus. $110.00.

The origin of American firearms engraving motifs in the decorative art of the Middle East. Illustrated with magnificent color photographs.

Firearms Pressure Factors, by Dr. Lloyd Brownell, Wolfe Publishing Co., Prescott, AZ, 1990. 200 pp., illus. $14.00.

The only book available devoted entirely to firearms and pressure. Contains chapters on secondary explosion effect, modern pressure measuring techniques in revolvers and rifles, and Dr. Brownell's series on pressure factors.

*****Flayderman's Guide to Antique American Firearms...and Their Values, 6th Edition,** by Norm Flayderman, DBI Books, Inc., Northbrook, IL, 1994. 624 pp., illus. Paper covers. $29.95.

Updated edition of this bible of the antique gun field. (September, 1994)

.45 ACP Super Guns, by J.M. Ramos, Paladin Press, Boulder, CO, 1991. 144 pp., illus. Paper covers. $20.00.

Modified .45 automatic pistols for competition, hunting and personal defense.

The .45, The Gun Digest Book of by Dean A. Grennell, DBI Books, Inc., Northbrook, IL, 1989. 256 pp., illus. Paper covers. $16.95.

Definitive work on one of America's favorite calibers.

German Military Pistols 1904-1930, by Fred A. Datig, Michael Zomber Co., Culver City, CA, 1990. 88 pp., illus. Paper covers. $14.95.

Monograph #2 in the series "The Luger Pistol Its History & Development from 1893-1945."

German Military Rifles and Machine Pistols, 1871-1945, by Hans Dieter Gotz, Schiffer Publishing Co., West Chester, PA, 1990. 245 pp., illus. $35.00.

This book portrays in words and pictures the development of the modern German weapons and their ammunition including the scarcely known experimental types.

German Pistols and Holsters 1934-1945, Vol. 2, by Robert Whittington, Brownlee Books, Hooks, TX, 1990. 312 pp., illus. $55.00.

This volume addresses pistols only: military (Heer, Luftwaffe, Kriegsmarine & Waffen-SS), captured, commercial, police, NSDAP and government.

German Pistols and Holsters, 1934-1945, Volume 4, by Lt. Col. Robert D. Whittington, 3rd, U.S.A.R., Brownlee Books, Hooks, TX, 1991. 208 pp. $30.00.

Pistols and holsters issued in 412 selected armed forces, army and Waffen-SS units including information on personnel, other weapons and transportation.

*****Glock: The New Wave in Combat Handguns,** by Peter Alan Kasler, Paladin Press, Boulder, CO, 1993. 304 pp., illus. $25.00.

In this book the author debunks the myths that surround what is the most innovative handgun to be introduced in some time.

*****Great Combat Handguns,** by Leroy Thompson and Rene Smeets, Sterling Publishing Co., New York, NY, 1993. 256 pp., illus. $29.95.

Fully revised, updated and newly designed edition of the successful classic in handgun use and reference.

Guide to Ruger Single Action Revolvers Production Dates, 1953-73, by John C. Dougan, Blacksmith Corp., Chino Valley, AZ, 1991. 22 pp., illus. Paper covers. $9.95.

A unique pocket-sized handbook providing production information for the popular Ruger single-action revolvers manufactured during the first 20 years.

Gun Collecting, by Geoffrey Boothroyd, Sportsman's Press, London, 1989. 208 pp., illus. $29.95.

The most comprehensive list of 19th century British gunmakers and gunsmiths ever published.

Gun Collector's Digest, 5th Edition, edited by Joseph J. Schroeder, DBI Books, Inc., Northbrook, IL, 1989. 224 pp., illus. Paper covers. $16.95.

The latest edition of this sought-after series.

*Gun Digest, 1995, 49th Edition, edited by Ken Warner, DBI Books, Inc., Northbrook, IL 1994. 544 pp., illus. Paper covers. $21.95.

All-new edition of the world's best selling gun book; the only one to make the *USA Today* list of best-selling sports books.

*Gun Digest Treasury, 7th Edition, edited by Harold A. Murtz, DBI Books, Inc., Northbrook, IL, 1994. 320 pp., illus. Paper covers. $16.95.

A collection of some of the most interesting articles which have appeared in Gun Digest over its first 45 years.

*Guns Illustrated, 1995, 27th Edition, edited by Harold A. Murtz, DBI Books, Inc., Northbrook, IL, 1994. 336 pp., illus. Paper covers. $19.95.

Truly the Journal of Gun Buffs, this all-new edition consists of articles of interest to every shooter as well as a complete catalog of all U.S. and imported firearms with latest specs and prices.

Guns of the Wild West, by George Markham, Arms & Armour Press, London, England, 1991. 160 pp., illus. $19.95.

The handguns, longarms and shotguns of the Gold Rush, the American Civil War, and the Armed Forces.

*Guns of the Wild West, by George Markham, Sterling Publishing Co., New York, NY, 1993. 160 pp., illus. Paper covers. $19.95.

Firearms of the American Frontier, 1849-1917.

Gun Talk, edited by Dave Moreton, Winchester Press, Piscataway, NJ, 1973. 256 pp., illus. $9.95.

A treasury of original writing by the top gun writers and editors in America. Practical advice about every aspect of the shooting sports.

Gun Trader's Guide, 16th Edition, published by Stoeger Publishing Co., S. Hackensack, NJ, 1993. 528 pp., illus. Paper covers. $18.95.

Complete guide to identification of modern firearms with current values.

The Gunfighter, Man or Myth? by Joseph G. Rosa, Oklahoma Press, Norman, OK, 1969. 229 pp., illus. (including weapons). Paper covers. $12.95.

A well-documented work on gunfights and gunfighters of the West and elsewhere. Great treat for all gunfighter buffs.

Gunproof Your Children/Handgun Primer, by Massad Ayoob, Police Bookshelf, Concord, NH, 1989. Paper covers. $4.95.

Two books in one. The first, keeping children safe from unauthorized guns in their hands; the second, a compact introduction to handgun safety.

Guns & Shooting: A Selected Bibliography, by Ray Riling, Ray Riling Arms Books Co., Phila., PA, 1982. 434 pp., illus. Limited, numbered edition. $75.

A limited edition of this superb bibliographical work, the only modern listing of books devoted to guns and shooting.

Guns of the First World War, Rifle, Handguns and Ammunition from the Text Book of Small Arms, 1909, edited by John Walter, Presidio Press, Novato, CA, 1991. $30.00.

Details of the Austro-Hung. Mann., French Lebels, German Mausers, U.S. Springfields, etc.

Guns of the Reich, by George Markham, Arms & Armour Press, London, England, 1989. 175 pp., illus. $24.95.

The pistols, rifles, submachine guns, machineguns and support weapons of the German armed forces, 1939-1945.

Gunshot Wounds, by Vincent J.M. DiMaio, M.D., Elsevier Science Publishing Co., New York, NY, 1985. 331 pp., illus. $70.00.

Practical aspects of firearms, ballistics, and forensic techniques.

Gunsmith Kinks, by F.R. (Bob) Brownell, F. Brownell & Son, Montezuma, IA, 1st ed., 1969. 496 pp., well illus. $18.95.

A widely useful accumulation of shop kinks, short cuts, techniques and pertinent comments by practicing gunsmiths from all over the world.

Gunsmith Kinks 2, by Bob Brownell, F. Brownell & Son, Publishers, Montezuma, IA, 1983. 496 pp., illus. $18.95.

A collection of gunsmithing knowledge, shop kinks, new and old techniques, shortcuts and general know-how straight from those who do them best—the gunsmiths.

*Gunsmith Kinks 3, edited by Frank Brownell, Brownells Inc., Montezuma, IA, 1993. 504 pp., illus. $19.95.

Tricks, knacks and "kinks" by professional gunsmiths and gun tinkerers. Hundreds of valuable ideas are given in this expanded volume.

The Gunsmith's Manual, by J.P. Stelle and Wm. B. Harrison, The Gun Room Press, Highland Park, NJ, 1982. 376 pp., illus. $19.95.

For the gunsmith in all branches of the trade.

Gunsmithing, by Roy F. Dunlap, Stackpole Books, Harrisburg, PA, 1990. 742 pp., illus. $29.95.

A manual of firearm design, construction, alteration and remodeling. For amateur and professional gunsmiths and users of modern firearms.

Gunsmithing at Home, by John E. Traister, Stoeger Publishing Co., So. Hackensack, NJ, 1985. 256 pp., illus. Paper covers. $14.95.

Over 25 chapters of explicit information on every aspect of gunsmithing.

Gunsmithing Tips and Projects, a collection of the best articles from the *Handloader* and *Rifle* magazines, by various authors, Wolfe Publishing Co., Prescott, AZ, 1992. 443 pp., illus. Paper covers. $25.00.

Includes such subjects as shop, stocks, actions, tuning, triggers, barrels, customizing, etc.

Handbook of Bullet Swaging No. 7, by David R. Corbin, Corbin Manufacturing and Supply Co., White City, OR, 1986. 199 pp., illus. Paper covers. $10.00.

This handbook explains the most precise method of making quality bullets.

Handbook of Metallic Cartridge Reloading, by Edward Matunas, Winchester Press, Piscataway, NJ, 1981. 272 pp., illus. $19.95.

Up-to-date, comprehensive loading tables prepared by four major powder manufacturers.

The Handgun, by Geoffrey Boothroyd, David and Charles, North Pomfret, VT, 1989. 566 pp., illus. $60.00.

Every chapter deals with an important period in handgun history from the 14th century to the present.

Handgun Digest, 2nd Edition, by Dean A. Grennell, DBI Books, Inc., Northbrook, IL, 1991. 256 pp., illus. Paper covers. $16.95.

Full coverage of all aspects of handguns and handgunning from a highly readable, knowledgeable author.

Handgun Reloading, The Gun Digest Book of, by Dean A. Grennell and Wiley M. Clapp, DBI Books, Inc., Northbrook, IL, 1987. 256 pp., illus. Paper covers. $15.95.

Detailed discussions of all aspects of reloading for handguns, from basic to complex. New loading data.

*Handguns '95, 7th Edition, Edited by Hal Swiggett, DBI Books, Inc., Northbrook, IL, 1994. 352 pp., illus. Paper covers. $19.95

What's new in handguns plus informative and interesting articles on all aspects of handguns plus a complete catalog on all handguns currently on the market with prices.

*Handloader's Digest 1995, 14th Edition, edited by Bob Bell, DBI Books, Inc., Northbrook, IL, 1994. 480 pp., illus. Paper covers. $21.95

Top writers in the field contribute helpful information on techniques and components. Greatly expanded and fully indexed catalog of all currently available tools, accessories and components for metallic cartridge, black powder cartridge, shotshell reloading and bullet swaging.

Handloader's Guide, by Stanley W. Trzoniec, Stoeger Publishing Co., So. Hackensack, NJ, 1985. 256 pp., illus. Paper covers. $14.95.

The complete step-by-step fully illustrated guide to handloading ammunition.

Handloading, by Bill Davis, Jr., NRA Books, Wash., D.C., 1980. 400 pp., illus. Paper covers. $15.95.

A complete update and expansion of the NRA Handloader's Guide.

"Hell, I Was There!," by Elmer Keith, Petersen Publishing Co., Los Angeles, CA, 1979. 308 pp., illus. $24.95.

Adventures of a Montana cowboy who gained world fame as a big game hunter.

High Standard: A Collector's Guide to the Hamden & Hartford Target Pistols, by Tom Dance, Andrew Mowbray, Inc., Lincoln, RI, 1991. 192 pp., illus. Paper covers. $24.00.

From Citation to Supermatic, all of the production models and specials made from 1951 to 1984 are covered according to model number or series.

High Standard Automatic Pistols 1932-1950, by Charles E. Petty, The Gunroom Press, Highland Park, NJ, 1989. 124 pp., illus. $19.95.

A definitive source for the collector of High Standard arms.

Hi-Standard Autoloading Pistols 1951-1984, by James V. Spacek, Jr., James V. Spacek, Jr., Berlin, CT, 1993. 60 pp., illus. Paper covers. $10.00.

Takedown styles, serial numbers, production numbers, model charts and magazine references. Includes a price guide.

Historic Pistols: The American Martial Flintlock 1760-1845, by Samuel E. Smith and Edwin W. Bitter, The Gun Room Press, Highland Park, NJ, 1986. 353 pp., illus. $45.00.

Covers over 70 makers and 163 models of American martial arms.

Historical Hartford Hardware, by William W. Dalrymple, Colt Collector Press, Rapid City, SD, 1976. 42 pp., illus. Paper covers. $5.50.

Historically associated Colt revolvers.

The History of Smith and Wesson, by Roy G. Jinks, Willowbrook Enterprises, Springfield, MA, 1988. 290 pp., illus. $27.95.

Revised 10th Anniversary edition of the definite book on S&W firearms.

Hornady Handbook of Cartridge Reloading, 4th Edition Hornady Mfg. Co., Grand Island, NE, 1991. 1200 pp., illus. $28.50.

New edition of this famous reloading handbook. Latest loads, ballistic information, etc.

Hornady Handbook of Cartridge Reloading, Abridged Edition Hornady Mfg. Co., Grand Island, NE, 1991. $19.95.

Ballistic data for 25 of the most popular cartridges.

Hornady Load Notes Hornady Mfg. Co., Grand Island, NE, 1991. $4.95.

Complete load data and ballistics for a single caliber. Eight pistol 9mm-45ACP; 16 rifle, 222-45-70.

How to Become a Master Handgunner: The Mechanics of X-Count Shooting, by Charles Stephens, Paladin Press, Boulder, CO, 1993. 64 pp., illus. Paper covers. $10.00.

Offers a simple formula for success to the handgunner who strives to master the technique of shooting accurately.

How to Buy and Sell Used Guns, by John Traister, Stoeger Publishing Co., So. Hackensack, NJ, 1984. 192 pp., illus. Paper covers. $10.95.

A new guide to buying and selling guns.

Hunting for Handgunners, by Larry Kelly and J.D. Jones, DBI Books, Inc., Northbrook, IL, 1990. 256 pp., illus. Paper covers. $16.95.

Covers the entire spectrum of hunting with handguns in an amusing, easy-flowing manner that combines entertainment with solid information.

The Ideal Handbook of Useful Information for Shooters, No. 15, originally published by Ideal Manufacturing Co., reprinted by Wolfe Publishing Co., Prescott, AZ, 1991. 142 pp., illus. Paper covers. $10.95.

A facsimile reprint of one of the early Ideal Handbooks.

The Ideal Handbook, No. 5, Facsimile reprint by Armory Publications, Oceanside, CA, 1993. 80 pp., illus. Paper covers. $12.95.

A limited reprinting of the rare 1893 edition of the handbook issued by the Ideal manufacturing Co., of New Haven, CT.

Illustrations of United States Military Arms 1776-1903 and Their Inspector's Marks, compiled by Turner Kirkland, Pioneer Press, Union City, TN, 1988. 37 pp., illus. Paper covers. $4.95.

Reprinted from the 1949 Bannerman catalog. Valuable information for both the advanced and beginning collector.

Instinct Combat Shooting, by Chuck Klein, Chuck Klein, The Goose Creek, IN, 1989. 49 pp., illus. Paper covers. $12.00.

Defensive handgunning for police.

An Introduction the Civil War Small Arms, by Earl J. Coates and Dean S. Thomas, Thomas Publishing Co., Gettysburg, PA, 1990. 96 pp., illus. Paper covers. $6.95.

The small arms carried by the individual soldier during the Civil War.

Iver Johnson's Arms & Cycle Works Handguns, 1871-1964, by W.E. "Bill" Goforth, Blacksmith Corp., Chino Valley, AZ, 1991. 160 pp., illus. Paper covers. $14.95.

Covers all of the famous Iver Johnson handguns from the early solid-frame pistols and revolvers to optional accessories, special orders and patents.

James Reid and His Catskill Knuckledusters, by Taylor Brown, Andrew Mowbray Publishers, Lincoln, RI, 1990. 288 pp., illus. $24.95.

A detailed history of James Reid, his factory in the picturesque Catskill Mountains, and the pistols which he manufactured there.

Japanese Handguns, by Frederick E. Leithe, Borden Publishing Co., Alhambra, CA, 1985. 160 pp., illus. $19.95.

This book is an identification guide to all models and variations of Japanese handguns.

Know Your Broomhandle Mausers, by R.J. Berger, Blacksmith Corp., Southport, CT, 1985. 96 pp., illus. Paper covers. $9.95.

An interesting story on the big Mauser pistol and its variations.

Know Your Czechoslovakian Pistols, by R.J. Berger, Blacksmith Corp., Chino Valley, AZ, 1989. 96 pp., illus. Soft covers. $9.95.

A comprehensive reference which presents the fascinating story of Czech pistols.

Know Your 45 Auto Pistols—Models 1911 & A1, by E.J. Hoffschmidt, Blacksmith Corp., Southport, CT, 1974. 58 pp., illus. Paper covers. $9.95.

A concise history of the gun with a wide variety of types and copies.

Know Your Walther P.38 Pistols, by E.J. Hoffschmidt, Blacksmith Corp., Southport, CT, 1974. 77 pp., illus. Paper covers. $9.95.

Covers the Walther models Armee, M.P., H.P., P.38—history and variations.

Know Your Walther PP & PPK Pistols, by E.J. Hoffschmidt, Blacksmith Corp., Southport, CT, 1975. 87 pp., illus. Paper covers. $9.95.

A concise history of the guns with a guide to the variety and types.

The Krieghoff Parabellum, by Randall Gibson, Midland, TX, 1988. 279 pp., illus. $40.00.

A comprehensive text pertaining to the Lugers manufactured by H. Krieghoff Waffenfabrik.

Lasers and Night Vision Devices, by Duncan Long, Desert Publications, El Dorado, AZ, 1993. 150 pp., illus. Paper covers. $29.95.

A comprehensive look at the evolution of devices that allow firearms to be operated in low light conditions and at night.

Luger Holsters and Accessories of the 20th Century, by Eugene J. Bender, Eugene J. Bender, Margate, FL, 1993. 640 pp., illus. $65.00.

A major new book for collectors, dealers, and historians, with over 1,000 photographs.

Lugers at Random, by Charles Kenyon, Jr., Handgun Press, Glenview, IL, 1990. 420 pp., illus. $39.95.

A new printing of this classic and sought-after work on the Luger pistol. A boon to the Luger collector/shooter.

The Luger Pistol Its History & Development From 1893 to 1947; Monograph IV: The Swiss Variations 1897-1947, by Fred A. Datig, Fred A. Datig, Los Angeles, CA, 1992. 88 pp., illus. Paper covers. $14.95.

A definitive work on the Swiss variations of this most collectible pistol.

Luger: The Multi-National Pistol, by Charles Kenyon, Jr., Richard Ellis Publications, Moline, IL, 1991. 192 pp., illus. $69.95 (hardcover); $150.00 (leather bound).

A fresh approach to this historical handgun. A must for the serious collector.

Luger Variations, by Harry E. Jones, Harry E. Jones, Torrance, CA, 1975. 328 pp., 160 full page illus., many in color. $45.00.

A rev. ed. of the book known as "The Luger Collector's Bible."

Lyman Cast Bullet Handbook, 3rd Edition, edited by C. Kenneth Ramage, Lyman Publications, Middlefield, CT, 1980. 416 pp., illus. Paper covers. $18.95.

Information on more than 5000 tested cast bullet loads and 19 pages of trajectory and wind drift tables for cast bullets.

Lyman Black Powder Handbook, ed. by C. Kenneth Ramage, Lyman Products for Shooters, Middlefield, CT, 1975. 239 pp., illus. Paper covers. $14.95.

Comprehensive load information for the blackpowder shooter.

Lyman Pistol & Revolver Handbook, edited by C. Kenneth Ramage, Lyman Publications, Middlefield, CT, 1978. 280 pp., illus. Paper covers. $14.95.

An extensive reference of handgun load and trajectory data.

Lyman Reloading Handbook No. 47, edited by Edward A. Matunas, Lyman Publications, Middlefield, CT, 1992. 480 pp., illus. Paper covers. $21.95.

"The world's most comprehensive reloading manual." Complete "How to Reload" information. Expanded data section with all the newest rifle and pistol calibers.

*Making Loading Dies and Bullet Molds, by Harold Hoffman, H&P Publishing, San Angelo, TX, 1993. 230 pp., illus. Paper covers. $22.95.

A good book for learning tool and die making.

Manual of Pistol and Revolver Cartridges, Volume 2, Centerfire U.S. and British Calibers, by Hans A. Erlmeier and Jakob H. Brandt, Journal-Verlag, Wiesbaden, Germany, 1981. 270 pp., illus. $34.95.

Catalog system allows cartridges to be traced by caliber or alphabetically.

Master Tips, by J. Winokur, Potshot Press, Pacific Palisades, CA, 1985. 96 pp., illus. Paper covers. $11.95.

Basics of practical shooting.

Mauser Rifles and Pistols, by Walter H.B. Smith, Wolfe Publishing Co., Prescott, AZ, 1990. 234 pp., illus. $30.00.

A handbook covering Mauser history and the amrs Mauser manufactured.

The Mauser Self-Loading Pistol, by Belford & Dunlap, Borden Publ. Co., Alhambra, CA. Over 200 pp., 300 illus., large format. $24.95.

The long-awaited book on the "Broom Handles," covering their inception in 1894 to the end of production. Complete and in detail: pocket pistols, Chinese and Spanish copies, etc.

Metallic Cartridge Reloading, 2nd Edition, by Edward A. Matunas, DBI Books, Inc., Northbrook, IL., 1988. 320 pp., illus. Paper covers. $17.95.

A true reloading manual with a wealth of invaluable technical data provided by a recognized expert.

Metallic Silhouette Shooting, 2nd Edition, The Gun Digest Book of, by Elgin Gates, DBI Books, Inc., Northbrook, IL, 1988. 256 pp., illus. Paper covers. $16.95.

All about the rapidly growing sport. With a history and rules of the International Handgun Metallic Silhouette Association.

*Military Handguns of France 1858-1958, by Eugene Medlin and Jean Huon, Excaliber Publications, Latham, NY, 1993. 128 pp., illus. Paper covers. $24.95.

The first book in English on the subject, providing students of arms with a thorough history of French service handguns.

Military Pistols of Japan, by Fred L. Honeycutt, Jr., Julin Books, Palm Beach Gardens, FL, 1991. 168 pp., illus. $34.00.

Covers every aspect of military pistol production in Japan through WWII.

Military Small Arms of the 20th Century, 6th Edition, by Ian V. Hogg, DBI Books, Inc., Northbrook, IL, 1991. 352 pp., illus. Paper covers. $19.95.

Fully revised and updated edition of the standard reference in its field.

Modern American Pistols and Revolvers, by A.C. Gould, Wolfe Publishing Co., Prescott, AZ, 1988. 222 pp., illus. $37.00.

A limited edition reprint. An account of the development of those arms as well as the manner of shooting them.

Modern Gun Values, The Gun Digest Book of 9th Edition, Edited by Jack Lewis, DBI Books, Inc., Northbrook, IL, illus. Paper covers. $20.95

Updated and expanded edition of the book that has become the standard for valuing modern firearms.

*Modern Gun Values, The Gun Digest Book of 10th Edition, Edited by Joe Schroeder, DBI Books, Inc., Northbrook, IL., illus. Paper covers.

Updated and expanded edition of the book that has become the standard for valuing modern firearms. (February '95)

Modern Handloading, by Maj. Geo. C. Nonte, Winchester Press, Piscataway, NJ, 1972. 416 pp., illus. $15.00.

Covers all aspects of metallic and shotshell ammunition loading, plus more loads than any book in print.

Modern Law Enforcement Weapons & Tactics, 2nd Edition, by Tom Ferguson, DBI Books, Inc., Northbrook, IL, 1991. 256 pp., illus. Paper covers. $17.95.

An in-depth look at the weapons and equipment used by law enforcement agencies of today.

Modern Practical Ballistics, by Art Pejsa, Pejsa Ballistics, Minneapolis, MN, 1990. 150 pp., illus. $24.95.

Covers all aspects of ballistics and new, simplified methods. Clear examples illustrate new, easy but very accurate formulas.

The Modern Technique of the Pistol, by Gregory Boyce Morrison, Gunsite Press, Paulden, AZ, 1991. 153 pp., illus. $45.00.

The theory of effective defensive use of modern handguns.

The Navy Luger, by Joachim Gortz and John Walter, Handgun Press, Glenview, IL, 1988. 128 pp., illus. $24.95.

The 9mm Pistole 1904 and the Imperial German Navy. A concise illustrated history.

9mm Handguns, 2nd Edition, The Gun Digest Book of, edited by Steve Comus, DBI Books, Inc., Northbrook, IL, 1993. 256 pp., illus. Paper covers. $17.95.

Covers the 9mmP cartridge and the guns that have been made for it in greater depth than any other work available.

9mm Parabellus; The History & Developement of the World's 9mm Pistols & Ammunition, by Klaus-Peter Konig and Martin Hugo, Schiffer Publishing Ltd., Atglen, PA, 1993. 304 pp., illus. $39.95.

Detailed history of 9mm weapons from Belguim, Italy, Germany, Israel, France, USA, Czechoslovakia, Hungary, Poland, Brazil, Finland and Spain.

Nosler Reloading Manual No. 3, edited by Gail Root, Nosler Bullets, Inc., Bend, OR, 1989. 516 pp., illus. $21.95.

All-new book. New format including featured articles and cartridge introductions by well-known shooters, gun writers and editors.

The NRA Gunsmithing Guide—Updated, by Ken Raynor and Brad Fenton, National Rifle Association, Wash., DC, 1984. 336 pp., illus. Paper covers. $15.95.

Material includes chapters and articles on all facets of the gunsmithing art.

The P-08 Parabellum Luger Automatic Pistol, edited by J. David McFarland, Desert Publications, Cornville, AZ, 1982. 20 pp., illus. Paper covers. $8.00.

Covers every facet of the Luger, plus a listing of all known Luger models.

P-38 Automatic Pistol, by Gene Gangarosa, Jr., Stoeger Publishing Co., S. Hackensack, NJ, 1993. 272 pp., illus. Paper covers. $16.95

This book traces the origins and development of the P-38, including the momentous political forces of the World War II era that caused its near demise and, later, its rebirth.

*Packing Iron, by Richard C. Rattenbury, Zon International Publishing, Millwood, NY, 1993. 216 pp., illus. $45.00.

The best book yet produced on pistol holsters and rifle scabbards. Over 300 variations of holster and scabbards are illustrated in large, clear plates.

*Patents for Inventions, Class 119 (Small Arms), 1855-1930. British Patent Office, Armory Publications, Oceanside, CA, 1993. 7 volume set. $350.00.

Contains 7980 abridged patent descriptions and their sectioned line drawings, plus a 37-page alphabetical index of the patentees.

Paterson Colt Pistol Variations, by R.L. Wilson and R. Phillips, Jackson Arms Co., Dallas, TX, 1979. 250 pp., illus. $35.00.

A book about the different models and barrel lengths in the Paterson Colt story.

Pin Shooting: A Complete Guide, by Mitchell A. Ota, Wolfe Publishing Co., Prescott, AZ, 1992. 145 pp., illus. Paper covers. $14.95.

Traces the sport from its humble origins to today's thoroughly enjoyable social event, including the mammoth eight-day Second Chance Pin Shoot in Michigan.

Pistol & Revolver Guide, 3rd Ed., by George C. Nonte, Stoeger Publ. Co., So. Hackensack, NJ, 1975. 224 pp., illus. Paper covers. $11.95.

The standard reference work on military and sporting handguns.

Pistol Guide, by George C. Nonte, Jr., Stoeger Publishing Co., So. Hackensack, NJ, 1991. 280 pp., illus. Paper covers. $13.95.

Covers handling and marksmanship, care and maintenance, pistol ammunition, how to buy a used gun, military pistols, air pistols and repairs.

Pistols of the World, 3rd Edition, by Ian Hogg and John Weeks, DBI Books, Inc., Northbrook, IL, 1992. 320 pp., illus. Paper covers. $19.95.

A totally revised edtion of one of the leading studies of small arms.

Pistolsmithing, The Gun Digest Book of, by Jack Mitchell, DBI Books, Inc., Northbrook, IL, 1980. 256 pp., illus. Paper covers. $15.95.

An expert's guide to the operation of each of the handgun actions with all the major functions of pistolsmithing explained.

Pistolsmithing, by George C. Nonte, Jr., Stackpole Books, Harrisburg, PA, 1974. 560 pp., illus. $29.95.

A single source reference to handgun maintenance, repair, and modification at home, unequaled in value.

Police Handgun Manual, by Bill Clede, Stackpole Books, Inc., Harrisburg, PA, 1985. 128 pp., illus. $18.95.

How to get street-smart survival habits.

Powerhouse Pistols—The Colt 1911 and Browning Hi-Power Source

book, by Duncan Long, Paladin Press, Boulder, CO, 1989. 152 pp., illus. Soft covers. $19.95.

The author discusses internal mechanisms, outward design, test-firing results, maintenance and accessories.

Practical Gunsmithing, by Edward A. Matunas, Stackpole Books, Harrisburg, PA, 1989. 352 pp., illus. $31.95.

A complete guide to maintaining, repairing, and improving firearms.

Precision Handloading, by John Withers, Stoeger Publishing Co., So. Hackensack, NJ, 1985. 224 pp., illus. Paper covers. $12.95.

An entirely new approach to handloading ammunition.

Propellant Profiles New and Expanded, 3rd Edition, Wolfe Publishing Co., Prescott, AZ, 1991. Paper covers. $16.95.

The Rare and Valuable Antique Arms, by James E. Serven, Pioneer Press, Union City, TN, 1976. 106 pp., illus. Paper covers. $4.95.

A guide to the collector in deciding which direction his collecting should go, investment value, historic interest, mechanical ingenuity, high art or personal preference.

Reloader's Guide, 3rd Edition, by R.A. Steindler, Stoeger Publishing Co., So. Hackensack, NJ, 1984. 224 pp., illus. Paper covers. $11.95.

Complete, fully illustrated step-by-step guide to handloading ammunition.

The very latest in reloading information for the shotgunner.

Report of Board on Tests of Revolvers and Automatic Pistols. From the Annual Report of the Chief of Ordnance, 1907. Reprinted by J.C. Tillinghast, Marlow, NH, 1969. 34 pp., 7 plates, paper covers. $9.95.

A comparison of handguns, including Luger, Savage, Colt, Webley-Fosbery and other makes.

Revolver Guide, by George C. Nonte, Jr., Stoeger Publishing Co., So. Hackensack, NJ, 1991. 288 pp., illus. Paper covers. $10.95.

A detailed and practical encyclopedia of the revolver, the most common handgun to be found.

Revolvers of the British Services 1854-1954, by W.H.J. Chamberlain and A.W.F. Taylerson, Museum Restoration Service, Ottawa, Canada, 1989. 80 pp., illus. $27.50.

Covers the types issued among many of the United Kingdom's naval, land or air services.

Ruger, edited by Joseph Roberts, Jr., the National Rifle Association of America, Washington, D.C., 1991. 109 pp. illus. Paper covers. $14.95.

The story of Bill Ruger's indelible imprint in the history of sporting firearms.

*Ruger Automatic Pistols and Single Action Revolvers, by Hugo A. Lueders, edited by Don Findley, Blacksmith Corp., Chino Valley, AZ, 1993. 79 pp., illus. Paper covers. $14.95.

The definitive work on Ruger automatic pistols and single action revolvers.

Ruger Double Action Revolvers, Vol. 1, Shop Manual, by Jerry Kuhnhausen, VSP Publishers, McCall, ID, 1989. 176 pp., illus. Soft covers. $18.95.

Covers the Ruger Six series of revolvers: Security-Six, Service-Six, and Speed-Six. Includes step-by-step function checks, disassembly, inspection, repairs, rebuilding, reassembly, and custom work.

*The Ruger "P" Family of Handguns, by Duncan Long, Desert Publications, El Dorado, AZ, 1993. 128 pp., illus. Paper covers. $14.95.

A full-fledged documentary on a remarkable series of Sturm Ruger handguns.

The Ruger .22 Automatic Pistol, Standard/Mark I/Mark II Series, by Duncan Long, Paladin Press, Boulder, CO, 1989. 168 pp., illus. Paper covers. $12.00.

The definitive book about the pistol that has served more than 1 million owners so well.

The S&W Revolver: A Shop Manual, by Jerry Kuhnhausen, VSP Publishers, McCall, ID, 1987. 152 pp., illus. Paper covers. $17.95.

Covers accurizing, trigger jobs, action tuning, rebarreling, barrel setback, forcing cone angles, polishing and rebluing.

Sam Colt's Own Record 1847, by John Parsons, Wolfe Publishing Co., Prescott, AZ, 1992. 167 pp., illus. $24.50.

Chronologically presented, the correspondence published here completes the account of the manufacture, in 1847, of the Walker Model Colt revolver.

The Semiautomatic Pistols in Police Service and Self Defense, by Massad Ayoob, Police Bookshelf, Concord, NH, 1990. 25 pp., illus. Soft covers. $9.95.

First quantitative, documented look at actual police experience with 9mm and 45 police service automatics.

The Sharpshooter—How to Stand and Shoot Handgun Metallic Silhouettes, by Charles Stephens, Yucca Tree Press, Las Cruces, NM, 1993. 86 pp., illus. Paper covers. $10.00.

A narration of some of the author's early experiences in silhouette shooting, plus how-to information.

Shoot a Handgun, by Dave Arnold, PVA Books, Canyon County, CA, 1983. 144 pp., illus. Paper covers. $11.95.

A complete manual of simplified handgun instruction.

Shoot to Win, by John Shaw, Blacksmith Corp., Southport, CT, 1985. 160 pp., illus. Paper covers. $11.95.

The lessons taught here are of interest and value to all handgun shooters.

Shooter's Bible, 1940, Stoeger Arms Corp., Stoeger, Inc., So. Hackensack, NJ, 1990. 512 pp., illus. Soft covers. $16.95.

Reprint of the Stoeger Arms Corp. catalog No. 33 of 1940.

*Shooter's Bible 1995, No. 86, edited by William S. Jarrett, Stoeger Publishing Co., So. Hackensack, NJ, 1993. 576 pp., illus. Paper covers. $19.95.

"The world's standard firearms reference book."

*Shooting, by J.H. FitzGerald, Wolfe Publishing Co., Prescott, AZ, 1993. 421 pp., illus. $29.00.

This is a classic book and reference for anyone interested in pistol and revolver shooting.

Shooting, by Edward A. Matunas, Stackpole Books, Harrisburg, PA, 1986. 416 pp., illus. $31.95.

How to become an expert marksman with rifle, shotgun, handgun, muzzle loader and bow.

Sierra Handgun Manual, 3rd Edition, edited by Kenneth Ramage, Sierra Bullets, Santa Fe Springs, CA, 1990. 704 pp., illus. 3-ring binder. $19.95.

New listings for XP-100 and Contender pistols and TCU cartridges...part of a new single shot section. Covers the latest loads for 10mm Auto, 455 Super Mag, and Accurate powders.

Sixgun Cartridges and Loads, by Elmer Keith, reprint edition by The Gun Room Press, Highland Park, NJ, 1984. 151 pp., illus. $24.95.

A manual covering the selection, use and loading of the most suitable and popular revolver cartridges.

Sixguns, by Elmer Keith, Wolfe Publishing Company, Prescott, AZ, 1992. 336 pp. Hardcover. $34.95.

The history, selection, repair, care, loading, and use of this historic frontiersman's friend–the one-hand firearm.

Skeeter Skelton on Handguns, by Skeeter Skelton, PJS Publications, Peoria, IL, 1980. 122 pp., illus. Soft covers. $5.00.

A treasury of facts, fiction and fables.

*Small Arms: Pistols & Rifles, by Ian V. Hogg, Greenhill Books, London, England, 1994. 160 pp., illus. $19.95.

An in-depth description of small arms, focusing on pistols and rifles, with detailed information about all small arms used by the world's armed forces.

*Smith & Wesson Hand Guns, by Roy C. McHenry and Walter F. Roper, Wolfe Publishing Co., Prescott, AZ, 1994. 244 pp., illus. $32.00.

Originally published in 1945, this is simply the bible on the subject.

*Speer Reloading Manual Number 12, edited by members of the Speer research staff, Omark Industries, Lewiston, ID, 1987. 621 pp., illus.

Reloading manual for rifles and pistols.

The Sporting Ballistics Book, by Charles W. Matthews, Bill Matthews, Inc., Lakewood, CO, 1992. 182 pp. Wirebound. $19.95.

A useful book for those interested in doing their own exterior-ballistic calculations without the aid of a computer.

Southern Derringers of the Mississippi Valley, by Turner Kirkland, Pioneer Press, Tenn., 1971. 80 pp., illus., paper covers. $5.00.

A guide for the collector, and a much-needed study.

Soviet Russian Postwar Military Pistols and Cartridges, by Fred A. Datig, Handgun Press, Glenview, IL, 1988. 152 pp., illus. $29.95.

Thoroughly researched, this definitive sourcebook covers the development and adoption of the Makarov, Stechkin and the new PSM pistols. Also included in this source book is coverage on Russian clandestine weapons and pistol cartridges.

*Soviet Russian Tokarev "TT" Pistols and Cartridges 1929-1953,** by Fred Datig, Graphic Publishers, Santa Ana, CA, 1993. 168 pp., illus. $39.95.

Details of rare arms and their accessories are shown in hundreds of photos. It also contains a complete bibliography and index.

*Standard Catalog of Firearms, 4th Edition,** by Ned Schwing and Herbert Houze, Krause Publications, Iola, WI, 1994. 720 pp., illus. Paper covers. $24.95.

This updated and expanded edition includes proper physical descriptions for over 11,000 guns from more than 1000 manufacturers with accurate prices.

Steindler's New Firearms Dictionary, by R.A. Steindler, Stackpole Books, Inc., Harrisburg, PA, 1985. 320 pp., illus. $24.95.

Completely revised and updated edition of this standard work.

Stevens Pistols & Pocket Rifles, by K.L. Cope, Museum Restoration Service, Alexandria Bay, NY, 1992. 114 pp., illus. $24.50.

This is the story of the guns and the man who designed them and the company which he founded to make them.

Successful Pistol Shooting, by Frank and Paul Leatherdale, The Crowood Press, Ramsbury, England, 1988. 144 pp., illus. $34.95.

Easy-to-follow instructions to help you achieve better results and gain more enjoyment from both leisure and competitive shooting.

Survival Guns, by Mel Tappan, Desert Publications, El Dorado, AZ, 1993. 456 pp., illus. Paper covers. $21.95.

Discusses in a frank and forthright manner which handguns, rifles and shotguns to buy for personal defense and securing food, and the ones to avoid.

Survival Gunsmithing, by J.B. Wood, Desert Publications, Cornville, AZ, 1986. 92 pp., illus. Paper covers. $9.95.

A guide to repair and maintenance of the most popular rifles, shotguns and handguns.

Textbook of Automatic Pistols, by R.K. Wilson, Wolfe Publishing Co., Prescott, AZ, 1990. 349 pp., illus. $54.00.

Reprint of the 1943 classic being a treatise on the history, development and functioning of modern military self-loading pistols.

U.S. Marine Corp Rifle and Pistol Marksmanship, 1935, reprinting of a government publication, Lancer Militaria, Mt. Ida, AR, 1991. 99 pp., illus. Paper covers. $11.95.

The old corps method of precision shooting.

U.S. Naval Handguns, 1808-1911, by Fredrick R. Winter, Andrew Mowbray Publishers, Lincoln, RI, 1990. 128 pp., illus. $26.00.

The story of U.S. Naval Handguns spans an entire century—included are sections on each of the important naval handguns within the period.

Walther Models PP and PPK, 1929-1945, by James L. Rankin, assisted by Gary Green, James L. Rankin, Coral Gables, FL, 1974. 142 pp., illus. $35.00.

Complete coverage on the subject as to finish, proofmarks and Nazi Party inscriptions.

Walther P-38 Pistol, by Maj. George Nonte, Desert Publications, Cornville, AZ, 1982. 100 pp., illus. Paper covers. $9.95.

Complete volume on one of the most famous handguns to come out of WWII. All models covered.

Walther Volume II, Engraved, Presentation and Standard Models, by James L. Rankin, J.L. Rankin, Coral Gables, FL, 1977. 112 pp., illus. $35.00.

The new Walther book on embellished versions and standard models. Has 88 photographs, including many color plates.

Walther, Volume III, 1908-1980, by James L. Rankin, Coral Gables, FL, 1981. 226 pp., illus. $35.00.

Covers all models of Walther handguns from 1908 to date, includes holsters, grips and magazines.

Webley & Scott Automatic Pistols, by Gordon Bruch, Stocker-Schmid Publishing Co., Dietikon, Switzerland, 1992. 256 pp., illus. $69.50.

The fundamental representation of the history and development of all Webley & Scott automatic pistols.

Webley Revolvers, by Gordon Bruce and Christien Reinhart, Stocker-Schmid, Zurich, Switzerland, 1988. 256 pp., illus. $69.50.

A revised edition of Dowell's "Webley Story."

Why Not Load Your Own? by Col. T. Whelen, A. S. Barnes, New York, 1957, 4th ed., rev. 237 pp., illus. $10.95.

A basic reference on handloading, describing each step, materials and equipment. Loads for popular cartridges are given.

Wildcat Cartridges, Volume I, Wolfe Publishing Company, Prescott, AZ, 1992. 125 pp. Soft cover. $16.95.

From *Handloader* magazine, the more popular and famous wildcats are profiled.

Wildcat Cartridges, Volume II, compiled from *Handloader* and *Rifle* magazine articles written by featured authors, Wolfe Publishing Co., Prescott, AZ, 1992. 971 pp., illus. Paper covers. $34.95.

This volume details rifle and handtgun cartridges from the 14-221 to the 460 Van Horn. A comprehensive work containing loading tables and commentary.

World's Deadliest Rimfire Battleguns, by J.M. Ramos, Paladin Press, Boulder, CO, 1990. 184 pp., illus. Paper covers. $14.00.

This heavily illustrated book shows international rimfire assault weapon innovations from World War II to the present.

You Can't Miss, by John Shaw and Michael Bane, John Shaw, Memphis, TN, 1983. 152 pp., illus. Paper covers. $12.95.

The secrets of a successful combat shooter; how to better defensive shooting skills.

ARMS ASSOCIATIONS

UNITED STATES

ALABAMA

Alabama Gun Collectors Assn.
Secretary, P.O. Box 70965, Tuscaloosa, AL 35407

ALASKA

Alaska Gun Collectors Assn., Inc.
C.W. Floyd, Pres., 5240 Little Tree, Anchorage, AK 99507

ARIZONA

Arizona Arms Assn.
Don DeBusk, President, 4837 Bryce Ave., Glendale, AZ 85301

CALIFORNIA

California Waterfowl Assn.
4630 Northgate Blvd., #150, Sacramento, CA 95834
Greater Calif. Arms & Collectors Assn.
Donald L. Bullock, 8291 Carburton St., Long Beach, CA 90808-3302
Los Angeles Gun Ctg. Collectors Assn.
F.H. Ruffra, 20810 Amie Ave., Apt. #9, Torrance, CA 90503

COLORADO

Colorado Gun Collectors Assn.
L.E.(Bud) Greenwald, 2553 S. Quitman St., Denver, CO 80219/303-935-3850

CONNECTICUT

Ye Connecticut Gun Guild, Inc.
Dick Fraser, P.O. Box 425, Windsor, CT 06095

FLORIDA

Unified Sportsmen of Florida
P.O. Box 6565, Tallahassee, FL 32314

GEORGIA

Georgia Arms Collectors Assn., Inc.
Michael Kindberg, President, P.O. Box 277, Alpharetta, GA 30239-0277

ILLINOIS

Illinois State Rifle Assn.
P.O. Box 637, Chatsworth, IL 60921
Illinois Gun Collectors Assn.
T.J. Curl, Jr., P.O. Box 971, Kankakee, IL 60901
Mississippi Valley Gun & Cartridge Coll. Assn.
Bob Filbert, P.O. Box 61, Port Byron, IL 61275/309-523-2593
Sauk Trail Gun Collectors
Gordell M. Matson, P.O. Box 1113, Milan, IL 61264
Wabash Valley Gun Collectors Assn., Inc.
Roger L. Dorsett, 2601 Willow Rd., Urbana, IL 61801/217-284-7302

INDIANA

Indiana State Rifle & Pistol Assn.
Thos. Glancy, P.O. Box 552, Chesterton, IN 46304
Southern Indiana Gun Collectors Assn., Inc.
Sheila McClary, 309 W. Monroe St., Boonville, IN 47601/812-897-3742

IOWA

Beaver Creek Plainsmen Inc.
Steve Murphy, Secy., P.O. Box 298, Bondurant, IA 50035

Central States Gun Collectors Assn.
Avery Giles, 1104 S. 1st Ave., Marshtown, IA 50158

KANSAS

Kansas Cartridge Collectors Assn.
Bob Linder, Box 84, Plainville, KS 67663

KENTUCKY

Kentuckiana Arms Collectors Assn.
Charles Billips, President, Box 1776, Louisville, KY 40201
Kentucky Gun Collectors Assn., Inc.
Ruth Johnson, Box 64, Owensboro, KY 42302/502-729-4197

LOUISIANA

Washitaw River Renegades
Sandra Rushing, P.O. Box 256, Main St., Grayson, LA 71435

MARYLAND

Baltimore Antique Arms Assn.
Mr. Cillo, 1034 Main St., Darlington, MD 21304

MASSACHUSETTS

Bay Colony Weapons Collectors, Inc.
John Brandt, Box 111, Hingham, MA 02043
Massachusetts Arms Collectors
Bruce E. Skinner, P.O. Box 31, No. Carver, MA 02355/508-866-5259

MISSISSIPPI

Mississippi Gun Collectors Assn.
Jack E. Swinney, P.O. Box 16323, Hattiesburg, MS 39402

MISSOURI

Mineral Belt Gun Collectors Assn.
D.F. Saunders, 1110 Cleveland Ave., Monett, MO 65708
Missouri Valley Arms Collectors Assn., Inc.
L.P Brammer II, Membership Secy., P.O. Box 33033, Kansas City, MO 64114

MONTANA

Montana Arms Collectors Assn.
Lewis E. Yearout, 308 Riverview Dr. East, Great Falls, MT 59404
The Winchester Arms Collectors Assn.
Richard Berg, P.O. Box 6754, Great Falls, MT 59406

NEW HAMPSHIRE

New Hampshire Arms Collectors, Inc.
Frank H. Galeucia, Rt. 28, Box 44, Windham, NH 03087

NEW JERSEY

Englishtown Benchrest Shooters Assn.
Michael Toth, 64 Cooke Ave., Carteret, NJ 07008
Jersey Shore Antique Arms Collectors
Joe Sisia, P.O. Box 100, Bayville, NJ 08721-1950
New Jersey Arms Collectors Club, Inc.
Angus Laidlaw, President, 230 Valley Rd., Montclair, NJ 07042/201-746-0939

NEW YORK

Iroquois Arms Collectors Assn.
Bonnie Robinson, Show Secy., P.O. Box 142, Ransomville, NY 14131/716-791-4096

Mid-State Arms Coll. & Shooters Club
Jack Ackerman, 24 S. Mountain Terr., Binghamton, NY 13903

NORTH CAROLINA

North Carolina Gun Collectors Assn.
Jerry Ledford, 3231-7th St. Dr. NE, Hickory, NC 28601

OHIO

Ohio Gun Collectors Assn.
P.O. Box 24170, Cincinnati, OH 45224-0170
The Stark Gun Collectors, Inc.
William I. Gann, 5666 Waynesburg Dr., Waynesburg, OH 44688

OKLAHOMA

Indian Territory Gun Collector's Assn.
P.O. Box 4491, Tulsa, OK 74159/918-745-9141

OREGON

Oregon Arms Collectors Assn., Inc.
Phil Bailey, P.O. Box 13000-A, Portland, OR 97213
Oregon Cartridge Collectors Assn.
Gale Stockton, 52 N.W. 2nd, Gresham, OR 97030

PENNSYLVANIA

Presque Isle Gun Collectors Assn.
James Welch, 156 E. 37 St., Erie, PA 16504

SOUTH CAROLINA

Belton Gun Club, Inc.
J.K. Phillips, 195 Phillips Dr., Belton, SC 29627
South Carolina Shooting Assn.
P.O. Box 12658, Columbia, SC 29211-2658
Membership Div.: William Strozier, Secretary, P.O. Box 70, Johns Island, SC 29457-0070

SOUTH DAKOTA

Dakota Territory Gun Coll. Assn., Inc.
Curt Carter, Castlewood, SD 57223

TENNESSEE

Smoky Mountain Gun Coll. Assn., Inc.
Hugh W. Yabro, President, P.O. Box 23225, Knoxville, TN 37933
Tennessee Gun Collectors Assn., Inc.
M.H. Parks, 3556 Pleasant Valley Rd., Nashville, TN 37204

TEXAS

Houston Gun Collectors Assn., Inc.
P.O. Box 741429, Houston, TX 77274-1429
Texas Cartridge Collectors Assn., Inc.
Peter E. Davis, Memb. Contact, 14738 C Perthshire Rd., Houston, TX 77079
Texas Gun Collectors Assn.
13201 Wells Fargo Trail, Austin, TX 78737
Texas State Rifle Assn.
P.O. Drawer 710549, Dallas, TX 75371

WASHINGTON

Washington Arms Collectors, Inc.
J. Dennis Cook, P.O. Box 7335, Tacoma, WA 98407/206-752-2268

WISCONSIN

Great Lakes Arms Collectors Assn., Inc.
Edward C. Warnke, 2913 Woodridge Lane, Waukesha, WI 53188

Wisconsin Gun Collectors Assn., Inc.
Lulita Zellmer, P.O. Box 181, Sussex, WI 53089
WYOMING
Wyoming Weapons Collectors
P.O. Box 284, Laramie, WY 82070/307-745-4652
or 745-9530

NATIONAL ORGANIZATIONS

Amateur Trapshooting Assn.
601 W. National Rd., Vandalia, OH 45377
American Coon Hunters Assn.
Opal Johnston, P.O. Cadet, Route 1, Box 492, Old Mines, MO 63630
American Custom Gunmakers Guild
Jan Billeb, Exec. Director, P.O. Box 812, Burlington, IA 52601-0812/319-752-6114 (Phone or Fax)
American Defense Preparedness Assn.
Two Colonial Place, 2101 Wilson Blvd., Suite 400, Arlington, VA 22201-3061
American Pistolsmiths Guild
Hamilton S. Bowen, President, P.O. Box 67, Louisville, TN 37777
American Police Pistol & Rifle Assn.
3801 Biscayne Blvd., Miami, FL 33137
American Single Shot Rifle Assn.
Gary Staup, Secy., 709 Carolyn Dr., Delphos, OH 45833/419-692-3866
American Society of Arms Collectors
George E. Weatherly, P.O. Box 2567, Waxahachie, TX 75165
Association of Firearm and Toolmark Examiners
Eugenia A. Bell, Secy., 7857 Esterel Dr., LaJolla, CA 92037; Membership Secy., Andrew B. Hart, 80 Mountain View Ave., Rensselaer, NY 12144
Boone & Crockett Club
250 Station Dr., Missoula, MT 59801-2753
Browning Collectors Assn.
Bobbie Hamit, P.O. Box 526, Aurora, NE 68818/402-694-6602
The Cast Bullet Assn., Inc.
Ralland J. Fortier, Membership Director, 4103 Foxcraft Dr., Traverse City, MI 49684
Citizens Comm. for the Right to Keep and Bear Arms
Natl. Hq., Liberty Park, 12500 NE Tenth Pl., Bellevue, WA 98005
Colt Collectors Assn.
3200 Westminster, Dallas, TX 75205
Ducks Unlimited, Inc.
One Waterfowl Way, Memphis, TN 38120
Fifty Caliber Shooters Assn.
11469 Olive St. Rd., Suite 50, St. Louis, MO 63141
Firearms Coalition
Box 6537, Silver Spring, MD 20906/301-871-3006
Firearms Engravers Guild of America
Robert Evans, Secy., 332 Vine St., Oregon City, OR 97045
Foundation for North American Wild Sheep
720 Allen Ave., Cody, WY 82414
Garand Collectors Assn.
P.O. Box 181, Richmond, KY 40475
Golden Eagle Collectors Assn.
Chris Showler, 11144 Slate Creek Rd., Grass Valley, CA 95945
Gun Owners of America
8001 Forbes Place, Suite 102, Springfield, VA 22151/703-321-8585
Handgun Hunters International
J.D. Jones, Director, P.O. Box 357 MAG, Bloomingdale, OH 43910
Harrington & Richardson Gun Coll. Assn.
George L. Cardet, 330 S.W. 27th Ave., Suite 603, Miami, FL 33135
Hopkins & Allen Arms & Memorabilia Society
1309 Pamela Circle, Delphos, OH 45833
International Benchrest Shooters
Joan Borden, RD 1, Box 244A, Tunkhannock, PA 18657
International Blackpowder Hunting Assn.
P.O. Box 1180, Glenrock, WY 82637/307-436-9817
International Cartridge Coll. Assn., Inc.
Charles Spano, P.O. Box 5297, Ormond Beach, FL 32174-5297
IHMSA (Intl. Handgun Metallic Silhouette Assn.)
Frank Scotto, P.O. Box 5038, Meriden, CT 06450

International Handloading Assn.
6471 Airpark Dr., Prescott, AZ 86301
IPPA (International Paintball Players Assn.)
P.O. Box 26669, San Diego, CA 92196-0669/619-695-8882
Jews for the Preservation of Firearms Ownership (JPFO)
2872 S. Wentworth Ave., Milwaukee, WI 53207/414-769-0760
The Mannlicher Collectors Assn.
Rev. Don L. Henry, Secy., P.O. Box 7144, Salem, OR 97303
Marlin Firearms Collectors Assn., Ltd.
Dick Paterson, Secy., 407 Lincoln Bldg., 44 Main St., Champaign, IL 61820
Miniature Arms Collectors/Makers Society, Ltd.
Ralph Koebbeman, Pres., 4910 Kilburn Ave., Rockford, IL 61101/815-963-1466
M1 Carbine Collectors Assn. (M1-CCA)
P.O. Box 4895, Stateline, NV 89449
National Association of Buckskinners
Tim Pray, 1981 E. 94th Ave., Thornton, CO 80229
The National Assoc. of Derringer ollec-tors
P.O. Box 20572, San Jose, CA 95160
National Assn. of Fed. Licensed Firearms Dealers
Andrew Molchan, 2455 E. Sunrise, Ft. Lauderdale, FL 33304
National Association to Keep and Bear Arms
P.O. Box 78336, Seattle, WA 98178
National Automatic Pistol Collectors Assn.
Tom Knox, P.O. Box 15738, Tower Grove Station, St. Louis, MO 63163
National Bench Rest Shooters Assn., Inc.
Pat Baggett, 2027 Buffalo, Levelland, TX 79336
National Firearms Assn.
P.O. Box 160038, Austin, TX 78716/403-439-1094; FAX: 403-439-4091
National Muzzle Loading Rifle Assn.
Box 67, Friendship, IN 47021
National Reloading Manufacturers Assn.
One Centerpointe Dr., Suite 300, Lake Oswego, OR 97035
National Rifle Assn. of America
11250 Waples Mill Rd., Fairfax, VA 22030
National Shooting Sports Foundation, Inc.
Robert T. Delfay, President, Flintlock Ridge Office Center, 11 Mile Hill Rd., Newtown, CT 06470-2359/203-426-1320; FAX: 203-426-1087
National Skeet Shooting Assn.
Mike Hampton, Exec. Director, P.O. Box 680007, San Antonio, TX 78268-0007
National Sporting Clays Association
P.O. Box 680007, San Antonio, TX 78268/800-877-5338
National Wild Turkey Federation, Inc.
P.O. Box 530, Edgefield, SC 29824
North American Hunting Club
P.O. Box 3401, Minnetonka, MN 55343
North-South Skirmish Assn., Inc.
Stevan F. Meserve, Exec. Secretary, 204 W. Holly Ave., Sterling, VA 20164-4006
Remington Society of America
Leon W. Wier Jr., President, 8268 Lone Feather Ln., Las Vegas, NV 89123
Rocky Mountain Elk Foundation
P.O. Box 8249, Missoula, MT 59807-8249
Ruger Collector's Assn., Inc.
P.O. Box 1441, Yazoo City, MS 39194
Safari Club International
Philip DeLone, Executive Dir., 4800 W. Gates Pass Rd., Tucson, AZ 85745/602-620-1220
Sako Collectors Assn., Inc.
Karen Reed, 1725 Woodhill Ln., Bedford, TX 76021
Second Amendment Foundation
James Madison Building, 12500 NE 10th Pl., Bellevue, WA 98005
Smith & Wesson Collectors Assn.
George Linne, 2711 Miami St., St. Louis, MO 63118
The Society of American Bayonet Collectors
P.O. Box 234, East Islip, NY 11730-0234
Southern California Schuetzen Society
Dean Lillard, 34657 Ave. E., Yucaipa, CA 92399
Sporting Arms & Ammo Manufacturers Institute
Flintlock Ridge Office Center, 11 Mile Hill Rd., Newtown, CT 06470-2359/203-426-1320; FAX: 203-426-1087

Sporting Clays of America (SCA)
Ellen McCormick, Director of Membership Services, 9 Mott Ave., Suite 103, Norwalk, CT 06850/203-831-8483; FAX: 203-831-8497
The Thompson/Center Assn.
Joe Wright, President, Box 792, Northboro, MA 01532/508-393-3834
U.S. Practical Shooting Assn./IPSC
Marilyn Stanford, P.O. Box 811, Sedro Woolley, WA 98284/206-855-2245
U.S. Revolver Assn.
Brian J. Barer, 40 Larchmont Ave., Taunton, MA 02780
The Varmint Hunters Assn., Inc.
Box 759, Pierre, SD 57501/Member Services 800-528-4868
Weatherby Collectors Assn., Inc.
P.O. Box 128, Moira, NY 12957
The Wildcatters
P.O. Box 170, Greenville, WI 54942
Winchester Arms Collectors Assn.
Richard Berg, Executive Secy., P.O. Box 6754, Great Falls, MT 59406
The Women's Shooting Sports Foundation (WSSF)
1505 Highway 6 South, Suite 101, Houston, TX 77077

AUSTRALIA

Sporting Shooters Assn. of Australia, Inc.
P.O. Box 2066, Kent Town, SA 5071, Australia

CANADA

ALBERTA

Canadian Historical Arms Society
P.O. Box 901, Edmonton, Alb., Canada T5J 2L8
National Firearms Assn.
Natl. Hq: P.O. Box 1779, Edmonton, Alb., Canada T5J 2P1

ONTARIO

Tri-County Antique Arms Fair
P.O. Box 122, RR #1, North Lancaster Ont., Canada K0C 1Z0

EUROPE

ENGLAND

Arms and Armour Society
E.J.B. Greenwood, Field House, Upper Dicker, Hailsham, East Sussex, BN27 3PY, England
Historical Breechloading Smallarms Assn.
D.J. Penn M.A., Imperial War Museum, Lambeth Rd., London SE 1 6HZ, England.
Journal and newsletter are $13 a yr., plus surcharge for airmail.
National Rifle Assn.
(Great Britain) Bisley Camp, Brookwood, Woking Surrey GU24 OPB, England/0483.797777
FRANCE
Syndicat National de l'Arquebuserie du Commerce de l'Arme Historique
B.P. No. 3, 78110 Le Vesinet, France
GERMANY
Bund Deutscher Sportschützen e.v. (BDS)
Borsigallee 10, 53125 Bonn 1, Germany

NEW ZEALAND

New Zealand Deerstalkers Assn.
Michael Watt, P.O. Box 6514, Wellington, New Zealand

SOUTH AFRICA

Historical Firearms Soc. of South Africa
P.O. Box 145, 7725 Newlands, Republic of South Africa
SAGA (S.A. Gunowners' Assn.)
P.O. Box 35204, Northway 4065, Republic of South Africa

HANDGUNS 95

DIRECTORY
OF THE
HANDGUNNER'S TRADE

PRODUCT DIRECTORY

AMMUNITION, COMMERCIAL

Action Arms Ltd.
American Ammunition
Amtech International, Inc.
Amtech-Overseas, Inc.
Black Hills Ammunition
Blammo Ammo
Blount, Inc.
Buck-X, Inc.
California Magnum
CBC
Cherokee Gun Accessories
ChinaSports, Inc.
Cor-Bon Bullet & Ammo Co.
Daisy Mfg. Co.
Diana
DKT, Inc.
Dynamit Nobel-RWS, Inc.
Eley Ltd.
Elite Ammunition
Federal Cartridge Co.
Fiocchi of America, Inc.
FN Herstal
Gamo
GDL Enterprises
Glaser Safety Slug, Inc.
"Gramps" Antique Cartridges
Hansen & Co.
Hansen Cartridge Co.
Hirtenberger Aktiengesellschaft
Hornady Mfg. Co.
ICI-America
IMI
IMI Services USA, Inc.
Jones, J.D.
Keng's Firearms Specialty, Inc.
Kent Cartridge Mfg. Co. Ltd.
Lapua Ltd.
Lethal Force Institute
Lomont Precision Bullets
M&D Munitions Ltd.
Magnum Research, Inc.

MagSafe Ammo Co.
MAGTECH Recreational
    Products, Inc.
Maionchi-L.M.I.
Markell, Inc.
Master Class Bullets
Men-Metallwerk
    Elisenhuette, GmbH
Mullins Ammo
NECO
Neutralizer Police Munitions
New England Ammunition Co.
Oklahoma Ammunition Co.
Old Western Scrounger, Inc.
Omark Industries
Patriot Manufacturing
PMC/Eldorado Cartridge Corp.
Police Bookshelf
Pony Express Reloaders
Precision Delta Corp.
Pro Load Ammunition, Inc.
Ravell Ltd.
Remington Arms Co., Inc.
Rocky Fork Enterprises
Royal Arm International Products
Rucker Ammunition Co.
RWS
Sherwood Intl. Export Corp.
Speer Products
SSK Industries
Star Reloading Co., Inc.
The BulletMakers Workshop
3-D Ammunition & Bullets
3-Ten Corp.
True Flight Bullet Co.
USAC
Valor Corp.
Victory USA
Winchester Div., Olin Corp.
Zero Ammunition Co., Inc.

AMMUNITION, CUSTOM

Accuracy Unlimited (Littleton, CO)
AFSCO Ammunition
All American Bullets
American Derringer Corp.
Ballistica Maximus North
Bear Arms
Beeline Custom Bullets
Black Hills Ammunition
Brynin, Milton
BulletMakers Workshop, The
Christman Jr., David
Country Armourer, The
Custom Hunting Ammo & Arms
Custom Tackle & Ammo
C.W. Cartridge Co.
Deadeye Sport Center
DKT, Inc.
Eagle Flight Bullet Co.
Eley Ltd.
Elite Ammunition
Elko Arms
Ellis Sport Shop, E.W.
Epps "Orillia" Ltd., Ellwood
Fitz Pistol Grip Co.
Fox Cartridge Division
Freedom Arms, Inc.
Gammog, Gregory B. Gally
Gonzalez Guns, Ramon B.
"Gramps" Antique Cartridges
Granite Custom Bullets
Green Bay Bullets
Heidenstrom Bullets
Hindman, Ace
Hirtenberger Aktiengesellschaft
Hoelscher, Virgil

Horizons Unlimited
Hornady Mfg. Co.
Jackalope Gun Shop
Jaro Manufacturing
Jensen Bullets
Jensen's Custom Ammunition
Jensen's Firearm Academy
Jett & Co., Inc.
Jones, J.D.
Kaswer Custom, Inc.
Keeler, R.H.
Kent Cartridge Mfg. Co. Ltd.
KJM Fabritek, Inc.
Kortz, Dr. L.
Lindsley Arms Cartridge Co.
Lomont Precision Bullets
M&D Munitions Ltd.
Marple & Associates, Dick
Master Class Bullets
McMurdo, Lynn
Men-Metallwerk
    Elisenhuette, GmbH
Mullins Ammo
NECO
Oklahoma Ammunition Co.
Old Western Scrounger, Inc.
Parts & Surplus
Pasadena Gun Center
Personal Protection Systems Ltd.
Precision Delta Corp.
Precision Munitions, Inc.
Professional Hunter Supplies
Sanders Custom Gun Service
Sandia Die & Cartridge Co.
Slings & Arrows

Specialty Gunsmithing
Spence, George W.
SSK Industries
Star Custom Bullets
State Arms Gun Co.
Stewart's Gunsmithing
Three-Ten Corp.
True Flight Bullet Co.

Vulpes Ventures, Inc.
Warren Muzzleloading Co., Inc.
Weaver Arms Corp.
Worthy Products, Inc.
Wyoming Armory, Inc.
Wyoming Bonded Bullets
Zero Ammunition Co., Inc.

AMMUNITION, FOREIGN

Action Arms Ltd.
AFSCO Ammunition
Ammunition Consulting
    Services, Inc.
Armscorp USA, Inc.
BulletMakers Workshop, The
B-West Imports, Inc.
Century International Arms, Inc.
Deadeye Sport Center
Diana
DKT, Inc.
Dynamit Nobel-RWS, Inc.
Fiocchi of America, Inc.
FN Herstal
Gamo
Gonzalez Guns, Ramon B.
"Gramps" Antique Cartridges
Hirtenberger Aktiengesellschaft
Hornady Mfg. Co.

IMI
Jackalope Gun Shop
Kassnar
K.B.I., Inc.
Maionchi-L.M.I.
Merkuria Ltd.
New England Arms Co.
Oklahoma Ammunition Co.
Old Western Scrounger, Inc.
Paragon Sales & Services, Inc.
Precision Delta Corp.
R.E.T. Enterprises
RWS
Samco Global Arms, Inc.
Sherwood Intl. Export Corp.
Southern Ammunition Co., Inc.
Spence, George W.
Talon Mfg. Co., Inc.
T.F.C. S.p.A.

AMMUNITION COMPONENTS— BULLETS, POWDER, PRIMERS, CASES

Acadian Ballistic Specialties
Accuracy Unlimited (Littleton, CO)
Accurate Arms Co., Inc.
Action Bullets, Inc.
Advance Car Mover Co.,
    Rowell Div.
Alaska Bullet Works
Allred Bullet Co.
American Bullets
American Products Co.
Ames Metal Products Co.
Badger Shooters Supply, Inc.
Ballard Built
Banaczkowski Bullets
Barnes Bullets, Inc.
Beartooth Bullets
Bell Reloading, Inc.
Bergman & Williams
Berry's Bullets
Bitterroot Bullet Co.
Black Hills Shooters Supply
Black Mountain Bullets
Blount, Inc.
Briese Bullet Co., Inc.
Brown Co., E. Arthur
Brownells, Inc.
BRP, Inc.
Buck Stix
Buckeye Custom Bullets
Buffalo Bullet Co., Inc.
Buffalo Rock Shooters Supply
Bullet, Inc.
Bullet Mills
Bullseye Bullets
Bull-X, Inc.
Butler Enterprises
Calhoon Varmint Bullets, James
Canadian Custom Bullets
Canyon Cartridge Corp.
Carnahan Bullets
Carroll Bullets
Cascade Bullet Co., Inc.
CBC
CCI
CFVentures

Champion's Choice, Inc.
Cheddite France S.A.
CheVron Bullets
Circle M Custom Bullets
Competitor Corp., Inc.
Cook Engineering Service
Cor-Bon Bullet & Ammo Co.
Crawford Co., Inc., R.M.
Creative Cartridge Co.
Cummings Bullets
Curtis Gun Shop
Custom Bullets by Hoffman
D&J Bullet Co. & Custom
    Gun Shop, Inc.
Dakota Arms
Deadeye Sport Center
Dohring Bullets
DuPont
Enguix Import-Export
Federal Cartridge Co.
Finch Custom Bullets
Fiocchi of America, Inc.
Fitz Pistol Grip Co.
Foy Custom Bullets
Freedom Arms, Inc.
G&C Bullet Co., Inc.
Gehmann, Walter
GOEX, Inc.
Gotz Bullets
"Gramps" Antique Cartridges
Grand Falls Bullets
Granite Custom Bullets
Green Bay Bullets
Grizzly Bullets
Gun City
Hardin Specialty Dist.
Haselbauer Products, Jerry
Hawk Co.
Heidenstrom Bullets
Hercules, Inc.
HH Engineering
Hirtenberger Aktiengesellschaft
Hobson Precision
    Manufacturing Co.
Hodgdon Powder Co., Inc.

Hornady Mfg. Co.
Huntington Die Specialties
Idaho Bullets
IMI
IMI Services USA, Inc.
IMR Powder Co.
J-4, Inc.
J&D Components
J&L Superior Bullets
Jaro Manufacturing
Jensen Bullets
Jensen's Firearms Academy
Jester Bullets
Jones, J.D.
Ka Pu Kapili
Kasmarsnik Bullets
Kaswer Custom, Inc.
Keith's Bullets
Ken's Kustom Kartridge
Kent Cartridge Mfg. Co. Ltd.
KJM Fabritek, Inc.
Kodiak Custom Bullets
Lachaussee, S.A.
Lane Bullets, Inc.
Lapua Ltd.
Lathrop's, Inc.
Liberty Shooting Supplies
Lightfield Ammunition Corp.,
    The Slug Group
Lindsley Arms Cartridge Co.
Lomont Precision Bullets
M&D Munitions Ltd.
Magnus Bullets
Maine Custom Bullets
Maionchi-L.M.I.
Marchmon Bullets
Master Class Bullets
McKenzie Bullet Co.
McMurdo, Lynn
MCRW Associates
    Shooting Supplies
Men-Metallwerk
    Elisenhuette, GmbH
Merkuria Ltd.
Miller Enterprises, Inc.
Miller Enterprises, Inc., R.P.
Mi-Te Bullets
MoLoc Bullets
Mushroom Express Bullet Co.
Nagel's Bullets
National Bullet Co.
Necromancer Industries, Inc.
Norma
Nosler, Inc.
Oklahoma Ammunition Co.
Old Wagon Bullets
Old Western Scrounger, Inc.
Omark Industries
Pace Marketing, Inc.
Page Custom Bullets
Paragon Sales & Services, Inc.
Pasadena Gun Center

Patrick Bullets
Peerless Alloy, Inc.
Petro-Explo, Inc.
Phillippi Custom Bullets, Justin
Pomeroy, Robert
Precision Ballistics Co.
Precision Components
Precision Components & Guns
Precision Delta Corp.
Precision Munitions, Inc.
Prescott Projectile Co.
Price Bullets, Patrick W.
Rainier Ballistic Corp.
Ravell Ltd.
Redwood Bullet Works
Remington Arms Co., Inc.
Rencher Bullets
Renner Co., R.J./Radical
    Concepts
Robinson H.V. Bullets
Rolston, Jr., Fred W.
Rucker Ammunition Co.
Sabertooth Industries
Schmidtman Custom Ammunition
Scot Powder Co. of Ohio, Inc.
Shappy Bullets
Sinclair International, Inc.
Sioux Bullets
SOS Products Co.
Southern Ammunition Co., Inc.
Specialty Gunsmithing
Speer Products
SSK Industries
Stanley Bullets
Stark's Bullets Manufacturing
Stewart's Gunsmithing
Swift Bullet Co.
Talon Mfg. Co., Inc.
TCCI
TCSR
T.F.C. S.p.A.
Thompson Precision
3-D Ammunition & Bullets
TMI Products
Trophy Bonded Bullets, Inc.
True Flight Bullet Co.
USAC
Vann Custom Bullets
Vihtavuori Oy
Vihtavuori Oy/Kaltron-Pettibone
Vincent's Shop
Watson Trophy Match Bullets
Widener's Reloading &
    Shooting Supply
Williams Bullet Co., J.R.
Winchester Div., Olin Corp.
Winkle Bullets
Woodleigh
Wyant Bullets
Wyoming Armory, Inc.
Zero Ammunition Co., Inc.

Pony Express Sport Shop, Inc.
Pre-Winchester 92-90-62
    Parts Co.
P.S.M.G. Gun Co.
Ravell Ltd.
Retting, Inc., Martin B.
Rutgers Gun & Boat Center

Scott Fine Guns, Inc., Thad
Semmer, Charles
Sherwood Intl. Export Corp.
Steves House of Guns
Vintage Arms, Inc.
Wood, Frank S.
Yearout, Lewis E.

APPRAISERS—GUNS, ETC.

Ahlman Guns
Ammunition Consulting
    Services, Inc.
Amodei, Jim
Antique Arms Co.
Armoury, Inc., The
Beeman Precision Airguns, Inc.
Behlert Precision
Blue Book Publications, Inc.
Bustani Appraisers, Leo
Butterfield & Butterfield
Camilli, Lou
Cannons Guns
Cape Outfitters
Chadick's Ltd.
Champlin Firearms, Inc.
Christie's East
Clark Firearms Engraving
Classic Guns, Inc.
Clements' Custom
    Leathercraft, Chas
Condon, Inc., David
Corry, John
Cullity Restoration, Daniel
Custom Tackle & Ammo
D&D Gunsmiths, Ltd.
Dixon Muzzleloading Shop, Inc.
D.O.C. Specialists, Inc.
Ed's Gun House
Ellis Sport Shop, E.W.
Epps "Orillia" Ltd., Ellwood
Fagan & Co., William
Fish, Marshall F.
Flayderman & Co., Inc., N.
Forgett, Valmore J., Jr.
Fredrick Gun Shop
Frontier Arms Co., Inc.
Goergen's Gun Shop, Inc.
Golden Age Arms Co.
Gonzalez Guns, Ramon B.
Goodwin, Fred
Greenwald, Leon E. "Bud"
Griffin & Howe, Inc.
Gun City
Gun Shop, The
Gun Works, The
Guncraft Sports, Inc.
Hallowell & Co.
Hank's Gun Shop
Hansen & Co.
Hughes, Steven Dodd
Irwin, Campbell H.
Jaeger, Inc., Paul/Dunn's

Jonas Appraisers &Taxidermy, Jack
Kelley's
Ledbetter Airguns, Riley
LeFever Arms Co., Inc.
Lock's Philadelphia Gun Exchange
Lynx-Line, The
Mac's .45 Shop
Mack's Sport Shop
Madis, George
Marple & Associates, Dick
Martin's Gun Shop
McGowan Rifle Barrels
Montana Outfitters
Moreton/Fordyce Enterprises
Mowreys Guns & Gunsmithing
Muzzleloaders Etcetera, Inc.
Oakland Custom Arms, Inc.
Orvis Co., The
Parke-Bernet
Pentheny de Pentheny
Perazzi U.S.A., Inc.
Pettinger Books, Gerald
Pioneer Guns
Pony Express Sport Shop, Inc.
Precision Arms International, Inc.
Pre-Winchester 92-90-62
    Parts Co.
P.S.M.G. Gun Co.
R.E.T. Enterprises
Richards, John
Rutgers Gun & Boat Center
Safari Outfitters Ltd.
Scott Fine Guns, Inc., Thad
Shell Shack
Silver Ridge Gun Shop
S.K. Guns, Inc.
Sotheby's
Stratco, Inc.
300 Gunsmith Service, Inc.
Thurston Sports, Inc.
Tillinghast, James C.
Ulrich, Doc & Bud
Unick's Gunsmithing
Vic's Gun Refinishing
Wayne Firearms for Collectors and
    Investors, James
Wells Custom Gunsmith, R.A.
Whildin & Sons Ltd., E.H.
Whitestone Lumber Corp.
Wiest, M.C.
Williams Shootin' Iron Service
Wood, Frank S.
Yearout, Lewis E.

ANTIQUE ARMS DEALERS

Ad Hominem
Antique American Firearms
Antique Arms Co.
Aplan Antiques & Art, James O.
Armoury, Inc., The
Arms, Jackson
Bear Mountain Gun & Tool
Beeman Precision Airguns, Inc.
Big 45 Frontier Gun Shop
Boggs, Wm.
British Arms Co. Ltd.
Buckskin Machine Works
Bustani Appraisers, Leo
Cannons Guns
Cape Outfitters
Carlson, Douglas R.
Chadick's Ltd.
Champlin Firearms, Inc.
Chuck's Gun Shop
Classic Guns, Inc.
Cole's Gun Works
Colonial Repair
Condon, Inc., David
Cullity Restoration, Daniel
D&D Gunsmiths, Ltd.
Dyson & Son Ltd., Peter
Ed's Gun House
Epps "Orillia" Ltd., Ellwood
Fagan & Co., William
Fish, Marshall F.
Flayderman & Co., N.

Flintlock Muzzle Loading
    Gun Shop, The
Forty Five Ranch Enterprises
Frielich Police Equipment
Fulmer's Antique Firearms, Chet
Galazan Shotgun Mfg. Co.
Glass, Herb
Goergen's Gun Shop, Inc.
Golden Age Arms Co.
Gun Works, The
Guncraft Sports, Inc.
Hallowell & Co.
Hansen & Co.
Hunkeler, A.
Johns, Bill
Kelley's
Ledbetter Airguns, Riley
LeFever Arms Co., Inc.
Lever Arms Service Ltd.
Lock's Philadelphia Gun Exchange
Log Cabin Sport Shop
McCann's Muzzle-Gun Works
Mendez, John A.
Montana Outfitters
Museum of Historical Arms, Inc.
Muzzleloaders Etcetera, Inc.
Navy Arms Co.
New England Arms Co.
New Orleans Arms Co.
Parker-Hale
Pioneer Guns

AUCTIONEERS—GUNS, ETC.

Ammunition Consulting
    Services, Inc.
Bourne Co., Inc., Richard A.
Butterfield & Butterfield
Christie's East
Fagan & Co., William
Goodwin, Fred

Kelley's
"Little John's" Antique Arms
Parke-Bernet
Silver Ridge Gun Shop
Sotheby's
Tillinghast, James C.

BOOKS (Publishers and Dealers)

American Handgunner Magazine
Armory Publications
Arms & Armour Press
Ballistic Products, Inc.
Barnes Bullets, Inc.
Beeman Precision Airguns, Inc.
Bellm Contenders
Blackhawk East
Blackhawk Mountain
Blackhawk West
Blacksmith Corp.
Blacktail Mountain Books
Blue Book Publications, Inc.
Brown Co., E. Arthur
Brownell's, Inc.
Calibre Press, Inc.
Colorado Sutlers Arsenal
Corbin, Inc.

DBI Books, Inc.
Flores Publications, Inc., J.
Golden Age Arms Co.
"Gramps" Antique Cartridges
Gun City
Gun Hunter Books
Gun List
Gun Room Press, The
Gunnerman Books
GUNS Magazine
H&P Publishing
Handgun Press
Haydon Shooters' Supply, Russ
Hodgdon Powder Co., Inc.
Home Shop Machinist, The
Hornady Mfg. Co.
Hungry Horse Books
Ironside International Publishers, Inc.

King & Co.
Krause Publications
Lane Publishing
Lapua Ltd.
Lyman Instant Targets, Inc.
Lyman Products Corp.
Madis, David
Magma Engineering Co.
Martin Bookseller, J.
McKee Publications
Mountain South
New Win Publishing, Inc.
Old Western Scrounger, Inc.
Outdoorsman's Bookstore, The
Pejsa Ballistics
Petersen Publishing Co.
Pettinger Books, Gerald
Pointing Dog Journal
Precision Shooting, Inc.

Ravell Ltd.
Reloading Specialties, Inc.
Riling Arms Books Co., Ray
Rutgers Book Center
Rutgers Gun & Boat Center
Safari Press, Inc.
Shootin' Accessories, Ltd.
Stackpole Books
Stoeger Publishing Co.
Survival Books/The Larder
Thomas, Charles C.
Trafalgar Square
Trotman, Ken
Vom Hofe
VSP Publishers
WAMCO-New Mexico
Weisz Antique Gun Parts
Wilderness Sound Products Ltd.
Wolfe Publishing Co.

BULLET AND CASE LUBRICANTS

Blackhawk East
Blackhawk Mountain
Blackhawk West
Blount, Inc.
Brown Co., E. Arthur
Camp-Cap Products
CFVentures
C-H Tool & Die Corp.
Chem-Pak, Inc.
Cooper-Woodward
Corbin, Inc.
Cunard & Co., J.
Dillon Precision Prods., Inc.
Eezox, Inc.
Elkhorn Bullets
E-Z-Way Systems
Fitz Pistol Grip Co.
Forster Products
4-D Custom Die Co.
GAR
Guardsman Products
HEBB Resources
Hollywood Engineering
Hornady Mfg. Co.
INTEC International, Inc.

Javelina Products
Jonad Corp.
Lee Precision, Inc.
Lithi Bee Bullet Lube
M&N Bullet Lube
Magma Engineering Co.
Micro-Lube
NECO
Old Western Scrounger, Inc.
Paco's
Ravell Ltd.
RCBS
Reardon Products
Redding Reloading, Inc.
Rooster Laboratories
SAECO
Shay's Gunsmithing
Slipshot MTS Group
Small Custom Mould & Bullet Co.
SPG Lubricants
Tamarack Products, Inc.
Thompson Bullet Lube Co.
Vom Hofe
Warren Muzzleloading Co., Inc.
Young Country Arms

BULLET SWAGE DIES AND TOOLS

Berger Bullets
Blount, Inc.
Bruno Shooters Supply
Brynin, Milton
Bullet Swaging Supply, Inc.
C-H Tool & Die Corp.
Corbin, Inc.
Fitz Pistol Grip Co.
4-D Custom Die Co.
"Gramps" Antique Cartridges

Holland's
Hollywood Engineering
King & Co.
Lachaussee, S.A.
Necromancer Industries, Inc.
Niemi Engineering, W.B.
Rorschach Precision Products
Speer Products
Sport Flite Manufacturing Co.
Vega Tool Co.

CARTRIDGES FOR COLLECTORS

Ad Hominem
Ammunition Consulting
   Services, Inc.
Baekgaard Ltd.
Big 45 Frontier Gun Shop
Cameron's
Campbell, Dick
Dakota Arms
Duffy, Chas. E.
Ed's Gun House
Eichelberger Bullets, Wm.
Enguix Import-Export
Epps "Orillia" Ltd., Ellwood
First Distributors, Inc., Jack
Forty Five Ranch Enterprises
"Gramps" Antique Cartridges

Idaho Ammunition Service
Kelley's
Michael's Antiques
Montana Outfitters
Mountain Bear Rifle Works, Inc.
Muzzleloaders Etcetera, Inc.
Naval Ordnance Works
Old Western Scrounger, Inc.
Ravell Ltd.
Rifle Works & Armory
San Francisco Gun Exchange
Tillinghast, James C.
Vom Hofe
Ward & Van Valkenburg
Weatherby, Inc.
Yearout, Lewis E.

CHRONOGRAPHS AND PRESSURE TOOLS

Brown Co., E. Arthur
Canons Delcour
Chronotech
Competition Electronics, Inc.
Custom Chronograph, Inc.
D&H Precision Tooling
Dedicated Systems
Hornady Mfg. Co.

Lachaussee, S.A.
Oehler Research, Inc.
Old Western Scrounger, Inc.
P.A.C.T., Inc.
Shooting Chrony, Inc.
Stratco, Inc.
Tepeco
Vom Hofe

CLEANING AND REFINISHING SUPPLIES

Acculube II, Inc.
Accupro Gun Care
Accuracy Products, S.A.
ADCO International
American Gas &
   Chemical Co., Ltd.
American Import Co., The
Armoloy Co. of Ft. Worth
Ballistic Products, Inc.
Barnes Bullets, Inc.
Belltown, Ltd.
Beretta, Dr. Franco
Big 45 Frontier Gun Shop
Bill's Gun Repair
Birchwood Casey
Blount, Inc.
Blue and Gray Products, Inc.
Break-Free, Inc.
Bridgers Best
Brobst, Jim
Brown Co., E. Arthur
Brown Precision, Inc.
Bruno Shooters Supply
Camp-Cap Products
Chem-Pak, Inc.
Chopie Mfg., Inc.
Clenzoil Corp.
Clymer Manufacturing Co., Inc.
Corbin, Inc.
Crane & Crane Ltd.
Creedmoor Sports, Inc.
Crouse's Country Cover
Custom Products
Dara-Nes, Inc.
Decker Shooting Products
Deepeeka Exports Pvt. Ltd.
Dewey Mfg. Co., Inc., J.
Du-Lite Corp.
Dutchman's Firearms, Inc., The
Dykstra, Doug
E&L Mfg., Inc.
E.A.A. Corp.
Eezox, Inc.
Ekol Leather Care
Faith Associates, Inc.
Flaig's
Flitz International Ltd.
Flouramics, Inc.
Forster Products
Forty Five Ranch Enterprises
Frontier Products Co.
G96 Products Co., Inc.
G.B.C. Industries, Inc.
Goddard, Allen
Golden Age Arms Co.
Gozon Corp.
Graves Co.
Guardsman Products
Half Moon Rifle Shop
Hart & Son, Inc., Robert W.
Heatbath Corp.
Hoppe's Div.
Hornady Mfg. Co.
Hydrosorbent Products
INTEC International, Inc.
Iosso Products
Jackalope Gun Shop
Jantz Supply
J-B Bore Cleaner
Johnston Bros.
Jonad Corp.
Jones Custom Products, Neil

Kesselring Gun Shop
Koppco Industries
Lee Supplies, Mark
LEM Gun Specialties, Inc.
LPS Laboratories, Inc.
Marble Arms Corp.
MCRW Associates
   Shooting Supplies
Micro Sight Co.
Minute Man High Tech Industries
Mountain View Sports, Inc.
MTM Molded Products Co., Inc.
Muscle Products Corp.
Nesci Enterprises, Inc.
Northern Precision Custom
   Swaged Bullets
Nygord Precision Products
Old World Oil Products
Omark Industries
Original Mink Oil, Inc.
Outers Laboratories, Div. of Blount
Ox-Yoke Originals, Inc.
P&M Sales and Service
Pachmayr Ltd.
Parker Gun Finishes
Pendleton Royal
Penguin Industries, Inc.
Precision Reloading, Inc.
Prolix
Pro-Shot Products, Inc.
R&S Industries Corp.
Radiator Specialty Co.
Ravell Ltd.
Raytech
Richards Classic Oil Finish, John
Rickard, Inc., Pete
RIG Products Co.
Rod Guide Co.
Rooster Laboratories
Rusteprufe Laboratories
Rusty Duck Premium
   Gun Care Products
San Angelo Sports Products, Inc.
Sharp Shooter, Inc.
Sheridan USA, Inc., Austin
Shiloh Creek
Shooter's Choice
Shootin' Accessories, Ltd.
Slipshot MTS Group
Speer Products
Stock Shop, The
Stoney Point Products, Inc.
Svon Corp.
TDP Industries, Inc.
Tetra Gun Lubricants
Texas Platers Supply Co.
T.F.C. S.p.A.
Treso, Inc.
Tyler Scott, Inc.
United States Products Co.
Valor Corp.
Van Gorden & Son, Inc., C.S.
Venco Industries, Inc.
Verdemont Fieldsports
Warren Muzzleloading Co., Inc.
WD-40 Co.
Whitestone Lumber Corp.
Williams Shootin' Iron Service
Willow Bend
World of Targets
Young Country Arms
Z-Coat Industrial Coatings, Inc.

COMPUTER SOFTWARE—BALLISTICS

Action Target, Inc.
ADC, Inc./PC Bullet
AmBr Software Group Ltd.
Arms, Peripheral Data Systems
Ballistic Products, Inc.
Ballistic Program Co., Inc., The
Barnes Bullets, Inc.
Beartooth Bullets
BestLoad, Inc.
Blackwell, W.
Blount, Inc.
Canons Delcour
Corbin, Inc.
Corbin Applied Technology
Country Armourer, The
Data Tech Software Systems
Exe, Inc.

Ford, Jack
JBM Software
Jensen Bullets
J.I.T. Ltd.
Lachaussee, S.A.
Lee Precision, Inc.
Load From A Disk
Magma Engineering Co.
Maionchi-L.M.I.
Oehler Research, Inc.
P.A.C.T., Inc.
Pejsa Ballistics
Precision Ballistics Co.
Ravell Ltd.
Regional Associates
Sierra Bullets
Tioga Engineering Co., Inc.

CUSTOM METALSMITHS

Ahlman Guns
Aldis Gunsmithing &
    Shooting Supply
Amrine's Gun Shop
Armurier Hiptmayer
Artistry In Wood
Baron Technology, Inc.
Bear Mountain Gun & Tool
Beitzinger, George
Bellm Contenders
Benchmark Guns
Biesen, Al
Billingsley & Brownell
Brace, Larry D.
Briganti & Co., A.
Brown Precision, Inc.
Campbell, Dick
Carter's Gun Shop
Checkmate Refinishing
Classic Guns, Inc.
Craftguard
Crandall Tool & Machine Co.
Cullity Restoration, Daniel
Custom Gun Products
Custom Gunsmiths
D&D Gunsmiths, Ltd.
D&H Precision Tooling
Duncan's Gunworks, Inc.
Dyson & Son Ltd., Peter
Eyster Heritage
    Gunsmiths, Inc., Ken
First Distributors, Inc., Jack
Forster, Larry L.
Francesca, Inc.
Fullmer, Geo. M.
Gilman-Mayfield, Inc.
Goodwin, Fred
Graybill's Gun Shop
Green, Roger M.
Gun Shop, The
Guns
Gunsmithing Ltd.
Hallberg Gunsmith, Fritz
Hamilton, Alex B.
Hecht, Hubert J.
Heilmann, Stephen
Highline Machine Co.
Hiptmayer, Klaus
Hoag, James W.
Hobaugh, Wm. H.
Hoelscher, Virgil
Hollands
Hollis Gun Shop
Home Shop Machinist, The
Hyper-Single, Inc.
Intermountain Arms & Tackle
Ivanoff, Thomas G.
J&S Heat Treat
Jaeger, Inc., Paul/Dunn's
Jamison's Forge Works
Jeffredo Gunsight
Johnston, James
Kilham & Co.
Klein Custom Guns, Don
Kleinendorst, K.W.
Lampert, Ron
Lawson Co., Harry
Long, George F.
Mac's .45 Shop
Mains Enterprises, Inc.

Makinson, Nicholas
Marek, George
McCament, Jay
McCormick's Custom Gun Bluing
McFarland, Stan
Mid-America Recreation, Inc.
Morrow, Bud
Mullis Guncraft
Nastoff's 45 Shop, Inc., Steve
Nettestad Gun Works
New England Custom Gun Service
Nicholson Custom
Noreen, Peter H.
North Fork Custom Gunsmithing
Olson, Vic
Ozark Gun Works
Pagel Gun Works, Inc.
Parker Gun Finishes
Pasadena Gun Center
Penrod Precision
Precision Metal Finishing
Precise Metalsmithing Enterprises
Precision Specialties
Pre-Winchester 92-90-62
    Parts Co.
Rice, Keith
Rifle Shop, The
RMS Custom Gunsmithing
Robar Co.'s, Inc., The
Roberts, J.J.
Robinson, Don
Shell Shack
Shirley Co. Gun &
    Riflemakers Ltd., J.A.
Silver Ridge Gun Shop
S.K. Guns, Inc.
Skeoch, Brian R.
Smith, Art
Snapp's Gunshop
Societa Armi Bresciane Srl.
Sportsmatch Ltd.
Sportsmen's Exchange & Western
    Gun Traders, Inc.
Stalwart Corp.
Steffens, Ron
Stiles Custom Guns
Szweda, Robert
Talley, Dave
Ten-Ring Precision, Inc.
Thompson, Randall
Tom's Gun Repair
T.S.W. Conversions, Inc.
Unick's Gunsmithing
Van Horn, Gil
Vic's Gun Refinishing
Waffen-Weber Custom Gunsmithing
Waldron, Herman
Wells, Fred F.
Welsh, Bud
Werth, T.W.
Wessinger Custom Guns & Engraving
West, Robert G.
Westchester Carbide
Western Design
Westrom, John
White Rock Tool & Die
Wiebe, Duane
Wilson's Gun Shop
Wisner's Gun Shop, Inc.
Wood, Frank S.

ENGRAVERS, ENGRAVING TOOLS

Adair Custom Shop, Bill
Adams, John J.
Ahlman Guns
Alfano, Sam
Allard, Gary
Allen, Richard L.
Altamont Co.
Anthony and George Ltd.
Armurier Hiptmayer
Artistic Engraving
Baron Technology, Inc.
Bates Engraving, Billy
Bledsoe, Weldon
Bleile, C. Roger
Boessler, Erich
Bone Engraving, Ralph
Bratcher, Dan
Brgoch, Frank
Brooker, Dennis
Brownell Checkering Tools, W.E.
CAM Enterprises

Churchill, Winston
Clark, Frank
Clark Firearms Engraving
Collings, Ronald
Creek Side Metal & Woodcrafters
Davidson, Jere
Delorge, Ed
Dolbare, Elizabeth
Drain, Mark
Dubber, Michael W.
Dyson & Son Ltd., Peter
EMF Co., Inc.
Engraving Artistry
Evans Engraving, Robert
Eyster Heritage
    Gunsmiths, Inc., Ken
Fanzoj GesmbH
Firearms Engraver's
    Guild of America
Flannery Engraving Co., Jeff W.
Floatstone Mfg. Co.

Fogle, James W.
Fountain Products
Francolini, Leonard
Frank Knives
French, J.R.
Gene's Custom Guns
George, Tim and Christy
Glimm, Jerome C.
Golden Age Arms Co.
Gournet, Geoffroy
Grant, Howard V.
Griffin & Howe, Inc.
GRS Corp.
Gun Room, The
Gurney, F.R.
Gwinnell, Bryson J.
Hale, Peter
Hand Engravers Supply Co.
Hands, Barry Lee
Harris Hand Engraving, Paul A.
Harwood, Jack O.
Hendricks, Frank E.
Herrett's Stocks, Inc.
Hiptmayer, Heidemarie
Horst, Alan K.
Ingle, Ralph W.
Jaeger, Inc., Paul/Dunn's
Johns, Bill
Kamyk Engraving Co., Steve
Kehr, Roger L.
Kelly, Lance
Klingler Woodcarving
Koevenig's Engraving Service
Kudlas, John M.
Lebeau-Courally
LeFever Arms Co., Inc.
Leibowitz, Leonard
Letschnig, Franz
Lindsay, Steve
Little Trees Ramble
Lutz Engraving, Ron
Mains Enterprises, Inc.
Maki School of Engraving,
    Robert E.
Marek, George
Master Engravers, Inc.
McCombs, Leo
McDonald, Dennis
McKenzie, Lynton
Mele, Frank
Mid-America Recreation, Inc.
Mittermeier, Inc., Frank
Montgomery Community College
Moschetti, Mitchell R.

Mountain States Engraving
Nelson, Gary K.
New Orleans Arms Co.
New Orleans Jewelers Supply Co.
NgraveR Co., The
Oker's Engraving
Old Dominion Engravers
P&S Gun Service
Palmgren Steel Products
Pedersen, C.R.
Pedersen, Rex C.
Pilkington, Scott
Piquette, Paul R.
Potts, Wayne E.
Rabeno, Martin
Ravell Ltd.
Reed, Dave
Reno, Wayne
Riggs, Jim
Roberts, J.J.
Rohner, Hans
Rohner, John
Rosser, Bob
Rundell's Gun Shop
Runge, Robert P.
Sampson, Roger
Schiffman, Mike
Sheffield Knifemakers Supply
Sherwood, George
Sinclair, W.P.
Singletary, Kent
Skaggs, R.E.
Smith, Mark A.
Smith, Ron
Smokey Valley Rifles
Theis, Terry
Thiewes, George W.
Thirion Hand Engraving, Denise
Tuscano, Tony
Valade, Robert B.
Vest, John
Viramontez, Ray
Vorhes, David
Waffen-Weber Custom Gunsmithing
Wagoner, Vernon G.
Wallace, Terry
Warenski, Julie
Warren, Kenneth W.
Welch, Sam
Wells, Rachel
Wessinger Custom Guns & Engraving
Willig Custom Engraving, Claus
Wood, Mel

GUN PARTS, U.S. AND FOREIGN

Ad Hominem
Ahlman Guns
Amherst Arms
Armscorp USA, Inc.
Bear Mountain Gun & Tool
Bob's Gun Shop
Briese Bullet Co., Inc.
British Arms Co. Ltd.
Bushmaster Firearms
Can Am Enterprises
Cape Outfitters
Caspian Arms
Century International Arms, Inc.
Chuck's Gun Shop
Colonial Repair
Costa, David
Cylinder & Slide, Inc.
Defense Moulding Enterprises
Delta Arms Ltd.
Dibble, Derek A.
Dragun Enterprises
Duffy, Charles E.
E&L Mfg., Inc.
Eagle International, Inc.
EMF Co., Inc.
Fabian Bros. Sporting Goods, Inc.
FAPA Corp.
First Distributors, Inc., Jack
Fleming Firearms
Forrest, Inc., Tom
Greider Precision
Gun Parts Corp., The
Gun Shop, The
Gun-Tec
Hastings Barrels
High Performance International
Irwin, Campbell H.
Island Pond Gun Shop
Jaeger, Inc., Paul/Dunn's

J.O. Arms & Ammunition Co.
Johnson Gunsmithing, Inc.,
    Neal G.
K&T Co.
Kimber, Inc.
K.K. Arms Co.
Krico/Kriegeskorte GmbH, A.
Laughridge, William R.
Liberty Antique Gunworks
Lodewick, Walter H.
Mac's .45 Shop
Markell, Inc.
McCormick Corp., Chip
Merkuria Ltd.
Moreton/Fordyce Enterprises
Morrow, Bud
Mountain Bear Rifle Works, Inc.
MPI Stocks
North American Specialties
Nu-Line Guns, Inc.
Oakland Custom Arms, Inc.
Old Western Scrounger, Inc.
Pace Marketing, Inc.
Pachmayr Ltd.
Parts & Surplus
Peacemaker Specialists
Pennsylvania Gun Parts
Perazzi U.S.A., Inc.
Pre-Winchester 92-90-62
    Parts Co.
Quality Firearms of Idaho, Inc.
Quality Parts Co.
Ranch Products
Randco UK
Ravell Ltd.
Retting, Inc., Martin B.
Rizzini Battista
Rutgers Gun & Boat Center
Safari Arms, Inc./SGW

Sarco, Inc.
Scherer
Shell Shack
Sheridan USA, Inc., Austin
Sherwood Intl. Export Corp.
Smires, C.
Southern Ammunition Co., Inc.
Southern Armory, The
Sportsmen's Exchange & Western
  Gun Traders, Inc.
Springfield, Inc.
Springfield Sporters, Inc.
"Su-Press-On," Inc.
Tank's Rifle Shop
Tapco, Inc.
Tradewinds, Inc.

T.S.W. Conversions, Inc.
Twin Pine Armory
Uberti USA, Inc.
Vintage Arms, Inc.
Vintage Industries, Inc.
Vom Hofe
Walker Arms Co., Inc.
Wardell Precision Handguns Ltd.
Weaver's Gun Shop
Weigand Combat Handguns, Inc.
Weisz Antique Gun Parts
Westfield Engineering
Wilson's Gun Shop
Wisner's Gun Shop, Inc.
Wolff Co., W.C.

GUNS, AIR

Action Arms Ltd.
Air Venture
Airgun Repair Centre
Anschutz GmbH
Beeman Precision Airguns, Inc.
Benjamin/Sheridan Co.
Brass Eagle, Inc.
Century International Arms, Inc.
Champion's Choice, Inc.
Component Concepts, Inc.
Crawford Co., Inc., R.M.
Crosman Airguns
Crosman Products of Canada Ltd.
Daisy Mfg. Co.
Diana
Dynamit Nobel-RWS, Inc.
FAS
Frankonia Jagd
FWB
Gamo
GFR Corp. Great Lakes Airguns
Hammerli Ltd.
Hartmann & Weiss GmbH
Hebard Guns, Gil
Hofmann & Co.
Hy-Score Arms Co. Ltd.
Interarms
I.S.S.
Mac-1 Distributors

Marksman Products
Merkuria Ltd.
National Survival Game, Inc.,
Nationwide Airgun Repairs
Nygord Precision
P&S Gun Service
Pardini Armi Commerciale Srl
Penguin Industries, Inc.
Precision Airgun Sales, Inc.
Precision Saltes Int'l, Inc.
Ravell Ltd.
Rossi S.A., Amadeo
RWS
Savana Sports, Inc.
S.G.S. Sporting Guns Srl
Sheridan USA, Inc., Austin
Sportsmatch Ltd.
Syeyr-Mannlicher AG
Stone Enterprises Ltd.
Swivel Machine Works, Inc.
Taurus, S.A., Forjas
Tippman Pneumatics, Inc.
Uberti, Aldo
UltraSport Arms, Inc.
Valor Corp.
Walther GmbH, Carl
Webley and Scott Ltd.
Weihrauch KG, Hermann

GUNS, FOREIGN—IMPORTERS (Manufacturers)

• Action Arms Ltd. (BRNO; CZ)
• American Arms, Inc. (Fausti & Figlie
  s.n.c., Stefano; Franchi S.p.A., Luigi;
  Grulla Armes; INDESAL; Norica,
  Avnda Otaloa; Uberti, Aldo; Zabala
  Hermanos S.A.; blackpowder arms)
• Armscorp USA, Inc.
  Armsport, Inc. (airguns;
  blackpowder arms)
• Beeman Precision Airguns, Inc.
  (Beeman Precision Airguns, Inc.; FWB;
  Hammerli Ltd.; Webley & Scott Ltd.;
  Weihrauch KG, Hermann)
• Beretta U.S.A. Corp. (Beretta Firearms,
  Pietro)
• Browning Arms Co. (Browning
  Arms Co.)
  B-West Imports, Inc.
• Cabela's (Pedersoli, Davide & C.;
  blackpowder arms)
• Century International Arms, Inc.
  (Famas; FEG; Norinco)
• ChinaSports, Inc. (Norinco)
• Cimarron Arms (Uberti, Aldo;
  blackpowder arms)
• CVA (blackpowder arms)
• Daisy Mfg. Co. (Daisy Mfg. Co.; Gamo)
• Dixie Gun Works (Pedersoli, Davide &
  C.; Uberti, Aldo; blackpowder arms)
• Dynamit Nobel-RWS, Inc. (Brenneke
  KG, Wilhelm; Diana; Gamo; RWS)
• E.A.A. Corp. (Astra-Unceta Y Cia, S.A.;
  Benelli Armi S.p.A.; Fabrica D'Armi
  Sabatti S.r.l.; Tanfoglio S.r.l.,
  Fratelli/Witness; Weihrauch KG,
  Hermann)
• Eagle Imports, Inc. (Bersa S.A.)
• EMF Co., Inc. (Dakota; Pedersoli,
  Davide & C.; San Marco; Uberti, Aldo;
  blackpowder arms)
• Euroarms of America, Inc. (blackpowder
  arms)
• Glock, Inc. (Glock GmbH)
• Great Lakes Airguns

• Hammerli USA (Hammerli Ltd.)
• Heckler & Koch, Inc. (Benelli Armi
  S.p.A.; Heckler & Koch, GmbH)
• Interarms (Helwan; Howa Machinery
  Ltd.; Interarms; Norinco; Rossi,
  Amadeo; Star Bonifacio Echeverria
  S.A.; Walther GmbH, Carl)
• Ithaca Acquisition Corp. (Fabarm S.p.A.)
• J.O. Arms & Ammunition Co. (J.O. Arms
  & Ammunition Co.)
• K.B.I., Inc. (Baikal; FEG; Kassnar;
  K.B.I., Inc.)
• Magnum Research, Inc. (IMI)
• Mandall Shooting Supplies, Inc.
  (Arizaga; Bretton; Cabanas;
  Crucelegoi, Hermanos; Erma Werke
  GmbH; Firearms Co. Ltd./Alpine;
  Gaucher Armes S.A.; Hammerli Ltd.;
  Korth; Krico/Kriegeskorte GmbH, A.;
  Morini; SIG; Tanner; Techni-Mec;
  Ugartechea S.A., Ignacio; Zanoletti,
  Pietro; blackpowder arms)
• Marksman Products (Marksman
  Products)
• McMillan Gunworks, Inc. (Peters
  Stahl GmbH)
• Mitchell Arms, Inc. (Mitchell Arms, Inc.;
  Uberti, Aldo;
  blackpowder arms)
• Nationwide Sports Distributors (Daewoo
  Precision Industries)
• Navy Arms Co. (Navy Arms Co;
  Pedersoli, Davide & C.; Uberti, Aldo;
  blackpowder arms)
• Nygord Precision Products (FAS;
  Pardini Armi Commerciale Srl; Steyr;
  Unique/M.A.P.F.)
• Olympic Arms (Peters Stahl GmbH)
• Para-Ordnance, Inc. (Para-Ordnance
  Mfg., Inc.)
• Precision Sales International, Inc.
  (Anschutz GmbH; Erma Werke GmbH;
  Marocchi F.lli)
• SGS Importers International, Inc.

(Llama Gabilondo Y Cia)
• Sigarms, Inc. (SIG-Sauer)
• Sile Distributors (Benelli Armi S.p.A.;
  Marocchi F.lli S.p.A.; Solothurn)
• Sportarms of Florida (Schmidt, Herbert)
• Springfield, Inc. (Springfield, Inc.)

• Stoeger Industries (IGA; Sako Ltd.;
  Tikka)
  Stone Enterprises Ltd. (airguns)
• Taurus Firearms, Inc. (Taurus
  International Firearms)
• Uberti USA, Inc. (Uberti, Aldo;
  blackpowder arms)

GUNS, FOREIGN—MANUFACTURERS (Importers)

• Anschutz GmbH (Precision Sales
  International, Inc.)
• Astra-Unceta Y Cia, S.A. (E.A.A. Corp.)
• Baikal (K.B.I., Inc.)
• Beeman Precision Airguns, Inc.
  (Beeman Precision Airguns, Inc.)
• Beretta Firearms, Pietro (Beretta U.S.A.
  Corp.)
• Bernardelli S.p.A., Vincenzo
• Bersa S.A. (Eagle Imports, Inc.)
• BRNO (Action Arms Ltd.; Bohemia
  Arms Co.)
• Browning Arms Co. (Browning
  Arms Co.)
• CVA (blackpowder arms)
• CZ (Action Arms Ltd.)
• Daewoo Precision Industries Ltd.
  (Nationwide Sports Distributors)
• Daisy Mfg. Co. (Daisy Mfg. Co.)
• Diana (Dynamit Nobel-RWS, Inc.)
• Erma Werke GmbH (Mandall Shooting
  Supplies, Inc.; Precision Sales
  International)
• FAS (Nygord Precision Products)
• Fausti & Figlie s.n.c., Stefano (American
  Arms, Inc.)
• FEG (Century International Arms, Inc.;
  K.B.I., Inc.)
  FN Herstal
• FWB (Beeman Precision Airguns, Inc.)
• Gaucher Armes S.A. (Mandall Shooting
  Supplies, Inc.)
• Glock GmbH (Glock, Inc.)
• Hammerli Ltd. (Beeman Precision
  Airguns, Inc.; Hammerli USA; Mandall
  Shooting Supplies, Inc.)
• Heckler & Koch, GmbH (Heckler &
  Koch, Inc.)
• Helwan (Interarms)
• IMI (Magnum Research, Inc.)
• Interarms (Interarms)
• J.O. Arms & Ammunition Co. (J.O. Arms
  & Ammunition Co.)
• Kassnar (K.B.I., Inc.)
• K.B.I., Inc. (K.B.I., Inc.)
• Korth (Mandall Shooting
  Supplies, Inc.)
• Llama Gabilondo Y Cia (SGS Importers
  International, Inc.)
• Marksman Products (Marksman
  Products)
• Mitchell Arms, Inc. (Mitchell
  Arms, Inc.)
• Morini (Mandall Shooting Supplies)

• Navy Arms Co. (Navy Arms Co.)
• Norinco (Century International Arms,
  Inc.; ChinaSports, Inc.; Interarms)
• Para-Ordnance Mfg., Inc.
  (Para-Ordnance, Inc.)
• Pardini Armi Commerciale Srl (MCS,
  Inc.; Nygord Precision Products)
• Peters Stahl GmbH (McMillan
  Gunworks, Inc.; Olympic Arms)
• Poly Technologies, Inc. (Keng's
  Firearms Specialty, Inc.)
• Powell & Son Ltd., William (Bell's
  Legendary Country Wear)
• Rossi, Amadeo (Interarms)
• RWS (Dynamit Nobel-RWS, Inc.)
  Sardius Industries Ltd.
• Sauer (Paul Co., The)
• Schmidt, Herbert (Sportarms of Florida)
• SIG (Mandall Shooting
  Supplies, Inc.)
• SIG-Sauer (Sigarms, Inc.)
• Societa Armi Bresciane Srl. (Cape
  Outfitters)
• Solothurn (Sile Distributors)
• Springfield, Inc. (Springfield, Inc.)
• Star Bonifacio Echeverria S.A.
  (Interarms)
• Steyr (GSI, Inc.; Nygord Precision
  Products)
• Steyr-Daimler-Puch (GSI, Inc.)
• Tanfoglio S.r.l., Fratelli/Witness
  (E.A.A. Corp.)
• Taurus International Firearms (Taurus
  Firearms, Inc.)
• Techni-Mec (Mandall Shooting
  Supplies, Inc.)
  T.F.C. S.p.A.
• Theoben Engineering (Air Rifle
  Specialists)
• Uberti, Aldo (American Arms, Inc.;
  Christopher Firearms Co., Inc., E.;
  Cimarron Arms; Dixie Gun Works;
  EMF Co., Inc.; Mitchell Arms, Inc.;
  Navy Arms Co.; Uberti USA, Inc.)
• Unique/M.A.P.F. (Nygord Precision
  Products)
  USA Sporting (Armas Kemen)
• Walther GmbH, Carl (Interarms)
• Webley & Scott Ltd. (Beeman Precision
  Airguns, Inc.)
• Weihrauch KG, Hermann (Beeman
  Precision Airguns, Inc.; E.A.A. Corp.)
• Zabala, Hermanos S.A. (American
  Arms, Inc.)

GUNS, U.S.-MADE

• Accu-Tek
• American Arms, Inc.
• American Derringer Corp.
• AMT
• Auto-Ordnance Corp.
• Beretta U.S.A. Corp.
• Brown Co., E. Arthur
• Browning (Parts & Service)
• Bryco Arms
• Bushmaster Firearms
• Calico Light Weapon Systems
• Century Gun Dist., Inc.
• Century International Arms, Inc.
• CHARCO
• Charter Arms
• Colt Blackpowder Arms Co.
• Colt's Mfg. Co., Inc.
• Competitor Corp., Inc.
• Coonan Arms, Inc.
• CVA
• Davis Industries
• Desert Industries, Inc.
• Dixie Gun Works
• Dragun Enterprises
• EMF Co., Inc.
• Essex Arms
• Feather Industries, Inc.
• Freedom Arms, Inc.

• Grendel, Inc.
• H&R 1871, Inc.
  Hi-Point Firearms
• HJS Arms, Inc.
  Holston Ent. Inc.
• Intratec
• Ithaca Aquisition Corp./Ithaca Gun Co.
• Jennings Firearms, Inc.
• J.O. Arms & Ammunition Co.
• Jones, J.D.
• Kahr Arms
• L.A.R. Manufacturing, Inc.
• Laseraim Arms
• Lorcin Engineering Co., Inc.
• Magnum Research, Inc.
• McMillan Gunworks, Inc.
• Mitchell Arms, Inc.
• M.O.A. Corp.
• New Advantage Arms Corp.
• New England Firearms
• North American Arms
• Olympic Arms, Inc.
• Phelps Mfg. Co.
• Phoenix Arms
• Ram-Line, Inc.
• Remington Arms Co., Inc.
  Rocky Mountain Arms, Inc.
• RPM

• See page 293 for Warranty Service Center addresses

- Safari Arms/SGW
- Seecamp Co., Inc., L.W.
- Smith & Wesson
- Springfield, Inc.
  SSK Industries
- Sturm, Ruger & Co., Inc.
- Sundance Industries, Inc.
- Swivel Machine Works, Inc.
- Taurus Firearms, Inc.

- Texas Arms
- Texas Longhorn Arms, Inc.
- Thompson/Center Arms
- Ultra Light Arms, Inc.
- Wesson Firearms Co., Inc.
  Wichita Arms, Inc.
- Wildey, Inc.
- Wilkinson Arms

GUNS AND GUN PARTS, REPLICA AND ANTIQUE

Ahlman Guns
Armi San Paolo
Armsport, Inc.
Bear Mountain Gun & Tool
Beauchamp & Son, Inc.
Bill's Gun Repair
British Arms Co. Ltd.
Buckskin Machine Works
Burgess & Son Gunsmiths, R.W.
Century International Arms, Inc.
Cogar's Gunsmithing
Cole's Gun Works
Colonial Repair
Dangler, Homer L.
Day & Sons, Inc., Leonard
D.B.A. Flintlocks, Etc.
Delhi Gun House
Delta Arms Ltd.
Dixon Muzzleloading Shop, Inc.
Dragun Enterprises
Dyson & Son Ltd., Peter
Ed's Gun House
EMF Co., Inc.
First Distributors, Inc., Jack
Flintlocks, Inc.
Forgett, Valmore J., Jr.
Golden Age Arms Co.
Goodwin, Fred
Gun Parts Corp., The
Gun Works, The
Gun-Tec
Hunkeler, A.

Ken's Gun Specialties
Liberty Antique Gunworks
Lodewick, Walter H.
Log Cabin Sport Shop
Lucas, Edw. E.
Mountain State Muzzleloading Supplies
Munsch Gunsmithing, Tommy
Muzzleloaders Etcetera, Inc.
Navy Arms Co.
Neumann GmbH
OMR Feinmechanik, Jagd-und
    Sportwaffen, GmbH
Parker Gun Finishes
PEM's Mfg. Co.
P.M. Enterprises, Inc.
Pony Express Sport Shop, Inc.
Precise Metalsmithing Enterprises
Quality Firearms of Idaho, Inc.
Randco UK
Ravell Ltd.
Rutgers Gun & Boat Center
S&S Firearms
Sarco, Inc.
Silver Ridge Gun Shop
Sklany, Steve
Taylor's & Co., Inc.
Track of the Wolf, Inc.
Upper Missouri Trading Co.
Vintage Industries, Inc.
Weihrauch KG, Hermann
Wescombe

GUNS, SURPLUS—PARTS AND AMMUNITION

Armscorp USA, Inc.
Aztec International Ltd.
Ballistica Maximus North
Bohemia Arms Co.
Bondini Paolo
Braun, M.
Century International Arms, Inc.
ChinaSports, Inc.
Colonial Repair
Combat Military Ordnance Ltd.
Delta Arms Ltd.
Ed's Gun House
First Distributors, Inc., Jack
Fleming Firearms
Forgett, Valmore J., Jr.
Forrest, Inc., Tom
Fulton Armory
Garcia National Gun Traders, Inc.
Gibbs Rifle Co., Inc.
Gun Parts Corp., The
Interarms
Lever Arms Service Ltd.

Moreton/Fordyce Enterprises
Navy Arms Co.
Nu-Line Guns, Inc.
Oil Rod and Gun Shop
Old Western Scrounger, Inc.
Paragon Sales & Services, Inc.
Parker-Hale
Parts & Surplus
Quality Firearms of Idaho, Inc.
Randall Firearms Research
Ravell Ltd.
Rutgers Gun & Boat Center
Sarco, Inc.
Shell Shack
Sherwood Intl. Export Corp.
Southern Ammunition Co., Inc.
Springfield Sporters, Inc.
T.F.C. S.p.A.
Thurston Sports, Inc.
Westfield Engineering
Whitestone Lumber Corp.

GUNSMITH SCHOOLS

Brooker, Dennis
Colorado School of Trades
Cylinder & Slide, Inc.
Lassen Community College,
    Gunsmithing Dept.
Laughridge, William R.
Modern Gun Repair School
Montgomery Community
    College
Murray State College

North American Correspondence
    Schools
Pennsylvania Gunsmith School
Piedmont Community College
Pine Technical College
Professional Gunsmiths of America, Inc.
Ravell Ltd.
Southeastern Community College
Trinidad State Junior College,
    Gunsmithing Dept.
Yavapai College

GUNSMITH SUPPLIES, TOOLS, SERVICES

Advance Car Mover Co.,
    Rowell Div.
Aldis Gunsmithing & Shooting Supply
Alley Supply Co.
Atlantic Mills, Inc.
Badger Shooters Supply, Inc.
Bald Eagle Precision Machine Co.

Bear Mountain Gun & Tool
Behlert Precision
Bellm Contenders
Bengtson Arms Co., L.
Biesen, Al
Biesen, Roger
Birchwood Laboratories, Inc.

Blue Ridge Machinery & Tools, Inc.
Brown Products, Inc., Ed
Brownells, Inc.
B-Square Co.
Buehler Scope Mounts
Can Am Enterprises
Carbide Checkering Tools
C-H Tool & Die Corp.
Chapman Manufacturing Co.
Chem-Pak, Inc.
Choate Machine & Tool Co., Inc.
Chopie Mfg., Inc.
Clymer Manufacturing Co., Inc.
Colonial Arms, Inc.
Conetrol Scope Mounts
Crouse's Country Cover
Cumberland Arms
Custom Checkering Service
Custom Gun Products
D&J Bullet Co. & Custom Gun Shop, Inc.
Davidson Products
Dayton Traister
Decker Shooting Products
Dem-Bart Hand Checkering
    Tools, Inc.
Dremel Mfg. Co.
Duffy, Charles E.
Du-Lite Corp.
Dutchman's Firearms, Inc., The
Echols & Co., D'Arcy
Ed's Gun House
EGW Evolution Gun Works
Eilan S.A.L.
Faith Associates, Inc.
Ferris Firearms
First Distributors, Inc., Jack
Fisher, Jerry A.
Forgreens Tool Mfg., Inc.
Forster, Kathy
Forster Products
4-D Custom Die Co.
Frazier Brothers Enterprises
G.B.C. Industries, Inc.
Grace Metal Products, Inc.
GRS Corp.
Gunline Tools
Gun-Tec
Half Moon Rifle Shop
Hastings Barrels
Henriksen Tool Co., Inc.
Hoehn Sales, Inc.
Hoelscher, Virgil
Holland's
Hoppe's Div.
Huey Gun Cases, Marvin
Iosso Products
Ivanoff, Thomas G.
Jantz Supply
JGS Precision Tool Mfg.
K&M Services
Kasenit Co., Inc.
KenPatable Ent., Inc.
Kimball, Gary
Kleinendorst, K.W.
Kmount
Koppco Industries
Korzinek Riflesmith, J.
Kwik Mount Corp.
LaRocca Gun Works, Inc.

Lea Mfg. Co.
Lee Supplies, Mark
Lock's Philadelphia Gun Exchange
London Guns Ltd.
Lortone, Inc.
Mag-Na-Port Int'l, Inc.
Marsh, Mike
MCRW Associates Shooting Supplies
Menck, Thomas W.
Metalife Industries
Michael's Antiques
Millett Sights
Milliron Custom Machine Carving, Earl
MMC
Morrow, Bud
Mowrey's Guns & Gunsmithing
N&J Sales
Nitex, Inc.
Ole Frontier Gunsmith Shop
Palmgren Steel Products
PanaVise Products, Inc.
PEM's Mfg. Co.
Penguin Industries, Inc.
Power Custom, Inc.
Practical Tools, Inc.
Precision Metal Finishing
Precision Arms International, Inc.
Precision Specialties
Pre-Winchester 92-90-62 Parts Co.
Pro-Port Ltd.
Ravell Ltd.
Reardon Products
Rice, Keith
Riggs, Jim
Roto Carve
Ruvel & Co., Inc.
Scott, McDougall & Associates
Sharp Shooter, Inc.
Sheridan USA, Inc., Austin
Shirley Co. Gun & Riflemakers Ltd.
Shooter's Choice
S.K. Guns, Inc.
Smith Whetstone Co., Inc.
Stalwart Corp.
Starrett Co., L.S.
Stoney Point Products, Inc.
Stuart Products, Inc.
Sullivan, David S.
Sure Shot of LA, Inc.
TDP Industries, Inc.
Texas Platers Supply
Tom's Gun Repair
Trulock Tool
Turnbull Restoration, Doug
Venco Industries, Inc.
Washita Mountain Whetstone Co.
Weaver's Gun Shop
Weigand Combat Handguns, Inc.
Welsh, Bud
Wessinger Custom Guns & Engraving
Westfield Engineering
Westrom, John
White Rock Tool & Die
Wilcox All-Pro Tools & Supply
Will-Burt Co.
Williams Gun Sight Co.
Wilson's Gun Shop
World of Targets

HANDGUN ACCESSORIES

Action Arms Ltd.
ADCO International
Adventurer's Outpost
Aimtech Mount Systems
Ajax Custom Grips, Inc.
American Bullets
American Derringer Corp.
Armite Laboratories
Auto-Ordnance Corp.
Baer Custom, Inc., Les
Bar-Sto Precision Machine
Baumannize Custom
Behlert Precision
Black Sheep Brand
Blue and Gray Products, Inc.
Boonie Packer Products
Boyds', Inc.
Broken Gun Ranch
Brown Products, Inc., Ed
Brownells, Inc.
Bucheimer, J.M.
Bullberry Barrel Works, Ltd.
Bushmaster Firearms
C3 Systems

Centaur Systems, Inc.
Central Specialties, Inc.
Clymer Manufacturing Co., Inc.
Cobra Gunskin
Dade Screw Machine Products
Desert Industries, Inc.
Doskocil Mfg. Co., Inc
E.A.A. Corp.
Eagle International, Inc.
EGW Evolution Gun Works
Emerging Technologies, Inc.
Faith Associates, Inc.
Feather Industries, Inc.
Feminine Protection, Inc.
Fleming Firearms
Frielich Police Equipment
Glock, Inc.
Greider Precision
Gremmel Enterprises
Gun-Alert
Gunfitters, The
Gun-Ho Sports Cases
Haselbauer Products, Jerry
Hebard Guns, Gil

Heinie Specialty Products
Hill Speed Leather, Ernie
H.K.S. Products
Hunter Co., Inc.
Jeffredo Gunsight
Jett & Co., Inc.
J.O. Arms & Ammunition Co.
Jones, J.D.
J.P. Enterprises, Inc.
Jumbo Sports Products
K&K Ammo Wrist Band
KeeCo Impressions
Keller Co., The
King's Gun Works
L&S Technologies, Inc.
Lakewood Products, Inc.
LaRocca Gun Works, Inc.
Laseraim, Inc.
Lee's Red Ramps
Leupold
Loch Leven Industries
Lock's Philadelphia Gun Exchange
Lohman Mfg. Co., Inc.
Mac's .45 Shop
Magnolia Sports, Inc.
Mag-Pack Corp.
Markell, Inc.
Masen Co., John
Master Products, Inc.
McCormick Corp., Chip
MEC-Gar S.R.L.
Merkuria Ltd.
Michaels of Oregon Co.
Monte Kristo Pistol Grip Co.
MPC (McMinnville, TN)
MTM Molded Products Co., Inc.
Mustra's Custom Guns, Inc., Carl
N.C. Ordnance Co.
North American Specialties
No-Sho Mfg. Co.

Outa-Site Gun Carriers
Owen, Harry
Ox-Yoke Originals, Inc.
Pace Marketing, Inc.
Pardini Armi Commerciale Srl
PAST Sporting Goods, Inc.
Power Custom, Inc.
Practical Tools, Inc.
Precision Arms International, Inc.
Protector Mfg. Co., Inc., The
Quality Parts Co.
Ram-Line, Inc.
Ranch Products
Ravell Ltd.
Round Edge, Inc.
RPM
Rutgers Gun & Boat Center
Sheridan USA, Inc., Austin
Sile Distributors, Inc.
Slings 'N Things, Inc.
Sonderman, Robert
Southwind Sanctions
Sport Specialties
SSK Industries
"Su-Press-On," Inc.
TacTell, Inc.
Tapco, Inc.
Taurus S.A., Forjas
T.F.C. S.p.A.
Trijicon, Inc.
Triple-K Mfg. Co.
Tyler Mfg.-Dist., Melvin
Valor Corp.
Volquartsen Custom Ltd.
Weigand Combat Handguns, Inc.
Wessinger Custom Guns & Engraving
Western Design
Whitestone Lumber Corp.
Wichita Arms, Inc.

HANDGUN GRIPS

African Import Co.
Ahrends, Kim
Ajax Custom Grips, Inc.
Altamont Co.
American Derringer Corp.
American Gripcraft
Art Jewel Enterprises Ltd.
Artistry In Wood
Barami Corp.
Bear Hug Grips, Inc.
Behlert Precision
Bob's Gun Shop
Boone's Custom Ivory Grips, Inc.
CAM Enterprises
Cobra Gunskin
Cole-Grip
Custom Firearms
Desert Industries, Inc.
Eagle Mfg. & Engineering
EMF Co., Inc.
Eyears Insurance
Fisher Custom Firearms
Fitz Pistol Grip Co.
Forrest, Inc., Tom
Greene, M.L.
Herrett's Stocks, Inc.
Hogue Grips
IMI Services USA, Inc.
KeeCo Impressions

Linebaugh Custom Sixguns
  & Rifle Works
Logan Security Products Co.
Mac's .45 Shop
Masen Co., John
N.C. Ordnance Co.
Newell, Robert H.
North American Specialties
Old Western Scrounger, Inc.
Pardini Armi Commerciale Srl
Peacemaker Specialists
Pilgrim Pewter, Inc.
Ravell Ltd.
Renner Co., R.J./Radical Concepts
Rosenberg & Sons, Jack A.
Roy's Custom Grips
Rutgers Gun & Boat Center
Safariland Ltd., Inc.
Savana Sports, Inc.
Sheridan USA, Inc., Austin
Sile Distributors, Inc.
Spegel, Craig
Taurus S.A., Forjas
Taurus Firearms, Inc.
Tirelli
Tyler Mfg.-Dist., Melvin
Valor Corp.
Vintage Industries, Inc.
Volquartsen Custom Ltd.
Vom Hofe
Wayland Precision Wood Products

HEARING PROTECTORS

Behlert Precision
Bilsom Intl., Inc.
Blount, Inc.
Brown Co., E. Arthur
Browning Arms Co.
Clark Co., Inc., David
Cobra Gunskin
Dragun Enterprises
E-A-R, Inc.
Fitz Pistol Grip Co.
Flents Products Co., Inc.
Hoppe's Div.
Kesselring Gun Shop
Marble Arms Corp.
North American Specialties

North Specialty Products
Paterson Gunsmithing
Peltor, Inc.
Penguin Industries, Inc.
R.E.T. Enterprises
Rutgers Gun & Boat Center
Safariland Ltd., Inc.
Safesport Manufacturing Co.
Silencio/Safety Direct
Smith & Wesson
Stock Shop, The
Tyler Mfg.-Dist., Melvin
Valor Corp.
Willson Safety Prods. Div.

HOLSTERS AND LEATHER GOODS

A&B Industries, Inc.
Action Products, Inc.
Aker Leather Products
Alessi Holsters, Inc.
American Import Co., The
American Sales & Mfg. Co.
Arratoonian, Andy
Artistry in Leather
Baker's Leather Goods, Roy
Bandcor Industries
Bang-Bang Boutique
Barami Corp.
Bear Hug Grips, Inc.
Beeman Precision Airguns, Inc.
Behlert Precision
Bianchi International, Inc.
Black Sheep Brand
Blocker's Holsters, Inc., Ted
Brauer Bros. Mfg. Co.
Brown, H.R.
Browning Arms Co.
Bucheimer, J.M.
Bushmaster Hunting & Fishing
Bushwacker Backpack &
  Supply Co.
Carvajal Belts & Holsters
Cathey Enterprises, Inc.
Chace Leather Products
Cimarron Arms
Clements' Custom Leathercraft, Chas
Cobra Gunskin
Cobra Line SRL
Cobra Sport
Crawford Co., Inc., R.M.
Creedmoor Sports, Inc.
Davis Leather Co., G. Wm.
Delhi Gun House
DeSantis Holster & Leather Goods
Dragun Enterprises
Easy Pull Outlaw Products
Ekol Leather Care
El Dorado Leather
El Paso Saddlery Co.
EMF Co., Inc.
Epps "Orillia" Ltd., Ellwood
Eutaw Co., Inc., The
Faust, Inc., T.G.
Flores Publications, Inc., J.
Fobus International Ltd.
Fury Cutlery
Galati International
GALCO International Ltd.
Glock, Inc.
GML Products, Inc.
Gould & Goodrich
Gun Leather Limited
Gunfitters, The
Gusty Winds Corp.
Gutmann Cutlery Co., Inc.
Hafner Creations, Inc.
Hebard Guns, Gil
Hellweg Ltd.
Henigson & Associates, Steve
Hill Speed Leather, Ernie
Holster Outpost
Holster Shop, The
Horseshoe Leather Products
Hoyt Holster Co., Inc.

Hume, Don
Hunter Co., Inc.
J.O. Arms & Ammunition Co.
John's Custom Leather
Joy Enterprises
Jumbo Sports Products
Kane Products, Inc.
Keller Co., The
Kirkpatrick Leather Co.
Kolpin Mfg., Inc.
Kramer Handgun Leather, Inc.
L.A.R. Manufacturing, Inc.
Law Concealment Systems, Inc.
Lawrence Leather Co.
Leather Arsenal
Lethal Force Institute
Lone Star Gunleather
Magnolia Sports, Inc.
Markell, Inc.
Michaels of Oregon Co.
Minute Man High Tech Industries
Mixson Leathercraft, Inc.
Nelson Combat Leather, Bruce
Noble Co., Jim
North American Arms
No-Sho Mfg. Co.
Null Holsters Ltd., K.L.
Ojala Holsters, Arvo
Oklahoma Leather Products, Inc.
Old West Reproductions, Inc.
Pathfinder Sports Leather
Police Bookshelf
PWL Gunleather
Red River Frontier Outfitters
Renegade
Ringler Custom Leather Co.
Rutgers Gun & Boat Center
Rybka Custom Leather Equipment, Thad
Safariland Ltd., Inc.
Safety Speed Holster, Inc.
Savana Sports, Inc.
Schulz Industries
Shadow Concealment Systems
Sheridan USA, Inc., Austin
Shoemaker & Sons, Inc., Tex
Shurkatch Corp.
Silhouette Leathers
Smith Saddlery, Jesse W.
Southwind Sanctions
Sparks, Milt
Stalker, Inc.
Strong Holster Co.
Stuart, V. Pat
Tabler Marketing
Texas Longhorn Arms, Inc.
Top-Line USA, Inc.
Torel, Inc.
Triple-K Mfg. Co., Inc.
Tyler Mfg.-Dist., Melvin
Valor Corp.
Venus Industries
Viking Leathercraft, Inc.
Walt's Custom Leather
Whinnery, Walt
Whitestone Lumber Corp.
Wild Bill's Originals
Winchester Sutler, Inc., The

LABELS, BOXES, CARTRIDGE HOLDERS

Accuracy Products, S.A.
Advance Car Mover Co.,
  Rowell Div.
Anderson Manufacturing Co., Inc.
Ballistic Products, Inc.
Berry's Mfg. Inc.
Brown Co., E. Arthur
Cabinet Mountain Outfitters Scents &
  Lures
Del Rey Products
Fitz Pistol Grip Co.
Flambeau Products Corp.
Flintlock Muzzle Loading Gun Shop, The

Hornady Mfg. Co.
J&J Products Co.
King & Co.
Lakewood Products, Inc.
Loadmaster
Lyman Instant Targets, Inc.
Lyman Products Corp.
Midway Arms, Inc.
MTM Molded Products Co., Inc.
Precision Reloading, Inc.
Ravell Ltd.
Scharch Mfg., Inc.
Zero Ammunition Co., Inc.

LOAD TESTING AND PRODUCT TESTING,
(Chronographing, Ballistic Studies)

Ammunition Consulting
  Services, Inc.
Arms, Peripheral Data Systems
A-Square Co., Inc.
Ballistic Research

BestLoad, Inc.
Briese Bullet Co., Inc.
Buck Stix
Bustani Appraisers, Leo
Clerke Co., J.A.

D&H Precision Tooling
Dever Co., Jack
Farr Studio, Inc.
Fusilier Bullets
Hank's Gun Shop
Hensler, Jerry
High Performance International
Hoelscher, Virgil
Jackalope Gun Shop
Jensen Bullets
Jones, J.D.
Jurras, L.E.
Lachaussee, S.A.
Lomont Precision Bullets
Maionchi-L.M.I.
McMurdo, Lynn
Multiplex International

Neutralizer Police Munitions
Oil Rod and Gun Shop
Pace Marketing, Inc.
Pejsa Ballistics
Ransom International Corp.
R.I.S. Co., Inc.
Romain's Custom Guns
RPM
Rupert's Gun Shop
SOS Products Co.
SSK Industries
Stock Shop, The
Tioga Engineering Co., Inc.
Vulpes Ventures, Inc.
White Laboratory, Inc., H.P.
Whitestone Lumber Corp.
X-Spand Target Systems

MUZZLE-LOADING GUNS, BARRELS AND EQUIPMENT

Accuracy Unlimited (Littleton, CO)
Ackermann & Co.
Adkins, Luther
All American Bullets
Allen Manufacturing
American Pioneer Video
• Anderson Manufacturing Co., Inc.
Armi San Paolo
• Armoury, Inc., The
• Armsport, Inc.
Barton, Michael D.
Bauska Barrels
• Beauchamp & Son, Inc.
Beaver Lodge
Bentley, John
Birdsong & Associates, W.E.
Blackhawk East
Blackhawk Mountain
Blackhawk West
Blake Affiliates
• Blount, Inc.
Blue and Gray Products, Inc.
Bridgers Best
Buckskin Machine Works
Buffalo Bullet Co., Inc.
Burgess and Son Gunsmiths, R.W.
Butler Creek Corp.
Cache La Poudre Rifleworks
Camas Hot Springs Mfg.
• Cape Outfitters
Cash Manufacturing Co., Inc.
CenterMark
Chambers Flintlocks, Ltd., Jim
Chopie Mfg., Inc.
• Cimarron Arms
Cogar's Gunsmithing
• Colt Blackpowder Arms Co.
Cousin Bob's Mountain Products
• Cumberland Arms
• Cumberland Knife & Gun Works
• CVA
Dangler, Homer L.
Day & Sons, Inc., Leonard
• Dayton Traister
deHaas Barrels
Delhi Gun House
• Denver Arms, Ltd.
• Dixie Gun Works
Dixon Muzzleloading Shop, Inc.
Eades' Muzzleloader Builders' Supply
Ed's Gun House
• EMF Co., Inc.
• Euroarms of America, Inc.
Eutaw Co., Inc., The
Fautheree, Andy
Feken, Dennis
Fellowes, Ted
Fish, Marshall F.
Flintlock Muzzle Loading Gun Shop, The
Flintlocks, Etc.
• Forster Products
Fort Hill Gunstocks
Frontier
• Gibbs Rifle Co., Inc.
Golden Age Arms Co.
• Gonic Arms, Inc.
Hastings Barrels
• Hatfield Gun Co., Inc.
• Hawken Shop, The
Hege Jagd-u. Sporthandels, GmbH
• Hornady Mfg. Co.
House of Muskets, Inc., The
Hunkeler, A.
Jamison's Forge Works
Jedediah Starr Trading Co.
Jones Co., Dale

• JSL (Hereford) Ltd.
K&M Industries, Inc.
Kennedy Firearms
Kolpin Mfg., Inc.
Kwik-Site Co.
L&R Lock Co.
Laurel Mountain Forge
Lite Tek International
• Log Cabin Sport Shop
Lutz Engraving, Ron
Lyman Instant Targets, Inc.
• Lyman Products Corp.
McCann's Muzzle-Gun Works
MMP
• Modern MuzzleLoading, Inc.
• Montana Armory, Inc.
Montana Precision Swaging
• Mossberg & Sons, Inc., O.F.
Mountain State Muzzleloading Supplies
• Mowrey Gun Works
MSC Industrial Supply Co.
Mt. Alto Outdoor Products
Mushroom Express Bullet Co.
Muzzleloaders Etcetera, Inc.
Newman Gun Shop
North Star West
October Country
Oklahoma Leather Products, Inc.
Olde Pennsylvania
Olson, Myron
Orion Rifle Barrel Co.
Ox-Yoke Originals, Inc.
Parker Gun Finishes
Pecatonica River Longrifle
• Pedersoli, Davide & C.
Phyl-Mac
• Pioneer Arms Co.
Rapine Bullet Mould Mfg. Co.
R.E. Davis
Rusty Duck Premium Gun Care
   Products
R.V.I.
S&B Industries
S&S Firearms
Selsi Co., Inc.
• Sharps Arms Co., Inc., C.
Shooter's Choice
• Sile Distributors, Inc.
Single Shot, Inc.
Slings 'N Things, Inc.
Smokey Valley Rifles
South Bend Replicas, Inc.
Southern Bloomer Mfg. Co.
SPG Bullet Lubricant
• Sturm, Ruger & Co., Inc.
TDP Industries, Inc.
Tennessee Valley Mfg.
Thompson Bullet Lube Co.
Thompson/Center Arms
• Thunder Mountain Arms
Tiger-Hunt
Track of the Wolf, Inc.
• Traditions
Tyler Scott, Inc.
• Uberti, Aldo
• Uberti USA, Inc.
• Upper Missouri Trading Co.
Venco Industries, Inc.
Warren Muzzleloading Co., Inc.
Wescombe
White Owl Enterprises
• White Shooting Systems, Inc.
Wideview Scope Mount Corp.
Winchester Sutler, Inc., The
Woodworker's Supply
Young Country Arms

PISTOLSMITHS

Accuracy Gun Shop
Accuracy Unlimited (Glendale, AZ)
Accurate Plating & Weaponry, Inc.
Ahlman Guns
Ahrends, Kim
Aldis Gunsmithing & Shooting Supply
Alpha Precision, Inc.
Alpine's Precision Gunsmithing & Indoor
   Shooting Range
American Pistolsmiths Guild
Amodei, Jim
Armament Gunsmithing Co., Inc.
Bain & Davis, Inc.
Baity's Custom Gunworks
Banks, Ed
Bar-Sto Precision Machine
Bengtson Arms Co., L.
Bowen Classic Arms Corp.
Boyd's Inc.
Brian, C.T.
Broken Gun Ranch
Brown Products, Inc., Ed
Cannons Guns
Caraville Manufacturing
Cellini, Inc., Vito Francesca
Clark Custom Guns, Inc.
Corkys Gun Clinic
Curtis Custom Shop
Custom Firearms
Custom Gunsmiths
D&D Gunsmiths, Ltd.
D&L Sports
Davis Service Center, Bill
D.O.C. Specialists, Inc.
Ellicott Arms Inc./Woods Pistolsmithing
EMF Co., Inc.
Ferris Firearms
First Distributors, Inc., Jack
Fisher Custom Firearms
Francesca, Inc.
Frielich Police Equipment
Frontier Arms Co., Inc.
Garthwaite, Jim
Giron, Robert E.
Greider Precision
Guncraft Sports, Inc.
Gunsite Gunsmithy
Gunsmithing Ltd.
Hamilton, Alex B.
Hamilton, Keith
Hank's Gun Shop
Hanson's Gun Center, Dick
Hardison, Charles
Hebard Guns, Gil
Heinie Specialty Products
High Bridge Arms, Inc.
Highline Machine Co.
Hindman, Ace
Hoag, James W.
Intermountain Arms & Tackle, Inc.
Irwin, Campbell H.
Ivanoff, Thomas G.
Jarvis Gunsmithing, Inc.
Johnston, James
Jones, J.D.
J.P. Enterprises, Inc.
Jungkind, Reeves C.
K-D, Inc.
Ken's Gun Specialties
Kilham & Co.
Kimball, Gary
Kopec Enterprises, John
Kopp, Terry K.
La Clinique du .45
LaFrance Specialties
LaRocca Gun Works, Inc.

Lawson, John G.
Lee's Red Ramps
Linebaugh Custom Sixguns & Rifle
   Works
Long, George F.
Mac's .45 Shop
Mahony, Philip Bruce
Martin's Gun Shop
Marvel, Alan
Mathews & Son, Inc., George E.
McMillan Gunworks, Inc.
Mid-America Recreation, Inc.
Middlebrooks Custom Shop
Miller Custom
Mitchell's Accuracy Shop
MJK Gunsmithing, Inc.
Moran, Jerry
Mountain Bear Rifle Works, Inc.
Mullis Guncraft
Mustra's Custom Guns, Inc., Carl
Nicholson Custom
North Fork Custom Gunsmithing
Novak's, Inc.
Nowlin Custom Barrels Mfg.
Oglesby & Oglesby Gunmakers, Inc.
Pace Marketing, Inc.
Pardini Armi Commerciale Srl
Paris, Frank J.
Peacemaker Specialists
PEM's Mfg. Co.
Performance Specialists
Peterson Gun Shop, Inc., A.W.
Pierce Pistols
Plaxco, J. Michael
Practical Tools, Inc.
Precision Arms International, Inc.
Precision Specialties
Randco UK
Ravell Ltd.
Ries, Chuck
Rim Pac Sports, Inc.
Roberts, J.J.
Rogers Gunsmithing, Bob
Rutgers Gun & Boat Center
Scott, McDougall & Associates
Seecamp Co., Inc., L.W.
Shell Shack
Shooters Supply
Sight Shop, The
Sipes Gun Shop
S.K. Guns, Inc.
Spokhandguns, Inc.
Springfield, Inc.
SSK Industries
Steger, James R.
Swampfire Shop, The
Swenson's 45 Shop, A.D.
Ten-Ring Precision, Inc.
Thompson, Randall
300 Gunsmith Service, Inc.
Thurston Sports, Inc.
Tom's Gun Repair
T.S.W. Conversions, Inc.
Ulrich, Doc & Bud
Unick's Gunsmithing
Vic's Gun Refinishing
Volquartsen Custom Ltd.
Walker Arms Co., Inc.
Walters Industries
Wardell Precision Handguns Ltd.
Weigand Combat Handguns, Inc.
Wessinger Custom Guns & Engraving
Wichita Arms, Inc.
Williamson Precision Gunsmithing
Wilson's Gun Shop

REBORING AND RERIFLING

Bellm Contenders
Blackstar Barrel Accurizing
Colonial Repair
D&D Gunsmiths, Ltd.
Flaig's
H&S Liner Service
Hart & Son, Inc., Robert W.
Home Shop Machinist, The
Ivanoff, Thomas G.
Jackalope Gun Shop
K-D, Inc.
LaBounty Precision Reboring
Matco, Inc.
Mid-America Recreation, Inc.
Nicholson Custom

Pac-Nor Barreling
Pence Precision Barrels
Redman's Rifling & Reboring
Rice, Keith
Ridgetop Sporting Goods
Schumakers Gun Shop, William
Sharon Rifle Barrel Co.
Shaw, Inc., E.R.
Siegrist Gun Shop
300 Gunsmith Service, Inc.
Tom's Gun Repair
Van Patten, J.W.
Wells, Fred F.
West, Robert G.
White Rock Tool & Die

• **See page 293 for Warranty Service Center addresses**

RELOADING TOOLS AND ACCESSORIES

Accuracy Components Co.
American Products Co.
• Ammo Load, Inc.
• AMT
Andela Tool & Machinery, Inc.
• ASI
Ballistic Products, Inc.
Ballisti-Cast, Inc.
Barlett, J.
Bear Reloaders
Ben's Machines
Berry's Mfg. Inc.
• Blount, Inc.
• Brown Co., E. Arthur
Brynin, Milton
Buck Stix
Bullet Swaging Supply, Inc.
C&D Special Products
• Camdex, Inc.
Carbide Die & Mfg. Co., Inc.
Case Sorting System
CCI
• C-H Tool & Die Corp.
Chem-Pak, Inc.
CheVron Case Master
Claybuster
Coats, Mrs. Lester
Colorado Shooter's Supply
Competitor Corp., Inc.
CONKKO
• Corbin, Inc.
D.C.C. Enterprises
• Denver Instrument Co.
Dever Co., Jack
Dewey Mfg. Co., Inc., J.
• Dillon Precision Prods., Inc.
E&L Mfg., Inc.
Eagan, Donald V.
Efemes Enterprises
Engineered Accessories
Enguix Import-Export
Feken, Dennis
Fisher Enterprises
Fitz Pistol Grip Co.
Flambeau Products Corp.
Forgreens Tool Mfg., Inc.
• Forster Products
• 4-D Custom Die Co.
• Fremont Tool Works
G&C Bullet Co., Inc.
Gehmann, Walter
Goddard, Allen
"Gramps" Antique Cartridges
Graphics Direct
Green, Arthur S.
Hanned Line, The
Hanned Precision
Harrell's Precision
• Hart & Son, Inc., Robert W.
Haydon Shooters' Supply, Russ
Heidenstrom Bullets
Hensley & Gibbs
Hindman, Ace
Hoch Custom Bullet Moulds
Hoehn Sales, Inc.
Hoelscher, Virgil
• Hollywood Engineering
Hondo Industries
• Hornady Mfg. Co.
• Huntington Die Specialties
INTEC International, Inc.
Iosso Marine Products
J&L Superior Bullets
JGS Precision Tool Mfg.
Jones Custom Products, Neil
Jones Moulds, Paul
• K&M Services
King & Co.
Lachaussee, S.A.
LAP Systems Group, N.A.
LBT
• Lee Precision, Inc.
Liberty Metals
Liberty Shooting Supplies
Lortone, Inc.
Loweth Firearms, Richard
Lyman Instant Targets, Inc.
• Lyman Products Corp.
MA Systems
• Magma Engineering Co.
Marquart Precision Co., Inc.
Match Prep
McKillen & Heyer, Inc.
MCRW Assoc. Shooting Supplies

• MCS, Inc.
• MEC, Inc.
Midway Arms, Inc.
Miller Engineering
MMP
Mountain South
Mt. Baldy Bullet Co.
MTM Molded Products Co., Inc.
Multi-Scale Charge Ltd.
Necromancer Industries, Inc.
NEI Handtools, Inc.
Niemi Enterprises, W.B.
OK Weber, Inc.
Old West Bullet Moulds
• Old Western Scrounger, Inc.
Omark Industries
Pace Marketing, Inc.
Pattern Control
Pend Oreille Sport Shop
Plum City Ballistic Range
Policlips North America
• Ponsness/Warren
Precision Castings & Equip.
• Precision Reloading, Inc.
Protector Mfg. Co., Inc., The
Quinetics Corp.
R&D Engineering & Manufacturing
Ransom International Corp.
Rapine Bullet Mould Mfg. Co.
Ravell Ltd.
Raytech
• RCBS
• R.D.P. Tool Co., Inc.
• Redding Reloading, Inc.
R.E.I.
Rice, Keith
Riebe Co., W.J.
Roberts Products
Rochester Lead Works, Inc.
Rooster Laboratories
Rorschach Precision Products
Rosenthal, Brad and Sallie
Rucker Ammunition Co.
SAECO
Sandia Die & Cartridge Co.
• Scharch Mfg., Inc.
Scot Powder Co. of Ohio, Inc.
Scott, Dwight
Sierra Bullets
Sierra Specialty Prod. Co.
Silver Eagle Machining
Simmons, Jerry
Sinclair International, Inc.
Skip's Machine
S.L.A.P. Industries
Slipshot MTS Group
Small Custom Mould & Bullet Co.
SOS Products Co.
• Speer Products
Sportsman Supply Co.
• Stalwart Corp.
• Star Machine Works
Stoney Point Products, Inc.
Taracorp Industries
TCSR
Tetra Gun Lubricants
Thompson Bullet Lube Co.
• Thompson/Center Arms
Timber Heirloom Products
Trammco, Inc.
Tru-Square Metal Prods., Inc.
Varner's Service
Vega Tool Co.
VibraShine, Inc.
Vibra-Tek Co.
Vom Hofe
Walters, John
Webster Scale Mfg. Co.
Welsh, Bud
Werner, Carl
Westfield Engineering
Wheel Weights Corp.
White Rock Tool & Die
Whitestone Lumber Corp.
Whitetail Design & Engineering Ltd.
Widener's Reloading & Shooting Supply
Wilcox All-Pro Tools & Supply
• William's Gun Shop, Ben
Wilson, Inc., L.E.
Wolf's Western Traders
Woodleigh
Yesteryear Armory & Supply
Young Country Arms

SCOPES, MOUNTS, ACCESSORIES, OPTICAL EQUIPMENT

Accuracy Innovations, Inc.
• Action Arms Ltd.
ADCO International
Adventurer's Outpost
• Aimpoint, Inc.
• Aimtech Mount Systems
• Air Venture
Ajax Custom Grips, Inc.
Alley Supply Co.
American Import Co. The
• Anderson Manufacturing Co., Inc.
Applied Laser Systems, Inc.
• Bausch & Lomb, Inc.
Beaver Park Products, Inc.
• Beeman Precision Airguns, Inc.
Bellm Contenders
• Blount, Inc.
B.M.F. Activator, Inc.
• Bohemia Arms Co.
• Brown Co., E. Arthur
Brownells, Inc.
• Browning
• B-Square Co.
• Burris
• Bushnell
Butler Creek Corp.
California Grip
Center Lock Scope Rings
Champion's Choice, Inc.
Combat Military Ordnance Ltd.
Conetrol Scope Mounts
D&H Prods. Co., Inc.
D.C.C. Enterprises
DHB Products
Eagle Mfg. & Engineering
Eggleston, Jere D.
Farr Studio, Inc.
• Forster Products
Galati International
Gonzalez Guns, Ramon B.
Grace Tool, Inc.
Guns, Gear & Gadgets, L.L.C.
• Hammerli USA
Hermann Leather Co., H.J.
Holden Co., J.B.
• Jackalope Gun Shop
• Jason Empire, Inc.
Jeffredo Gunsight
Jewell, Arnold W.
Jones, J.D.
J.P. Enterprises, Inc.
• JSL (Hereford) Ltd.
• Kahles USA
• Keng's Firearms Specialty, Inc.
• Kesselring Gun Shop
Kmount
Kris Mounts
KVH Industries, Inc.
Kwik Mount Corp.
Kwik-Site Co.
• L&S Technologies, Inc.
• Laser Devices, Inc.
Laseraim
Lectro Science, Inc.
Lee Co., T.K.
Lee Supplies, Mark
• Leupold
Lightforce USA
Lite Tek International
Lohman Mfg. Co., Inc.
Mac's .45 Shop
Maxi-Mount
MDS
Meier Works
Merit Corp.

Military Armament Corp.
Millett Sights
• Mirador Optical Corp.
Morrow, Bud
Muzzle-Nuzzle Co.
New Democracy, Inc.
New England Custom Gun Svc.
• Nichols Sports Optics
• Nikon, Inc.
North American Specialties
Nygord Precision Products
Oakshore Electronic Sights, Inc.
• Old Western Scrounger, Inc.
Olympic Optical Co.
OMR Feinmechanik, Jagd-und
    Sportwaffen, GmbH
Optolyth-USA, Inc.
Orchard Park Enterprise
Outdoor Connection, Inc., The
Pace Marketing, Inc.
• Pentax Corp.
Pilkington Gun Co.
Precise Metalsmithing Enterprises
• Precision Sport Optics
Premier Reticles
Protektor Model
• Ram-Line, Inc.
Ranch Products
Randolph Engineering, Inc.
• Ranging, Inc.
Ravell Ltd.
• Redfield, Inc.
Rice, Keith
Rockwood Corp., Speedwell Div.
Rocky Mountain High Sports Glasses
Royal Arm International Products
• RPM
Rutgers Gun & Boat Center
S&K Mfg. Co.
• Sanders Custom Gun Service
Scope Control Inc.
ScopLevel
Seattle Binocular & ScopeRepair Co.
Selsi Co., Inc.
• Shepherd Scope Ltd.
• Sheridan USA, Inc., Austin
Sightron, Inc.
Silencio/Safety Direct
• Simmons Enterprises, Ernie
• Simmons Outdoor Corp.
• Speer Products
Sportsmatch Ltd.
• Springfield, Inc.
SSK Industries
Stock Shop, The
Sure Shot of LA, Inc.
• Swift Instruments, Inc.
• Tapco, Inc.
• Tasco Sales, Inc.
Tele-Optics
• Thompson/Center Arms
• Trijicon, Inc.
United States Optics
    Technologies, Inc.
Warne Manufacturing Co.
Warren Muzzleloading Co., Inc.
WASP Shooting Systems
Weaver Products
• Weaver Scope Repair Service
Weigand Combat Handguns, Inc.
Western Design
Westfield Engineering
White Rock Tool & Die
Wideview Scope Mount Corp.
• Williams Gun Sight Co.

SHOOTING/TRAINING SCHOOLS

Alpine Precision Gunsmithing & Indoor
    Shooting Range
American Small Arms Academy
Auto Arms
Bob's Tactical Indoor Shooting Range &
    Gun Shop
Chapman Academy of Practical
    Shooting
Chelsea Gun Club of New York City, Inc.
CQB Training
Daisy Mfg. Co.
Defense Training International, Inc.
Dowtin Gunworks
Executive Protection Institute
Firearm Training Center, The
Firearms Academy of Seattle

G.H. Enterprises Ltd.
Gunfitters, The
Gunsite Training Center
InSights Training Center, Inc.
International Shootists, Inc.
Jensen's Firearms Acadamy
Lethal Force Institute
McMurdo, Lynn
Mendez, John A.
North Mountain Pines
    Training Center
Pacific Pistolcraft
Police Bookshelf
Quack Decoy & Sporting Clays
Quigley's Personal Protection
    Strategies, Paxton

• **See page 293 for Warranty Service Center addresses**

PRODUCT DIRECTORY

River Road Sporting Clays
SAFE
Scott, McDougall & Associates
Shooter's World
Shooting Gallery, The
Shotgun Shop, The
Sipes Gun Shop

Specialty Gunsmithing
Starlight Training Center, Inc.
S.W.I.F.T.
Tactical Training Center
Western Missouri Shooters Alliance
Yavapai Firearms Academy Ltd.

SIGHTS, METALLIC

Alley Supply Co.
Alpec Team, Inc.
Armurier Hiptmayer
Bo-Mar Tool & Mfg. Co.
Bradley Gunsight Co.
Brown Co., E. Arthur
Carter's Gun Shop
Champion's Choice, Inc.
C-More Systems
Colonial Repair
DHB Products
Engineered Accessories
Evans Gunsmithing
Fautheree, Andy
Gun Doctor, The
Hart & Son, Inc., Robert W.
Heinie Specialty Products
Hesco-Meprolight
Hiptmayer, Klaus
IMI Services USA, Inc.
Innovative Weaponry, Inc.
Jackalope Gun Shop
J.O. Arms & Ammunition Co.
Lee's Red Ramps
Lofland, James W.
L.P.A. Snc
Lyman Products Corp.
Mac's .45 Shop
Marble Arms Corp.

MCS, Inc.
Meadow Industries
MEC-Gar S.R.L.
Meier Works
Meprolight
Merit Corp.
Mid-America Recreation, Inc.
Millett Sights
MMC
Montana Vintage Arms
North American Specialties
Novak's, Inc.
Oakshore Electronic Sights, Inc.
Omega Sales, Inc.
OMR Feinmechanik, Jagd-und
  Sportwaffen, GmbH
Pachmayr Ltd.
P.M. Enterprises, Inc.
Ravell Ltd.
RPM
Sheridan USA, Inc., Austin
Stoeger Industries
Tanfoglio S.r.l., Fratelli
T.F.C. S.p.A.
Thompson/Center Arms
Trijicon, Inc.
Wichita Arms, Inc.
Williams Gun Sight Co.

TARGETS AND BULLET TRAPS

Action Target, Inc.
American Target
American Whitetail Target Systems
Armor Metal Products
A-Tech Corp.
Barsotti, Bruce
Birchwood Laboratories, Inc.
Blount, Inc.
Blue and Gray Products, Inc.

Caswell International Corp.
Champion Target Co.
Champion's Choice, Inc.
Cunningham Co., Eaton
Dapkus Co., J.G.
Datumtech Corp.
D.C.C. Enterprises
Detroit-Armor Corp.
Diamond Mfg. Co.

Dutchman's Firearms, Inc., The
Epps "Orillia" Ltd., Ellwood
Federal Champion Target Co.
Freeman Animal Targets
G.H. Enterprises Ltd.
Gozon Corp.
Hart & Son, Inc., Robert W.
Hiti-Schuch, Atelier Wilma
Hoppe's Div.
Hornady Mfg. Co.
Hunterjohn
Innovision Enterprises
Jackalope Gun Shop
Kennebec Journal
Littler Sales Co.
Lyman Instant Targets, Inc.
M&D Munitions Ltd.
Marksman Products
National Target Co.
North American Shooting Systems
Nu-Teck
Old Western Scrounger, Inc.
Outers Laboratories

Ox-Yoke Originals, Inc.
Parker Reproductions
Pease Accuracy, Bob
Penguin Industries, Inc.
Primos Wild Game Calls, Inc.
Protektor Model
Quack Decoy & Sporting Clays
Red Star Target Co.
Remington Arms Co., Inc.
Richards, John
Rockwood Corp., Speedwell Div.
Rocky Mountain Target Co.
Schaefer Shooting Sports
Seligman Shooting Products
Shooters Supply
Shooting Arts Ltd
Shotgun Shop, The
Stoney Baroque Shooters Supply
Stoney Point Products, Inc.
Thompson Target Technology
Verdemont Fieldsports
World of Targets
X-Spand Target Systems

TAXIDERMY

Jonas Appraisers &Taxidermy, Jack
Kulis Freeze Dry Taxidermy
Parker, Mark D.

Piedmont Community College
Shell Shack
World Trek, Inc.

TRIGGERS, RELATED EQUIPMENT

B&D Trading Co., Inc.
Canjar Co., M.H.
Central Specialties Ltd.
Costa, David
Cycle Dynamics, Inc.
Dayton Traister
E.A.A. Corp.
Electronic Trigger Systems, Inc.
Eversull Co., Inc., K.
Forster Products
Grace Tool, Inc.
Hart & Son, Inc., Robert W.
Hoelscher, Virgil
Hollands
Home Shop Machinist, The
Island Pond Gun Shop
Jackalope Gun Shop
Jaeger, Inc., Paul/Dunn's
Jewell, Arnold W.

Jones Custom Products, Neil
Krieger Barrels, Inc.
Mahony, Philip Bruce
Master Lock Co.
Mid-America Recreation, Inc.
Miller Single Trigger Mfg. Co.
Morrow, Bud
Pace Marketing, Inc.
Pease Accuracy, Bob
PEM's Mfg. Co.
Penrod Precision
Perazzi U.S.A., Inc.
S&B Industries
Sheridan USA, Inc., Austin
Shilen Rifles, Inc.
Stock Shop, The
Timney Mfg., Inc.
Tyler Mfg.-Dist., Melvin
Voere-KGH m.b.H.

MANUFACTURERS' DIRECTORY

A

A&B Industries, Inc. (See Top-Line USA, Inc.)

A.A. Arms, Inc., 4811 Persimmont Ct., Monroe, NC 28110/704-289-5356; FAX: 704-289-5859

AAL Optics, Inc., 2316 NE 8th Rd., Ocala, FL 34470/904-629-3211

A.B.S. III, 9238 St. Morritz Dr., Fern Creek, KY 40291

Acadian Ballistic Specialties, P.O. Box 61, Covington, LA 70434

Acculube II, Inc., 4366 Shackleford Rd., Norcross, GA 30093-2912

Accupro Gun Care, 15512-109 Ave., Surrey, BC U3R 7E8, CANADA/604-583-7807

Accuracy Components Co., P.O. Box 60034, Renton, WA 98058/206-255-4577

Accuracy Den, The, 25 Bitterbrush Rd., Reno, NV 89523/702-345-0225

Accuracy Gun Shop, 3651 University Ave., San Diego, CA 92104/619-282-8500

Accuracy Innovations, Inc., P.O. Box 376, New Paris, PA 15554/814-839-4517; FAX: 814-839-2601

Accuracy Products, S.A., 14 rue de Lawsanne, Brussels, 1060 BELGIUM/32-2-539-34-42; FAX: 32-2-539-39-60

Accuracy Unlimited, 7479 S. DePew St., Littleton, CO 80123

Accuracy Unlimited, 16036 N. 49 Ave., Glendale, AZ 85306/602-978-9089

Accura-Site (See All's, The Jim Tembellis, Inc.)

Accurate Arms Co., Inc., Rt. 1, Box 167, McEwen, TN 37101/615-729-4207; FAX 615-729-4217

Accurate Plating & Weaponry, Inc., 1937 Calumet St., Clearwater, FL 34625/813-449-9112

Accuright, 119 E. Main, Belgrade, MT 59714/406-388-7234; FAX: 406-388-7234

Accu-Tek, 4525 Carter Ct., Chino, CA 91710/909-627-2404; FAX: 909-627-7817

Ackerman & Co., 16 Cortez St., Westfield, MA 01085/413-568-8008

Ackerman, Bill, 10236 Woodway, El Paso, TX 79925/915-592-5338

Action Ammo Ltd. (See Action Arms Ltd.)

Action Arms Ltd., P.O. Box 9573, Philadelphia, PA 19124/215-744-0100; FAX: 215-533-2188

Action Bullets, Inc., 1811 W. 13th Ave., Denver, CO 80204/303-595-9636; FAX: 303-893-9161

Action Products, Inc., 22 N. Mulberry St., Hagerstown, MD 21740/301-797-1414

Action Target, Inc., P.O. Box 636, Provo, UT 84603/801-377-8033; FAX: 801-377-8096

Actions by "T", Teddy Jacobson, 16315 Redwood Forest Ct., Sugarland, TX 77478/713-277-4008

ACTIV Industries, Inc., 1000 Zigor Rd., P.O. Box 339, Kearneysville, WV 25430/304-725-0451; FAX: 304-725-2080

Ad Hominem, RR 3, Orillia, Ont. L3V 6H3, CANADA/705-689-5303

Adair Custom Shop, Bill, 2886 Westridge, Carrollton, TX 75006

Adams, John J., P.O. Box 467, Corinth, VT 05039-0467/802-439-5904

Adaptive Technology, 939 Barnum Ave., Bridgeport, CT 06609/800-643-6735; FAX: 800-643-6735

ADC, Inc./PC Bullet, 32654 Coal Creek Rd., Scappoose, OR 97056-2601/503-543-5088; FAX: 503-543-5990

ADCO International, 10 Cedar St., Woburn, MA 01801-2341/617-935-1799; FAX: 617-932-4807

Adkins, Luther, 1292 E. McKay Rd., Shelbyville, IN 46176-9353/317-392-3795

Advance Car Mover Co., Rowell Div., P.O. Box 1, 240 N. Depot St., Juneau, WI 53039/414-386-4464; FAX: 414-386-4416

Adventurer's Outpost, P.O. Box 70, Cottonwood, AZ 86326/800-762-7471; FAX: 602-634-8781

African Import Co., 20 Braunecker Rd., Plymouth, MA 02360/508-746-8552

AFSCO Ammunition, 731 W. Third St., P.O. Box L, Owen, WI 54460/715-229-2516

Ahlman Guns, Rt. 1, Box 20, Morristown, MN 55052/507-685-4243; FAX: 507-685-4247

Ahrends, Kim, Custom Firearms, Box 203, Clarion, IA 50525/515-532-3449

Aimpoint, Inc., 580 Herndon Parkway, Suite 500, Herndon, VA 22070/703-471-6828; FAX: 703-689-0575

Aimtech Mount Systems, P.O. Box 223, Thomasville, GA 31799/912-226-4313; FAX: 912-227-0222

Air Arms (See U.S. importer—Air Rifle Specialists)

Air Rifle Specialists, 311 East Water St., Elmira, NY 14901/607-734-7340; FAX: 607-733-3261

Air Venture, 9752 E. Flower St., Bellflower, CA 90706/310-867-6355

Airgun Repair Centre, 3227 Garden Meadows, Lawrenceburg, IN 47025/812-637-1463

Airrow (See Swivel Machine Works, Inc.)

Ajax Custom Grips, Inc., Div. of A. Jack Rosenberg & Sons, 9130 Viscount Row, Dallas, TX 75247/214-630-8893; FAX: 214-630-4942

Aker Leather Products, 2248 Main St., Suite 6, Chula Vista, CA 91911/619-423-5182

Alaska Bullet Works, P.O. Box 54, Douglas, AK 99824/907-789-3834

Aldis Gunsmithing & Shooting Supply, 502 S. Montezuma St., Prescott, AZ 86303/602-445-6723; FAX: 602-445-6763

Alessandri & Son, Lou, 24 French St., Rehoboth, MA 02769/508-252-5590, 800-248-5652; FAX: 508-252-3436

Alessi Holsters, Inc., 2465 Niagara Falls Blvd., Amherst, NY 14228-3527/716-691-5615

Alfano, Sam, 36180 Henry Gaines Rd., Pearl River, LA 70452/504-863-3364; FAX: 504-863-7715

All American Bullets, 889 Beatty St., Medford, OR 97501/503-770-5649

All American Lead Shot Corp., P.O. Box 224566, Dallas, TX 75062

All's, The Jim J. Tembelis Co., Inc., 280 E. Fernau Ave., Oshkosh, WI 54901/414/426/1080; FAX: 414-426-1080

Allard, Gary, Creek Side Metal & Woodcrafters, Fishers Hill, VA 22626/703-465-3903

Allen, Richard L., 339 Grove Ave., Prescott, AZ 86301/602-778-1237

Allen Mfg., 6449 Hodgson Rd., Circle Pines, MN 55014/612-429-8231

Alley Supply Co., P.O. Box 848, Gardnerville, NV 89410/702-782-3800

Allred Bullet Co., 932 Evergreen Drive, Logan, UT 84321/801-752-6983

Alpec Team, Inc., 55 Oak Ct., Danville, CA 94526/510-820-1763; FAX: 510-820-8738

Alpha LaFranck Enterprises, P.O. Box 81072, Lincoln, NE 68501/402-466-3193

Alpha Precision, Inc., 2765-B Preston Rd. NE, Good Hope, GA 30641/404-267-6163

Alpine's Precision Gunsmithing & Indoor Shooting Range, 2401 Government Way, Coeur d'Alene, ID 83814/208-765-3559; FAX: 208-765-3559

Altamont Co., 901 N. Church St., P.O. Box 309, Thomasboro, IL 61878/217-643-3125; FAX: 217-643-7973

Alumna Sport by Dee Zee, 1572 NE 58th Ave., P.O. Box 3090, Des Moines, IA 50316/800-798-9899

AmBr Software Group Ltd., The, 2205 Maryland Ave., Baltimore, MD 21218/410-243-7717; FAX: 410-366-8742

American Ammunition, 3545 NW 71st St., Miami, FL 33147/FAX: 305-638-1014

American Arms & Ordnance, Inc., P.O. Box 2691, 1303 S. College Ave., Bryan, TX 77805/409-822-4983

American Arms, Inc., 715 E. Armour Rd., N. Kansas City, MO 64116/816-474-3161; FAX: 816-474-1225

American Bullets, 2190 C. Coffee Rd., Lithonia, GA 30058/404-482-4253

American Derringer Corp., 127 N. Lacy Dr., Waco, TX 76705/800-642-7817, 817-799-9111; FAX: 817-799-7935

American Gas & Chemical Co., Ltd., 220 Pegasus Ave., Northvale, NJ 07647/201-767-7300

American Gripcraft, 3230 S. Dodge 2, Tucson, AZ 85713/602-790-1222

American Handgunner Magazine, 591 Camino de la Reina, Suite 200, San Diego, CA 92108/619-297-5350; FAX: 619-297-5353

American Import Co., The, 1453 Mission St., San Francisco, CA 94103/415-863-1506; FAX: 415-863-0939

American Pioneer Video, P.O. Box 50049, Bowling Green, KY 42102-2649/800-743-4675

American Pistol Institute (See Gunsite Training Center)

American Pistolsmiths Guild, P.O. Box 67, Louisville, TN 37777/615-984-3583

American Products Co., 14729 Spring Valley Road, Morrison, IL 61270/815-772-3336; FAX: 815-772-7921

American Sales & Mfg. Co., P.O. Box 677, Laredo, TX 78042/210-723-6893; FAX: 210-725-0672

American Small Arms Academy, P.O. Box 12111, Prescott, AZ 86304/602-778-5623

American Whitetail Target Systems, P.O. Box 41, 106 S. Church St., Tennyson, IN 47637/812-567-4527

Ames Metal Products Co., 4324 S. Western Blvd., Chicago, IL/312-523-3230; FAX: 312-523-3854

Amherst Arms, P.O. Box 1457, Englewood, FL 34295/813-475-2020

Ammo Load, Inc., 1560 East Edinger, Suite G., Santa Ana, CA 92705/714-558-8858; FAX: 714-569-0319

Amm-O-Mart, Ltd., P.O. Box 125, Hawkesbury, Ont., K6A 2R8 CANADA/613-632-9300

Ammunition Consulting Services, Inc., P.O. Box 701084, San Antonio, TX 78270-1084/201-646-9624; FAX: 210-646-0141

Amodei, Jim (See D.O.C. Specialists, Inc.)

Amrine's Gun Shop, 937 La Luna, Ojai, CA 93023/805-646-2376

Amsec, 11925 Pacific Ave., Fontana, CA 92337

AMT, 6226 Santos Diaz St., Irwindale, CA 91702/818-334-6629; FAX: 818-969-5247

Amtech International, Inc., 4942 Industrial Ave. E., Coeur D'Alene, ID 83814

Amtech-Overseas, Inc., 1015 15th St. NW, Suite 402, Washington, D.C. 20005/202-408-4760; FAX: 202-408-4746

Analog Devices, Box 9106, Norwood, MA 02062

Andela Tool & Machine, Inc., RD3, Box 246, Richfield Springs, NY 13439

Anderson Manufacturing Co., Inc., P.O. Box 2640, 2741 N. Crosby Rd., Oak Harbor, WA 98277/206-675-7300; FAX: 206-675-3939

Anschutz GmbH, Postfach 1128, D-89001 Ulm, Donau, GERMANY (U.S. importer—PSI, Inc.)

Anthony and George Ltd., Rt. 1, P.O. Box 45, Evington, VA 24550/804-821-8117

Antique American Firearms (See Carlson, Douglas R.)

Antique Arms Co., 1110 Cleveland Ave., Monett, MO 65708/417-235-6501

AO Safety Products, Div. of American Optical Corp. (See E-A-R, Inc.)

Aplan Antiques & Art, James O., HC 80, Box 793-25, Piedmont, SD 57769/605-347-5016

Applied Laser Systems, 2160 NW Vine St., Grants Pass, OR 97526/503-479-0484; FAX: 503-476-5105

Applied Laser Systems, Inc., 2160 NW Vine St., Grants Pass, OR 97526/503-479-0484; FAX: 503-476-5105

Arcadia Machine & Tool, Inc. (See AMT)

Arizaga (See U.S. importer—Mandall Shooting Supplies, Inc.)

Armament Gunsmithing Co., Inc., 525 Rt. 22, Hillside, NJ 07205/908-686-0960

Armas Kemen (See U.S. importer—USA Sporting)

Armes de Chasse, P.O. Box 827, Chadds Ford, PA 19317/215-388-1146; FAX: 215-388-1147

Armfield Custom Bullets, 4775 Caroline Drive, San Diego, CA 92115/619-582-7188; FAX: 619-287-3238

Armi San Paolo, via Europa 172-A, I-25062 Concesio, 030-2751725 (BS) ITALY

Armite Laboratories, 1845 Randolph St., Los Angeles, CA 90001/213-587-7768; FAX: 213-587-5075

Armoloy Co. of Ft. Worth, 204 E. Daggett St., Fort Worth, TX 76104/817-332-5604; FAX: 817-335-6517

Armor Metal Products, P.O. Box 4609, Helena, MT 59604/406-442-5560

Armory Publications, P.O. Box 4206, Oceanside, CA 92052-4206/619-757-3930; FAX: 619-722-4108

Armoury, Inc., The, Rt. 202, Box 2340, New Preston, CT 06777/203-868-0001

Arms & Armour Press, Villiers House, 41-47 Strand, London WC2N 5JE ENGLAND/071-839-4900; FAX: 071-839-1804

A.R.M.S., Inc., 375 West St., West Bridgewater, MA 02379/508-584-7816; FAX: 508-588-8045

Arms Corp. of the Phillipines, 550E Delos Santos Ave., Cubau, Quezon City, PHILLIPINES

Arms, Peripheral Data Systems, P.O. Box 1526, Lake Oswego, OR 97035/800-366-5559, 503-697-0533; FAX: 503-697-3337

Armscor (See U.S. importer—Ruko Products)

Armscor Precision, 225 Lindbergh St., San Mateo, CA 94401/415-347-9556; FAX: 415-347-7634

Armscorp USA, Inc., 4424 John Ave., Baltimore, MD 21227/410-247-6200

Armsport, Inc., 3950 NW 49th St., Miami, FL 33142/305-635-7850; FAX: 305-633-2877

Armurier Hiptmayer, RR 112 750, P.O. Box 136, Eastman, Quebec J0E 1P0, CANADA/514-297-2492

Aro-Tek, Ltd., 201 Frontage Rd. North, Suite C, Pacific, WA 98047/206-351-2984

Arratoonian, Andy (See Horseshoe Leather Products)

Art Jewel Enterprises Ltd., Eagle Business Ctr., 460 Randy Rd., Carol Stream, IL 60188/708-260-0400

Artistry in Leather (See Stuart, V. Pat)

Artistry in Wood, 134 Zimmerman Rd., Kalispell, MT 59901/406-257-9003

ASI, 6226 Santos Dias St., Irwindale, CA 91706/818-334-6629

Aspen Outdoors, 1059 W. Market St., York, PA 17404/717-846-0255; FAX: 717-845-7747

A-Square Co., Inc., One Industrial Park, Bedford, KY 40006-9667/502-255-7456; FAX: 502-255-7657

Astra-Unceta Y Cia, S.A., Apartado 3, 48300 Guernica, Espagne, SPAIN/34-4-6250100; FAX: 34-4-6255186 (U.S. importer—E.A.A. Corp.)

A-Tech Corp., P.O. Box 1281, Cottage Grove, OR 97424

ATIS Armi S.A.S., via Gussalli 24, Zona Industriale-Loc. Fornaci, 25020 Brescia, ITALY

Atlantic Mills, Inc., 1325 Washington Ave., Asbury Park, NJ 07712/201-774-4882

Atlantic Research Marketing Systems (See A.R.M.S., Inc.)

Atsko/Sno-Seal, Inc., 2530 Russell SE, Orangeburg, SC 29115/803-531-1820; FAX: 803-531-2139

Audette, Creighton, 19 Highland Circle, Springfield, VT 05156/802-885-2331

Austin's Calls, Bill, Box 284, Kaycee, WY 82639/307-738-2552

Auto Arms, 738 Clearview, San Antonio, TX 78228/512-434-5450

Automatic Equipment Sales, 627 E. Railroad Ave., Salesburg, MD 21801

Automatic Weaponry (See Scattergun Technologies, Inc.)

Auto-Ordnance Corp., Williams Lane, West Hurley, NY 12491/914-679-7225; FAX: 914-679-2698

Autumn Sales, Inc. (Blaser), 1320 Lake St., Fort Worth, TX 76102/817-335-1634; FAX: 817-338-0119

Avtac, 489 Rt. 32, Highland Mills, NY 10930-0522/800-348-9127

AYA (See U.S. importer—Armes de Chasse)

A Zone Bullets, 2039 Walter Rd., Billings, MT 59105/800-252-3111

Aztec International Ltd., P.O. Box 1384, Clarkesville, GA 30523/706-754-7263

B

B&D Trading Co., Inc., 3935 Fair Hill Rd., Fair Oaks, CA 95628/916-967-9366

B&G Bullets, P.O. Box 14313, Oklahoma City, OK 73114/405-840-2353

Badger Shooters Supply, Inc., 202 N. Harding, Owen, WI 54460/715-229-2101; FAX: 715-229-2332

Baekgaard Ltd., 1855 Janke Dr., Northbrook, IL 60062/708-498-3040; FAX: 708-493-3106

Baer Custom, Inc., Les, 29601 34th Ave., Hillsdale, IL 61257/309-794-1166; FAX: 309-794-9882

Bagmaster Mfg., Inc., 2731 Sutton Ave., St. Louis, MO 63143/314-781-8002

Baikal (See U.S. importer—K.B.I., Inc.)

Bain & Davis, Inc., 307 E. Valley Blvd., San Gabriel, CA 91776-3522/818-573-4241, 213-283-7449

Baity's Custom Gunworks, 414 2nd St., N. Wilkesboro, NC 28659/919-667-8785

Baker's Leather Goods, Roy, P.O. Box 893, Magnolia, AR 71753/501-234-0344

Balaance Co., 340-39 Ave. S.E. Box 505, Calgary, AB, T2G 1X6 CANADA

Bald Eagle Precision Machine Co., 101 Allison St., Lock Haven, PA 17745/717-748-6772; FAX: 717-748-4443

Ballard Built, P.O. Box 1443, Kingsville, TX 78364/512-592-0853

Ballentine's Scopes Unlimited, 22525 Ballentine Lane, Onaga, KS 66521/913-889-4859

Ballistic Engineering & Software, Inc., 2440 Freeman Dr., Lake Orion, MI 48360/313-391-1074

Ballistic Products, Inc., 20015 75th Ave. North, Corcoran, MN 55340-9456/612-494-9237; FAX: 612-494-9236

Ballistic Program Co., Inc., The, 2417 N. Patterson St., Thomasville, GA 31792/912-228-5739, 800-368-0835

Ballistic Research, 1108 W. May Ave., McHenry, IL 60050/815-385-0037

Ballistica Maximus North, 107 College Park Plaza, Johnstown, PA 15904/814-266-8380

Ballisti-Cast, Inc., Box 383, Parshall, ND 58770/701-862-3324; FAX: 701-862-3331

Banaczkowski Bullets, 56 Victoria Dr., Mount Barker, S.A. 5251 AUSTRALIA

Bancorr Industries, Div. of Man-Sew Corp., 6108 Sherwin Dr., Port Richey, FL 34668/813-848-0432

Bang-Bang Boutique (See Holster Shop, The)

Banks, Ed, 2762 Hwy. 41 N., Ft. Valley, GA 31030/912-987-4665

Barami Corp., 6689 Orchard Lake Rd. No. 148, West Bloomfield, MI 48322/810-738-0462; FAX: 810-855-4084

Barlett, J., 6641 Kaiser Ave., Fontana, CA 92336-3265

Barnes Bullets, Inc., P.O. Box 215, American Fork, UT 84003/801-756-4222; FAX: 801-756-2465

Baron Technology, 62 Spring Hill Rd., Trumbull, CT 06611/203-452-0515; FAX: 203-452-0663

Barrett Firearms Mfg., Inc., P.O. Box 1077, Murfreesboro, TN 37133/615-896-2938; FAX: 615-896-7313

Barsotti, Bruce (See River Road Sporting Clays)

Bar-Sto Precision Machine, 73377 Sullivan Rd., P.O. Box 1838, Twentynine Palms, CA 92277/619-367-2747; FAX: 619-367-2407

Barteaux Machete, 1916 SE 50th Ave., Portland, OR 97215-3238/503-233-5880

Barton, Michael D. (See Tiger-Hunt)

Bates Engraving, Billy, 2302 Winthrop Dr., Decatur, AL 35603/205-355-3690

Baumannize Custom, 4784 Sunrise Hwy., Bohemia, NY 11716/800-472-4387; FAX: 516-567-0001

Baumgartner Bullets, 3011 S. Alane St., W. Valley City, UT 84120

Bausch & Lomb, Inc., 42 East Ave., Rochester, NY 14603/800-828-5423

Bausch & Lomb Sports Optics Div., 9200 Cody, Overland Park, KS 66214/913-752-3400, 800-423-3537; FAX: 913-752-3550

Bauska Barrels, 105 9th Ave. W., Kalispell, MT 59901/406-752-7706

Bear Arms, 121 Rhodes St., Jackson, SC 29831/803-471-9859

Bear Hug Grips, Inc., 17230 County Rd. 338, Buena Vista, CO 81211/800-232-7710

Bear Mountain Gun & Tool, 120 N. Plymouth, New Plymouth, ID 83655/208-278-5221; FAX: 208-278-5221

Bear Reloaders, P.O. Box 1613, Akron, OH 44309-1613/216-920-1811

Beartooth Bullets, P.O. Box 491, Dept. HLD, Dover, ID 83825-0491/208-448-1865

Beauchamp & Son, Inc., 160 Rossiter Rd., Richmond, MA 01254/413-698-3822; FAX: 413-698-3866

Beaver Lodge (See Fellowes, Ted)

Beaver Park Products, Inc., 840 J St., Penrose, CO 81240/719-372-6744

Bedford Technologies, Inc., P.O. Box 820, Fairland, OK 74343/800-467-7233

Beeline Custom Bullets, P.O. Box 85, Yarmouth, Nova Scotia CANADA B5A 4B1/902-648-3494; FAX: 902-648-0253

Beeman Precision Airguns, 5454 Argosy Dr., Huntington Beach, CA 92649/714-890-4800; FAX: 714-890-4808

Behlert Precision, P.O. Box 288, 7067 Easton Rd., Pipersville, PA 18947/215-766-8681; FAX: 215-766-8681

Beitzinger, George, 116-20 Atlantic Ave., Richmond Hill, NY 11419/718-847-7661

Bell Originals, Sid, Inc., 7776 Shackham Rd., Tully, NY 13159-9333/607-842-6431

Bell Reloading, Inc., 1725 Harlin Lane Rd., Villa Rica, GA 30180

Bell's Gun & Sport Shop, 3309-19 Mannheim Rd, Franklin Park, IL 60131

Bell's Legendary Country Wear, 22 Circle Dr., Bellmore, NY 11710/516-679-1158

Belltown, Ltd., 11 Camps Rd., Kent, CT 06757/203-354-5750

Ben's Machines, 1151 S. Cedar Ridge, Duncanville, TX 75137/214-780-1807

Benchmark Guns, 12593 S. Ave. 5 East, Yuma, AZ 85365

Benelli Armi, S.p.A., Via della Stazione, 61029 Urbino, ITALY/39-722-328633; FAX: 39-722-327427 (U.S. importers—E.A.A. Corp.; Heckler & Koch, Inc.; Sile Distributors)

Bengtson Arms Co., L., 6345-B E. Akron St., Mesa, AZ 85205/602-981-6375

Benjamin/Sheridan Co., Crossman, Rts. 5 and 20, E. Bloomfield, NY 14443/716-657-6161; FAX: 716-657-5405

Bentley, John, 128-D Watson Dr., Turtle Creek, PA 15145

Beretta, Dr. Franco, via Rossa, 4, Concesio (BC), Italy I-25062/030-2751955; FAX: 030-218-0414 (U.S. importer—Nevada Cartridge Co.)

Beretta Firearms, Pietro, 25063 Gardone V.T., ITALY (U.S. importer—Beretta U.S.A. Corp.)

Beretta U.S.A. Corp., 17601 Beretta Drive, Accokeek, MD 20607/301-283-2191

Berger Bullets, Ltd., 5342 W. Camelback Rd., Suite 500, Glendale, AZ 85301/602-842-4001; FAX: 602-934-9083

Bergman & Williams, 2450 Losee Rd., Suite F, Las Vegas, NV 89030/702-642-1901; FAX: 702-642-1540

Bernardelli Vincenzo S.p.A., 125 Via Matteotti, P.O. Box 74, 25063 Gardone, V.T. (Brescia) ITALY/39-30-8912851/2/3; FAX: 39-30-8910249 (U.S. importer—Armsport, Inc.)

Berry's Bullets, Div. of Berry's Mfg., Inc., Box 100, Bloomington, CA 92316/801-634-1682

Berry's Mfg., Inc., 401 North 3050 East, St. George, UT 84770

Bersa S.A., Gonzales Castillo 312, 1704 Ramos Mejia, ARGENTINA/541-656-2377; FAX: 541-656-2093 (U.S. importer—Eagle Imports, Inc.)

Bertram Bullet Co., P.O. Box 313, Seymour, Victoria 3660, AUSTRALIA/61-57-922912; FAX: 61-57-991650

Bertuzzi (See U.S. importers—Moore & Co., Wm. Larkin; New England Arms Co.)

Bestload, Inc., P.O. Box 4354, Stamford, CT 06907/FAX: 203-978-0796

Bianchi International, Inc., 100 Calle Cortez, Temecula, CA 92590/909-676-5621

Biesen, Al, 5021 Rosewood, Spokane, WA 99208/509-328-9340

Biesen, Roger, 5021 W. Rosewood, Spokane, WA 99208/509-328-9340

Big 45 Frontier Gun Shop, P.O. Box 70, Hill City, SD 57745/800-342-1548; FAX: 800-342-1548

Big Bear Arms & Sporting Goods, 2714 Fairmount St., Dallas, TX 75201/214-871-7061; FAX: 214-754-0449

Bill's Gun Repair, 1007 Burlington St., Mendota, IL 61342/815-539-5786

Billingsley & Brownell, P.O. Box 25, Dayton, WY 82836/307-655-9344

Bilsom Intl., Inc., 109 Carpenter Dr., Sterling, VA 20164/703-834-1070

Birchwood Casey, 7900 Fuller Rd., Eden Prairie, MN 55344/800-328-6156; FAX: 612-937-7979

Birdsong & Assoc., W.E., 4832 Windermere, Jackson, MS 39206/601-366-8270

Bismuth Cartridge Co., 3500 Maple Ave., Suite 1650, Dallas, TX 75129/800-759-3333; 214-521-5882

Bitterroot Bullet Co., Box 412, Lewiston, ID 83501-0412/208-743-5635

Black Hills Ammunition, P.O. Box 3090, Rapid City, SD 57709-3090/605-348-5150; FAX: 605-348-9827

Black Hills Shooters Supply, P.O. Box 4220, Rapid City, SD 57709

Black Mountain Bullets, Rt. 7, Box 297, Warrenton, VA 22186/703-347-1199

Black Sheep Brand, 3220 W. Gentry Parkway, Tyler, TX 75702/903-592-3853

Blackhawk East, Box 2274, Loves Park, IL 61131

Blackhawk Mountain, Box 210, Conifer, CO 80433

Blackhawk West, Box 285, Hiawatha, KS 66434

Blacksmith Corp., 830 N. Road 1 E.,Box 1752, Chino Valley, AZ 86323/602-636-4456; FAX: 602-636-4457

BlackStar Barrel Accurizing, 11609 Galayda St., Houston, TX 77086/713-448-5300; FAX: 713-448-7298

Blacktail Mountain Books, 42 First Ave. West, Kalispell, MT 59901/406-257-5573

Blackwell, W., Load From A Disk, Dept. GD, 9826 Sagedale, Houston, TX 77089/713-484-0935

Blake Affiliates, Box 133, Roscoe, IL 61073

Blammo Ammo, P.O. Box 1677, Seneca, SC 29679/803-882-1768

Blaser Jagdwaffen GmbH, D-88316 Isny Im Allgau, GERMANY (U.S. importer—Autumn Sales, Inc.)

Bledsoe, Weldon, 6812 Park Place Dr., Fort Worth, TX 76118/817-589-1704

Bleile, C. Roger, 5040 Ralph Ave., Cincinnati, OH 45238/513-251-0249

Blocker's Holsters, Inc., Ted, 5360 NE 112, Portland, OR 97220/503-254-9950

Blount, Inc., Sporting Equipment Div., 2299 Snake River Ave., P.O. Box 856, Lewiston, ID 83501/800-627-3640, 208-746-2351

Blue and Gray Products, Inc. (See Ox-Yoke Originals, Inc.)

Blue Book Publications, Inc., One Appletree Square, Minneapolis, MN 55425/800-877-4867; FAX: 612-853-1486

Blue Mountain Bullets, HCR 77, P.O. Box 231, John Day, OR 97845/503-820-4594

Blue Point Mfg. Co., P.O. Box 722, Massena, NY 13662

Blue Ridge Machinery & Tools, Inc., P.O. Box 536-GD, Hurricane, WV 25526/800-872-6500; FAX: 304-562-5311

Bluebonnet Specialty, P.O. Box 737, Palestine, TX 75802/214-723-2075

BMC Supply, Inc., 26051 - 179th Ave. S.E., Kent, WA 98042

B.M.F. Activator, Inc., 803 Mill Creek Run, Plantersville, TX 77363/409-894-2005, 800-527-2881

Bob's Coins & Guns, Inc., 24 Defense St., Annapolis, MD 21401/301-224-8683

Bob's Gun Shop, P.O. Box 200, Royal, AR 71968/501-767-1970

Bob's Tactical Indoor Shooting Range & Gun Shop, 122 Lafayette Rd., Salisbury, MA 01952/508-465-5561

Boessler, Erich, Am Vogeltal 3, 8732 Munnerstadt, GERMANY/9733-9443

Boggs, Wm., 1816 Riverside Dr. C, Columbus, OH 43212/614-486-6965

Bohemia Arms Co., 17101 Los Modelos, Fountain Valley, CA 92708/714-963-0809; FAX: 714-963-0809

Bo-Mar Tool & Mfg. Co., Rt. 12, Box 405, Longview, TX 75605/903-759-4784; FAX: 903-759-9141

Bondini Paolo, Via Sorrento, 345, San Carlo di Cesena, ITALY I-47020/0547 663 240; FAX: 0547 663 780

Bone Engraving, Ralph, 718 N. Atlanta, Owasso, OK 74055/918-272-9745

Boono's Custom Ivory Grips, Inc., 562 Coyote Rd., Brinnon, WA 98320/206-796-4330

Boonie Packer Products, P.O. Box 12204, Salem, OR 97309/800-477-3244; FAX: 503-581-3191

Bourne Co., Inc., Richard A., P.O. Box 141, Hyannis Port, MA 02647/508-775-0797

Bowen Classic Arms Corp., P.O. Box 67, Louisville, TN 37777/615-984-3583

Bowen Knife Co., Inc., P.O. Box 590, Blackshear, GA 31516/912-449-4794

Bowlin, Gene, Rt. 1, Box 890, Snyder, TX 79549

Boyds', Inc., 3rd & Main, Geddes, SD 57342/605-337-2125; FAX: 605-337-3363

Brace, Larry D., 771 Blackfoot Ave., Eugene, OR 97404/503-688-1278

Bradley Gunsight Co., P.O. Box 140, Plymouth, VT 05056/203-589-0531; FAX: 203-582-6294

Brass and Bullet Alloys, P.O. Box 1238, Sierra Vista, AZ 85636/602-458-5321; FAX: 602-458-9125

Brass Eagle, Inc., 7050A Bramalea Rd., Unit 19, Mississauga, Ont. L4Z 1C7, CANADA/416-848-4844

Bratcher, Dan, 311 Belle Air Pl., Carthage, MO 64836/417-358-1518

Brauer Bros. Mfg. Co., 2020 Delmar Blvd., St. Louis, MO 63103/314-231-2864; FAX: 314-249-4952

Braun, M., 32, rue Notre-Dame, 2440 LUXEMBURG

Break-Free, Inc., P.O. Box 25020, Santa Ana, CA 92799/714-953-1900; FAX: 714-953-0402

Brenneke KG, Wilhelm, Ilmenauweg 2, D-30551 Langenhagen, GERMANY/0511/97262-0; FAX: 0511/9726262 (U.S. importer—Dynamit Nobel-RWS, Inc.)

Bretton, 19, rue Victor Grignard, F-42026 St.-Etienne (Cedex 1) FRANCE/77-93-54-69; FAX: 77-93-57-98 (U.S. importer—Mandall Shooting Supplies, Inc.)

Brgoch, Frank, 1580 S. 1500 East, Bountiful, UT 84010/801-295-1885

Brian, C.T., 1101 Indiana Ct., Decatur, IL 62521/217-429-2290

Bridgers Best, P.O. Box 1410, Berthoud, CO 80513

Briese Bullet Co., Inc., RR1, Box 108, Tappen, ND 58487/701-327-4578; FAX: 701-327-4579

Briganti & Co., A., 475 Rt. 32, Highland Mills, NY 10930/914-928-9573

British Arms Co. Ltd., P.O. Box 7, Latham, NY 12110/518-783-0773

British Sporting Arms, RR1, Box 130, Millbrook, NY 12545/914-677-8303

BRNO (See U.S. importers—Action Arms Ltd.; Bohemia Arms Co.)

Brobst, Jim, 299 Poplar St., Hamburg, PA 19526/215-562-2103

Broken Gun Ranch, RR2, Box 92, Spearville, KS 67876/316-385-2587

Brooker, Dennis, Rt. 1, Box 12A, Derby, IA 50068/515-533-2103

Brown, H.R. (See Silhouette Leathers)

Brown Co., E. Arthur, 3404 Pawnee Dr., Alexandria, MN 56308/612-762-8847

Brown Precision, Inc., 7786 Molinos Ave., Los Molinos, CA 96055/916-384-2506; FAX: 916-384-1638

Brown Products, Inc., Ed, Rt. 2, Box 2922, Perry, MO 63462/314-565-3261; FAX: 565-2791

Brownell Checkering Tools, W.E., 9390 Twin Mountain Circle, San Diego, CA 92126/619-695-2479; FAX: 619-695-2479

Brownells, Inc., 200 S. Front St., Montezuma, IA 50171/515-623-5401; FAX: 515-623-3896

Browning Arms Co. (Gen. Offices), One Browning Place, Morgan, UT 84050/801-876-2711; FAX: 801-876-3331

Browning Arms Co. (Parts & Service), 3005 Arnold Tenbrook Rd., Arnold, MO 63010-9406/314-287-6800; FAX: 314-287-9751

BRP, Inc. High Performance Cast Bullets, 1210 Alexander Rd., Colorado Springs, CO 80909/719-633-0658

Bruno Shooters Supply, 106 N. Wyoming St., Hazleton, PA 18201/717-455-2211; FAX: 717-455-2211

Bryco Arms (See U.S. distributor—Jennings Firearms, Inc.)

Brynin, Milton, P.O. Box 383, Yonkers, NY 10710/914-779-4333

B-Square Company, Inc., P.O. Box 11281, 2708 St. Louis Ave., Ft. Worth, TX 76110/817-923-0964, 800-433-2909; FAX: 817-926-7012

Bucheimer, J.M., Jumbo Sports Products, 721 N. 20th St., St. Louis, MO 63103/314-241-1020

Buck Stix—SOS Products Co., Box 3, Neenah, WI 54956

Buckeye Custom Bullets, 6490 Stewart Rd., Elida, OH 45807/419-641-4463

Buckskin Machine Works, A. Hunkeler, 3235 S. 358th St., Auburn, WA 98001/206-927-5412

Buehler Scope Mounts, 17 Orinda Way, Orinda, CA 94563/510-254-3201; FAX: 510-254-9720

Buffalo Arms, 123 S. Third, Suite 6, Sandpoint, ID 83864/208-263-6953; FAX: 208-265-2096

Buffalo Bullet Co., Inc., 12637 Los Nietos Rd. Unit A, Santa Fe Springs, CA 90670/310-944-0322; FAX: 310-944-5054

Buffalo Rock Shooters Supply, R.R. 1, Ottawa, IL 61350/815-433-2471

Bullberry Barrel Works, Ltd., 2430 W. Bullberry Ln. 67-5, Hurricane, UT 84737/801-635-9866

Bullet, Inc., 3745 Hiram Alworth Rd., Dallas, GA 30132

Bullet Mills, P.O. Box 102, Port Carbon, PA 17965/717-622-0657

Bullet Swaging Supply, Inc., P.O. Box 1056, 303 McMillan Rd, West Monroe, LA 71291/318-387-7257; FAX: 318-387-7779

Bullet Traps, Springdale RD., Westfield, MA 01085/413-568-7001

BulletMakers Workshop, The, RFD 1 Box 1755, Brooks, ME 04921

Bullseye Bullets, 1610 State Road 60, No. 12, Valrico, FL 33594/813-654-6563

Bull-X, Inc., P.O. Box 182, Farmer City, IL 61842/309-928-2574, 800-248-3845 orders only

Burgess & Son Gunsmiths, R.W., P.O. Box 3364, Warner Robins, GA 31099/912-328-7487

Burnham Bros., P.O. Box 1148, Menard, TX 78659/915-396-4572; FAX: 915-396-4574

Burris, P.O. Box 1747, Greeley, CO 80631/303-356-1670; FAX: 303-356-8702

Busch Metal Merchants, Roger, 48861 West Rd., Wixon, MI 48393/800-876-5337

Bushmann Hunters & Safaris, P.O. Box 293088, Lewisville, TX 75029/214-317-0768

Bushmaster Hunting & Fishing, 451 Alliance Ave., Toronto, Ont. M6N 2J1 CANADA/416-763-4040; FAX: 416-763-0623

Bushnell (See Bausch & Lomb)

Bustani Appraisers, Leo, P.O. Box 8125, W. Palm Beach, FL 33407/305-622-2710

Butler Creek Corp., 290 Arden Dr., Belgrade, MT 59714/800-423-8327, 406-388-1356; FAX: 406-388-7204

Butler Enterprises, 834 Oberting Rd., Lawrenceburg, IN 47025/812-537-3584

Butterfield & Butterfield, 220 San Bruno Ave., San Francisco, CA 94103/415-861-7500

Buzztail Brass, 5306 Bryant Ave., Klamath Falls, OR 97603/503-884-1072

B-West Imports, Inc., 2425 N. Huachuca Dr., Tucson, AZ 85745-1201/602-628-1990; FAX: 602-628-3602

C

C3 Systems, 678 Killingly St., Johnston, RI 02919

C&D Special Products (Claybuster), 309 Sequoya Dr., Hopkinsville, KY 42240/800-922-6287, 800-284-1746

Cabanas (See U.S. importer—Mandall Shooting Supplies, Inc.)

Cabela's, 812-13th Ave., Sidney, NE 69160/308-254-5505; FAX: 308-254-7809

Cabinet Mtn. Outfitters Scents & Lures, P.O. Box 766, Plains, MT 59859/406-826-3970

Cache La Poudre Rifleworks, 140 N. College, Ft. Collins, CO 80524/303-482-6913

Cadre Supply (See Parts & Surplus)

Calhoon Varmint Bullets, James, Shambo Rt., Box 304, Havre, MT 59501

Calibre Press, Inc., 666 Dundee Rd., Suite 1607, Northbrook, IL 60062-2760/800-323-0037; FAX: 708-498-6869

Cali'co Hardwoods, Inc., 1648 Airport Blvd., Windsor, CA 95492/707-546-4045; FAX: 707-546-4027

Calico Light Weapon Systems, 405 E. 19th St., Bakersfield, CA 93305/805-323-1327; FAX: 805-323-7844

California Grip, 1323 Miami Ave., Clovis, CA 93612/209-299-1316

California Magnum, 20746 Dearborn St., Chatsworth, CA 91313/818-341-7302; FAX: 818-341-7304

California Sight, P.O. Box 4607, Pagosa Springs, CO 81157/303-731-5003

CAM Enterprises, 5090 Iron Springs Rd., Box 2, Prescott, AZ 86301/602-776-9640

Camas Hot Springs Mfg., P.O. Box 639, Hot Springs, MT 59845/406-741-3756

Camdex, Inc., 2330 Alger, Troy, MI 48083/313-528-2300

Cameron's, 16690 W. 11th Ave., Golden, CO 80401/303-279-7365; FAX: 303-628-5413

Cammi, Lou, 4700 Oahu Dr. NE, Albuquerque, NM 87111/505-293-5259
Campbell, Dick, 20,000 Silver Ranch Rd., Conifer, CO 80433/303-697-0150
Camp-Cap Products, P.O. Box 173, Chesterfield, MO 63006/314-532-4340
Can Am Enterprises, 350 Jones Rd., Fruitland, Ont. LOR ILO, CANADA/416-643-4357
Canadian Custom Bullets, Box 52, Anola Man. R0E 0A0 CANADA
Canjar Co., M.H., 500 E. 45th Ave., Denver, CO 80216/303-295-2638
Cannon's Guns, Box 1036, 320 Main St., Polson, MT 59860/406-887-2048
Canons Delcour, Rue J.B. Cools, B-4040 Herstal, BELGIUM 32.(0)41.40.13.40; FAX:
    32(0)412.40.22.88
Canyon Cartridge Corp., P.O. Box 152, Albertson, NY 11507/FAX: 516-294-8946
Cape Outfitters, Rt. 2, Box 437C, Cape Girardeau, MO 63701/314-335-4103; FAX:
    314-335-1555
Caraville Manufacturing, P.O. Box 4545, Thousand Oaks, CA 91359/805-499-1234
Carbide Checkering Tools, P.O. Box 77, 200 Lyons Hill Rd., Athol, MA
    01331/508-249-9241
Carbide Die & Mfg. Co., Inc., 15615 E. Arrow Hwy., Irwindale, CA 91706/818-337-2518
Carlson, Douglas R., Antique American Firearms, P.O. Box 71035, Dept. GD, Des Moines,
    IA 50325/515-224-6552
Carnahan Bullets, 17645 110th Ave. SE, Renton, WA 98055
Carolina Precision Rifles, 1200 Old Jackson Hwy., Jackson, SC 29831/803-827-2069
Carrell's Precision Firearms, P.O. Box 232, 201 S. Park, Joliet, MT 59041/406-962-3593
Carroll Bullets (See Precision Reloading, Inc.)
Carter's Gun Shop, 225 G St., Penrose, CO 81240/719-372-6240
Carvajal Belts & Holsters, 422 Chestnut, San Antonio, TX 78202/210-222-1634
Cascade Bullet Co., Inc., 312 Main St., Klamath Falls, OR 97601/503-884-9316
Cascade Shooters, 2155 N.W. 12th St., Redwood, OR 97756
Case Sorting System, 12695 Cobblestone Creek Rd., Poway, CA 92064/619-486-9340
Cash Mfg. Co., Inc., P.O. Box 130, 201 S. Klein Dr., Waunakee, WI
    53597-0130/608-849-5664
Caspian Arms, 14 North Main St., Hardwick, VT 05843/802-472-6454
Caswell International Corp., 1221 Marshall St. NE, Minneapolis, MN 55413/612-379-2000;
    FAX: 612-379-2367
Catco-Ambush, Inc., P.O.Box 300, Corte Madera, CA 94926
Cathey Enterprises, Inc., P.O. Box 2202, Brownwood, TX 76804/915-643-2553; FAX:
    915-643-3653
CBC, Avenida Humberto de Campos, 3220, 09400-000 Ribeirao
    Pires-SP-BRAZIL/55-11-742-7500; FAX: 55-11-459-7385 (U.S. importer—MAGTECH
    Recreational Products, Inc.)
C.C.G. Enterprises, 5217 E. Belknap St., Halton City, TX 76117/817-834-9554
CCI, Div. of Blount, Inc., 2299 Snake River Ave., P.O. Box 856, Lewiston, ID
    83501/800-627-3640, 208-746-2351
Celestron International, P.O. Box 3578, Torrance, CA 90503/310-328-9560; FAX:
    310-212-5835
Centaur Systems, Inc., 1602 Foothill Rd., Kalispell, MT 59901/406-755-8609; FAX:
    406-755-8609
Center Lock Scope Rings, 9901 France Ct., Lakeville, MN 55044/612-461-2114
CenterMark, P.O. Box 4066, Parnassus Station, New Kensington, PA
    15068/412-335-1319
Central Specialties Ltd., 1122 Silver Lake Road, Cary, IL 60013/708-537-3300; FAX:
    708-537-3615
Century Gun Dist., Inc., 1467 Jason Rd., Greenfield, IN 46140/317-462-4524
Century International Arms, Inc., 48 Lower Newton St., St. Albans, VT
    05478/802-527-1252; FAX: 802-527-0470
C-H Tool & Die Corp. (See 4-D Custom Die Co.)
Chace Leather Products, 507 Alden St., Fall River, MA 02722/508-678-7556; FAX:
    508-675-9666
Chadick's Ltd., P.O. Box 100, Terrell, TX 75160/214-563-7577
Chambers Flintlocks Ltd., Jim, Rt. 1, Box 513-A, Candler, NC 28715/704-667-8361
Champion Target Co., 232 Industrial Parkway, Richmond, IN 47374/800-441-4971
Champion's Choice, Inc., 201 International Blvd., LaVergne, TN 37086/615-793-4066;
    FAX: 615-793-4070
Champlin, R. MacDonald, P.O. Box 132, Candia, NH 03034
Champlin Firearms, Inc., P.O. Box 3191, Woodring Airport, Enid, OK 73701/405-237-7388;
    FAX: 405-242-6922
Chapman Academy of Practical Shooting, 4350 Academy Rd., Hallsville, MO
    65255/314-696-5544; FAX: 314-696-2266
Chapman Manufacturing Co., 471 New Haven Rd., P.O. Box 250, Durham, CT
    06422/203-349-9228; FAX: 203-349-0408
Chapuis Armes, 21 La Gravoux, BP15, 42380 St. Bonnet-le-Chateau,
    FRANCE/(33)77.50.06.96 (U.S. importer—Chapuis USA)
Chapuis USA, 416 Business Park, Bedford, KY 40006
CHARCO, 26 Beaver St., Ansonia, CT 06401/203-735-4686; 203-735-6569
Charter Arms (See CHARCO)
Checkmate Refinishing, 8232 Shaw Rd., Brooksville, FL 34602/904-799-5774
Cheddite France, S.A., 99 Route de Lyon, F-26500 Bourg Les Valence, FRANCE/75 56 45
    45; FAX: 75 56 98 89
Chelsea Gun Club of New York City, Inc., 237 Ovington Ave., Apt. D53, Brooklyn, NY
    11209/718-836-9422, 718-833-2704
Chem-Pak, Inc., 11 Oates Ave., P.O. Box 1685, Winchester, VA 22601/800-336-9828;
    FAX: 703-722-3993
Cherokee Gun Accessories (See Glaser Safety Slug, Inc.)
Cherry's Fine Guns, P.O. Box 5307, Greensboro, NC 27435-0307/919-854-4182
CheVron Bullets, RR1, Ottawa, IL 61350/815-433-2471
CheVron Case Master (See CheVron Bullets)
ChinaSports, Inc., 2010 S. Lynx Place, Ontario, CA 91761/714-923-1411; FAX:
    714-923-0775
Choate Machine & Tool Co., Inc., P.O. Box 218, Bald Knob, AR 72010/501-724-6193,
    800-972-6390; FAX: 501-724-5873
Chopie Mfg., Inc., 700 Copeland Ave., LaCrosse, WI 54603/608-784-0926
Christie's East, 219 E. 67th St., New York, NY 10021/212-606-0400

Christman Jr., David, 937 Lee Hedrick Rd., Colville, WA 99114/509-684-5686 days;
    509-684-3314 evenings
Chronotech, 1655 Siamet Rd. Unit 6, Mississauga, Ont. L4W 1Z4 CANADA/416-625-5200;
    FAX: 416-625-5190
Chu Tani Ind., Inc., Box 3782, Chula Vista, CA 92011
Chuck's Gun Shop, P.O. Box 597, Waldo, FL 32694/904-468-2264
Churchill (See U.S. importer—Ellett Bros.)
Churchill, Winston, Twenty Mile Stream Rd., RFD P.O. Box 29B, Proctorsville, VT
    05153/802-226-7772
Ciener, Inc., Jonathan Arthur, 8700 Commerce St., Cape Canaveral, FL
    32920/407-868-2200; FAX: 407-868-2201
Cimarron Arms, P.O. Box 906, Fredericksburg, TX 78624-0906/210-997-9090; FAX:
    210-997-0802
Circle M Custom Bullets, 29 Avenida de Silva, Abilene, TX 79602-7509/915-698-3106
Claridge Hi-Tec, Inc., 19350 Business Center Dr., Northridge, CA 91324/818-700-9093;
    FAX: 818-700-0026
Clark, Frank, 3714-27th St., Lubbock, TX 79410/806-799-1187
Clark Co., Inc., David, P.O. Box 15054, Worcester, MA 01615-0054/508-756-6216; FAX:
    508-753-5827
Clark Custom Guns, Inc., P.O. Box 530, 11462 Keatchie Rd., Keithville, LA
    71047/318-925-0836; FAX: 318-925-9425
Clark Firearms Engraving, P.O. Box 80746, San Marino, CA 91118/818-287-1652
Classic Arms Corp., P.O. Box 106, Dunsmuir, CA 96025-0106/916-235-2000
Classic Brass, 14 Grove St., Plympton, MA 02367/FAX: 617-585-5673
Classic Guns, Inc., Frank S. Wood, 3230 Medlock Bridge Rd., Suite 110, Norcross, GA
    30092/404-242-7944
Clay Target Enterprises, 300 Railway Ave., Campbell, CA 95008/408-379-4829
Clearview Mfg. Co., Inc., 413 S. Oakley St., Fordyce, AR 71742/501-352-8557; FAX:
    501-352-8557
Cleland's Gun Shop, Inc., 10306 Airport Hwy., Swanton, OH 43558/419-865-4713
Clements' Custom Leathercraft, Chas, 1741 Dallas St., Aurora, CO
    80010-2018/303-364-0403
Clenzoil Corp., P.O. Box 80226, Sta. C, Canton, OH 44708-9998/216-833-9758
Clerke Co., J.A., P.O. Box 627, Pearblossom, CA 93553-0627/805-945-0713
Clift Mfg., L.R., 3821 Hammonton Rd., Marysville, CA 95901/916-755-3390; FAX:
    916-755-3393
Clift Welding Supply & Cases, 1332-A Colusa Hwy., Yuba City, CA 95993/916-755-3390;
    FAX: 916-755-3393
Clymer Manufacturing Co., Inc., 1645 W. Hamlin Rd., Rochester Hills, MI
    48309-3312/810-853-5555; FAX: 810-853-1530
C-More Systems, 7806 Sudley Rd., Suite 200, Manassas, VA 22110/703-361-2663; FAX:
    703-361-5881
Coats, Mrs. Lester, 300 Luman Rd., Space 125, Phoenix, OR 97535/503-535-1611
Cobra Gunskin, 133-30 32nd Ave., Flushing, NY 11354/718-762-8181; FAX:
    718-762-0890
Cobra Sport s.r.l., Via Caduti Nei Lager No. 1, 56020 San Romano, Montopoli v/Arno (Pi),
    ITALY/0039-571-450490; FAX: 0039-571-450492
Cogar's Gunsmithing, P.O. Box 755, Houghton Lake, MI 48629/517-422-4591
Cole's Gun Works, Rt. 3, Box 159-A, Moyock, NC 27958/919-435-2345
Cole-Grip, 16135 Cohasset St., Van Nuys, CA 91406/818-782-4424
Coleman's Custom Repair, 4035 N. 20th Rd., Arlington, VA 22207/703-528-4486
Collings, Ronald, 1006 Cielta Linda, Vista, CA 92083
Colonial Arms, Inc., P.O. Box 636, Selma, AL 36702-0636/205-872-9455; FAX:
    205-872-9540
Colonial Repair, P.O. Box 372, Hyde Park, MA 02136-9998/617-469-4951
Colorado School of Trades, 1575 Hoyt St., Lakewood, CO 80215/800-234-4594; FAX:
    303-233-4723
Colorado Shooter's Supply, 138 S. Plum, P.O. Box 132, Fruita, CO 81521/303-858-9191
Colorado Sutlers Arsenal, Box 991, Granby, CO 80446-9998/303-887-3813
Colt Blackpowder Arms Co., 5 Centre Market Place, New York, NY 10013/212-925-2159;
    FAX: 212-966-4986
Colt's Mfg. Co., Inc., P.O. Box 1868, Hartford, CT 06144-1868/800-962-COLT,
    203-236-6311; FAX: 203-244-1449
Combat Military Ordnance Ltd., 3900 Hopkins St., Savannah, GA 31405/912-238-1900;
    FAX: 912-236-7570
Companhia Brasileira de Cartuchos (See CBC)
Competition Electronics, Inc., 3469 Precision Dr., Rockford, IL 61109/815-874-8001; FAX:
    815-874-8181
Competitive Edge Dynamics Ltd., P.O. Box 1123, 85 Bliss Rd., White River Junction, VT
    05001/802-295-1334; FAX: 802-295-1965
Competitor Corp., Inc., P.O. Box 244, 293 Townsend Rd., West Groton, MA
    01472/508-448-3521; FAX: 603-673-4540
Complete Handloader, The, P.O. Box 5264, Arvada, CO 80005/303-460-9489
Component Concepts, Inc., 10240 SW Nimbus Ave., Suite L-8, Portland, OR
    97223/503-684-9262; FAX: 503-620-4285
Condon, Inc., David, 109 E. Washington St., Middleburg, VA 22117/703-687-5642
Condon, Inc., David, P.O. Box 312, 14502-G Lee Rd., Chatilly, VA 22021/703-631-7748
Conetrol Scope Mounts, 10225 Hwy. 123 south, Seguin, TX 78155/210-379-3030,
    800-CONETROL
CONKKO, P.O. Box 40, Broomall, PA 19008/215-356-0711
Connecticut Valley Arms Co. (See CVA)
Connecticut Valley Classics, P.O. Box 2068, 12 Taylor Lane, Westport, CT
    06880/203-435-4600
Continental Kite & Key (See CONKKO)
Cook Bullets, 1846 Rosemeade Parkway 188, Carrollton, TX 75007/214-394-8725
Cook Engineering Service, 891 Highbury Rd., Vermont VICT 3133 AUSTRALIA
Coonan Arms, Inc., 1465 Selby Ave., St. Paul, MN 55104/612-646-6672; FAX:
    612-646-0902
Cooper Arms, P.O. Box 114, Stevensville, MT 59870/406-777-5534
Cooper-Woodward, 3800 Pelican Rd., Helena, MT 59601/406-458-3800

Corbin, Inc., 600 Industrial Circle, P.O. Box 2659, White City, OR 97503/503-826-5211; FAX: 503-826-8669

Corbin Applied Technology, P.O. Box 2171, White City, OR 97503/503-826-5211

Cor-Bon, Inc., 4828 Michigan Ave., P.O. Box 10126, Detroit, MI 48210/313-894-2373

Corkys Gun Clinic, 111 North 11th Ave., Greeley, CO 80631/303-330-0516

Corry, John, 861 Princeton Ct., Neshanic Station, NJ 08853/308-369-8019

Cosmi Americo & Figlio s.n.c., Via Flaminia 307, Ancona, ITALY I-60020/071-888208; FAX: 071-887008 (U.S. importer—New England Arms Co.)

Costa, David, Island Pond Gun Shop, P.O. Box 428, Cross St., Island Pond, VT 05846/802-723-4546

Country Armourer, The, P.O. Box 308, Ashby, MA 01431-0308/508-386-7590; FAX: 508-386-7789

Cousin Bob's Mountain Products, 7119 Ohio River Blvd., Ben Avon, PA 15202/412-766-5114; FAX: 412-766-5114

CP Specialties, 1814 Mearns Rd., Warminster, PA 18974

CQB Training, P.O. Box 1739, Manchester, MO 63011

Craftguard, 3624 Logan Ave., Waterloo, IA 50703/319-232-2959

Craig Custom Guns, 629 E. 10th, Hutchinson, KS 67501/316-669-0601

Crandall Tool & Machine Co., 1545 N. Mitchell St., P.O. Box 569, Cadillac, MI 49601/616-775-5562

Crane & Crane Ltd., 105 N. Edison Way 6, Reno, NV 89502-2355/702-856-1516; FAX: 702-856-1616

Cravener's Gun Shop, 1627-5th Ave., Ford City, PA 16226/412-763-8312

Crawford Co., Inc., R.M., P.O. Box 277, Everett, PA 15537/814-652-6536; FAX: 814-652-9526

CRDC Technologies, 3972 Barranca Parkway, Ste. J-484, Irvine, CA 92714/714-730-8835

Creative Cartridge Co., 56 Morgan Rd., Canton, CT 06019/203-693-2529

Creedmoor Sports, Inc., P.O. Box 1040, Oceanside, CA 92051/619-757-5529

Creek Side Metal & Woodcrafters (See Allard, Gary)

Crit'R Call, Box 999V, La Porte, CO 80535/303-484-2768

Crosman Airguns, Rt. 5 and 20, E. Bloomfield, NY 14443/716-657-6161; FAX: 716-657-5405

Crosman Products of Canada Ltd., 1173 N. Service Rd. West, Oakville, Ontario, L6M 2V9 CANADA/905-827-1822

Crouse's Country Cover, P.O. Box 160, Storrs, CT 06268/203-429-4715

Crucelegui Hermanos (See U.S. importer—Mandall Shooting Supplies, Inc.)

CRW Products, Inc., Box 2123, Des Moines, IA 50310

Cubic Shot Shell Co., Inc., 98 Fatima Dr., Campbell, OH 44405/216-755-0349; FAX: 216-755-0349

Cullity Restoration, Daniel, 209 Old County Rd., East Sandwich, MA 02537/508-888-1147

Cumberland, Dave, Dept. MCA, 12924 Highway A-12, Montague, CA 96064/916-459-5445

Cumberland Arms, Rt. I, Box 1150 Shafer Rd., Blantons Chapel, Manchester, TN 37355

Cumberland Knife & Gun Works, 5661 Bragg Blvd., Fayetteville, NC 28303/919-867-0009

Cummings Bullets, 1417 Esperanza Way, Escondido, CA 92027

Cunard & Co., J., P.O. Box 755, Newark, OH 43058-0755/614-345-6646

Cunningham Co., Eaton, 607 Superior St., Kansas City, MO 64106/816-842-2600

Curtis Custom Shop, RR1, Box 193A, Wallingford, KY 41093/703-659-4265

Curtis Gun Shop, Dept. ST, 119 W. College, Bozeman, MT 59715

Custom Barreling & Stocks, 937 Lee Hedrick Rd., Colville, WA 99114/509-684-5686 (days), 509-684-3314 (evenings)

Custom Bullets by Hoffman, 2604 Peconic Ave., Seaford, NY 11783

Custom Checkering Service, Kathy Forster, 2124 SE Yamhill St., Portland, OR 97214/503-236-5874

Custom Chronograph, Inc., 5305 Reese Hill Rd., Sumas, WA 98295/206-988-7801

Custom Firearms (See Ahrends, Kim)

Custom Gun Products, 5021 W. Rosewood, Spokane, WA 99208/509-328-9340

Custom Gunsmiths, 4303 Friar Lane, Colorado Springs, CO 80907/719-599-3366

Custom Hunting Ammo & Arms, 2900 Fisk Rd., Howell, MI 48843/517-546-9498

Custom Products (See Jones Custom Products, Neil)

Custom Tackle and Ammo, P.O. Box 1886, Farmington, NM 87499/505-632-3539

Cutsinger Bench Rest Bullets, RR 8, Box 161-A, Shelbyville, IN 46176/317-729-5360

CVA, 5988 Peachtree Corners East, Norcross, GA 30071/404-449-4687; FAX: 404-242-8546

C.W. Cartridge Co., 71 Hackensack St., Wood Ridge, NJ 07075

C.W. Cartridge Co., 242 Highland Ave., Kearney, NJ 07032/201-998-1030

Cycle Dynamics, Inc., 74 Garden St., Feeding Hills, MA 01030/413-786-0141

Cylinder & Slide, Inc., William R. Laughridge, 245 E. 4th St., Fremont, NE 68025/402-721-4277; FAX: 402-721-0263

CZ (See U.S. importer—Action Arms Ltd.)

D

D&D Gunsmiths, Ltd., 363 E. Elmwood, Troy, MI 48083/313-583-1512

D&H Precision Tooling, 7522 Barnard Mill Rd., Ringwood, IL 60072/815-653-4011

D&H Prods. Co., Inc., 465 Denny Rd., Valencia, PA 16059/412-898-2840

D&J Bullet Co. & Custom Gun Shop, Inc., 426 Ferry St., Russell, KY 41169/606-836-2663; FAX: 606-836-2663

D&L Sports, P.O. Box 651, Gillette, WY 82717/307-686-4008

D&R Distributing, 308 S.E. Valley St., Myrtle Creek, OR 97457/503-863-6850

Dade Screw Machine Products, 2319 NW 7th Ave., Miami, FL 33127/305-573-5050

Daewoo Precision Industries Ltd., 34-3 Yeoeuido-Dong, Yeongdeungoo-GU, 15th, Fl./Seoul, KOREA (U.S. importer—Nationwide Sports Distributors)

Daisy Mfg. Co., P.O. Box 220, Rogers, AR 72756/501-636-1200; FAX: 501-636-1601

Dakota (See U.S. importer—EMF Co., Inc.)

Dakota Arms, HC55, Box 326, Sturgis, SD 57785/605-347-4686; FAX: 605-347-4459

Daly, Charles (See Miroku, B.C./Charles Daly)

Dangler, Homer L., Box 254, Addison, MI 49220/517-547-6745

Dapkus Co., J.G., P.O. Box 293, Durham, CT 06422

Dara-Nes, Inc. (See Nesci Enterprises, Inc.)

Data Tech Software Systems, 19312 East Eldorado Drive, Aurora, CO 80013

Datumtech Corp., 2275 Wehrle Dr., Buffalo, NY 14221

Davidson, Jere, Rt. 1, Box 132, Rustburg, VA 24588/804-821-3637

Davidson Products, 2020 Huntington Dr., Las Cruces, NM 88801/505-522-5612

Davidson's, 2703 High Point Rd., Greensboro, NC 27403/800-367-4867, 919-292-5161; FAX: 919-252-2552

Davis Co., R.E., 3450 Pleasantville NE, Pleasantville, OH 43148/614-654-9990

Davis Industries, 11186 Venture Dr., Mira Loma, CA 91752/909-360-5598

Davis Leather Co., G. Wm., 3990 Valley Blvd., Unit D, Walnut, CA 91789/714-598-5620

Davis Products, Mike, 643 Loop Dr., Moses Lake, WA 98837/509-765-6178, 800-765-6178 orders only

Davis Service Center, Bill, 10173 Croydon Way 9, Sacramento, CA 95827/916-369-6789

Day & Sons, Inc., Leonard, P.O. Box 122, Flagg Hill Rd., Heath, MA 01346/413-337-8369

Dayton Traister, P.O. Box 593, Oak Harbor, WA 98277/206-679-4657; FAX:206-675-1114

DBASE Consultants (See Arms, Peripheral Data Systems)

DBI Books, Inc., 4092 Commercial Ave., Northbrook, IL 60062/708-272-6310; FAX: 708-272-2051

D.C.C. Enterprises, 259 Wynburn Ave., Athens, GA 30601

Deadeye Sport Center, RD 1, Box 147B, Shickshinny, PA 18655/717-256-7432

Decker Shooting Products, 1729 Laguna Ave., Schofield, WI 54476/715-359-5873

Dedicated Systems, 105-B Cochrane Circle, Morgan Hill, CA 95037/408-629-1796; FAX: 408-779-2673

Deepeeka Exports Pvt. Ltd., D-78, Saket, Meerut-250-006, INDIA/0121-74483; FAX: 0121-74483

Defense Moulding Enterprises, 16781 Daisey Ave., Fountain Valley, CA 92708/714-842-5062

Defense Training International, Inc., 749 S. Lemay, Ste. A3-337, Ft. Collins, CO 80524/303-482-2520; FAX: 303-482-0548

deHaas Barrels, RR 3, Box 77, Ridgeway, MO 64481/816-872-6308

Del Rey Products, P.O. Box 91561, Los Angeles, CA 90009/213-823-0494

Del-Sports, Inc., Box 685, Main St., Margaretville, NY 12455/914-586-4103; FAX: 914-586-4105

Delhi Gun House, 1374 Kashmere Gate, Delhi, INDIA 110 006/(011)237375 239116; FAX: 91-11-2917344

Delorge, Ed, 2231 Hwy. 308, Thibodaux, LA 70301/504-447-1633

Delta Arms Ltd., P.O. Box 68, Sellers, SC 29592-0068/803-752-7426, 800-677-0641; 800-274-1611

Delta Co. Ammo Bunker, 1209 16th Place, Yuma, AZ 85364/602-783-4563

Delta Enterprises, 284 Hagemann Drive, Livermore, CA 94550

Dem-Bart Checkering Tools, Inc., 6807 Hwy. 2, Bickford Ave., Snohomish, WA 98290/206-568-7356; FAX: 206-568-3134

Denver Arms, Ltd., P.O. Box 4640, Pagosa Springs, CO 81157/303-731-2295

Denver Bullets, Inc., 1811 W. 13th Ave., Denver, CO 80204/303-893-3146; FAX: 303-893-9161

Denver Instrument Co., 6542 Fig St., Arvada, CO 80004/800-321-1135, 303-431-7255; FAX: 303-423-4831

DeSantis Holster & Leather Goods, P.O. Box 2039, New Hyde Park, NY 11040-0701/516-354-8000; FAX: 516-354-7501

Desert Industries, Inc., 3245 E. Patrick Ln., Suite H, Las Vegas, NV 89120/702-597-1066; FAX: 702-434-9495

Desert Mountain Mfg., Box 184, Coram, MT 59913/800-477-0762, 406-387-5361

Detroit-Armor Corp., 720 Industrial Dr. No. 112, Cary, IL 60013/708-639-7666; FAX: 708-639-7694

Dever Co., Jack, 8590 NW 90, Oklahoma City, OK 73132/405-721-6393

Dewey Mfg. Co., Inc., J., P.O. Box 2014, Southbury, CT 06488/203-598-7912; FAX: 203-598-3119

DHB Products, P.O. Box 3092, Alexandria, VA 22302/703-836-2648

Diamond Machining Technology, Inc. (See DMT)

Diamond Mfg. Co., P.O. Box 174, Wyoming, PA 18644/800-233-9601

Diana (See U.S. importer—Dynamit Nobel-RWS, Inc.)

Dibble, Derek A., 555 John Downey Dr., New Britain, CT 06051/203-224-2630

Dietz Gun Shop & Range, Inc., 421 Range Rd., New Braunfels, TX 78132/210-885-4662

Dillon, Ed, 1035 War Eagle Dr. N., Colorado Springs, CO 80919/719-598-4929; FAX: 719-598-4929

Dillon Precision Products, Inc., 7442 E. Butherus Dr., Scottsdale, AZ 85260/602-948-8009, 800-762-3845; FAX: 602-998-2786

Dina Arms Corp., P.O. Box 46, Royersford, PA 19468/215-287-0266

Division Lead Co., 7742 W. 61st Pl., Summit, IL 60502

Dixie Gun Works, Hwy. 51 South, Union City, TN 38261/901-885-0700, order 800-238-6785; FAX: 901-885-0440

Dixon Muzzleloading Shop, Inc., RD 1, Box 175, Kempton, PA 19529/215-756-6271

DKT, Inc., 14623 Vera Drive, Union, MI 49130-9744/616-641-7120; FAX: 616-641-2015

D-Max, Inc., Rt. 1, Box 473, Bagley, MN 56621

DMT, 85 Hayes Memorial Dr., Marlborough, MA 01752/508-481-5944; FAX: 508-485-3924

D.O.C. Specialists, Inc.; Doc & Bud Ulrich, Jim Amodei, 2209 S. Central Ave., Cicero, IL 60650/708-652-3606; FAX: 708-652-2516

Dohring Bullets, 100 W. 8 Mile Rd., Ferndale, MI 48220

Dolbare, Elizabeth, 39 Dahlia, Casper, WY 82604/307-266-5924

Double A Ltd., Dept. ST, Box 11036, Minneapolis, MN 55411

Dowtin Gunworks, Rt. 4, Box 930A, Flagstaff, AZ 86001/602-779-1898

Dragun Enterprises, P.O. Box 222, Murfreesboro, TN 37133-2222/615-895-7373, 800-467-7375; FAX: 800-829-7536

Drain, Mark, SE 3211 Kamilche Point Rd., Shelton, WA 98584/206-426-5452

Dremel Mfg. Co., 4915-21st St., Racine, WI 53406

Dri-Slide, Inc., 411 N. Darling, Fremont, MI 49412/616-924-3950

Dubber, Michael W., P.O. Box 312, Evansville, IN 47702/812-424-9000; FAX: 812-424-6551

Duffy, Charles E., Williams Lane, West Hurley, NY 12491/914-679-2997

Du-Lite Corp., 171 River Rd., Middletown, CT 06457/203-347-2505

Dumoulin, Ernest, Rue Florent Boclinville 8-10, 13-4041 Votten, BELGIUM/41 27 78 92

Dunphy, Ted, W. 5100 Winch Rd., Rathdrum, ID 83858/208-687-1399; FAX: 208-687-1399
DuPont (See IMR Powder Co.)
Durward, John, 448 Belgreen Way, Waterloo, Ontario N2L 5X5 CANADA
Dutchman's Firearms, Inc., The, 4143 Taylor Blvd., Louisville, KY 40215/502-366-0555
Dybala Gun Shop, P.O. Box 1024, FM 3156, Bay City, TX 77414/409-245-0866
Dykstra, Doug, 411 N. Darling, Fremont, MI 49412/616-924-3950
Dynamit Nobel-RWS, Inc., 81 Ruckman Rd., Closter, NJ 07624/201-767-1995; FAX: 201-767-1589
Dyson & Son Ltd., Peter, 29-31 Church St., Honley, Huddersfield, W. Yorkshire HDL7 2AH, ENGLAND/0484-661062; FAX: 0484 663709

E

E&L Mfg., Inc., 39042 N. School House Rd., Cave Creek, AZ 85331/602-488-2598; FAX: 602-488-0813
E.A.A. Corp., P.O. Box 1299, Sharpes, FL 32959/407-639-7006
Eades' Muzzleloader Builders' Supply, Don, 201-J Beasley Dr., Franklin, TN 37064/615-791-1731
Eagan, Donald V., P.O. Box 196, Benton, PA 17814/717-925-6134
Eagle Arms, Inc., 128 E. 23rd Ave., Coal Valley, IL 61240/309-799-5619; FAX: 309-799-5150
Eagle Flight Bullet Co., 925 Lakeville St., Suite 123, Petaluma, CA 94954/707-762-6955
Eagle Grips, Eagle Business Center, 460 Randy Rd., Carol Stream, IL 60188/800-323-6144
Eagle Imports, Inc., 1750 Brielle Ave., Unit B1, Wanamassa, NJ 07712/908-493-0333; FAX: 908-493-0301
Eagle International, Inc., 5195 W. 58th Ave., Suite 300, Arvada, CO 80002/303-426-8100
Eagle Mfg. & Engineering, 2648 Keen Dr., San Diego, CA 92139/619-479-4402; FAX: 619-472-5585
Eagle Products Co., 1520 Adelia Ave., S. El Monte, CA 91733
E-A-R, Inc., Div. of Cabot Safety Corp., 5457 W. 79th St., Indianapolis, IN 46268/800-327-3431; FAX: 800-488-8007
Easy Pull Outlaw Products, 316 1st St. East, Polson, MT 59860/406-883-6822
E.A.W. GmbH, Am Kirschberg 3, D-97218 Gerbrunn, GERMANY/0(931)70 71 92
Echols & Son, D'Arcy, 164 W. 580 S., Providence, UT 84332/801-753-2367
Ed's Gun House, Rt. 1, Box 62, Minnesota City, MN 55959/507-689-2925
Edenpine, Inc. c/o Six Enterprises, Inc., 320 D Turtle Creek Ct., San Jose, CA 95125/408-999-0201; FAX: 408-999-0216
Edmisten Co., P.O. Box 1293, Boone, NC 28607
Edmund Scientific Co., 101 E. Gloucester Pike, Barrington, NJ 08033/609-543-6250
Ednar, Inc., 2-4-8 Kayabacho, Nihonbashi, Chuo-ku, Tokyo, JAPAN/81(Japan)-3-3667-1651
Eezox, Inc., P.O. Box 772, Waterford, CT 06385-0772/203-447-8282; FAX: 203-447-3484
Efemes Enterprises, P.O. Box 691, Colchester, VT 05446
Eggleston, Jere D., 400 Saluda Ave., Columbia, SC 29205/803-799-3402
EGW Evolution Gun Works, 4050 B-8 Skyron Dr., Doylestown, PA 18901/215-348-9892; FAX: 215-348-1056
Eichelberger Bullets, Wm., 158 Crossfield Rd., King of Prussia, PA 19406
Eilan S.A.L., Paseo San Andres N8, Eibar, SPAIN 20600/(34)43118916; FAX: (34)43 114038
Eiland Custom Bullets, P.O. Box 688, Buena Vista, CO 81211/719-395-2952
Ekol Leather Care, P.O. Box 2652, West Lafayette, IN 47906/317-463-2250; FAX: 317-463-7004
El Dorado Leather, P.O. Box 2603, Tucson, AZ 85702/602-623-0606; FAX: 602-623-0606
El Paso Saddlery Co., P.O. Box 27194, El Paso, TX 79926/915-544-2233; FAX: 915-544-2535
Eldorado Cartridge Corp. (See PMC/Eldorado Cartridge Corp.)
Electro Prismatic Collimators, Inc., 1441 Manatt St., Lincoln, NE 68521
Electronic Trigger Systems, Inc., P.O. Box 13, Hector, MN 55342/612-848-2760
Eley Ltd., P.O. Box 705, Witton, Birmingham, B6 7UT, ENGLAND/21-356-8899; FAX: 21-331-4173
Elite Ammunition, P.O. Box 3251, Oakbrook, IL 60522/708-366-9006
Elkhorn Bullets, P.O. Box 5293, Central Point, OR 97502/503-826-7440
Elko Arms, Dr. L. Kortz, 28 rue Ecole Moderne, B-7060 Soignies, BELGIUM/(32)67-33-29-34
Ellett Bros., P.O. Box 128, Columbia, SC 29036/803-345-3751, 800-845-3711; FAX: 803-345-1820
Ellicott Arms, Inc./Woods Pistolsmithing, 3840 Dahlgren Ct., Ellicott City, MD 21042/410-465-7979
Ellis Sport Shop, E.W., RD 1, Route 9N, P.O. Box 315, Corinth, NY 12822/518-654-6444
Emerging Technologies, Inc., P.O. Box 3548, Little Rock, AR 72203/501-375-2227; FAX: 501-372-1445
EMF Co., Inc., 1900 E. Warner Ave. Suite 1-D, Santa Ana, CA 92705/714-261-6611; FAX: 714-956-0133
Engineered Accessories, 1307 W. Wabash Ave., Effingham, IL 62401/217-347-7700; FAX: 217-347-7737
Englishtown Sporting Goods Co., Inc., David J. Maxham, 38 Main St., Englishtown, NJ 07726/201-446-7717
Engraving Artistry, 36 Alto Rd., RFD 2, Burlington, CT 06013/203-673-6837
Enguix Import-Export, Alpujarras 58, Alzira, Valencia, SPAIN 46600/(96) 241 43 95; FAX: (96) 241 43 95
Enlow, Charles, 895 Box, Beaver, OK 73932/405-625-4487
Ensign-Bickford Co., The, 660 Hopmeadow St., Simsbury, CT 06070
EPC, 1441 Manatt St., Lincoln, NE 68521/402-476-3946
Epps "Orillia" Ltd., Ellwood, RR 3, Hwy. 11 North, Orillia, Ont. L3V 6H3, CANADA/705-689-5333
Erma Werke GmbH, Johan Ziegler St., 13/15/FeldiglSt., D-8060 Dachau, GERMANY (U.S. importers—Mandall Shooting Supplies, Inc.; PSI, Inc.)
Essex Arms, P.O. Box 345, Island Pond, VT 05846/802-723-4313

Essex Metals, 1000 Brighton St., Union, NJ 07083/800-282-8369
Estate Cartridge, Inc., 2778 FM 830, Willis, TX 77378/409-856-7277; FAX: 409-856-5486
Euroarms of America, Inc., 208 E. Piccadilly St., Winchester, VA 22601/703-662-1863; FAX: 703-662-4464
European American Armory Corp. (See E.A.A. Corp.)
Europtik Ltd., P.O. Box 319, Dunmore, PA 18512/717-347-6049, 800-873-5362; FAX: 717-969-4330
Eutaw Co., Inc., The, P.O. Box 608, U.S. Hwy. 176 West, Holly Hill, SC 29059/803-496-3341
Evans Engraving, Robert, 332 Vine St., Oregon City, OR 97045/503-656-5693
Evans Gunsmithing, 47532 School St., Oakridge, OR 97463/503-782-4432
Eversull Co., Inc., K., 1 Tracemont, Boyce, LA 71409/318-793-8728; FAX: 318-793-5483
Excaliber Enterprises, P.O. Box 400, Fogelsville, OA 18051-0400/610-391-9106; FAX: 610-391-9223
Exe, Inc., 18830 Partridge Circle, Eden Prairie, MN 55346/612-944-7662
Executive Protection Institute, Rt. 2, Box 3645, Berryville, VA 22611/703-955-1128
Eyears Insurance, 4926 Annhurst Rd., Columbus, OH 43228-1341
Eyster Heritage Gunsmiths, Inc., Ken, 6441 Bishop Rd., Centerburg, OH 43011/614-625-6131
E-Z-Way Systems, Box 700, Newark, OH 43058-0700/614-345-6645, 800-848-2072; FAX: 614-345-6600

F

Fabarm S.p.A., Via Averolda 31, 25039 Travagliato (Brescia) ITALY/(030)6863631; FAX: (030)6863684 (U.S. importer—Ithaca Acquisition Corp.)
Fabian Bros. Sporting Goods, Inc., 1510 Morena Blvd., Suite "G", San Diego, CA 92110/619-275-0816; FAX: 619-276-8733
Fabrica D'Armi Sabatti S.R.L., via Dante 179, 25068 Sarezzo, Brescia, ITALY/030-8900590; FAX: 030-8900598 (U.S. importer—E.A.A. Corp.)
Fagan & Co., William, 22952 15 Mile Rd., Mt. Clemens, MI 48043/313-465-4637; FAX: 313-792-6996
F.A.I.R. Techni-Mec s.n.c. Di Isidoro Rizzini & C., Via Gitti 41, 25060 Marcheno (BS), ITALY
Faith Associates, Inc., 1139 S. Greenville Hwy., Hendersonville, NC 28739/704-692-1916; FAX: 704-697-6827
Famas (See U.S. importer—Century International Arms, Inc.)
FAPA Corp., P.O. Box 1439, New London, NH 03257/603-735-5652; FAX: 603-735-5154
Far North Outfitters, Box 1252, Bethel, AK 99559
Farr Studio, Inc., 1231 Robinhood Rd., Greeneville, TN 37743/615-638-8825
Farrar Tool Co., Inc., 12150 Bloomfield Ave. Suite E, Santa Fe Springs, CA 90670/310-863-4367; FAX: 310-863-5123
FAS, Via E. Fermi, 8, 20019 Settimo Milanese, Milano, ITALY/02-3285846; FAX: 02-33500196 (U.S. importer—Nygord Precision Products)
Faust, Inc., T.G., 544 Minor St., Reading, PA 19602/215-375-8549; FAX: 215-375-4488
Fausti & Figlie s.n.c., Stefano, Via Martiri Dell Indipendenza, 70, Marcheno, ITALY 25060 (U.S. importer—American Arms, Inc.)
Fautheree, Andy, P.O. Box 4607, Pagosa Springs, CO 81157/303-731-5003
Feather Industries, Inc., 2300 Central Ave. K, Boulder, CO 80301/303-442-7021; FAX: 303-447-0944
Federal Cartridge Co., 900 Ehlen Dr., Anoka, MN 55303/612-422-2840
Federal Champion Target Co., 232 Industrial Parkway, Richmond, IN 47374/800-441-4971; FAX: 317-966-7747
Federal Engineering Corp., 1090 Bryn Mawr, Bensenville, IL 60106/708-860-1938
Federated-Fry, 6th Ave., 41st St., Altuna, PA 16602/814-946-1611
FEG, Budapest, Soroksariut 158, H-1095 HUNGARY (U.S. importers—Century International Arms, Inc.; K.B.I., Inc.)
Feinwerkbau Westinger & Altenburger GmbH & Co. KG (See FWB)
Feken, Dennis, Rt. 2 Box 124, Perry, OK 73077/405-336-5611
Fellowes, Ted, Beaver Lodge, 9245 16th Ave. SW, Seattle, WA 98106/206-763-1698
Feminine Protection, Inc., 10514 Shady Trail, Dallas, TX 75220/214-351-4500
Ferdinand, Inc., P.O. Box 5, 201 Main St., Harrison, ID 83833/208-689-3012; FAX: 208-689-3142
Ferguson, Bill, P.O. Box 1238, Sierra Vista, AZ 85636
FERLIB, Via Costa 46, 25063 Gardone V.T. (Brescia) ITALY/30 89 12 586; FAX: 30 89 12 586 (U.S. importers—Wm. Larkin Moore & Co.; New England Arms Co., Pachmayr Co.; Quality Arms, Inc.)
Ferris Firearms, HC 51, Box 1255, Suite 158, Bulverde, TX 78163/210-980-4811
Final Option Enterprises, P.O. Box 1128, Easthampton, MA 01027/413-548-8119
Finch Custom Bullets, 40204 La Rochelle, Prairieville, LA 70769
Fiocchi of America, Inc., 5030 Fremont Rd., Ozark, MO 65721/417-725-4118; FAX: 417-725-1039
Firearm Training Center, The, 9555 Blandville Rd., West Paducah, KY 42086/502-554-5886
Firearms Academy of Seattle, P.O. Box 2814, Kirkland, WA 98083/206-820-4853
Firearms Co. Ltd./Alpine (See U.S. importer—Mandall Shooting Supplies, Inc.)
Firearms Engraver's Guild of America, 332 Vine St., Oregon City, OR 97045/503-656-5693
Firearms Safety Products, Inc. (See FSPI)
First Distributors, Inc., Jack, 1201 Turbine, Rapid City, SD 55701/605-343-8481
Fish, Marshall F., Rt. 22 N., P.O. Box 2439, Westport, NY 12993/518-962-4897
Fisher, Jerry A., 535 Crane Mt. Rd., Big Fork, MT 59911/406-837-2722
Fisher Custom Firearms, 2199 S. Kittredge Way, Aurora, CO 80013/303-755-3710
Fisher Enterprises, 655 Main St. 305, Edmonds, WA 98020/206-776-4365
Fitz Pistol Grip Co., P.O. Box 610, Douglas City, CA 96024/916-623-4019
Flaig's, 2200 Evergreen Rd., Millvale, PA 15209/412-821-1717
Flambeau Products Corp., 15981 Valplast Rd., Middlefield, OH 44062/216-632-1631; FAX: 216-632-1581
Flannery Engraving Co., Jeff W., 11034 Riddles Run Rd., Union, KY 41091/606-384-3127
Flayderman & Co., Inc., N., P.O. Box 2446, Ft. Lauderdale, FL 33303/305-761-8855

Fleming Firearms, 9525-J East 51st St., Tulsa, OK 74145/918-665-3624

Flents Products Co., Inc., P.O. Box 2109, Norwalk, CT 06852/203-866-2581; FAX: 203-854-9322

Flintlock Muzzle Loading Gun Shop, The, 1238 "G" S. Beach Blvd., Anaheim, CA 92804/714-821-6655

Flintlocks, Etc. (See Beauchamp & Son, Inc.)

Flitz International Ltd., 821 Mohr Ave., Waterford, WI 53185/414-534-5898; FAX: 414-534-2991

Floatstone Mfg. Co., 106 Powder Mill Rd., P.O. Box 765, Canton, CT 06019/203-693-1977

Flores Publications, Inc., J., P.O. Box 830131, Miami, FL 33283/305-559-4652

Flouramics, Inc., 18 Industrial Ave., Mahwah, NJ 07430/800-922-0075; FAX: 201-825-7035

FN Herstal, Voie de Liege 33, Herstal 4040, BELGIUM/(32)41.40.82.83; FAX: (32)40.86.79

Fobus International Ltd., Kfar Hess, ISRAEL 40692/972-9-911716; FAX: 972-9-911716

Fogle, James W., RR 2, P.O. Box 258, Herrin, IL 62948/618-988-1795

Ford, Jack, 1430 Elkwood, Missouri City, TX 77489/713-499-9984

Forgett Jr., Valmore J., 689 Bergen Blvd., Ridgefield, NJ 07657/201-945-2500; FAX: 201-945-6859

Forgreens Tool Mfg., Inc., P.O. Box 990, Robert Lee, TX 76945/915-453-2800

Forrest, Inc., Tom, P.O. Box 326, Lakeside, CA 92040/619-561-5800; FAX: 619-561-0227

Forster, Kathy (See Custom Checkering Service)

Forster, Larry L., P.O. Box 212, 220 First St. NE, Gwinner, ND 58040-0212/701-678-2475

Forster Products, 82 E. Lanark Ave., Lanark, IL 61046/815-493-6360; FAX: 815-493-2371

Fort Hill Gunstocks, 12807 Fort Hill Rd., Hillsboro, OH 45133/513-466-2763

Forty Five Ranch Enterprises, Box 1080, Miami, OK 74355-1080/918-542-5875

Fouling Shot, The, 6465 Parfet St., Arvada, CO 80004

Fountain Products, 492 Prospect Ave., West Springfield, MA 01089/413-781-4651; FAX: 413-733-8217

4-D Custom Die Co., 711 N. Sandusky St., P.O. Box 889, Mt. Vernon, OH 43050-0889/614-397-7214; FAX: 614-397-6600

4W Ammunition, Rt. 1, P.O. Box 313, Tioga, TX 76271/817-437-2458; FAX: 817-437-2228

Fowler Bullets, 806 Dogwood Dr., Gastonia, NC 28054/704-867-3259

Foy Custom Bullets, 104 Wells Ave., Daleville, AL 36322

Francesca, Inc., 3115 Old Ranch Rd., San Antonio, TX 78217/512-826-2584; FAX: 512-826-8211

Franchi S.p.A., Luigi, Via del Serpente, 12, 25020 Fornaci, ITALY (U.S. importer—American Arms, Inc.)

Francolini, Leonard, 106 Powder Mill Rd., P.O. Box 765, Canton, CT 06019/203-693-1977

Frank Knives, Box 984, Whitefish, MT 59937/406-862-2681; FAX: 406-862-2681

Frankonia Jagd, Hofmann & Co., D-97064 Wurzburg, GERMANY/09302-200; FAX: 09302-20200

Frazier Brothers Enterprises, 1118 N. Main St., Franklin, IN 46131/317-736-4000; FAX: 317-736-4000

Fredrick Gun Shop, 10 Elson Dr., Riverside, RI 02915/401-433-2805

Freedom Arms, Inc., P.O. Box 1776, Freedom, WY 83120/307-883-2468; FAX: 307-883-2005

Freeman Animal Targets, 2559 W. Morris St., Plainsfield, IN 46168/317-271-5314; FAX: 317-271-9106

Fremont Tool Works, 1214 Prairie, Ford, KS 67842/316-369-2338

French, J.R., 1712 Creek Ridge Ct., Irving, TX 75060/214-254-2654

Frielich Police Equipment, 211 East 21st St., New York, NY 10010/212-254-3045

From Jena, Europtik Ltd., P.O. Box 319, Dunmore, PA 18512/717-347-6049, 800-873-5362; FAX: 717-969-4330

Frontier, 2910 San Bernardo, Laredo, TX 78040/512-723-5409

Frontier Arms Co., Inc., 401 W. Rio Santa Cruz, Green Valley, AZ 85614-3932

Frontier Products Co., 164 E. Longview Ave., Columbus, OH 43202/614-262-9357

FSPI, 5885 Glenridge Dr. Suite 220A, Atlanta, GA 30328/404-843-2881; FAX: 404-843-0271

Fujinon, Inc., 10 High Point Dr., Wayne, NJ 07470/201-633-5600

Fullmer, Geo M., 2499 Mavis St., Oakland, CA 94601/510-533-4193

Fulmer's Antique Firearms, Chet, P.O. Box 792, Rt. 2 Buffalo Lake, Detroit Lakes, MN 56501/218-847-7712

Fulton Armory, 8725 Bollman Place No. 1, Savage, MD 20763/301-490-9485; FAX: 301-490-9547

Fury Cutlery, 801 Broad Ave., Ridgefield, NJ 07657/201-943-5920; FAX: 201-943-1579

Fusilier Bullets, 10010 N. 6000 W., Highland, UT 84003/801-756-6813

FWB, Neckarstrasse 43, 78727 Oberndorf a. N., GERMANY/07423-814-0; FAX: 07423-814-89 (U.S. importer—Beeman Precision Airguns, Inc.)

G

G3 & Co., 18 Old Northville Rd., New Milford, CT 06776/203-354-7500

G96 Products Co., Inc., 237 River St., Paterson, NJ 07524/201-684-4050; FAX: 201-684-3848

G&C Bullet Co., Inc., 8835 Thornton Rd., Stockton, CA 95209

Gage Manufacturing, 663 W. 7th St., San Pedro, CA 90731

Galati International, P.O. Box 326, Catawissa, MO 63015/314-257-4837; FAX: 314-257-2268

Galazan, Div. of Connecticut Shotgun Mfg. Co., P.O. Box 622, 35 Woodland St., New Britain, CT 06051-0622/203-225-6581; FAX: 203-832-8707

GALCO International Ltd., 2019 W. Quail Ave., Phoenix, AZ 85027/602-258-8295; FAX: 602-582-6854

Gamba S.p.A., Renato, Via Artigiani, 93, 25063 Gardone V.T. (Brescia), ITALY (U.S. importers—Giacomo Sporting, Inc.; New England Arms Co.)

Gammog, Gregory B. Gally, 16009 Kenny Rd., Laurel, MD 20707/301-725-3838

Gamo (See U.S. importers—Daisy Mfg. Co.; Dynamit Nobel-RWS, Inc.)

GAR, 139 Park Lane, Wayne, NJ 07470/201-256-7641

Garbi, Armas Urki, 12-14, 20.600 Eibar (Guipuzcoa) SPAIN/43-11 38 73 (U.S. importer—Moore & Co., Wm. Larkin)

Garcia National Gun Traders, Inc., 225 SW 22nd Ave., Miami, FL 33135/305-642-2355

Garrett Cartridges, Inc., P.O. Box 178, Chehalis, WA 98532/206-736-0702

Garthwaite, Jim, Rt. 2, Box 310, Watsontown, PA 17777/717-538-1566

Gaucher Armes, S.A., 46, rue Desjoyaux, 42000 Saint-Etienne, FRANCE/77 33 38 92; FAX: 767 41 95 72 (U.S. importer—Mandall Shooting Supplies, Inc.)

G.B.C. Industries, Inc., P.O. Box 1602, Spring, TX 77373/713-350-9690; FAX: 713-350-0601

G.C.C.T., 4455 Torrance Blvd., Ste. 453, Torrance, CA 90509-2806

GDL Enterprises, 409 Le Gardeur, Slidell, LA 70460/504-649-0693

Gehmann, Walter (See Huntington Die Specialties)

Genco, P.O. Box 5704, Asheville, NC 28803

Gene's Custom Guns, P.O. Box 10534, White Bear Lake, MN 55110/612-429-5105

Gene's Gun Shop, Rt. 1 Box 890, Snyder, TX 79549/915-573-2323

General Lead, Inc., 1022 Grand Ave., Phoenix, AZ 85007

George & Roy's, 2950 NW 29th, Portland, OR 97210/800-553-3022; FAX: 503-225-9409

George, Tim, Rt. 1, P.O. Box 45, Evington, VA 24550/804-821-8117

GFR Corp., P.O. Box 430, Andover, NH 03216/603-735-5300

G.H. Enterprises Ltd., Bag 10, Okotoks, Alberta T0L 1T0 CANADA/403-938-6070

Giacomo Sporting, Inc., Delta Plaza, Rt. 26N, Rome, NY 13440

Gibbs Rifle Co., Inc., Cannon Hill Industrial Park, Rt. 2, Box 214 Hoffman, Rd./Martinsburg, WV 25401/304-274-0458; FAX: 304-274-0078

Gilbert Equipment Co., Inc., 960 Downtowner Rd., Mobile, AL 36609/205-344-3322

Gilman-Mayfield, Inc., 3279 E. Shields, Fresno, CA 93703/209-221-9415; FAX: 209-221-9419

Gilmore, 5949 S. Garnett, Tulsa, OK 74146/918-250-4867; FAX: 918-250-3845

Giron, Robert E., 1328 Pocono St., Pittsburgh, PA 15218/412-731-6041

Glaser Safety Slug, Inc., P.O. Box 8223, Foster City, CA 94404/800-221-3489, 415-345-7677; FAX: 415-345-8217

Glass, Herb, P.O. Box 25, Bullville, NY 10915/914-361-3021

Glimm, Jerome C., 19 S. Maryland, Conrad, MT 59425/406-278-3574

Glock, Inc., 6000 Highlands Parkway, Smyrna, GA 30082/404-433-8719

Glock GmbH, P.O. Box 50, A-2232 Deutsch Wagram, AUSTRIA (U.S. importer—Glock, Inc.)

GML Products, Inc., 394 Laredo Dr., Birmingham, AL 35226/205-979-4867

Goddard, Allen, 716 Medford Ave., Hayward, CA 94541/510-276-6830

Goergen's Gun Shop, Inc., Rt. 2, Box 182BB, Austin, MN 55912/507-433-9280

GOEX, Inc., 1002 Springbrook Ave., Moosic, PA 18507/717-457-6724; FAX: 717-457-1130

Golden Age Arms Co., 115 E. High St., Ashley, OH 43003/614-747-2488

Gonic Arms, Inc., 134 Flagg Rd., Gonic, NH 03839/603-332-8456, 603-332-8457

Gonzalez Guns, Ramon B., P.O. Box 370, Monticello, NY 12701/914-794-4515

Goodwin, Fred, Silver Ridge Gun Shop, Sherman Mills, ME 04776/207-365-4451

Gotz Bullets, 7313 Rogers St., Rockford, IL 61111

Gould & Goodrich, P.O. Box 1479, Lillington, NC 27546/919-893-2071; FAX: 919-893-4742

Gournet, Geoffroy, 820 Paxinosa Ave., Easton, PA 18042/215-559-0710

Gozon Corp., P.O. Box 6278, 152 Bittercreek Dr., Folsom, CA 95630/916-983-1807; FAX: 916-983-9500

Grace Metal Products, Inc., P.O. Box 67, Elk Rapids, MI 49629/616-264-8133

Grace Tool, Inc., 3661 E. 44th St., Tucson, AZ 85713/602-747-0213

"Gramps" Antique Cartridges, Box 341, Washago, Ont. L0K 2B0 CANADA/705-689-5348

Grand Falls Bullets, Inc., 1120 Forest Dr., Blue Springs, MO 64015/816-229-0112

Granger, Georges, 66 cours Fauriel, 42100 Saint Etienne, FRANCE/(77)25 14 73

Granite Custom Bullets, Box 190, Philipsburg, MT 59858/406-859-3245

Grant, Howard V., Hiawatha 15, Woodruff, WI 54568/715-356-7146

Graphics Direct, 18336 Gault St., Reseda, CA 91335/818-344-9002

Graves Co., 1800 Andrews Av., Pompano Beach, FL 33069/800-327-9103; FAX: 305-960-0301

Graybill's Gun Shop, 1035 Ironville Pike, Columbia, PA 17512/717-684-2739

Great Lakes Airguns, 6175 S. Park Ave., Hamburg, NY 14075/716-648-6666; FAX: 716-648-5279

Green, Arthur S., 485 S. Robertson Blvd., Beverly Hills, CA 90211/310-274-1283

Green, Roger M., P.O. Box 984, 435 E. Birch, Glenrock, WY 82637/307-436-9804

Green Bay Bullets, 1638 Hazelwood Dr., Sobieski, WI 54171/414-826-7760

Green Genie, Box 114, Cusseta, GA 31805

Greene, M.L., 17200 W. 57th Ave., Golden, CO 80403/303-279-2383

Greenwald, Leon E. "Bud", 2553 S. Quitman St., Denver, CO 80219/303-935-3850

Greg's Superior Products, P.O. Box 46219, Seattle, WA 98146

Greider Precision, 431 Santa Marina Ct., Escondido, CA 92029/619-480-8892

Gremmel Enterprises, 271 Sterling Dr., Eugene, OR 97404/503-688-3319

Grendel, Inc., P.O. Box 560909, Rockledge, FL 32956-0909/800-274-7427, 407-636-1211; FAX: 407-633-6710

Griffin & Howe, Inc., 33 Claremont Rd., Bernardsville, NJ 07924/908-766-2287; FAX: 908-766-1068

Griffin & Howe, Inc., 36 W. 44th St., Suite 1011, New York, NY 10036/212-921-0980

Grifon, Inc., 58 Guinam St., Waltham, MS 02154

Grip-Master, P.O. Box 32, Westbury, NY 11490/800-752-0164; FAX: 516-997-5142

Grizzly Bullets, 2137 Hwy. 200, Trout Creek, MT 59874/406-847-2627

Group Tight Bullets, 482 Comerwood Court, San Francisco, CA 94080/415-583-1550

GRS Corp., Glendo, P.O. Box 1153, 900 Overlander St., Emporia, KS 66801/316-343-1084

Grulla Armes, Apartado 453, Avda Otaloa, 12, Eiber, SPAIN (U.S. importer—American Arms, Inc.)

GSI, Inc., 108 Morrow Ave., P.O. Box 129, Trussville, AL 35173/205-655-8299; FAX: 205-655-7078

G.U., Inc., 4325 S. 120th St., Omaha, NE 68137/402-330-4492

Guardsman Products, 411 N. Darling, Fremont, MI 49412/616-924-3950

Gun City, 212 W. Main Ave., Bismarck, ND 58501/701-223-2304

Gun Doctor, The, 435 East Maple, Roselle, IL 60172/708-894-0668

Gun Doctor, The, P.O. Box 39242, Downey, CA 90242/310-862-3158

Gun Hunter Books, Div. of Gun Hunter Trading Co., 5075 Heisig St., Beaumont, TX 77705/409-835-3006

Gun Leather Limited, 116 Lipscomb, Ft. Worth, TX 76104/817-334-0225; 800-247-0609

Gun List (See Krause Publications)

Gun Parts Corp., The, 226 Williams Lane, West Hurley, NY 12491/914-679-2417; FAX: 914-679-5849

Gun Room Press, The, 127 Raritan Ave., Highland Park, NJ 08904/908-545-4344; FAX: 908-545-6686

Gun Room, The, 1121 Burlington, Muncie, IN 47302/317-282-9073; FAX: 317-282-9073

Gun Shop, The, 5550 S. 900 East, Salt Lake City, UT 84117/801-263-3633

Gun Shop, The, 62778 Spring Creek Rd., Montrose, CO 81401

Gun South, Inc. (See GSI, Inc.)

Gun Works, The, 236 Main St., Springfield, OR 97477/503-741-4118

Gun-Alert/Master Products, Inc., 1010 N. Maclay Ave., San Fernando, CA 91340/818-365-0864; FAX: 818-365-1308

Guncraft Books (See Guncraft Sports, Inc.)

Guncraft Sports, Inc., 10737 Dutchtown Rd., Knoxville, TN 37932/615-966-4545; FAX: 615-966-4500

Gunfitters, The, P.O. 426, Cambridge, WI 53523-0426/608-764-8128

Gun-Ho Sports Cases, 110 E. 10th St., St. Paul, MN 55101/612-224-9491

Gunline Tools, P.O. Box 478, Placentia, CA 92670/714-528-5252; FAX: 714-572-4128

Gunnerman Books, P.O. Box 214292, Auburn Hills, MI 48321/810-879-2779

Guns, 81 E. Streetsboro St., Hudson, OH 44236/216-650-4563

Guns, Div. of D.C. Engineering, Inc., 8633 Southfield Fwy., Detroit, MI 48228/313-271-7111, 800-886-7623 (orders only); FAX: 313-271-7112

Guns, Gear & Gadgets, L.L.C., P.O. Box 35722, Tucson, AZ 85240-5222/602-747-9578; FAX: 602-747-9715

GUNS Magazine, 591 Camino de la Reina, Suite 200, San Diego, CA 92108/619-297-5350; FAX: 619-297-5353

Guns Unlimited, Inc. (See G.U., Inc.)

Gunsight, The, 1712 North Placentia Ave., Fullerton, CA 92631

Gunsite Gunsmithy, P.O. Box 451, Paulden, AZ 86334/602-636-4565; FAX: 602-636-1236

Gunsite Training Center, P.O. Box 700, Paulden, AZ 86334/602-636-4565; FAX: 602-636-1236

Gunsmith in Elk River, The, 14021 Victoria Lane, Elk River, MN 55330/612-441-7761

Gunsmithing Ltd., 57 Unquowa Rd., Fairfield, CT 06430/203-254-0436

Gun-Tec, P.O. Box 8125, W. Palm Beach, FL 33407

Gurney, F.R., Box 13, Sooke, BC V0S 1N0 CANADA/604-642-5282

Gusty Winds Corp., 2950 Bear St., Suite 120, Costa Mesa, CA 92626/714-536-3587

Gutmann Cutlery Co., Inc., 120 S. Columbus Ave., Mt. Vernon, NY 10553/914-699-4044

Gwinnell, Bryson J., P.O. Box 248C, Maple Hill Rd., Rochester, VT 05767/802-767-3664

GZ Paintball Sports Products, P.O. Box 430, Andover, NH 03216/603-735-5300; FAX: 603-735-5154

H

H&P Publishing, 7174 Hoffman Rd., San Angelo, TX 76905/915-655-5953

H&R 1871, Inc., 60 Industrial Rowe, Gardner, MA 01440/508-632-9393; FAX: 508-632-2300

H&S Liner Service, 515 E. 8th, Odessa, TX 79761/915-332-1021

Hakko Co. Ltd., 5F Daini-Tsunemi Bldg., 1-13-12, Narimasu, Itabashiku Tokyo 175, JAPAN/(03)5997-7870-2

Hale, Peter, 800 E. Canyon Rd., Spanish Fork, UT 84660/801-798-8215

Half Moon Rifle Shop, 490 Halfmoon Rd., Columbia Falls, MT 59912/406-892-4409

Hallberg Gunsmith, Fritz, 33 S. Main, Payette, ID 83661

Hallowell & Co., 340 W. Putnam Ave., Greenwich, CT 06830/203-869-2190; FAX: 203-869-0692

Hamilton, Alex B. (See Ten-Ring Precision, Inc.)

Hamilton, Keith, P.O. Box 871, Gridley, CA 95948/916-846-2316

Hämmerli Ltd., Seonerstrasse 37, CH-5600 Lenzburg, SWITZERLAND/064-50 11 44; FAX: 064-51 38 27
   (U.S. importers—Beeman Precision Ariguns, Inc.; Hammerli USA; Mandall Shooting Supplies, Inc.)

Hammerli USA, 19296 Oak Grove Circle, Groveland, CA 95321/209-962-5311; FAX: 209-962-5931

Hammets VLD Bullets, P.O. Box 479, Rayville, LA 71269/318-728-2019

Hammonds Rifles, RD 4, Box 504, Red Lion, PA 17356/717-244-7879

Hand Engravers Supply Co., 601 Springfield Dr., Albany, GA 31707/912-432-9683

Handgun Press, P.O. Box 406, Glenview, IL 60025/708-657-6500; FAX: 708-724-8831

HandiCrafts Unltd. (See Clements' Custom Leathercraft, Chas)

Handloader's Journal, 60 Cottage St. 11, Hughesville, PA 17737

Hands, Barry Lee, 26184 E. Shore Route, Bigfork, MT 59911/406-837-0035

Hank's Gun Shop, Box 370, 50 West 100 South, Monroe, UT 84754/801-527-4456

Hanned Line, The, P.O. Box 161565, Cupertino, CA 95016-1565/408-345-3414

Hanned Precision (See Hanned Line, The)

Hansen & Co. (See Hansen Cartridge Co.)

Hansen Cartridge Co., 244 Old Post Rd., Southport, CT 06490/203-259-5424 ext. 260

Hanson's Gun Center, Dick, 233 Everett Dr., Colorado Springs, CO 80911

Hardin Specialty Dist., P.O. Box 338, Radcliff, KY 40159-0338/502-351-6649

Hardison, Charles, P.O. Box 356, 200 W. Baseline Rd., Lafayette, CO 80026-0356/303-666-5171

Harold's Custom Gun Shop, Inc., Rt. 1, Box 447, Big Spring, TX 79720/915-394-4430

Harrell's Precision, 5756 Hickory Dr., Salem, VA 24153/703-380-2683

Harrington & Richardson (See H&R 1871, Inc.)

Harris Engineering, Inc., Rt. 1, Barlow, KY 42024/502-334-3633; FAX: 502-334-3000

Harris Enterprises, P.O. Box 105, Bly, OR 97622/503-353-2625

Harris Hand Engraving, Paul A., 10630 Janet Lee, San Antonio, TX 78230/512-391-5121

Hart & Son, Inc., Robert W., 401 Montgomery St., Nescopeck, PA 18635/717-752-3655; FAX: 717-752-1088

Hartmann & Weiss GmbH, Rahlstedter Bahnhofstr. 47, 22143 Hamburg, GERMANY/(40) 677 55 85; FAX: (40) 677 55 92

Harwood, Jack O., 1191 S. Pendlebury Lane, Blackfoot, ID 83221/208-785-5368

Haselbauer Products, Jerry, P.O. Box 27629, Tucson, AZ 85726/602-792-1075

Hastings Barrels, 320 Court St., Clay Center, KS 67432/913-632-3169; FAX: 913-632-6554

Hatfield Gun Co., Inc., 224 N. 4th St., St. Joseph, MO 64501/816-279-8688; FAX: 816-279-2716

Hawk Co., P.O. Box 1689, Glenrock, WY 82637/307-436-5561

Hawken Shop, The (See Dayton Traister)

Haydon Shooters' Supply, Russ, 15018 Goodrich Dr. NW, Gig Harbor, WA 98329/206-857-7557

Heatbath Corp., P.O. Box 2978, Springfield, MA 01101/413-543-3381

Hebard Guns, Gil, 125-129 Public Square, Knoxville, IL 61448

HEBB Resources, P.O. Box 999, Mead, WA 99021-09996/509-466-1292

Hecht, Hubert J., Waffen-Hecht, P.O. Box 2635, Fair Oaks, CA 95628/916-966-1020

Heckler & Koch, Inc., 21480 Pacific Blvd., Sterling, VA 20166/703-450-1900; FAX: 703-450-8160

Heckler & Koch GmbH, Postfach 1329, D-7238 Oberndorf, Neckar, GERMANY (U.S. importer—Heckler & Koch, Inc.)

Hege Jagd-u. Sporthandels, GmbH, P.O. Box 101461, W-7770 Ueberlingen a. Bodensee, GERMANY

Heidenstrom Bullets, Urds GT 1 Heroya, 3900 Porsgrunn, NORWAY

Heilmann, Stephen, P.O. Box 657, Grass Valley, CA 95945/916-272-8758

Heinie Specialty Products, 323 W. Franklin St., Havana, IL 62644/309-543-4535; FAX: 309-543-2521

Heintz, David, 800 N. Hwy. 17, Moffat, CO 81143/719-256-4194

Hellweg Ltd., 40356 Oak Park Way, Suite H, Oakhurst, CA 93644/209-683-3030; FAX: 209-683-3422

Helwan (See U.S. importer—Interarms)

Hendricks, Frank E., Master Engravers, Inc., HC03, Box 434, Dripping Springs, TX 78620/512-858-7828

Henigson & Associates, Steve, 2049 Kerwood Ave., Los Angeles, CA 90025/213-305-8288

Henriksen Tool Co., Inc., 8515 Wagner Creek Rd., Talent, OR 97540/503-535-2309

Hensler, Jerry, 6614 Country Field, San Antonio, TX 78240/210-690-7491

Hensley & Gibbs, Box 10, Murphy, OR 97533/503-862-2341

Hercules, Inc., Hercules Plaza, 1313 N Market St., Wilmington, DE 19894/800-276-9337

Heritage Firearms, 4600 NW 135th St., Opa Locka, FL 33054/305-685-5966; FAX: 305-687-6721

Hermann Leather Co., H.J., Rt. 1, P.O. Box 525, Skiatook, OK 74070/918-396-1226

Herrett's Stocks, Inc., P.O. Box 741, Twin Falls, ID 83303/208-733-1498

Hertel & Reuss, Werk für Optik und Feinmechanik GmbH, Quellhofstrabe 67, 34 127 Kassel, GERMANY/0561-83006; FAX: 0561-893308

Hesco-Meprolight, 2821 Greenville Rd., LaGrange, GA 30240/706-884-7967; FAX: 706-882-4683

Heym GmbH & Co. KG, Friedrich Wilh, Coburger Str.8, D-97702 Muennerstadt, GERMANY (U.S. importers—JägerSport, Ltd.; Swarovski Optik North America Ltd.)

HH Engineering, Box 642, Dept. HD, Narberth, PA 19072-0642

Hickman, Jaclyn, Box 1900, Glenrock, WY 82637

Hidalgo, Tony, 12701 SW 9th Pl., Davie, FL 33325/305-476-7645

High Bridge Arms, Inc., 3185 Mission St., San Francisco, CA 94110/415-282-8358

High Performance International, 5734 W. Florist Ave., Milwaukee, WI 53218/414-466-9040

Highline Machine Co., 654 Lela Place, Grand Junction, CO 81504/303-434-4971

Hi-Grade Imports, 8655 Monterey Rd., Gilroy, CA 95021/408-842-9301; FAX: 408-842-2374

Hill Speed Leather, Ernie, 4507 N. 195th Ave., Litchfield Park, AZ 85340/602-853-9222; FAX: 602-853-9235

Hindman, Ace, 1880 ½ Upper Turtle Creek Rd., Kerrville, TX 78028/512-257-4290

Hi-Point Firearms, 174 South Mulberry, Manfield, OH 44902/419-522-8830

Hiptmayer, Heidemarie, RR 112 750, P.O. Box 136, Eastman, Quebec J0E 1PO, CANADA/514-297-2492

Hiptmayer, Klaus, RR 112 750, P.O. Box 136, Eastman, Quebec J0E 1P0, CANADA/514-297-2492

Hirtenberger Aktiengesellschaft, Leobersdorferstrasse 31, A-2552 Hirtenberg, AUSTRIA/43(0)2256 81184; FAX: 43(0)2256 81807

HiTek International, 490 El Camino Real, Redwood City, CA 94063/800-54-NIGHT; FAX: 415-363-1408

Hiti-Schuch, Atelier Wilma, A-8863 Predlitz, Pirming Y1 AUSTRIA/0353418278

HJS Arms, Inc., P.O. Box 3711, Brownsville, TX 78523-3711/800-453-2767, 210-542-2767

H.K.S. Products, 7841 Founion Dr., Florence, KY 41042/606-342-7841

Hoag, James W., 8523 Canoga Ave., Suite C, Canoga Park, CA 91304/818-998-1510

Hobaugh, Wm. H. (See Rifle Shop, The)

Hobson Precision Mfg. Co., Rt. 1, Box 220-C, Brent, AL 35034/205-926-4662

Hoch Custom Bullet Moulds (See Colorado Shooter's Supply)

Hodgdon Powder Co., Inc., P.O. Box 2932, Shawnee Mission, KS 66201/913-362-9455; FAX: 913-362-1307

Hoehn Sales, Inc., 75 Greensburg Ct., St. Charles, MO 63304/314-441-4231

Hoelscher, Virgil, 11047 Pope Ave., Lynwood, CA 90262/310-631-8545

Hoffman New Ideas, 821 Northmoor Rd., Lake Forest, IL 60045/312-234-4075

Hogue Grips, P.O. Box 1138, Paso Robles, CA 93446/800-438-4747; FAX: 805-466-7329

Holden Co., J.B., P.O. Box 700320, 975 Arthur, Plymouth, MI 48170/313-455-4850; FAX: 313-455-4212

Holland's, Box 69, Powers, OR 97466/503-439-5155; FAX: 503-439-5155

Hollis Gun Shop, 917 Rex St., Carlsbad, NM 88220/505-885-3782

Hollywood Engineering, 10642 Arminta St., Sun Valley, CA 91352/818-842-8376

Holster Outpost, 950 Harry St., El Cajon, CA 92020/619-588-1222

Holster Shop, The, 720 N. Flagler Dr., Ft. Lauderdale, FL 33304/305-463-7910; FAX: 305-761-1483

Holston Ent., Inc., P.O. Box 493, Piney Flats, TN 37686

Home Shop Machinist, The, Village Press Publications, P.O. Box 1810, Traverse City, MI 49685/800-447-7367; FAX: 616-946-3289

Hondo Ind., 510 S. 52nd St.,|04, Tempe, AZ 85281

Hoppe's Div., Penguin Industries, Inc., Airport Industrial Mall, Coatesville, PA

19320/251-384-6000

Horizons Unlimited, P.O. Box 426, Warm Springs, GA 31830/706-655-3603; FAX: 706-655-3603

Hornady Mfg. Co., P.O. Box 1848, Grand Island, NE 68801/800-338-3220, 308-382-1390

Horseshoe Leather Products, Andy Arratoonian, The Cottage Sharow, Ripon HG4 5BP ENGLAND/0765-605858

Horst, Alan K., 3221 2nd Ave. N., Great Falls, MT 59401/406-454-1831

Horton Dist. Co., Inc., Lew, 15 Walkup Dr., Westboro, MA 01581/508-366-7400

House of Muskets, Inc., The, P.O. Box 4640, Pagosa Springs, CO 81157/303-731-2295

Howa Machinery, Ltd., Sukaguchi, Shinkawa-cho, Nishikasugai-gun, Aichi 452, JAPAN (U.S. importer—Interarms)

Howell Machine, 815 1/2 D St., Lewiston, ID 83501/208-743-7418

Hoyt Holster Co., Inc., P.O. Box 69, Coupeville, WA 98239-0069/206-678-6640; FAX: 206-678-6549

HT Bullets, 244 Belleville Rd., New Bedford, MA 02745/508-999-3338

Huey Gun Cases, Marvin, P.O. Box 22456, Kansas City, MO 64113/816-444-1637

Hughes, Steven Dodd, P.O. Box 11455, Eugene, OR 97440/503-485-8869

Hume, Don, P.O. Box 351, Miami, OK 74355/918-542-6604

Hungry Horse Books, 4605 Hwy. 93 South, Whitefish, MT 59937/406-862-7997

Hunkeler, A. (See Buckskin Machine Works)

Hunter Co., Inc., 3300 W. 71st Ave., Westminster, CO 80030/303-427-4626

Hunterjohn, P.O. Box 477, St. Louis, MO 63166/314-531-7250

Huntington Die Specialties, 601 Oro Dam Blvd., Oroville, CA 95965/916-534-1210; FAX: 916-534-1212

Hydrosorbent Products, P.O. Box 437, Ashley Falls, MA 01222/413-229-2967; FAX: 413-229-8743

Hyper-Single, Inc., 520 E. Beaver, Jenks, OK 74037/918-299-2391

Hy-Score Arms Co. Ltd., 40 Stonar Industrial Estate, Sandwich, Kent CT13 9LN, ENGLAND/0304-61.12.21

I

IAI, 6226 Santos Diaz St., Irwindale, CA 91702/818-334-1200

ICI-America, P.O. Box 751, Wilmington, DE 19897/302-575-3000

Idaho Ammunition Service, 2816 Mayfair Dr., Lewiston, ID 83501/208-743-0270; FAX: 208-743-4930

Idaho Bullets, 4344 Cavendish Hwy., Lenore, ID 83541/208-476-5046

IGA (See U.S. importer—Stoeger Industries)

Illinois Lead Shop, 7742 W. 61st Place, Summit, IL 60501

IMI, P.O. Box 1044, Ramat Hasharon 47100, ISRAEL/972-3-5485222 (U.S. importer—Magnum Research, Inc.)

IMI Services USA, Inc., 2 Wisconsin Circle, Suite 420, Chevy Chase, MD 20815/301-215-4800; FAX: 301-657-1446

IMR Powder Co., 1080 Military Turnpike, Suite 2, Plattsburgh, NY 12901/518-563-2253; FAX: 518-563-6916

Incor, Inc., P.O. Box 132, Addison, TX 75001/214-931-3500; FAX: 214-458-1626

Independent Machine & Gun Shop, 1416 N. Hayes, Pocatello, ID 83201

INDESAL, P.O. Box 233, Eibar, SPAIN 20600/43-751800; FAX: 43-751962 (U.S. importer—American Arms, Inc.)

Industria de la Escopeta S.A.L. (See INDESAL)

Info-Arm, P.O. Box 1262, Champlain, NY 12919

Ingle, Ralph W., 4 Missing Link, Rossville, GA 30741/404-866-5589

Innovative Weaponry, Inc., 337 Eubank NE, Albuquerque, NM 87123/800-334-3573, 505-296-4645; FAX: 505-271-2633

Innovision Enterprises, 728 Skinner Dr., Kalamazoo, MI 49001/616-382-1681; FAX: 616-382-1830

InSights Training Center, Inc., 240 NW Gilman Blvd., Issaquah, WA 98027/206-391-4834

INTEC International, Inc., P.O. Box 5828, Sparks, NV 89432-5828/602-483-1708

Interarms, 10 Prince St., Alexandria, VA 22314/703-548-1400

Intermountain Arms & Tackle, Inc., 105 E. Idaho St., Meridian, ID 83642/208-888-4911; FAX: 208-888-4381

International Shooters Service (See I.S.S.)

International Shootists, Inc., P.O. Box 5354, Mission Hills, CA 91345/818-891-1723

Intratec, 12405 SW 130th St., Miami, FL 33186/305-232-1821; FAX: 305-253-7207

Iosso Products, 1485 Lively Blvd., Elk Grove Village, IL 60007/708-437-8400

Ironside International Publishers, Inc., P.O. Box 55, 800 Slaters Lane, Alexandria, VA 22313/703-684-6111; FAX: 703-683-5486

Irwin, Campbell H., 140 Hartland Blvd., East Hartland, CT 06027/203-653-3901

Irwindale Arms, Inc. (See IAI)

Israel Military Industries Ltd. (See IMI)

I.S.S., P.O. Box 185234, Ft. Worth, TX 76181/817-595-2090

I.S.W., 106 E. Cairo Dr., Tempe, AZ 85282

Ithaca Aquisition Corp., Ithaca Gun Co., 891 Route 34B, King Ferry, NY 13081/315-364-7171; FAX: 315-364-5134

Ivanoff, Thomas G. (See Tom's Gun Repair)

J

J-4, Inc., 1700 Via Burton, Anaheim, CA 92806

J&D Components, 75 East 350 North, Orem, UT 84057-4719/801-225-7007

J&J Products, Inc., 9240 Whitmore, El Monte, CA 91731/818-571-5228; FAX: 818-571-8704

J&L Superior Bullets (See Huntington Die Specialties)

J&R Enterprises, 4550 Scotts Valley Rd., Lakeport, CA 95453

J&S Heat Treat, 803 S. 16th St., Blue Springs, MO 64015/816-229-2149; FAX: 816-228-1135

Jackalope Gun Shop, 1048 S. 5th St., Douglas, WY 82633/307-358-3441

JACO Precision Co., 11803 Indian Head Dr., Austin, TX 78753/512-836-4418

Jaeger, Inc. Paul, /Dunn's, P.O. Box 449, 1 Madison Ave., Grand Junction, TN 38039/901-764-6909; FAX: 901-764-6503

JägerSport, Ltd., One Wholesale Way, Cranston, RI 02920/800-426-3089, 401-944-9682; FAX: 401-946-2587

Jamison's Forge Works, 4527 Rd. 6.5 NE, Moses Lake, WA 98837/509-762-2659

Jansma, Jack J., 4320 Kalamazoo Ave., Grand Rapids, MI 49508/616-455-7810; FAX: 616-455-5212

Jantz Supply, P.O. Box 584, Davis, OK 73030/405-369-2316; FAX: 405-369-3082

Jarvis Gunsmithing, Inc., 1123 Cherry Orchard Lane, Hamilton, MT 59840/406-961-4392

JAS, Inc., P.O. Box 0, Rosemount, MN 55068/612-890-7631

Jason Empire, Inc., 9200 Cody, Overland Park, KS 66214-3259/913-888-0220; FAX: 913-888-0222

Javelina Products, P.O. Box 337, San Bernardino, CA 92402/714-882-5847; FAX: 714-434-6937

J/B Adventures & Safaris, Inc., P.O. Box 3397, Englewood, CO 80155/303-771-0977

J-B Bore Cleaner, 299 Poplar St., Hamburg, PA 19526/610-562-2103

JBM Software, P.O. Box 3648, University Park, NM 88003

Jedediah Starr Trading Co., P.O. Box 2007 Farmington Hills, MO 48333/810-683-4343; FAX: 810-474-9277

Jeffredo Gunsight, P.O. Box 669, San Marcos, CA 92079/619-728-2695

Jennings Firearms, Inc., 17692 Cowan, Irvine, CA 92714/714-252-7621; FAX: 714-252-7626

Jensen Bullets, 86 North, 400 West, Blackfoot, ID 83221/208-785-5590

Jensen's Custom Ammunition, 5146 E. Pima, Tucson, AZ 85712/602-325-3346; FAX: 602-322-5704

Jensen's Firearms Academy, 1280 W. Prince, Tucson, AZ 85705/602-293-8516

Jester Bullets, Rt. 1 Box 27, Orienta, OK 73737

Jett & Co., Inc., 104 W. Water St., Litchfield, IL 62056-2464/217-324-3779

Jewell, Arnold W., 1490 Whitewater Rd., New Braunfels, TX 78132/210-620-0971

J-Gar Co., 183 Turnpike Rd., Dept. 3, Petersham, MA 01366-9604

JGS Precision Tool Mfg., 1141 S. Summer Rd., Coos Bay, OR 97420/503-267-4331; FAX:503-267-5996

Jim's Precision, Jim Ketchum, 1725 Moclips Dr., Petaluma, CA 94952/707-762-3014

J.I.T., Ltd., P.O. Box 749, Glenview, IL 60025/708-998-0937

JLK Bullets, RR1, Box 310C, Dover, AR 72837/501-331-4194

J.O. Arms & Ammunition Co., 5709 Hartsdale, Houston, TX 77036/713-789-0745; FAX: 713-789-7513

John's Custom Leather, 523 S. Liberty St., Blairsville, PA 15717/412-459-6802

Johns, Bill, 1412 Lisa Rae, Round Rock, TX 78664/512-255-8246

Johnson Gunsmithing, Inc., Neal G., 111 Marvin Dr., Hampton, VA 23666/804-838-8091; FAX: 804-838-8157

Johnston, James (See North Fork Custom Gunsmithing)

Johnston Bros., 1889 Rt. 9, Unit 22, Toms River, NJ 08755/800-257-2595; FAX: 800-257-2534

Jonad Corp., 2091 Lakeland Ave., Lakewood, OH 44107/216-226-3161

Jonas Appraisals & Taxidermy, Jack, 1675 S. Birch, Suite 506, Denver, CO 80222/303-757-7347

Jones Co., Dale, 680 Hoffman Draw, Kila, MT 59920/406-755-4684

Jones Custom Products, Neil, RD 1, Box 483A, Saegertown, PA 16433/814-763-2769; FAX: 814-763-4228

Jones, J.D. (See SSK Industries)

Jones Moulds, Paul, 4901 Telegraph Rd., Los Angeles, CA 90022/213-262-1510

Joy Enterprises (See Fury Cutlery)

J.P. Enterprises, Inc., P.O. Box 26324, Shoreview, MN 55126/612-486-9064, 800-528-9886; FAX: 612-482-0970

JP Sales, Box 307, Anderson, TX 77830

JRW, 2425 Taffy Ct., Nampa, ID 83687

JSL (Hereford) Ltd., 35 Church St., Hereford HR1 2LR ENGLAND/0432-355416; FAX: 0432-355242 (U.S. importer—Specialty Shooters Supply, Inc.)

Jumbo Sports Products (See Bucheimer, J.M.)

Jungkind, Reeves C., 5001 Buckskin Pass, Austin, TX 78745/512-442-1094

Jurras, L.E., P.O. Box 680, Washington, IN 47501/812-254-7698

K

K&K Ammo Wrist Band, R.D. 1, P.O. Box 448-CA18, Lewistown, PA 17044/717-242-2329

K&M Industries, Inc., Box 66, 510 S. Main, Troy, ID 83871/208-835-2281; FAX: 208-835-5211

K&M Services, 5430 Salmon Run Rd., Dover, PA 17315

K&P Gun Co., 1024 Central Ave., New Rockford, ND 58356/701-947-2248

K&T Co., Div. of T&S Industries, Inc., 1027 Skyview Dr., W. Carrollton, OH 45449/513-859-8414

Ka Pu Kapili, P.O. Box 745, Honokaa, HI 96727/808-776-1644; FAX: 808-776-1731

Kahles U.S.A., P.O. Box 81071, Warwick, RI 02888/800-752-4537; FAX: 401-946-2587

Kahr Arms, P.O. Box 220, Blauvelt, NY 10913/914-353-5996; FAX: 914-353-7833

Kamyk Engraving Co., Steve, 9 Grandview Dr., Westfield, MA 01085-1810/413-568-0457

Kane Products, Inc., 5572 Brecksville Rd., Cleveland, OH 44131/216-524-9962

Kapro Mfg. Co., Inc. (See R.E.I.)

Kasenit Co., Inc., 13 Park Ave., Highland Mills, NY 10930/914-928-9595; FAX: 914-928-7292

Kasmarsik Bullets, 152 Crstler Rd., Chehalis, WA 98532

Kassnar (See U.S. importer—K.B.I., Inc.)

Kaswer Custom, Inc., 13 Surrey Drive, Brookfield, CT 06804/203-775-0564; FAX: 203-775-6872

K.B.I., Inc., P.O. Box 5440, Harrisburg, PA 17110-0440/717-540-8518; FAX: 717-540-8567

K-D, Inc., Box 459, 585 N. Hwy. 155, Cleveland, UT 84518/801-653-2530

KeeCo Impressions, Inc., 346 Wood Ave., North Brunswick, NJ 08902/800-468-0546

Keeler, R.H., 817 "N" St., Port Angeles, WA 98362/206-457-4702

Kehr, Roger, 2131 Agate Ct. SE, Lacy, WA 98503/206-456-0831

Keith's Bullets, 942 Twisted Oak, Algonquin, IL 60102/708-658-3520

Kelbly, Inc., 7222 Dalton Fox Lake Rd., North Lawrence, OH 44666/216-683-4674; FAX: 216-683-7349

Keller Co., The, 4215 McEwen Rd., Dallas, TX 75244/214-770-8585

Kelley's, P.O. Box 125, Woburn, MA 01801/617-935-3389

Kelly, Lance, 1723 Willow Oak Dr., Edgewater, FL 32132/904-423-4933

Ken's Gun Specialties, Rt. 1, Box 147, Lakeview, AR 72642/501-431-5606

Ken's Kustom Kartridges, 331 Jacobs Rd., Hubbard, OH 44425/216-534-4595

Keng's Firearms Specialty, Inc., 875 Wharton Dr. SW, Atlanta, GA 30336/404-691-7611; FAX: 404-505-8445

Kennebec Journal, 274 Western Ave., Augusta, ME 04330/207-622-6288

Kennedy Firearms, 10 N. Market St., Muncy, PA 17756/717-546-6695

KenPatable Ent., Inc., P.O. Box 19422, Louisville, KY 40259/502-239-5447

Kent Cartridge Mfg. Co. Ltd., Unit 16, Branbridges Industrial Estate, East, Peckham/Tonbridge, Kent, TN12 5HF ENGLAND/622-872255; FAX: 622-872645

Kesselring Gun Shop, 400 Hwy. 99 North, Burlington, WA 98233/206-724-3113; FAX: 206-724-7003

Kilham & Co., Main St., P.O. Box 37, Lyme, NH 03768/603-795-4112

Kimball, Gary, 1526 N. Circle Dr., Colorado Springs, CO 80909/719-634-1274

Kimber of America, Inc., 9039 SE Jannsen Rd., Clackamas, OR 97015/503-656-1704; FAX: 503-657-5695

Kimel Industries, 3800 Old Monroe Rd., P.O. Box 335, Matthews, NC 28105/800-438-9288; FAX: 704-821-6339

King & Co., Box 1242, Bloomington, IL 61701/309-473-3964

King's Gun Works, 1837 W. Glenoaks Blvd., Glendale, CA 91201/818-956-6010

Kirk Game Calls, Inc., Dennis, RD1, Box 184, Laurens, NY 13796/607-433-2710; FAX: 607-433-2711

Kirkpatrick Leather Co., 1910 San Bernardo, Laredo, TX 78040/512-723-6631; FAX: 512-725-0672

KJM Fabritek, Inc., P.O. Box 162, Marietta, GA 30061

K.K. Arms Co., Star Route Box 671, Kerrville, TX 78028/210-257-4718; FAX: 210-257-4891

Klein Custom Guns, Don, 433 Murray Park Dr., Ripon, WI 54971/414-748-2931

Kleinendorst, K.W., RR 1, Box 1500, Hop Bottom, PA 18824/717-289-4687; FAX: 717-289-4687

Klingler Woodcarving, P.O. Box 141, Thistle Hill, Cabot, VT 05647/802-426-3811

Kmount, P.O. Box 19422, Louisville, KY 40259/502-239-5447

Kneiper Custom Guns, Jim, 334 Summit Vista, Carbondale, CO 81623/303-963-9880

Knight's Mfg. Co., 7750 9th St. SW, Vero Beach, FL 32968/407-778-3700; FAX: 407-569-2955

Kodiak Custom Bullets, 8261 Henry Circle, Anchorage, AK 99507/907-349-2282

Koevenig's Engraving Service, Box 55 Rabbit Gulch, Hill City, SD 57745

Kokolus, Michael M., 7005 Herber Rd., New Tripoli, PA 18066/215-298-3013

Kolpin Mfg., Inc., P.O. Box 107, 205 Depot St., Fox Lake, WI 53933/414-928-3118; FAX: 414-928-3687

Kopec Enterprises, John (See Peacemaker Specialists)

Kopp, Terry K., 1301 Franklin, Lexington, MO 64067/816-259-2636

Koppco Industries, 1301 Franklin, Lexington, MO 64067/816-259-3239

Korth, Robert-Bosch-Str. 4, P.O. Box 1320, 23909 Ratzeburg, GERMANY/0451-4991497; FAX: 0451-4993230 (U.S. importer—Mandall Shooting Supplies, Inc.)

Korzinek Riflesmith, J., RD 2, Box 73, Canton, PA 17724/717-673-8512

Kowa Optimed, Inc., 20001 S. Vermont Ave., Torrance, CA 90502/310-327-1913; FAX: 310-327-4177

Kramer Designs, 302 Lump Gulch, Clancy, MT 59634/406-933-8658; FAX: 406-933-8658

Kramer Handgun Leather, P.O. Box 112154, Tacoma, WA 98411/206-564-6652; FAX: 206-564-1214

Krause Publications, 700 E. State St., Iola, WI 54990/715-445-2214; FAX: 715-445-4087

Krico/Kriegeskorte GmbH, A., Kronacherstr. 63, 85 W. Fürth-Stadeln, D-8510 GERMANY/0911-796092; FAX: 0911-796074 (U.S. importer—Mandall Shooting Supplies, Inc.)

Krieger Barrels, Inc., N114 W18697 Clinton Dr., Germantown, WI 53022/414-255-9593; FAX: 414-255-9586

Kriegeskorte GmbH, A. (See Krico/Kriegeskorte GmbH., A.)

Krieghoff Gun Co., H., Bosch Str. 22, 7900 Ulm, GERMANY (U.S. importer—Krieghoff International, Inc.)

Krieghoff International, Inc., 7528 Easton Rd., Ottsville, PA 18942/215-847-5173; FAX: 215-847-8691

Kris Mounts, 108 Lehigh St., Johnstown, PA 15905/814-539-9751

K-Sports Imports, Inc., 2755 Thompson Creek Rd., Pomona, CA 91767/909-392-2345; FAX: 909-392-2354

Kudlas, John M., 622 14th St. SE, Rochester, MN 55904/507-288-5579

Kulis Freeze Dry Taxidermy, 725 Broadway Ave., Bedford, OH 44146/216-232-8352; FAX: 216-232-7305

KVH Industries, Inc., 110 Enterprise Center, Middletown, RI 02842/401-847-3327; FAX: 401-849-0045

Kwik Mount Corp., P.O. Box 19422, Louisville, KY 40259/502-239-5447

Kwik-Site Co., 5555 Treadwell, Wayne, MI 48184/313-326-1500; FAX: 313-326-4120

L

L&R Lock Co., 1137 Pocalla Rd., Sumter, SC 29150/803-775-6127

L&S Technologies, Inc. (See Aimtech Mount Systems)

LaBounty Precision Reboring, P.O. Box 186, 7968 Silver Lk. Rd., Maple Falls, WA 98266/206-599-2047

Lachaussee, S.A., 29 Rue Kerstenne, Ans, B-4430 BELGIUM/041-63 88 77

La Clinique du .45, 1432 Rougemont, Chambly, Quebec, J3L 2L8 CANADA/514-658-1144

LaFrance Specialties, P.O. Box 178211, San Diego, CA 92117/619-293-3373

Lage Uniwad, Inc., P.O. Box 446, Victor, IA 52327/319-647-3232

Lake Center, P.O. Box 38, St. Charles, MO 63302/314-946-7500

Lakefield Arms Ltd., 248 Water St., Lakefield, Ont. K0L 2H0, CANADA/705-652-6735, 705-652-8000; FAX: 705-652-8431

Lakewood Products, Inc., P.O. Box 1527, 1445 Eagle St., Rhinelander, WI 54501/715-369-3445

Lampert, Ron, Rt. 1, Box 177, Guthrie, MN 56461/218-854-7345

Lan Orchards, 3601 10th St. SE, Ewenatchee, WA 98801

Lanber Armes S.A., Calle Zubiaurre 5, Zaldibar, SPAIN/34-4-6827702; FAX: 34-4-6827999

Lane Bullets, Inc., 1011 S. 10th St., Kansas City, KS 66105/913-621-6113, 800-444-7468

Lane Publishing, P.O. Box 759, Hot Springs, AR 71902/501-525-7514; FAX: 501-525-7519

LAP Systems Groups, N.A., P.O. Box 162, Marietta, GA 30061

Lapua Ltd., P.O. Box 5, Lapua, FINLAND SF-62101/64-310111; FAX: 64-4388951

L.A.R. Manufacturing, Inc., 4133 W. Farm Rd., West Jordan, UT 84088/801-255-7106; FAX: 801-569-1972

LaRocca Gun Works, Inc., 51 Union Place, Worcester, MA 01608/508-754-2887; FAX: 508-754-2887

Laser Devices, Inc., 2 Harris Ct. A-4, Monterey, CA 93940/408-373-0701; FAX: 408-373-0903

Laseraim, Inc. (See Emerging Technologies, Inc.)

Laseraim Arms, Inc., Sub. of Emerging Technologies, Inc., P.O. Box 3548, Little Rock, AR 72203/501-375-2227; FAX: 501-372-1445

LaserMax, 3495 Winton Place, Bldg. B, Rochester, NY 14623/716-272-5420

Lassen Community College, Gunsmithing Dept., P.O. Box 3000, Hwy. 139, Susanville, CA 96130/916-257-6181 ext. 109; FAX: 916-257-8964

Lathrop's, Inc., 5146 E. Pima, Tucson, AZ 85712/602-881-0226, 800-875-4867

Laughridge, William R. (See Cylinder & Slide, Inc.)

Laurel Mountain Forge, P.O. Box 224, Romeo, MI 48065/313-749-5742

Laurona Armas S.A., P.O. Box 260, 20600 Eibar, SPAIN/34-43-700600; FAX: 34-43-700616 (U.S. importer—Galaxy Imports Ltd., Inc.)

Law Concealment Systems, Inc., P.O. Box 3952, Wilmington, NC 28406/919-791-6656, 800-373-0116 orders

Lawrence Brand Shot (See Precision Reloading, Inc.)

Lawrence Leather Co., P.O. Box 1479, Lillington, NC 27546/910-893-2071; FAX: 910-893-4742

Lawson, John G. (See Sight Shop, The)

Lawson Co., Harry, 3328 N. Richey Blvd., Tucson, AZ 85716/602-326-1117

LBT, HCR 62, Box 145, Moyie Springs, ID 83845/208-267-3588

Lea Mfg. Co., 237 E. Aurora St., Waterbury, CT 06720/203-753-5116

Lead Bullets Technology (See LBT)

Leather Arsenal, 27549 Middleton Rd., Middleton, ID 83644/208-585-6212

Leatherwood-Meopta, Inc., 751 W. Lamar Blvd. Suite 102, Arlington, TX 76012-2010/817-965-3253

Lebeau-Courally, Rue St. Gilles, 386, 4000 Liege, BELGIUM/041 52 48 43; FAX: 041 52 20 08 (U.S. importer—New England Arms Co.

Lectro Science, Inc., 6410 W. Ridge Rd., Erie, PA 16506/814-833-6487; FAX: 814-833-0447

Ledbetter Airguns, Riley, 1804 E. Sprague St., Winston Salem, NC 27107-3521/919-784-0676

Leding Loader, RR 1, Box 645, Ozark, AR 72949

Lee Co., T.K., One Independence Plaza, Suite 520, Birmingham, AL 35209/205-913-5222

Lee Precision, Inc., 4275 Hwy. U, Hartford, WI 53027/414-673-3075

Lee Supplies, Mark, 9901 France Ct., Lakeville, MN 55044/612-461-2114

Lee's Red Ramps, Box 291240, Phelan, CA 92329-1240/619-868-5731

LeFever Arms Co., Inc., 6234 Stokes, Lee Center Rd., Lee Center, NY 13363/315-337-6722; FAX: 315-337-1543

Leibowitz, Leonard, 1205 Murrayhill Ave., Pittsburgh, PA 15217/412-361-5455

Leica USA, Inc., 156 Ludlow Ave., Northvale, NJ 07647/201-767-7500; FAX: 201-767-8666

LEM Gun Specialties, Inc., P.O. Box 2855, Peachtree City, GA 30269-2024

Lem Sports, Inc., P.O. Box 2107, Aurora, IL 60506/708-897-7382, 800-688-8801 (orders only)

Lenahan Family Enterprise, P.O. Box 46, Manitou Springs, CO 80829

Lethal Force Institute (See Police Bookshelf)

Letschnig, Franz, RR 1, Martintown, Ont. K0C 1S0, CANADA/613-528-4843

Lett, Mfg., W.F., Box 479A Currier Rd., Contoocook NH 03229

Leupold, P.O. Box 688, Beaverton, OR 97075/503-526-1491; FAX: 503-526-1475

Lever Arms Service Ltd., 2131 Burrard St., Vancouver, B.C. V6J 3H7 CANADA/604-736-0004; FAX: 604-738-3503

Lewis, Ed, P.O. Box 875, Pico Rivera, CA 90660

Liberty Antique Gunworks, 19 Key St., P.O. Box 183, Eastport, ME 04631/207-853-4116

Liberty Metals, 2233 East 16th St., Los Angeles, CA 90021/213-581-9171; FAX: 213-581-9351

Liberty Shooting Supplies, P.O. Box 357, Hillsboro, OR 97123/503-640-5518

Lightfield Ammunition Corp., The Slug Group, P.O. Box 376, Paris, PA 15554/814-839-4517; FAX: 814-839-2601

Lightforce U.S.A., P.O. Box 488, Vaughn, WA 98394/206-876-3225; FAX: 206-876-3249

Lincoln, Dean, Box 1886, Farmington, NM 87401

Lindner Custom Bullets, 325 Bennetts Pond La., Mattituck, NY 11952

Lindsay, Steve, RR 2 Cedar Hills, Kearney, NE 68847/308-236-7885

Lindsley Arms Ctg. Co., P.O. Box 757, 20 College Hill Rd., Henniker, NH 03242/603-428-3127

Linebaugh Custom Sixguns & Rifle Works, P.O. Box 1263, Cody, WY 82414/307-587-8010

Lite Tek International, 133-30 32nd Ave., Flushing, NY 11354/718-463-0650; FAX: 718-762-0890

Lithi Bee Bullet Lube, 1885 Dyson St., Muskegon, MI 49442/616-726-3400

"Little John's" Antique Arms, 1740 W. Laveta, Orange, CA 92668

Littler Sales Co., 20815 W. Chicago, Detroit, MI 48228/313-273-6888; FAX: 313-273-1099

Ljutic Industries, Inc., 732 N. 16th Ave., Yakima, WA 98902/509-248-0476; FAX: 509-457-5141

Llama Gabilondo Y Cia, Apartado 290, E-01080, Victoria, SPAIN (U.S. importer—SGS Importers International, Inc.)

Load From A Disk, 9826 Sagedale, Houston, TX 77089/713-484-0935

Loadmaster, P.O. Box 1209, Warminster, Wilts. BA12 9XJ ENGLAND//(0985)218544; FAX: (0985)214111

Loch Leven Industries, P.O. Box 2751, Santa Rosa, CA 95405/707-573-8735; FAX: 707-573-6369

Lock's Philadelphia Gun Exchange, 6700 Rowland Ave., Philadelphia, PA 19149/215-332-6225; FAX: 215-332-4800

Lodewick, Walter H., 2816 NE Halsey St., Portland, OR 97232/503-284-2554

Lofland, James W., 2275 Larkin Rd., Boothwyn, PA 19061/610-485-0391

Log Cabin Sport Shop, 8010 Lafayette Rd., Lodi, OH 44254/216-948-1082

Logan, Harry M., Box 745, Honokaa, HI 96727/808-776-1644

Logan Security Products Co., 4926 Annhurst Rd., Columbus, OH 43228-1341

Lohman Mfg. Co., Inc., 4500 Doniphan Dr., P.O. Box 220, Neosho, MO 64850/417-451-4438; FAX: 417-451-2576

Lomont Precision Bullets, 4236 W. 700 South, Poneto, IN 46781/219-694-6792; FAX: 219-694-6797

London Guns Ltd., Box 3750, Santa Barbara, CA 93130/805-683-4141; FAX: 805-683-1712

Lone Star Gunleather, 1301 Brushy Bend Dr., Round Rock, TX 78681/512-255-1805

Long, George F., 1500 Rogue River Hwy., Ste. F, Grants Pass, OR 97527/503-476-7552

Lorcin Engineering Co., Inc., 10427 San Sevaine Way, Ste. A, Mira Loma, CA 91752/909-360-1406; FAX: 909-360-0623

Lortone, Inc., 2856 NW Market St., Seattle, WA 98107/206-789-3100

Loweth, Richard, 29 Hedgegrow Lane, Kirby Muxloe, Leics. LE9 9BN ENGLAND

L.P.A. Snc, Via V. Alfieri 26, Gardone V.T. BS, ITALY 25063/(30)8911481; FAX: (30)8910951

LPS Laboratories, Inc., 4647 Hugh Howell Rd., P.O. Box 3050, Tucker, GA 30084/404-934-7800

Lucas, Edward E., 32 Garfield Ave., East Brunswick, NJ 08816/201-251-5526

Lucas, Mike, 1631 Jessamine Rd., Lexington, SC 29073/803-356-0282

Lutz Engraving, Ron, E. 1998 Smokey Valley Rd., Scandinavia, WI 54977/715-467-2674

Lyman Instant Targets, Inc. (See Lyman Products Corp.)

Lyman Products Corporation, Rt. 147, Middlefield, CT 06455/800-22-LYMAN, 203-349-3421; FAX: 203-349-3586

M

M&D Munitions Ltd., 127 Verdi St., Farmingdale, NY 11735/516-752-1038; FAX: 516-752-1905

M&M Engineering (See Hollywood Engineering)

M&N Bullet Lube, P.O. Box 495, 151 NE Jefferson St., Madras, OR 97741/503-255-3750

MA Systems, P.O. Box 1143, Chouteau, OK 74337/918-479-6378

Mac-1 Distributors, 13974 Van Ness Ave., Gardena, CA 90249/310-327-3582

Mac's .45 Shop, P.O. Box 2028, Seal Beach, CA 90740/310-438-5046

Madis, David, 2453 West Five Mile Pkwy., Dallas, TX 75233/214-330-7168

Madis, George, P.O. Box 545, Brownsboro, TX 75756

Magma Engineering Co., P.O. Box 161, Queen Creek, AZ 85242/602-987-9008; FAX: 602-987-0148

Mag-Na-Port International, Inc., 41302 Executive Dr., Harrison Twp., MI 48045-3448/810-469-6727; FAX: 810-469-0425

Magnolia Sports, Inc., 211 W. Main, Magnolia, AR 71753/800-530-7816; FAX: 501-234-8117

Magnum Grips, Box 801G, Payson, AZ 85547

Magnum Power Products, Inc., P.O. Box 17768, Fountain Hills, AZ 85268

Magnum Research, Inc., 7110 University Ave., Minneapolis, MN 55432/612-574-1868; FAX: 612-574-0109

Magnus Bullets, P.O.Box 239, Toney, AL 35773/205-828-5089; FAX: 205-828-7756

Mag-Pack Corp., P.O. Box 846, Chesterland, OH 44026

MagSafe Ammo Co., 2725 Friendly Grove Rd NE, Olympia, WA 98506/206-357-6383

MAGTECH Recreational Products, Inc., 5030 Paradise Rd., Suite C211, Las Vegas, NV 89119/702-795-7191, 800-466-7191; FAX: 702-795-2769

Mahony, Philip Bruce, 67 White Hollow Rd., Lime Rock, CT 06039-2418/203-435-9341

Maine Custom Bullets, RFD 1, Box 1755, Brooks, ME 04921

Mains Enterprises, Inc., 3111 S. Valley View Blvd., Suite B120, Las Vegas, NV 89102-7790/702-876-6278; FAX: 702-876-1269

Maionchi-L.M.I., Via Di Coselli-Zona Industriale Di Guamo, Lucca, ITALY 55060/011 39-583 94291

Maki School of Engraving, Robert E., P.O. Box 947, Northbrook, IL 60065/708-724-8238

Makinson, Nicholas, RR 3, Komoka, Ont. N0L 1R0 CANADA/519-471-5462

Malcolm Enterprises, 1023 E. Prien Lake Rd., Lake Charles, LA 70601

Mandall Shooting Supplies, Inc., 3616 N. Scottsdale Rd., Scottsdale, AZ 85252/602-945-2553; FAX: 602-949-0734

Manufacture D'Armes Des Pyrenees Francaises (See Unique/M.A.P.F.)

Marble Arms Corp., 420 Industrial Park, P.O. Box 111, Gladstone, MI 49837/906-428-3710; FAX: 906-428-3711

Marchmon Bullets, 8191 Woodland Shore Dr., Brighton, MI 48116

Marek, George, 55 Arnold St., Westfield, MA 01085/413-562-5673

Markell, Inc., 422 Larkfield Center 235, Santa Rosa, CA 95403/707-573-0792; FAX: 707-573-9867

Marksman Products, 5482 Argosy Dr., Huntington Beach, CA 92649/714-898-7535, 800-822-8005; FAX: 714-891-0782

Marlin Firearms Co., 100 Kenna Dr., New Haven, CT 06473/203-239-5621; FAX: 203-234-7991

Marocchi F.lli S.p.A., Via Galileo Galilei, I-25068 Zanano di Sarezzo, ITALY (U.S. importers—PSI, Inc.; Sile Distributors)

Marple & Associates, Dick, 21 Dartmouth St., Hooksett, NH 03106/603-627-1837; FAX: 603-641-4837

Marquart Precision Co., Inc., Rear 136 Grove Ave., Box 1740, Prescott, AZ 86302/602-445-5646

Marsh, Mike, Croft Cottage, Main St., Elton, Derbyshire DE4 2BY, ENGLAND/0629 650 669

Marshall Enterprises, 792 Canyon Rd., Redwood City, CA 94062

Martin Bookseller, J., P.O. Drawer AP, Beckley, WV 25802/304-255-4073; FAX: 304-255-4077

Martin's Gun Shop, 937 S. Sheridan Blvd., Lakewood, CO 80226/303-922-2184

Marvel, Alan, 3922 Madonna Rd., Jarretsville, MD 21084/301-557-6545

Maryland Munitions, P.O. Box 1711, Ellicott City, MD 21041-1711/410-744-3533

Masen Co., John, P.O. Box 5050, Suite 165, Lewisville, TX 75057/817-430-8732

MAST Technology, P.O. Box 97274, Las Vegas, NV 89193/702-362-5043

Master Class Bullets, 4110 Alder St., Eugene, OR 97405/503-687-1263

Master Engravers, Inc. (See Hendricks, Frank E.)

Master Lock Co., 2600 N. 32nd St., Milwaukee, WI 53245/414-444-2800

Master Products, Inc. (See Gun-Alert/Master Products, Inc.)

Match Prep, P.O. Box 155, Tehachapi, CA 93581/805-822-5383

Matco, Inc., 1003-2nd St., N. Manchester, IN 46962/219-982-8282

Mathews & Son, Inc., George E., 10224 S. Paramount Blvd., Downey, CA 90241/310-862-6719; FAX: 310-862-6719

Mauser-Werke Oberndorf GmbH, P.O. Box 1349   1360, 78722 Oberndorf/Neckar GERMANY

Maverick Arms, Inc., 7 Grasso Ave., P.O. Box 497, North Haven, CT 06473/203-230-5300; FAX: 203-230-5420

Maxi-Mount, P.O. Box 291, Willoughby Hills, OH 44094-0291/216-946-3105

Mayville Engineering Co. (See MEC, Inc.)

MCA Sports, P.O. Box 8868, Palm Springs, CA 92263/619-770-2005

McCament, Jay, 1730-134th St. Ct. S., Tacoma, WA 98444/206-531-8832

McCann's Muzzle-Gun Works, 14 Walton Dr., New Hope, PA 18938/215-862-9180

McCombs, Leo, 1862 White Cemetery Rd., Patriot, OH 45658/614-256-1714

McCormick Corp., Chip, 1825 Fortview Rd., Ste. 115, Austin, TX 78704/800-328-CHIP, 512-462-0004; FAX: 512-462-0009

McCormick's Custom Gun Bluing, 609 NE 104th Ave., Vancouver, WA 98664/206-896-4232

McDonald, Dennis, 8359 Brady St., Peosta, IA 52068/319-556-7940

McFarland, Stan, 2221 Idella Ct., Grand Junction, CO 81505/303-243-4704

McKee Publications, 121 Eatons Neck Rd., Northport, NY 11768/516-575-8850

McKenzie, Lynton, 6940 N. Alvernon Way, Tucson, AZ 85718/602-299-5090

McKillen & Heyer, Inc., 35535 Euclid Ave. Suite 11, Willoughby, OH 44094/216-942-2044

McMillan Bros. Rifle Co., Inc., P.O. Box 86549, Phoenix, AZ 85080/602-780-2115; FAX: 602-581-3825

McMillan Gunworks, Inc., 302 W. Melinda Lane, Phoenix, AZ 85027/602-582-9627; FAX: 602-582-5178

McMillan Optical Gunsight Co., 28638 N. 42nd St., Cave Creek, AZ 85331/602-585-7868; FAX: 602-585-7872

McMurdo, Lynn (See Specialty Gunsmithing)

MCRW Associates Shooting Supplies, R.R. 1 Box 1425, Sweet Valley, PA 18656/717-864-3967; FAX: 717-864-2669

MCS, Inc., 34 Delmar Dr., Brookfield, CT 06804/203-775-1013; FAX: 203-775-9462

MDS, P.O. Box 1441, Brandon, FL 33509-1441/813-894-3512; FAX: 813-684-5953

Meadow Industries, P.O. Box 754, Locust Grove, VA 22508/703-972-2175; FAx: 703-972-2175

Measurement Group, Inc., Box 27777, Raleigh, NC 27611

MEC, Inc., 715 South St., Mayville, WI 53050/414-387-4500

MEC-Gar S.R.L., Via Madonnina 64, Gardone V.T. (BS), ITALY 25063/39-30-8911719; FAX: 39-30-8910065 (U.S. importer—MEC-Gar U.S.A., Inc.)

MEC-Gar U.S.A., Inc., Box 112, 500B Monroe Turnpike, Monroe, CT 06468/203-635-8662; FAX: 203-635-8662

Meier Works, P.O. Box 423, Tijeras, NM 87059/505-281-3783

Mele, Frank, 201 S. Wellow Ave., Cookeville, TN 38501/615-526-4860

Menck, Thomas W., 5703 S. 77th St., Ralston, NE 68127-4201

Mendez, John A., P.O. Box 620984, Orlando, FL 32862/407-282-2178

Men-Metallwerk Elisenhuette, GmbH, P.O. Box 1263, D-56372 Nassau/Lahn, GERMANY/2604-7819

Meprolight (See Hesco-Meprolight)

Merit Corp., Box 9044, Schenectady, NY 12309/518-346-1420

Merkel Freres, Strasse 7 October, 10, Suhl, GERMANY (U.S. importer—GSI, Inc.)

Merkuria Ltd., Argentinska 38, 17005 Praha 7, CZECH REPUBLIC/422-875117; FAX: 422-809152

Metal Products Co. (See MPC/McMinnville, TN)

Metalife Industries, Box 53 Mong Ave., Reno, PA 16343/814-436-7747; FAX: 814-676-5662

Michael's Antiques, Box 591, Waldoboro, ME 04572

Michaels of Oregon Co., P.O. Box 13010, Portland, OR 97213/503-255-6890; FAX: 503-255-0746

Micro Sight Co., 242 Harbor Blvd., Belmont, CA 94002/415-591-0769; FAX: 415-591-7531

Micro-Lube, Rt. 2, P.O. Box 201, Deming, NM 88030/505-546-9116

Mid-America Recreation, Inc., 1328 5th Ave., Moline, IA 52807/309-764-5089; FAX: 309-764-2722

Middlebrooks Custom Shop, 7366 Colonial Trail East, Surry, VA 23883/804-357-0881; FAX: 804-365-0442

Midway Arms, Inc., P.O. Box 1483, Columbia, MO 65205/800-243-3220, 314-445-6363; FAX: 314-446-1018

Midwest Gun Sport, 1108 Herbert Dr., Zebulon, NC 27597/919-269-5570

Midwest Sport Distributors, Box 129, Fayette, MO 65248

Military Armament Corp., P.O. Box 120, Mt. Zion Rd., Lingleville, TX 76461/817-965-3253

Miller Arms, Inc., P.O. Box 260 Purl St., St. Onge, SD 57779/605-642-5160; FAX: 605-642-5160

Miller Custom, 210 E. Julia, Clinton, IL 61727/217-935-9362

Miller Engineering, R&D Engineering & Manufacturing, P.O. Box 6342, Virginia Beach, VA 23456/804-468-1402

Miller Enterprises, Inc., R.P., 1557 E. Main St., P.O. Box 234, Brownsburg, IN 46112/317-852-8187

Miller Single Trigger Mfg. Co., R.D.1, P.O. Box 99, Millersburg, PA 17061/717-692-3704
Millett Sights, 16131 Gothard St., Huntington Beach, CA 92647/800-645-5388; FAX: 714-843-5707
Milliron Custom Machine Carving, Earl, 1249 NE 166th Ave., Portland, OR 97230/503-252-3725
Miniature Machine Co. (See MMC)
Minute Man High Tech Industries, 3005B 6th Ave., Tacoma, WA 98406/800-233-2734
Mirador Optical Corp., P.O. Box 11614, Marina Del Rey, CA 90295-7614/310-821-5587; FAX: 310-305-0386
Miroku, B.C./Daly, Charles (See U.S. importers—Bell's Legendary Country Wear; British Sporting Arms; U.S. distributor—Outdoor Sports Headquarters, Inc.)
Mitchell Arms, Inc., 3400 W. MacArthur Blvd., Ste. 1, Santa Ana, CA 92704/714-957-5711; FAX: 714-957-5732
Mitchell Bullets, R.F., 430 Walnut St., Westernport, MD 21562
Mitchell Leatherworks, 1220 Black Brook Rd., Dunbarton, NH 03045/603-774-6283
Mitchell's Accuracy Shop, 68 Greenridge Dr., Stafford, VA 22554/703-659-0165
Mi-Te Bullets, R.R. 1 Box 230, Ellsworth, KS 67439/913-472-4575
Mittermeier, Inc., Frank, P.O. Box 2G, 3577 E. Tremont Ave., Bronx, NY 10465/718-828-3843
Mixson Leathercraft, Inc., 7435 W. 19th Ct., Hialeah, FL 33014/305-821-5190; FAX: 305-558-9318
MJK Gunsmithing, Inc., 417 N. Huber Ct., E. Wenatchee, WA 98802/509-884-7683
MJM Mfg., 3283 Rocky Water Ln. Suite B, San Jose, CA 95148/408-270-4207
MKL Service Co., 610 S. Troy St., P.O. Box D, Royal Oak, MI 48068/810-548-5453
MKS Supply, Inc., 174 S. Mulberry St., Mansfield, OH 44902/419-522-8330
MMC, 606 Grace Ave., Ft. Worth, TX 76111/817-831-0837
MMP, Rt. 6, Box 384, Harrison, AR 72601/501-741-5019; FAX: 501-741-3104
Mo's Competitor Supplies (See MCS, Inc.)
M.O.A. Corp., 2451 Old Camden Pike, Eaton, OH 45320/513-456-3669
M.O.A. Maximum, P.O. Box 185, Dayton, OH 45404/513-456-3669
Modern Gun Repair School, 2538 N. 8th St., P.O. Box 5338, Dept. GNX95, Phoenix, AZ 85010/602-990-8346
Modern MuzzleLoading, Inc., 234 Airport Rd., P.O. Box 130, Centerville, IA 52544/515-856-2626; FAX: 515-856-2628
MoLoc Bullets, P.O. Box 2810, Turlock, CA 95381-2810/209-632-1644
Montana Armory, Inc., 100 Centennial Dr., Big Timber, MT 59011/406-932-4353
Montana Outfitters, Lewis E. Yearout, 308 Riverview Dr. E., Great Falls, MT 59404/406-761-0859
Montana Precision Swaging, P.O. Box 4746, Butte, MT 59702/406-782-7502
Montana Vintage Arms, 2354 Bear Canyon Rd., Bozeman, MT 59715
Monte Kristo Pistol Grip Co., P.O. Box 85, Whiskeytown, CA 96095/916-623-4019
Montgomery Community College, P.O. Box 787, Troy, NC 27371/919-572-3691
Moore & Co., Wm. Larkin, 31360 Via Colinas, Suite 109, Westlake Village, CA 91361/818-889-4160
Moran, Jerry, P.O. Box 357, Mt. Morris, MI 45458-0357
Moreton/Fordyce Enterprises, P.O. Box 940, Saylorsburg, PA 18353/717-992-5742; FAX: 717-992-8775
Morini (See U.S. importer—Mandall Shooting Shpplies, Inc.)
Moschetti, Mitchell R., P.O. Box 27065, Denver, CO 80227/303-733-9593
Mossberg & Sons, Inc., O.F, 7 Grasso Ave., North Haven, CT 06473/203-288-6491; FAX: 203-288-2404
Mountain Bear Rifle Works, Inc., 100 B Ruritan Rd., Sterling, VA 20164/703-430-0420
Mountain South, P.O. Box 381, Barnwell, SC 29812/FAX: 803-259-3227
Mountain State Muzzleloading Supplies, Box 154-1, Rt. 2, Williamstown, WV 26187/304-375-7842; FAX: 304-375-3737
Mountain States Engraving, Kenneth W. Warren, P.O. Box 2842, Wenatchee, WA 98802/509-663-6123
Mountain View Sports, Inc., Box 188, Troy, NH 03465/603-357-9690; FAX: 603-357-9691
Mowrey Gun Works, P.O. Box 246, Waldron, IN 46182/317-525-6181; FAX: 317-525-6181
Mowrey's Guns & Gunsmithing, RR1, Box 82, Canajoharie, NY 13317/518-673-3483
MPC, P.O. Box 450, McMinnville, TN 37110-0450
MPI Stocks, P.O. Box 83266, Portland, OR 97283-0266/503-226-1215; FAX: 503-216-2661
MSC Industrial Supply Co., 151 Sunnyside Blvd., Plainview, NY 11803-9915/516-349-0330
Mt. Alto Outdoor Products, Rt. 735, Howardsville, VA 24562
Mt. Baldy Bullet Co., HC 87, Box 10A, Keystone, SD 57751/605-666-4725
MTM Molded Products Co., Inc., 3370 Obco Ct., Dayton, OH 45414/513-890-7461; FAX: 513-890-1747
Mulhern, Rick, Rt. 5, Box 152, Rayville, LA 71269/318-728-2688
Mullins Ammo, Rt. 2, Box 304K, Clintwood, VA 24228/703-926-6772
Mullis Guncraft, 3523 Lawyers Road E., Monroe, NC 28110/704-283-6683
Multipax, 8086 S. Yale, Suite 286, Tulsa, OK 74136/918-496-1999; FAX: 918-492-7465
Multiplex International, 26 S. Main St., Concord, NH 03301/FAX: 603-796-2223
Multi-Scale Charge Ltd., 3269 Niagara Falls Blvd., N. Tonawanda, NY 14120/905-566-1255; FAX: 416-276-6295
Mundy, Thomas A., 69 Robbins Road, Somerville, NJ 08876/201-722-2199
Munsch Gunsmithing, Tommy, Rt. 2, P.O. Box 248, Little Falls, MN 56345/612-632-6695
Murmur Corp., 2823 N. Westmoreland Ave., Dallas, TX 75222/214-630-5400
Murray State College, 100 Faculty Dr., Tishomingo, OK 73460/405-371-2371
Muscle Products Corp., 188 Freeport Rd., Butler, PA 16001/800-227-7049, 412-283-0567; FAX: 412-283-8310
Museum of Historical Arms, Inc., 1038 Alton Rd., Miami Beach, FL 33139/305-672-7480
Mushroom Express Bullet Co., 601 W. 6th St., Greenfield, IN 46140/317-462-6332
Mustra's Custom Guns, Inc., Carl, 1002 Pennsylvania Ave., Palm Harbor, FL 34683/813-785-1403
Muzzlelite Corp., P.O. Box 987, DeLeon Springs, FL 32130
Muzzleload Magnum Products (See MMP)
Muzzleloaders Etcetera, Inc., 9901 Lyndale Ave. S., Bloomington, MN 55420/612-884-1161
Muzzle-Nuzzle Co., 609 N. Virginia Ave., Roswell, NM 88201/505-624-1260

N

N&J Sales, Lime Kiln Rd., Northford, CT 06472/203-484-0247
Nagel's Bullets, 9 Wilburn, Baytown, TX 77520
Nastoff's 45 Shop, Inc., Steve, 12288 Mahoning Ave., P.O. Box 446, North Jackson, OH 44451/216-538-2977
National Bullet Co., 1585 E. 361 St., Eastlake, OH 44095/216-951-1854; FAX: 216-951-7761
National Survival Game, Inc., P.O. Box 1439, New London, NH 03257/603-735-6165; FAX: 603-735-5154
National Target Co., 4690 Wyaconda Rd., Rockville, MD 20852/800-827-7060, 301-770-7060; FAX: 301-770-7892
Nationwide Airgun Repairs (See Airgun Repair Centre)
Nationwide Sports Distributors, 70 James Way, Southampton, PA 18966/215-322-2050; FAX: 215-322-5972
Naval Ordnance Works, Rt. 2, Box 919, Sheperdstown, WV 25443/304-876-0998
Navy Arms Co., 689 Bergen Blvd., Ridgefield, NJ 07657/201-945-2500; FAX: 201-945-6859
N.C. Ordnance Co., P.O. Box 3254, Wilson, NC 27895/919-237-2440
NCP Products, Inc., 721 Maryland Ave. SW, Canton, OH 44710
NECO, 1316-67th St., Emeryville, CA 94608/510-450-0420
Necromancer Industries, Inc., 14 Communications Way, West Newton, PA 15089/412-872-8722
NEI Handtools, Inc., 51583 Columbia River Hwy., Scappoose, OR 97056/503-543-6776; FAX: 503-543-6799
Nelson, Gary K., 975 Terrace Dr., Oakdale, CA 95361/209-847-4590
Nelson Combat Leather, Bruce, P.O. Box 8691 CRB, Tucson, AZ 85738/602-825-9047
Nesci Enterprises, Inc., P.O. Box 119, Summit St., East Hampton, CT 06424/203-267-2588
Nesika Bay Precision, 22239 Big Valley Rd., Poulsbo, WA 98370/206-697-3830
Nettestad Gun Works, RR 1, Box 160, Pelican Rapids, MN 56572/218-863-4301
Neumann GmbH, Am Galgenberg 6, 90575 Langenzenn, GERMANY/09101/8258; FAX: 09101/6356
Neutralizer Police Munitions, 5029 Middle Rd., Horseheads, NY 14845-9568/607-739-8362; FAX: 607-594-3900
Nevada Cartridge Co., 44 Montgomery St., Suite 500, San Francisco, CA 94104/415-925-9394; FAX: 415-925-9396
New Advantage Arms Corp., 2843 N. Alvernon Way, Tucson, AZ 85712/602-881-7444; FAX: 602-323-0949
New Democracy, Inc., 751 W. Lamar Blvd., Suite 102, Arlington, TX 76012-2010
New England Ammunition Co., 1771 Post Rd. East, Suite 223, Westport, CT 06880/203-254-8048
New England Arms Co., Box 278, Lawrence Lane, Kittery Point, ME 03905/207-439-0593; FAX: 207-439-6726
New England Custom Gun Service, Brook Rd., RR2, Box 122W, W. Lebanon, NH 03784/603-469-3450; FAX: 603-469-3471
New England Firearms, 60 Industrial Rowe, Gardner, MA 01440/508-632-9393; FAX: 508-632-2300
New Orleans Arms Co., 5001 Treasure St., New Orleans, LA 70186/504-944-3371
New Orleans Jewelers Supply Co., 206 Charters St., New Orleans, LA 70130/504-523-3839
New Win Publishing, Inc., Box 5159, Clinton, NJ 08809/201-735-9701; FAX: 201-735-9703
Newark Electronics, 4801 N. Ravenswood Ave., Chicago, IL 60640
Newell, Robert H., 55 Coyote, Los Alamos, NM 87544/505-662-7135
Newman Gunshop, 119 Miller Rd., Agency, IA 52530/515-937-5775
NgraveR Co., The, 67 Wawecus Hill Rd., Bozrah, CT 06334/203-823-1533
Nichols Sports Optics, P.O. Box 37669, Omaha, NE 68137/402-339-3530; FAX: 402-330-8029
Nicholson Custom, Rt. 1, Box 176-3, Sedalia, MO 65301/816-826-8746
Niemi Engineering, W.B., Box 126 Center Road, Greensboro, VT 05841/802-533-7180 days, 802-533-7141 evenings
Nikon, Inc., 1300 Walt Whitman Rd., Melville, NY 11747/516-547-4200
Nitex, Inc., P.O. Box 1706, Uvalde, TX 78801/512-278-8843
Noble Co., Jim, 1305 Columbia St., Vancouver, WA 98660/206-695-1309
Noreen, Peter H., 5075 Buena Vista Dr., Belgrade, MT 59714/406-586-7383
Norica, Avnda Otaola, 16, Apartado 68, 20600 Eibar, SPAIN (U.S. importers—American Arms, Inc.)
Norinco, 7A, Yun Tan N Beijing, CHINA (U.S. importers—Century International Arms, Inc.; ChinaSports, Inc.; Interarms)
Norma (See U.S. importer—Paul Co., The)
North American Arms, 2150 South 950 East, Provo, UT 84606-6285/800-821-5783, 801-374-9990; FAX: 801-374-9998
North American Correspondence Schools, The Gun Pro School, Oak & Pawney St., Scranton, PA 18515/717-342-7701
North American Shooting Systems, P.O. Box 306, Osoyoos, B.C. V0H 1V0 CANADA/604-495-3131; FAX: 604-495-2816
North American Specialties, 25442 Trabuco Rd., 105-328, Lake Forest, CA 92630/714-837-4867
North Devon Firearms Services, 3 North St., Braunton, EX33 1AJ ENGLAND
North Fork Custom Gunsmithing, James Johnston, 428 Del Rio Rd., Roseburg, OR 97470/503-673-4467
North Mountain Pine Training Center (See Executive Protection Institute)
North Specialty Products, 2664-B Saturn St., Brea, CA 92621/714-524-1665
North Star West, P.O. Box 488, Glencoe, CA 95232/209-293-7010
Northern Precision Custom Swaged Bullets, 329 S. James St., Carthage, NY 13619/315-493-1711
No-Sho Mfg. Co., 10727 Glenfield Ct., Houston, TX 77096/713-723-5332
Nosler, Inc., P.O. Box 671, Bend, OR 97709/800-285-3701, 503-382-3921; FAX: 503-388-4667
Novak's, Inc., 1206 1/2 30th St., P.O. Box 4045, Parkersburg, WV 26101/304-485-9295; FAX: 304-428-6722

Nowlin Custom Mfg., Rt. 1, Box 308, Claremore, OK 74017/918-342-0689; FAX: 918-342-0624

NRI Schools, 4401 Connecticut Ave. NW, Washington, D.C. 20008

Nu-Line Guns, Inc., 1053 Caulks Hill Rd., Harvester, MO 63304/314-441-4500; FAX: 314-447-5018

Null Holsters Ltd., K.L., 161 School St. NW, Hill City Station, Resaca, GA 30735/706-625-5643; FAX: 706-625-9392

Numrich Arms Corp., 203 Broadway, W. Hurley, NY 12491

Nu-Teck, 30 Industrial Park Rd., Box 37, Centerbrook, CT 06409/203-767-3573; FAX: 203-767-9137

NW Sinker and Tackle, 380 Valley Dr., Myrtle Creek, OR 97457-9717

Nygord Precision Products, P.O. Box 8394, La Crescenta, CA 91224/818-352-3027; FAX: 818-352-3378

O

Oakland Custom Arms, Inc., 4690 W. Walton Blvd., Waterford, MI 48329/810-674-8261

Oakshore Electronic Sights, Inc., P.O. Box 4470, Ocala, FL 32678-4470/904-629-7112; FAX: 904-629-1433

O'Connor Rifle Products Co., Ltd., 2008 Maybank Hwy., Charleston, SC 29412/803-795-8894

Ociober Country, P.O. Box 969, Dept. GD, Hayden Lake, ID 83835/208-772-2068

Oehler Research, Inc., P.O. Box 9135, Austin, TX 78766/208-772-2068, 800-531-5125

Oglesby & Oglesby Gunmakers, Inc., RR 5, Springfield, IL 62707/217-487-7100

Oil Rod and Gun Shop, 69 Oak St., East Douglas, MA 01516/508-476-3687

Ojala Holsters, Arvo, P.O. Box 98, N. Hollywood, CA 91603/503-669-1404

OK Weber, Inc., P.O. Box 7485, Eugene, OR 97401/503-747-0458; FAX: 503-747-5927

Oker's Engraving, 365 Bell Rd., P.O. Box 126, Shawnee, CO 80475/303-838-6042

Oklahoma Ammunition Co., 4310 W. Rogers Blvd., Shiatook, OK 74070/918-396-3187; FAX: 918-396-4270

Oklahoma Leather Products, Inc., 500 26th NW, Miami, OK 74354/918-542-6651

Old Dominion Engravers, 100 Progress Drive, Lynchburg, VA 24502/804-237-4450

Old Wagon Bullets, 32 Old Wagon Rd., Wilton, CT 06897

Old West Bullet Moulds, P.O. Box 519, Flora Vista, NM 87415/505-334-6970

Old West Reproductions, Inc., 446 Florence S. Loop, Florence, MT 59833/406-273-2615

Old Western Scrounger, Inc., 12924 Hwy. A-l2, Montague, CA 96064/916-459-5445; FAX: 916-459-3944

Old World Oil Products, 3827 Queen Ave. N., Minneapolis, MN 55412/612-522-5037

Olde Pennsylvania, P.O. Box 912, New Kensington, PA 15068/412-337-1552

Ole Frontier Gunsmith Shop, 2617 Hwy. 29 S., Cantonment, FL 32533/904-477-8074

Olsen Development Lab, 111 Lakeview Ave., Blackwood, NJ 08012

Olson, Myron, 989 W. Kemp, Watertown, SD 57201/605-886-9787

Olson, Vic, 5002 Countryside Dr., Imperial, MO 63052/314-296-8086

Olympic Arms, Inc., 624 Old Pacific Hwy. SE, Olympia, WA 98503/206-456-3471; FAX: 206-491-3447

Olympic Optical Co., P.O. Box 752377, Memphis, TN 38175-2377/901-794-3890, 800-238-7120; FAX: 901-794-0676

Omark Industries, Div. of Blount, Inc., 2299 Snake River Ave., P.O. Box 856, Lewiston, ID 83501/800-627-3640, 208-746-2351

Omniohook, 2219 Verde Oak Drive, Hollywood, CA 90068

OMR Feinmechanik, Jagd-und Sportwaffen, GmbH, Postfach 1231, Schutzenstr. 20, D-5400 Koblenz, GERMANY/0261-31865-15351

Op-Tec, P.O. Box L632, Langhorn, PA 19047/215-757-5037

Optolyth-USA, Inc., 18805 Melvista Lane, Hillsboro, OR 97123/503-628-0246; FAX: 503-628-0797

Orchard Park Enterprise, P.O. Box 563, Orchard Park, NY 14227/616-656-0356

Ordnance Works, The, 2969 Pidgeon Point Road, Eureka, CA 95501/707-443-3252

Original Mink Oil, Inc., P.O. Box 20191, 11021 NE Beach St., Portland, OR 97220/503-255-2814, 800-547-5895; FAX: 503-255-2487

Orion Rifle Barrel Co., RR2, 137 Cobler Village, Kalispell, MT 59901/406-257-5649

Orvis Co., The, Rt. 7, Manchester, VT 05254/802-362-3622 ext. 283; FAX: 802-362-3525

Outa-Site Gun Carriers, 219 Market, Laredo, TX 78040/210-722-4678, 800-880-9715; FAX: 210-726-4858

Outdoor Connection, Inc., The, 201 Douglas, P.O. Box 7751, Waco, TX 76712/800-533-6076; 817-772-5575; FAX: 817-776-6076

Outdoor Sports Headquarters, Inc., 967 Watertower Lane, Dayton, OH 45449/513-865-5855; FAX: 513-865-5962

Outdoorsman's Bookstore, The, Llangorse, Brecon, Powys LD3 7UE, U.K./44-87484-660; FAX: 44-87484-650

Outers Laboratories, Div. of Blount, Inc., Route 2, Onalaska, WI 54650/608-781-5800

Owen, Harry, Sport Specialties, 100 N. Citrus Ave. 412, W. Covina, CA 91791-1614/818-968-5806

Ox-Yoke Originals, Inc., 34 Main St., Milo, ME 04463/501-631-6944; FAX: 501-631-6944

Ozark Gun Works, 11830 Cemetery Rd., Rogers, AR 72756/501-631-6944; FAX: 501-631-6944

P

P&M Sales and Service, 5724 Gainsborough Pl., Oak Forest, IL 60452/708-687-7149

P&S Gun Service, 2138 Old Shepardsville Rd., Louisville, KY 40218/502-456-9346

Pace Marketing, Inc., 9474 NW 48th St., Sunrise, FL 33351-5137/305-741-4361; FAX: 305-741-2901

Pachmayr Ltd., 1875 S. Mountain Ave., Monrovia, CA 91016/818-357-7771, 800-423-9704; FAX: 818-358-7251

Pacific Pistolcraft, 1810 E. Columbia Ave., Tacoma, WA 98404/206-474-5465

Pacific Tool Co., P.O. Box 2048, Ordnance Plant Rd., Grand Island, NE 68801

Pac-Nor Barreling, 99299 Overlook Rd., P.O. Box 6188, Brookings, OR 97415/503-469-7330; FAX: 503-469-7331

Paco's (See Small Custom Mould & Bullet Co.)

P.A.C.T., Inc., P.O. Box 531525, Grand Prairie, TX 75053/214-641-0049

Page Custom Bullets, P.O. Box 25, Port Moresby Papua, NEW GUINEA

Pagel Gun Works, Inc., 1407 4th St. NW, Grand Rapids, MN 55744/218-326-3003

Palmer Metal Products, 2930 N. Campbell Ave., Chicago, IL 60618/800-788-7725; FAX: 312-267-8080

Palmgren Steel Products, 8383 S. Chicago Ave., Chicago, IL 60617/312-721-9675; FAX: 312-721-9739

PanaVise Products, Inc., 1485 Southern Way, Sparks, NV 89431/702-353-2900; FAX: 702-353-2929

Para-Ordnance, Inc., 1919 NE 45th St., Ft. Lauderdale, FL 33308

Para-Ordnance Mfg., Inc., 3411 McNicoll Ave., Unit 14, Scarborough, Ont. M1V 2V6, CANADA/416-297-7855; FAX: 416-297-1289 (U.S. importer—Para-Ordnance, Inc.)

Paragon Sales & Services, Inc., P.O. Box 2022, Joliet, IL 60434/815-725-9212; FAX: 815-725-8974

Pardini Armi Commerciale Srl, Via Italica 154, 55043 Lido Di Camaiore Lu, ITALY/584-90121; FAX: 584-90122 (U.S. importers—MCS, Inc.; Nygord Precision Products)

Paris, Frank J., 17417 Pershing St., Livonia, MI 48152-3822

Parke-Bernet (See Sotheby's)

Parker, Mark D., 1240 Florida Ave. 7, Longmont, CO 80501/303-772-0214

Parker Div. Reageant Chemical (See Parker Reproductions)

Parker Gun Finishes, 9337 Smokey Row Rd., Strawberry Plains, TN 37871/615-933-3286

Parker Reproductions, 124 River Rd., Middlesex, NJ 08846/908-469-0100; FAX: 908-469-9692

Parker-Hale (See U.S. distributor—Navy Arms Co.)

Parsons Optical Mfg. Co., P.O. Box 192, Ross, OH 45061/513-867-0820

Parts & Surplus, P.O. Box 22074, Memphis, TN 38122/901-683-4007

Pasadena Gun Center, 206 E. Shaw, Pasadena, TX 77506/713-472-0417; FAX: 713-472-1322

PAST Sporting Goods, Inc., P.O. Box 1035, Columbia, MO 65205/314-445-9200

Paterson Gunsmithing, 438 Main St., Paterson, NJ 07502/201-345-4100

Pathfinder Sports Leather, 2920 E. Chambers St., Phoenix, AZ 85040/602-276-0016

Patrick Bullets, P.O. Box 172, Warwick QSLD 4370 AUSTRALIA

Patriot Manufacturing, P.O. Box 50065, Lighthouse Point, FL 33074/305-783-4849

Pattern Control, 114 N. Third St., Garland, TX 75040/214-494-3551

Paul Co., The, 27385 Pressonville Rd., Wellsville, KS 66092/913-883-4444; FAX: 913-883-2525

Peacemaker Specialists, John Kopec Enterprises, P.O. Box 157, Whitmore, CA 96096/916-472-3438

Pease Accuracy, Bob, P.O. Box 310787, New Braunfels, TX 78131/210-625-1342

Peasley, David, P.O. Box 604, 2067 S. Hiway 17, Alamosa, CO 81101

PECAR Herbert Schwarz, GmbH, Kreuzbergstrasse 6, 10965 Berlin, GERMANY/004930-785-7383; FAX: 004930-785-1934

Pecatonica River Longrifle, 5205 Noddingham Dr., Rockford, IL 61111/815-968-1995; FAX: 815-968-1996

Pedersen, C.R., 2717 S. Pere Marquette Hwy., Ludington, MI 49431/616-843-2061

Pedersen, Rex C., 2717 S. Pere Marquette Hwy., Ludington, MI 49431/616-843-2061

Pedersoli Davide & C., Via Artigiani 53, Gardone V.T. (BS) ITALY 25063/030-8912402; FAX: 030-0911019 (U.S. importers—Beauchamp & Son, Inc.; Cabela's; Dixie Gun Works; EMF Co., Inc.; Navy Arms Co.)

Peerless Alloy, Inc., 1445 Osage St., Denver, CO 80204/303-825-6394, 800-253-1278

Pejsa Ballistics, 2120 Kenwood Pkwy., Minneapolis, MN 55405/612-374-3337; FAX: 612-374-3337

Peltor, Inc., 41 Commercial Way, E. Providence, RI 02914/401-438-4800; FAX: 800-EAR-FAX1

PEM's Mfg. Co., 5063 Waterloo Rd., Atwater, OH 44201/216-947-3721

Pence Precision Barrels, 7567 E. 900 S., S. Whitley, IN 46787/219-839-4745

Pend Oreille Sport Shop, 3100 Hwy. 200 East, Sandpoint, ID 83864/208-263-2412

Pendleton Royal, 4/7 Highgate St., Birmingham, ENGLAND B12 0X5/44 21 440 3060; FAX: 44 21 446 4165

Penguin Industries, Inc., Airport Industrial Mall, Coatesville, PA 19320/215-384-6000

Penn Bullets, P.O. Box 756, Indianola, PA 15051

Pennsylvania Gun Parts, 638 Whiskey Spring Rd., Boiling Springs, PA 17007/717-258-5683

Pennsylvania Gunsmith School, 812 Ohio River Blvd., Avalon, Pittsburgh, PA 15202/412-766-1812

Penrod Precision, 312 College Ave., P.O. Box 307, N. Manchester, IN 46962/219-982-8385

Pentax Corp., 35 Inverness Dr. E., Englewood, CO 80112/303-799-8000

Pentheny de Pentheny, 2352 Baggett Ct., Santa Rosa, CA 95401/707-573-1390; FAX: 707-573-1390

Perazzi m.a.p. S.P.A., Via Fontanelle 1/3, 1-25080 Botticino Mattina, ITALY (U.S. importer—Perazzi USA, Inc.)

Perazzi USA, Inc., 1207 S. Shamrock Ave., Monrovia, CA 91016/818-303-0068

Performance Specialists, 308 Eanes School Rd., Austin, TX 78746/512-327-0119

Peripheral Data Systems (See Arms)

Personal Protection Systems, RD 5, Box 5027-A, Moscow, PA 18444/717-842-1766

Perugini Visini & Co. s.r.l., Via Camprelle, 126, 25080 Nuvolera (Bs.), ITALY

Peters Stahl GmbH, Stettiner Str. 42, D-4790 Paderborn, GERMANY/05251-750025-27; FAX: 05251-75611 (U.S. importers—McMillan Gunworks, Inc.; Olympic Arms)

Petersen Publishing Co., 6420 Wilshire Blvd., Los Angeles, CA 90048

Peterson Gun Shop, A.W., Inc., 4255 W. Old U.S. 441, Mt. Dora, FL 32757-3299/904-383-4258

Petro-Explo, Inc., 7650 U.S. Hwy. 287, Suite 100, Arlington, TX 76017/817-478-8888

Pettinger Books, Gerald, Rt. 2, Box 125, Russell, IA 50238/515-535-2239

PFRB Co., P.O. Box 1242, Bloomington, IL 61701/309-473-3964

Phelps Mfg. Co., Box 2266, Evansville, IN 47714/812-476-8791

Phil-Chem, Inc., 2950 NW 29th, Portland, OR 97210/800-553-3022

Phillippi Custom Bullets, Justin, P.O. Box 773, Ligonier, PA 15658/412-238-9671

Phoenix Arms, 1420 S. Archibald Ave., Ontario, CA 91761/909-947-4843; FAX: 909-947-6798

Phoenix Arms Co. Ltd. (See Hy-Score Arms Co. Ltd.)

Photronic Systems Engineering Company, 6731 Via De La Reina, Bonsall, CA 92003/619-758-8000

Phyl-Mac, 609 NE 104th Ave., Vancouver, WA 98664/206-256-0579

Piedmont Community College, P.O. Box 1197, Roxboro, NC 27573/910-599-1181

Pierce Pistols, 2326 E. Hwy. 34, Newnan, GA 30263/404-253-8192

Pilgrim Pewter, Inc. (See Bell Originals, Sid)

Pilkington, Scott, Little Trees Ramble, P.O. Box 97, Monteagle, TN 37356/615-924-3475; FAX: 615-924-3489

Pilkington Gun Co., P.O. Box 1296, Muskogee, OK 74402/918-683-9418

Pine Technical College, 1100 4th St., Pine City, MN 55063/800-521-7463; FAX: 612-629-6766

Pioneer Arms Co., 355 Lawrence Rd., Broomall, OA 19008/215-356-5203

Pioneer Guns, 5228 Montgomery Rd., Norwood, OH 45212/513-631-4871

Pioneer Research, Inc., 216 Haddon Ave., Westmont, NJ 08108/609-854-2424, 800-257-7742; FAX: 609-858-8695

Piotti (See U.S. importer—Moore & Co., Wm. Larkin)

Piquette, Paul R., 80 Bradford Dr., Feeding Hills, MA 01030/413-781-8300, Ext. 682

Plaxco, J. Michael, Rt. 1, P.O. Box 203, Roland, AR 72135/501-868-9787

Plum City Ballistic Range, N2162 80th St., Plum City, WI 54761-8622/715-647-2539

P.M. Enterprises, Inc., 146 Curtis Hill Rd., Chehalis, WA 98532/206-748-3743; FAX: 206-748-1802

PMC/Eldorado Cartridge Corp., P.O. Box 62508, 12801 U.S. Hwy. 95 S., Boulder City, NV 89006-2508/702-294-0025; FAX: 702-294-0121

Pointing Dog Journal, Village Press Publications, P.O. Box 968, Dept. PGD, Traverse City, MI 49685/800-272-3246; FAX: 616-946-3289

Police Bookshelf, P.O. Box 122, Concord, NH 03301/603-224-6814; FAX: 603-226-3554

Policlips North America, 59 Douglas Crescent, Toronto, Ont. CANADA M4W 2E6/800-229-5089, 416-924-0383; FAX: 416-924-4375

Poly Technologies, Inc. (See U.S. importer—Keng's Firearms Specialty, Inc.)

Polywad, Inc., P.O. Box 7916, Macon, GA 31209/912-477-0669

Pomeroy, Robert, RR1, Box 50, E. Corinth, ME 04427/207-285-7721

Ponsness/Warren, P.O. Box 8, Rathdrum, ID 83858/208-687-2231; FAX: 208-687-2233

Pony Express Reloaders, 608 E. Co. Rd. D, Suite 3, St. Paul, MN 55117/612-483-9406; FAX: 612-483-9884

Pony Express Sport Shop, Inc., 16606 Schoenborn St., North Hills, CA 91343/818-895-1231

Portus, Robert, 130 Ferry Rd., Grants Pass, OR 97526/503-476-4919

Potts, Wayne E., 912 Poplar St., Denver, CO 80220/303-355-5462

Powder Horn, Inc., The, P.O. Box 114 Patty Drive, Cusseta, GA 31805/404-989-3257

Powder Horn Antiques, P.O. Box 4196, Ft. Lauderdale, FL 33338/305-565-6060

Power Custom, Inc., RR 2, P.O. Box 756AB, Gravois Mills, MO 65037/314-372-5684

PPC Corp., 627 E. 24th St., Paterson, NJ 07514/201-278-5428

Practical Tools, Inc., Div. Behlert Precision, 7067 Easton Rd., P.O. Box 133, Pipersville, PA 18947/215-766-7301; FAX: 215-766-8681

Pragotrade, 307 Humberline Dr., Rexdale, Ontario, CANADA M9W 5V1/416-675-1322

Precise Metal Finishing, John Westrom, P.O. Box 3186, Des Moines, IA 50316/515-288-8680; FAX: 515-244-3925

Precise Metalsmithing Enterprises, 146 Curtis Hill Rd., Chehalis, WA 98532/206-748-3743; FAX: 206-748-8102

Precision, Jim, 1725 Moclip's Dr., Petaluma, CA 94952/707-762-3014

Precision Airgun Sales, Inc., 5139 Warrensville Center Rd., Maple Hts., OH 44137-1906/216-587-5005

Precision Ballistics Co., P.O. Box 4374, Hamden, CT 06514/203-373-2293

Precision Bullet Co., 5200 A. Florence Loop, Dunsmuir, CA 96025/916-235-0565

Precision Cartridge, 176 Eastside Rd., Deer Lodge, MT 59722/800-397-3901, 406-846-3900

Precision Cast Bullets, 101 Mud Creek Lane, Ronan, MT 59864/406-676-5135

Precision Castings & Equipment, Inc., P.O. Box 326, Jasper, IN 47547-0135/812-634-9167

Precision Components and Guns, Rt. 55, P.O. Box 337, Pawling, NY 12564/914-855-3040

Precision Components, 3177 Sunrise Lake, Milford, PA 18337/717-686-4414

Precision Delta Corp., P.O. Box 128, Ruleville, MS 38771/601-756-2810; FAX: 601-756-2590

Precision Metal Finishing, John Westrom, P.O. Box 3186, Des Moines, IA 50316/515-288-8680; FAX: 515-244-3925

Precision Munitions, Inc., P.O. Box 326, Jasper, IN 47547

Precision Ordnance, 1316 E. North St., Jackson, MI 49202

Precision Reloading, Inc., P.O. Box 122, Stafford Springs, CT 06076/203-684-7979; FAX: 203-684-6788

Precision Rifles, Inc., 9814 Harney Bkwy. N., Omaha, NE 68114/402-397-3009; FAX: 402-393-7705

Precision Rifles, Inc., 19303 Ossenfort Ct., St. Louis, MO 63038/314-273-5159; FAX: 314-273-5149

Precision Sales International, Inc., P.O. Box 1776, Westfield, MA 01086/413-562-5055; FAX: 413-562-5056

Precision Shooting, Inc., 5735 Sherwood Forest Dr., Akron, OH 44319/216-882-2515; FAX: 216-882-2214

Precision Small Parts, Inc., 155 Carlton Rd., Charlottesville, VA 22902/804-293-6124

Precision Specialties, 131 Hendom Dr., Feeding Hills, MA 01030/413-786-3365; FAX: 413-786-3365

Precision Sport Optics, 15571 Producer Lane, Unit G, Huntington Beach, CA 92649/714-891-1309; FAX: 714-892-6920

Premier Reticles, 920 Breckinridge Lane, Winchester, VA 22601-6707

Prescott Projectile Co., 1808 Meadowbrook Road, Prescott, AZ

Preslik's Gunstocks, 4245 Keith Ln., Chico, CA 95926/916-891-8236

Pre-Winchester 92-90-62 Parts Co., P.O. Box 8125, W. Palm Beach, FL 33407

Price Bullets, Patrick W., 16520 Worthley Drive, San Lorenzo, CA 94580/510-278-1547

Prime Reloading, 30 Chiswick End, Meldreth, Royston SG8 6LZ UK

Primos Wild Game Calls, Inc., P.O. Box 12785, Jackson, MS 39236-2785/601-366-1288; FAX: 601-362-3274

Pro Load Ammunition, Inc., 5180 E. Seltice Way, Post Falls, ID 83854/208-773-9444; FAX: 208-773-9441

Pro-Port Ltd., 41302 Executive Dr., Harrison Twp., MI 48045-3448/810-469-7323; FAX: 810-469-0425

Pro-Shot Products, Inc., P.O. Box 763, Taylorville, IL 62568/217-824-9133; FAX: 217-824-8861

Professional Firearms Record Book Co. (See PFRB Co.)

Professional Gunsmiths of America, Inc., 1301 Franklin, Lexington, MO 64067/816-259-2636

Professional Hunter Supplies (See Star Custom Bullets)

Prolix, P.O. Box 1348, Victorville, CA 92393/800-248-LUBE, 619-243-3129; FAX: 619-241-0148

Protector Mfg. Co., Inc., The, 443 Ashwood Place, Boca Raton, FL 33431/407-394-6011

Protektor Model, 1-11 Bridge St., Galeton, PA 16922/814-435-2442

ProWare, Inc., 15847 NE Hancock St., Portland, OR 97230/503-239-0159

P.S.M.G. Gun Co., 10 Park Ave., Arlington, MA 02174/617-646-8845; FAX: 617-646-2133

PWL Gunleather, P.O. Box 450432, Atlanta, GA 31145/404-822-1640; FAX: 404-822-1704

Q

Quack Decoy & Sporting Clays, 4 Ann & Hope Way, P.O. Box 98, Cumberland, RI 02864/401-723-8202; FAX: 401-722-5910

Qualigraphics, Inc., 25 Ruta Ct., P.O. Box 2306, S. Hackensack, NJ 07606/201-440-9200

Quality Firearms of Idaho, Inc., 114 13th Ave. S., Nampa, ID 83651/208-466-1631

Quality Parts Co./Bushmaster Firearms, 999 Roosevelt Trail, Bldg. 3, Windham, ME 04062/800-998-7928, 207-892-2005; FAX: 207-892-8068

Quartz-Lok, 13137 N. 21st Lane, Phoenix, AZ 85029

Quigley's Personal Protection Strategies, Paxton, 9903 Santa Monica Blvd.,, 300/Beverly Hills, CA 90212/310-281-1762

Quinetics Corp., P.O. Box 13237, San Antonio, TX 78213/512-684-8561; FAX: 512-684-2912

R

R&S Industries Corp., 8255 Brentwood Industrial Dr., St. Louis, MO 63144/314-781-5400

Rabeno, Martin, 92 Spook Hole Rd., Ellenville, NY 12428/914-647-4567

Radiator Specialty Co., 1900 Wilkinson Blvd., P.O. Box 34689, Charlotte, NC 28234/800-438-6947; FAX: 800-421-9525

Radical Concepts, P.O. Box 10731, Canoga Park, CA 91309-1731

Rainier Ballistics Corp., 4500 15th St. East, Tacoma, WA 98424/800-638-8722, 206-922-7589; FAX: 206-922-7854

Ram-Line, Inc., 545 Thirty-One Rd., Grand Junction, CO 81504/303-434-4500; FAX: 303-434-4004

Ranch Products, P.O. Box 145, Malinta, OH 43535/313-277-3118; FAX: 313-565-8536

Randall Firearms Research, P.O. Box 1586, Lomita, CA 90717-5586/310-325-0102; FAX: 310-325-0298

Randco UK, 286 Gipsy Rd., Welling, Kent DA16 1JJ, ENGLAND/44 81 303 4118

Randolph Engineering, Inc., 26 Thomas Patten Dr., Randolph, MA 02368/800-541-1405; FAX: 617-986-0337

Ranger Shooting Glasses, 26 Thomas Patten Dr., Randolph, MA 02368/800-541-1405; FAX: 617-986-0337

Ranging, Inc., Routes 5 & 20, East Bloomfield, NY 14443/716-657-6161

Ransom International Corp., P.O. Box 3845, 1040-A Sandretto Dr., Prescott, AZ 86302/602-778-7899; FAX: 602-778-7993

Rapine Bullet Mould Mfg. Co., 9503 Landis Lane, East Greenville, PA 18041/215-679-5413; FAX: 215-679-9795

Ravell Ltd., 289 Diputacion St., 08009, Barcelona SPAIN

Raytech, Div. of Lyman Products Corp., Rt. 32 Stafford Ind. Park, Box 6, Stafford Springs, CT 06076/203-684-4273; FAX: 203-684-7938

RCBS, Div. of Blount, Inc., 605 Oro Dam Blvd., Oroville, CA 95965/800-533-5000, 916-533-5191

R.D.P. Tool Co., Inc., 49162 McCoy Ave., East Liverpool, OH 43920/216-385-5129

Reagent Chemical & Research, Inc. (See Calico Hardwoods, Inc.)

Reardon Products, P.O. Box 126, Morrison, IL 61270/815-772-3155

Red Diamond Dist. Co., 1304 Snowdon Dr., Knoxville, TN 37912

Red River Frontier Outfitters, P.O. Box 241, Dept. GD, Tujunga, CA 91043/818-821-3167

Red Star Target Co., 4519 Brisebois Dr. NW, Calgary AB T2L 2G3 CANADA/403-289-7939; FAX: 403-289-3275

Redding Reloading Equipment, 1089 Starr Rd., Cortland, NY 13045/607-753-3331; FAX: 607-756-8445

Redfield, Inc., 5800 E. Jewell Ave., Denver, CO 80224/303-757-6411; FAX: 303-756-2338

Redman's Rifling & Reboring, Rt. 3, Box 330A, Omak, WA 98841/509-826-5512

Redmist Rifles, 316 W. Olive, Fresno, CA 93728/209-266-6363; FAX: 209-266-4638

Redwood Bullet Works, 3559 Bay Rd., Redwood City, CA 94063/415-367-6741

Reed, Dave, Rt. 1, Box 374, Minnesota City, MN 55959/507-689-2944

Reedy & Assoc., C.L., 2485 Grassmere Dr., Melbourne, FL 32904

Regional Associates, 6932 Little River Turnpike, Annandale, VA 22003/703-914-9338

R.E.I., P.O. Box 88, Tallevast, FL 34270/813-755-0085

Reloaders Equipment Co., 4680 High St., Ecorse, MI 48229

Reloading Specialties, Inc., Box 1130, Pine Island, MN 55963/507-356-8500; FAX: 507-356-8800

Remington Arms Co., Inc., 1007 Market St., Wilmington, DE 19898/302-773-5291

Rencher Bullets, 5161 NE 5th St., Redmond, OR 97756

Renegade, P.O. Box 31546, Phoenix, AZ 85046/602-482-6777; FAX: 602-482-1952

Renner Co., R.J./Radical Concepts, P.O. Box 10731, Canoga Park, CA 91309/818-700-8131
Reno, Wayne, 2808 Stagestop Rd., Jefferson, CO 80456/719-836-3452
R.E.T. Enterprises, 2608 S. Chestnut, Broken Arrow, OK 74012/918-251-GUNS; FAX: 918-251-0587
Retting, Inc., Martin B., 11029 Washington, Culver City, CA 90232/213-837-2412
Reynolds, Lois M., 321 Lindenwood Ln. S., Hewitt, TX 76643/817-669-9686
Rice, Keith (See White Rock Tool & Die)
Richards Classic Oil Finish, John, Rt. 2, Box 325, Bedford, KY 40006/502-255-7222
Rickard, Inc., Pete, RD 1, Box 292, Cobleskill, NY 12043/800-282-5663; FAX: 518-234-2454
Ridgetop Sporting Goods, P.O. Box 306, 42907 Hilligoss Ln. East, Eatonville, WA 98328/206-832-6422
Riebe Co., W.J., 3434 Tucker Rd., Boise, ID 83703
Ries, Chuck, 415 Ridgecrest Dr., Grants Pass, OR 97527/503-476-5623
Rifle Shop, The, Wm. H. Hobaugh, P.O. Box M, Philipsburg, MT 59858/406-859-3515
Rifle Works & Armory, 707 N 12 St., Cody, WY 82414/307-587-4914
RIG Products, 87 Coney Island Dr., Sparks, NV 89431-6334/702-331-5666; FAX: 702-331-5669
Riggs, Jim, 206 Azalea, Boerne, TX 78006/210-249-8567
Riling Arms Books Co., Ray, 6844 Gorsten St., P.O. Box 18925, Philadelphia, PA 19119/215-438-2456
Rim Pac Sports, Inc., 1034 N. Soldano Ave., Azusa, CA 9170222-2135
Ringler Custom Leather Co., P.O. Box 206, Cody, WY 82414/307-645-3255
R.I.S. Co., Inc., 718 Timberlake Circle, Richardson, TX 75080/214-235-0933
River Road Sporting Clays, Bruce Barsotti, P.O. Box 3016, Gonzales, CA 93926/408-675-2473
Rizzini, F.LLI (See U.S. importers—Moore & Co., Wm. Larkin; New England Arms Co.)
Rizzini Battista, Via 2 Giugno, 7/7Bis-25060 Marcheno (Brescia), ITALY (U.S. importer—Alessandri & Son, Lou)
RLCM Enterprises, 110 Hill Crest Drive, Burleson, TX 76028
RMS Custom Gunsmithing, 4120 N. Bitterwell, Prescott Valley, AZ 86314/602-772-7626
Robar Co.'s, Inc., The, 21438 N. 7th Ave., Suite B, Phoenix, AZ 85027/602-581-2648; FAX: 602-582-0059
Roberts, J.J., 7808 Lake Dr., Manassas, VA 22111/703-330-0448
Roberts Products, 25238 SE 32nd, Issaquah, WA 98027/206-392-8172
Robinson, Don, Pennsylvania Hse., 36 Fairfax Crescent, Southowram, Halifax, W. Yorkshire HX3 9SQ, ENGLAND/0422-364458
Robinson H.V. Bullets, 3145 Church St., Zachary, LA 70791/504-654-4029
Rochester Lead Works, 76 Anderson Ave., Rochester, NY 14607/716-442-8500
Rockwood Corp., Speedwell Division, 136 Lincoln Blvd., Middlesex, NJ 08846/908-560-7171
Rocky Fork Enterprises, P.O. Box 427, 878 Battle Rd., Nolensville, TN 37135/615-941-1307
Rocky Mountain Arms, Inc., 600 S. Sunset, Unit C, Longmont, CO 80501/303-768-8522; FAX: 303-678-8766
Rocky Mountain High Sports Glasses, 8121 N. Central Park Ave., Skokie, IL 60076/708-679-1012; FAX: 708-679-0184
Rocky Mountain Target Co., 3 Aloe Way, Leesburg, FL 34788/904-365-9598
Rocky Shoes & Boots, 294 Harper St., Nelsonville, OH 45764/800-421-5151, 614-753-1951; FAX: 614-753-4042
Rod Guide Co., Box 1149, Forsyth, MO 65653/800-952-2774
Rogers Gunsmithing, Bob, P.O. Box 305, 344 S. Walnut St., Franklin Grove, IL 61031/815-456-2685; FAX: 815-288-7142
Rohner, Hans, 1148 Twin Sisters Ranch Rd., Nederland, CO 80466-9600
Rohner, John, 710 Sunshine Canyon, Boulder, CO 80302/303-444-3841
Rolston Jr., Fred W., 210 E. Cummins St., Tecumseh, MI 49286/517-423-6002; FAX: 517-423-6002
Romain's Custom Guns, RD 1, Whetstone Rd., Brockport, PA 15823/814-265-1948
Rooster Laboratories, P.O. Box 412514, Kansas City, MO 64141/816-474-1622; FAX: 816-474-1307
Rorschach Precision Products, P.O. Box 151613, Irving, TX 75015/214-790-3487
Rosenberg & Sons, Jack A., 12229 Cox Lane, Dallas, TX 75234/214-241-6302
Rosenthal, Brad and Sallie, 19303 Ossenfort Ct., St. Louis, MO 63038/314-273-5159; FAX: 314-273-5149
Ross, Don, 12813 West 83 Terrace, Lenexa, KS 66215/913-492-6982
Rosser, Bob, 267 W. Valley Ave., Suite 158, Birmingham, AL 35209/205-870-4422
Rossi S.A., Amadeo, Rua: Amadeo Rossi, 143, Sao Leopoldo, RS, BRAZIL 93030-220/051-592-5566 (U.S. importer—Interarms)
Roto Carve, 2754 Garden Ave., Janesville, IA 50647
Round Edge, Inc., P.O. Box 723, Lansdale, PA 19446/215-361-0859
Rowe Engineering, Inc. (See R.E.I.)
Roy's Custom Grips, Rt. 3, Box 174-E, Lynchburg, VA 24504/804-993-3470
RPM, 15481 N. Twin Lakes Dr., Tucson, AZ 85737/602-825-1233; FAX: 602-825-3333
Rubright Bullets, 1008 S. Quince Rd., Walnutport, PA 18088/215-767-1339
Rucker Ammunition Co., P.O. Box 479, Terrell, TX 75160
Rudnicky, Susan, 8714 Center St., Holland, NY 14080/716-941-3259
Ruger (See Sturm, Ruger & Co.)
Ruko Products, Inc., P.O. Box 1181, Buffalo NY 14240-1181/905-874-2707; FAX: 905-826-1353
Rundell's Gun Shop, 6198 Frances Rd., Clio, MI 48420/313-687-0559
Runge, Robert P., 94 Grove St., Ilion, NY 13357/315-894-3036
Rupert's Gun Shop, 2202 Dick Rd., Suite B, Fenwick, MI 48834/517-248-3252
Rusteprufe Laboratories, 1319 Jefferson Ave., Sparta, WI 54656/608-269-4144
Rusty Duck Premium Gun Care Products, 7785 Founion Dr., Florence, KY 41042/606-342-5553
Rutgers Book Center, 127 Raritan Ave., Highland Park, NJ 08904/908-545-4344; FAX: 908-545-6686
Rutgers Gun & Boat Center, 127 Raritan Ave., Highland Park, NJ 08904/908-545-4344; FAX: 908-545-6686

Ruvel & Co., Inc., 4128-30 W. Belmont Ave., Chicago, IL 60641/312-286-9494
R.V.I., P.O. Box 8019-56, Blaine, WA 98230/206-595-2933
RWS (See U.S. importer—Dynamit Nobel-RWS, Inc.)
Rybka Custom Leather Equipment, Thad, 32 Havilah Hill, Odenville, AL 35120

S

S&B Industries, 11238 McKinley Rd., Montrose, MI 48457/313-639-5491
S&K Mfg. Co., P.O. Box 247, Pittsfield, PA 16340/814-563-7808; FAX: 814-563-7808
S&S Firearms, 74-11 Myrtle Ave., Glendale, NY 11385/718-497-1100; FAX: 718-497-1105
Sabertooth Industries, P.O. Box 772, Santa Clara, CA 95052
SAECO (See Redding Reloading Equipment)
Safari Arms/SGW (See Olympic Arms, Inc.)
Safari Outfitters Ltd., 71 Ethan Allan Hwy., Ridgefield, CT 06877/203-544-9505
Safari Plus, 218 Quinlan, Suite 322, Kerrville, TX 78028-5314/210-367-5209
Safari Press, Inc., 15621 Chemical Lane B, Huntington Beach, CA 92649/714-894-9080; FAX: 714-894-4949
Safariland Ltd., Inc., 3120 E. Mission Blvd., P.O. Box 51478, Ontario, CA 91761/909-923-7300; FAX: 909-923-7400
SAFE, P.O. Box 864, Post Falls, ID 83854/208-773-3624
Safesport Manufacturing Co., 1100 W. 45th Ave., Denver, CO 80211/303-433-6506; FAX: 303-433-4112
Safety Speed Holster, Inc., 910 S. Vail Ave., Montebello, CA 90640/213-723-4140; FAX: 213-726-6973
Sako Ltd., P.O. Box 149, SF-11101, Riihimaki, FINLAND (U.S. importer—Stoeger Industries)
Samco Global Arms, Inc., 6995 NW 43rd St., Miami, FL 33166/305-593-9782
Sampson, Roger, 430 N. Grove, Mora, MN 55051/612-679-4868
San Angelo Sports Products, Inc., 909 W. 14th St., San Angelo, TX 76903/915-655-7126; FAX: 915-653-6720
San Francisco Gun Exchange, 124 Second St., San Francisco, CA 94105/415-982-6097
San Marco (See U.S. importers—Cape Outfitters; EMF Co., Inc.)
Sanders Custom Gun Service, 2358 Tyler Ln., Louisville, KY 40205/502-454-3338
Sanders Gun and Machine Shop, 145 Delhi Road, Manchester, IA 52057
Sandia Die & Ctg. Co., 37 Atancacio Rd. NE, Albuquerque, NM 87123/505-298-5729
Sarco, Inc., 323 Union St., Stirling, NJ 07980/908-647-3800
Sauer (See U.S. importer—Paul Co., The)
Sauer Sporting Rifles, P.O. Box 37669, Omaha, NE 68137
Saunders Gun & Machine Shop, R.R. 2, Delhi Road, Manchester, IA 52057
Savage Arms, Inc., Springdale Rd., Westfield, MA 01085/413-568-7001; FAX: 413-562-7764
Savana Sports, Inc., 5763 Ferrier St., Montreal, Quebec, CANADA/514-739-1753; FAX: 514-739-1755
Scattergun Technologies, Inc., 518 3rd Ave. S., Nashville, TN 37210/615-254-1441
Schaefer Shooting Sports, 2280 Grand Ave., Baldwin, NY 11510/516-379-4900; FAX: 516-379-6701
Scharch Mfg., Inc., 10325 Co. Rd. 120, Unit C, Salida, CO 81201/719-539-7242
Scherer, Box 250, Ewing, VA 24248/615-733-2615; FAX: 615-733-2073
Schiffman, Mike, 8233 S. Crystal Springs, McCammon, ID 83250/208-254-9114
Schmidpke, Karl, P.O. Box 51692, New Berlin, WI 53151
Schmidt & Bender, Inc., Brook Rd., P.O. Box 134, Meriden, NH 03770/603-469-3565, 800-468-3450; FAX: 603-469-3471
Schmidt, Herbert (See U.S. importer—Sportarms of Florida)
Schmidtman Custom Ammunition, 6 Gilbert Court, Cotati, CA 94931
Schneider Bullets, 3655 West 214th St., Fairview Park, OH 44126
School of Gunsmithing, The, 6065 Roswell Rd., Atlanta, GA 30328/800-223-4542
Schulz Industries, 16247 Minnesota Ave., Paramount, CA 90723/213-439-5903
Schumakers Gun Shop, William, 512 Prouty Corner Lp. A, Colville, WA 99114/509-684-4848
Scope Control, Inc., 5775 Co. Rd. 23 SE, Alexandria, MN 56308/612-762-7295
ScopLevel, 977 E. Stanley Blvd. 365, Livermore, CA 94550/510-449-5052; FAX: 510-373-0861
Scot Powder Co., Rt. 1, Box 167, McEwen, TN 37101/615-729-4207; FAX: 615-729-4217
Scott, Dwight, 23089 Englehardt St., Clair Shores, MI 48080/313-779-4735
Scott, McDougall & Associates, 7950 Redwood Dr., Cotati, CA 94931/707-546-2264
Scott Fine Guns, Inc., Thad, P.O. Box 412, Indianola, MS 38751/601-887-5929
Seattle Binocular & Scope Repair Co., P.O. Box 46094, Seattle, WA 98146/206-932-3733
Security Awareness & Firearms Education (See SAFE)
Seebeck Assoc., R.E., P.O. Box 59752, Dallas, TX 75229
Seecamp Co., Inc., L.W., P.O. Box 255, New Haven, CT 06502/203-877-3429
Seligman Shooting Products, Box 133, Seligman, AZ 86337/602-422-3607
Selsi Co., Inc., 40 Veterans Blvd., Carlstadt, NJ 07072-0497/201-935-5851
Semmer, Charles, 7885 Cyd Dr., Denver, CO 80221/303-429-6947
Serva Arms Co., Inc., RD 1, Box 483A, Greene, NY 13778/607-656-4764
Service Armament, 689 Bergen Blvd., Ridgefield, NJ 07657
SGS Importers International, Inc., 1750 Brielle Ave., Unit B1, Wanamassa, NJ 07712/908-493-0302; FAX: 908-493-0301
S.G.S. Sporting Guns Srl., Via Della Resistenza, 37, 20090 Buccinasco (MI) ITALY/2-45702446; FAX: 2-45702464
Shappy Bullets, 76 Milldale Ave., Plantsville, CT 06479/203-621-3704
Sharon Rifle Barrel Co., 14396 D. Tuolumne Rd., Sonora, CA 95370/209-532-4139
Sharp Shooter, Inc., P.O. Box 21362, St. Paul, MN 55121/612-452-4687
Sharps Arms Co., Inc., C. (See Montana Armory, Inc.)
Shay's Gunsmithing, 931 Marvin Ave., Lebanon, PA 17042
Sheffield Knifemakers Supply, P.O. Box 141, Deland, FL 32721/904-775-6453; FAX: 904-774-5754
Shell Shack, 113 E. Main, Laurel, MT 59044/406-628-8986
Shepherd Scope Ltd., Box 189, Waterloo, NE 68069/402-779-2424; FAX: 402-779-4010
Sheridan USA, Inc., Austin, P.O. Box 577, Durham, CT 06422

Sherwood, George, 46 N. River Dr., Roseburg, OR 97470/503-672-3159
Sherwood Intl. Export Corp., 18714 Parthenia St., Northridge, CA 91324/818-349-7600
Shilen Rifles, Inc., P.O. Box 1300, 205 Metro Park Blvd., Ennis, TX 75120/214-875-5318; FAX: 214-875-5402
Shiloh Creek, Box 357, Cottleville, MO 63338/314-447-2900; FAX: 314-447-2900
Shiloh Rifle Mfg., P.O. Box 279, Big Timber, MT 59011/406-932-4454; FAX: 406-932-5627
Shirley Co. Gun & Riflemakers Ltd., J.A., P.O. Box 368, High Wycombe, Bucks. HP13 6YN, ENGLAND/0494-446883; FAX: 0494-463685
Shoemaker & Sons, Inc., Tex, 714 W. Cienega Ave., San Dimas, CA 91750/714-592-2071; FAX: 714-592-2378
Shooter's Choice, 16770 Hilltop Park Place, Chagrin Falls, OH 44023/216-543-8808; FAX: 216-543-8811
Shooter's Edge, Inc., P.O.Box 769, Trinidad, CO 81082
Shooter's Supply, RR1, Box 333B, Rt. 55, Poughquag, NY 12570/914-724-3088; FAX: 914-724-3454
Shooter's World, 3828 N. 28th Ave., Phoenix, AZ 85017/602-266-0170
Shooters Supply, 1120 Tieton Dr., Yakima, WA 98902/509-452-1181
Shootin' Accessories, Ltd., P.O. Box 6810, Auburn, CA 95604/916-889-2220
Shooting Arts Ltd., Box 621399, Littleton, CO 80162/303-933-2539
Shooting Chrony, Inc., 3269 Niagara Falls Blvd., N. Tonawanda, NY 14120/905-276-6292; FAX: 416-276-6295
Shooting Gallery, The, 8070 Southern Blvd., Boardman, OH 44512/216-726-7788
Shooting Star, 1825 Fortview Rd., Ste. 115, Austin, TX 78747/512-462-0009
Shoptask, P.O. Box 591, Montesano, WA 98563/800-343-5775
Shotgun Bullets Mfg., Rt. 3, Box 41, Robinson, IL 62454/618-546-5043
Shotgun Shop, The, 14145 Proctor Ave., Suite 3, Industry, CA 91746/818-855-2737; FAX: 818-855-2735
Shurkatch Corp., P.O. Box 850, Richfield Springs, NY 13439/315-858-1470; FAX: 315-858-2969
Siegrist Gun Shop, 8754 Turtle Road, Whittemore, MI 48770
Sierra Bullets, 1400 W. Henry St., Sedalia, MO 65301/816-827-6300; FAX: 816-827-4999
Sierra Specialty Prod. Co., 1344 Oakhurst Ave., Los Altos, CA 94024
SIG, CH-8212 Neuhausen, SWITZERLAND (U.S. importer—Mandall Shooting Supplies, Inc.)
Sigarms, Inc., Industrial Drive, Exeter, NH 03833/603-772-2302; FAX: 603-772-9082
Sight Shop, The, John G. Lawson, 1802 E. Columbia Ave., Tacoma, WA 98404/206-474-5465
Sightron, Inc., 9000 W. Sheridan St., Pembroke Pines, FL 33024/305-438-4227; FAX: 305-438-3465
Signet Metal Corp., 551 Stewart Ave., Brooklyn, NY 11222/718-384-5400; FAX: 718-388-7488
SIG-Sauer (See U.S. importer—Sigarms, Inc.)
Sile Distributors, Inc., 7 Centre Market Pl., New York, NY 10013/212-925-4389; FAX: 212-925-3149
Silencio/Safety Direct, 56 Coney Island Dr., Sparks, NV 89431/800-648-1812, 702-354-4451; FAX: 702-359-1074
Silhouette Leathers, P.O. Box 1161, Gunnison, CO 81230/303-641-6639
Silver Eagle Machining, 18007 N. 69th Ave., Glendale, AZ 85308
Silver Ridge Gun Shop (See Goodwin, Fred)
Silver-Tip Corp., RR2, Box 184, Gloster, MS 39638-9520
Simmons, Jerry, 715 Middlebury St., Goshen, IN 46526/219-533-8546
Simmons Enterprises, Ernie, 709 East Elizabethtown Rd., Manheim, PA 17545/717-664-4040
Simmons Outdoor Corp., 2120 Killearney Way, Tallahassee, FL 32308-3402/904-878-5100; FAX: 904-878-0300
Sinclair, W.P., Box 1209, Warminster, Wiltshire BA12 9XJ, ENGLAND/01044-985-218544; FAX: 01044-985-214111
Sinclair International, Inc., 2330 Wayne Haven St., Fort Wayne, IN 46803/219-493-1858; FAX: 219-493-2530
Single Shot, Inc. (See Montana Armory, Inc.)
Singletary, Kent, 7516 W. Sells, Phoenix, AZ 85033/602-849-5917
Sioux Bullets, P.O. Box 3696, Midland, TX 79702
Sipes Gun Shop, 7415 Asher Ave., Little Rock, AR 72204/501-565-8480
S.K. Guns, Inc., 3041A Main Ave., Fargo, ND 58103/701-293-4867; FAX: 701-232-0001
Skaggs, R.E., 1217 S. Church St., Princeton, IL 61356/815-875-8207
SKB Arms Co., C.P.O. Box 1401, Tokyo, JAPAN (U.S. importer—G.U., Inc.)
Skeoch, Brian R., P.O. Box 279, Glenrock, WY 82637/307-436-9804; FAX: 307-436-9804
Skip's Machine, 364 29 Road, Grand Junction, CO 81501/303-245-5417
Sklany, Steve, 566 Birch Grove Dr., Kalispell, MT 59901/406-755-4257
SKR Industries, POB 1382, San Angelo, TX 76902/915-658-3133
S.L.A.P. Industries, P.O. Box 1121, Parklands 2121, SOUTH AFRICA/27-11-788-0030; FAX: 27-11-788-0030
Slings & Arrows, RR1, Box 95, Derby Line, VT 05830
Slings 'N Things, Inc., 8909 Bedford Circle, Suite 11, Omaha, NE 68134/402-571-6954; FAX: 402-571-7082
Slipshot MTS Group, P.O. Box 5, Postal Station D, Etobicoke, Ont., CANADA M9A 4X1/FAX: 416-762-0962
Slug Site Co., Ozark Wilds, Rt. 2, Box 158, Versailles, MO 65084/314-378-6430
Small Custom Mould & Bullet Co., Box 17211, Tucson, AZ 85731
Small Group Bullets, P.O. Box 20, Mertzon, TX 76941/915-835-4751
Smires, C.L., 28269 Old Schoolhouse Rd., Columbus, NJ 08022/609-298-3158
Smith & Wesson, 2100 Roosevelt Ave., Springfield, MA 01102/413-781-8300
Smith, Art, P.O. Box 13, Hector, MN 55342/612-848-2760
Smith, Mark A., 200 N. 9th, Sinclair, WY 82334/307-324-7929
Smith, Ron, 5869 Straley, Ft. Worth, TX 76114/817-732-6768
Smith Saddlery, Jesse W., 3601 E. Boone Ave., Spokane, WA 99202-4501/509-325-0622
Smith Whetstone Co., Inc., 1700 Sleepy Valley Rd., P.O. Box 5095, Hot Springs, AR 71901-5095/501-321-2244; FAX: 501-321-9232
Smokey Valley Rifles (See Lutz Engraving, Ron)
Snapp's Gunshop, 6911 E. Washington Rd., Clare, MI 48617/517-386-9226

Sno-Seal (See Atsko/Sno-Seal)
Societa Armi Bresciane Srl., Via Artigiani 93, Gardone Val Trompia, ITALY 25063/30-8911640, 30-8911648 (U.S. importer—Cape Outfitters)
Solothurn (See U.S. importer—Sile Distributors)
Sonderman, Robert, 735 Kenton Dr., Charleston, IL 61920/217-345-5429
SOS Products Co. (See Buck Stix—SOS Products Co.)
Sotheby's, 1334 York Ave. at 72nd St., New York, NY 10021
South Bend Replicas, Inc., 61650 Oak Rd., South Bend, IN 46614/219-289-4500
Southeastern Community College, 1015 S. Gear Ave., West Burlington, IA 52655/319-752-2731
Southern Ammunition Co., Inc., Rt. 1, Box 6B, Latta, SC 29565/803-752-7751; FAX: 803-752-2022
Southern Armory, The, Rt. 2, Box 134, Woodlawn, VA 24381/703-236-7835; FAX: 703-236-3714
Southern Bloomer Mfg. Co., P.O. Box 1621, Bristol, TN 37620/615-878-6660; FAX: 615-878-8761
Southern Security, 1700 Oak Hills Dr., Kingston, TN 37763/615-376-6297; 800-251-9992
Southwest Institute of Firearms Training (See S.W.I.F.T.)
Southwind Sanctions, P.O. Box 445, Aledo, TX 76008/817-441-8917
Sparks, Milt, 605 E. 44th St. No. 2, Boise, ID 83714-4800
Spartan-Realtree Products, Inc., 1390 Box Circle, Columbus, GA 31907/706-569-9101; FAX: 706-569-0042
Specialty Gunsmithing, Lynn McMurdo, P.O. Box 404, Afton, WY 83110/307-886-5535
Speer Products, Div. of Blount, Inc., P.O. Box 856, Lewiston, ID 83501/208-746-2351; FAX: 208-746-2915
Spegel, Craig, P.O. Box 108, Bay City, OR 97107/503-377-2697
Spence, George W., 115 Locust St., Steele, MO 63877/314-695-4926
Spencer's Custom Guns, Rt. 1, Box 546, Scottsville, VA 24590/804-293-6836
SPG Lubricants, Box 761-H, Livingston, MT 59047
Sphinx Engineering SA, Ch. des Grandes-Vies 2, CH-2900 Porrentruy, SWITZERLAND/41 66 66 73 81; FAX: 41 66 66 30 90
Spokhandguns, Inc., 1206 Fig St., Benton City, WA 99320/509-588-5255
Sport Flite Manufacturing Co., P.O. Box 1082, Bloomfield Hills, MI 48303/818-647-3747
Sport Specialties (See Owen, Harry)
Sportarms of Florida, 5555 NW 36 Ave., Miami, FL 33142/305-635-2411; FAX: 305-634-4536
Sporting Arms Mfg., Inc., 801 Hall Ave., Littlefield, TX 79339/806-385-5665; FAX: 806-385-3394
Sports Support Systems, Inc., 28416 Pacheco, Mission Viejo, CA 92692/714-472-1105
Sportsman Safe Mfg. Co., 6309-6311 Paramount Blvd., Long Beach, CA 90805/800-266-7150, 310-984-5445
Sportsman Supply Co., 714 East Eastwood, P.O. Box 650, Marshall, MO 65340/816-886-9393
Sportsmatch Ltd., 16 Summer St., Leighton Buzzard, Bedfordshire, LU7 8HT ENGLAND/0525-381638; FAX: 0525-851236
Sportsmen's Exchange & Western Gun Traders, Inc., 560 S. "C" St., Oxnard, CA 93030/805-483-1917
Springfield, Inc., 420 W. Main St., Geneseo, IL 61254/309-944-5631; FAX: 309-944-3676
Springfield Sporters, Inc., RD 1, Penn Run, PA 15765/412-254-2626; FAX: 412-254-9173
SSK Co., 220 N. Belvidere Ave., York, PA 17404/717-854-2897
SSK Industries, 721 Woodvue Lane, Wintersville, OH 43952/614-264-0176; FAX: 614-264-2257
St. Lawrence Sales, Inc., 12 W. Fint St., Lake Orion, MI 48035/313-693-7760; 313-693-7718
Stackpole Books, P.O. Box 1831, Harrisburg, PA 17105/717-234-5041; FAX: 717-234-1359
Stafford Bullets, 1920 Tustin Ave., Philadelphia, PA 19152
Stalker, Inc., P.O. Box 21, Fishermans Wharf Rd., Malakoff, TX 75148/903-489-1010
Stalwart Corporation, P.O. Box 357, Pocatello, ID 83204/208-232-7899; FAX: 208-232-0815
Stanley Bullets, 2085 Heatheridge Ln., Reno, NV 89509
Star Bonifacio Echeverria S.A., Torrekva 3, Eibar, SPAIN 20600/43-117340; FAX: 43-111524 (U.S. importer—Interarms)
Star Custom Bullets, P.O. Box 608, 468 Main St., Ferndale, CA 95536/707-786-9140; FAX: 707-786-9117
Star Machine Works, 418 10th Ave., San Diego, CA 92101/619-232-3216
Star Reloading Co., Inc., 5520 Rock Hampton Ct., Indianapolis, IN 46268/317-872-5840
Stark's Bullet Mfg., 2580 Monroe St., Eugene, OR 97405
Starlight Training Center, Inc., Rt. 1, P.O. Box 88, Bronaugh, MO 64728/417-843-3555
Starline, 1300 W. Henry St., Sedalia, MO 65301/816-827-6640; FAX: 816-827-6650
Starrett Co., L.S., 121 Crescent St., Athol, MA 01331/617-249-3551
Starshot Holduxa, Bolognise 125, Miraflores, Lima PERU
State Arms Gun Co., 815 S. Division St., Waunakee, WI 53597/608-849-5800
Steel Reloading Components, Inc., P.O. Box 812, Washington, IN 47501/812-254-3775; FAX: 812-254-7269
Steffens, Ron, 18396 Mariposa Creek Rd., Willits, CA 95490/707-485-0873
Stegall, James B., 26 Forest Rd., Wallkill, NY 12589
Steger, James R., 1131 Dorsey Pl., Plainfield, NJ 07062
Steves House of Guns, Rt. 1, Minnesota City, MN 55959/507-689-2573
Stewart's Gunsmithing, P.O. Box 5854, Pietersburg North 0750, Transvaal, SOUTH AFRICA/01521-89401
Steyr Mannlicher AG, Mannlicherstrasse 1, P.O.B. 1000, A-4400 Steyr, AUSTRIA/0043-7252-896-0; FAX: 0043-7252-68621 (U.S. importer—GSI, Inc.)
Steyr-Daimler-Puch, Schonauerstrasse 5, A-4400 Steyr AUSTRIA (U.S. importer—GSI, Inc.)
Stiles Custom Guns, RD3, Box 1605, Homer City, PA 15748/412-479-9945, 412-479-8666
Stillwell, Robert, 421 Judith Ann Dr., Schertz, TX 78154
Stock Shop, The, 134 Zimmerman Rd., Kalispell, MT 59901/406-257-9003
Stoeger Industries, 55 Ruta Ct., S. Hackensack, NJ 07606/201-440-2700, 800-631-0722; FAX: 201-440-2707

Stoeger Publishing Co. (See Stoeger Industries)

Stone Enterprises Ltd., Rt. 609, P.O. Box 335, Wicomico Church, VA 22579/804-580-5114; FAX: 804-580-8421

Stoney Baroque Shooters Supply, John Richards, Rt. 2, Box 325, Bedford, KY 40006/502-255-7222

Stoney Point Products, Inc., 124 Stoney Point Rd., P.O. Box 5, Courtland, MN 56021-0005/507-354-3360; FAX: 507-354-7236

Storage Tech, 1254 Morris Ave., N. Huntingdon, PA 15642/800-437-9393

Storm, Gary, P.O. Box 5211, Richardson, TX 75083/214-385-0862

Stratco, Inc., 200 E. Center St., Kalispell, MT 59901/406-755-4034; FAX: 406-257-4753

Strong Holster Co., 105 Maplewood Ave., Gloucester, MA 01930/508-281-3300; FAX: 508-281-6321

Stuart, V. Pat, Rt. 1, Box 447-S, Greenville, VA 24440/804-556-3845

Stuart Products, Inc., P.O. Box 1587, Easley, SC 29641/803-859-9360

Sturm, Ruger & Co., Inc., Lacey Place, Southport, CT 06490/203-259-7843

Sullivan, David S. (See Westwind Rifles, Inc.)

Sun Jammer Products, Inc., 9600 N. IH-35, Austin, TX 78753/512-837-8696

Sundance Industries, Inc., 25163 W. Avenue Stanford, Valencia, CA 91355/805-257-4807

"Su-Press-On," Inc., P.O. Box 09161, Detroit, MI 48209/313-842-4222 7:30-11p.m. Mon-Thurs.

Sure Shot of LA, Inc., 103 Coachman Dr., Houma, LA 70360/504-876-6709

Survival Arms, Inc., 4500 Pine Cone Place, Cocoa, FL 32922/407-633-4880; FAX: 407-633-4975

Survival Books/The Larder, 11106 Magnolia Blvd., North Hollywood, CA 91601/818-763-0804

Svon Corp., 280 Eliot St., Ashland, MA 01721/508-881-8852

Swampfire Shop, The (See Peterson Gun Shop, Inc., A.W.)

SwaroSports, Inc. (See JägerSports, Ltd.)

Swarovski Optik North America Ltd., One Wholesale Way, Cranston, RI 02920/401-946-2220, 800-426-3089; FAX: 401-946-2587

Swenson's 45 Shop, A.D., P.O. Box 606, Fallbrook, CA 92028

S.W.I.F.T., 4610 Blue Diamond Rd., Las Vegas, NV 89118/702-897-1100

Swift Bullet Co., P.O. Box 27, 201 Main St., Quinter, KS 67752/913-754-3959; FAX: 913-754-2359

Swift Instruments, Inc., 952 Dorchester Ave., Boston, MA 02125/617-436-2960; FAX: 617-436-3232

Swivel Machine Works, Inc., 167 Cherry St., Suite 286, Milford, CT 06460/203-926-1840; FAX: 203-874-9212

Synchronized Shooting Systems, P.O. Box 52481, Knoxville, TN 37950-2481/800-952-8649

Szweda, Robert (See RMS Custom Gunsmithing)

T

Tabler Marketing, 2554 Lincoln Blvd. 555, Marina Del Rey, CA 90291-5082/818-366-7485; FAX: 818-831-3441

TacStar Industries, Inc., P.O. Box 70, Cottonwood, AZ 86326/800-762-7471

TacTell, Inc., P.O. Box 5654, Maryville, TN 37802/615-982-7855; FAX: 615-558-8294

Tactical Training Center, 574 Miami Bluff Ct., Loveland, OH 45140/513-677-8229

Talley, Dave, P.O. Box 821, Glenrock, WY 82637/307-436-8724

Talon Mfg. Co., Inc., 575 Bevans Industrial Ln., Paw Paw, WV 25434

Tamarack Products, Inc., P.O. Box 625, Wauconda, IL 60084/708-526-9333; FAX: 708-526-9353

Tanfoglio S.r.l., Fratelli, via Valtrompia 39, 41, 25068 Gardone V.T., Brescia, ITALY/30-8910361; FAX: 30-8910183 (U.S. importer—E.A.A. Corp.)

Tank's Rifle Shop, 1324 Ohio St., P.O. Box 474, Fremont, NE 68025/402-727-1317; FAX: 402-721-2573

Tanner (See U.S. importer—Mandall Shooting Supplies, Inc.)

Tapco, Inc., P.O. Box 818, Smyrna, GA 30081/404-435-9782, 800-359-6195; FAX: 404-333-9798

Taracorp Industries, Inc., 16th & Cleveland Blvd., Granite City, IL 62040/618-451-4400

Targot Man, Inc., 49 Gerald Dr., Manchester, CT 06040/203-646-8335; FAX: 203-646-8335

Tar-Hunt Custom Rifles, Inc., RR3, Box 572, Bloomsburg, PA 17815/717-784-6368; FAX: 717-784-6368

Tasco Sales, Inc., 7600 NW 84th Ave., Miami, FL 33122/305-591-3670; FAX: 305-592-5895

Taurus Firearms, Inc., 16175 NW 49th Ave., Miami, FL 33014/305-624-1115; FAX: 305-623-7506

Taurus International Firearms (See U.S. importer—Taurus Firearms, Inc.)

Taurus S.A., Forjas, Avenida Do Forte 511, Porto Alegre, BRAZIL 91360/55-51-340-22-44; FAX: 55-51-340-49-81

Taylor's & Co., Inc., 299 Broad Ave., Winchester, VA 22602/703-722-2017; FAX: 703-722-2018

TCCI, P.O. Box 302, Phoenix, AZ 85001/602-237-3823; FAX: 602-237-3858

TCSR, 3998 Hoffman Rd., White Bear Lake, MN 55110-4626/800-328-5323; FAX: 612-429-0526

TDP Industries, Inc., 603 Airport Blvd., Doylestown, PA 18901/215-345-8687

Techni-Mec, Via Gitti s.n., 25060 Marcheno, ITALY (U.S. importer—Mandall Shooting Supplies, Inc.)

Tejas Resource, 104 Tejas Dr., Terrell, TX 75160/214-563-1220

Tele-Optics, 5514 W. Lawrence Ave., Chicago, IL 60630/312-283-7757; FAX: 312-283-7757

Tennessee Valley Mfg., P.O. Box 1175, Corinth, MS 38834/601-286-5014

Ten-Ring Precision, Inc., Alex B. Hamilton, 1449 Blue Crest Lane, San Antonio, TX 78232/512-494-3063; FAX: 512-494-3066

Tepeco, P.O. Box 342, Friendswood, TX 77546/713-482-2702

Testing Systems, Inc., 220 Pegasus Ave., Northvale, NJ 07647

Teton Arms, Inc., P.O. Box 411, Wilson, WY 83014/307-733-3395

Tetra Gun Lubricants, 1812 Margaret Ave., Annapolis, MD 21401/410-268-6451; FAX: 410-268-8377

Texas Arms, P.O. Box 154906, Waco, TX 76715/817-867-6972

Texas Longhorn Arms, Inc., 5959 W. Loop South, Suite 424, Bellaire, TX 77401/713-668-0631; FAX: 713-660-0493

Texas Platers Supply Co., 2453 W. Five Mile Parkway, Dallas, TX 75233/214-330-7168

T.F.C. S.p.A., Via G. Marconi 118, B, Villa Carcina, Brescia 25069, ITALY/030-881271; FAX: 030-881826

Theis, Terry, P.O. Box 535, Fredericksburg, TX 78624/210-997-6778

Theoben Engineering (See U.S. importer—Air Rifle Specialists)

Thiewes, George W., 1846 Allen Lane, St. Charles, IL 60174/708-584-1383

Things Unlimited, 235 N. Kimbau, Casper, WY 82601/307-234-5277

Thirion Hand Engraving, Denise, P.O. Box 408, Graton, CA 95444/707-829-1876

Thomas, Charles C., 2600 S. First St., Springfield, IL 62794/217-789-8980; FAX: 217-789-9130

Thompson, Randall (See Highline Machine Co.)

Thompson Bullet Lube Co., P.O. Box 472343, Garland, TX 75047/214-271-8063; FAX: 214-840-6743

Thompson Precision, 110 Mary St., P.O. Box 251, Warren, IL 61087/815-745-3625

Thompson Target Technology, 618 Roslyn Ave., SW, Canton, OH 44710/216-453-7707; FAX: 216-478-4723

Thompson/Center Arms, P.O. Box 5002, Rochester, NH 03867/603-332-2394; FAX: 603-332-5133

3-D Ammunition & Bullets, 112 W. Plum St., P.O. Box J, Doniphan, NE 68832/402-845-2285; FAX: 402-845-6546

300 Gunsmith Service, Inc., 6850 S. Yosemite Ct., Englewood, CO 80112/303-773-0300

3-Ten Corp., P.O. Box 269, Feeding Hills, MA 01030/413-789-2086

Thunder Mountain Arms, P.O. Box 593, Oak Harbor, WA 98277/206-679-4657; FAX: 206-675-1114

Thunderbird Cartridge Co., Inc. (See TCCI)

Thurston Sports, Inc., RD 3 Donovan Rd., Auburn, NY 13021/315-253-0966

Tiger-Hunt, Michael D. Barton, Box 379, Beaverdale, PA 15921/814-472-5161

Tikka (See U.S. importer—Stoeger Industries)

Tillinghast, James C., P.O. Box 405DG, Hancock, NH 03449/603-525-4049

Timber Heirloom Products, 618 Roslyn Ave. SW, Canton, OH 44710/216-453-7707; FAX: 216-478-4723

Time Precision, Inc., 640 Federal Rd., Brookfield, CT 06804/203-775-8343

Timney Mfg., Inc., 3065 W. Fairmont Ave., Phoenix, AZ 85017/602-274-2999; FAX: 602-241-0361

Tioga Engineering Co., Inc., P.O. Box 913, 13 Cone St., Wellsboro, PA 16901/717-724-3533, 717-662-3347

Tippman Pneumatics, Inc., 3518 Adams Center Rd., Fort Wayne, IN 46806/219-749-6022; FAX: 219-749-6619

Tirelli, Snc Di Tirelli Primo E.C., Via Matteotti No. 359, Gardone V.T., Brescia, ITALY 25063/030-8912819; FAX: 030-8832240

TM Stockworks, 6355 Maplecrest Rd., Fort Wayne, IN 46835/219-485-5389

TMI Products, 930 S. Plumer Ave., Tucson, AZ 85719/602-792-1075; FAX: 602-792-0093

Tom's Gun Repair, Thomas G. Ivanoff, 76-6 Rt. Southfork Rd., Cody, WY 82414/307-587-6949

Tom's Gunshop, 3601 Central Ave., Hot Springs, AR 71913/501-624-3856

Tomboy, Inc., P.O. Box 846, Dallas, OR 97338/503-623-6955

Tonoloway Tack Drives, HCR 81, Box 100, Needmore, OA 17238

Top-Line USA, Inc., 7920-28 Hamilton Ave., Cincinnati, OH 45231/513-522-2992, 800-346-6699; FAX: 513-522-0916

Torel, Inc., 1053 N. South St., P.O. Box 592, Yoakum, TX 77995/512-293-2341; FAX: 512-293-3413

Totally Dependable Products (See TDP Industries, Inc.)

Track of the Wolf, Inc., P.O. Box 6, Osseo, MN 55369-0006/612-424-2500; FAX: 612-424-9860

Tradewinds, Inc., P.O. Box 1191, 2339-41 Tacoma Ave. S., Tacoma, WA 98401/206-272-4887

Traditions, P.O. Box 235, Deep River, CT 06417/203-526-9555; FAX: 203-526-4564

Trafalgar Square, P.O. Box 257, N. Pomfret, VT 05053/802-457-1911

Traft Gunshop, P.O. Box 1078, Buena Vista, CO 81211

Trail Guns Armory, 1422 E. Main St., League City, TX 77573

Trammco, 839 Gold Run Rd., Boulder, CO 80302

Trappers Trading, P.O. Box 26946, Austin, TX 78755/800-788-9334

Treadlok Gun Safe, Inc., 1764 Granby St. NE, Roanoke, VA 24012/800-729-8732, 703-982-6881; FAX: 703-982-1059

Treso, Inc., P.O. Box 4640, Pagosa Springs, CO 81157/303-731-2295

Trico Plastics, 590 S. Vincent Ave., Azusa, CA 91702

Trijicon, Inc., P.O. Box 6029, Wixom, MI 48393-6029/810-960-7700; FAX: 810-960-7725

Trinidad State Junior College, Gunsmithing Dept., 600 Prospect St., Trinidad, CO 81082/719-846-5631; FAX: 719-846-5667

Triple-K Mfg. Co., Inc., 2222 Commercial St., San Diego, CA 92113/619-232-2066; FAX: 619-232-7675

Trophy Bonded Bullets, Inc., 900 S. Loop W., Suite 190, Houston, TX 77054/713-645-4499; FAX: 713-741-6393

Trotman, Ken, 135 Ditton Walk, Unit 11, Cambridge CB5 8QD, ENGLAND/0223-211030; FAX: 0223-212317

Tru-Square Metal Prods., Inc., 640 First St. SW, P.O. Box 585, Auburn, WA 98001/206-833-2310

True Flight Bullet Co., 5581 Roosevelt St., Whitehall, PA 18052/800-875-3625; FAX: 215-262-7806

Trulock Tool, Broad St., Whigham, GA 31797/912-762-4678

T.S.W. Conversions, Inc., E. 115 Crain Rd., Paramus, NJ 07650-4017/201-265-1618

Turkish Firearms Corp., 8487 Euclid Ave., Suite 1, Manassas Park, VA 22111/703-369-6848; FAX: 703-257-7709

Turnbull Restoration, Doug, 6426 County Rd. 30, Bloomfield, NY 14469/716-657-6338

Tuscano, Tony, P.O. Box 461, Wickliffe, OH 44092/216-943-1175

Twin Pine Armory, P.O. Box 58, Hwy. 6, Adna, WA 98522/206-748-4590; FAX: 206-748-7011

Tyler Mfg.-Dist., Melvin, 1326 W. Britton Rd., Oklahoma City, OK 73114/405-842-8044

Tyler Scott, Inc., 313 Rugby Ave., Terrace Park, OH 45174/513-831-7603; FAX: 513-831-7417

U

Uberti, Aldo, Casella Postale 43, I-25063 Gardone V.T., ITALY (U.S. importers—American Arms, Inc.; Christopher Firearms Co., Inc., E.; Cimarron Arms; Dixie Gun Works; EMF Co., Inc.; Mitchell Arms, Inc.; Navy Arms Co; Uberti USA, Inc.)

Uberti USA, Inc., 362 Limerock Rd., P.O. Box 469, Lakeville, CT 06039/203-435-8068; FAX: 203-435-8146

U.F.A., Inc., 7655 Evans Rd. Suite Z, Scottsdale, AZ 85260/602-998-3941; FAX: 602-998-3941

Ugartechea S.A., Ignacio, Chonta 26, Eibar, SPAIN 20600/43-121257; FAX: 43-121669 (U.S. importer—Mandall Shooting Supplies, Inc.)

Ulrich, Doc & Bud (See D.O.C. Specialists, Inc.)

Ultimate Accuracy, 121 John Shelton Rd., JAcksonville, AR 72076/501-985-2530

Ultra Light Arms, Inc., P.O. Box 1270, 214 Price St., Granville, WV 26534/304-599-5687

UltraSport Arms, Inc., 1955 Norwood Ct., Racine, WI 53403/414-554-3237; FAX: 414-554-9731

Uncle Mike's (See Michaels of Oregon Co.)

Unertl Optical Co., Inc., John, 308 Clay Ave., P.O. Box 818, Mars, PA 16046-0818/412-625-3810

Unick's Gunsmithing, 5005 Center Rd., Lowellville, OH 44436/216-536-8015

Unique/M.A.P.F., 10, Les Allees, 64700 Hendaye, FRANCE 64700/33-59 20 71 93 (U.S. importer—Nygord Precision Products)

UniTec, 1250 Bedford SW, Canton, OH 44710/216-452-4017

United Binocular Co., 9043 S. Western Ave., Chicago, IL 60620

United States Ammunition Co. (See USAC)

United States Optics Technologies, Inc., 1501 E. Chapman Ave. 306, Fullerton, CA 92631/714-879-8922; FAX: 714-449-0941

United States Products Co., 518 Melwood Ave., Pittsburgh, PA 15213/412-621-2130

Upper Missouri Trading Co., 304 Harold St., Crofton, NE 68730/402-388-4844

U.S. General Technologies, Inc., 145 Mitchell Ave., South San Francisco, CA 94080/415-634-8440; FAX: 415-634-8452

U.S. Optics Technologies, Inc., Div. of Zeitz Optics, U.S.A., 1501 E. Chapman Ave. Suite 306/Fullerton, CA 92631/714-944-4901; FAX: 714-944-4904

U.S. Repeating Arms Co., Inc., 275 Winchester Ave., New Haven, CT 06511/203-789-5000; FAX: 203-789-5071

USA Magazines, P.O. Box 39115, Downey, CA 90241/800-872-2577

USA Sporting, 1330 N. Glassell, Suite M, Orange, CA 92667/714-538-3109, 800-538-3109; FAX: 714-538-1334

USAC, 4500-15th St. East, Tacoma, WA 98424/206-922-7589

Uvalde Machine & Tool, P.O. Box 1604, Uvalde, TX 78802

V

Valade, Robert B., 931 3rd Ave., Seaside, OR 97138/503-738-7672

Valmet (See Tikka/U.S. importer—Stoeger Industries)

Valor Corp., 5555 NW 36th Ave., Miami, FL 33142/305-633-0127

Van Gorden & Son, Inc., C.S., 1815 Main St., Bloomer, WI 54724/715-568-2612

Van Horn, Gil, P.O. Box 207, Llano, CA 93544

Van Patten, J.W., P.O. Box 145, Foster Hill, Milford, PA 18337/717-296-7069

Vann Custom Bullets, 330 Grandview Ave., Novato, CA 94947

Varner's Service, 102 Shaffer Rd., Antwerp, OH 45813/419-258-8631

Vega Tool Co., 1840 Commerce St. Unit H, Boulder, CO 80301/303-443-4750

Venco Industries, Inc. (See Shooter's Choice)

Venus Industries, P.O. Box 246, Sialkot-1, PAKISTAN/FAX: 92 432 85579

Verdemont Fieldsports, 3035 Jo An Dr., San Bernardino, CA 92407-2022/714-880-8255; FAX: 714-880-8255

Vest, John, P.O. Box 1552, Susanville, CA 96130/916-257-7228

VibraShine, Inc., Rt. 1, P.O. Box 64, Mt. Olive, MS 39119/601-733-5614; FAX: 601-733-2226

Vibra-Tek Co., 1844 Arroya Rd., Colorado Springs, CO 80906/719-634-8611; FAX: 719-634-6886

Vic's Gun Refinishing, 6 Pineview Dr., Dover, NH 03820-6422/603-742-0013

Victory USA, P.O. Box 1021, Pine Bush, NY 12566/914-744-2060; FAX: 914-744-5181

Vihtavuori Oy, FIN-41330 Vihtavuori, FINLAND/358-41-3779211; FAX: 358-41-3771643

Vihtavuori Oy/Kaltron-Pettibone, 1241 Ellis St., Bensenville, IL 60106/708-350-1116; FAX: 708-350-1606

Viking Leathercraft, Inc., 1579A Jayken Way, Chula Vista, CA 91911/800-262-6666; FAX: 619-429-8268

Viking Video Productions, P.O. Box 251, Roseburg, OR 97470

Vincent's Shop, 210 Antoinette, Fairbanks, AK 99701

Vintage Arms, Inc., 6003 Saddle Horse, Fairfax, VA 22030/703-968-0779; FAX: 703-968-0780

Vintage Industries, Inc., 781 Big Tree Dr., Longwood, FL 32750/407-831-8949; FAX: 407-831-5346

VIP Products, 488 East 17th St., Ste. A-101, Costa Mesa, CA 92627/714-722-5986

Viramontez, Ray, 601 Springfield Dr., Albany, GA 31707/912-432-9683

Visible Impact Targets, Rts. 5 & 20, E. Bloomfield, NY 14443/716-657-6161

Vitt/Boos, 2178 Nichols Ave., Stratford, CT 06497/203-375-6859

Voere-KGH m.b.H., P.O. Box 416, A-6333 Kufstein, Tirol, AUSTRIA/0043-5372-62547; FAX: 0043-5372-65752 (U.S. importers—JägerSport, Ltd.; Swarovski Optik North America Ltd.)

Volquartsen Custom Ltd., RR 1, Box 33A, P.O. Box 271, Carroll, IA 51401/712-792-4238; FAX: 712-792-2542

Vom Hofe (See Old Western Scrounger, Inc., The)

Von Minden Gunsmithing Services, 2403 SW 39 Terrace, Cape Coral, FL 33914/813-542-8946

Vorhes, David, 3042 Beecham St., Napa, CA 94558/707-226-9116

VSP Publishers, P.O. Box 887, McCall, ID 83638/208-634-4104

Vulpes Ventures, Inc., Fox Cartridge Division, P.O. Box 1363, Bolingbrook, IL 60440-7363/708-759-1229

W

Waffen-Weber Custom Gunsmithing, 4-1691 Powick Rd., Kelowna, B.C. CANADA V1X 4L1/604-762-7575; FAX: 604-861-3655

Wagoner, Vernon G., 2325 E. Encanto, Mesa, AZ 85213/602-835-1307

Waldron, Herman, Box 475, 80 N. 17th St., Pomeroy, WA 99347/509-843-1404

Walker Arms Co., Inc., 499 County Rd. 820, Selma, AL 36701/205-872-6231

Walker Mfg., Inc., 8296 S. Channel, Harsen's Island, MI 48028

Wallace, Terry, 385 San Marino, Vallejo, CA 94589/707-642-7041

Walt's Custom Leather, Walt Whinnery, 1947 Meadow Creek Dr., Louisville, KY 40218/502-458-4361

Walters, John, 500 N. Avery Dr., Moore, OK 73160/405-799-0376

Walters Industries, 6226 Park Lane, Dallas, TX 75225/214-691-6973

Walther GmbH, Carl, B.P. 4325, D-89033 Ulm, GERMANY (U.S. importer—Interarms)

WAMCO—New Mexico, P.O. Box 205, Peralta, NM 87042-0205/505-869-0826

Ward & Van Valkenburg, 114 32nd Ave. N., Fargo, ND 58102/701-232-2351

Wardell Precision Handguns Ltd., 48851 N. Fig Springs Rd., New River, AZ 85027-8513/602-465-7995

Warenski, Julie, 590 E. 500 N., Richfield, UT 84701/801-896-5319; FAX: 801-896-5319

Warne Manufacturing Co., 9039 SE Jannsen Rd., Clackamas, OR 97015/503-657-5590; FAX: 503-657-5695

Warren, Kenneth W. (See Mountain States Engraving)

Warren Muzzleloading Co., Inc., Hwy. 21 North, P.O. Box 100, Ozone, AR 72854/501-292-3268

Washita Mountain Whetstone Co., P.O. Box 378, Lake Hamilton, AR 71951/501-525-3914

WASP Shooting Systems, Rt. 1, Box 147, Lakeview, AR 72642/501-431-5606

Watson Trophy Match Bullets, 2404 Wade Hampton Blvd., Greenville, SC 29615/803-244-7948

Watsontown Machine & Tool Co., 309 Dickson Ave., Watsontown, PA 17777/717-538-3533

Wayland Precision Wood Products, P.O. Box 1142, Mill Valley, CA 94942/415-381-3543

Wayne Firearms for Collectors and Investors, James, 2608 N. Laurent, Victoria, TX 77901/512-578-1258; FAX: 512-578-3559

Wayne Specialty Services, 260 Waterford Drive, Florissant, MO 63033/413-831-7083

W.C. Wolff Co., P.O. Box I, Newtown Square, PA 19073/610-359-9600, 800-545-0077

WD-40 Co., P.O. Box 80607, San Diego, CA 92138-0607/619-275-1400; FAX: 619-275-5823

Weatherby, Inc., 2781 Firestone Blvd., South Gate, CA 90280/213-569-7186, 800-227-2023; FAX: 213-569-5025

Weaver Arms Corp., P.O. Box 8, Dexter, MO 63841/314-568-3101

Weaver Products, Div. of Blount, Inc., P.O. Box 39, Onalaska, WI 54650/800-635-7656; FAX: 608-781-0368

Weaver Scope Repair Service, 1121 Larry Mahan Dr., Suite B, El Paso, TX 79925/915-593-1005

Weaver's Gun Shop, P.O. Box 8, Dexter, MO 63841/314-568-3101

Webb, Bill, 6504 North Bellefontaine, Kansas City, MO 64119/816-453-7431

Webley and Scott Ltd., Frankley Industrial Park, Tay Rd., Rubery Rednal, Birmingham B45 OPA, U.K./021-453-1864; FAX: 021-457-7846 (U.S. importer—Beeman Precision Airguns, Inc.)

Webster Scale Mfg. Co., P.O. Box 188, Sebring, FL 33870/813-385-6362

Weigand Combat Handguns, Inc., P.O. Box 239, Crestwood Industrial Park, Mountain Top, PA 18707/717-474-9804; FAX: 717-474-9987

Weihrauch KG, Hermann, Industriestrasse 11, 8744 Mellrichstadt, GERMANY/09776-497-498 (U.S. importers—Beeman Precision Airguns; E.A.A. Corp.)

Weisz Parts, P.O. Box 20038, Columbus, OH 43220-0038/614-457-0500; FAX: 614-846-8585

Welch, Sam, CVSR 2110, Moab, UT 84532/801-259-8131

Wells, Fred F., Wells Sport Store, 110 N. Summit St., Prescott, AZ 86301/602-445-3655

Wells, Rachel, 110 N. Summit St., Prescott, AZ 86301/602-445-3655

Wells Creek Knife & Gun Works, 32956 State Hwy. 38, Scottsburg, OR 97473/503-587-4202

Wells Custom Gunsmith, R.A., 3452 1st Ave., Racine, WI 53402/414-639-5223

Welsh, Bud, 80 New Road, E. Amherst, NY 14051/716-688-6344

Wentling Co., S.A., 546 W. Chocolate Ave., P.O. Box 355P, Hershey, PA 17033/717-533-2468; FAX: 717-534-1252

Werner, Carl, P.O. Box 492, Littleton, CO 80160

Werth, T.W., 1203 Woodlawn Rd., Lincoln, IL 62656/217-732-1300

Wescombe, P.O. Box 488, Glencoe, CA 95232/209-293-7010

Wessinger Custom Guns & Engraving, 268 Limestone Rd., Chapin, SC 29036/803-345-5677

Wesson Firearms Co., Inc., Maple Tree Industrial Center, Rt. 20, Wilbraham, Rd./Palmer, MA 01069/413-267-4081; FAX: 413-267-3601

West, Robert G., 3973 Pam St., Eugene, OR 97402/503-344-3700

Westchester Carbide, 148 Wheeler Ave., Pleasantville, NY 10570/914-769-1445

Western Design, 1629 Via Monserate, Fallbrook, CA 92028/619-723-9279

Western Missouri Shooters Alliance, P.O. Box 11144, Kansas City, MO 64119/816-597-3950; FAX: 816-229-7350

Westfield Engineering, 6823 Watcher St., Commerce, CA 90040/FAX: 213-928-8270

Westrom, John (See Precise Metal Finishing)

MANUFACTURERS' DIRECTORY

Westwind Rifles, Inc., David S. Sullivan, P.O. Box 261, 640 Briggs St., Erie, CO 80516/303-828-3823

Wheel Weights Corp., 2611 Hwy. 40 East, Inglis, FL 34449/904-447-3571

Whildin & Sons Ltd., E.H., RR2, Box 119, Tamaqua, PA 18252/717-668-6743; FAX: 717-668-6745

Whinnery, Walt (See Walt's Custom Leather)

White Flyer, Div. of Reagent Chemical & Research, Inc., 9139 W. Redfield Rd., Peoria, AZ 85381/800-647-2898

White Flyer Targets, 124 River Rd., Middlesex, NJ 08846/908-469-0100; FAX: 908-469-9692

White Laboratory, Inc., H.P., 3114 Scarboro Rd., Street, MD 21154/410-838-6550; FAX: 410-838-2802

White Owl Enterprises, 2583 Flag Rd., Abilene, KS 67410/913-263-2613; FAX: 913-263-2613

White Rock Tool & Die, 6400 N. Brighton Ave., Kansas City, MO 64119/816-454-0478

White Shooting Systems, Inc., P.O. Box 277, Roosevelt, UT 84066/801-722-3085; FAX: 801-722-3054

Whitehead, James D., 204 Cappucino Way, Sacramento, CA 95838

Whitestone Lumber Corp., 148-02 14th Ave., Whitestone, NY 11357/718-746-4400; FAX: 718-767-1748

Whitetail Design & Engineering Ltd., 9421 E. Mannsiding Rd., Clare, MI 48617/517-386-3932

Whits Shooting Stuff, Box 1340, Cody, WY 82414

Wichita Arms, Inc., 923 E. Gilbert, P.O. Box 11371, Wichita, KS 67211/316-265-0661; FAX: 316-265-0760

Wick, David E., 1504 Michigan Ave., Columbus, IN 47201/812-376-6960

Widener's Reloading & Shooting Supply, Inc., P.O. Box 3009 CRS, Johnson City, TN 37602/615-282-6786; FAX: 615-282-6651

Wideview Scope Mount Corp., 26110 Michigan Ave., Inkster, MI 48141/313-274-1238; FAX: 313-274-2814

Wiebe, Duane, 3715 S. Browns Lake Dr. 106, Burlington, WI 53105-7931

Wiest, M.C., 10737 Dutchtown Rd., Knoxville, TN 37932/615-966-4545

Wilcox All-Pro Tools & Supply, RR 1, Montezuma, IA 50171/515-623-3138

Wild Bill's Originals, P.O. Box 13037, Burton, WA 98013/206-463-5738

Wilderness Sound Products Ltd., 4015 Main St. A, Springfield, OR 97478/503-741-0263; FAX: 503-741-7648

Wildey, Inc., P.O. Box 475, Brookfield, CT 06804/203-355-9000; FAX: 203-354-7759

Wilkinson Arms, 26884 Pearl Rd., Parma, ID 83660/208-722-6771; FAX: 208-722-5197

Will-Burt Co., 169 S. Main, Orrville, OH 44667

William's Gun Shop, Ben, 1151 S. Cedar Ridge, Duncanville, TX 75137/214-780-1807

Williams Bullet Co., J.R., 2008 Tucker Rd., Perry, GA 31069/912-987-0274

Williams Gun Sight Co., 7389 Lapeer Rd., Box 329, Davison, MI 48423/810-653-2131, 800-530-9028; FAX: 810-658-2140

Williams Mfg. of Oregon, P.O. Box 98, 561 Upper Smith River Rd., Drain, OR 97435/503-836-7461; FAX: 503-836-7245

Williams Shootin' Iron Service, The Lynx-Line, 8857 Bennett Hill Rd., Central Lake, MI 49622/616-544-6615

Williamson Precision Gunsmithing, 117 W. Pipeline, Hurst, TX 76053/817-285-0064; FAX: 817-285-0064

Willig Custom Engraving, Claus, D-97422 Schweinfurt, Siedlerweg 17, GERMANY/01149-9721-41446; FAX: 01149-9721-44413

Willow Bend, P.O. Box 203, Chelmsford, MA 01824/508-256-8508; FAX: 508-256-9765

Willson Safety Prods. Div., P.O. Box 622, Reading, PA 19603-0622/610-376-6161; FAX: 610-371-7725

Wilson, Inc., L.E., Box 324, 404 Pioneer Ave., Cashmere, WA 98815/509-782-1328

Wilson's Gun Shop, Box 578, Rt. 3, Berryville, AR 72616/501-545-3635; FAX: 501-545-3310

Winchester (See U.S. Repeating Arms Co., Inc.)

Winchester Div., Olin Corp., 427 N. Shamrock, E. Alton, IL 62024/618-258-3566; FAX: 618-258-3599

Winchester Press (See New Win Publishing, Inc.)

Winchester Sutler, Inc., The, 270 Shadow Brook Lane, Winchester, VA 22603/703-888-3595

Windjammer Tournament Wads, Inc., 750 W. Hampden Ave. Suite 170, Englewood, CO 80110/303-781-6329

Wingshooting Adventures, 4320 Kalamazoo Ave. SE, Grand Rapids, MI 49508/616-455-7810; FAX: 616-455-5212

Winkle Bullets, R.R. 1 Box 316, Heyworth, IL 61745

Winter & Associates (See Olde Pennsylvania)

Wiseman and Co., Bill, P.O. Box 3427, Bryan, TX 77805/409-690-3456; FAX: 409-690-0156

Wisner's Gun Shop, Inc., 287 NW Chehalis Ave., Chehalis, WA 98532/206-748-8942; FAX: 206-748-7011

Wolf's Western Traders, 40 E. Works #3F, Sheridan, WY 82801/307-674-5352

Wolfe Publishing Co., 6471 Airpark Dr., Prescott, AZ 86301/602-445-7810, 800-899-7810; FAX: 602-778-5124

Wolverine Boots & Outdoor Footwear Div., Wolverine World Wide, 9341 Cour, land Dr./Rockford, MI 49351/616-866-5500

Wood, Frank (See Classic Guns)

Wood, Mel, P.O. Box 1255, Sierra Vista, AZ 85636/602-455-5541

Woodleigh (See Huntington Die Specialties)

Woodworker's Supply, 1108 North Glenn Rd., Casper, WY 82601/307-237-5354

World of Targets (See Birchwood Casey)

World Trek, Inc., P.O. Box 11670, Pueblo, CO 81001-0670/719-546-2121; FAX: 719-543-6886

Worthy Products, Inc., RR 1, P.O. Box 213, Martville, NY 13111/315-324-5298

Wosenitz VHP, Inc., Box 741, Dania, FL 33004/305-923-3748; FAX: 305-925-2217

Wyant Bullets, Gen. Del., Swan Lake, MT 59911

Wyoming Armory, Inc., Box 28, Farson, WY 82932/307-273-5556

Wyoming Bonded Bullets, Box 91, Sheridan, WY 82801/307-674-8091

Wyoming Custom Bullets, 1626 21st St., Cody, WY 82414

X, Y

X-Spand Target Systems, 26-10th St. SE, Medicine Hat, AB T1A 1P7 CANADA/403-526-7997; FAX: 403-526-7997

Yavapai College, 1100 E. Sheldon St., Prescott, AZ 86301/602-776-2359; FAX: 602-776-2193

Yavapai Firearms Academy Ltd., P.O. Box 27290, Prescott Valley, AZ 86312/602-772-8262

Yearout, Lewis E. (See Montana Outfitters)

Yesteryear Armory & Supply, P.O. Box 408, Carthage, TN 37030

Young Country Arms, P.O. Box 3615, Simi Valley, CA 93093

Z

Zabala Hermanos S.A., P.O. Box 97, Eibar, SPAIN 20600/43-768085, 43-768076; FAX: 43-768201 (U.S. importer—American Arms, Inc.)

Zanoletti, Pietro, Via Monte Gugielpo, 4, I-25063 Gardone V.T., ITALY (U.S. importer—Mandall Shooting Supplies, Inc.)

Z-Coat Industrial Coatings, Inc., 3375 U.S. Hwy. 98 S. No. A, Lakeland, FL 33803-8365/813-665-1734

Zeiss Optical, Carl, 1015 Commerce St., Petersburg, VA 23803/804-861-0033; FAX: 804-733-4024

Zero Ammunition Co., Inc., 1601 22nd St. SE, P.O. Box 1188, Cullman, AL 35056-1188/800-545-9376; FAX: 205-739-4683

Zim's Inc., 4370 S. 3rd West, Salt Lake City, UT 84107/801-268-2505

Zoli, Antonio, Via Zanardelli 39, Casier Postal 21, I-25063 Gardone V.T., ITALY

Zufall, Joseph F., P.O. Box 304, Golden, CO 80402-0304